# Exam Ref 70-762
# Developing SQL
# Databases

Louis Davidson
Stacia Varga

**Exam Ref 70-762 Developing SQL Databases**

**Published with the authorization of Microsoft Corporation by:**
**Pearson Education, Inc.**

**Copyright © 2017 by Pearson Education Inc.**

ISBN-13: 978-1-5093-0491-2
ISBN-10: 1-5093-0491-6

Library of Congress Control Number: 2016962647

**Trademarks**

Microsoft and the trademarks listed at https://www.microsoft.com on the "Trademarks" webpage are trademarks of the Microsoft group of companies. All other marks are property of their respective owners.

**Warning and Disclaimer**

Every effort has been made to make this book as complete and as accurate as possible, but no warranty or fitness is implied. The information provided is on an "as is" basis. The authors, the publisher, and Microsoft Corporation shall have neither liability nor responsibility to any person or entity with respect to any loss or damages arising from the information contained in this book or programs accompanying it.

**Special Sales**

For information about buying this title in bulk quantities, or for special sales opportunities (which may include electronic versions; custom cover designs; and content particular to your business, training goals, marketing focus, or branding interests), please contact our corporate sales department at corpsales@pearsoned.com or (800) 382-3419.

For government sales inquiries, please contact governmentsales@pearsoned.com.

For questions about sales outside the U.S., please contact intlcs@pearson.com.

| | |
|---|---|
| **Editor-in-Chief** | Greg Wiegand |
| **Acquisitions Editor** | Trina MacDonald |
| **Development Editor** | Rick Kughen |
| **Managing Editor** | Sandra Schroeder |
| **Senior Project Editor** | Tracey Croom |
| **Editorial Production** | Backstop Media |
| **Copy Editor** | Jordan Severns |
| **Indexer** | Julie Grady |
| **Proofreader** | Christina Rudloff |
| **Technical Editor** | Christopher Ford |
| **Cover Designer** | Twist Creative, Seattle |

11 2019

# Contents at a glance

# Contents

---

### What do you think of this book? We want to hear from you!

Microsoft is interested in hearing your feedback so we can continually improve our books and learning resources for you. To participate in a brief online survey, please visit:

**https://aka.ms/tellpress**

**What do you think of this book? We want to hear from you!**

Microsoft is interested in hearing your feedback so we can continually improve our
books and learning resources for you. To participate in a brief online survey, please visit:

**https://aka.ms/tellpress**

# Introduction

The 70-762 exam tests your knowledge about developing databases in Microsoft SQL Server 2016. To successfully pass this exam, you should know how to create various types of database objects, such as disk-based and memory-optimized tables, indexes, views, and stored procedures, to name a few. Not only must you know how and why to develop specific types of database objects, but you must understand how to manage database concurrency by correctly using transactions, assigning isolation levels, and troubleshooting locking behavior. Furthermore, you must demonstrate familiarity with techniques to optimize database performance by reviewing statistics and index usage, using tools to troubleshoot and optimize query plans, optimizing the configuration of SQL Server and server resources, and monitoring SQL Server performance metrics. You must also understand the similarities and differences between working with databases with SQL Server on-premises and Windows Azure SQL Database in the cloud.

The 70-762 exam is focused on measuring skills of database professionals, such as developers or administrators, who are responsible for designing, implementing, or optimizing relational databases by using SQL Server 2016 or SQL Database. In addition to reinforcing your existing skills, it measures what you know about new features and capabilities in SQL Server and SQL Database.

To help you prepare for this exam and reinforce the concepts that it tests, we provide many different examples that you can try for yourself. Some of these examples require only that you have installed SQL Server 2016 or have created a Windows Azure subscription. Other examples require that you download and restore a backup of the Wide World Importers sample database for SQL Server 2016 from *https://github.com/Microsoft/sql-server-samples/releases/tag/wide-world-importers-v1.0*. The file to download from this page is WideWorldImporters-Full.bak. You can find documentation about this sample database at Wide World Importers documentation, *https://msdn.microsoft.com/library/mt734199(v=sql.1).aspx*.

This book covers every major topic area found on the exam, but it does not cover every exam question. Only the Microsoft exam team has access to the exam questions, and Microsoft regularly adds new questions to the exam, making it impossible to cover specific questions. You should consider this book a supplement to your relevant real-world experience and other study materials. If you encounter a topic in this book that you do not feel completely comfortable with, use the "Need more review?" links you'll find in the text to find more information and take the time to research and study the topic. Great information is available on MSDN, TechNet, and in blogs and forums.

## Organization of this book

This book is organized by the "Skills measured" list published for the exam. The "Skills measured" list is available for each exam on the Microsoft Learning website: *https://aka.ms/examlist*. Each chapter in this book corresponds to a major topic area in the list, and the technical tasks in each topic area determine a chapter's organization. If an exam covers six major topic areas, for example, the book will contain six chapters.

## Microsoft certifications

Microsoft certifications distinguish you by proving your command of a broad set of skills and experience with current Microsoft products and technologies. The exams and corresponding certifications are developed to validate your mastery of critical competencies as you design and develop, or implement and support, solutions with Microsoft products and technologies both on-premises and in the cloud. Certification brings a variety of benefits to the individual and to employers and organizations.

> *MORE INFO*  **ALL MICROSOFT CERTIFICATIONS**
>
> For information about Microsoft certifications, including a full list of available certifications, go to *https://www.microsoft.com/learning*.

## Acknowledgments

**Louis Davidson** I would like to dedicate my half of this book to my wife Valerie, who put up with me writing my half of this book (a few times) while simultaneously finishing my Database Design book.

Technically speaking, I would like to thank my colleagues in the MVP community and program at Microsoft. I have learned so much from them for the many years I have been an awardee and would never have accomplished so much without them. Far more than one is referenced for additional material.

Thank you, Stacia, for your work on the book. I appreciate your involvement more than you can imagine.

**Stacia Varga** I am grateful to have a community of SQL Server professionals that are always ready to share their experience and insights related with me, whether through informal conversations or more extensive reviews of any content that I write. The number of people with whom I have had informal conversations are too numerous to mention, but they know who they are. I would like to thank a few people in particular for the more in-depth help they provided: Joseph D'Antoni, Grant Fritchey, and Brandon Leach. And thanks to Louis as well. We have been on stage together, we have worked together, and now we have written together!

Behind the scenes of the publishing process, there are many other people involved that help us bring this book to fruition. I'd like to thank Trina McDonald for her role as the acquisitions editor and Troy Mott as the managing editor for his incredible patience with us and his efforts to make the process as easy as possible. I also appreciate the copyediting by Christina Rudloff and technical editing by Christopher Ford to ensure that the information we provide in this book is communicated as clearly as possible and technically accurate.

Last, I want to thank my husband, Dean Varga, not only for tolerating my crazy work hours during the writing of this book, but also for doing his best to create an environment conducive to writing on many different levels.

# Free ebooks from Microsoft Press

From technical overviews to in-depth information on special topics, the free ebooks from Microsoft Press cover a wide range of topics. These ebooks are available in PDF, EPUB, and Mobi for Kindle formats, ready for you to download at:

*https://aka.ms/mspressfree*

Check back often to see what is new!

# Microsoft Virtual Academy

Build your knowledge of Microsoft technologies with free expert-led online training from Microsoft Virtual Academy (MVA). MVA offers a comprehensive library of videos, live events, and more to help you learn the latest technologies and prepare for certification exams. You'll find what you need here:

*https://www.microsoftvirtualacademy.com*

# Quick access to online references

Throughout this book are addresses to webpages that the author has recommended you visit for more information. Some of these addresses (also known as URLs) can be painstaking to type into a web browser, so we've compiled all of them into a single list that readers of the print edition can refer to while they read.

Download the list at *https://aka.ms/examref762/downloads*.

The URLs are organized by chapter and heading. Every time you come across a URL in the book, find the hyperlink in the list to go directly to the webpage.

# Errata, updates, & book support

We've made every effort to ensure the accuracy of this book and its companion content. You can access updates to this book—in the form of a list of submitted errata and their related corrections—at:

*https://aka.ms/examref762/detail*

If you discover an error that is not already listed, please submit it to us at the same page.

If you need additional support, email Microsoft Press Book Support at *mspinput@microsoft.com*.

Please note that product support for Microsoft software and hardware is not offered through the previous addresses. For help with Microsoft software or hardware, go to *https://support.microsoft.com*.

# We want to hear from you

At Microsoft Press, your satisfaction is our top priority, and your feedback our most valuable asset. Please tell us what you think of this book at:

*https://aka.ms/tellpress*

We know you're busy, so we've kept it short with just a few questions. Your answers go directly to the editors at Microsoft Press. (No personal information will be requested.) Thanks in advance for your input!

# Stay in touch

Let's keep the conversation going! We're on Twitter: *http://twitter.com/MicrosoftPress*.

# Important: How to use this book to study for the exam

Certification exams validate your on-the-job experience and product knowledge. To gauge your readiness to take an exam, use this Exam Ref to help you check your understanding of the skills tested by the exam. Determine the topics you know well and the areas in which you need more experience. To help you refresh your skills in specific areas, we have also provided "Need more review?" pointers, which direct you to more in-depth information outside the book.

The Exam Ref is not a substitute for hands-on experience. This book is not designed to teach you new skills.

We recommend that you round out your exam preparation by using a combination of available study materials and courses. Learn more about available classroom training at *https://www.microsoft.com/learning*. Microsoft Official Practice Tests are available for many exams at *https://aka.ms/practicetests*. You can also find free online courses and live events from Microsoft Virtual Academy at *https://www.microsoftvirtualacademy.com*.

This book is organized by the "Skills measured" list published for the exam. The "Skills measured" list for each exam is available on the Microsoft Learning website: *https://aka.ms/examlist*.

Note that this Exam Ref is based on this publicly available information and the author's experience. To safeguard the integrity of the exam, authors do not have access to the exam questions.

## CHAPTER 1

# Design and implement database objects

Developing and implementing a database for SQL Server starts with understanding both the process of designing a database and the basic structures that make up a database. A firm grip on those fundamentals is a must for an SQL Server developer, and is even more important for taking this exam.

We begin with the fundamentals of a typical database meant to store information about a business. This is generally referred to as online transaction processing (OLTP), where the goal is to store data that accurately reflects what happens in the business in a manner that works well for the applications. For this pattern, we review the relational database design pattern, which is covered in Skill 1.1. OLTP databases can be used to store more than business transactions, including the ability to store any data about your business, such as customer details, appointments, and so on.

> **IMPORTANT**
>
> **Have you read page xv?**
>
> It contains valuable information regarding the skills you need to pass the exam.

Skills 1.2 and 1.3 cover some of the basic constructs, including indexes and views, that go into forming the physical database structures (Transact-SQL code) that applications use to create the foundational objects your applications use to do business.

In Skill 1.4 we explore columnstore indexes that focus strictly on analytics. While discussing analytics, we look at the de facto standard for building reporting structures called dimensional design. In dimensional design, the goal is to format the data in a form that makes it easier to extract results from large sets of data without touching a lot of different structures.

## Skills in this chapter:

- Design and implement a relational database schema
- Design and implement indexes
- Design and implement views
- Implement columnstore indexes

# Skill 1.1: Design and implement a relational database schema

In this section, we review some of the factors that go into creating the base tables that make up a relational database. The process of creating a relational database is not tremendously difficult. People build similar structures using Microsoft Excel every day. In this section, we are going to look at the basic steps that are needed to get started creating a database in a professional manner.

> **This section covers how to:**
> - Design tables and schemas based on business requirements
> - Improve the design of tables by using normalization
> - Write create table statements
> - Determine the most efficient data types to use

## Designing tables and schemas based on business requirements

A very difficult part of any project is taking the time to gather business requirements. Not because it is particularly difficult in terms of technical skills, but because it takes lots of time and attention to detail. This exam that you are studying for is about developing the database, and the vast majority of topics center on the mechanical processes around the creation of objects to store and manipulate data via Transact-SQL code. However, the first few sections of this skill focus on required skills prior to actually writing Transact-SQL.

Most of the examples in this book, and likely on the exam, are abstract, contrived, and targeted to a single example; either using a sample database from Microsoft, or using examples that include only the minimal details for the particular concept being reviewed. There are, however, a few topics that require a more detailed narrative. To review the topic of designing a database, we need to start out with some basic requirements, using them to design a database that demonstrates database design concepts and normalization.

We have a scenario that defines a database need, including some very basic requirements. Questions on the exam can easily follow this pattern of giving you a small set of requirements and table structures that you need to match to the requirements. This scenario will be used as the basis for the first two sections of this chapter.

Imagine that you are trying to write a system to manage an inventory of computers and computer peripherals for a large organization. Someone has created a document similar in scope to the following scenario (realistic requirements are often hundreds or even thousands of pages long, but you can learn a lot from a single paragraph):

*We have 1,000 computers, comprised of laptops, workstations, and tablets. Each computer has items associated with it, which we will list as mouse, keyboard, etc. Each computer has a tag number associated with it, and is tagged on each device with a tag graphic that can be read by tag readers manufactured by "Trey Research" (http://www.treyresearch.net/) or "Litware, Inc" (http://www.litwareinc.com/). Of course tag numbers are unique across tag readers. We don't know which employees are assigned which computers, but all computers that cost more than $300 are inventoried for the first three years after purchase using a different software system. Finally, employees need to have their names recorded, along with their employee number in this system.*

Let's look for the tables and columns that match the needs of the requirements. We won't actually create any tables yet, because this is just the first step in the process of database design. In the next section, we spend time looking at specific tests that we apply to our design, followed by two sections on creating the table structures of a database.

The process of database design involves scanning requirements, looking for key types of words and phrases. For tables, you look for the nouns such as "computers" or "employee." These can be tables in your final database. Some of these nouns you discover in the requirements are simply subsets of one another: "computer" and "laptop." For example, laptop is not necessarily its own table at all, but instead may be just a type of computer. Whether or not you need a specific table for laptops, workstations, or tablets isn't likely to be important. The point is to match a possible solution with a set of requirements.

After scanning for nouns, you have your list of likely objects on which to save data. These will typically become tables after we complete our design, but still need to be refined by the normalization process that we will cover in the next section:

1. Computer
2. Employee

The next step is to look for attributes of each object. You do this by scanning the text looking for bits of information that might be stored about each object. For the Computer object, you see that there is a Type of Computer (laptop, workstation, or tablet), an Associated Item List, a Tag, a Tag Company, and a Tag Company URL, along with the Cost of the computer and employee that the computer is assigned to. Additionally, in the requirements, we also have the fact that they keep the computer inventoried for the first three years after purchase if it is > $300, so we need to record the Purchase Date. For the Employee object we are required to capture their Name and Employee Number.

Now we have the basic table structures to extract from the requirements, (though we still require some refinement in the following section on normalization) and we also define *schemas*, which are security/organizational groupings of tables and code for our implemented database. In our case, we define two schemas: Equipment and HumanResources.

Our design consists of the following possible tables and columns:

1. Equipment.Computer: (ComputerType, AssociatedItemList, Tag, TagCompany, TagCompanyURL, ComputerCost, PurchaseDate, AssignedEmployee)

2. HumanResources.Employee: (Name, EmployeeNumber)

The next step in the process is to look for how you would uniquely identify a row in your potential database. For example, how do you tell one computer from another. In the requirements, we are told that, "Each computer has a tag number," so we will identify that the Tag attribute must be unique for each Computer.

This process of designing the database requires you to work through the requirements until you have a set of tables that match the requirements you've been given.

In the real world, you don't alter the design from the provided requirements unless you discuss it with the customer. And in an exam question, you do whatever is written, regardless of whether it makes perfect sense. Do you need the URL of the TagCompany,for instance? If so, why? For the purposes of this exam, we will focus on the process of translating words into tables.

> **NOTE** **LOGICAL DATABASE MODEL**
>
> Our progress so far in designing this sample database is similar to what is referred to as a logical database model. For brevity, we have skipped some of the steps in a realistic design process. We continue to refine this example in upcoming sections.

# Improving the design of tables by using normalization

Normalization is a set of "rules" that cover some of the most fundamental structural issues with relational database designs (there are other issues beyond normalization—for example, naming—that we do not talk about.) All of the rules are very simple at their core and each will deal with eliminating some issue that is problematic to the users of a database when trying to store data with the least redundancy and highest potential for performance using SQL Server 2016's relational engine.

The typical approach in database design is to work instinctively and then use the principles of normalization as a test to your design. You can expect questions on normalization to be similar, asking questions like, "is this a well-designed table to meet some requirement?" and any of the normal forms that might apply.

However, in this section, we review the normal forms individually, just to make the review process more straightforward. The rules are stated in terms of *forms*, some of which are numbered, and some which are named for the creators of the rule. The rules form a progression, with each rule becoming more and more strict. To be in a stricter normal form, you need to also conform to the lesser form, though none of these rules are ever followed one hundred percent of the time.

The most important thing to understand will be the concepts of normalization, and particularly how to verify that a design is normalized. In the following sections, we will review two families of normalization concepts:

- Rules covering the shape of a table
- Rules covering the relationship of non-key attributes to key attributes

## Rules covering the shape of a table

A table's structure—based on what SQL Server (and most relational database management systems, or RDBMSs) allow—is a very loose structure. Tables consist of rows and columns. You can put anything you want in the table, and you can have millions, even billions of rows. However, just because you *can* do something, doesn't mean it is correct.

The first part of these rules is defined by the mathematical definition of a relation (which is more or less synonymous with the proper structure of a table). Relations require that you have no duplicated rows. In database terminology, a column or set of columns that are used to uniquely identify one row from another is called a *key*. There are several types of keys we discuss in the following section, and they are all columns to identify a row (other than what is called a foreign key, which are columns in a table that reference another table's key attributes). Continuing with the example we started in the previous section, we have one such example in our design so far with: HumanResources.Employee: (Name, EmployeeNumber).

Using the Employee table definition that we started with back in the first section of this chapter, it would be allowable to have the following two rows of data represented:

```
Name                                EmployeeNumber
----------------------------------- ----------------
Harmetz, Adam                       000010012
Harmetz, Adam                       000010012
```

This would not be a proper table, since you cannot tell one row from another. Many people try to fix this by adding some random bit of data (commonly called an *artificial key* value), like some auto generated number. This then provides a structure with data like the following, with some more data that is even more messed up, but still legal as the structure allows:

```
EmployeeId Name                            EmployeeNumber
---------- ------------------------------- ------------------------
         1 Harmetz, Adam                   000010012
         2 Harmetz, Adam                   000010012
         3 Popkova, Darya                  000000013
         4 Popkova, Darya                  000000013
```

In the next section on creating tables, we begin the review of ways we can enforce the uniqueness on data in column(s), but for now, let's keep it strictly in design mode. While this seems to make the table *better*, unless the EmployeeId column actually has some meaning to the user, all that has been done is to make the problem worse because someone looking for

Adam's information can get one row or the other. What we really want is some sort of data in the table that makes the data unique based on data the user chooses. Name is not the correct choice, because two people can have the same name, but EmployeeNumber is data that the user knows, and is used in an organization to identify an employee. A key like this is commonly known as a *natural key*. When your table is created, the artificial key is referred to as a *surrogate key*, which means it is a stand-in for the natural key for performance reasons. We talk more about these concepts in the "Determining the most efficient data types to use" section and again in Chapter 2, Skill 2.1 when choosing UNIQUE and PRIMARY KEY constraints.

After defining that EmployeeNumber must be unique, our table of data looks like the following:

```
EmployeeId Name                                 EmployeeNumber
---------- ------------------------------- ---------------------
         1 Harmetz, Adam                        000010012
         2 Popkova, Darya                       000000013
```

The next two criteria concerning row shape are defined in the First Normal Form. It has two primary requirements that your table design must adhere to:

1. All columns must be atomic—that is, each column should represent one value
2. All rows of a table must contain the same number of values—no arrays

Starting with atomic column values, consider that we have a column in the Employee table we are working on that probably has a non-atomic value (*probably* because it is based on the requirements). Be sure to read the questions carefully to make sure you are not assuming things. The name column has values that contain a delimiter between what turns out to be the last name and first name of the person. If this is always the case then you need to record the first and last name of the person separately. So in our table design, we will break 'Harmetz, Adam' into first name: 'Adam' and last name: 'Harmetz'. This is represented here:

```
EmployeeId LastName         FirstName        EmployeeNumber
---------- ---------------- ---------------- ----------------
         1 Harmetz          Adam             000010012
         2 Popkova          Darya            000000013
```

For our design, let's leave off the EmployeeId column for clarity in the design. So the structure looks like:

```
HumanResources.Employee (EmployeeNumber [key], LastName, FirstName)
```

Obviously the value here is that when you need to search for someone named 'Adam,' you don't need to search on a partial value. Queries on partial values, particularly when the partial value does not include the leftmost character of a string, are not ideal for SQL Server's indexing strategies. So, the desire is that every column represents just a single value. In reality, names are always more complex than just last name and first name, because people have suffixes and titles that they really want to see beside their name (for example, if it was Dr. Darya Popkova, feelings could be hurt if the Dr. was dropped in correspondence with them.)

The second criteria for the first normal form is the rule about no repeating groups/arrays. A lot of times, the data that doesn't fit the atomic criteria is not the same item, such as parts of a name, but rather it's a list of items that are the same types of things. For example, in our requirements, there is a column in the Computer table that is a list of items named AssociatedItemList and the example: 'mouse, keyboard.' Looking at this data, a row might look like the following:

```
Tag    AssociatedItemList
------ ------------------------------------
 s344  mouse, keyboard
```

From here, there are a few choices. If there are always two items associated to a computer, you might add a column for the first item, and again for a second item to the structure. But that is not what we are told in the requirements. They state: "Each computer has items associated with it." This can be any number of items. Since the goal is to make sure that column values are atomic, we definitely want to get rid of the column containing the delimited list. So the next inclination is to make a repeating group of column values, like:

```
Tag    AssociatedItem1 AssociatedItem2 … AssociatedItemN
------ --------------- --------------- … ----------------
 s344  mouse           keyboard        … not applicable
```

This however, is not the desired outcome, because now you have created a fixed array of associated items with an index in the column name. It is very inflexible, and is limited to the number of columns you want to add. Even worse is that if you need to add something like a tag to the associated items, you end up with a structure that is very complex to work with:

```
Tag    AssociatedItem1 AssociatedItem1Tag AssociatedItem2 AssociatedItem2Tag
------ --------------- ------------------ --------------- ------------------
 s344  mouse           r232               keyboard        q472
```

Instead of this structure, create a new table that has a reference back to the original table, and the attributes that are desired:

```
Tag    AssociatedItem
------ ----------------
 s344  mouse
 s344  keyboard
```

So our object is: Equipment.ComputerAssociatedItem (Tag [Reference to Computer], AssociatedItem, [key Tag, AssociatedItem]).

Now, if you need to search for computers that have keyboards associated, you don't need to either pick it out of a comma delimited list, nor do you need to look in multiple columns. Assuming you are reviewing for this exam, and already know a good deal about how indexes and queries work, you should see that everything we have done in this first section on normalization is going to be great for performance. The entire desire is to make scalar values that index well and can be searched for. It is never wrong to do a partial value search (if you can't remember how keyboard is spelled, for example, looking for associated items LIKE '%k%' isn't a violation of any moral laws, it just isn't a design goal that you are be trying to attain.

## Rules covering the relationship of non-key attributes to key attributes

Once your data is shaped in a form that works best for the engine, you need to look at the relationship between attributes, looking for redundant data being stored that can get out of sync. In the first normalization section covering the shape of attributes, the tables were formed to ensure that each row in the structure was unique by choosing keys. For our two primary objects so far, we have:

```
HumanResources.Employee (EmployeeNumber)

Equipment.Computer (Tag)
```

In this section, we are going to look at how the other columns in the table relate to the key attributes. There are three normal forms that are related to this discussion:

- **Second Normal Form**    All attributes must be a fact about the entire primary key and not a subset of the primary key.
- **Third Normal Form**    All attributes must be a fact about the entire primary key, and not any non-primary key attributes

  For the second normal form to be a concern, you must have a table with multiple columns in the primary key. For example, say you have a table that defines a car parked in a parking space. This table can have the following columns:

  - **CarLicenseTag** (Key Column1)
  - **SpaceNumber** (Key Column2)
  - **ParkedTime**
  - **CarColor**
  - **CarModel**
  - **CarManufacturer**
  - **CarManufacturerHeadquarters**

  Each of the non-key attributes should say something about the combination of the two key attributes. The ParkedTime column is the time when the car was parked. This attribute makes sense. The others are all specifically about the car itself. So you need another table that looks like the following where all of the columns are moved to (the CarLicenseTag column stays as a reference to this new table. Now you have a table that represents the details about a car with the following columns:

  - **CarLicenseTag** (Key Column)
  - **CarColor**
  - **CarModel**
  - **CarManufacturer**
  - **CarManufacturerHeadquarters**

  Since there is a single key column, this must be in second normal form (like how the table we left behind with the CarLicenseTag, SpaceNumber and ParkedTime since

ParkedTime references the entire key.) Now we turn our attention to the third normal form. Here we make sure that each attribute is solely focused on the primary key column. A car has a color, a model, and a manufacturer. But does it have a CarManufacturerHeadquarters? No, the manufacturer does. So you would create another table for that attribute and the key CarManufacturer. Progress through the design making more tables until you have eliminated redundancy.

The redundancy is troublesome because if you were to change the headquarter location for a manufacturer, you might need to do so for more than the one row or end up with mismatched data. Raymond Boyce and Edgar Codd (the original author of the normalization forms), refined these two normal forms into the following normal form, named after them:

- **Boyce-Codd Normal Form**   Every candidate key is identified, all attributes are fully dependent on a key, and all columns must identify a fact about a key and nothing but a key.

All of these forms are stating that once you have set what columns uniquely define a row in a table, the rest of the columns should refer to what the key value represents. Continuing with the design based on the scenario/requirement we have used so far in the chapter, consider the Equipment.Computer table. We have the following columns defined (Note that AssociatedItemList was removed from the table in the previous section):

Tag (key attribute), ComputerType, TagCompany, TagCompanyURL, ComputerCost, PurchaseDate, AssignedEmployee

In this list of columns for the Computer table, your job is to decide which of these columns describes what the Tag attribute is identifying, which is a computer. The Tag column value itself does not seem to describe the computer, and that's fine. It is a number that has been associated with a computer by the business in order to be able to tell two physical devices apart. However, for each of the other attributes, it's important to decide if the attribute describes something about the computer, or something else entirely. It is a good idea to take each column independently and think about what it means.

- **ComputerType**   Describes the type of computer that is being inventoried.
- **TagCompany**   The tag has a tag company, and since we defined that the tag number was unique across companies, this attribute is violating the Boyce-Codd Normal Form and must be moved to a different table.
- **TagCompanyURL**   Much like TagCompany, the URL for the company is definitely not describing the computer.
- **ComputerCost**   Describes how much the computer cost when purchased.
- **PurchaseDate**   Indicates when the computer was purchased.
- **AssignedEmployee**   This is a reference to the Employee structure. So while a computer doesn't really have an assigned employee in the real world, it does make sense

in the overall design as it describes an attribute of the computer as it stands in the business.

Now, our design for these two tables looks like the following:

Equipment.Computer (Tag [key, ref to Tag], ComputerType, ComputerCost, PurchaseDate, AssignedEmployee [Reference to Employee])

Equipment.Tag (Tag [key], TagCompany, TagCompanyURL)

If the tables have the same key columns, do we need two tables? This depends on your requirements, but it is not out of the ordinary that you have two tables that are related to one another with a cardinality of one-to-one. In this case, you have a pool of tags that get created, and then assigned, to a device, or tags could have more than one use. Make sure to always take your time and understand the requirements that you are given with your question.

So we now have:

Equipment.Computer (Tag [key, Ref to Tag], ComputerType, ComputerCost, PurchaseDate, AssignedEmployee [Reference to Employee]

Equipment.TagCompany (TagCompany [key], TagCompanyURL)

Equipment.Tag (Tag [key], TagCompany [Reference to TagCompany])

And we have this, in addition to the objects we previously specified:

Equipment.ComputerAssociatedItem (Tag [Reference to Computer], AssociatedItem, [key Tag, AssociatedItem])

HumanResources.Employee (EmployeeNumber [key], LastName, FirstName)

Generally speaking, the third normal form is referred to as the most important normal form, and for the exam it is important to understand that each table has one meaning, and each scalar attribute refers to the entire natural key of the final objects. Good practice can be had by working through tables in your own databases, or in our examples, such as the WideWorldImporters (the newest example database they have created), AdventureWorks, Northwind, or even Pubs. None of these databases are perfect, because doing an excellent job designing a database sometimes makes for really complex examples. Note that we don't have the detailed requirements for these sample databases. Don't be tricked by thinking you know what a system should look like by experience. The only thing worse than having no knowledge of your customer's business is having too much knowledge of their business.

> **NEED MORE REVIEW?** **DATABASE DESIGN AND NORMALIZATION**
>
> What has been covered in this book is a very small patterns and techniques for database design that exist in the real world, and does not represent all of the normal forms that have been defined. Boyce-Codd/Third normal form is generally the limit of most writers. For more information on the complete process of database design, check out "Pro SQL Server Relational Database Design and Implementation," written by Louis Davidson for Apress in 2016. Or, for a more academic look at the process, get the latest edition of "An Introduction to Database Systems" by Chris Date with Pearson Press.

One last term needs to be defined: *denormalization*. After you have normalized your database, and have tested it out, there can be reasons to undo some of the things you have done for performance. For example, later in the chapter, we add a formatted version of an employee's name. To do this, it duplicates the data in the LastName and FirstName columns of the table (in order to show a few concepts in implementation). A poor design for this is to have another column that the user can edit, because they might not get the name right. Better implementations are available in the implementation of a database.

## Writing table create statements

The hard work in creating a database is done at this point of the process, and the process now is to simply translate a design into a physical database. In this section, we'll review the basic syntax of creating tables. In Chapter 2 we delve a bit deeper into the discussion about how to choose proper uniqueness constraints but we cover the mechanics of including such objects here.

Before we move onto CREATE TABLE statements, a brief discussion on object naming is useful. You sometimes see names like the following used to name a table that contain rows of purchase orders:

- PurchaseOrder
- PURCHASEORDER
- PO
- purchase_orders
- tbl_PurchaseOrder
- A12
- [Purchase Order] or "Purchase Order"

Of these naming styles, there are a few that are typically considered sub-optimal:

- **PO**   Using abbreviations, unless universally acceptable tend to make a design more complex for newcomers and long-term users alike.
- **PURCHASEORDER**   All capitals tends to make your design like it is 1970, which can hide some of your great work to make a modern computer system.
- **tbl_PurchaseOrder**   Using a clunky prefix to say that this is a table reduces the documentation value of the name by making users ask what tbl means (admittedly this could show up in exam questions as it is not universally disliked).
- **A12**   This indicates that this is a database where the designer is trying to hide the details of the database from the user.
- **[Purchase Order] or "Purchase Order"**   Names that require delimiters, [brackets], or "double-quotes" are terribly hard to work with. Of the delimiter types, double-quotes are more standards-oriented, while the brackets are more typical SQL Server coding. Between the delimiters you can use any Unicode characters.

The more normal, programmer friendly naming standards are using Pascal-casing (Leading character capitalized, words concatenated: PurchaseOrder), Camel Casing (leading character lower case: purchaseOrder), or using underscores as delimiters (purchase_order).

> **NEED MORE REVIEW?** **DATABASE NAMING RULES**
>
> This is a very brief review of naming objects. Object names must fall in the guidelines of a database identifier, which has a few additional rules. You can read more about database identifiers here in this MSDN article: *https://msdn.microsoft.com/en-us/library/ms175874.aspx*.

Sometimes names are plural, and sometimes singular, and consistency is the general key. For the exam, there are likely to be names of any format, plural, singular, or both. Other than interpreting the meaning of the name, naming is not listed as a skill.

To start with, create a schema to put objects in. Schemas allow you to group together objects for security and logical ordering. By default, there is a schema in every database called dbo, which is there for the database owner. For most example code in this chapter, we use a schema named Examples located in a database named ExamBook762Ch1, which you see referenced in some error messages.

```
CREATE SCHEMA Examples;
GO --CREATE SCHEMA must be the only statement in the batch
```

The CREATE SCHEMA statement is terminated with a semicolon at the end of the statement. All statements in Transact-SQL can be terminated with a semicolon. While not all statements must end with a semicolon in SQL Server 2016, not terminating statements with a semicolon is a deprecated feature, so it is a good habit to get into. GO is not a statement in Transact-SQL it is a batch separator that splits your queries into multiple server communications, so it does not need (or allow) termination.

To create our first table, start with a simple structure that's defined to hold the name of a widget, with attributes for name and a code:

```
CREATE TABLE Examples.Widget
(
    WidgetCode  varchar(10) NOT NULL
         CONSTRAINT PKWidget PRIMARY KEY,
    WidgetName  varchar(100) NULL
);
```

Let's break down this statement into parts:

```
CREATE TABLE Examples.Widget
```

Here we are naming the table to be created. The name of the table must be unique from all other object names across its database schema, including tables, views, constraints, procedures, etc. Note that it is a best practice to reference all objects explicitly by at least their two-part names, which includes the name of the object prefixed with a schema name, so most of the code in this book will use two-part names. In addition, object names that a user may reference directly such as tables, views, stored procedures, etc. have a total of four possible parts. For example, Server.Database.Schema.Object has the following parts:

- **Server**   The local server, or a linked server name that has been configured. By default, the local server from which you are executing the query.
- **Database**   The database where the object you are addressing resides. By default, this is the database that to which you have set your context.
- **Schema**   The name of the schema where the object you are accessing resides within the database. Every login has a default schema which defaults to dbo. If the schema is not specified, the default schema will be searched for a matching name.
- **Object**   The name of the object you are accessing, which is not optional.

In the CREATE TABLE statement, if you omit the schema, it is created in the default schema. So the CREATE TABLE Widget would, by default, create the table dbo.Widget in the database of context. You can create the table in a different database by specifying the database name: CREATE TABLE Tempdb..Widget or Tempdb.dbo.Widget. There is an article here: (*https://technet.microsoft.com/en-us/library/ms187879.aspx*.) from an older version of books online that show you the many different forms of addressing an object.

The next line:

```
WidgetCode  varchar(10) NOT NULL
```

This specifies the name of the column, then the data type of that column. There are many different data types, and we examine their use and how to make the best choice in the next section. For now, just leave it as this determines the format of the data that is stored in this column. NOT NULL indicates that you must have a known value for the column. If it simply said NULL, then it indicates the value of the column is allowed to be NULL.

NULL is a special value that mathematically means UNKNOWN. A few simple equations that can help clarify NULL is that: UNKNOWN + any value = UNKNOWN, and NOT(UNKNOWN) = UNKNOWN. If you don't know a value, adding any other value to it is still unknown. And if you don't know if a value is TRUE or FALSE, the opposite of that is still not known. In comparisons, A NULL expression is never equivalent to a NULL expression. So if you have the following conditional: IF (NULL = NULL); the expression would not be TRUE, so it would not succeed.

If you leave off the NULL specification, whether or not the column allows NULL values is based on a couple of things. If the column is not part of a PRIMARY KEY constraint that is being added in the CREATE TABLE statement (like in the next line of code), or the setting: SET ANSI_NULL_DFLT_ON, then NULL values are allowed.

> **NOTE   NULL SPECIFICATION**
>
> For details on the SET ANSI_NULL_DFLT_ON setting, go to *https://msdn.microsoft.com/en-us/library/ms187375.aspx*.). It is considered a best practice to always specify a NULL specification for columns in your CREATE and ALTER table statements.

The following line of code is a continuation of the previous line of code, since it was not terminated with a comma (broken out to make it easier to explain):

```
CONSTRAINT PKWidget PRIMARY KEY,
```

This is how you add a constraint to a single column. In this case, we are defining that the WidgetCode column is the only column that makes up the primary key of the table. The CONSTRAINT PKWidget names the constraint. The constraint name must be unique within the schema, just like the table name. If you leave the name off and just code it as PRIMARY KEY, SQL Server provides a name that is guaranteed unique, such as PK__Widget__1E5F7A7F7A139099. Such a name changes every time you create the constraint, so it's really only suited to temporary tables (named either with # or ## as a prefix for local or global temporary objects, respectively).

Alternatively, this PRIMARY KEY constraint could have been defined independently of the column definition as (with the leading comma there for emphasis):

```
,CONSTRAINT PKWidget PRIMARY KEY (WidgetCode),
```

This form is needed when you have more than one column in the PRIMARY KEY constraint, like if both the WidgetCode and WidgetName made up the primary key value:

```
,CONSTRAINT PKWidget PRIMARY KEY (WidgetCode, WidgetName),
```

This covers the simple version of the CREATE TABLE statement, but there are a few additional settings to be aware of. First, if you want to put your table on a file group other than the default one, you use the ON clause:

```
CREATE TABLE Examples.Widget
(
    WidgetCode  varchar(10) NOT NULL
            CONSTRAINT PKWidget PRIMARY KEY,
    WidgetName  varchar(100) NULL
) ON FileGroupName;
```

There are also table options for using temporal extensions, as well as partitioning. These are not a part of this exam, so we do not cover them in any detail, other than to note their existence.

In addition to being able to use the CREATE TABLE statement to create a table, it is not uncommon to encounter the ALTER TABLE statement on the exam to add or remove a constraint. The ALTER TABLE statement allows you to add columns to a table and make changes to some settings.

For example, you can add a column using:

```
ALTER TABLE Examples.Widget
    ADD NullableColumn int NULL;
```

If there is data in the table, you either have to create the column to allow NULL values, or create a DEFAULT constraint along with the column (which is covered in greater detail in Chapter 2, Skill 2.1).

```
ALTER TABLE Examples.Widget
    ADD NotNullableColumn int NOT NULL
        CONSTRAINT DFLTWidget_NotNullableColumn DEFAULT ('Some Value');
```
To drop the column, you need to drop referencing constraints, which you also do with the ALTER TABLE statement:

```
ALTER TABLE Examples.Widget
    DROP DFLTWidget_NotNullableColumn;
```

Finally, we will drop this column (because it would be against the normalization rules we have discussed to have this duplicated data) using:

```
ALTER TABLE Examples.Widget
    DROP COLUMN NotNullableColumn;
```

> **NEED MORE REVIEW?**   **CREATING AND ALTERING TABLES**
>
> We don't touch on everything about the CREATE TABLE or ALTER TABLE statement, but you can read more about the various additional settings you can see in Books Online in the CREATE TABLE (*https://msdn.microsoft.com/en-us/library/ms174979.aspx*) and ALTER TABLE (*https://msdn.microsoft.com/en-us/library/ms190273.aspx*) topics.

# Determining the most efficient data types to use

Every column in a database has a data type, which is the first in a series of choices to limit what data can be stored. There are data types for storing numbers, characters, dates, times, etc., and it's your job to make sure you have picked the very best data type for the need. Choosing the best type has immense value for the systems implemented using the database.

- **It serves as the first limitation of domain of data values that the columns can store.**   If the range of data desired is the name of the days of the week, having a column that allows only integers is completely useless. If you need the values in a column to be between 0 and 350, a tinyint won't work because it has a maximum of 256, so a better choice is smallint, that goes between −32,768 and 32,767, In Chapter 2, we look at several techniques using CONSTRAINT and TRIGGER objects to limit a column's value even further.

- **It is important for performance**   Take a value that represents the 12th of July, 1999. You could store it in a char(30) as '12th of July, 1999', or in a char(8) as '19990712'. Searching for one value in either case requires knowledge of the format, and doing ranges of date values is complex, and even very costly, performance-wise. Using a date data type makes the coding natural for the developer and the query processor.

When handled improperly, data types are frequently a source of interesting issues for users. Don't limit data enough, and you end up with incorrect, wildly formatted data. Limit too much, like only allowing 35 letters for a last name, and Janice "Lokelani" Keihanaikukauakahihuliheeka-haunaele has to have her name truncated on her driver's license (true story, as you can see in the following article on USA Today *http://www.usatoday.com/story/news/nation/2013/12/30/hawaii-long-name/4256063/*).

SQL Server has an extensive set of data types that you can choose from to match almost any need. The following list contains the data types along with notes about storage and purpose where needed.

- **Precise Numeric** Stores number-based data with loss of precision in how it stored.

  - **bit** Has a domain of 1, 0, or NULL; Usually used as a pseudo-Boolean by using 1 = True, 0 = False, NULL = Unknown. Note that some typical integer operations, like basic math, cannot be performed. (1 byte for up to 8 values)

  - **tinyint** Integers between 0 and 255 (1 byte).

  - **smallint** Integers between –32,768 and 32,767 (2 bytes).

  - **int** Integers between -2,147,483,648 to 2,147,483,647 (–2^31 to 2^31 – 1) (4 bytes).

  - **bigint** Integers between -9,223,372,036,854,775,808 to 9,223,372,036,854,775,807 (-2^63 to 2^63 – 1) (8 bytes).

  - **decimal   (or numeric which are functionally the same, with decimal the more standard type)**: All numbers between –10^38 – 1 and 10^38 – 1, with a fixed set of digits up to 38. decimal(3,2) would be a number between -9.99 and 9.99. And decimal(38,37), with be a number with one digit before the decimal point, and 37 places after it. Uses between 5 and 17 bytes, depending on precision.

  - **money** Monetary values from –922,337,203,685,477.5808 through 922,337,203,685,477.5807 (8 bytes).

  - **smallmoney** Money values from –214,748.3648 through 214,748.3647 (4 bytes).

- **Approximate numeric data** Stores approximations of numbers based on IEEE 754 standard, typically for scientific usage. Allows a large range of values with a high amount of precision but you lose precision of very large or very small numbers.

  - **float(N)** Values in the range from –1.79E + 308 through 1.79E + 308 (storage varies from 4 bytes for N between 1 and 24, and 8 bytes for N between 25 and 53).

  - **real** Values in the range from –3.40E + 38 through 3.40E + 38. real is an ISO synonym for a float(24) data type, and hence equivalent (4 bytes).

- **Date and time values** Stores values that deal storing a point in time.

  - **date** Date-only values from January 1, 0001, to December 31, 9999 (3 bytes).

  - **time(N)** Time-of-day-only values with N representing the fractional parts of a second that can be stored. time(7) is down to HH:MM:SS.0000001 (3 to 5 bytes).

  - **datetime2(N)** This type stores a point in time from January 1, 0001, to December 31, 9999, with accuracy just like the *time* type for seconds (6 to 8 bytes).

  - **datetimeoffset** Same as datetime2, plus includes an offset for time zone offset (does not deal with daylight saving time) (8 to 10 bytes).

- **smalldatetime**   A point in time from January 1, 1900, through June 6, 2079, with accuracy to 1 minute (4 bytes).

- **datetime**   Points in time from January 1, 1753, to December 31, 9999, with accuracy to 3.33 milliseconds (so the series of fractional seconds starts as: .003, .007, .010, .013, .017 and so on) (8 bytes).

- **Binary data**   Strings of bits used for storing things like files, encrypted values, etc. Storage for these data types is based on the size of the data stored in bytes, plus any overhead for variable length data.

  - **binary(N)**   Fixed-length binary data with a maximum value of N of 8000, for an 8,000 byte long binary value.

  - **varbinary(N)**   Variable-length binary data with maximum value of N of 8,000.

  - **varbinary(max)**   Variable-length binary data up to $(2^{31}) - 1$ bytes (2GB) long. Values are often stored using filestream filegroups, which allow you to access files directly via the Windows API, and directly from the Windows File Explorer using filetables.

- **Character (or string) data**   String values, used to store text values. Storage is specified in number of characters in the string.

  - **char(N)**   Fixed-length character data up to 8,000 characters long. When using fixed length data types, it is best if most of the values in the column are the same, or at least use most of the column.

  - **varchar(N)**   Variable-length character data up to 8,000 characters long.

  - **varchar(max)**   Variable-length character data up to $(2^{31}) - 1$ bytes (2GB) long. This is a very long string of characters, and should be used with caution as returning rows with 2GB per row can be hard on your network connection.

  - **nchar, nvarchar, nvarchar(max)**   Unicode equivalents of char, varchar, and varchar(max). Unicode is a double (and in some cases triple) byte character set that allows for more than the 256 characters at a time that the ASCII characters do. Support for Unicode is covered in detail in this article: *https://msdn.microsoft.com/ en-us/library/ms143726.aspx*. It is generally accepted that it is best to use Unicode when storing any data where you have no control over the data that is entered. For example, object names in SQL Server allow Unicode names, to support most any characters that a person might want to use for names. It is very common that columns for people's names are stored in Unicode to allow for a full range of characters to be stored.

- **Other data types**   Here are a few more data types:

  - **sql_variant**   Stores nearly any data type, other than CLR based ones like hierarchyId, spatial types, and types with a maximum length of over 8016 bytes. Infrequently used for patterns where the data type of a value is unknown before design time.

- **rowversion** (**timestamp** is a synonym)   Used for optimistic locking to version-stamp in a row. The value in the rowversion data type-based column changes on every modification of the row. The name of this type was timestamp in all SQL Server versions before 2000, but in the ANSI SQL standards, the timestamp type is equivalent to the datetime data type. Stored as a 16-byte binary value.

- **uniqueidentifier**   Stores a globally unique identifier (GUID) value. A GUID is a commonly used data type for an artificial key, because a GUID can be generated by many different clients and be almost 100 percent assuredly unique. It has downsides of being somewhat random when being sorted in generated order, which can make it more difficult to index. We discuss indexing in Skill 1.2. Represented as a 36-character string, but is stored as a 16-byte binary value.

- **XML**   Allows you to store an XML document in a column value. The XML type gives you a rich set of functionality when dealing with structured data that cannot be easily managed using typical relational tables.

- **Spatial types**   (geometry, geography, circularString, compoundCurve, and curve-Polygon)   Used for storing spatial data, like for shapes, maps, lines, etc.

- **heirarchyId**   Used to store data about a hierarchy, along with providing methods for manipulating the hierarchy.

---

***NEED MORE REVIEW*** **DATA TYPE OVERVIEW**

**This is just an overview of the data types. For more reading on the types in the SQL Server Language Reference, visit the following URL:** *https://msdn.microsoft.com/en-us/library/ms187752.aspx.*

---

The difficultly in choosing the data type is that you often need to consider not just the requirements given, but real life needs. For example, say we had a table that represents a company and all we had was the company name. You might logically think that the following makes sense:

```
CREATE TABLE Examples.Company
(
        CompanyName     varchar(50) NOT NULL
                        CONSTRAINT PKCompany PRIMARY KEY
);
```

There are a few concerns with this choice of data type. First let's consider the length of a company name. Almost every company name will be shorter than 50 characters. But there are definitely companies that exist with much larger names than this, even if they are rare. In choosing data types, it is important to understand that you have to design your objects to allow the maximum size of data *possible*. If you could ever come across a company name that is greater than 50 characters and need to store it completely, this will not do. The second concern is character set. Using ASCII characters is great when all characters will be from A-Z (upper or lower case), and numbers. As you use more special characters, it becomes very difficult because there are only 256 ASCII characters per code page.

In an exam question, if the question was along the lines of "the 99.9 percent of the data that goes into the CompanyName column is 20 ASCII characters or less, but there is one row that has 2000 characters with Russian and Japanese characters, what data type would you use?" the answer would be nvarchar(2000). varchar(2000) would not have the right character set, nchar(2000) would be wasteful, and integer would be just plain silly.

---

> **NOTE   COLUMN DETAILS**
>
> For the exam, expect more questions along the lines of whether a column should be one version of a type or another, like varchar or nvarchar. Most any column where you are not completely in control of the values for the data (like a person's name, or external company names) should use Unicode to give the most flexibility regarding what data can go into the column.

---

There are several groups of data types to learn in order to achieve a deep understanding. For example, consider a column named Amount in a table of payments that holds the amount of a payment:

```
CREATE TABLE Examples.Payment
(
        PaymentNumber char(10) NOT NULL
                      CONSTRAINT PKPayment PRIMARY KEY,
        Amount int NOT NULL
);
```

Does the integer hold an amount? Definitely. But in most countries, monetary units are stored with a fractional part, and while you could shift the decimal point in the client, that is not the best design. What about a real data type? Real types are meant for scientific amounts where you have an extremely wide amount of values that could meet your needs, not for money where fractional parts, or even more, could be lost in precision. Would decimal(30,20) be better? Clearly. But it isn't likely that most organizations are dealing with 20 decimal places for monetary values. There is also a money data type that has 4 decimal places, and something like decimal(10,2) also works for most monetary cases. Actually, it works for any decimal or numeric types with a scale of 2 (in decimal(10,2), the 10 is the precision or number of digits in the number; and 2 is the scale, or number of places after the decimal point).

The biggest difficulty with choosing a data type goes back to the requirements. If there are given requirements that say to store a company name in 10 characters, you use 10 characters. The obvious realization is that a string like 'Blue Yonder Airlines' takes more than 10 characters (even if it is fictitious, you know real company names that won't fit in 10 characters). You should default to what the requirements state (and in the non-exam world verify it with the customer.) All of the topics in this Skill 1.1 section, and on the exam should be taken from the requirements/question text. If the client gives you specific specifications to follow, you follow them. If the client says "store a company name" and gives you no specific limits, then you use the best data type. The exam is multiple choice, so unlike a job interview where you might be asked to give your reasoning, you just choose a *best* answer.

In Chapter 2, the first of the skills covered largely focuses on refining the choices in this section. For example, say the specification was to store a whole number between -20 and 2,000,000,000. The int data type stores all of those values, but also stores far more value. The goal is to make sure that 100 percent of the values that are stored meet the required range. Often we need to limit a value to a set of values in the same or a different table. Data type alone doesn't do it, but it gets you started on the right path, something you could be asked.

Beyond the basic data type, there are a couple of additional constructs that extend the concept of a data type. They are:

- **Computed Columns**   These are columns that are based on an expression. This allows you to use any columns in the table to form a new value that combines/reformats one or more columns.

- **Dynamic Data Masking**   Allows you to mask the data in a column from users, allowing data to be stored that is private in ways that can show a user parts of the data.

## Computed columns

Computed columns let you manifest an expression as a column for usage (particularly so that the engine maintains values for you that do not meet the normalization rules we discussed earlier). For example, say you have a table with columns FirstName and LastName, and want to include a column named FullName. If FullName was a column, it would be duplicated data that we would need to manage and maintain, and the values could get out of sync. But adding it as a computed column means that the data is either be instantiated at query time or, if you specify it and the expression is deterministic, persisted.  (A deterministic calculation is one that returns the same value for every execution. For example, the COALESCE() function, which returns the first non-NULL value in the parameter list, is deterministic, but the GETDATE() function is not, as every time you perform it, you could get a different value.)

So we can create the following:

```
CREATE TABLE Examples.ComputedColumn
(
    FirstName   nvarchar(50) NULL,
    LastName    nvarchar(50) NOT NULL,
    FullName AS CONCAT(LastName,',' + FirstName)
);
```

Now, in the FullName column, we see either LastName or LastName, FirstName for each person in our table. If you added PERSISTED to the end of the declaration, as in:

```
ALTER TABLE Examples.ComputedColumn DROP COLUMN FullName;
```

```
ALTER TABLE Examples.ComputedColumn
   ADD FullName AS CONCAT(LastName,', ' + FirstName) PERSISTED;
```

Now the expression is not evaluated during access in a statement, but is saved in the physical table storage structure along with the rest of the data. It is read only to the programmer's touch, and it's maintained by the engine. Throughout this book, one of the most important tasks for you as an exam taker is to be able to predict the output of a query, based on structures and code. Hence, when we create an object, we provide a small example explaining it. This does not replace having actually attempted everything in the book on your own (many of which you will have done professionally, but certainly not all.) These examples should give you reproducible examples to start from. In this case, consider you insert the following two rows:

```
INSERT INTO Examples.ComputedColumn
VALUES (NULL,'Harris'),('Waleed','Heloo');
```

Then query the data to see what it looks like with the following SELECT statement.

```
SELECT *
FROM    Examples.ComputedColumn;
```

You should be able to determine that the output of the statement has one name for Harris, but two comma delimited names for Waleed Heloo.

```
FirstName     LastName        FullName
------------  -------------   ---------------------
NULL          Harris          Harris
Waleed        Heloo           Heloo, Waleed
```

## Dynamic data masking

Dynamic data masking lets you mask data in a column from the view of the user. So while the user may have all rights to a column, (INSERT, UPDATE, DELETE, SELECT), when they use the column in a SELECT statement, instead of showing them the actual data, it masks it from their view. For example, if you have a table that has email addresses, you might want to mask the data so most users can't see the actual data when they are querying the data. In Books Online, the topic of Dynamic Data Masking falls under security (*https://msdn.microsoft.com/en-us/library/mt130841.aspx*), but as we will see, it doesn't behave like classic security features, as you will be adding some code to the DDL of the table, and there isn't much fine tuning of the who can access the unmasked value.

As an example, consider the following table structure, with three rows to use to show the feature in action:

```
CREATE TABLE Examples.DataMasking
(
    FirstName     nvarchar(50) NULL,
    LastName      nvarchar(50) NOT NULL,
    PersonNumber  char(10) NOT NULL,
    Status        varchar(10), --domain of values ('Active','Inactive','New')
    EmailAddress  nvarchar(50) NULL, --(real email address ought to be longer)
    BirthDate     date NOT NULL, --Time we first saw this person.
    CarCount      tinyint NOT NULL --just a count we can mask
);
```

```
INSERT INTO Examples.DataMasking(FirstName,LastName,PersonNumber, Status,
                        EmailAddress, BirthDate, CarCount)
VALUES('Jay','Hamlin','0000000014','Active','jay@litwareinc.com','1979-01-12',0),
    ('Darya','Popkova','0000000032','Active','darya.p@proseware.net','1980-05-22', 1),
    ('Tomasz','Bochenek','0000000102','Active',NULL, '1959-03-30', 1);
```

There are four types of data mask functions that we can apply:

- **Default**   Takes the default mask of the data type (not of the DEFAULT constraint of the column, but the data type).

- **Email**   Masks the email so you only see a few meaningful characters.

- **Random**   Masks any of the numeric data types (int, smallint, decimal, etc) with a random value within a range.

- **Partial**   Allows you to take values from the front and back of a value, replacing the center with a fixed string value.

Once applied, the masking function emits a masked value unless the column value is NULL, in which case the output is NULL.

Who can see the data masked or unmasked is controlled by a database level permission called UNMASK. The dbo user always has this right, so to test this, we create a different user to use after applying the masking. The user must have rights to SELECT data from the table:

```
CREATE USER MaskedView WITHOUT LOGIN;
GRANT SELECT ON Examples.DataMasking TO MaskedView;
```

The first masking type we apply is default. This masks the data with the default for the particular data type (not the default of the column itself from any DEFAULT constraint if one exists). It is applied using the ALTER TABLE...ALTER COLUMN statement, using the following syntax:

```
ALTER TABLE Examples.DataMasking ALTER COLUMN FirstName
    ADD MASKED WITH (FUNCTION = 'default()');
ALTER TABLE Examples.DataMasking ALTER COLUMN BirthDate
    ADD MASKED WITH (FUNCTION = 'default()');
```

Now, when someone without the UNMASK database right views this data, it will make the FirstName column value look like the default for string types which is 'XXXX', and the date value will appear to all be '1900-01-01'. Note that care should be taken that when you use a default that the default value isn't used for calculations. Otherwise you could send a birthday card to every customer on Jan 1, congratulating them on being over 116 years old.

> **NOTE**  **THE MASKED WITH CLAUSE**
>
> To add masking to a column in the CREATE TABLE statement, the MASKED WITH clause goes between the data type and NULL specification. For example: LastName   nvarchar(50) MASKED WITH (FUNCTION = 'default()') NOT NULL

Next, we add masking to the EmailAddress column. The email filter has no configuration, just like default(). The email() function uses fixed formatting to show the first letter of an email address, always ending in the extension .com:

```
ALTER TABLE Examples.DataMasking ALTER COLUMN EmailAddress
    ADD MASKED WITH (FUNCTION = 'email()');
```

Now the email address: darya.p@proseware.net will appear as dXXX@XXXX.com. If you wanted to mask the email address in a different manner, you could also use the following masking function.

The partial() function is by far the most powerful. It let's you take the number of characters from the front and the back of the string. For example, in the following data mask, we make the PersonNumber show the first and last characters. This column is of a fixed width, so the values will show up as the same size as previously.

```
--Note that it uses double quotes in the function call
ALTER TABLE Examples.DataMasking ALTER COLUMN PersonNumber
    ADD MASKED WITH (FUNCTION = 'partial(2,"*******",1)');
```

The size of the mask is up to you. If you put fourteen asterisks, the value would look fourteen wide. Now, PersonNumber: '0000000102' looks like '00*******2', as does: '0000000032'. Apply the same sort of mask to a non-fixed length column, the output will be fixed width if there is enough data for it to be:

```
ALTER TABLE Examples.DataMasking ALTER COLUMN LastName
    ADD MASKED WITH (FUNCTION = 'partial(3,"_____",2)');
```

Now 'Hamlin' shows up as 'Ham_____n'. Partial can be used to default the entire value as well, as if you want to make a value appear as unknown. The partial function can be used to default the entire value as well. In our example, you default the Status value to 'Unknown':

```
ALTER TABLE Examples.DataMasking ALTER COLUMN Status
    ADD MASKED WITH (Function = 'partial(0,"Unknown",0)');
```

Finally, to the CarCount column, we will add the random() masking function. It will put a random number of the data type of the column between the start and end value parameters:

```
ALTER TABLE Examples.DataMasking ALTER COLUMN CarCount
    ADD MASKED WITH (FUNCTION = 'random(1,3)');
```

Viewing the data as dbo (which you typically will have when designing and building a database):

```
SELECT *
FROM    Examples.DataMasking;
```

There is no apparent change:

```
FirstName LastName  PersonNumber  Status      EmailAddress            BirthDate  CarCount
--------- --------- ------------- ----------  ----------------------  ---------- --------
Jay       Hamlin    0000000014    Active      jay@litwareinc.com      1979-01-12 0
```

```
Darya    Popkova    0000000032    Active    darya.p@proseware.net    1980-05-22 1
Tomasz   Bochenek   0000000102    Active    NULL                     1959-03-30 1
```

Now, using the EXECUTE AS statement to impersonate this MaskedView user, run the following statement:

```
EXECUTE AS USER = 'MaskedView';
SELECT *
FROM    Examples.DataMasking;
```

```
FirstName LastName     PersonNumber Status  EmailAddress              BirthDate  CarCount
--------- ------------ ------------ ------- ------------------------- ---------- --------
xxxx      Hamlin       00****14     Unknown jXXX@XXXX.com             1900-01-01 2
xxxx      Popkova      00****32     Unknown dXXX@XXXX.com             1900-01-01 1
xxxx      Bochenek     00****02     Unknown NULL                     1900-01-01 1
```

Run the statement multiple times and you will see the CarCount value changing multiple times. Use the REVERT statement to go back to your normal user context, and check the output of USER_NAME() to make sure you are in the correct context, which should be dbo for these examples:

```
REVERT; SELECT USER_NAME();
```

# Skill 1.2: Design and implement indexes

In this section, we examine SQL Server's B-Tree indexes on on-disk tables. In SQL Server 2016, we have two additional indexing topics, covered later in the book, those being columnstore indexes (Skill 1.4) and indexes on memory optimized tables (Skill 3.4). A term that will be used for the B-Tree based indexes is *rowstore*, in that their structures are designed to contain related data for a row together. Indexes are used to speed access to rows using a *scan* of the values in a table or index, or a *seek* for specific row(s) in an index.

Indexing is a very complex topic, and a decent understanding of the internal structures makes understanding when to and when not to use an index easier. Rowstore indexes on the on-disk tables are based on the concept of a B-Tree structure, consisting of index nodes that sort the data to speed finding one value. Figure 1-1 shows the basic structure of all of these types of indexes.

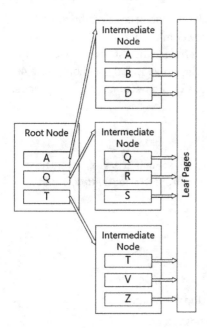

**FIGURE 1-1** The base structure of a B-Tree Index

In the index shown in Figure 1-1, when you search for an item, if it is between A and Q, you follow the pointer to the first intermediate node of the tree. This structure is repeated for as many levels as there are in the index. When you reach the last intermediate node (which may be the root node for smaller indexes), you go to the leaf node.

There are two types of indexes in SQL Server: *clustered* and *non-clustered*. Clustered indexes are indexes where the leaf node in the tree contains the actual data in the table (A table without a clustered index is a *heap* which is made up of non-sequential, 8K pages of data.) A non-clustered index is a separate structure that has a copy of data in the leaf node that is in the keys, along with a pointer to the heap or clustered index.

The structure of the non-clustered leaf pages depends on whether the table is a heap or a clustered table. For a heap, it contains a pointer to the physical structure where the data resides. For a clustered table, it contains the value of the clustered index keys (referred to as the *clustering key*.) Last, for a clustered columnstore index, it is the position in the columnstore index (covered in Skill 1.4).

When the index key is a single column, it is referred to as a *simple index*, and when there are multiple columns, it is called a *composite index*. The index nodes (and leaf pages) will be sorted in the order of the leading column first, then the second column, etc. For a composite index it is best to choose the column that is the most *selective* for the lead column, which is to say, it has the most unique values amongst the rows of the table.

The limit on the size of index key (for the data in all of the columns declared for the index) is based on the type of the index. The maximum key size for a non-clustered index is 1700 bytes, and 900 for a clustered index. Note that the smaller the index key size, the more that fits on each index level, and the fewer index levels, the fewer reads per operation. A page contains a maximum of 8060 bytes, and there is some overhead when storing variable length column values. If your index key values are 1700 bytes, which means you could only have 4 rows per page. In a million row table, you can imagine this would become quite a large index structure.

> **NEED MORE REVIEW?**  **INDEXING**
>
> For more details on indexes that we will use in this skill, and some that we will cover later in the book, MSDN has a set of articles on indexes lined to from this page: *https://msdn. microsoft.com/en-us/library/ms175049.aspx.*

> **This section covers how to:**
> - Design new indexes based on provided tables, queries, or plans
> - Distinguish between indexed columns and included columns
> - Implement clustered index columns by using best practices
> - Recommend new indexes based on query plans

## Design new indexes based on provided tables, or plans

There are two phases of a project where you typically add indexes during the implementation process:

- During the database design phase
- During the coding phase, continuing throughout the lifecycle of your implementation

The primary difference between the two phases is need. During the design phase, there are constraints that create indexes as part of their creation, and a few situations where it is essential to create an index without even executing a query. After you have configured your tables, the goal of indexes is almost completely aligned to how well your queries work, and you must add indexes where the need arises, and not just because it seems like a good idea.

> **NOTE**  **CONCURRENCY CONCEPTS**
>
> Chapter 3 reviews the concepts of concurrency, and the first step to building highly concurrent database systems is to get the design right, and match the indexing of the database to the user's queries, so queries only access the minimum amount of data needed to answer queries.

## Indexing during the database design phase

Indexing during the design phase of a database project generally fits a very small range of needs. There is only so much guesswork about user behavior that you can make. There are specifically two situations where it is essential to define indexes in your design:

- **Uniqueness Constraints**  PRIMARY KEY and UNIQUE constraints automatically create an index.
- **Foreign Key Columns**  Columns that reference a FOREIGN KEY constraint are often, but not always a likely target for an index.

Let's explore these two situations.

### UNIQUENESS CONSTRAINTS

In Skill 1.1, we created PRIMARY KEY constraints on all of the tables in our design. PRIMARY KEY constraints are enforced by creating a unique index on the columns to speed the search for the duplicated value, plus a unique index does not allow duplicated data. By default, they create a unique clustered index (where the leaf pages of the B-Tree structure are the actual data pages as opposed to just pointers to the data pages), but there are situations where the clustered index is best served on a different column (This will be covered later in "Implement clustered index columns by using best practices").

As an example, consider the following table structure:

```
CREATE TABLE Examples.UniquenessConstraint
(
    PrimaryUniqueValue int NOT NULL,
    AlternateUniqueValue1 int NULL,
    AlternateUniqueValue2 int NULL
);
```

When you have a value that you need to be the primary key value, you can use a PRIMARY KEY constraint. So, using ALTER TABLE (or inline as part of the initial CREATE TABLE statement) you can add:

```
ALTER TABLE Examples.UniquenessConstraint
    ADD CONSTRAINT PKUniquenessContraint PRIMARY KEY (PrimaryUniqueValue);
```

A PRIMARY KEY constraint cannot be placed on a column that allows NULL values, and you get an error if you try (or in a CREATE TABLE statement it sets the column to not allow NULL values). In cases where you have alternate columns that are used to identify a row (typical when you use an artificial surrogate value like a meaningless integer for a primary key, which is covered in Chapter 2 in more detail, you can add a UNIQUE constraint that can be placed on columns that allow NULL values, something demonstrated later in this section):

```
ALTER TABLE Examples.UniquenessConstraint
    ADD CONSTRAINT AKUniquenessContraint UNIQUE
        (AlternateUniqueValue1, AlternateUniqueValue2);
```

The uniqueness constraints created indexes with the same name as the constraints behind the scenes, which you can see in sys.indexes:

```
SELECT type_desc, is_primary_key, is_unique, is_unique_constraint
FROM   sys.indexes
WHERE  OBJECT_ID('Examples.UniquenessConstraint') = object_id;
```

This shows you that the index is clustered, and is unique.

| name | type_desc | is_primary_key | is_unique | is_unique_constraint |
|------|-----------|----------------|-----------|----------------------|
| PKUniquenessContraint | CLUSTERED | 1 | 1 | 0 |
| AKUniquenessContraint | NONCLUSTERED | 0 | 1 | 1 |

When you have constraints on all of the data that needs to be unique for an OLTP database, you often have a large percentage of the indexes you need. OLTP databases are generally characterized by short transactions and simple queries, usually looking for one row (even if the query sometimes looks for a range of data because the user doesn't know how to spell a given value.)

In Chapter 4, Skill 4.1, we discuss optimizing indexes, including how to determine if indexes are being used. However, indexes that are created by uniqueness constraints should not be considered for removal. Even if the index is never used to improve the performance of a query, it is essential to your data integrity to make sure that if a value is supposed to be unique, that a constraint ensures that values are unique. NULL values behave differently in UNIQUE indexes than in almost any other place in SQL Server. A PRIMARY KEY constraint does not allow any NULL values in columns, but a UNIQUE constraint and a unique index does. So, using the table we created, if we try creating the following rows:

```
INSERT INTO Examples.UniquenessConstraint
            (PrimaryUniqueValue, AlternateUniqueValue1, AlternateUniqueValue2)
VALUES (1, NULL, NULL), (2, NULL, NULL);
```

We then receive the following error message:

```
Msg 2627, Level 14, State 1, Line 95
Violation of UNIQUE KEY constraint 'AKUniquenessContraint'. Cannot insert duplicate key
in object 'Examples.UniquenessConstraint'. The duplicate key value is (<NULL>, <NULL>)
```

What is initially confusing about this is that we said earlier that NULL never was equal to NULL. This is still true, but in the index keys, two NULL values are treated as duplicate missing values.

### FOREIGN KEY COLUMNS

When implementing a FOREIGN KEY constraint, it is generally a good idea to index the key columns in the referencing tables. For example, consider the following three tables:

```
--Represents an order a person makes, there are 10,000,000 + rows in this table
CREATE TABLE Examples.Invoice
(
    InvoiceId   int NOT NULL CONSTRAINT PKInvoice PRIMARY KEY,
    --Other Columns Omitted
);
--Represents a type of discount the office gives a customer,
--there are 200 rows in this table
```

```
CREATE TABLE Examples.DiscountType
(
    DiscountTypeId    int NOT NULL CONSTRAINT PKDiscountType PRIMARY KEY,
    --Other Columns Omitted
)
--Represents the individual items that a customer has ordered, There is an average of
--3 items ordered per invoice, so there are over 30,000,000 rows in this table
CREATE TABLE Examples.InvoiceLineItem
(
    InvoiceLineItemId int NOT NULL CONSTRAINT PKInvoiceLineItem PRIMARY KEY,
    InvoiceId int NOT NULL
        CONSTRAINT FKInvoiceLineItem$Ref$Invoice
            REFERENCES Examples.Invoice (InvoiceId),
    DiscountTypeId int NOT NULL
        CONSTRAINT FKInvoiceLineItem$Ref$DiscountType
            REFERENCES Examples.DiscountType (DiscountTypeId)
    --Other Columns Omitted
);
```

There are two foreign key columns in the InvoiceLineItem table to cover. The InvoiceId column has mostly unique values, with an average of 3 rows per invoice. It is also a typical thing a user might do; grabbing all of the invoice items for an invoice. Hence, that is a column that almost certainly benefits from an index (and as we discuss later in the section "Implement clustered index columns by using best practices", perhaps even a clustered index if the reference is used frequently enough.) Create that index as a non-clustered index for now as:

```
CREATE INDEX InvoiceId ON Examples.InvoiceLineItem (InvoiceId);
```

When creating an index on a not-very selective column, like perhaps the DiscountTypeId, where out of 30 million rows, there are just 20 distinct values in 100000 rows. This column could benefit from a filtered index, which is an index that has a WHERE clause. So if almost all rows were NULL, it could be that searching for a row with the value of NULL in the index would be useless. However, a search for other values actually could use the index. So you could create a filtered index as:

```
CREATE INDEX DiscountTypeId ON Examples.InvoiceLineItem(DiscountTypeId)
                                    WHERE DiscountTypeId IS NOT NULL;
```

Filtered indexes can have any columns in the WHERE clause, even if not represented in the index keys or included columns (which we use later in this chapter in the section: "Distinguish between indexed columns and included columns").

When creating an INDEX, if the data in the key columns is always unique (such as if the columns of the index are a superset of a UNIQUE and/or PRIMARY KEY constraint columns,) declare the index as UNIQUE, as in:

```
CREATE UNIQUE INDEX InvoiceColumns ON Examples.InvoiceLineItem(InvoiceId,
                                                InvoiceLineItemId);
```

It is typically desirable to have indexes that enforce uniqueness to be based on a constraint, but this is not a requirement. Any UNIQUE index, even a filtered one, can be declared as only allowing unique values which will disallow duplicated index key values.

In the WideWorldImporters database, there are indexes on all of the foreign keys that were generated when creating that database. Beyond guessing what one can do to decide whether an index would be useful, it is essential to understand a query plan. Most of the figures in this chapter are query plans to demonstrate what is going on in the query optimizer and query processor. As an example, use one of the relationships in the WideWorldImporters database, between the Sales.CustomerTransactions and Application.PaymentMethods tables.

In the Sales.CustomerTransactions table, there are 97147 rows. The index on the foreign key column is non-clustered, so every use of the non-clustered index requires a probe of the clustered index to fetch the data (referred to as a *bookmark lookup*), so it is very unlikely the index is used for a predicate. Take a look at the data in the PaymentMethodId column:

```
SELECT PaymentMethodId, COUNT(*) AS NumRows
FROM   Sales.CustomerTransactions
GROUP  BY PaymentMethodID;
```

You can see that there are just two values in use:

```
PaymentMethodId NumRows
--------------- -----------
4               26637
NULL            70510
```

Take a look at the plan of the following query that the system might perform, searching for CustomerTransactions rows where the PaymentMethodId = 4:

```
SELECT *
FROM   Sales.CustomerTransactions
WHERE PaymentMethodID = 4;
```

This returns the expected 26637 rows, and has the actual plan shown in Figure 1-2. The Compute Scalar operator is there because we returned all columns, and there is a computed column in the table named IsFinalized.

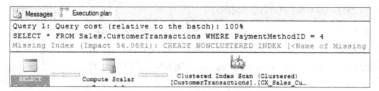

**FIGURE 1-2** The plan from the query for PaymentMethodId = 4

There are three ways using the GUI to get the query plan. From the Query Menu, select:

1. **Display Estimated Plan**   This shows you the plan that is likely to be used to perform the query. The plan can change when the query is performed, due to many factors such as query load, memory available, etc. All row counts and costs are guesses based on the statistics of the index, and it does not require the query to be performed. Whether or not parallelism can be used is determined during execution based on system settings (such as the sp_configure setting 'cost threshold for parallelism' and 'max degree of parallelism') and the load on the system at execution time.

2. **Include Actual Execution Plan**   This represents the plan that is used, including actual row counts, use of parallelism, etc. You get the actual plan after the query has completed in its entirety.

3. **Include Live Query Statistics**   When you are working with a complex, long-running query, you can see data moving through the actual query plan operators live. It can help you diagnose issues with a large query by letting you see the problem spots in real time.

> **NOTE   TEXTUAL PLAN OPTIONS**
>
> Additionally, there are several ways to get a textual plan when you need it. Two examples are SET SHOWPLAN_TEXT to get the estimated plan, and SET STATISTICS PROFILE to get the actual query plan.

For now, we ignore the Missing Index listed in the plan (and for future cases edit them out until we get to the section on "Included Columns"), but the point here is that the index was not used. However, it is important to note that while an index is not generally useful, there are scenarios where the index actually turns out to be useful:

- If the only column that was returned from the query was the PaymentMethodId since all of the data is there in the index, then it is useful.

- An index is also useful when you are searching for a value that does not exist in the table. The statistics of the index do not tell the optimizer that no rows are returned from the query, only that very few are returned, so using the index should be fast enough. We review managing statistics in more detail in Chapter 4, but they are basically structures that help the optimizer to guess how many rows are returned by a given query based on a sampling of the data at a given point in time.

These scenarios are why foreign key indexes are often applied to all foreign key columns, even if the indexes applied are not generally useful.

## Indexing once data is in your tables

Although the indexing you might do to your tables before adding data is essentially part of the structure, and the rest of the indexes are strictly intended to improve performance. In this section, we cover several scenarios to consider when adding indexes to tables. Some of these scenarios crop up during development, even when you have very little data in your tables. Some do not show up until the data grows during performance testing or production loads. All of Chapter 4 delves more into the ongoing tuning of your system, but for now we look at some common query types to tune, no matter how you discover the need.

- Common search paths
- Joins
- Sorting data

Unless you have very simplistic needs, it is hard to know exactly how queries behave in a real scenario, so in most cases it is better to test out your expectations rather than guess about performance.

**EXAM TIP**

While tuning a real database should generally be done with real data, seeing real needs, this is not the case for the exam. The situations more likely follow a very deliberate pattern similar to the ones we discuss in the next sections. The upcoming examples are not exhaustive as there are many different scenarios that can use an index to improve performance.

### COMMON SEARCH PATHS DISCOVERED DURING DEVELOPMENT

In order to optimize common search criteria, the process of adding indexes starts during the development phase of the project. Many indexes will correspond to the uniqueness constraints created during table design. However, as the application is developed, there are typically search arguments used that are not handled by the uniqueness constraints. For example, consider the CustomerPurchaseOrderNumber from the WideWorldImporters.Sales. Orders table. It is not a key value, and the sample data has duplicated values, even for a single customer. Once the application is created, the following query is executed from the application code:

```
SELECT CustomerID, OrderID, OrderDate, ExpectedDeliveryDate
FROM Sales.Orders
WHERE CustomerPurchaseOrderNumber = '16374';
```

The query runs quickly in the default set of rows in the Sales.Orders table, returning only 6 rows. The amount of time the query takes, using the small-sized dataset, seems adequate. However, to dig deeper and find out how well the query actually performs, you can use two commands in Transact-SQL to see some very important statistics. The statistics, along with the query plan will give you deeper insight into how the query is operating.

```
SET STATISTICS TIME ON;
SET STATISTICS IO ON;

SELECT CustomerID, OrderId, OrderDate, ExpectedDeliveryDate
FROM  Sales.Orders
WHERE CustomerPurchaseOrderNumber = '16374';

SET STATISTICS TIME OFF;
SET STATISTICS IO OFF;
```

The plan returns what is shown in Figure 1-3.

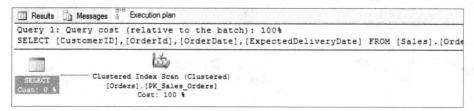

**FIGURE 1-3** Query plan that does not use an index

Along with the query results, there are a few additional messages. We are reducing to the pertinent ones here in our output, but you can see the compile and parse times, and the overall execution time in addition to the following:

```
Table 'Orders'. Scan count 1, logical reads 692, physical reads 0, read-ahead reads 0,
lob logical reads 0, lob physical reads 0, lob read-ahead reads 0.

 SQL Server Execution Times:
   CPU time = 15 ms,  elapsed time = 20 ms.:
```

The query only takes around 20 milliseconds (ms) on my VM (Surface Pro 4 with 16 GB of RAM, and 8GB for the VM), scanning the entire table, and touching all 692 pages containing 73595 rows. The pages are all in RAM, so there are no physical reads. This is very common when testing individual queries, so there is no memory pressure. (You can clear the cache using DBCC DROPCLEANBUFFERS, but the most important number for indexing is logical reads. Consistent readings of a large number of physical reads are more indicative of not enough RAM to cache data). However, if this is a table to which data is being actively written, scanning those 692 pages means that every single row is touched, and therefore locked for some amount of time, causing concurrency issues that are covered in more detail in Chapter 3, "Manage Database Concurrency."

Next, add an index to the Sales.Orders table on just the CustomerPurchaseOrderNumber column, in attempt to make the query perform better.

```
CREATE INDEX CustomerPurchaseOrderNumber ON Sales.Orders(CustomerPurchaseOrderNumber);
```

Now, perform the same query on CustomerPurchaseOrderNumber = '16374', and the following query plan is used, as shown in Figure 1-4.

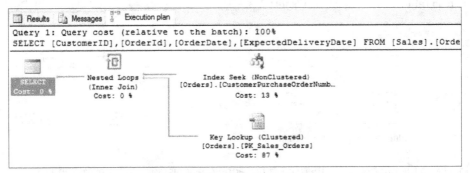

**FIGURE 1-4** Query plan after adding an index on the CustomerPurchaseOrderNumber

The query plan looks more complex. There is a join, even though the query uses a single table. SQL Server now uses the index-seek operation to find the six matching rows, but all it has are the CustomerPurchaseOrderNumber and the OrderID from the index keys. So it needs to use a JOIN operator to join to the clustered index to get the rest of the data. While the plan is more complex, the results are a lot better statistically, as you can see:

```
Table 'Orders'. Scan count 1, logical reads 20, physical reads 0, read-ahead reads 0,
lob logical reads 0, lob physical reads 0, lob read-ahead reads 0.
 SQL Server Execution Times:
   CPU time = 0 ms,  elapsed time = 0 ms.
```

It took only 20 logical reads, and less than 1 millisecond to perform. The reduction in 672 reads, means 672 less physical resources touched, and locked by default. As a result, it is very useful to check out all of the queries that are used by your applications, either (ideally) from stored procedures, or as ad-hoc queries performed from your external interfaces.

Note that you can index a computed column as long as it is deterministic. You can tell if a column can be indexed, even if it is computed by using the COLUMNPROPERTYEX function:

```
SELECT CONCAT(OBJECT_SCHEMA_NAME(object_id), '.', OBJECT_NAME(object_id)) AS TableName,
       name AS ColumnName, COLUMNPROPERTY(object_id, name, 'IsIndexable') AS Indexable
FROM sys.columns
WHERE is_computed = 1;
```

Search conditions are typically the most obvious to index because they affect people directly. When a user searches on an unindexed column in a large table (relative to hardware capabilities), you may see locking, blocking, or using some settings (such as the database setting READ COMMITTED SNAPSHOT): high tempdb utilization. The needs are more random than in the following situation we will cover.

### JOINS

While simple index needs often manifest themselves as table scans, when joining data in two tables, the need for an index instead may show up as a different join operator than a nested-loops join. Nested loops work best when one set is very small, or the cost of seeking for a row in that set is inexpensive. It works by going row by row in one of the inputs, and seeking for a matching value in the other. When the cost of seeking in both sets is too costly, a Hash Match operator is used. This operator makes a pseudo hash index by segmenting values into buckets of values that can be easier to scan using a hash function. It does not need any order to the operation, so it can work to join two really large sets together.

As an example, drop the foreign key index from the Sales.Orders table named FK_Sales_Orders_ContactPersonID using the following command:

```
DROP INDEX FK_Sales_Orders_ContactPersonID ON Sales.Orders;
```

Now, search for the Sales.Orders rows for any person with a preferred name of 'Aakriti:'

```
SELECT OrderId, OrderDate, ExpectedDeliveryDate, People.FullName
FROM   Sales.Orders
       JOIN Application.People
          ON People.PersonID = Orders.ContactPersonID
WHERE  People.PreferredName = 'Aakriti';
```

The PreferredName column is not indexed. Figure 1-5 shows the actual query plan, along with the typical query stats output.

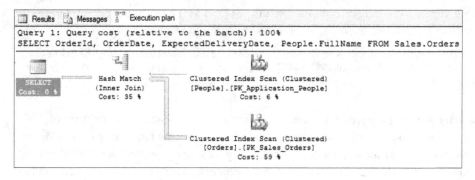

```
    Results    Messages    Execution plan
Query 1: Query cost (relative to the batch): 100%
SELECT OrderId, OrderDate, ExpectedDeliveryDate, People.FullName FROM Sales.Orders

  SELECT          Hash Match          Clustered Index Scan (Clustered)
  Cost: 0 %       (Inner Join)        [People].[PK_Application_People]
                  Cost: 35 %                  Cost: 6 %

                                      Clustered Index Scan (Clustered)
                                      [Orders].[PK_Sales_Orders]
                                              Cost: 59 %
```

**FIGURE 1-5** Query plan and statistic output for unindexed foreign key index in join

Figure 1-5 has the following output:

Table 'Workfile'. Scan count 0, logical reads 0, physical reads 0, read-ahead reads 0, lob logical reads 0, lob physical reads 0, lob read-ahead reads 0.

Table 'Worktable'. Scan count 0, logical reads 0, physical reads 0, read-ahead reads 0, lob logical reads 0, lob physical reads 0,

lob read-ahead reads 0.

Table 'Orders'. Scan count 1, logical reads 692, physical reads 0, read-ahead reads 0, lob logical reads 0, lob physical reads 0,

lob read-ahead reads 0.

Table 'People'. Scan count 1, logical reads 80, physical reads 0, read-ahead reads 0, lob logical reads 0, lob physical reads 0,

lob read-ahead reads 0.

CPU time = 15 ms,   elapsed time = 53 ms.

Hovering your mouse over the Clustered Index Scan operator for the PK_Application_People index (the clustered index on the table), you see (as depicted in Figure 1-6) the costs, but also that the predicate of PreferredName = 'Aakriti' is handled as part of this scan.

**Clustered Index Scan (Clustered)**
Scanning a clustered index, entirely or only a range.

| | |
|---|---|
| Physical Operation | Clustered Index Scan |
| Logical Operation | Clustered Index Scan |
| Actual Execution Mode | Row |
| Estimated Execution Mode | Row |
| Storage | RowStore |
| Number of Rows Read | 1111 |
| Actual Number of Rows | 2 |
| Actual Number of Batches | 0 |
| Estimated Operator Cost | 0.0615411 (6%) |
| Estimated I/O Cost | 0.060162 |
| Estimated CPU Cost | 0.0013791 |
| Estimated Subtree Cost | 0.0615411 |
| Number of Executions | 1 |
| Estimated Number of Executions | 1 |
| Estimated Number of Rows | 1.33333 |
| Estimated Row Size | 79 B |
| Actual Rebinds | 0 |
| Actual Rewinds | 0 |
| Ordered | False |
| Node ID | 1 |

**Predicate**
[WideWorldImporters].[Application].[People].
[PreferredName]=N'Askrib'
**Object**
[WideWorldImporters].[Application].[People].
[PK_Application_People]
**Output List**
[WideWorldImporters].[Application].[People].PersonID,
[WideWorldImporters].[Application].[People].FullName

**FIGURE 1-6** Operator costs for the Clustered Index Scan operator for the PK_Application_People index

As you can see, the query optimizer scans the two indexes, and the Hash Match operator builds a hash index structure, and then matches the rows together. Adding back the index on the foreign key columns:

```
CREATE INDEX FK_Sales_Orders_ContactPersonID ON Sales.Orders
--Note that USERDATA is a filegroup where the index was originally
            (ContactPersonID ASC ) ON USERDATA;
```

Executing the query again shows a better result, though not tremendously, as shown in Figure 1-7.

**FIGURE 1-7** Query plan after adding back the foreign key index

Figure 1-7 has the following output:

Table 'Orders'. Scan count 2, logical reads 695, physical reads 0, read-ahead reads 0, lob logical reads 0, lob physical reads 0,

lob read-ahead reads 0.

Table 'People'. Scan count 1, logical reads 80, physical reads 0, read-ahead reads 0, lob logical reads 0, lob physical reads 0,

lob read-ahead reads 0.

CPU time = 0 ms,  elapsed time = 17 ms.

The big cost here is the Key Lookup operator to fetch the rest of the Sales.Orders columns in our query. This cost is what the missing index hint has been suggesting for nearly every query, and is the topic of the next section of this chapter. The query can be improved upon one more time by indexing the PreferredName column, so the query processor doesn't have to test every single row in the Application.People table to see if it matches PreferredName = 'Aakriti'.

```
CREATE INDEX PreferredName ON Application.People (PreferredName) ON USERDATA;
```

Finally, perform the query again to see the plan and statistics shown in Figure 1-8.

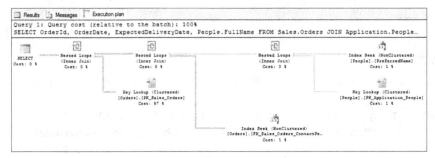

**FIGURE 1-8** Query plan after adding index on `Application.People.PreferredName`

Figure 1-8 has the following output:

```
Table 'Orders'. Scan count 2, logical reads 695, physical reads 0, read-ahead reads 0,
lob logical reads 0, lob physical reads 0,

lob read-ahead reads 0.

Table 'People'. Scan count 1, logical reads 6, physical reads 0, read-ahead reads 0, lob
logical reads 0, lob physical reads 0, lob read-ahead reads 0.

CPU time = 0 ms,  elapsed time = 19 ms.
```

This is not a tremendous improvement, and is just 74 less accessed pages, and execution times are typically the same. Generally speaking though, the fewer pages read in the process of executing the query, the better, particularly as the number of queries increase in an active system.

Note the Key Lookup operator that is 97 percent of the cost of this query. In a following section on included columns, we review how to erase that cost, and lower the logical reads to very few.

### SORTS

The final query situation we look at is sorts. When you need to sort data, either for an ORDER BY clause or for some operation in the query where sorting data would make query operation quicker (the last join operator that we haven't mentioned yet, called the Merge Join operator, requires sorted inputs to match rows from one large input set to another large set, in a quicker manner than using the Hash Merge algorithm previously mentioned).

A part of the CREATE INDEX statement we have not yet looked at is sorting of the index keys, particularly useful with composite index keys. By default, the data in the index is sorted in ascending order, so the indexes created so far have been ascending by default. The query processor can scan the index in either direction, so for a *simple index* (one with a single key column), this is generally not a problem. For *composite indexes* (those with greater than a single key column) it can be an issue.

As an example, consider the following query of the entire Sales.Orders table, sorted in SalespersonPersonID and OrderDate order. Both are explicitly spelled out as ASC, meaning ascending, which is the default. Note too that we only return the columns that are being sorted on to make the example simpler.

```
SELECT SalespersonPersonId, OrderDate
FROM Sales.Orders
ORDER BY SalespersonPersonId ASC, OrderDate ASC;
```

Figure 1-9 shows the plan, which includes a scan through the data, a sort, and it even shows that the query used parallelism, since we're running on a VM with 2 CPUs allocated. In other words, this was not a trivial query.

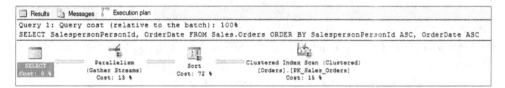

**FIGURE 1-9** Sorting results prior to adding index

Figure 1-9 has the following output:

```
Table 'Worktable'. Scan count 0, logical reads 0, physical reads 0, read-ahead reads 0,
lob logical reads 0, lob physical reads 0,

lob read-ahead reads 0.

Table 'Orders'. Scan count 3, logical reads 758, physical reads 0, read-ahead reads 0,
lob logical reads 0, lob physical reads 0,

lob read-ahead reads 0.

CPU time = 94 ms,  elapsed time = 367 ms.
```

Now, add an index to support this query, as we know that this query is performed very often in our enterprise. Add a composite index, and explicitly show that we are sorting the keys in ascending order, for the query:

```
CREATE INDEX SalespersonPersonID_OrderDate ON Sales.Orders
                        (SalespersonPersonID ASC, OrderDate ASC);
```

Perform the query just as we did in the first attempt. Figure 1-10, shows that the plan has changed, as now it can get the data in a pre-sorted manner, with the primary cost of the query now embedded in the bookmark lookup.

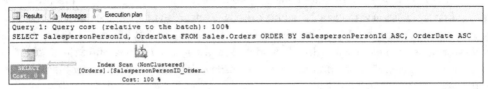

**FIGURE 1-10** Query plan after adding the index to the table

Figure 1-10 has the following output:

```
Table 'Orders'. Scan count 1, logical reads 157, physical reads 0, read-ahead reads 0,
lob logical reads 0, lob physical reads 0, lob read-ahead reads 0.
```

```
CPU time = 47 ms,  elapsed time = 217 ms.
```

If the order you request is completely opposite of how the index is sorted, you will find that nothing in the plan will change:

```
SELECT SalespersonPersonId, OrderDate
FROM Sales.Orders
ORDER BY SalespersonPersonId DESC, OrderDate DESC;
```

If your sorting needs don't match the index exactly, it's still useful to the query, but only until there is a mismatch. For example, change the ORDER BY to either of the following (DESC is descending):

- ORDER BY SalespersonPersonId DESC, OrderDate ASC;
- ORDER BY SalespersonPersonId ASC, OrderDate DESC;

And you see the plan changes to what is shown in Figure 1-11.

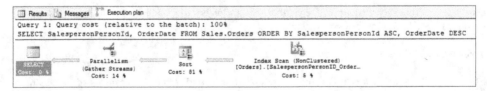

**FIGURE 1-11** Query plan when the sort order does not match

The query processor was able to skip sorting the data based on the first column by using the index, but then it had to sort the second column using a separate operator, rather than just scanning the data in order. As such, it is important to note the order of the columns in the ORDER BY clause, if you were given a question matching the index with the ORDER BY clause.

One place where sorting often is helped by indexes is when joining two large sets. The query plan can use a Merge Join operator to join two sorted sets together, by matching item after item, since they are in sorted order. As an example, take a join of two tables, the Sales. Orders and the Application.People, returning all of the rows in the tables, but just their key values:

```
SELECT Orders.ContactPersonID, People.PersonID
FROM   Sales.Orders
           INNER JOIN Application.People
             ON Orders.ContactPersonID = People.PersonID;
```

Executing this, you see that since there is an index on the foreign key column in Sales. Orders, and the PRIMARY KEY constraint on the Application.People table, the data is sorted, so it can use a Merge Join operator, as seen in Figure 1-12.

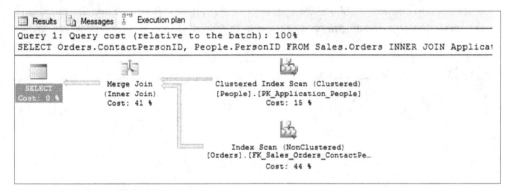

**FIGURE 1-12** Merge Join operator due to large output and sorted inputs

To be entirely fair, the output of this query is nonsensical because it returns two columns that are equivalent in all 72,595 rows. However, when you are doing joins between multiple tables, you often see a Merge Join operator appear in plans when nothing but indexed columns are accessed from the tables that are being joined.

Carefully consider how you use non-clustered indexes to support sorts, as the cost of the bookmark lookup often tips the plan towards using a scan of the base structure.

## Distinguish between indexed columns and included columns

When fetching only a few rows (as you generally do when you are querying an OLTP database), the overhead of this lookup is not terribly costly. It requires reading two or three extra pages in the clustered index, but this cost is extremely minimal compared to reading every physical page of data for an entire table.

However, as the number of rows you return grows, the bookmark lookup operations become more and more of a drag on performance. When you need to run a query that returns a lot of rows, but doesn't need all of the data in the table, there is a feature known as *included columns* that allows you to use an index to *cover* the entire needs of the query. When an index has all of the data that is needed to return the results of a query, either in the key columns, or included columns, it is referred to as a *covering index* for a query.

As an example, take a look back at this query we have used previously:

```
SELECT OrderId, OrderDate, ExpectedDeliveryDate, People.FullName
FROM   Sales.Orders
         JOIN Application.People
            ON People.PersonID = Orders.ContactPersonID
WHERE  People.PreferredName = 'Aakriti';
```

Remember back in Figure 1-11, this query was very efficient in terms of finding the rows that needed to be returned in the Sales.Orders table, but had one operator that was 97 percent of the cost of execution, and required 695 pages to be read in the Sales.Orders table.

Now perform the query, and see the plan that is output. In the plan shown in Figure 1-13, the Key Lookup operator is 97% of the overall cost of the query. There are two Key Lookup operators in the plan, so remove both of them in the simplest case.

**FIGURE 1-13** Query plan with a very high costs for the Key Lookup operators of 98%

Figure 1-13 has the following output:

```
Table 'Orders'. Scan count 2, logical reads 695, physical reads 0, read-ahead reads 0,
lob logical reads 0, lob physical reads 0,

lob read-ahead reads 0.

Table 'People'. Scan count 1, logical reads 6, physical reads 0, read-ahead reads 0, lob
logical reads 0, lob physical reads 0,

lob read-ahead reads 0.

CPU time = 0 ms,  elapsed time = 141 ms.
```

As a first step, if we simplify our query to just use the columns that are indexed, the Sales.Orders.ContactPersonID column from the foreign key index that was created by the database designer, and the Application.People.PreferredName column (which also includes the PersonId since it is the clustering key), you see that all of the data you need for your query (for all clauses, SELECT, FROM, WHERE, etc) can be found in the index keys. Executing the query:

```
SELECT Orders.ContactPersonId, People.PreferredName
FROM   Sales.Orders
```

```
      JOIN Application.People
            ON People.PersonID = Orders.ContactPersonID
WHERE  People.PreferredName = 'Aakriti';
```

Now the query plan looks wonderful, and the number of logical reads are down dramatically, as you can see in Figure 1-14. The indexes that are being sought are covering the query processor's needs. There is only one small problem. The query results are not even vaguely what the customer needs.

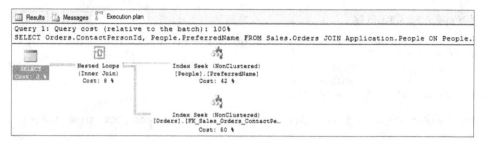

FIGURE 1-14 The Key Lookup operators have been eliminated from the plan

Figure 1-14 has the following output:

```
Table 'Orders'. Scan count 2, logical reads 4, physical reads 0, read-ahead reads 0, lob
logical reads 0, lob physical reads 0,

lob read-ahead reads 0.

Table 'People'. Scan count 1, logical reads 2, physical reads 0, read-ahead reads 0, lob
logical reads 0, lob physical reads 0,

lob read-ahead reads 0.

CPU time = 0 ms,  elapsed time = 38 ms.
```

In order to keep this performance with the minimum overhead, but providing results that were requested, you can use what is referred to as a *covering index*. The leaf nodes of a non-clustered index contains the value being indexed, along with a row locator. A covering index uses the INCLUDE keyword on the CREATE INDEX statement to include additional information on the leaf nodes. You can include any data type (even the large types like nvarchar(max), though the larger the data type, the less fits on a page, or it could even overflow to multiple pages.

For our two queries, we add another index to the Sales.Orders table (since the foreign key index came as part of the base installation) and replace the PreferredName index that is part of the original WideWorldImporters database.

```
CREATE NONCLUSTERED INDEX ContactPersonID_Include_OrderDate_ExpectedDeliveryDate
ON Sales.Orders ( ContactPersonID )
INCLUDE ( OrderDate,ExpectedDeliveryDate)
ON USERDATA;
GO
```

And to the PreferredName index we include the column the customer wanted, the Full-
Name column.

```
DROP INDEX PreferredName ON Application.People;
GO
CREATE NONCLUSTERED INDEX PreferredName_Include_FullName
ON Application.People (   PreferredName )
INCLUDE (FullName)
ON USERDATA;
```

Now, perform the query:

```
SELECT OrderId, OrderDate, ExpectedDeliveryDate, People.FullName
FROM   Sales.Orders
       JOIN Application.People
          ON People.PersonID = Orders.ContactPersonID
WHERE  People.PreferredName = 'Aakriti';
```

And the plan now looks great, and returns what the customer needs. You can see the plan
in Figure 1-15.

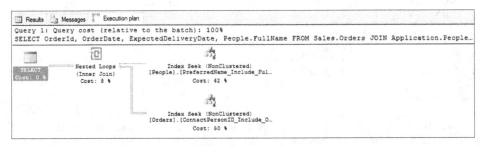

**FIGURE 1-15** The query plan of the query execution after adding the covering index

Figire 1-15 has the following output:

```
Table 'Orders'. Scan count 2, logical reads 6, physical reads 0, read-ahead reads 0, lob
logical reads 0, lob physical reads 0,

lob read-ahead reads 0.

Table 'People'. Scan count 1, logical reads 2, physical reads 0, read-ahead reads 0, lob
logical reads 0, lob physical reads 0,

lob read-ahead reads 0.

CPU time = 0 ms,  elapsed time = 79 ms.
```

Covering indexes are fantastic tools for tuning queries where you are dealing with costly
Key Lookup operators. However, restraint should be taken when considering whether or not
to apply them. When checking the plan of a query, you are frequently given a missing index
hint that encourages you to add an index with a long list of included columns. Figure 1-5
showed the plan of the following query:

```
SELECT *
```

```
FROM    Sales.CustomerTransactions
WHERE PaymentMethodID = 4;
```

When looking at the plan, there was a missing index hint as shown in Figure 1-16.

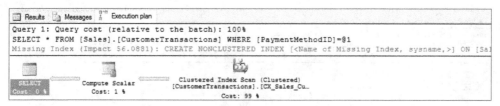

**FIGURE 1-16** Showing the Missing Index hint on query plan

Hovering your cursor over the missing index shows you details in a tool-tip, or right click the plan and choose "Missing Index Details..." and you see the following index:

```
CREATE NONCLUSTERED INDEX [<Name of Missing Index, sysname,>]
ON [Sales].[CustomerTransactions] ([PaymentMethodID])
INCLUDE ([CustomerTransactionID],[CustomerID],[TransactionTypeID], [InvoiceID],[Transact
ionDate],[AmountExcludingTax],[TaxAmount],[TransactionAmount],
[OutstandingBalance],[FinalizationDate],[IsFinalized],[LastEditedBy],[LastEditedWhen])
```

Adding this index definitely increases the performance of your query. It reduces logical reads from 1126 to 312. This is not a tremendous savings, and likely doesn't merit adding in a strict OLTP system, as for every change to the Sales.CustomerTransactions table, all of these column values are copied again to the index pages. For a reporting database, missing indexes can be great things to add, but you always need to take caution.

The Missing Indexes tip is basically where the optimizer was working through what it was looking for to perform the query the fastest, and an index that would have helped was discovered. In Chapter 4, "Optimize database objects and SQL infrastructure," we explore the missing indexes dynamic management view (DMV) where you can see indexes that SQL Server would like to have had for the queries that have been optimized over time. Many of them overlap with other indexes that it has suggested. If you added all of the indexes that it suggested to a busy system, it would be brought to its knees maintaining indexes.

One last property of included columns is important to understand. Included columns in an index can never be used to seek for rows or for ordered scans (since they are not ordered at all), but they can be used to cover a query even if the key columns are not involved. For example, consider the following query that uses the columns that we indexed in the index named ContactPersonID_Include_OrderDate_ExpectedDeliveryDate. If we only reference the OrderDate and ExpectedDeliveryDate in a query, even as a predicate, the index can be scanned instead of the (typically) much larger data in the base table. Take the following query:

```
SELECT OrderDate, ExpectedDeliveryDate
```

```
FROM  Sales.Orders
WHERE OrderDate > '2015-01-01';
```

Figure 1-17 shows that it uses the index with included columns:

**FIGURE 1-17** Query plan showing an index scan of the included columns of the index

Of course, this is not the optimum index for the query, so the query plan suggests the following index, which orders the data on the OrderDate, and includes the ExpectedDelivery-Date as an included column:

```
CREATE NONCLUSTERED INDEX [<Name of Missing Index, sysname,>]
ON [Sales].[Orders] ([OrderDate])
INCLUDE ([ExpectedDeliveryDate]);
```

Take caution when using the missing index hints (or missing indexes DMV that are re-viewed in Chapter 4.) They are not the best for your system's overall performance, which certainly could be a topic on the exam. Still, covering queries using the INCLUDE feature is a great way to improve situations where a read-intensive workload is using scans to resolve queries because of a few columns that could be added to the index leaf nodes.

## Implement clustered index columns by using best practices

The choice of the clustered index can be a complex one as you consider the possibilities. As we have seen throughout the chapter, for various reasons the clustered index is the most important index on your objects. The following are a few characteristics that we need to con-sider when choosing the clustered index:

- The clustered index contains all of the data of the table on the leaf index pages (or at least the base structures, as data can overflow onto multiple pages for very large rows), so when the clustered index optimally satisfies the query's needs, the performance of the query is going to be better than otherwise.

- The *clustering key* (the term used for the key column(s) of the clustered index) affects the other row store indexes in the table. Picking a larger clustering key could be ter-rible for performance of all of the other indexes since every non-clustered index key carries this value around.

- If the clustered index is not created as unique, when a duplicate key value is created, it has a four-byte *uniqueifier* attached to duplicated values to make it unique so it makes a proper row locator.

- If you change the value of the clustering key, you change the data on every non-clustered rowstore index.

- The best clustering key is an increasing value, as it is inserted at the end of the structure that is sorted, leading to minimized page splits. When a new row is created in the middle of the clustering key sequence, a large row causes the page split.

- There is also a clustered columnstore index that we cover in Skill 1.4.

> **NEED MORE REVIEW?** **MORE INFORMATION ABOUT CLUSTERED INDEXES**
>
> An excellent, if slightly older, resource to study more about clustered indexes is Kimberly Tripp's blog series here: *http://www.sqlskills.com/blogs/kimberly/category/clustering-key/*.

So with all of these limitations, what should you choose for the clustered index? There are a few key scenarios to look for:

- **The column(s) that are used for single row fetches, often for modifications**   Many OLTP databases operate by fetching a set of rows to a client, and then updating the rows, one at a time. Watching the patterns of usage can help, but almost all of the time the primary key fits this usage, whether the database is using a natural key as primary key, or an artificial surrogate key. An IDENTITY or SEQUENCE based artificial key meets all of the points we started out with, so when implementing a system with artificial keys, it is often the best choice.

- **Range queries**   Having all the data in a particular order can be essential to performance when the data that you often need to get a range. Even a range of 1 distinct value makes sense, for a situation like a child row, such as Invoice and InvoiceLineItem where you are constantly fetching InvoiceLineItem rows by the InvoiceId for the invoice.

- **Queries that return large result sets**   If you have a situation where a particular query (or set of queries) is run frequently and returns a lot of rows, performing these searches by clustered index can be beneficial.

The typical default that most designers use is to use the clustered index on columns of the primary key. It is always unique, and is almost certainly where the largest percentage of rows are fetched or the PRIMARY KEY constraint is likely misused. In a real database, this requires testing to see how it affects overall performance.

Instinctively, it seems that you want to use the value that the user does most searches on, but the reason that the index that backs the PRIMARY KEY constraint is chosen is because beyond searches, you see lots of fetches by the primary key since singleton SELECTs, UPDATEs, and DELETEs all typically use the primary key for access. Add to that how JOIN operations are done using the primary key, and there needs to be a very compelling case to use something other than the primary key.

What data type you choose for the clustering key is a matter of opinion and tooling. For the exam, it is good to understand the different possibilities and some of the characteristics of each, particularly when creating an artificial value for a key. Two choices stand out as very common approaches:

- Integer Data types
- GUIDs

It isn't impossible to use different approaches to these, but these are very common in almost any database. In the WideWorldImporters database, all of the primary keys are based on integers. Integers are generally the favored method because they are very small, and are easy to create in a monotonically increasing sequence using the IDENTITY property on a column, or using a SEQUENCE object applied using a DEFAULT constraint.

While integer-based data types generally fit the pattern of a great clustering key, there is another possibility that is very common. Using the uniqueidentifier data type, you can store a standard GUID (Globally Unique Identifier). A major advantage of these values are that they can be generated outside of the database server by any client, unlike an integer value, due to concurrency concerns. However, a major downside is indexing them. They have a 16-byte binary value with a 36-character representation (which can be needed if you have a client that can't handle a GUID), and they are random in nature in terms of sorting. This leads to data being spread around the indexing structures, causing fragmentation, which can reduce the system's ability to scan the data (though this is a bit less of a concern when you have fast SSD drives). You can generate GUID values in the database using NEWID(), or, if you almost never have new values coming from the client, you can use NEWSEQUENTIALID() to generate GUID values that are always increasing, making it a slightly better clustering key than a normal GUID. (However, NEWSEQUENTIALID() even can't be trusted completely because the sequence of GUIDs is not guaranteed to be sequential with other GUIDs created after a reboot.)

In the end, the question of clustering key is very much centered on performance of your queries. Using a natural key can be difficult due to the size of many natural keys, but at the same time, a lot matters about how the application works, and how it turns out that data is used.

**NEED MORE REVIEW?**  **THE CREATE INDEX STATEMENT**

Indexes are a complex topic, and there are a lot of settings that we do not touch on or even mention. It would be very good to review the many settings of the CREATE INDEX statement here in the MSDN library: *https://msdn.microsoft.com/en-us/library/ms188783.aspx*.

# Recommend new indexes based on query plans

In the preceding sections on indexing, we used query plans to show that an index made a difference in the performance of one or more queries. The process of reviewing a query plan to determine what the optimizer is doing, or planning to do to optimize a query, is an important one. In this section, we review some of the factors you need to look for in a query plan.

In the code shown in Listing 1-1, we make a copy of a couple of tables from the WideWorldImporters database, with limited indexes to serve as an example.

**LISTING 1-1** Setting up a scenario for demonstrating query plans and indexes

```
CREATE SCHEMA Examples AUTHORIZATION dbo;
GO
--2074 Rows
SELECT *
INTO Examples.PurchaseOrders
FROM WideWorldImporters.Purchasing.PurchaseOrders;

ALTER  TABLE Examples.PurchaseOrders
    ADD CONSTRAINT PKPurchaseOrders PRIMARY KEY (PurchaseOrderId);

--8367 Rows
SELECT *
INTO   Examples.PurchaseOrderLines
FROM   WideWorldImporters.Purchasing.PurchaseOrderLines;

ALTER  TABLE Examples.PurchaseOrderLines
    ADD CONSTRAINT PKPurchaseOrderLines PRIMARY KEY (PurchaseOrderLineID);

ALTER TABLE Examples.PurchaseOrderLines
    ADD CONSTRAINT FKPurchaseOrderLines_Ref_Examples_PurchaseOrderLines
        FOREIGN KEY (PurchaseOrderId) REFERENCES
                                    Examples.PurchaseOrders(PurchaseOrderId);
```

Then we execute the following two queries:

```
SELECT *
FROM   Examples.PurchaseOrders
WHERE  PurchaseOrders.OrderDate BETWEEN '2016-03-10' AND '2016-03-14';

SELECT PurchaseOrderId, ExpectedDeliveryDate
FROM   Examples.PurchaseOrders
WHERE  EXISTS (SELECT *
               FROM  Examples.PurchaseOrderLines
               WHERE PurchaseOrderLines.PurchaseOrderId =
                                       PurchaseOrders.PurchaseOrderID)
  AND  PurchaseOrders.OrderDate BETWEEN '2016-03-10' AND '2016-03-14' ;
```

Executing these queries returns two sets of 5 rows each, and will probably take much less than a second on any computer as there are not very many rows in these tables at all. Since the query executes so quickly, the developer may get the idea that the query's performance is optimum, even though there will be many users, and much more data in the production version. Using the Query; Display Estimated Query Plan menu in SQL Server Management Studio, we view the estimated plan in Figure 1-18 for this query, to help determine if the query is optimum.

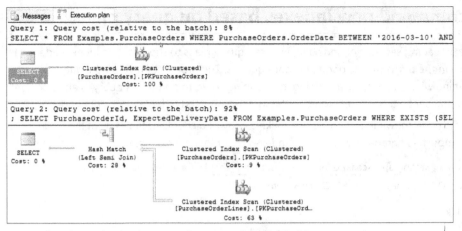

FIGURE 1-18 Query plan for the untuned query on the pair of tables

**NOTE   AN ESTIMATED PLAN**

Earlier in the "Indexing once data is in your tables" section, we covered the multiple ways to see the query plan for a query. For this section we simply look at the estimated plan for the queries.

Even though the first query would have appeared to be the costliest from looking at the results (or at least the equivalent amount of cost, it returned all of the data in the table, while the other just two small columns, all from the same rows), we can see that the first query was considerably less costly. Note how there are hidden costs, such as using user-defined functions that may not show up in a query plan.

For an exam question, you might be asked what you can tell about the indexes on the table from the plan given. We can tell that both queries are scanning the entire physical structures they reference due to the Clustered Index Scan operators. This certainly means that no index is available on the OrderDate column of the Examples.PurchaseOrders table that can help make this query execute faster. Knowing the row counts, there must be statistics on the OrderDate column that tells the optimizer how many rows will likely match the predicate because the line from PKPurchaseOrders is much smaller than that from PKPurchaseOrder-Lines. You can see the row counts by hovering over the lines, as shown in Figure 1-19, which is a composite from both lines. (Statistics, their meaning, and how they can be incorrect at times is covered in Skill 4.1).

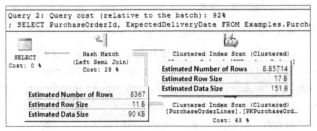

FIGURE 1-19 Query plan for the untuned pair of tables showing number of rows for each operator

Even though it was estimated that approximately 9 rows met the criteria, the optimizer still chose to scan the Examples.PurchaseOrderLines table and use a Hash Match join operator. This is an indication that there is no index on the PurchaseOrderLines.PurchaseOrderId column. Notice that the Hash Match operator is a Left Semi Join. A semi join means that data is returned from the left input, and not the right. This tells you that the Hash Match operator is most likely implementing a filter via a subquery, and not a JOIN in the FROM clause of the query.

Another question you might be asked is what index or indexes are useful to optimize a query based on the plan. From the evidence presented in our example, we can possibly add two indexes. One of them is simple:

```
CREATE INDEX PurchaseOrderId ON Examples.PurchaseOrderLines (PurchaseOrderId);
```

This index is definite since the only data that is used in the Examples.PurchaseOrderLines table is the PurchaseOrderId. What is more complex is whether the following index would be valuable on OrderDate in Examples.PurchaseOrders.:

```
CREATE INDEX OrderDate ON Examples.PurchaseOrders (OrderDate);
```

Because of the bookmark lookup factor, and the smaller table, this index is not used for this query, and even more importantly for taking the exam. Without executing the query we could not accurately predict this. However, a better index that will be useful on any size table will include the ExpectedDeliveryDate column along with the OrderDate:

```
CREATE INDEX OrderDate_Incl_ExpectedDeliveryDate
    ON Examples.PurchaseOrders (OrderDate) INCLUDE (ExpectedDeliveryDate);
```

This is because it covers all of the data needed to answer the conditions of the query. On the exam, it will be important to watch for conditions like this, where you are looking for the best answer that is always correct.

Reading a query plan is an essential developer skill, and should be expected on the exam since it is called out specifically in the indexes skill, and skill 4.2 is entitled "Analyze and troubleshoot query plans." All throughout this chapter you will find query plans to demonstrate multiple scenarios you can see from the query plan. It is the primary way that we can tell how well a query is tuned.

---

**NOTE  QUERY PLANS**

For deep detail on query plans, one of the best resources is "SQL Server Execution Plans, Second Edition" by Grant Fritchey: *https://www.simple-talk.com/books/sql-books/sql-server-execution-plans,-second-edition,-by-grant-fritchey/.*

# Skill 1.3: Design and implement views

A view is a single SELECT statement that is compiled into a reusable object. Views can be used in a variety of situations, for a variety of purposes. To the user, views more or less appear the same as tables, and have the same security characteristics as tables. They are objects just like tables (and procedure, sequences, etc.) and as such cannot have the same name as any other object. The query can be very complex, or very simple. Just like a table, it does not have parameters. Also like a table, there is no guaranteed order of the data in a view, even if you have an ORDER BY clause in the view to support the TOP phrase on the SELECT clause.

The basic form of a view is very straightforward:

```
CREATE VIEW SchemaName.ViewName
[WITH OPTIONS]
AS SELECT statement
[WITH CHECK OPTION]
```

The SELECT statement can be as complex as you desire, and can use CTEs, set operators like UNION and EXCEPT, and any other constructs you can use in a single statement.

The options you can specify are:

- **SCHEMABINDING**   Protects the view from changes to the objects used in the SELECT statement.  For example, if you reference Table1.Column1, the properties of that Column1 cannot be changed, nor can Table1 be dropped. Columns not referenced can be removed, or new columns added.

- **VIEW_METADATA**   Alters how an application that accesses the VIEW sees the metadata. Typically, the metadata is based on the base tables, but VIEW_METADATA returns the definition from the VIEW object. This can be useful when trying to use a view like a table in an application.

- **ENCRYPTION**   Encrypts the text of the VIEW object. Has the side effect of preventing the view from being published as part of replication.

THE WITH CHECK OPTION will be covered in more detail later in this skill, but it basically limits what can be modified in the VIEW to what could be returned by the VIEW object.

> **This section covers how to:**
> - Design a view structure to select data based on user or business requirements
> - Identify the steps necessary to design an updateable view
> - Implement partitioned views
> - Implement indexed views

# Design a view structure to select data based on user or business requirements

There are a variety of reasons for using a view to meet user requirements, though some reasons have changed in SQL Server 2016 with the new Row-Level Security feature (such as hiding data from a user, which is better done using the Row-Level Security feature, which is not discussed in this book as it is not part of the objectives of the exam.)

For the most part, views are used for one specific need: to query simplification to encapsulate some query, or part of query, into a reusable structure. As long as they are not layered too deeply and complexly, this is a great usage. The following are a few specific scenarios to consider views for:

- **Hiding data for a particular purpose**   A view can be used to present a projection of the data in a table that limits the rows that can be seen with a WHERE clause, or by only returning certain columns from a table (or both).

- **Reformatting data**   In some cases, there is data in the source system that is used frequently, but doesn't match the need as it stands. Instead of dealing with this situation in every usage, a view can provide an object that looks like the customer needs.

- **Reporting**   Often to encapsulate a complex query that needs to perform occasionally, and even some queries that aren't exactly complicated, but they are performed repeatedly. This can be for use with a reporting tool, or simply for ad-hoc usage.

- **Providing a table-like interface for an application that can only use tables**   Sometimes a stored procedure makes more sense, but views are a lot more general purpose than are stored procedures. Almost any tool that can ingest and work with tables can use a view.

Let's examine these scenarios for using a VIEW object, except the last one. That particular utilization is shown in the next section on updatable views. Of course, all of these scenarios can sometimes be implemented in the very same VIEW, as you might just want to see sales for the current year, with backordered and not shipped products grouped together for a report, and you might even want to be able to edit some of the data using that view. While this might be possible, we look at them as individual examples in the following sections.

## Using views to hide data for a particular purpose

One use for views is to provide access to certain data stored in a table (or multiple tables). For example, say you have a customer requirement that states: "We need to be able to provide access to orders made in the last 12 months (to the day), where there were more than one-line items in that order. They only need to see the Line items, Customer, SalesPerson, Date of Order, and when it was likely to be delivered by."

A view might be created as shown in Listing 1-2.

**LISTING 1-2** Creating a view that meets the user requirements

```
CREATE VIEW Sales.Orders12MonthsMultipleItems
AS
SELECT OrderId, CustomerID, SalespersonPersonID, OrderDate, ExpectedDeliveryDate
FROM   Sales.Orders
WHERE  OrderDate >= DATEADD(Month,-12,SYSDATETIME())
  AND (SELECT COUNT(*)
       FROM   Sales.OrderLines
       WHERE  OrderLines.OrderID = Orders.OrderID) > 1;
```

Now the user can simply query the data using this view, just like a table:

```
SELECT TOP 5 *
FROM   Sales.Orders12MonthsMultipleItems
ORDER BY ExpectedDeliveryDate desc;
```

Using TOP this returns 5 rows from the table:

| OrderId | CustomerID | SalespersonPersonID | OrderDate | ExpectedDeliveryDate |
| --- | --- | --- | --- | --- |
| 73550 | 967 | 15 | 2016-05-31 | 2016-06-01 |
| 73549 | 856 | 16 | 2016-05-31 | 2016-06-01 |
| 73548 | 840 | 3 | 2016-05-31 | 2016-06-01 |
| 73547 | 6 | 14 | 2016-05-31 | 2016-06-01 |
| 73546 | 810 | 3 | 2016-05-31 | 2016-06-01 |

Note that this particular usage of views is not limited to security like using row-level security might be. A user who has access to all of the rows in the table can still have a perfectly valid reason to see a specific type of data for a purpose.

## Using a view to reformatting data in the output

Database designers are an interesting bunch. They often try to store data in the best possible format for space and some forms of internal performance that can be gotten away with. Consider this subsection of the Application.People table in WideWorldImporters database.

```
SELECT PersonId, IsPermittedToLogon, IsEmployee, IsSalesPerson
FROM   Application.People;
```

What you see is 1111 rows of kind of cryptic data to look at (showing the first four rows):

| PersonId | IsPermittedToLogon | IsEmployee | IsSalesPerson |
| --- | --- | --- | --- |
| 1 | 0 | 0 | 0 |
| 2 | 1 | 1 | 1 |
| 3 | 1 | 1 | 1 |
| 4 | 1 | 1 | 0 |

A common request from a user that needs to look at this data using Transact-SQL could be: "I would like to see the data in the People table in a more user friendly manner. If the user can logon to the system, have a textual value that says 'Can Logon', or 'Can't Logon' otherwise. I would like to see employees typed as 'SalesPerson' if they are, then as 'Regular' if they are an employee, or 'Not Employee' if they are not an employee."

In Listing 1-3 is a VIEW object that meets these requirements.

**LISTING 1-3** Creating the view reformat some columns in the Application.People table

```
CREATE VIEW Application.PeopleEmployeeStatus
AS
SELECT PersonId, FullName,
       IsPermittedToLogon, IsEmployee, IsSalesPerson,
       CASE WHEN IsPermittedToLogon = 1 THEN 'Can Logon'
            ELSE 'Can''t Logon' END AS LogonRights,
       CASE WHEN IsEmployee = 1 and IsSalesPerson = 1
                THEN 'Sales Person'
            WHEN IsEmployee = 1
                THEN 'Regular'
            ELSE 'Not Employee' END AS EmployeeType
FROM   Application.People;
```

Now, querying the data in the same manner (leaving off names), you see something more pleasant to work with:

```
SELECT PersonId, LogonRights, EmployeeType
FROM   Application.PeopleEmployeeStatus;
```

Which returns:

```
PersonId    LogonRights EmployeeType
----------- ----------- -------------
1           Can't Logon Not Employee
2           Can Logon   Sales Person
3           Can Logon   Sales Person
4           Can Logon   Regular
```

There is one serious downside to this method of reformatting. While this looks better, and is easier to see, queries that use the reformatted values to filter on the new columns never use an index since the data does not match what is in the index. For a smaller table, this isn't an issue, but it is a concern. We included the columns in the view that had the original data for that reason.

A final concern is not to use views as layers of encapsulation in your application code for that same reason. The more layers of views you have, the less likely you get a great plan of execution. Views are definitely useful to have for morphing a set for many reasons, particularly when a user is repeatedly doing the same kinds of transformations in their code.

## Using a view to provide a reporting interface

A very useful pattern to apply with a view is building a reporting interface, to format some data for a reporting tool.

Requirements might be given to "Build a simple reporting interface that allows us to see sales profit or net income broken down by city, state, or territory customer category for the current week, up to the most current data". If the system is normalized, there are quite a few tables involved in the query. Note that an important part of these requirements is that it be up to the most current data. If it did not include the most recent data, a data warehousing solution with a separate database would likely be more efficient.

In Listing 1-4, the code for the view that gives you a structure that can easily be used for providing these answers is included. The object is in a new schema named Reports to segregate it from other bits of code, and the view is suffixed "Basis" because this view could be the basis of several reports.

There are not any locking or isolation hints, and it is generally not a good practice to do so in your code unless using the SNAPSHOT isolation level in your database. Chapter 3 covers concurrency, isolation levels, in more detail.

**LISTING 1-4** Creating the view that is the basis of an Invoice Summary report

```
CREATE SCHEMA Reports;
GO
CREATE VIEW Reports.InvoiceSummaryBasis
AS
SELECT Invoices.InvoiceId, CustomerCategories.CustomerCategoryName,
       Cities.CityName, StateProvinces.StateProvinceName,
       StateProvinces.SalesTerritory,
       Invoices.InvoiceDate,
       --the grain of the report is at the invoice, so total
       --the amounts for invoice
       SUM(InvoiceLines.LineProfit) as InvoiceProfit,
       SUM(InvoiceLines.ExtendedPrice) as InvoiceExtendedPrice
FROM   Sales.Invoices
         JOIN Sales.InvoiceLines
            ON Invoices.InvoiceID = InvoiceLines.InvoiceID
         JOIN Sales.Customers
             ON Customers.CustomerID = Invoices.CustomerID
         JOIN Sales.CustomerCategories
             ON Customers.CustomerCategoryID =
                           CustomerCategories.CustomerCategoryID
         JOIN Application.Cities
             ON Customers.DeliveryCityID = Cities.CityID
         JOIN Application.StateProvinces
             ON StateProvinces.StateProvinceID = Cities.StateProvinceID
GROUP BY Invoices.InvoiceId, CustomerCategories.CustomerCategoryName,
       Cities.CityName, StateProvinces.StateProvinceName,
       StateProvinces.SalesTerritory,
       Invoices.InvoiceDate;
```

Now you can create a report of the top 5 Sales by SalesTerritory pretty simply:

```
SELECT TOP 5 SalesTerritory, SUM(InvoiceProfit) AS InvoiceProfitTotal
FROM Reports.InvoiceSummaryBasis
WHERE InvoiceDate > '2016-05-01'
GROUP BY SalesTerritory
ORDER BY InvoiceProfitTotal DESC;
```

This returns:

```
SalesTerritory              InvoiceProfitTotal
-------------------------   --------------------
Southeast                   536367.60
Great Lakes                 366182.65
Mideast                     344703.00
Southwest                   344386.95
Plains                      288766.20
```

Or, using the same structure, the top five sales by state and customer category:

```
SELECT TOP 5 StateProvinceName, CustomerCategoryName,
        SUM(InvoiceExtendedPrice) AS InvoiceExtendedPriceTotal
FROM Reports.InvoiceSummaryBasis
WHERE InvoiceDate > '2016-05-01'
GROUP BY StateProvinceName, CustomerCategoryName
ORDER BY InvoiceExtendedPriceTotal DESC;
```

This returns:

```
StateProvinceName    CustomerCategoryName    InvoiceExtendedPriceTotal
-------------------  ----------------------  -------------------------------------
Texas                Novelty Shop            229966.31
Pennsylvania         Novelty Shop            210254.62
Ohio                 Novelty Shop            201242.59
New York             Novelty Shop            197664.32
California           Novelty Shop            178698.48
```

Clearly, novelty shops are a big business for WideWorldImporters. Looking at the plans of both queries, you should notice a couple of things. The plans are pretty large, not surprising since we joined a lot of tables. Nothing stands out as too terrible, and both plans suggest the same index:

```
CREATE NONCLUSTERED INDEX [<Name of Missing Index, sysname,>]
        ON [Sales].[Invoices] ([InvoiceDate]) INCLUDE ([InvoiceID],[CustomerID]);
```

There is no need to actually apply the index, but as we have discussed frequently, having a covering index for almost every query is a very common desire of the optimizer, and is not always a bad idea when you are doing ranges queries on the table (which was one of the strengths of the clustered index, because it had all of the data sorted for the range. Covering the data needs of queries make a non-clustered index with included columns behave like a clustered index for queries such as this.)

# Identify the steps necessary to design an updateable view

In the previous section, we identified four scenarios where views are frequently useful (not an exhaustive list). The fourth scenario (providing a table-like interface for an application that can only use tables) was put off until this section because for the most part, the goal is to make objects that behave exactly like tables in regards to SELECT, INSERT, UPDATE, and DELETE statements with no special modifications.

To provide interfaces with views there are some special configurations that you need to know. We look at the following scenarios for using views to modify tables.

- Modifying views that reference one table
- Limiting what data can be added to a table through a view through DDL
- Modifying data in views with more than one table

## Modifying views that reference one table

Generally speaking, any view that references a single table is going to be editable. For example, create a VIEW on the HumanResources.Employee table. To keep it simple, say the requirements are: "The user needs a view to allow the interface to only be able to modify rows where the type of gadget is 'Electronic', but not any other value." The table is shown in Listing 1-5.

**LISTING 1-5** Creating the table and some data that is the basis of the updatable view example

```
CREATE TABLE Examples.Gadget
(
    GadgetId     int NOT NULL CONSTRAINT PKGadget PRIMARY KEY,
    GadgetNumber char(8) NOT NULL CONSTRAINT AKGadget UNIQUE,
    GadgetType   varchar(10) NOT NULL
);
INSERT INTO Examples.Gadget(GadgetId, GadgetNumber, GadgetType)
VALUES  (1,'00000001','Electronic'),
        (2,'00000002','Manual'),
        (3,'00000003','Manual');
```

When building a view to be editable, the simpler the view, the easier it is when you're working with it. In the code that you see in Listing 1-6, there is a column that is the uppercase version of the gadget type to show how a non-executable column behaves.

**LISTING 1-6** Creating the view that is the basis of an Invoice Summary report

```
CREATE VIEW Examples.ElectronicGadget
AS
    SELECT GadgetId, GadgetNumber, GadgetType,
           UPPER(GadgetType) AS UpperGadgetType
    FROM    Examples.Gadget
    WHERE GadgetType = 'Electronic';
```

> **NOTE**  **USING VIEW_METADATA**
>
> When using views to provide an interface for an application, you can use the VIEW_META-DATA to alter how an application that accesses the view sees the metadata. Typically, the metadata is based on the base tables, but VIEW_METADATA returns the definition from the VIEW object. This can be useful when trying to use a view like a table in an application.

Now, any user who is granted access to this view can only see rows that meet the WHERE clause of GadgetType = 'Electronic'.

**EXAM TIP**

It's very useful to know all of the comparison operators that are used in SQL, such as LIKE, IN, =, <,>,<> (or !=), etc. While there aren't necessarily questions on how to use LIKE, base knowledge of logical and comparison operators is necessary to get a question correct.

Next, perform the following query that shows you the data in the table, seeing what data the user sees:

```
SELECT ElectronicGadget.GadgetNumber AS FromView, Gadget.GadgetNumber AS FromTable,
       Gadget.GadgetType, ElectronicGadget.UpperGadgetType
FROM   Examples.ElectronicGadget
           FULL OUTER JOIN Examples.Gadget
               ON ElectronicGadget.GadgetId = Gadget.GadgetId;
```

You can see that for rows where the GadgetType <> 'Electronic':

```
FromView FromTable GadgetType UpperGadgetType
-------- --------- ---------- ---------------
00000001 00000001  Electronic ELECTRONIC
NULL     00000002  Manual     NULL
NULL     00000003  Manual     NULL
```

Now we run three statements to create some new rows, delete two rows, and update two rows in the table. In the comments on the code, include details of what you're doing. First, try creating two new rows, referencing the derived column:

```
INSERT INTO Examples.ElectronicGadget(GadgetId, GadgetNumber,
                                      GadgetType, UpperGadgetType)
VALUES (4,'00000004','Electronic','XXXXXXXXXX'), --row we can see in view
       (5,'00000005','Manual','YYYYYYYYYY'); --row we cannot see in view
```

This fails, as you would expect:

```
Msg 4406, Level 16, State 1, Line 433
Update or insert of view or function 'Examples.ElectronicGadget' failed because
it contains a derived or constant field.
```

**EXAM TIP**

As you are studying for the exam, it is a great idea to try different syntaxes and scenarios everything to see what happens. While the question writers are not writing tricky questions, they can test you on scenarios that are atypical based on your experience. By pushing the boundaries of what you might normally try, you learn new concepts.

Now, try again, not referencing the calculated column:

```
INSERT INTO Examples.ElectronicGadget(GadgetId, GadgetNumber, GadgetType)
VALUES (4,'00000004','Electronic'),
       (5,'00000005','Manual');
```

This succeeds, so now use the query with the FULL OUTER JOIN from before, but limit it to the rows you created.

```
SELECT ElectronicGadget.GadgetNumber as FromView, Gadget.GadgetNumber as FromTable,
       Gadget.GadgetType, ElectronicGadget.UpperGadgetType
FROM   Examples.ElectronicGadget
          FULL OUTER JOIN Examples.Gadget
             ON ElectronicGadget.GadgetId = Gadget.GadgetId;

WHERE Gadget.GadgetId in (4,5);
```

Both rows were created, even though you cannot see the row in the view after the operation:

```
FromView FromTable GadgetType UpperGadgetType
-------- --------- ---------- ---------------
00000004 00000004  Electronic ELECTRONIC
NULL     00000005  Manual     NULL
```

Next, update two rows:

```
--Update the row we could see to values that could not be seen
UPDATE Examples.ElectronicGadget
SET    GadgetType  = 'Manual'
WHERE  GadgetNumber = '00000004';

--Update the row we could see to values that could actually see
UPDATE Examples.ElectronicGadget
SET    GadgetType  = 'Electronic'
WHERE  GadgetNumber = '00000005';
```

When looking at the data (using the same query as before,) see that the row you could see has change to be not visible from the view, but the row we could not see was not updated:

```
FromView FromTable GadgetType UpperGadgetType
-------- --------- ---------- ---------------
NULL     00000004  Manual     NULL
NULL     00000005  Manual     NULL
```

Since you cannot see the row in the results of a query of the view, you cannot update the row either. Hence, the same would be true of the DELETE operation. The FROM clause of the SELECT, DELETE, and UPDATE all work the same, and only give us access to the rows that are visible through the view. What is interesting though is that you are able to update a row from a name you could see, to a name you could not. The following section demonstrates how to make that not the case using DDL. Change the E1111111 row back to the original value:

```
UPDATE Examples.Gadget
SET    GadgetType  = 'Electronic'
WHERE  GadgetNumber = '00000004';
```

## Limiting what data can be added to a table through a view through DDL

When using a view as an interface like we are doing in this section, one of the things that you generally don't want to occur is to have a DML statement affect the view of the data that is not visible to the user of the view, as we saw in the previous section.

In order to stop this from occurring, there is a clause on the creation of the view called WITH CHECK OPTION that checks to make sure that the result of the INSERT or UPDATE statement is still visible to the user of the view. In Listing 1-7, modify the Examples.ElectronicGadget view to include this clause:

**LISTING 1-7** Altering the view to use the WITH CHECK OPTION

```
ALTER VIEW Examples.ElectronicGadget
AS
    SELECT GadgetId, GadgetNumber, GadgetType,
           UPPER(GadgetType) AS UpperGadgetType
    FROM   Examples.Gadget
    WHERE GadgetType = 'Electronic'
    WITH CHECK OPTION;
```

Now, when you attempt to create a new row that would not be visible, you get an error. As an example, try the following:

```
INSERT INTO Examples.ElectronicGadget(GadgetId, GadgetNumber, GadgetType)
VALUES (6,'00000006','Manual');
```

This returns the following error now:

```
Msg 550, Level 16, State 1, Line 482
The attempted insert or update failed because the target view either specifies
WITH CHECK OPTION or spans a view that specifies WITH CHECK OPTION and one or more
rows resulting from the operation did not qualify under the CHECK OPTION constraint.
```

This UPDATE worked earlier, but it shouldn't because it does not match the view definition and it gives you back the same error message as the previous one.

```
UPDATE Examples.ElectronicGadget
SET    GadgetType  = 'Manual'
WHERE  GadgetNumber = '00000004';
```

While this is definitely different than a normal table, it usually makes more sense because the view has carved out a slice of an object's domain, and it is generally illogical that a change to a row in a table should be able to move data out of the table's domain (be it a table or a view, which is commonly referred to as a *virtual table*).

## Modifying data in views with more than one table

So far, the view we have worked with only contained one table. In this section we look at how things are affected when you have greater than one table in the view. Listing 1-8 adds a table to the Examples.Gadget table we have been using in this section on modifying data in views, including data, and a foreign key constraint.

**LISTING 1-8** Adding a table to go with the Examples.Gadget table to show a view with more than one table

```
CREATE TABLE Examples.GadgetType
(
    GadgetType  varchar(10) NOT NULL CONSTRAINT PKGadgetType PRIMARY KEY,
    Description varchar(200) NOT NULL
)
INSERT INTO Examples.GadgetType(GadgetType, Description)
VALUES ('Manual','No batteries'),
       ('Electronic','Lots of bats');

ALTER TABLE Examples.Gadget
    ADD CONSTRAINT FKGadget$ref$Examples_GadgetType
        FOREIGN KEY (GadgetType) REFERENCES Examples.GadgetType (GadgetType);
```

In Listing 1-9 is the code for a view that references both of the tables we have created, with no WHERE clause to limit the rows returned. Note that we have duplicated the GadgetType column from both tables to allow access to both columns.

**LISTING 1-9** View that references multiple tables

```
CREATE VIEW Examples.GadgetExtension
AS
    SELECT Gadget.GadgetId, Gadget.GadgetNumber,
           Gadget.GadgetType, GadgetType.GadgetType As DomainGadgetType,
           GadgetType.Description as GadgetTypeDescription
    FROM   Examples.Gadget
             JOIN Examples.GadgetType
                ON Gadget.GadgetType = GadgetType.GadgetType;
```

Now try to insert a new gadget and gadget type simultaneously:

```
INSERT INTO Examples.GadgetExtension(GadgetId, GadgetNumber, GadgetType,
                     DomainGadgetType, GadgetTypeDescription)
VALUES(7,'00000007','Acoustic','Acoustic','Sound');
```

This ends with the following message:

```
Msg 4405, Level 16, State 1, Line 512
View or function 'Examples.GadgetExtension' is not updatable because the modification
affects multiple base tables.
```

However, if you know the internals of the view, and know which columns go with which tables, you can break this up into two statements:

```
INSERT INTO Examples.GadgetExtension(DomainGadgetType, GadgetTypeDescription)
VALUES('Acoustic','Sound');

INSERT INTO Examples.GadgetExtension(GadgetId, GadgetNumber, GadgetType)
VALUES(7,'00000007','Acoustic');
```

See that it works and, looking at the data, see that both rows have been created. Now, to see the UPDATE work, we update the description of one of the types. There are two rows where the GadgetType = 'Electronic'.

```
SELECT *
FROM    Examples.Gadget
            JOIN Examples.GadgetType
                ON Gadget.GadgetType = GadgetType.GadgetType
WHERE   Gadget.GadgetType = 'Electronic';
```

Two rows are returned:

```
GadgetId    GadgetNumber GadgetType GadgetType Description
----------- ------------ ---------- ---------- --------------
1           00000001     Electronic Electronic Lots of bats
4           00000004     Electronic Electronic Lots of bats
```

Update one of these rows, using the primary key column, and setting the description:

```
UPDATE Examples.GadgetExtension
SET    GadgetTypeDescription = 'Uses Batteries'
WHERE GadgetId = 1;
```

Look at the data again and see that both rows have changed:

```
GadgetId    GadgetNumber GadgetType GadgetType Description
----------- ------------ ---------- ---------- ----------------
1           00000001     Electronic Electronic Uses Batteries
4           00000004     Electronic Electronic Uses Batteries
```

There is no way to specify that a DELETE statement affects any certain columns, so DELETE from a view that touches multiple tables doesn't work by simply affecting a DELETE against the view.

## Implement partitioned views

A partitioned view is a view that is based on a query that uses a UNION ALL set operator to treat multiple tables as one. Before the feature of partitioning tables and indexes was created, it was the primary way to give an administrator the ability to manage multiple "slices" of a table as different physical resources.

The feature still exists, both for backward compatibility (since partitioning is the typical best way to implement partitioning since 2005), and to enable a VIEW object to work across multiple independent *federated* SQL Servers. Generally, the place where this feature is still the best practice is a case such as having two or more servers located in different corporate locations. Each location might have a copy of their data, and then a view is created that lets you treat the table as one on the local server.

Our example is located on a single server, but we will point out where you would address and configure the references to an external server. Listing 1-10 creates two tables and loads them from the Sales.Invoices table in the WideWordImporters database to build a local version of a partitioned view.

**LISTING 1-10** Tables and data to use as the basis of a Partitioned View

```
CREATE TABLE Examples.Invoices_Region1
(
    InvoiceId   int NOT NULL
        CONSTRAINT PKInvoices_Region1 PRIMARY KEY,
        CONSTRAINT CHKInvoices_Region1_PartKey
                        CHECK (InvoiceId BETWEEN 1 and 10000),
    CustomerId  int NOT NULL,
    InvoiceDate date NOT NULL
);
CREATE TABLE Examples.Invoices_Region2
(
    InvoiceId   int NOT NULL
        CONSTRAINT PKInvoices_Region2 PRIMARY KEY,
        CONSTRAINT CHKInvoices_Region2_PartKey
                        CHECK (InvoiceId BETWEEN 10001 and 20000),

        CustomerId  int NOT NULL,
        InvoiceDate date NOT NULL

    );

    INSERT INTO Examples.Invoices_Region1 (InvoiceId, CustomerId, InvoiceDate)
```

```
SELECT InvoiceId, CustomerId, InvoiceDate
FROM   WideWorldImporters.Sales.Invoices
WHERE  InvoiceId BETWEEN 1 and 10000;

INSERT INTO Examples.Invoices_Region2 (InvoiceId, CustomerId, InvoiceDate)
SELECT InvoiceId, CustomerId, InvoiceDate
FROM   WideWorldImporters.Sales.Invoices
WHERE  InvoiceId BETWEEN 10001 and 20000;
```

The PRIMARY KEY constraint of this table must be involved in the partitioning for this to work. In our case, we use a range of InvoiceId values, which is the primary key of both tables. You could use a SEQUENCE object with a pre-defined range to create your data, but the partitioning column cannot be a column with the IDENTITY property, and it cannot be loaded from a DEFAULT constraint. The partitioning range must be enforced with a CHECK constraint, and must be for a mutually-exclusive range of values.

There are several criteria beyond what you have seen thus far that you should understand, but note that not every source table needs the exact same shape, even if that is the more typical application.

> **NEED MORE REVIEW?**   **CONFIGURING PARTITIONED VIEWS**
>
> There is a complete list and more complete reading on the subject on the MSDN site here: *https://msdn.microsoft.com/en-us/library/ms187956.aspx*. There are several rules that make configuring a partitioned a complex operation. You cannot simply create a partitioned view with any set of similarly configured tables.

In Listing 1-11, we create a very simple, locally-partitioned view.

**LISTING 1-11**   Partitioned View created from the tables in Listing 1-10

```
CREATE VIEW Examples.InvoicesPartitioned
AS
    SELECT InvoiceId, CustomerId, InvoiceDate
    FROM   Examples.Invoices_Region1
    UNION ALL
    SELECT InvoiceId, CustomerId, InvoiceDate
    FROM   Examples.Invoices_Region2;
```

Using this VIEW object, and requesting data from only one of the TABLE objects by partitioning key only needs to fetch data from one of the partitions. As an example, fetch the row where InvoiceId = 1:

```
SELECT *
FROM   Examples.InvoicesPartitioned
WHERE  InvoiceId = 1;
```

See the following plan in figure 1-20 that only references the one index.

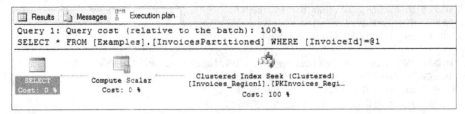

FIGURE 1-20 Plan from query that accesses data in one partition.

Even if you made the query access all 10000 rows in the Sales.Invoices_Region1 table by making the WHERE predicate BETWEEN 1 AND 10000, it would only access the one table. A predicate of IN (1,10001) however, accesses both tables.

More difficult for the user is that all queries need to specify the partitioning key(s) values(s) or the partitioning does not work. For the following query, use the InvoiceDate in the predicate:

```
SELECT InvoiceId
FROM    Examples.InvoicesPartitioned
WHERE   InvoiceDate = '2013-01-01';
```

The range of values in the results shows that only include data from the Sales.Invoices_Region1 table is returned.

```
InvoiceId
-----------
1
2
...
40
41
```

Looking at the plan shows the query accessed both physical tables, as seen in Figure 1-21. The Concatenation operator represents the UNION ALL in the query, as it is concatenating the two sets together. You can see from the size of the lines that the optimizer was expecting very few rows, but it still had to perform the scan.

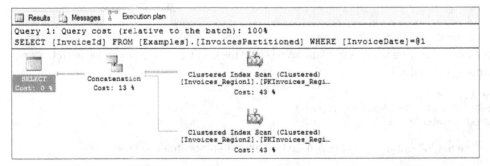

FIGURE 1-21 Plan from query that accesses data in both partitions, yet only returns data from one

When doing this on a local table, much like in a partitioned table, this is generally not so terrible. You could get some performance benefit by locating the tables being in different physical structures, or even different file groups. But what if this was on a different server? If the query that the VIEW object was based upon was changed:

```
SELECT InvoiceId, CustomerId, InvoiceDate
FROM    Sales.Invoices_Region1
UNION ALL
SELECT InvoiceId, CustomerId, InvoiceDate
FROM    ServerName.DatabaseName.Sales.Invoices_Region2;
```

And now that the database is on a *linked server,* this is more costly than local and could be very costly to execute the query. A linked server is a server that is registered in SQL Server's metadata with security to access data that is not located on the local server. An indication that a query is using a linked server is when you see the object referenced by a four-part name.

> **NEED MORE REVIEW?**  **LINKED SERVERS**
>
> Read more about linked servers here on MSDN: *https://msdn.microsoft.com/en-us/library/ms188279.aspx)*

# Implement indexed views

An indexed view (sometimes referred to as a *materialized* view), is a view that has been made into more than just a simple stored query by creating a clustered index on it. By doing this, it basically makes it into a copy of data in a physical structure much like a table.

The first benefit of using an indexed view is that when you use it Enterprise Edition of SQL Server, it uses the stored data in the index structure. For Standard Edition, it uses the code of the query unless you use a NOEXPAND table hint, in which case it uses the clustered index representation.

A second benefit, which is very important, is that it is recalculated for every modification of the underlying data. If you need up to the second aggregations extremely fast, it is better than managing copying data using a trigger. This can also be a detriment, depending on how busy the server is as the aggregations are done synchronously, meaning other users may need to wait for locks to be released.

Finally, and the benefit that can be the biggest help is that, when using Enterprise Edition, SQL Server considers using the aggregates that are stored in your view for queries that look like the query, but doesn't reference the view directly. Getting this to work depends on the needs being fairly limited. The limitations are pretty stiff. For example, a few common bits of coding syntax that are not allowed:

- SELECT * syntax—columns must be explicitly named
- UNION, EXCEPT, or INTERSECT

- Subqueries
- Outer joins or recursive join back to the same table
- TOP in the SELECT clause
- DISTINCT
- SUM() function referencing a nullable expression
- Almost any aggregate function against an expression that can return NULL
- Reference any other views, or use CTEs or derived tables
- Reference any nondeterministic functions
- Reference data outside the database.
- COUNT(*) – Must use COUNT_BIG(*)
- View not specifying SCHEMABINDING

> ***NEED MORE REVIEW?*** **MORE ON INDEXED REVIEWS**
>
> **For more information about indexed views, and a complete list of limitations, read this article in MSDN: *https://msdn.microsoft.com/en-us/library/ms191432.aspx*.**

In Listing 1-12, we create a view in the WideWorldImporters database that a customer needed. It is pretty typical, and gives the sum of the cost of what they have purchased, the profit, and the number of line items.

**LISTING 1-12** Typical VIEW object a customer may want to view some data

```
CREATE VIEW Sales.InvoiceCustomerInvoiceAggregates
WITH SCHEMABINDING
AS
SELECT Invoices.CustomerId,
       SUM(ExtendedPrice * Quantity) AS SumCost,
       SUM(LineProfit) AS SumProfit,
       COUNT_BIG(*) AS TotalItemCount
FROM   Sales.Invoices
          JOIN Sales.InvoiceLines
              ON  Invoices.InvoiceID = InvoiceLines.InvoiceID
GROUP  BY Invoices.CustomerID;
```

Run the following statement:

```
SELECT *
FROM   Sales.InvoiceCustomerInvoiceAggregates;
```

And, checking the plan, you see the plan as shown in Figure 1-22.

**FIGURE 1-22** Query plan from using the Sales.InvoiceCustomerInvoiceAggregates view before indexing

Add the following unique clustered index. The index needn't be unique, but since the data allows it, it is best to create it as unique. If duplicated data occurs in the source you receive an error (this is a way to bolt on a uniqueness constraint without changing the DML of a table).

```
CREATE UNIQUE CLUSTERED INDEX XPKInvoiceCustomerInvoiceAggregates on
                Sales.InvoiceCustomerInvoiceAggregates(CustomerID);
```

Then perform the same query of all data, and the plan changes to what is shown in Figure 1-23. You should also notice the query runs much faster, even with such a small data set.

**FIGURE 1-23** Query plan from using the Sales.InvoiceCustomerInvoiceAggregates view after adding index

As an example of how this feature can be used to speed up a system without changing the data, look at the plan of the following query:

```
SELECT Invoices.CustomerId,
       SUM(ExtendedPrice * Quantity) / SUM(LineProfit),
       COUNT(*) AS TotalItemCount
FROM   Sales.Invoices
          JOIN Sales.InvoiceLines
              ON  Invoices.InvoiceID = InvoiceLines.InvoiceID
GROUP  BY Invoices.CustomerID;
```

It uses the view that we created, because the building blocks used SUM(LineProfit), COUNT(*), and SUM(ExtendedPrice * Quantity) exist in the indexed view. In the plan, you see the same Clustered Index Scan operator, with two Compute Scalars, for the columns that are being output. Indexed views can be a useful tool to apply when you are dealing with a view that is costly and all or some of it can be put into an indexed view. Using indexed views in this manner is a niche use, but it is definitely possible and very powerful when needed. The typical use of indexed views is for reporting, and typically reporting in a reporting database where lots of data modifications are not taking place.

# Skill 1.4: Implement columnstore indexes

This final topic is different than what we have covered so far, but it will certainly be on the exam. We have focused primarily on OLTP table design and optimization using the technologies in SQL Server that have been around, in some fashion, since the early versions of the product. Most SQL Server professional developers and DBAs have created tables and applied indexes to them, clustered and non-clustered.

However, our focus now will be centered squarely on reporting, using this new technology in columnstore indexes. Columnstore indexes have changed considerably in each edition of SQL Server since they were introduced. While the basic internal structures are very similar to what was in SQL Server 2012 or 2014, their usage patterns have changed considerably.

### EXAM TIP

Be sure that if you have used columnstore indexes in earlier editions of the product that you review this topic in detail.

---

**This section covers how to:**

- Determine use cases that support the use of columnstore indexes
- Identify proper usage of clustered and non-clustered columnstore indexes
- Design standard non-clustered indexes in conjunction with clustered columnstore indexes
- Implement columnstore index maintenance

## Determine use cases that support the use of columnstore indexes

Columnstore indexes are purpose built for reporting scenarios, particularly when dealing with large quantities of data. Columnstore indexes are based on the concept of a *columnar database*, of which the concept is not a new one (if you would like a deeper explanation of columnar databases, the following paper provides as much and more than you may want: *http://db.csail.mit.edu/pubs/abadi-column-stores.pdf*). The base idea is that instead of storing all of the data for a row together, you store all of the data for a column together, as shown conceptually in Figure 1-24. Each column is stored independently, but the rows of the table are kept in the same order in each segment.

**FIGURE 1-24** Conceptual format of a columnar database

This format is particularly apt when you only need a small percentage of the columns from the table, particularly when you need a large percentage of the rows of the table. For example, a query of the format SELECT SUM(Col1) FROM TableName; would only need to scan the structure for Col1, and would never need to touch Col2, Col3, or Col4.

Column-oriented indexes, because they are not ordered, are not useful for picking only a few rows out of a table, so the implementation of columnstore indexes before SQL Server 2016 was not tremendously flexible in how it might be applied. Another limitation is that there are several data types that are not supported:

- varchar(max) and nvarchar(max)
- rowversion (also known as timestamp)
- sql_variant
- CLR based types (hierarchyid and spatial types)
- xml
- ntext, text, and image (though rightfully so as these data types have been deprecated for some time)

In SQL Server 2016, you can apply these indexes not only to tables that are only for strictly for reporting, but also to tables in your live OLTP database for real-time analytics. While the maintenance of these indexes is more costly and complex than rowstore indexes, one columnstore index can replace almost all of the indexes you may have applied for analytics.

Figure 1-25 is a conceptual drawing of the structure of a columnstore index as implemented by SQL Server. Each *row group* contains up to 1,048,576 rows each, broken down into *segments* that are all ordered physically the same, though in no logical order.

**FIGURE 1-25** Conceptual format of a columnstore index

In each row group, there is a set of *column segments*, that store the data for one single column. In Figure 1-25, note that the column segments are drawn as differently sized, because each of the segments is compressed, using similar constructs like can be done with page compression on classic row oriented structures, but instead of an 8K page, compression can take place over the single row group, or even all row groups for far greater compression. At the structure and segment, data is compressed using a process like normalization, where values that are duplicated over and over are replaced by a smaller value to look up the actual value.

Each of the segments have information stored about the values to let the query processor know if the segment can be skipped in processing, so if you have a WHERE clause that is looking for Col1 > 100, and the max value is 50, the segment can be skipped.

The *deltastore* structure comes into play when you are modifying the data in a table with a columnstore index. New rows are placed into the deltastore in a heap structure until the rows in the deltastore are compressed, and moved into a compressed row group in column segments. DELETE operations simply mark the row as removed from the column segment, telling the query processor to ignore the row. UPDATE operations in the columnstore index are a delete from the columnstore index, and then the row is added to the deltastore like a normal INSERT operation.

The process that moves rows from the deltastore to compressed rowgroups is called the *tuple mover.* It is a background process that runs periodically and does most of the management of your columnstore index maintenance. However, depending on how you use the table with the columnstore index, you need to do some maintenance as well (this is covered in the last section of the chapter: "Implement Columnstore Index Maintenance").

> **NEED MORE REVIEW?**   **MORE INFORMATION ABOUT COLUMNSTORE INDEXES**
>
> The introduction to columnstore indexes that is provided in this section has been strictly as a review of key concepts about how the indexes work. There is much more useful information in the MSDN: Columnstore Indexes Guide *https://msdn.microsoft.com/en-us/library/ gg492088.aspx.* It contains links and references to a lot of really great information, far more than we are able to provide in this chapter.

# Identify proper usage of clustered and non-clustered columnstore indexes

Much like rowstore indexes, the distinction between clustered and non-clustered indexes is whether it is a separate structure, or if it changes the physical structure of the table. A clustered columnstore index compresses the base rows, removing the row based storage altogether. The non-clustered columnstore leaves the heap or clustered rowstore index and adds a separate compressed structure. At a high level, columnstore indexes support two scenarios, one of which works with each type of index:

- **Dimensional formatted data warehouses (Clustered Columnstore Indexes)** Different than relational databases we have covered so far, we look at the pattern of how dimensional databases are structured, and how these indexes work well with them

- **Analytics on OLTP tables (Nonclustered Columnstore Indexes)** Due to how these indexes are maintained, it can be that when operational reporting is needed, a columnstore index performs better overall than a B-Tree index, particularly if multiple complex B-Tree indexes are needed, as the query processor only needs to synchronously maintain one analytical index.

These indexes are not used to improve performance of small row by row operations, but rather when one needs to work through large sets of data, touching most of the rows. In this section, we review how this need applies to the two identified scenarios, and how they differ calling for the different type of index.

One important thing about any use case for columnstore indexes is that they should have a large amount of data. As we have noted, the optimum amount of data in a row group is 1,048,576. If your tables only have a few thousand rows (or even a few hundred thousand rows) in them, columnstore indexes may not be what you need, though they can still be applied and used.

## Using clustered columnstore indexes on dimensional data warehouse structures

A data warehouse can mean many things to people, but one of the primary meanings is based on the pattern of a *star schema*. The following is a brief review of a star schema from the WideWordImportersDW sample database that is a companion to the WideWorldImporters sample database that we have been using so far for performance examples. The name star schema comes from the way a data model looks when the structure is implemented as shown in Figure 1-26.

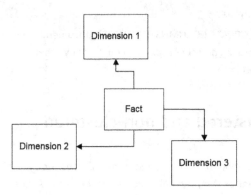

**FIGURE 1-26** Conceptual format of star schema

In some cases, a dimension links to other dimensions forming what is referred to as a *snowflake schema*, though ideally there is one join between fact and dimension. The concept of a star schema is that there is one central table that contains measurements (called a *fact table*) that needs to be reported on (typically the goal is to perform some aggregate), and a set of foreign key values that link to tables of values that the data can be summarized by (called *dimensions*). One such example in the WideWorldImportersDW is the Fact.[Order] table, shown in Listing 1-13.

**LISTING 1-13** Columns in the Fact.Order table in WideWorldImportersDW

```
CREATE TABLE Fact.[Order]
(
    [Order Key] bigint IDENTITY(1,1) NOT NULL,
    [City Key] int NOT NULL,
    [Customer Key] int NOT NULL,
    [Stock Item Key] int NOT NULL,
    [Order Date Key] date NOT NULL,
    [Picked Date Key] date NULL,
    [Salesperson Key] int NOT NULL,
    [Picker Key] int NULL,
    [WWI Order ID] int NOT NULL,
    [WWI Backorder ID] int NULL,
    [Description] nvarchar(100) NOT NULL,
    [Package] nvarchar(50) NOT NULL,
    [Quantity] int NOT NULL,
    [Unit Price] decimal(18, 2) NOT NULL,
    [Tax Rate] decimal(18, 3) NOT NULL,
    [Total Excluding Tax] decimal(18, 2) NOT NULL,
    [Tax Amount] decimal(18, 2) NOT NULL,
    [Total Including Tax] decimal(18, 2) NOT NULL,
    [Lineage Key] int NOT NULL
);
```

Breaking this table down, the [Order Key] column is a surrogate key. Column: [City Key] down to [Picker Key] are *dimension keys*, or dimension foreign key references. The cardinality of the dimension compared to the fact table is generally very low. You could have millions of fact rows, but as few as 2 dimension rows. There are techniques used to combine dimensions, but the most germane point to our discussion of columnstore indexes is that dimensions are lower cardinality tables with factors that one might group the data. Sometimes in data warehouses, FOREIGN KEY constraints are implemented, and sometimes not. Having them in the database when querying can be helpful, because they provide guidance to tools and the optimizer. Having them on during loading can hinder load performance.

Columns from [WWI BackorderID] to [Package] are referred to as *degenerate dimensions*, which means they are at, or are nearly at, the cardinality of the row and are more often used for finding a row in the table, rather than for grouping data.

Columns from [Quantity] down to [Total Including Tax] as called *measures*. These are the values that a person writing a query applies math to. Many measures are additive, meaning you can sum the values (such as [Quantity] in this example, and others are not, such as [Tax Rate]. If you add a 10 percent tax rate to a 10 percent tax rate, you don't get 20 percent, no matter your political affiliations.

The [Lineage Key] is used to track details of where data comes from during loads. The table Integration.Lineage contains information about what was loaded and when. In Listing 1-14, is the basic code for two dimensions that relate to the Fact.Orders table.

LISTING 1-14  Columns in the Customer and Date dimensions in WideWorldImportersDW

```
CREATE TABLE Dimension.Customer
(
    [Customer Key] int NOT NULL,
    [WWI Customer ID] int NOT NULL,
    [Customer] nvarchar(100) NOT NULL,
    [Bill To Customer] nvarchar(100) NOT NULL,
    [Category] nvarchar(50) NOT NULL,
    [Buying Group] nvarchar(50) NOT NULL,
    [Primary Contact] nvarchar(50) NOT NULL,
    [Postal Code] nvarchar(10) NOT NULL,
    [Valid From] datetime2(7) NOT NULL,
    [Valid To] datetime2(7) NOT NULL,
    [Lineage Key] int NOT NULL
);
CREATE TABLE Dimension.Date(
    Date date NOT NULL,
    [Day Number] int NOT NULL,
    [Day] nvarchar(10) NOT NULL,
    [Month] nvarchar(10) NOT NULL,
    [Short Month] nvarchar(3) NOT NULL,
    [Calendar Month Number] int NOT NULL,
    [Calendar Month Label] nvarchar(20) NOT NULL,
    [Calendar Year] int NOT NULL,
    [Calendar Year Label] nvarchar(10) NOT NULL,
    [Fiscal Month Number] int NOT NULL,
    [Fiscal Month Label] nvarchar(20) NOT NULL,
    [Fiscal Year] int NOT NULL,
    [Fiscal Year Label] nvarchar(10) NOT NULL,
    [ISO Week Number] int NOT NULL
);
```

We won't go into too much detail about all of these columns in the tables. But, the [Customer Key] and the Date columns are the columns that are referenced from the fact table. In the Dimensions.Customer table, the [Valid From] and [Valid To] columns set up a *slowly changing dimension*, where you could have multiple copies of the same customer over time, as attributes change. There are no examples of having multiple versions of a customer in the sample database, and it would not change our indexing example either.

> **NOTE  MORE ON FACT TABLES**
>
> Fact tables are generally designed to be of a minimal width, using integer types for foreign key values, and very few degenerate dimensions if at all possible. For demos, the cost savings you see could be fairly small. However, in a real fact table, the number of rows can be very large, in the billions or more, and the calculations attempted more complex than just straightforward aggregations.

All of the other columns in the dimensions (other than [Lineage Key], which provides the same sort of information as for the fact) can be used to group data in queries. Because the WideWorldImporterDW database starts out configured for examples, we can begin by dropping the columnstore index that is initially on all of the fact tables.

```
DROP INDEX [CCX_Fact_Order] ON [Fact].[Order];
```

The table starts out with indexes on all of the foreign keys, as well as primary keys on the dimension keys that the query uses. Perform the following query (there are 231,412 rows in the Fact.[Order] table), which you likely note runs pretty quickly without the columnstore index) :

```
SELECT Customer.Category, Date.[Calendar Month Number],
       COUNT(*) AS SalesCount,
       SUM([Total Excluding Tax]) as SalesTotal
FROM   Fact.[Order]
         JOIN Dimension.Date
           ON Date.Date = [Order].[Order Date Key]
         JOIN Dimension.Customer
           ON Customer.[Customer Key] = [Order].[Customer Key]
GROUP BY Customer.Category, Date.[Calendar Month Number]
ORDER BY Category, Date.[Calendar Month Number], SalesCount, SalesTotal;
```

The plan for this query, shown in Figure 1-27 is complicated by the cost of scanning the table, which pushes the query to use parallelism, even on my VM. The largest cost is the table scan of the heap structure that was left after removing the clustered columnstore index.

**FIGURE 1-27** Plan of the basic data warehousing style query, without a columnstore index

Figure 1-27 has the following output:

```
Table 'Customer'. Scan count 3, logical reads 40, physical reads 0, read-ahead reads 0,
lob logical reads 0, lob physical reads 0,

lob read-ahead reads 0.

Table 'Date'. Scan count 3, logical reads 79, physical reads 0, read-ahead reads 0, lob
logical reads 0, lob physical reads 0,

lob read-ahead reads 0.

Table 'Order'. Scan count 7, logical reads 5908, physical reads 0, read-ahead reads 0,
lob logical reads 0, lob physical reads 0,

lob read-ahead reads 0.

Table 'Workfile'. Scan count 0, logical reads 0, physical reads 0, read-ahead reads 0,
lob logical reads 0, lob physical reads 0,

lob read-ahead reads 0.

Table 'Worktable'. Scan count 0, logical reads 0, physical reads 0, read-ahead reads 0,
lob logical reads 0, lob physical reads 0,

lob read-ahead reads 0.

CPU time = 344 ms,  elapsed time = 276 ms.
```

Most of the plan is typical, as you often see Hash Match operators when joining two larger sets of data, which could not realistically be ordered in the same order as one another. Even with the smallish table structure for the fact table, there are 5908 logical reads (which is the same number of reads if it scanned the entire table once).

Prior to columnstore indexes, a suggested index to help this query would have been to use a covering index to cover the needs of this query so you didn't have to touch any data other than the query needed. The optimizer suggested such an index for our query:

```
CREATE NONCLUSTERED INDEX SpecificQuery ON [Fact].[Order] ([Customer Key])
INCLUDE ([Order Date Key],[Total Excluding Tax]);
```

After adding this suggested index, the plan for this query is very similar, without the parallelism, and instead of a Table Scan operator that is 60 percent of the cost, there is an index scan that is 23 percent. The logical reads are reduced to 871 instead of 5908. The processing still takes around 300 ms, and actually took a bit longer than the full table scan versions at times. The problem with indexes that are tailored to specific queries is, if you want to add another column to your query, this index stops being of value. Columnstore indexes basically give you great aggregate and scan performance for most of the combinations of attributes you might consider without custom pre-planning.

Now, add the clustered columnstore index back to the table.

```
CREATE CLUSTERED COLUMNSTORE INDEX [CCX_Fact_Order] ON [Fact].[Order];
```

As the name clustered implies, this changes the internal structure of the table to be the columnar structures. We did not remove any of the rowstore indexes, and we review why you would or would not want to use both in tandem in section later in this chapter entitled "Design standard non-clustered indexes in conjunction with clustered columnstore indexes".

The row locator for the rowstore indexes has been changed from the physical location in the heap, to the position in the columnstore structure (the row group, and the position in the row group). It is a bit more complex than this, and if you want more information, Niko Neugebauer has a great article about it here: *http://www.nikoport.com/2015/09/06/columnstore-indexes-part-65-clustered-columnstore-improvements-in-sql-server-2016/*.

For nearly all data warehousing applications, the clustered columnstore is a useful structure for fact tables when the table is large enough. Since the main copy of the data is compressed, you can see very large space savings, even having the table be 10 percent of the original size. Couple this with the usual stability of data in a data warehouse, with minimal changes to historical data, make the clustered columnstore typically ideal. Only cases where something does not work, like one of the data types that were mentioned in the introductory section (varchar(max) or nvarchar(max), for example) would you likely want to consider using a non-clustered columnstore index.

Whether or not a clustered columnstore index will be useful with a dimension will come down to how it is used. If the joins in your queries do not use a Nested Loop operator, there is a good chance it could be useful.

Perform the query again, and check the plan shown in Figure 1-28, which shows a tremendous difference:

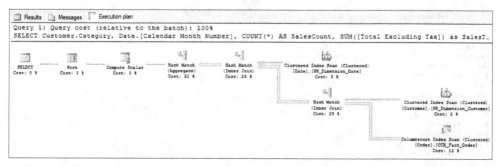

Results | Messages | Execution plan

Query 1: Query cost (relative to the batch): 100%
SELECT Customer.Category, Date.[Calendar Month Number], COUNT(*) AS SalesCount, SUM([Total Excluding Tax]) as SalesT...

**FIGURE 1-28** Plan of the basic data warehousing style query, after adding a columnstore index

Figure 1-28 has the following output:

Table 'Order'. Scan count 1, logical reads 0, physical reads 0, read-ahead reads 0, lob logical reads 256, lob physical reads 0,

lob read-ahead reads 0.

Table 'Order'. Segment reads 4, segment skipped 0.

Table 'Worktable'. Scan count 0, logical reads 0, physical reads 0, read-ahead reads 0, lob logical reads 0, lob physical reads 0,

lob read-ahead reads 0.

Table 'Customer'. Scan count 1, logical reads 15, physical reads 0, read-ahead reads 0, lob logical reads 0, lob physical reads 0,

lob read-ahead reads 0.

Table 'Date'. Scan count 1, logical reads 28, physical reads 0, read-ahead reads 0, lob logical reads 0, lob physical reads 0,

lob read-ahead reads 0.

CPU time = 15 ms,  elapsed time = 65 ms.

The logical reads are down to 256 in the lob reads for the segments, since the column segments are stored in a form of large varbinary storage. Note, too, that it took just 68ms rather than 286.

One thing that makes columnstore indexes better for queries such as those found in data warehouses is *batch execution mode*. When the query processor is scanning data in the columnstore index, it is possible for it to process rows in chunks of 900 rows at a time, rather than one row at a time in the typical row execution mode. Figure 1-29 displays the tool tip from hovering over the Columnstore Index Scan operator from Figure 1-28. The third and fourth lines down show you the estimated and actual execution mode. Batch execution mode can provide great performance improvements.

**Columnstore Index Scan (Clustered)**
Scan a columnstore index, entirely or only a range.

| | |
|---|---|
| **Physical Operation** | Columnstore Index Scan |
| **Logical Operation** | Clustered Index Scan |
| **Actual Execution Mode** | Batch |
| **Estimated Execution Mode** | Batch |
| **Storage** | ColumnStore |
| **Actual Number of Rows** | 231412 |
| **Actual Number of Batches** | 511 |
| **Estimated Operator Cost** | 0.0586584 (12%) |
| **Estimated I/O Cost** | 0.0322454 |
| **Estimated Subtree Cost** | 0.0586584 |
| **Estimated CPU Cost** | 0.026413 |
| **Estimated Number of Executions** | 1 |
| **Number of Executions** | 1 |
| **Estimated Number of Rows** | 231412 |
| **Estimated Row Size** | 23 B |
| **Actual Rebinds** | 0 |
| **Actual Rewinds** | 0 |
| **Partitioned** | True |
| **Actual Partition Count** | 0 |
| **Ordered** | False |
| **Node ID** | 7 |

**Object**
[WideWorldImportersDW].[Fact].[Order].[CCX_Fact_Order]
**Output List**
[WideWorldImportersDW].[Fact].[Order].Customer Key,
[WideWorldImportersDW].[Fact].[Order].Order Date Key,
[WideWorldImportersDW].[Fact].[Order].Total Excluding Tax

**FIGURE 1-29** Tooltip showing Columnstore Index Scan operator using Batch Execution Mode

Finally, just for comparison, let us drop the clustered columnstore index, and add a non-clustered columnstore index. When you are unable to use a clustered one due to some limitation, non-clustered columnstore indexes are just as useful to your queries, but the base table data is not compressed, giving you less overall value.

In our demo, include all of the columns except for [Lineage ID] and [Description], which have no real analytic value to our user:

```
CREATE NONCLUSTERED COLUMNSTORE INDEX [NCCX_Fact_Order] ON [Fact].[Order] (
      [Order Key] ,[City Key] ,[Customer Key] ,[Stock Item Key]
      ,[Order Date Key] ,[Picked Date Key] ,[Salesperson Key] ,[Picker Key]
      ,[WWI Order ID],[WWI Backorder ID],[Package]
      ,[Quantity],[Unit Price],[Tax Rate],[Total Excluding Tax]
      ,[Tax Amount],[Total Including Tax]);
```

Executing the query one more time, the plan looks exactly like the query did previously, other than it is using a non-clustered columnstore operator rather than a clustered one. The number of reads go up slightly in comparison to the clustered example, but not tremendously. The beauty of the columnstore indexes however is how well they adapt to the queries you are executing. Check the plan and IO/time statistics for the following query, that adds in a new grouping criteria, and a few additional aggregates:

```
SELECT Customer.Category, Date.[Calendar Year],
      Date.[Calendar Month Number],
      COUNT(*) as SalesCount,
      SUM([Total Excluding Tax]) AS SalesTotal,
      AVG([Total Including Tax]) AS AvgWithTaxTotal,
      MAX(Date.Date) AS MaxOrderDate
```

```
FROM   Fact.[Order]
          JOIN Dimension.Date
              ON Date.Date = [Order].[Order Date Key]
          JOIN Dimension.Customer
              ON Customer.[Customer Key] = [Order].[Customer Key]
GROUP BY Customer.Category, Date.[Calendar Year], Date.[Calendar Month Number]
ORDER BY Category, Date.[Calendar Month Number], SalesCount, SalesTotal;
```

You should see very little change, including the time required to perform the query. This ability to cover many analytical indexing needs is what truly makes the columnstore indexes a major difference when building data warehouse applications. Hence, both the clustered and non-clustered columnstore indexes can be used to greatly improve your data warehouse loads, and in a later section, we review some of the differences.

> **NEED MORE REVIEW?** **USING COLUMNSTORE INDEXES IN DATA WAREHOUSING**
>
> For more information about using columnstore indexes for data warehousing scenarios, the following page in MSDN's Columnstore Indexes Guide has more information: *https://msdn.microsoft.com/en-us/library/dn913734.aspx*.

## Using non-clustered columnstore indexes on OLTP tables for advanced analytics

The typical data warehouse is refreshed daily, as the goal of most analytics is to take some amount of past performance and try to replicate and prepare for it. "We sold 1000 lunches on average on Tuesdays following a big game downtown, and we have 500 plates, so as a company, we need to plan to have more in stock." However, there are definitely reports that need very up to date data. "How many lunches have we sold in the past 10 minutes? There are 100 people in line." At which point, queries are crafted to use the OLTP database.

By applying a non-clustered columnstore index to the table you wish to do real-time analytics on, you can enable tremendous performances with little additional query tuning. And depending on your concurrency needs, you can apply a few settings to tune how the columnstore index is maintained.

> **NOTE** **MEMORY OPTIMIZED TABLES**
>
> Memory optimized tables, which is covered in Skill 3.4, can also use columnstore indexes. While they are called clustered, and they must have all of the columns of the table; they are more similar in purpose and usage to non-clustered columnstore indexes because they do not change the physical storage of the table.

Columnstore indexes can be used to help greatly enhance reporting that accesses an OLTP database directly, certainly when paired with concurrency techniques that we cover in Chapter 3. Generally speaking, a few questions need to be considered: "How many reporting queries do you need to support?" and "How flexible does the reporting need to be?"

If, for example, the report is one, fairly rigid report that uses an index with included columns to cover the needs of that specific query could be better. But if the same table supports multiple reports, and particularly if there needs to be multiple indexes to support analytics, a columnstore index is a better tool.

In the WideWorldImporters database, there are a few examples of tables that have a non-clustered columnstore index, such as the OrderLines table, the abbreviated DDL of which is shown in Listing 1-15.

**LISTING 1-15** Abbreviated structure of the WideWorldImporters.Sales.InvoiceLines table with non-clustered columnstore index

```
CREATE TABLE Sales.InvoiceLines
(
    InvoiceLineID int NOT NULL,
    InvoiceID int NOT NULL,
    StockItemID int NOT NULL,
    Description nvarchar(100) NOT NULL,
    PackageTypeID int NOT NULL,
    Quantity int NOT NULL,
    UnitPrice decimal(18, 2) NULL,
    TaxRate decimal(18, 3) NOT NULL,
    TaxAmount decimal(18, 2) NOT NULL,
    LineProfit decimal(18, 2) NOT NULL,
    ExtendedPrice decimal(18, 2) NOT NULL,
    LastEditedBy int NOT NULL,
    LastEditedWhen datetime2(7) NOT NULL,
 CONSTRAINT PK_Sales_InvoiceLines PRIMARY KEY
            CLUSTERED ( InvoiceLineID )
 );
--Not shown: FOREIGN KEY constraints, indexes other than the PK

CREATE NONCLUSTERED COLUMNSTORE INDEX NCCX_Sales_OrderLines ON Sales.OrderLines
(
    OrderID,
    StockItemID,
    Description,
    Quantity,
    UnitPrice,
    PickedQuantity
) ON USERDATA;
```

Now, if you are reporting on the columns that are included in the columnstore index, only the columnstore index is used. The needs of the OLTP (generally finding and operating on just a few rows), are served from the typical rowstore indexes. There are a few additional ways to improve the utilization and impact of the columnstore index on the overall performance of the table, which we examine in the following sections:

- Targeting analytically valuable columns only in columnstore
- Delaying adding rows to compressed rowgroups
- Using filtered non-clustered columnstore indexes to target hot data

### TARGETING ANALYTICALLY VALUABLE COLUMNS ONLY IN COLUMNSTORE

As shown with the columnstore index that was created in the Sales.OrderLines table, only certain columns were part of the non-clustered columnstore index. This can reduce the amount of data duplicated in the index (much like you would usually not want to create a rowstore index with every column in the table as included columns), reducing the required amount of maintenance.

### DELAYING ADDING ROWS TO COMPRESSED ROWGROUPS

Columnstore indexes have to be maintained in the same transaction with the modification statement, just like normal indexes. However, modifications are done in a multi-step process that is optimized for the loading of the data. As described earlier, all modifications are done as an insert into the delta store, a delete from a column segment or the delta store, or both for an update to a row. The data is organized into compressed segments over time, which is a burden in a very busy system. Note that many rows in an OLTP system can be updated multiple times soon after rows are created, but in many systems are relatively static as time passes.

Hence there is a setting that lets you control the amount of time the data stays in the deltastore. The setting is: COMPRESSION_DELAY, and the units are minutes. This says that the data stays in the delta rowgroup for at least a certain number of minutes. The setting is added to the CREATE COLUMNSTORE INDEX statement, as seen in Listing 1-16.

**LISTING 1-16** Changing the non-clustered columnstore index to have COMPRESSION_DELAY = 5 minutes

```
CREATE NONCLUSTERED COLUMNSTORE INDEX NCCX_Sales_OrderLines ON Sales.OrderLines
(
        OrderID,
        StockItemID,
        Description,
        Quantity,
        UnitPrice,
        PickedQuantity
) WITH (DROP_EXISTING = ON, COMPRESSION_DELAY = 5) ON USERDATA;
```

Now, in this case, say the PickedQuantity is important to the analytics you are trying to perform, but it is updated several times in the first 5 minutes (on average) after the row has been created. This ensures that the modifications happens in the deltastore, and as such does not end up wasting space in a compressed rowgroup being deleted and added over and over.

## USING FILTERED NON-CLUSTERED COLUMNSTORE INDEXES TO TARGET COLDER DATA

Similar to filtered rowstore indexes, non-clustered columnstore indexes have filter clauses that allow you to target only data that is of a certain status. For example, Listing 1-17 is the structure of the Sales.Orders table. Say that there is a business rule that once the items have been picked by a person, it is going to be shipped. Up until then, the order could change in several ways. The user needs to be able to write some reports on the orders that have been picked.

**LISTING 1-17**  Base structure of the Sales.Orders Table

```
CREATE TABLE Sales.Orders
(
    OrderID int NOT NULL,
    CustomerID int NOT NULL,
    SalespersonPersonID int NOT NULL,
    PickedByPersonID int NULL,
    ContactPersonID int NOT NULL,
    BackorderOrderID int NULL,
    OrderDate date NOT NULL,
    ExpectedDeliveryDate date NOT NULL,
    CustomerPurchaseOrderNumber nvarchar(20) NULL,
    IsUndersupplyBackordered bit NOT NULL,
    Comments nvarchar(max) NULL,
    DeliveryInstructions nvarchar(max) NULL,
    InternalComments nvarchar(max) NULL,
    PickingCompletedWhen datetime2(7) NULL,
    LastEditedBy int NOT NULL,
    LastEditedWhen datetime2(7) NOT NULL,
    CONSTRAINT PK_Sales_Orders PRIMARY KEY CLUSTERED
    (
        OrderID ASC
    )
);
```

One could then, applying a few of the principles we have mentioned in these sections, choose only the columns we are interested in, though we should not need to add a compression delay for this particular case since once the PickedByPersonID is set, we are saying the data is complete.

So we might set up:

```
CREATE NONCLUSTERED COLUMNSTORE INDEX NCCI_Orders ON Sales.Orders
(
    PickedByPersonId,
    SalespersonPersonID,
    OrderDate,
    PickingCompletedWhen
)
WHERE PickedByPersonId IS NOT NULL;
```

One additional thing you can do, if you need your reporting to span the cold and hot data, and that is to cluster your data on the key that is use for the filtering. So in this case, if you clustered your table by PickedByPersonId, the optimizer would easily be able to split the set for your queries. This could seem counter to the advice given earlier about clustering keys and it generally is. However, in some cases this could make a big difference if the reporting is critical. It is covered in more detail by Sunil Agarwal in his blog here (*https://blogs.msdn. microsoft.com/sqlserverstorageengine/2016/03/06/real-time-operational-analytics-filtered-nonclustered-columnstore-index-ncci/*) when he suggested using the a column with a domain of order status values in his example to cluster on, even though it has only 6 values and the table itself has millions.

## Design standard non-clustered indexes in conjunction with clustered columnstore indexes

When using columnstore indexes in your database solution, it is important to know what their values and detriments are. To review, here are some of the attributes we have discussed so far:

- **Columnstore Indexes**   Great for working with large data sets, particularly for aggregation. Not great for looking up a single row, as the index is not ordered
    - **Clustered**   Compresses the table to greatly reduce memory and disk footprint of data.
    - **Nonclustered**   Addition to typical table structure, ideal when the columns included cover the needs of the query.
- **Rowstore Indexes**   Best used for seeking a row, or a set of rows in order.
    - **Clustered**   Physically reorders table's data in an order that is helpful. Useful for the primary access path where you fetch rows along with the rest of the row data, or for scanning data in a given order.
    - **Nonclustered**   Structure best used for finding a single row. Not great for scanning unless all of the data needed is in the index keys, or is in included in the leaf pages of the index.

If you have worked with columnstore indexes in SQL Server 2012 or 2014, it is necessary to change how you think about using these indexes. In 2012, SQL Server only had read only non-clustered columnstore indexes, and to modify the data in the index (and any of the rows in the table), the index needed to be dropped and completely rebuilt. In 2014, read/write clustered columnstore indexes were added, but there was no way to have a rowstore index on the same table with them. When you needed to fetch a single row, the query processor needed to scan the entire table. If your ETL did many updates or deletes, the operation was costly. So for many applications, sticking with the drop and recreating a non-clustered index made sense.

In SQL Server 2016, the version that you are studying for in this exam, both types of columnstore indexes are read/write, and both allow you to have complimentary rowstore indexes. In this section, we focus on adding non-clustered indexes to your clustered columnstore indexes, which in the previous section we have established as generally the best practice for data warehousing situations, mostly fact tables, and possibly very large dimensions. The columnstore indexes are there to aid in analytical queries, but there are a few other needs to consider.

To demonstrate, begin by making a copy of the Fact.Sale table in the WideWorldImport-ersDW database, and adding a clustered columnstore index.

```
SELECT *
INTO    Fact.SaleBase
FROM    Fact.Sale;

CREATE CLUSTERED COLUMNSTORE INDEX CColumnsStore ON Fact.SaleBase;
```

You see that if you perform an aggregation query, the columnstore index is used, and the performance is stellar:

```
SELECT Date.[Fiscal Year], Customer.Category,  Sum(Quantity) as NumSales
FROM    Fact.SaleBase
        JOIN Dimension.Customer
            on Customer.[Customer Key] = SaleBase.[Customer Key]
        JOIN Dimension.Date
            ON Date.Date = SaleBase.[Invoice Date Key]
GROUP BY Date.[Fiscal Year], Customer.Category
ORDER BY Date.[Fiscal Year], Customer.Category;
```

And the plan is shown in Figure 1-30.

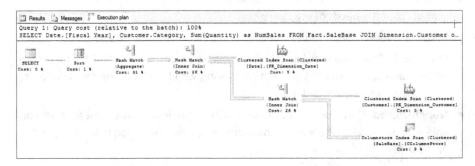

**FIGURE 1-30** The plan with the query aggregating data from the fact

Figure 1-30 has the following output:

```
Table 'Worktable'. Scan count 0, logical reads 0, physical reads 0, read-ahead reads 0,
lob logical reads 0, lob physical reads 0,

lob read-ahead reads 0.

Table 'Customer'. Scan count 1, logical reads 15, physical reads 0, read-ahead reads 0,
lob logical reads 0, lob physical reads 0,

lob read-ahead reads 0.

Table 'Date'. Scan count 1, logical reads 28, physical reads 0, read-ahead reads 0, lob
logical reads 0, lob physical reads 0,

lob read-ahead reads 0.

CPU time = 15 ms,  elapsed time = 22 ms.
```

What is likely unexpected is what happens when filtering on a single value in a column not yet referenced by adding to the statement the following WHERE clause (a common operation when doing ETL where data can change):

```
WHERE SaleBase.[Sale Key] = 26974
```

The plan changes to something that looks better, but actually takes more time and considerably more IO as seen in Figure 1-31.

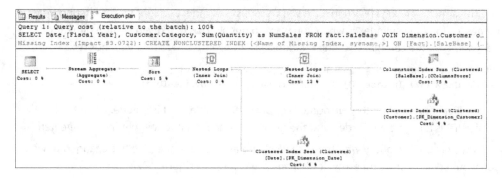

**FIGURE 1-31** The plan with the query aggregating one row based on the [Sale Key]

Figure 1-31 has the following output:

```
Table 'SaleBase'. Scan count 1, logical reads 0, physical reads 0, read-ahead reads 0,
lob logical reads 347, lob physical reads 0,

lob read-ahead reads 0.

Table 'SaleBase'. Segment reads 1, segment skipped 0.

Table 'Worktable'. Scan count 0, logical reads 0, physical reads 0, read-ahead reads 0,
lob logical reads 0, lob physical reads 0,

lob read-ahead reads 0.

Table 'Date'. Scan count 0, logical reads 2, physical reads 0, read-ahead reads 0, lob
logical reads 0, lob physical reads 0,

lob read-ahead reads 0.

Table 'Customer'. Scan count 0, logical reads 2, physical reads 0, read-ahead reads 0,
lob logical reads 0, lob physical reads 0,

lob read-ahead reads 0.

CPU time = 0 ms,   elapsed time = 40 ms.
```

Note that now the major cost is spent in the Columnstore Scan operator, which isn't surprising since the query processor has to touch all of the rows in the table; for the column segment for the [Sale Key] in any case. This cost isn't too much in this very small fact table (less than 300,000 rows), but it is very telling that you have an issue if you're needing to fetch rows one at a time for some reason, either to update data, or delete a row.

So next we add indexes to the table for any cases where you want to access rows one at a time. Examples in the Fact.SaleBase table are columns like the surrogate key: [Sale Key], and the degenerate key: [WWI Invoice ID]. Other uses of indexes might be for filtering date ranges, or foreign key indexes when you want to get all rows of a given related dimension, depending on the cardinality of the relationship. For example, let's add two indexes:

```
CREATE UNIQUE INDEX [Sale Key] ON Fact.SaleBase ([Sale Key]);
CREATE INDEX [WWI Invoice ID] ON Fact.SaleBase ([WWI Invoice ID]);
```

The [Sale Key] index is the surrogate key for the fact table, so it is unique, while the [WWI Invoice ID] is for the entire order, and the grain of the table is one row per invoice line item.

Now perform the query with the WHERE clause and you see the plan has changed to what you would desire for a single-row lookup, as you can see in Figure 1-32.

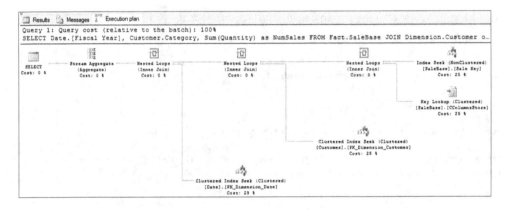

**FIGURE 1-32** The plan with the query aggregating one row based on the [Sale Key] after adding a non-clustered rowstore index to the column

Figure 1-32 has the following output:

```
Table 'Date'. Scan count 0, logical reads 2, physical reads 0, read-ahead reads 0, lob
logical reads 0, lob physical reads 0,

lob read-ahead reads 0.

Table 'Customer'. Scan count 0, logical reads 2, physical reads 0, read-ahead reads 0,
lob logical reads 0, lob physical reads 0,

lob read-ahead reads 0.

Table 'SaleBase'. Scan count 1, logical reads 3, physical reads 0, read-ahead reads 0,
lob logical reads 186, lob physical reads 0,
```

lob read-ahead reads 0.

Table 'SaleBase'. Segment reads 1, segment skipped 0.

CPU time = 0 ms,   elapsed time = 30 ms.

Now, while you never aggregate just a row at a time, other than perhaps in development, when you go to update a single row in the table during ETL, the operation of finding the rows is not cost prohibitive.

## Implement columnstore index maintenance

In this section we look at what maintenance you need to do with your columnstore indexes as you load them in various ways. To do the index maintenance, use the ALTER INDEX command, either using the REORGANIZE or REBUILD settings. REORGANIZE basically starts the tuple mover immediately rather than running it in the background, slowly. REORGANIZE is, like the tuple mover running natively, an ONLINE operation.  REBUILD on the other hand, is just like creating a new clean index, and compresses all of the data, but it is an offline process.

You need to decide whether to wait for the tuple mover to handle your structure, force the tuple mover to perform, or just rebuild your indexes, depending on the urgency of your needs. If this is a nightly-loaded data warehouse and you have the time, you want to just use REBUILD, but if it is a more active system, you want to check the configuration of the index and do a REORGANIZE. We look at a few examples in this section.

There are a few ways that data is loaded into a columnstore:

- **Bulk Load Into a Clustered Columnstore**   Different from bulk loading data into a rowstore table, you can load bulk amounts of data into a clustered columnstore index by using an INSERT...SELECT ... FROM <TableName> WITH (TABLOCK) statement.

- **Other Batch Operations**   Loading data where you don't meet the requirements of the Bulk Load pattern.

For each of the examples, use a pared-down version of the Fact.Sale table named Fact.SaleLimited, as shown in Listing 1-18

LISTING 1-18  Fact table code to be used for this section

```
CREATE TABLE [Fact].[SaleLimited](
      [City Key] [int] NOT NULL,
            [Customer Key] [int] NOT NULL,
      [Bill To Customer Key] [int] NOT NULL,
      [Stock Item Key] [int] NOT NULL,
      [Invoice Date Key] [date] NOT NULL,
      [Delivery Date Key] [date] NULL,
      [Salesperson Key] [int] NOT NULL,
      [WWI Invoice ID] [int] NOT NULL,
      [Description] [nvarchar](100) NOT NULL,
      [Package] [nvarchar](50) NOT NULL,
      [Quantity] [int] NOT NULL
);
```

## Bulk loading data into a clustered columnstore

To start with, add a clustered columnstore index to the Fact.SaleLimited table:

```
CREATE CLUSTERED COLUMNSTORE INDEX [CColumnStore] ON [Fact].[SaleLimited];
```

Next, load some data. The WITH (TABLOCK) allows this statement to run in parallel (for more information, the following blog has more details: *https://blogs.msdn.microsoft.com/sql-cat/2016/07/21/real-world-parallel-insert-what-else-you-need-to-know/*), so you could end up with more or less deltastores on your system:

```
INSERT INTO [Fact].[SaleLimited] WITH (TABLOCK)
    ([City Key], [Customer Key],  [Bill To Customer Key], [Stock Item Key],
     [Invoice Date Key], [Delivery Date Key],[Salesperson Key],
     [WWI Invoice ID], [Description], [Package], [Quantity])
SELECT TOP (100000) [City Key], [Customer Key],  [Bill To Customer Key],
        [Stock Item Key], [Invoice Date Key], [Delivery Date Key],[Salesperson Key],
        [WWI Invoice ID], [Description], [Package], [Quantity]
FROM Fact.Sale
GO 3 --run this statement 3 times
```

Next, go and look at the information from the DMV sys.dm_db_column_store_row_group_physical_stats, which gives you information about the physical characteristics of the rowgroups in your columnstore index. The query in Listing 1-19 is used throughout these maintenance sections to view the physical state of the columnstore indexes.

> **LISTING 1-19**  Query on sys.dm_db_column_store_row_group_physical_stats to see state of columnstore indexes
>
> ```
> SELECT state_desc, total_rows, deleted_rows,
>        transition_to_compressed_state_desc as transition
> FROM sys.dm_db_column_store_row_group_physical_stats
> WHERE object_id  = OBJECT_ID('Fact.SaleLimited');
> ```

The output of this query, right after execution is:

```
state_desc      total_rows deleted_rows transition
--------------- ---------- ------------ --------------------------------
OPEN            150000     0            NULL
OPEN            150000     0            NULL
```

Two deltastore rowgroups were created, since there are two processors in my VM, and the bulk insert performs in parallel. If the VM had 8 processors, there could have been as many as 8 groups created. Since the total_rows column value is less than the 1048576 rows that is optimum, executing simple ALTER INDEX REORGANIZE does not change anything. The transition column tells you what triggered the row group to transition to a compressed state. There are other good bits of information not shown here, like the trim_reason that tells you why less than the expected maximum number of rows are in the rowgroup.

However, if you are not going to be adding any additional rows, you can force the tuple mover to compress these rowgroups by executing:

```
ALTER INDEX CColumnStore ON Fact.SaleLimited REORGANIZE
                        WITH (COMPRESS_ALL_ROW_GROUPS = ON);
```

Then you see:

```
state_desc      total_rows deleted_rows transition
--------------- ---------- ------------ ------------------------------
COMPRESSED      150000     0            REORG_FORCED
COMPRESSED      150000     0            REORG_FORCED
TOMBSTONE       150000     0            NULL
TOMBSTONE       150000     0            NULL
```

The two deltastore rowgroups have been compressed, and have then been tombstoned. When and whether you want to do these tasks largely depends on the type of table. For an OLTP table, where data is being loaded constantly, it may not be advantageous to reorganize the table, particularly if you are rapidly reaching the million row point. Of course, it is possible that you want to run the reorganize prior to a large reporting task. For a data warehouse table that is loaded periodically, you want to either rebuild or reorganize, depending on time allotted, and how many UPDATE and DELETE operations have occurred. Once you have compressed filegroups, things happen automatically.

Forcing the tuple mover to start by running REORGANIZE has the process combine the two compressed row groups, as the larger the number of rows in the rowgroup, up to the maximum, is better.

```
ALTER INDEX CColumnStore ON Fact.SaleLimited REORGANIZE;
```

Now check the structure of the columnstore index:

```
state_desc      total_rows deleted_rows transition
--------------- ---------- ------------ ------------------------------
COMPRESSED      300000     0            MERGE
TOMBSTONE       150000     0            NULL
TOMBSTONE       150000     0            NULL
```

Note, if you directly bulk insert 102400 or more rows, the data goes directly into compressed rowgroups as rows are being added. To show what happens when you bulk load at least the minimum number of rows, perform:

```
TRUNCATE TABLE Fact.SaleLimited;
GO
INSERT INTO [Fact].[SaleLimited] WITH (TABLOCK)
    ([City Key], [Customer Key],  [Bill To Customer Key], [Stock Item Key],
     [Invoice Date Key], [Delivery Date Key],[Salesperson Key],
     [WWI Invoice ID], [Description], [Package], [Quantity])
SELECT TOP (102400) [City Key], [Customer Key],  [Bill To Customer Key],
```

```
                [Stock Item Key], [Invoice Date Key], [Delivery Date Key],[Salesperson Key],
                [WWI Invoice ID], [Description], [Package], [Quantity]
FROM Fact.Sale
OPTION (MAXDOP 1); --not in parallel
GO 3
```

You now see three compressed rowgroups in the output of the Listing 1-19 query. This is better for actually using the row groups immediately, but not as efficient as having them all in the same rowgroup:

```
state_desc      total_rows deleted_rows transition
--------------- ---------- ------------ ------------------------------
COMPRESSED      102400     0            BULKLOAD
COMPRESSED      102400     0            BULKLOAD
COMPRESSED      102400     0            BULKLOAD
```

Perform ALTER INDEX REORGANIZE, and these three rowgroups are combined into just 1.

```
state_desc      total_rows deleted_rows transition
--------------- ---------- ------------ ------------------------------
COMPRESSED      307200     0            MERGE
TOMBSTONE       102400     0            NULL
TOMBSTONE       102400     0            NULL
TOMBSTONE       102400     0            NULL
```

Using ALTER INDEX...REBUILD skips directly to having all of the rowgroups compressed in the best fashion possible, much like dropping and recreating the index, but it is an offline process just like initially recreating the index. This is true, even a minimal number of rows, as in this example:

```
TRUNCATE TABLE Fact.SaleLimited;
INSERT INTO [Fact].[SaleLimited] WITH (TABLOCK)
([City Key],      [Customer Key],
                [Bill To Customer Key], [Stock Item Key],
                [Invoice Date Key], [Delivery Date Key],[Salesperson Key],
                [WWI Invoice ID], [Description], [Package], [Quantity])

SELECT TOP (5000) [City Key],      [Customer Key],
                [Bill To Customer Key], [Stock Item Key],
                [Invoice Date Key], [Delivery Date Key],[Salesperson Key],
                [WWI Invoice ID], [Description], [Package], [Quantity]

FROM Fact.Sale;
```

Then rebuild the index:

```
ALTER INDEX [CColumnStore] ON [Fact].[SaleLimited] REBUILD;
```

And there is a compressed rowgroup with only 5000 rows:

```
state_desc      total_rows deleted_rows transition
--------------- ---------- ------------ ------------------------------
COMPRESSED      5000       0            INDEX_BUILD
```

## Non-bulk operations on a columnstore

For any columnstore index, when you load data and never reach the 1048576 rows to get the tuple mover to compress the data, you can do the exact same tasks as we looked at in the previous section. The following code demonstrates how the other, non-bulk operations show up, and what maintenance steps that one can take to clear things up. Using the same table we had in the previous section, load 100000 rows, and use ALTER INDEX REBUILD to set the index up in pristine shape.

```
TRUNCATE TABLE Fact.SaleLimited;
INSERT INTO [Fact].[SaleLimited]
([City Key],       [Customer Key],
                  [Bill To Customer Key], [Stock Item Key],
                  [Invoice Date Key], [Delivery Date Key],[Salesperson Key],
                  [WWI Invoice ID], [Description], [Package], [Quantity])

SELECT TOP (100000 ) [City Key],    [Customer Key],
                  [Bill To Customer Key], [Stock Item Key],
                  [Invoice Date Key], [Delivery Date Key],[Salesperson Key],
                  [WWI Invoice ID], [Description], [Package], [Quantity]

FROM Fact.Sale;
ALTER INDEX [CColumnStore] ON [Fact].[SaleLimited] REBUILD;
```

Now the structure looks like:

| state_desc | total_rows | deleted_rows | transition |
|---|---|---|---|
| COMPRESSED | 100000 | 0 | INDEX_BUILD |

Then delete some data:

```
DELETE FROM Fact.SaleLimited
WHERE   [Customer Key] = 21;
```

You now see what is sometimes thought of as fragmentation showing up. There are still 100000 rows in the rowgroup, but 135 rows are marked as deleted. As this number grows, the rowgroup becomes less and less useful:

| state_desc | total_rows | deleted_rows | transition |
|---|---|---|---|
| COMPRESSED | 100000 | 135 | INDEX_BUILD |

Next, update some data:

```
UPDATE Fact.SaleLimited
SET    [Customer Key] = 35
WHERE  [Customer Key] = 22;
```

Looking at the structure, you can now see that we have more deleted rows, and a new delta rowgroup for the inserted versions of the updated rows.

| state_desc | total_rows | deleted_rows | transition |
|---|---|---|---|
| OPEN | 98 | 0 | NULL |
| COMPRESSED | 100000 | 233 | INDEX_BUILD |

From here, there are three choices. Wait for the tuple mover to deal with this situation, though maybe not if more data isn't loaded. REBUILD, or REORGANIZE using the COMPRESS_ALL_ROW_GROUPS option as done in the previous section.

The steps done here are the same for non-clustered and clustered columnstore indexes, but the non-clustered version does not update the deleted_rows column, whereas the clustered does. Columnstore indexes are wonderful for many things, but they are definitely tuned for large quantities of data, particularly when the automated processes work after more than a million rows are inserted. This, plus the fact that they can get fragmented from just simple INSERT, UPDATE, and DELETE statements means you certainly want to keep up with how the load from your processes is affecting the rowgroups.

> **NEED MORE REVIEW?** **COLUMNSTORE INDEX MAINTENANCE RESOURCES**
>
> There are a lot of resources about maintaining columnstore indexes, and a few of the more useful ones that are definitely worth reviewing are:
>
> - **Columnstore Indexes Defragmentation**  *https://msdn.microsoft.com/en-us/library/dn935013.aspx*. Details on what fragments columnstore indexes, and links to Sunil Agarwal's blogs on the topics as well.
> - **Part 36 of Niko Neugebauer's blog series on clustered columnstore indexes**  *http://www.nikoport.com/2014/07/29/clustered-columnstore-indexes-part-36-maintenance-solutions-for-columnstore/.* Of course, the other many sections of his series on columnstore indexes are useful reading as well.
> - **An excellent blog on the Tuple Mover on the Rusanu Consulting Blog, mentioned by Sunil Agarwal**  *http://rusanu.com/2013/12/02/sql-server-clustered-columnstore-tuple-mover/.*
> - **Columnstore Data Loading**  *https://msdn.microsoft.com/en-us/library/dn935008.aspx* Covers how data is loaded into the columnstore index, and how this affects the need to maintain your indexes.

# Chapter summary

- Designing your database objects starts with requirements and understanding them. On the exam, if you are presented with a set of requirements to match to a table set, make sure you comprehend and match requirements precisely to the objects given.
- Understanding what normalization means is essential to the process of matching the needs of the user to the needs of the query optimizer and processor. The normal forms are very much about eliminated duplication in your structures to enhance data integrity,
- SQL Server provides you as a user with a tremendous number of data types, not all of which you need for any given design. Match the data type you need to the requirements

the user provides or, if no prescribed size is provided, to a size that is large enough to handle any reasonable value, but not so large as to allow unnecessarily large values. For example: nvarchar(3) for a person's name, too small, nvarchar(max) far too large. nvarchar(50) is probably more than you ever need, but not so large that it is ridiculous.

- Dynamic Data Masking can be added to the declaration for a column in the table create statement to mask data from database principals that do not have the UNMASK privilege in the database. There are several functions you can use to mask data.

- The clustered index of a table is a very important choice, as the key columns are used in all other rowstore indexes. The greater percentage of your queries can use the clustered index for seek operations to answer queries the better. The best clustered indexes are small in size, never changing, and monotonically increasing. A small clustering key size reduces the size of all nonclustered indexes; never changing values eliminates updates to non-clustered indexes; and monotonically increasing lets data be inserted at the end of the physical structures.

- An essential tool for designing indexes is the query plan. Use the graphical versions from the UI, or one of the SET SHOWPLAN commands to get a textual version of the estimated plan, or SET STATISTICS PROFILE ON for a textual version of the actual plan. Adding indexes without any real knowledge of how they are used often ends up creating useless indexes (something that is touched on in Chapter 4.)

- Index key columns can total 900 bytes or less for a clustered index, and up to 1700 bytes for a non-clustered index.

- There is only one clustered index, which makes it very important to choose what to put in the clustered index wisely for two reasons:

  - The data pages of the table are ordered by the clustering key
  - All non-clustered indexes use the clustering key for their row locators

- Providing summarized/denormalized data to the client by DML based automated means can be achieved using an indexed view.

- Columnstore indexes are specifically built for analytic purposes and typically need to be coupled with rowstore indexes to allow searches on a single row, unless you extremely rarely need to fetch a single row.

- Clustered columnstore indexes change your table's storage and compress your data considerably, reducing the amount of IO needed to perform queries on very large data sets. Nonclustered columnstore indexes can be added to a rowstore table to allow real-time analytics.

- In columnstore indexes, DELETE operations just mark compressed rows as deleted, and UPDATE operations mark the row to be updated deleted and perform and INSERT. Both INSERT operations add rows to a deltastore rowgroup. Unless your table is very active, you need to perform maintenance on your table using ALTER INDEX REORGANIZE or ALTER INDEX REBUILD to get the most out of your columnstore indexes, as the background tuple mover moves rows when there are 1048576 rows in the deltastore rowgroup.

# Thought experiment

In this thought experiment, demonstrate your skills and knowledge of the topics covered in this chapter. You can find the answer to this thought experiment in the next section.

You are taking over the table design for the invoicing system for a toy shop. The requirements state "Wingtip Toys want to track their customer's basic information, the orders they have placed for one or more products, and how much they have paid for each product on the order. The price of a toy can change for every order."

In the database, you see the following tables, with accompanying definitions:

- **Customer**   People and companies that have purchase toys from the shop
- **CustomerOwnedToys**   Toys that we know a customer owns
- **InvoiceItem**   The bill for the toys that a customer has purchased
- **Product**   The list of products that Wingtip Toys sells.

What are the potential issues with the design, based solely on the table names?

The original designer had created a column in the Customer table named: nickname, allowing you to store a name a person would prefer to be called. For example, a person named William might prefer to be called Bill, and Mariusz Wolodzko could prefer to be called "Captain Awesome." The data type for this column is int, and you realize that int is not really a desirable data type for storing a text value. You have the following five different data types that you are deciding from:

1. varchar (100)
2. nvarchar(50)
3. nvarchar(Max)
4. char(120)
5. varbinary(100)

For each type, evaluate in terms of A. Ability to store the data B. Appropriateness of the data type to meet the specified requirements.

Once the database has been created, the following query is written:

```
SELECT StockItemID, StockItemName, SupplierID, ColorID, UnitPackageID,
       OuterPackageID, Brand, Size
FROM   Examples.Product
WHERE  UnitPackageId = 9;
```

And the plan for this query is shown in Figure 1-33:

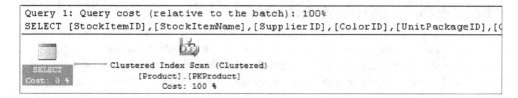

```
Query 1: Query cost (relative to the batch): 100%
SELECT [StockItemID],[StockItemName],[SupplierID],[ColorID],[UnitPackageID],[(

  SELECT            Clustered Index Scan (Clustered)
  Cost: 0 %              [Product].[PKProduct]
                            Cost: 100 %
```

**FIGURE 1-33** The plan for a simple query

From the information given, can you decide if adding either of the following indexes improves the query?

- CREATE INDEX UnitPackageId ON Examples.Product (UnitPackageId);

- CREATE INDEX UnitPackageIdPlus ON Examples.Product (UnitPackageId) INCLUDE (StockItemID, StockItemName, SupplierID, ColorID, OuterPackageID, Brand, Size);

Finally, in your review, you see the following table with over 5 million rows in it:

```
CREATE TABLE Sales.InvoiceItemFact
(
    InvoiceItemFactId int NOT NULL
        IDENTITY CONSTRAINT PKInvoiceItemFact PRIMARY KEY,
    ProductDimId int NOT NULL,
    CustomerDimId int NOT NULL,
    DateDimId int NOT NULL,
    SalesAmount money NOT NULL,
    SalesQuantity decimal(10,4)

);
```

There is also a table named Sales.ProductDim and Sales.CustomerDim, that contain data about the customer and product associated with the sale. Do all of the indexes work with the existing PRIMARY KEY constraint's index? For queries that aggregate a lot of data in the table, do the indexes help?

- CREATE INDEX ProductDimId ON Sales.InvoiceItemFact (ProductDimId);

- CREATE NONCLUSTERED COLUMNSTORE INDEX NCColumnstore ON Sales.InvoiceItemFact (InvoiceItemFactId, ProductDimId, CustomerDimId, DateDimId, SalesAmount, SalesQuantity);

- CREATE CLUSTERED COLUMNSTORE INDEX CColumnstore ON Sales.InvoiceItemFact;

# Thought experiment answer

This section contains the solution to the thought experiment. Each answer explains why the answer choice is correct. Users provide an email address when they sign up. However, sometimes the same person creates multiple accounts with the same email address, causing issues with the validity of a research results set.

There are several concerns in the design as given, both in terms of meeting the requirements given and basic normalization considerations. In terms of requirements, there is a table named CustomerOwnedToys, specifying a feature that was not requested by the customer. The normalization problem comes with just having an InvoiceItem table without a table named Invoice. This causes the columns to need to repeat information about the order that was placed. There was one answer included to possibly throw you off. "The price of a toy can change for every order" seems to indicate that we need a ProductPrice table. However, the requirements strictly ask "how much they have paid for each product on the order".

A column for a person's nickname is a typical need, and clearly int is not the proper solution. Let's look at each type mentioned, in terms of A. Ability to store the data, and B. Appropriateness of the data type to meet the specified requirements.

1. varchar (100)

    A. Since this is an ASCII type, it is acceptable for storing simple character data. However, real names contain special characters. It is best to use a Unicode type for names

    B. 100 characters of string data is likely too long of a string for name data, the width of text on this page is approximately 80 characters wide. If you are going to allow 100 characters in a column, usage should never cut it off. Since it is variably sized, it does not waste space, making it efficient enough.

2. nvarchar(50)

    A. This is a Unicode type, and as such it should handle any text.

    B. 50 characters is a typical length that people set names to be. Since it is variably sized, it does not waste space, making it efficient enough.

3. nvarchar(Max)

    A. This is a Unicode type, and as such it should handle any text.

    B. Much like other larger strings, this is too large of a string for a name at over 1 million characters. Some designers simply use nvarchar(max) because it is easy, and since it is variably sized, technically no less efficient than any other nvarchar type. However, this is generally not the best practice that is desirable.

4. char(120)

    A. Since this is an ASCII type, it is acceptable for storing simple character data. However, real names contain special characters. It is best to use a Unicode type for names.

**B.** 120 characters is too long, and in this case, since it is not variable sized, space is typically wasted when storing a short string. Even if using a compression setting (not covered in this exam), the string appears padded in all uses, which is not optimal.

5. varbinary(100)

   **A.** If you assumed that this would not work, you were incorrect. While it is definitely not the most efficient way to store a string, the following CAST expression results in a Unicode string of N'Bill': CAST (0x420069006C006C00 as nvarchar(100)).

   **B.** Clearly this is not optimum way of storing a string. However, this is something that could have been done in very old systems to give binary comparisons. Using a binary collation provides the same properties in modern versions of SQL Server.

Given the query we have been provided on the Examples.Product table, without any data to look at, it is not possible to be sure that either index that we are provided with gives any benefit (for example, what if the table had 1 row? The size of the line from the Clustered Index Scan to the SELECT operator is very thin. It also isn't stated if an index already exists on the UnitPackage column.) However, so this isn't just a trick question, let's assume that there is data in the table, there is not an index on UnitPackageId, and some data was returned from the query.

- **CREATE INDEX UnitPackageId ON Examples.Product (UnitPackageId);** This index has the least likelihood between the two to provide benefit. For it to be useful, there needs to be a lot of rows that don't match, and just a few that do, based on the statistics of the table. Because of the necessity of a Key Lookup operator to fetch additional columns that are not in the index, the value of this index has to be great to outweigh the costs.

- **CREATE INDEX UnitPackageIdPlus ON Examples.Product (UnitPackageId) INCLUDE (StockItemID, StockItemName, SupplierID, ColorID, OuterPackageID, Brand, Size);** There is no guarantee that this index tremendously improves the query, since we are not sure if there are columns in the table that are not included but the index, but since the index key matches the WHERE clause, and the INCLUDE columns match the SELECT clause, it can almost certainly be of some value to the query.

Finally, there were a few indexes that were to be applied to a fact table in a dimensional design.

All indexes listed work with the existing PRIMARY KEY constraint index.

- **CREATE INDEX ProductDimId ON Sales.InvoiceItemFact (ProductDimId);** This index is generally only be useful for queries only return a ProductDimId, such as counting the number of orders per ProductDimId. Generally, this is not a great, general-purpose index.

- **CREATE NONCLUSTERED COLUMNSTORE INDEX NCColumnstore ON Sales. InvoiceItemFact (InvoiceItemFactId, ProductDimId, CustomerDimId, DateDimId,**

**SalesAmount, SalesQuantity);**    Almost all queries that do analytical queries on the Sales.InvoiceItemFact table can benefit from this index. However, the non-clustered columnstore index is generally more appropriate for OLTP tables, where you want a minimal overhead for the OLTP users, and no change to the base table structures.

- **CREATE CLUSTERED COLUMNSTORE INDEX CColumnstore ON Sales.InvoiceItemFact;**    This is the best choice of index from the list. It compresses the base data in the table to make the IO impact the smallest for all queries. It works nicely with the PRIMARY KEY constraint index to allow singleton updates/seeks as needed for ETL and simple queries also. Note that you will need to change the existing primary key constraint to NONCLUSTERED before executing this statement, since by default a PRIMARY KEY constraint creates a CLUSTERED index.

## CHAPTER 2

# Implement programmability objects

In the previous chapter, we reviewed the basic data structure of a SQL Server database. First, we designed the structures of the database from requirements, and then we built a set of tables and views to access the data, with indexes to make the queries using these objects perform well. In this chapter, we further enhance this database by using more of the tools that SQL Server provides to enhance data integrity through constraints and Transact-SQL coded objects.

Skill 2.1 starts with constraints, a topic we brushed upon in Chapter 1, but we dive deeper into their use and configuration. Constraints help shape the data that can be placed in your tables in a few ways, such as keeping data unique, limiting the domain of columns to certain formats or lengths that can't be done with data type alone, and enforcing foreign key relationships. Using constraints, you take databases from simple data storage, to intelligent data filters that eliminate most data issues with very little performance impact.

In Skill 2.2 we cover stored procedures, which allow you as a programmer to bundle the execution of code together in a way that is generally much more convenient to use than ad-hoc Transact-SQL statements from the middle layer of an application. Almost any code can be performed from a stored procedure, and we cover several of the most useful scenarios.

In Skill 2.3, the final skill section of this chapter, there are two types of objects we deal with: triggers and User-Defined Functions (UDFs). TRIGGER objects are used to react to certain types of actions, such as a DML operation like an INSERT, a DDL operation like ALTER INDEX, CREATE TABLE, etc., or a user logging into the server. The most common use of triggers is to use a DML trigger to extend data integrity where constraints are not sufficient.

UDFs allow you to create modules of code that can be used as the building blocks of SQL statements. While Transact-SQL is not generally great at producing very modular code, UDFs allow you to build code that works much like SQL Server's system functions where it makes sense.

> **NOTE** **TRANSACT-SQL SOLUTIONS**
>
> This chapter focuses primarily on on-disk tables and interpreted Transact-SQL solutions exclusively. Skill 3.4 highlights the differences between these solutions and the memory-optimized tables and natively-compiled modules.

## Skills in this chapter:

- Ensure data integrity with constraints
- Create stored procedures
- Create triggers and user-defined functions

# Skill 2.1 Ensure data integrity with constraints

In Chapter 1, the first skill that we explored was designing a database. In that exercise, we designed a database that met some basic requirements. Many of the data integrity requirements for a database are covered by the table design and the physical implementation, but not all of them. In this skill section, we look at the declarative tools that are available to further constrain data to meet a set of requirements.

> **This section covers how to:**
> - Define table and foreign-key constraints to enforce business rules
> - Write Transact-SQL statements to add constraints to tables
> - Identify results of Data Manipulation Language (DML) statements given existing tables and constraints
> - Identify proper usage of PRIMARY KEY constraints

## Define table and foreign-key constraints to enforce business rules

PRIMARY KEY constraints are almost always used by even novice database implementers, but for the exam (and for implementing a proper database), the other types of constraints that are available are extremely important as well. Constraints can either be for a single column (referred to as column constraints), or for multiple columns (referred to as table constraints.) In this section, we review the following constraint types that you should be familiar with:

- **DEFAULT** Used to provide a value for a column when no value is provided by the user.
- **UNIQUE** Used to implement any uniqueness criteria (alternate/candidate keys) that are not chosen as the primary key.
- **CHECK** Used to apply a simple predicate check to the values in an INSERT or UPDATE operation.
- **FOREIGN KEY** Used to enforce foreign key relationships between tables, so that referenced data is always in existence for rows that reference it.

In addition to reviewing each of these types of constraint individually, we also examine a section on limiting a column value to a set of values, which makes use of a few of these items simultaneously.

## Using DEFAULT constraints to guide the user's input

DEFAULT constraints, at first look, don't seem like they have much value for enforcing business rules, and that is somewhat true. However, they are useful to give the user an idea of what value to put in a column. For example, say you have a column in a table that is called DisabledFlag, with a domain of 1, if what the row represents has been disabled, and 0 when not. More than likely, the typical value of this column is 0. So in the table definition, you might specify:

```
DisabledFlag bit NOT NULL CONSTRAINT DFLTTableName_DisabledFlag DEFAULT (0);
```

Now, if a user doesn't specify this value in the INSERT, it is automatically 0. Applications can access the metadata of the default value as well, so it can be useful that way as well (this can be accessed in sys.default_constraints). There are a few system uses of DEFAULT constraints as well that are commonly used. One is to make it easier to set columns that are used to denote when a row was modified, created, etc. such as RowLastModifiedTime (RowCreatedTime, RowCreatedByLogin, and others). For example, consider the following table, with just a simple integer primary key, and a column that is used to capture the last time the row was modified:

```
CREATE SCHEMA Examples;
GO
CREATE TABLE Examples.Widget
(
    WidgetId    int CONSTRAINT PKWidget PRIMARY KEY,
    RowLastModifiedTime datetime2(0) NOT NULL
);
```

Add the DEFAULT constraint as the default value for the column:

```
ALTER TABLE Examples.Widget
  ADD CONSTRAINT DFLTWidget_RowLastModifiedTime
        DEFAULT (SYSDATETIME()) FOR RowLastModifiedTime;
```

So if you insert a row, you can do one of two things. Either don't include the column in the INSERT statement, or use the DEFAULT keyword to have the value default itself, as in the following two statements:

```
INSERT INTO Examples.Widget(WidgetId)
VALUES (1),(2);
INSERT INTO Examples.Widget(WidgetId, RowLastModifiedTime)
VALUES (3,DEFAULT), (4,DEFAULT);
```

Checking the data that has been inserted:

```
SELECT *
FROM    Examples.Widget;
```

The values are all the same, as the statements were executed within the same second:

```
WidgetId     RowLastModifiedTime
-----------  ----------------------------
1            2016-09-14 18:08:28
2            2016-09-14 18:08:28
3            2016-09-14 18:08:28
4            2016-09-14 18:08:28
```

You can also use the DEFAULT keyword on an UPDATE operation. The following query would change every row's RowLastModifiedTime to the default value, which is the current time:

```
UPDATE Examples.Widget
SET RowLastModifiedTime = DEFAULT;
```

DEFAULT constraints are also useful for adding a new NOT NULL column to a table that already has data in it. As the column is being added to the table, it uses the DEFAULT constraints value. If you are adding a DEFAULT to an existing column, use the following syntax:

```
ALTER TABLE Examples.Widget
  ADD EnabledFlag BIT NOT NULL
      CONSTRAINT DFLTWidget_EnabledFlag DEFAULT (1);
```

> **NOTE  NULL COLUMNS**
>
> If the column is defined as NULL when creating it, all of the values are NULL in the column when you create the column even if you attach a DEFAULT constraint. When you are creating a NULL column and want to default all of the values in the new column regardless, use WITH VALUES after the DEFAULT specification DEFAULT (value) WITH VALUES.

One last interesting thing you should know about using DEFAULT constraints is that if every column either has the IDENTITY property or has a DEFAULT constraint, you can use DEFAULT VALUES to skip the entire VALUES clause. For example, consider the following table:

```
CREATE TABLE Examples.AllDefaulted
(
    AllDefaultedId int IDENTITY(1,1) NOT NULL,
    RowCreatedTime datetime2(0) NOT NULL
        CONSTRAINT DFLTAllDefaulted_RowCreatedTime DEFAULT (SYSDATETIME()),
    RowModifiedTime datetime2(0) NOT NULL
        CONSTRAINT DFLTAllDefaulted_RowModifiedTime DEFAULT (SYSDATETIME())
);
```

Now you can create a new row with all default values, by using DEFAULT VALUES:

```
INSERT INTO Examples.AllDefaulted
DEFAULT VALUES;
```

You can specify any of the columns in the table in the INSERT INTO clause that have a DEFAULT constraint:

```
INSERT INTO Examples.AllDefaulted(RowModifiedTime, RowCreatedTime)
DEFAULT VALUES;
INSERT INTO Examples.AllDefaulted(RowCreatedTime)
DEFAULT VALUES;
```

And the values are defaulted:

```
SELECT *
FROM    Examples.AllDefaulted;
```

This returns:

```
AllDefaultedId  RowCreatedTime                  RowModifiedTime
--------------  --------------------------      ---------------------------
1               2016-09-14 18:19:30             2016-09-14 18:19:30
2               2016-09-14 18:19:30             2016-09-14 18:19:30
3               2016-09-14 18:19:30             2016-09-14 18:19:30
```

As we mentioned previously, this does not work with the column with the IDENTITY property set. So if you were to include the column in the INSERT column list, you will get an error:

```
INSERT INTO Examples.AllDefaulted(AllDefaultedId)
DEFAULT VALUES;
```

This gets you an error message:

```
Msg 339, Level 16, State 1, Line 69
DEFAULT or NULL are not allowed as explicit identity values.
```

This is because not including the column in the INSERT list is telling the query processor to use DEFAULT constraint values, not to use the IDENTITY property.

## Using UNIQUE constraints to enforce secondary uniqueness criteria

A particularly important constraint to use when using surrogate keys for your primary keys is the UNIQUE constraint. We discuss choosing a PRIMARY KEY later in the chapter, but the purpose of the UNIQUE constraint is pretty straightforward: protect the uniqueness characteristics of column sets that need to be unique but were not chosen as the PRIMARY KEY.

Consider the following table that has two key columns, the GadgetId, and the Gadget-Code. Say that GadgetId has been chosen as the PRIMARY KEY:

```
CREATE TABLE Examples.Gadget
(
    GadgetId     int IDENTITY(1,1) NOT NULL CONSTRAINT PKGadget PRIMARY KEY,
    GadgetCode   varchar(10) NOT NULL
);
```

Now the following set of data is inserted:

```
INSERT INTO Examples.Gadget(GadgetCode)
VALUES ('Gadget'), ('Gadget'), ('Gadget');
```

The data in the table now looks like the following:

```
GadgetId    GadgetCode
----------- ----------
1           Gadget
2           Gadget
3           Gadget
```

It is not possible to tell one row from another except using a value that was system-generated, so we need to add a constraint to the table to make sure that this cannot happen. The UNIQUE constraint works very much like a PRIMARY KEY constraint, in that it enforces uniqueness and is implemented with an UNIQUE INDEX. There are a few subtle differences however:

- The index that is created to back the constraint is nonclustered by default.
- The columns of the key allow NULL values (yet, quite unusually, NULL values are treated as equal on this case).

On the GadgetCode column of the Examples.Gadget table, create a UNIQUE constraint, after deleting the logically duplicated data:

```
DELETE FROM Examples.Gadget WHERE GadgetId in (2,3);

ALTER TABLE Examples.Gadget
    ADD CONSTRAINT AKGadget UNIQUE (GadgetCode);
```

Now, an attempt to insert a row with the duplicated GadgetCode value of Gadget:

```
INSERT INTO Examples.Gadget(GadgetCode)
VALUES ('Gadget');
```

Instead of creating duplicated data in the column, this results in the following error:

```
Msg 2627, Level 14, State 1, Line 100
Violation of UNIQUE KEY constraint 'AKGadget'. Cannot insert duplicate key in object
'Examples.Gadget'. The duplicate key value is (Gadget).
```

Back in Chapter 1, when talking about indexes, we previously covered the concerns with having NULL columns in your UNIQUE constraints. UNIQUE (and PRIMARY KEY) constraints are objects that have properties of data integrity protection, which this skill section is about, as well as indexes.

> **NEED MORE REVIEW?**   **CREATING UNIQUE CONTSTRAINTS**
>
> See the following article on MSDN for more details about creating UNIQUE constraints:
> *https://msdn.microsoft.com/en-us/library/ms190024.aspx.*

## Using CHECK constraints to limit data input

The CHECK constraint is used to apply an expression predicate to data as it is inserted or updated. When evaluating the predicate of a CHECK constraint, the expression must evaluate to FALSE before the new or changed data is rejected. If a column allows NULL, and the expression does not explicitly reject NULL values, then if you need the constraint to fail on any condition, you must explicitly check for NULL.

Typical uses of CHECK constraints are to validate the format of a piece of data, limit the domain of data stricter than a data type, ensure data is in a valid range, and to coordinate multiple values make sense together (the last section of this skill review uses CHECK constraints as one method of choosing an explicit domain of values). The constraint can use a simple expression, and even use a user-defined function that accesses other tables, though that is not a typical use.

Using our sample database, there are several places where we need to limit the data that can be put into the tables. We look at:

- **Limiting data more than a data type** For example, the int data type is arguably the most common data type, but usually the desired range of a columns' value is not between approximately -2 billion to 2 billion. A CHECK constrain can limit the data in a column to a desired range.

- **Enforcing a format for data in a column** Some values, usually character data, needs to meet a predefined format. For example, an American Social Security Number is formatted NNN-NN-NNNN where N is a whole number.

- **Coordinate multiple values together** In some cases, multiple columns need to make logical sense together. For example, a composite foreign key reference that allows NULL values.

While the concept of a CHECK constraint is very simple, in practice there is one major thing to remember: in building a database (and possibly answering an exam question), if the requirement says "always" or "must" (as in "the maximum price of a widget must always be less than or equal to 100") this is a candidate for a constraint. If the requirement is less strict, (as in "the typical maximum price of a widget is 100"), a constraint cannot be used. This particular sort of constraint is more tailored to a user interface message box that asks: "Are you sure that they paid 200 for that widget?"

> **NEED MORE REVIEW? CHECK CONSTRAINTS**
>
> For more information about CHECK constraints than we can cover, check out this article on MSDN about UNIQUE Constraints and CHECK constraints: *https://msdn.microsoft.com/en-us/library/ms187550.aspx#Check*.

## LIMITING DATA MORE THAN A DATA TYPE

When creating initial database objects, a goal from Chapter 1, Skill 1.1 was to choose the best data type possible. If, for example, you need a data type that holds values between 1 and 10, you almost certainly choose a tinyint data type. The tinyint data type has a domain of 0 to 255, which is the data type with the best performance characteristics that is the smallest in range. You can use a decimal(2,0) to get to a domain of -99 to 99, but any integer type is better than a type that is implemented in the software of SQL Server rather than using the hardware as an integer would. In order to limit the values to between 1 and 10, we will use a CHECK constraint.

For example, let's say you have a table that captures the cost of a product in a grocery store. You can use the smallmoney data type, but the smallmoney data type has a range of - 214,748.3648 to 214,748.3647. There are concerns at the top and the bottom of the range. First, a product would not cost a negative amount, so the bottom limit should be at least 0. At the top you don't want to accidentally charge 200 thousand for a can of corn. For this example, we limit the cost to a range of greater than 0 to 999.9999.

```
CREATE TABLE Examples.GroceryItem
(
    ItemCost smallmoney NULL,
    CONSTRAINT CHKGroceryItem_ItemCostRange
        CHECK (ItemCost > 0 AND ItemCost < 1000)
);
```

> **NOTE  CHECKING A CONSTRAINT**
>
> You can determine if a constraint is a table or column level constraint by checking the parent_column_id in the sys.check_constraints system catalog view. If it is NULL, then it is a table constraint.

Now, any attempt to put a value outside of the range in the predicate:

```
INSERT INTO Examples.GroceryItem
VALUES (3000.95);
```

This causes an error:

```
Msg 547, Level 16, State 0, Line 286
The INSERT statement conflicted with the CHECK constraint
"CHKGroceryItem_ItemCostRange". The conflict occurred in database "ExamBook762Ch2",
table "Examples.GroceryItem", column 'ItemCost'.
```

But values in the allowable range are accepted:

```
INSERT INTO Examples.GroceryItem
VALUES (100.95);
```

Finally, note that since the column allows NULL values, an INSERT with a NULL for the ItemCost is allowed, even though the predicate was: ItemCost > 0 and ItemCost < 1000.

```
INSERT INTO Examples.GroceryItem
VALUES (NULL);
```

If, for some reason, you want this column to reject NULL values even though it is declared NULL, you can add AND ItemCost IS NOT NULL to the predicate.

### ENFORCING A FORMAT FOR DATA IN A COLUMN

Datatypes can be used to limit data to a maximum length, but they cannot limit data to a minimum length or a certain format (though XML and uniqueidentifier are examples where they have some formatting control). For example, it is a common desire to disallow a user from inputting only space characters for a value in a column, or to make sure that a corporate-standard-formatted value is input for a value.

As an example, consider the following table:

```
CREATE TABLE Examples.Message
(
    MessageTag  char(5) NOT NULL,
    Comment nvarchar(max) NULL
);
```

For these tables, we want to check the format of the two values. For the MessageTag, we want to make sure the format of the data is Alpha-NumberNumberNumber. For the Comment column, the requirement is to make sure that the value is either NULL, or a character string of 1 or more characters.

```
ALTER TABLE Examples.Message
   ADD CONSTRAINT CHKMessage_MessageTagFormat
      CHECK (MessageTag LIKE '[A-Z]-[0-9][0-9][0-9]');

ALTER TABLE Examples.Message
   ADD CONSTRAINT CHKMessage_CommentNotEmpty
       CHECK (LEN(Comment) > 0);
```

One of the primary difficulties regarding constraints (and really any of the declarative forms of data integrity checks we are reviewing) is that you only get one error, no matter how many errors are found. For example, say you break both rules in your statement:

```
INSERT INTO Examples.Message(MessageTag, Comment)
VALUES ('Bad','');
```

The only message you get back is for the MessageTag being poorly formatted (the order of error checking is not guaranteed or controllable.):

```
Msg 547, Level 16, State 0, Line 312
The INSERT statement conflicted with the CHECK constraint "CHKMessage_MessageTagFormat".
The conflict occurred in database "ExamBook762Ch2", table "Examples.Message",
column 'MessageTag'.
```

### COORDINATE MULTIPLE VALUES TOGETHER

As one last example, consider a case where two column values can influence the legal value for another. For example, say you have a Customer table, and it has a set of status flags. Two of them are ForcedDisabledFlag, manually saying that the customer has been disabled, and a ForcedEnabledFlag, manually saying that the customer has been enabled, likely overriding the normal business rules in each case. Typically, there might be a few other columns for the user to explain why they are overriding the rules, but for simplicity, just these two columns are needed for the example.

The following table implements these two columns and a CHECK constraint that makes sure the offending scenario does not occur:

```
CREATE TABLE Examples.Customer
(
    ForcedDisabledFlag bit NOT NULL,
    ForcedEnabledFlag bit NOT NULL,
    CONSTRAINT CHKCustomer_ForcedStatusFlagCheck
      CHECK (NOT (ForcedDisabledFlag = 1 AND ForcedEnabledFlag = 1))
);
```

## Using FOREIGN KEY constraints to enforce relationships

FOREIGN KEY constraints are used to ensure that when you set up a foreign key link between tables (by placing the key value of one table in another table as a reference), the values remain in sync. They are generally quite simple to set up, though there are a number of options you can use to control what occurs when a reference exists, and when you are changing one side to not exist. In the next sections, we cover:

- Creating a simple FOREIGN KEY constraint on a table with data in it
- Cascading Operations
- Relating a table to itself to form a hierarchy
- FOREIGN KEY constraints relating to a UNIQUE constraint instead of a PRIMARY KEY constraint

> **NEED MORE REVIEW?  FOREIGN KEY CONSTRAINTS**
>
> For more information about FOREIGN KEY constraints and their relationship to PRIMARY KEY constraints beyond what we can cover here, see the following article on MSDN: *https://msdn.microsoft.com/en-us/library/ms179610.aspx.*

### CREATING A SIMPLE FOREIGN KEY CONSTRAINT ON A TABLE WITH DATA IN IT

Most FOREIGN KEY constraints that are implemented are of the straightforward variety. We need to make sure the data in one column in a table matches the data in the primary of another. In later sections, we cover some more breadth of configurations, but in this first section we keep it very simple.

For example, consider the following two tables, named after the common names for their position in the relationship (the Child table in a relationship references the Parent table).

```
CREATE TABLE Examples.Parent
(
    ParentId   int NOT NULL CONSTRAINT PKParent PRIMARY KEY
);
CREATE TABLE Examples.Child
(
    ChildId int NOT NULL CONSTRAINT PKChild PRIMARY KEY,
    ParentId int NULL
);
```

At this point, the user can put any value into the ParentId column of the Child table, which makes using the data complicated. To make sure that the data is always in sync, we can add the following constraint:

```
ALTER TABLE Examples.Child
    ADD CONSTRAINT FKChild_Ref_ExamplesParent
      FOREIGN KEY (ParentId) REFERENCES Examples.Parent(ParentId);
```

In the declaration, you specify the column that references a given column in a table. While almost every FOREIGN KEY constraint references a PRIMARY KEY constraint, it can actually reference a UNIQUE constraint or even a UNIQUE index in the rare cases where that makes sense (more on that later in the section).

Now, after inserting a few rows into the Examples.Parent table:

```
INSERT INTO Examples.Parent(ParentId)
VALUES (1),(2),(3);
```

You are able to insert a row into Child where the ParentId does match:

```
INSERT INTO Examples.Child (ChildId, ParentId)
VALUES (1,1);
```

But if you try to use a ParentId that is not in the table:

```
INSERT INTO Examples.Child (ChildId, ParentId)
VALUES (2,100);
```

The following error is then thrown:

```
Msg 547, Level 16, State 0, Line 124
The INSERT statement conflicted with the FOREIGN KEY constraint
"FKChild_Ref_ExamplesParent". The conflict occurred in database "ExamBook762Ch2",
table "Examples.Parent", column 'ParentId'.
```

Finally, note that the ParentId column in the Child table was created to allow NULL values. The referenced PRIMARY KEY constraint does not allow NULL values by definition, so this could never have a match. This brings up an important point about constraints. Much like CHECK constraints, they fail only when the comparison is FALSE, and any comparison to NULL return UNKNOWN. Hence the following INSERT statement works:

```
INSERT INTO Examples.Child (ChildId, ParentId)
VALUES (3,NULL);
```

So far, we have dealt with simple keys only, but PRIMARY KEY constraints can easily have a composite key. For required, NOT NULL child table references, this is not a concern. However, where the referencing table's columns do allow NULL values, something more complex occurs. Consider the following tables, and a single row in the table that the FOREIGN KEY constraint is referencing:

```
CREATE TABLE Examples.TwoPartKey
(
    KeyColumn1  int NOT NULL,
    KeyColumn2  int NOT NULL,
    CONSTRAINT PKTwoPartKey PRIMARY KEY (KeyColumn1, KeyColumn2)
);

INSERT INTO Examples.TwoPartKey (KeyColumn1, KeyColumn2)

VALUES (1, 1);
CREATE TABLE Examples.TwoPartKeyReference
(
    KeyColumn1 int NULL,
    KeyColumn2 int NULL,
    CONSTRAINT FKTwoPartKeyReference_Ref_ExamplesTwoPartKey
        FOREIGN KEY (KeyColumn1, KeyColumn2)
            REFERENCES Examples.TwoPartKey (KeyColumn1, KeyColumn2)
);
```

Here you put in a row with 1,1 for the Examples.TwoPartKeyReference table or NULL, NULL:

```
INSERT INTO Examples.TwoPartKeyReference (KeyColumn1, KeyColumn2)
VALUES (1, 1), (NULL, NULL);
```

It is successful. If you try to put in 2,2, which is not in the referenced table:

```
INSERT INTO Examples.TwoPartKeyReference (KeyColumn1, KeyColumn2)
VALUES (2, 2);
```

This does not work, as expected:

```
Msg 547, Level 16, State 0, Line 157
The INSERT statement conflicted with the FOREIGN KEY constraint "FKTwoPartKeyReference_
Ref_ExamplesTwoPartKey". The conflict occurred in database
"ExamBook762Ch2", table "Examples.TwoPartKey".
```

However, what about 6 million (a value most certainly not in the parent table) and NULL?

```
INSERT INTO Examples.TwoPartKeyReference (KeyColumn1, KeyColumn2)
VALUES (6000000, NULL);
```

This actually works because of the NULL value in the KeyColumn2, since the comparison of NULL to the referenced table returns UNKNOWN (NULL), the row is accepted, regardless of whether the KeyColumn1 value exists or not. To prevent this condition from occurring, you can use a CHECK constraint to make sure both columns are either NULL or NOT NULL. In this case, we could add the following CHECK constraint to correct this:

```
ALTER TABLE Examples.TwoPartKeyReference
     ADD CONSTRAINT CHKTwoPartKeyReference_FKNULLs
         CHECK ((KeyColumn1 IS NULL and KeyColumn2 IS NULL)
             OR
             (KeyColumn1 IS NOT NULL and KeyColumn2 IS NOT NULL));
```

Now, the entire reference is NULL or NOT NULL, not one or the other, eliminating the concept that a KeyColumn1 or KeyColumn2 value might not exist in the referenced table.

### CASCADING OPERATIONS

We have seen already that a FOREIGN KEY constraint can be used to prevent rows being deleted from a table with referring data, or inserting or updating data into the referring table that doesn't match the referenced table. However, sometimes it is desirable to allow changes at the parent table to be reflected in the referencing child table. The following settings can be chosen when the row is deleted, or when the key columns in the parent are updated.

- **NO ACTION**   Prevent any updates or deletions where the end result would leave the data invalid. This behaves as seen in the previous section, as this is the default action.
- **CASCADE**   Repeat on the referencing table what occurs in the referenced. If the key column is changed, change it in the referencing table. If the row is deleted, remove it from the referencing table as well.
- **SET (NULL or DEFAULT)**   In these cases, if the referenced row is deleted or the key value is changed, the referencing data is set to either NULL or to the value from a DEFAULT constraint, respectively.

The most common use of this feature is to cascade a DELETE operation to remove all related rows from one table to a related table that is, in essence, part of the referenced table. This is usually the case when one table logically owns the rows in the second table. For example, an invoice and invoice line item. You would never need an invoice line item without the invoice.

```
CREATE TABLE Examples.Invoice
(
    InvoiceId    int NOT NULL CONSTRAINT PKInvoice PRIMARY KEY
);
CREATE TABLE Examples.InvoiceLineItem
(
    InvoiceLineItemId int NOT NULL CONSTRAINT PKInvoiceLineItem PRIMARY KEY,
    InvoiceLineNumber smallint NOT NULL,
    InvoiceId      int NOT NULL
       CONSTRAINT FKInvoiceLineItem_Ref_ExamplesInvoice
          REFERENCES Examples.Invoice(InvoiceId)
             ON DELETE CASCADE
             ON UPDATE NO ACTION,
    CONSTRAINT AKInvoiceLineItem UNIQUE (InvoiceId, InvoiceLineNumber)
);
```

Now create a few rows of data in both tables:

```
INSERT INTO Examples.Invoice(InvoiceId)
VALUES (1),(2),(3);
INSERT INTO Examples.InvoiceLineItem(InvoiceLineItemId, InvoiceId,InvoiceLineNumber)
VALUES (1,1,1),(2,1,2), (3,2,1);
```

View the data using the following query, which shows you the key of both tables (and the FULL OUTER JOIN insures that if we had a row in InvoiceLineItem without a referenced Invoice, it would still show up. This, however, is not possible, but if you were testing your code, this is the safest way to check the data.):

```
SELECT Invoice.InvoiceId, InvoiceLineItem.InvoiceLineItemId
FROM    Examples.Invoice
            FULL OUTER JOIN Examples.InvoiceLineItem
            ON Invoice.InvoiceId = InvoiceLineItem.InvoiceId;
```

This returns:

```
InvoiceId    InvoiceLineItemId
-----------  -----------------
1            1
1            2
2            3
3            NULL
```

Now delete InvoiceId number 1:

```
DELETE Examples.Invoice
WHERE  InvoiceId = 1;
```

Repeat the query of the data, and you see that the Invoice and InvoiceLineItem rows have gone away.

```
InvoiceId    InvoiceLineItemId
-----------  -----------------
2            3
3            NULL
```

When using surrogate keys for your primary key values (as we did with InvoiceId and InvoiceLineItemId), there are only a few scenarios for cascading update operations. Surrogate key values should never be updated. Sometimes this is technically possible, such as using a GUID for the key, but not needing to change the value is one of the main reasons why we use a surrogate key in the first place. However, if you choose to use natural keys for the primary key value, occasionally a value needs to be changed, either because of something like a company changing name, or perhaps because a
misspelled value caught after the value was used in multiple places.

As an example, consider the following tables. The second table is an example of creating a FOREIGN KEY constraint in the table declaration, where the Example.Code table sets up a domain of code values, and Example.CodedItem simulates a row that needs that code (though the only column in the table is the Code column to keep things very simple).

```
CREATE TABLE Examples.Code
(
    Code     varchar(10) NOT NULL CONSTRAINT PKCode PRIMARY KEY
);
CREATE TABLE Examples.CodedItem
(
    Code     varchar(10) NOT NULL
        CONSTRAINT FKCodedItem_Ref_ExampleCode
            REFERENCES Examples.Code (Code)
                ON UPDATE CASCADE
);
```

Now, create a row in each table, with a misspelled code value of 'Blacke':

```
INSERT INTO Examples.Code (Code)
VALUES ('Blacke');
INSERT INTO Examples.CodedItem (Code)
VALUES ('Blacke');
```

Now, looking at the data, you can see that the data in both tables are spelled incorrectly:

```
SELECT Code.Code, CodedItem.Code AS CodedItemCode
FROM    Examples.Code
            FULL OUTER JOIN Examples.CodedItem
                ON Code.Code = CodedItem.Code;
```

This returns:

```
Code        CodedItemCode
----------  -------------
Blacke      Blacke
```

Now, update the Alt.Code row with the proper spelling of Black:

```
UPDATE Examples.Code
SET   Code = 'Black';
```

Check the data again, and see that both items say Black, as the UPDATE operation cascaded.

```
Code        CodedItemCode
----------  -------------
Black       Black
```

### RELATING A TABLE TO ITSELF TO FORM A HIERARCHY

In many databases, there is need to define a hierarchy of items. A common example is an employee-to-manager relationship, where everyone in a company except for one (the CEO or President) has a simple manager relationship. In the next example, we create a table named Examples.Employee that includes the relationship structure that one might create for an employee hierarchy. In the table, note that the ManagerId FOREIGN KEY constraint references the EmployeeId column in this same table:

```
CREATE TABLE Examples.Employee
(
        EmployeeId int NOT NULL CONSTRAINT PKEmployee PRIMARY KEY,
        EmployeeNumber char(8) NOT NULL,
        ManagerId int NULL
            CONSTRAINT FKEmployee_Ref_ExamplesEmployee
                REFERENCES Examples.Employee (EmployeeId);

);
```

Now you can add some data to the table, and add four rows, including the top level manager, and two persons that work for the top-level manager. Finally, one person works for one of those two employees:

```
INSERT INTO Examples.Employee(EmployeeId, EmployeeNumber, ManagerId)
VALUES (1,'00000001',NULL), (2,'10000001',1),(3,'10000002',1), (4,'20000001',3);
```

Now, check the contents of the table:

```
SELECT *
FROM    Examples.Employee;
```

By following the relationships in the data, you can see that EmployeeId = 1 is the main manager, and EmployeeId in (2,3) reports to number 1, and EmployeeId = 4 reports to EmployeeId = 3.

```
EmployeeId  EmployeeNumber ManagerId
----------- -------------- -----------
1           00000001       NULL
2           10000001       1
3           10000002       1
4           20000001       3
```

There's no need to go into any detail since this is not a Transact-SQL focused exam, but note that this sort of structure is typically queried via a recursive common table expression (CTE) such as the following:

```
WITH EmployeeHierarchy AS
(
    SELECT EmployeeID,  CAST(CONCAT('\',EmployeeId,'\') AS varchar(1500)) AS Hierarchy
    FROM Examples.Employee
    WHERE ManagerId IS NULL
    UNION ALL
    SELECT Employee.EmployeeID, CAST(CONCAT(Hierarchy,Employee.EmployeeId,'\')
                                            AS varchar(1500)) AS Hierarchy
    FROM Examples.Employee
      INNER JOIN EmployeeHierarchy
        ON Employee.ManagerId = EmployeeHierarchy.EmployeeId
  )
SELECT *
FROM    EmployeeHierarchy;
GO
```

This returns:

```
EmployeeID  Hierarchy
```

```
----------- ---------------
1          \1\
2          \1\2\
3          \1\3\
4          \1\3\4\
```

The Hierarchy column is a delimited display of the path from the row with NULL for ManagerId to the EmployeeId in the row.

> **NEED MORE REVIEW**  **COMMON TABLE EXPRESSIONS**
>
> If you would like to read more about CTEs, the following article by Robert Shelton on Simple-Talk gives a very easy-to-follow description of using them, including recursive CTEs: *https://www.simple-talk.com/sql/t-sql-programming/sql-server-cte-basics/*.

**FOREIGN KEY CONSTRAINTS RELATING TO A UNIQUE CONSTRAINT INSTEAD OF A PRIMARY KEY CONSTRAINT**

Though it is definitely a fringe case, it is allowable for a FOREIGN KEY constraint to reference the columns in a UNIQUE constraint as well as a PRIMARY KEY one. This is often done for a code of some sort, which legitimately would have made a reasonable primary key, and you want to validate the code's value in a table.

As an example, consider a table of colors for products:

```
CREATE TABLE Examples.Color
(
     ColorId   int NOT NULL CONSTRAINT PKColor PRIMARY KEY,
     ColorName varchar(30) NOT NULL CONSTRAINT AKColor UNIQUE
);
INSERT INTO Examples.Color(ColorId, ColorName)
VALUES (1,'Orange'),(2,'White');
```

Now, a table is created that needs to use the natural key value:

```
CREATE TABLE Examples.Product
(
    ProductId int NOT NULL CONSTRAINT PKProduct PRIMARY KEY,
    ColorName varchar(30) NOT NULL
        CONSTRAINT FKProduct_Ref_ExamplesColor
            REFERENCES Examples.Color (ColorName)
);
```

Demonstrate now that everything works as expected:

```
INSERT INTO Examples.Product(ProductId,ColorName)
VALUES (1,'Orange');
```

That INSERT statement worked, but the following fails:

```
INSERT INTO Examples.Product(ProductId,ColorName)
VALUES (2,'Crimson');
```

This returns the following error:

```
Msg 547, Level 16, State 0, Line 266
The INSERT statement conflicted with the FOREIGN KEY constraint
"FKProduct_Ref_ExamplesColor". The conflict occurred in database "ExamBook762Ch2",
table "Examples.Color", column 'ColorName'.
```

Note that since you can reference a UNIQUE constraint, which can contain NULL column(s), the concerns noted in the previous section with composite indexes and NULL values goes both for the referenced and referencing key values in this case. No parent row with NULL is able to be referenced, and no child row with NULL ever fails.

## Limiting a column to a set of values

The one last scenario we cover in terms of using constraints is to implement a domain of a set of columns to a set of values. As our example, consider a column that has the size of shirt for a conference attendee. The values for this column would likely be something like S, M, L, XL, and XXL. There are two common methods of implementing this domain of values:

```
CREATE TABLE Examples.Attendee
(
     ShirtSize  varchar(8) NULL
);
```

The first is using a simple CHECK constraint:

```
ALTER TABLE Examples.Attendee
    ADD  CONSTRAINT CHKAttendee_ShirtSizeDomain
        CHECK  (ShirtSize in ('S', 'M','L','XL','XXL'));
```

Now, the value is checked on the INSERT or UPDATE operations, so if the user misspells 'XL' as 'LX:'

```
INSERT INTO Examples.Attendee(ShirtSize)
VALUES ('LX');
```

They are denied:

```
  Msg 547, Level 16, State 0, Line 346
The INSERT statement conflicted with the CHECK constraint "CHKAttendee_ ShirtSizeDo-
main".
The conflict occurred in database "ExamBook762Ch2", table "Examples.Attendee",
column 'ShirtSize'.
```

The problem is, how do you know what the legitimate values are? For many CHECK constraint conditions, this is not too big a deal as the goal is to limit really outlandish values. However, for a domain of values, it can be helpful to coordinate the domain of values with another table.

The second solution is to use a table of values. So you can create:

```
CREATE TABLE Examples.ShirtSize
(
    ShirtSize varchar(10) NOT NULL CONSTRAINT PKShirtSize PRIMARY KEY
);
INSERT INTO Examples.ShirtSize(ShirtSize)
VALUES ('S'),('M'),('L'),('XL'),('XXL');
```

Now drop the CHECK constraint and replace with a FOREIGN KEY constraint:

```
ALTER TABLE Examples.Attendee
    DROP CONSTRAINT CHKAttendee_ShirtSizeDomain;
ALTER TABLE Examples.Attendee
    ADD CONSTRAINT FKAttendee_Ref_ExamplesShirtSize
        FOREIGN KEY (ShirtSize) REFERENCES Examples.ShirtSize(ShirtSize);
```

Though the error message has changed, the result is the same:

```
INSERT INTO Examples.Attendee(ShirtSize)
VALUES ('LX');
```

It fails:

```
Msg 547, Level 16, State 0, Line 364
The INSERT statement conflicted with the FOREIGN KEY constraint
"FKAttendee_Ref_ExamplesShirtSize". The conflict occurred in database "ExamBook762Ch2",
table "Examples.ShirtSize", column 'ShirtSize'.
```

Even in systems that use surrogate keys for primary keys, it isn't atypical to use a natural key for a domain table, depending on how the tools used interact with the data. Using a foreign key gives you easy expandability (such as adding descriptive information to the values by adding additional columns to your domain table), as well as the ability to add new values to the domain without any coding changes.

# Write Transact-SQL statements to add constraints to tables

So far in the chapter, we have added many constraints to tables. In this section we review the basics of this process briefly, and then cover a few more advanced aspects of creating and managing constraints.

When creating a table, there are two ways to add a constraint: on the same line with a column declaration, denoting that the constraint pertains to that column, or delimited by a comma, meaning it could reference any of the columns in the table. As an example of the many ways you can add constraints in the declaration, consider the following:

```
CREATE TABLE Examples.CreateTableExample
(
    --Uniqueness constraint referencing single column
    SingleColumnKey int NOT NULL CONSTRAINT PKCreateTableExample PRIMARY KEY,

    --Uniqueness constraint in separate line
    TwoColumnKey1 int NOT NULL,
    TwoColumnKey2 int NOT NULL,
    CONSTRAINT AKCreateTableExample UNIQUE (TwoColumnKey1, TwoColumnKey2),

    --CHECK constraint declare as column constraint
    PositiveInteger int NOT NULL
        CONSTRAINT CHKCreateTableExample_PostiveInteger CHECK (PositiveInteger > 0),

    --CHECK constraint that could reference multiple columns
    NegativeInteger int NOT NULL,
    CONSTRAINT CHKCreateTableExample_NegativeInteger CHECK (NegativeInteger > 0),

    --FOREIGN KEY constraint inline with column
    FKColumn1 int NULL CONSTRAINT FKColumn1_ref_Table REFERENCES Tbl (TblId),

    --FOREIGN KEY constraint... Could reference more than one columns
    FKColumn2 int NULL,
    CONSTRAINT FKColumn2_ref_Table FOREIGN KEY (FKColumn2) REFERENCES Tbl (TblId)
);
```

In addition, every constraint has the ability to be dropped and added after the table has been created. With this table, we can drop and recreate the PRIMARY KEY constraint with:

```
ALTER TABLE Examples.CreateTableExample
    DROP PKCreateTableExample;
ALTER TABLE Examples.CreateTableExample
    ADD CONSTRAINT PKCreateTableExample PRIMARY KEY (SingleColumnKey);
```

You can do this for every one of the constraint types. However, for the ALTER TABLE commands for CHECK and FOREIGN KEY constraints, you have a few additional choices to deal with data that doesn't match the constraint. UNIQUE and PRIMARY KEY constraints behave like indexes when being enabled, so you can't violate the uniqueness characteristics. Disabling uniqueness constraints will remove the index.

Consider the following table and data:

```
CREATE TABLE Examples.BadData
(
        PositiveValue int NOT NULL
);
INSERT INTO Examples.BadData(PositiveValue)
VALUES (-1),(-2),(-3),(-4);
```

You want to add the following constraint:

```
ALTER TABLE Examples.BadData
    ADD CONSTRAINT CHKBadData_PostiveValue CHECK(PositiveValue > 0);
```

But you are greeted with the following message:

```
Msg 547, Level 16, State 0, Line 414
The ALTER TABLE statement conflicted with the CHECK constraint
CHKBadData_PostiveValue". The conflict occurred in database
ExamBook762Ch2", table "Examples.BadData", column 'PositiveValue'.
```

From here, you have two choices. You can (ideally) fix the data, or you can create the constraint and leave the bad data. This can be done by specifying WITH NOCHECK which bypasses the data check:

```
ALTER TABLE Examples.BadData WITH NOCHECK
    ADD CONSTRAINT CHKBadData_PostiveValue CHECK(PositiveValue > 0);
```

The problem with this approach is twofold. First, you have bad data in the table. So if you run the following statement that sets the value to an existing value, you get something that seems silly as a statement, but is technically done in user code all of the time:

```
UPDATE Examples.BadData
SET    PositiveValue = PositiveValue;
```

The data isn't granted immunity, even though it already exists in the table:

```
Msg 547, Level 16, State 0, Line 420
The UPDATE statement conflicted with the CHECK constraint "CHKBadData_PostiveValue".
The conflict occurred in database "ExamBook762Ch2", table "Examples.BadData",
column 'PositiveValue'.
```

It seems that if you just delete the data that would violate the constraint, and everything would be great:

```
DELETE FROM Examples.BadData
WHERE   PositiveValue <= 0;
```

And from a certain perspective, it is. If you try to insert a non-positive value, it fails. However, even though the constraint now does everything that you expect it to, because the data wasn't checked when you created the constraint, it is considered not *trusted*, which means that SQL Server has never checked to see that the data is correct. You can see if a CHECK constraint is trusted using the following query (note that CHECK constraints are owned by a schema, just like a table, even though you rarely reference them as such):

```
SELECT is_not_trusted, is_disabled
FROM    sys.check_constraints --for a FOREIGN KEY, use sys.foreign_keys
WHERE   OBJECT_SCHEMA_NAME(object_id) = 'Examples'
  and   OBJECT_NAME(object_id) = 'CHKBadData_PostiveValue';
```

Which returns:

```
is_not_trusted is_disabled
-------------- -----------
1              0
```

This shows you how the constraint is not trusted, but it is enabled. Now that you know the data in the table is correct, you can tell the constraint to check the data in the table using the following command:

```
ALTER TABLE Examples.BadData WITH CHECK CHECK
 CONSTRAINT CHKBadData _ PostiveValue;
```

If you check the constraint now to see if it is trusted, it is. If you want to disable (turn off) a CHECK or FOREIGN KEY constraint, you can use NOCHECK in the ALTER TABLE command:

```
ALTER TABLE Examples.BadData
      NOCHECK CONSTRAINT CHKBadData_PostiveValue;
```

After running this, you can see that the constraint has been disabled.

Having a trusted CHECK constraint can be useful for performance. The Query Optimizer can use a trusted constraint in optimizing queries. If a value that is searched for would be illegal for the CHECK constraint predicate, it does not need to even check the physical data (assuming there is enough data in the table to make it worth optimizing more than just a simple plan). For an example with a reasonable amount of data, we a table in the WideWorldImporters database. Consider that the domain of the OrderId column of the Sales.Invoices table should be 0 to 1,000,000. We might add a constraint such as the following:

```
ALTER TABLE Sales.Invoices
    ADD CONSTRAINT CHKInvoices_OrderIdBetween0and1000000
        CHECK (OrderId BETWEEN 0 AND 1000000);
```

Now, consider the following two queries are performed:

```
SELECT *
FROM    Sales.Invoices
WHERE   OrderID = -100;

SELECT *
FROM    Sales.Invoices
WHERE   OrderID = 100;
```

Notice that, despite how similar the queries appear, their query plans are quite different; as seen in Figure 2-1. The first query sees that the value is outside of the legal domain and returns immediately, while the other needs to look at the data.

FIGURE 2-1 Comparison of plans, where the first value is eliminated by the CHECK predicate, and the second is not

---

**NEED MORE REVIEW?** **ALTERING A TABLE'S CONSTRAINTS**

FOREIGN KEY constraints also have trusted and disabled status with you can find in sys.foreign_keys, and the same syntax that sets CHECK constraints trusted works the same way. There are many settings and uses of the ALTER TABLE command. For more information for review, check the MSDN article here: *https://msdn.microsoft.com/en-us/library/ms190273.aspx*.

---

# Identify results of Data Manipulation Language (DML) statements given existing tables and constraints

An important task for almost any database programmer is to be able to predict the outcome given some Transact-SQL Data Definition Language (DDL) code that sets up a scenario, followed by some DML (Data Manipulation Language) that you need to determine the outcome of. Every time we set up some new concept, the next thing to do is to show it working (one of the great things about working with a declarative interactive language like Transact-SQL).

In this example, we highlight the process of working through a given scenario. Fortunately, when you are taking the exam, questions are all multiple choice, and there is always one answer that is correct for a question of this variety. Imagine you have the following table structure.

```
CREATE TABLE Examples.ScenarioTestType
(
    ScenarioTestType varchar(10) NOT NULL CONSTRAINT PKScenarioTestType PRIMARY KEY
);
CREATE TABLE Examples.ScenarioTest
(
    ScenarioTestId int NOT NULL PRIMARY KEY,
    ScenarioTestType varchar(10) NULL CONSTRAINT CHKScenarioTest_ScenarioTestType
                                CHECK (ScenarioTestType IN ('Type1','Type2'))

);
ALTER TABLE Examples.ScenarioTest
    ADD CONSTRAINT FKScenarioTest_Ref_ExamplesScenarioTestType
        FOREIGN KEY (ScenarioTestType) REFERENCES Examples.ScenarioTestType;
```

Now, after contemplating what is going on in the DDL, you need to work through something like the following DML. As an exercise, consider how many rows are inserted into Examples.ScenarioTest when these statements are performed in a single batch:

```
INSERT INTO Examples.ScenarioTest(ScenarioTestId, ScenarioTestType)
VALUES (1,'Type1');
INSERT INTO Examples.ScenarioTestType(ScenarioTestType)
VALUES ('Type1');
INSERT INTO Examples.ScenarioTest(ScenarioTestId, ScenarioTestType)
VALUES (1,'Type1');
INSERT INTO Examples.ScenarioTest(ScenarioTestId, ScenarioTestType)
VALUES (1,'Type2');
INSERT INTO Examples.ScenarioTest(ScenarioTestId, ScenarioTestType)
VALUES (2,'Type1');
INSERT INTO Examples.ScenarioTests(ScenarioTestId, ScenarioTestType)
VALUES (3,'Type1');
```

Anything is possible, and while questions aren't created to trick you, they are tricky if you do not have a grasp on some of the finer details of the topics covered, and are set up to make you think and pay attention to details. In this batch, first you need to know that a CHECK or FOREIGN KEY constraint error does not stop the batch, so the answer is not just simply zero.

Next, you need to consider each statement in order. The first statement violates the FOREIGN KEY constraint, but not the CHECK constraint.

```
INSERT INTO Examples.ScenarioTest(ScenarioTestId, ScenarioTestType)
VALUES (1,'Type1');
```

The next line adds a row to the domain table, so doesn't change the number of rows in the ScenarioTest table.

```
INSERT INTO Examples.ScenarioTestType(ScenarioTestType)
VALUES ('Type 1')
```

The next INSERT statement now succeeds, as it passes the test of the FOREIGN KEY and the CHECK constraints, and the primary key value is not duplicate (since it is the first row). So you have 1 row in the table.

```
INSERT INTO Examples.ScenarioTest(ScenarioTestId, ScenarioTestType)
VALUES (1,'Type1');
```

The next INSERT statement violates the domain table's FOREIGN KEY constraint.

```
INSERT INTO Examples.ScenarioTest(ScenarioTestId, ScenarioTestType)
VALUES (1,'Type2');
```

The next insert is the same ScenarioTestType that worked prior, and the new ScenarioTestId does not violate the PRIMARY KEY constraint. So there are 2 rows in the table.

```
INSERT INTO Examples.ScenarioTest(ScenarioTestId, ScenarioTestType)
VALUES (2,'Type1');
```

The last INSERT statement looks like it works, but the table name is ScenarioTests (plural) in the INSERT statement, so it fails (or at least does not insert into the table that the question is about if there is a table by that name in the database):

```
INSERT INTO Examples.ScenarioTests(ScenarioTestId, ScenarioTestType)
VALUES (3,'Type1');
```

So, there are 2 rows that are returned from the DML. Admittedly, it is much easier when you can use Management Studio to test your expectations than under the stress of the exam timer.

# Identify proper usage of PRIMARY KEY constraints

Choosing a primary key during the design phase of a project is generally pretty straightforward. Many designers use the simplest candidate key chosen during design. For example, consider you have a table that defines companies that you do business with:

```
CREATE SCHEMA Examples;
GO
CREATE TABLE Examples.Company
(
    CompanyName    nvarchar(50) NOT NULL CONSTRAINT PKCompany PRIMARY KEY,
    CompanyURL nvarchar(max) NOT NULL
);
```

Insert a few rows into the table to show that the table works. This example is very straightforward, but as this section progresses and we start to alter the table to do interesting things, it becomes more and more interesting to test a few rows.

```
INSERT INTO Examples.Company(CompanyName, CompanyURL)
VALUES ('Blue Yonder Airlines','http://www.blueyonderairlines.com/'),
       ('Tailspin Toys','http://www.tailspintoys.com/');
```

Now, check out the data that has been created.

```
SELECT *
FROM    Examples.Company;
```

You see the rows you expected from the INSERT statement.

```
CompanyName              CompanyURL
-----------------------  ----------------------------------------
Blue Yonder Airlines     http://www.blueyonderairlines.com/
Tailspin Toys            http://www.tailspintoys.com/
```

Note that this, by default, makes the CompanyName the clustered index of the table. But is a value that has an upper limit on data size of 100 bytes (50 characters * 2 bytes per character for typical Unicode characters) really the best choice? This limits the number of index keys on a page for all indexes you add as well. And if this key is used as a foreign key, if this value needed changing, it would require changes to any child tables as well. The choice of how to use the PRIMARY KEY constraint is as much about performance as it is about the integrity of the data.

Another choice you might consider is a more derived key value, such as: CompanyCode that is either a strictly formatted value (such as char(3) and a domain of numbers or letters, like for a company named "Fourth Coffee" it might be "4CF", much like the stock exchange ticker code is for a company), or even a 10-20 character string value that is kept very short, like "4Coffee", or something similar). Of course while this solves the length issue, if the name of the company changes to "Tailspin Toys" you still need to change the value or end up with a confusing CompanyCode value.

In typical practice, most people tend to use something like an ever increasing integer type for their primary key, using this as a stand-in for the natural key (commonly referred to as a *surrogate key.*) This is generally great because what makes a great surrogate key overlaps nicely with what makes a great clustering key (monotonically increasing, never needs changing, small data size), works great for foreign keys references, and always ends up with a single key column.

So where CompanyName was the key of the PRIMARY KEY constraint before, we now make an integer-valued column named CompanyId. Using an integer surrogate key, it is typical to use either a column with the IDENTITY property, or a DEFAULT constraint that uses the result of a SEQUENCE object. For the Examples.Company table, first, use an IDENTITY column which you specify in the following manner:

```
DROP TABLE IF EXISTS Examples.Company;
CREATE TABLE Examples.Company
(
    CompanyId      int NOT NULL IDENTITY(1,1) CONSTRAINT PKCompany PRIMARY KEY,
    CompanyName    nvarchar(50) NOT NULL CONSTRAINT AKCompany UNIQUE,
    CompanyURL nvarchar(max) NOT NULL
);
```

The IDENTITY setting has two parameters, the first being the *seed* value, or the starting point when the values start generating. The second is the *step* value, which indicates the difference between the previous value and the next value. Now, let's create some sample data:

```
INSERT INTO Examples.Company(CompanyName, CompanyURL)
VALUES ('Blue Yonder Airlines','http://www.blueyonderairlines.com/'),
       ('Tailspin Toys','http://www.tailspintoys.com/');
```

Before we look at the data, let's take a look at what happens if a row fails to be created. So we violate the alternate key UNIQUE constraint.

```
INSERT INTO Examples.Company(CompanyName, CompanyURL)
VALUES ('Blue Yonder Airlines','http://www.blueyonderairlines.com/');
```

This gives the following error:

```
Msg 2627, Level 14, State 1, Line 53
Violation of UNIQUE KEY constraint 'AKCompany'. Cannot insert duplicate key in object
'Examples.Company'. The duplicate key value is (Blue Yonder Airlines).
```

Now insert another row that is not in violation:

```
INSERT INTO Examples.Company(CompanyName, CompanyURL)
VALUES ('Northwind Traders','http://www.northwindtraders.com/');
```

Looking at the rows in the table, you see that there is a value missing from the expected sequence of values. The IDENTITY value is generated before the value fails, and for concurrency purposes, the value is not returned to be reused.

If you need to get the value of the IDENTITY value after the insert, you can use SCOPE_IDENTITY() to get the value in the current scope, or @@IDENTITY to get the last value for the connection. SCOPE_IDENTITY() is generally preferred.

```
SELECT *
FROM   Examples.Company;
```

Which returns:

| CompanyId | CompanyName | CompanyURL |
| --- | --- | --- |
| 1 | Blue Yonder Airlines | http://www.blueyonderairlines.com/ |
| 2 | Tailspin Toys | http://www.tailspintoys.com/ |
| 4 | Northwind Traders | http://www.northwindtraders.com/ |

You cannot specify values for an IDENTITY column without using SET IDENTITY INSERT <tableName> ON first, then doing your INSERT and turning it off. So, you can go back and add CompanyId = 3, but the general goal of using a surrogate key is to not care about the value of the keys. You cannot modify the value in a column that has the IDENTITY property.

Note that you can add a column with the IDENTITY property, but you cannot control the data being inserted into the new column. If the value matters to you (typically because you are replacing another surrogate value), the typical method is to duplicate the table by renaming the table (using the sp_rename system stored procedure) and making a copy of the table and loading existing data.

A second method of generating a numeric surrogate key is to use a SEQUENCE object. Using the same base table structure, we use a DEFAULT constraint to get the next value for the SEQUENCE object.

```
DROP TABLE IF EXISTS Examples.Company;
DROP SEQUENCE IF EXISTS Examples.Company_SEQUENCE;

CREATE SEQUENCE Examples.Company_SEQUENCE AS INT START WITH 1;
CREATE TABLE Examples.Company
(
    CompanyId      int NOT NULL CONSTRAINT PKCompany PRIMARY KEY
                            CONSTRAINT DFLTCompany_CompanyId DEFAULT
                                        (NEXT VALUE FOR Examples.Company_SEQUENCE),
    CompanyName    nvarchar(50) NOT NULL CONSTRAINT AKCompany UNIQUE,
    CompanyURL nvarchar(max) NOT NULL
);
```

The same INSERT statement from before works great:

```
INSERT INTO Examples.Company(CompanyName, CompanyURL)
VALUES ('Blue Yonder Airlines','http://www.blueyonderairlines.com/'),
       ('Tailspin Toys','http://www.tailspintoys.com/');
```

But now you can insert your own value into the CompanyId column, ideally after fetching the value from the SEQUENCE object.

```
DECLARE @CompanyId INT = NEXT VALUE FOR Examples.Company_SEQUENCE;


INSERT INTO Examples.Company(CompanyId, CompanyName, CompanyURL)
VALUES (@CompanyId, 'Northwind Traders','http://www.northwindtraders.com/');
```

Using a SEQUENCE object to create surrogate key values has advantages over IDENTITY columns, but it does require some discipline around values. While IDENTITY values don't guarantee uniqueness, once you create the IDENTITY column, you only end up with duplicates by inserting the duplicate values or using DBCC CHECKIDENT to reseed the value. This method using a SEQUENCE object requires that you fetch the value using NEXT VALUE FOR, or use sp_sequence_get_range to get a range of values that you can work with.

A final alternative method of creating a surrogate primary key value is using a Globally Unique Identifier (GUID) using a uniqueidentier column. GUIDs are great surrogate key values in terms of programmability, but do have a couple of issues when used as a clustering key. First GUID values are fairly large, using 16 bytes of storage (and they are 36 characters when needing to type). They are not monotonically increasing, so they can tend to increase page splits (there is a NEWSEQUENTIALID() function you can use to generate sequential GUIDs, but they are not necessarily sequential with existing data after a server reboot). The code looks very much like the SEQUENCE example with a DEFAULT constraint:

```
DROP TABLE IF EXISTS Examples.Company;
CREATE TABLE Examples.Company
(
    CompanyId      uniqueidentifier NOT NULL CONSTRAINT PKCompany PRIMARY KEY
                            CONSTRAINT DFLTCompany_CompanyId DEFAULT (NEWID()),
    CompanyName    nvarchar(50) NOT NULL CONSTRAINT AKCompany UNIQUE,
    CompanyURL nvarchar(max) NOT NULL
);
```

Now you can use the DEFAULT constraint, create your own GUID, or let the client generate the GUID value.

The primary reason for using a surrogate key for your primary key is to make implementation simpler for tooling, and in some cases to make the database easier to follow. For example, say you had a table of driver's licenses:

```
CREATE TABLE Examples.DriversLicense
(
        Locality char(10) NOT NULL,
        LicenseNumber varchar(40) NOT NULL,
        CONSTRAINT PKDriversLicense PRIMARY KEY (Locality, LicenseNumber)

);
```

If you use this as a FOREIGN KEY reference, like in a table of employee driver licenses table:

```
CREATE TABLE Examples.EmployeeDriverLicense
(
        EmployeeNumber char(10) NOT NULL, --Ref to Employee table
        Locality char(10) NOT NULL, --Ref to DriversLicense table
        LicenseNumber varchar(40) NOT NULL, --Ref to DriversLicense table
        CONSTRAINT PKEmployeeDriversLicense PRIMARY KEY
                (EmployeeNumber, Locality, LicenseNumber)
);
```

Now, say you need to use this key in the key of another table, which has three key columns also. Not only is this messy, but it begins to get rather confusing. While some manner of role-naming helps (changing Locality to DriversLicenceLocality, for example), using a surrogate key changes the table to something easier to follow:

```
CREATE TABLE Examples.DriversLicense
(
        DriversLicenseId int CONSTRAINT PKDriversLicense PRIMARY KEY,
        Locality char(10) NOT NULL,
        LicenseNumber varchar(40) NOT NULL,
        CONSTRAINT AKDriversLicense UNIQUE (Locality, LicenseNumber)
);
CREATE TABLE Examples.EmployeeDriverLicense
(
        EmployeeDriverLicenseId int NOT NULL
                CONSTRAINT PKEmployeeDriverLicense PRIMARY KEY,
        EmployeeId int NOT NULL, --Ref to Employee table
        DriversLicenseId int NOT NULL, --Ref to DriversLicense table
        CONSTRAINT AKEmployeeDriverLicense UNIQUE (EmployeeId, DriversLicenseId)
);
```

It's easier to read, and easier to understand where the key columns come from at a glance. It is important to realize that the DriversLicenseId actually represents the Locality and LicenseNumber in the EmployeeDriverLicense table. The meaning of the table doesn't change, it is just implemented differently.

# Skill 2.2 Create stored procedures

Stored procedures are coded objects that are used to bundle together Transact-SQL calls into one simple call from a client. There are, in SQL Server 2016, three versions of stored procedures. All of them are compiled and stored on the server, but each have different coding and execution limitations:

- **Interpreted SQL**  These objects are compiled into a format that are then interpreted, one line at a time, by the execution engine. This is the classic version of a stored procedure that has been around since version 1.0.

- **CLR (Common Language Runtime)**  These are procedures that are written in a .NET language and have a Transact-SQL calling mechanism.

- **Natively Compiled SQL**  These stored procedures are written in Transact-SQL, but are compiled into a C language module. They can only access memory optimized TABLE objects and other natively compiled objects. Natively compiled objects are similar to interpreted SQL stored procedures in appearance, but have many limitations.

While each of the types of STORED PROCEDURE (and all coded object type) are different, they all look to Transact-SQL the same. You can run the code, or use the objects in queries in the same manner with few limitations.

This chapter is focused on interpreted SQL stored procedures, but it is important to understand what the CLR objects are. Using managed, .NET code you can create STORED PROCEDURE objects that behave and are called exactly like ones created in interpreted SQL. The .NET code used has access to everything that the interpreted code does as well. These objects are not created using Management Studio in Transact-SQL, but are built in Visual Studio like other .NET programs.

Natively compiled objects are reviewed in Skill 3.4, but many of the topics in this section apply.

We also limit our focus to user-managed stored procedures in a user database. There are system stored procedures in the master database, and in the resource database, which is a special, hidden read-only database with additional system objects.

# Design stored procedure components and structure based on business requirements

As this section moves forward, we cover several of the most important details about using stored procedures, parameters, and error handling. However, in this section, the focus is on why to use stored procedures, and a few examples that include one or more of the concepts that are covered in the rest of this section in more detail.

There are two common philosophies regarding the use of STORED PROCEDURE objects:

- Using stored procedures as a complete encapsulation layer between the user and the database. This is a prevalent way of thinking for many architects (and a smoother path to using the new natively compiled stored procedures).

- Using stored procedures only to encapsulate complex calls. This utilization is typical for people who use tools to generate their access layer, and only use stored procedures when it is impossible to do from the user interface. Other uses are in building a report interface when simple ad-hoc queries do not suffice.

The biggest difference between the philosophies is that in the complete encapsulation version, you end up with a mix of very simple and very complex stored procedures. Hence we look at some simple procedures as well as an example of a complex one.

The form of a stored procedure is generally quite straightforward. The basic structure is:

```
CREATE PROCEDURE SchemaName.ObjectName

[WITH options]
[FOR REPLICATION]
    @Parameter1 datatype,
    @Parameter2 datatype = 'Optional Default',
    @Parameter3 datatype = NULL
AS
    1 or more Transact-SQL statements;
```

STORED PROCEDURE objects are schema-bound, just like TABLE objects, and all of the constraint types, Hence they follow the same rules for naming objects and name space, with the addition that STORED PROCEDURE object names should not be prefixed with SP, as this denotes a system-stored procedure that SQL Server checks for in the master database first.

Parameters are for sending data to, and receiving data from, a stored procedure. Any data type can be used for a parameter, and only very few have limitations (table-valued parameters must be read-only, and cursors can only be output parameters.) Parameters behave for the most part just like variables do in the body of the procedure, with values provided either by the caller or the default, including being changeable by the code of the stored procedure. If no default is provided, the parameter must be specified.

There are very few limitations on what Transact-SQL can be used in a stored procedure. One example are statements that need to be the first statement in a batch, like CREATE SCHEMA, CREATE PROCEDURE, CREATE VIEW, etc. (and the ALTER versions of the same). You cannot use the USE command to change database context, and there are a few SET commands

pertaining to query execution. However, using dynamic SQL (putting your query into a string variable and using EXECUTE or sp_executesql to run the code) allows you to run any code at all.

The options you can specify are:

- **WITH ENCRYPTION**  Encrypts the entry in sys.syscomments that contains the text of the STORED PROCEDURE create statement.
- **WITH RECOMPILE**  Specifies that a plan is not cached for the procedure, so it is recompiled for every execution.
- **WITH EXECUTE AS**  Let's you change the security context that the procedure is executed under.
- **FOR REPLICATION**  Indicates that this is a procedure that is specifically created for replication.

> *NOTE*  **THE CREATE PROCEDURE STATEMENT**
>
> **For more details about the CREATE PROCEDURE statement, check here on the MSDN site: *https://msdn.microsoft.com/en-us/library/ms187926.aspx*. While we will not user the WITH EXECUTE AS clause in the stored procedure examples, it will be used when triggers are created in Skill 2.4.**

In the first example, consider the business requirement that the user needs to be able to create, and remove rows from a simple table. If the table is defined as:

```
CREATE TABLE Examples.SimpleTable
(
    SimpleTableId int NOT NULL IDENTITY(1,1)
            CONSTRAINT PKSimpleTable PRIMARY KEY,
    Value1    varchar(20) NOT NULL,
    Value2    varchar(20) NOT NULL
);
```

Then we could create the three stored procedures shown in Listing 2-1:

**LISTING 2-1**  Three simple stored procedures to insert, update, and delete data

```
CREATE PROCEDURE Examples.SimpleTable_Insert
    @SimpleTableId int,
    @Value1 varchar(20),
    @Value2 varchar(20)
AS
    INSERT INTO Examples.SimpleTable(Value1, Value2)
    VALUES (@Value1, @Value2);
GO

CREATE PROCEDURE Examples.SimpleTable_Update
    @SimpleTableId int,
    @Value1 varchar(20),
    @Value2 varchar(20)
AS
    UPDATE Examples.SimpleTable
    SET Value1 = @Value1,
        Value2 = @Value2
    WHERE SimpleTableId = @SimpleTableId;
GO
CREATE PROCEDURE Examples.SimpleTable_Delete
    @SimpleTableId int,
    @Value varchar(20)
AS
    DELETE Examples.SimpleTable
    WHERE SimpleTableId = @SimpleTableId
GO
```

As you can see, the body of code for each STORED PROCEDURE is just one simple Transact-SQL query. The power of STORED PROCEDURE objects we are applying here is providing a strict user interface that you have complete control over.

There are three ways you can return data to a user from a stored procedure. Output parameters and return codes are covered later, but the first and most common is by using one or more result sets (Generally one result set is desirable. You can get the metadata of the first result set using the system stored procedure: sp_describe_first_result_set).

For example, you could create a stored procedure to return all of the data in the Examples. SimpleTable, ordered by Value1:

```
CREATE PROCEDURE Examples.SimpleTable_Select
AS
    SELECT SimpleTableId, Value1, Value2
    FROM Examples.SimpleTable
    ORDER BY Value1;
```

You can also return multiple result sets to the client, though again, it is generally desirable to return a single result set:

```
CREATE PROCEDURE Examples.SimpleTable_SelectValue1StartWithQorZ
AS
    SELECT SimpleTableId, Value1, Value2
    FROM Examples.SimpleTable
```

```
WHERE Value1 LIKE 'Q%'
ORDER BY Value1;

SELECT SimpleTableId, Value1, Value2
FROM Examples.SimpleTable
WHERE Value1 LIKE 'Z%'
ORDER BY Value1 DESC;
```

Another ability is to return a variable number of result sets. For example, say the requirement is to allow a user to search the table for rows where Value1 starts with 'Q' or 'Z' and the query is performed on a weekday. Whereas we could have done the INSERT or UPDATE statements from Listing 2-1, without the stored procedure you could not fulfill the business requirement in Transact-SQL code. For this (obviously contrived) requirement, you could write the following stored procedure which returns either 1 or 0 result sets:

```
CREATE PROCEDURE Examples.SimpleTable_SelectValue1StartWithQorZ
AS
  IF DATENAME(weekday,getdate()) NOT IN ('Saturday','Sunday')
    SELECT SimpleTableId, Value1, Value2
    FROM Examples.SimpleTable
    WHERE  Value1 LIKE '[QZ]%';
```

There are more elegant ways of accomplishing this requirement, particularly by throwing an error to alert the user why nothing is returned, but we cover this later in this section. In the following sections covering the specific skills of writing a STORED PROCEDURE, the examples get more and more complex.

One interesting characteristic of STORED PROCEDURE code is that it can reference objects that do not exist. For example, you could code:

```
CREATE PROCEDURE Examples.ProcedureName
AS
SELECT ColumnName From Bogus.TableName;
```

This compiles, regardless of the existence of Bogus.TableName. The compilation process of creating the procedure stores the reference by name and by internal id values when available. When it doesn't have the internal id values, it tries to fetch them at execution time. If the object does not exist at runtime, you get an error telling you "Invalid object name 'Bogus.TableName'."

One last fundamental about developing STORED PROCEDURE objects to understand. Configurations you set on the connection using the SET command in the body of the STORED PROCEDURE only pertains to the statements in the STORED PROCEDURE. The most common example is the SET NOCOUNT ON setting that suppresses the "Rows Affected" messages, but others such as ANSI WARNINGS can definitely be useful. So in the following procedure:

```
CREATE PROCEDURE Examples.SimpleTable_Select
AS
    SET NOCOUNT ON;
    SELECT SimpleTableId, Value1, Value2
    FROM Examples.SimpleTable
    ORDER BY Value1;
```

If you perform this procedure, no "Rows Affected" would be returned, but if you did an IN-SERT statement in the same connection it would show the messages, unless you turned them off in the connection. However, silencing the messages from the calling connection silences them in STORED PROCEDURE calls. Because of this, you need to make sure and set any SET options that you rely on in the body of the object.

In this initial section, the main aspect of stored procedure writing we wanted to review was that stored procedures are just compiled batches of Transact-SQL code that you can use to do almost anything, allow you as the database developer to build a set of stored proce-dures to do almost any task.

# Implement input and output parameters

Parameters allow you to pass data in and out of a STORED PROCEDURE object. To the code, they are very similar to variables, and can have their values changed as needed. Whether or not you see the changes to the value of the parameters after running the procedure is based on how you declare, and then call, the STORED PROCEDURE.

The following examples use this table as reference.

```
CREATE TABLE Examples.Parameter
(
    ParameterId int NOT NULL IDENTITY(1,1) CONSTRAINT PKParameter PRIMARY KEY,
    Value1   varchar(20) NOT NULL,
    Value2   varchar(20) NOT NULL,
)
```

In the first iteration, it is simple input parameters for the two value columns:

```
CREATE PROCEDURE Examples.Parameter_Insert
    @Value1 varchar(20) = 'No entry given',
    @Value2 varchar(20) = 'No entry given'
AS
    SET NOCOUNT ON;
    INSERT INTO Examples.Parameter(Value1,Value2)
    VALUES (@Value1, @Value2);
```

Now, in the following code block, we show the various ways you can run this code in Transact-SQL:

```
--using all defaults
EXECUTE Examples.Parameter_Insert;

--by position, @Value1 parameter only
EXECUTE Examples.Parameter_Insert 'Some Entry';

--both columns by position
EXECUTE Examples.Parameter_Insert 'More Entry','More Entry';

-- using the name of the parameter (could also include @Value2);
EXECUTE Examples.Parameter_Insert @Value1 = 'Other Entry';

--starting positionally, but finishing by name
EXECUTE Examples.Parameter_Insert 'Mixed Entry', @Value2 = 'Mixed Entry';
```

Once you start filling in parameters by name, you must continue to or you will receive an error. For example, if you attempt:

```
EXECUTE Examples.Parameter_Insert @Value1 = 'Remixed Entry', 'Remixed Entry';
```

It causes the following error:

```
Msg 119, Level 15, State 1, Line 736
Must pass parameter number 2 and subsequent parameters as '@name = value'. After the
form '@name = value' has been used, all subsequent parameters must be passed in the form
'@name = value'.
```

If you want to get the value of a parameter after it has been modified in the STORED PROCEDURE, you define the parameter as OUTPUT. In the alteration of the Examples.Parameter_Insert stored procedure, use the UPPER and LOWER functions to modify the two @Value parameters, and then retrieve the value of SCOPE_IDENTITY() system function to get the key value of the ParameterId column that has been created:

```
ALTER PROCEDURE Examples.Parameter_Insert
    @Value1 varchar(20) = 'No entry given',
    @Value2 varchar(20) = 'No entry given' OUTPUT,
    @NewParameterId int = NULL OUTPUT
AS
    SET NOCOUNT ON;
    SET @Value1 = UPPER(@Value1);
    SET @Value2 = LOWER(@Value2);

    INSERT INTO Examples.Parameter(Value1,Value2)
    VALUES (@Value1, @Value2);

    SET @NewParameterId = SCOPE_IDENTITY();
```

Next we call the procedure using the variables as the parameter value. Set the @NewParameterId value to a value that could not be returned. Note that the parameter is configured as OUTPUT on the EXECUTE statement as well (and if you try to declare a non-OUTPUT parameter as OUTPUT, it gives you an error telling you that the parameter is not an OUTPUT parameter).

```
DECLARE @Value1 varchar(20) = 'Test',
        @Value2 varchar(20) = 'Test',
        @NewParameterId int = -200;

EXECUTE Examples.Parameter_Insert @Value1 = @Value1,
                                  @Value2 = @Value2 OUTPUT,
                                  @NewParameterId = @NewParameterId OUTPUT;

SELECT @Value1 as Value1, @Value2 as Value2, @NewParameterId as NewParameterId;

SELECT *
FROM Examples.Parameter
WHERE ParameterId = @newParameterId;
```

This returns the following, showing that the @Value2 parameters values did change, as the row inserted has an all uppercase, and all lowercase versions of the parameter values. However, the variable values did not change, unlike the @Value2 and @NewParameterId values.

```
Value1                Value2                NewParameterId
--------------------  --------------------  ---------------
Test                  test                  7


ParameterId Value1                Value2
----------- --------------------  --------------------
7           TEST                  test
```

Using output parameters is the only way to return data to a variable that is not an integer, and is the only way to return more than one value to a variable, no matter the type.

## Implement table-valued parameters

Table-valued parameters allow you need to pass more than a simple scalar value to a procedure. The reasons to do this generally fall into two categories:

- The user wants to pick a set of rows to filter a set that could not easily be done using scalar valued parameters.
- To create a procedure interface that allows you to create more than a single row in the table in a natural way.

For our example, we use a small table that has a few columns, and start with a few rows as well.

```
CREATE TABLE Examples.Machine
(
    MachineId    int NOT NULL CONSTRAINT PKMachine PRIMARY KEY,
    MachineNumber char(3) NOT NULL CONSTRAINT AKMachine UNIQUE,
    Description varchar(50) NOT NULL
);
INSERT INTO Examples.Machine(MachineId, MachineNumber, Description)
VALUES (1,'001','Thing1'),(2,'002','Thing2'),(3,'003','Thing3');
```

Now, consider the case where the user wants to target a few rows. One method that was used for many years was to pass in a comma-delimited list. There were many ways of splitting the string, but SQL Server 2016 added a new system function STRING_SPLIT(). So we could pass a variable value such as '1,3' to get three specific rows in the table.

```
CREATE PROCEDURE Examples.Machine_MultiSelect
    @MachineList varchar(200)
AS
    SET NOCOUNT ON;
    SELECT Machine.MachineId, Machine.MachineNumber
    FROM    Examples.Machine
            JOIN STRING_SPLIT(@MachineList,',') AS StringList
                ON StringList.value = Machine.MachineId;
```

While this works ,and it still a very useful way of passing a pseudo-table valued parameter in cases where the caller is not able to use a table-valued parameter, the more efficient method of passing in a table of values is to pass a table object.

> **NOTE**  **THE SQL SERVER 2016 DATABASE ENGINE**
>
> It is great to be up to date about the latest improvements in SQL Server 2016 database engine, particularly Transact-SQL, so if you see STRING_SPLIT(), you won't be confused as to whether it is a trick question or not. The entire list of improvements in the database engine is located here: *https://msdn.microsoft.com/en-us/library/bb510411.aspx.*

To use a table-valued parameter that is actually a true table object, we start by creating a USER DEFINED TYPE with the table data type. We use a generic structure, because this is a fairly generic usage to fetch a specific set of rows. Note that types are schema-owned, but they are not objects, so their names need not be different from the pool of objects.:

```
CREATE TYPE Examples.SurrogateKeyList AS table
(
    SurrogateKeyId int PRIMARY KEY --note you cannot name constraints for table types

);
```

Now you can use this table type as a parameter to the STORED PROCEDURE. You must define it as READONLY, which means that the rows in the table are static. Hence, unlike other parameter values, if you try to INSERT, UPDATE, or DELETE rows you receive an error. In the following procedure, join the TABLE variable to the permanent TABLE object for the output.

```
ALTER PROCEDURE Examples.Machine_MultiSelect
    @MachineList Examples.SurrogateKeyList READONLY
AS
    SET NOCOUNT ON;
    SELECT Machine.MachineId, Machine.MachineNumber
    FROM    Examples.Machine
            JOIN @MachineList AS MachineList
                ON MachineList.SurrogateKeyId = Machine.MachineId;
```

Calling this procedure is a bit more complex than using a string, but the code is far more straightforward. For parameter sets that are a little larger, you can even include PRIMARY KEY and UNIQUE constraints when defining the table USER DEFINED TYPE, so using the table in a JOIN will have a better chance of using an index.

```
DECLARE @MachineList Examples.SurrogateKeyList;
INSERT INTO @MachineList (SurrogateKeyId)
VALUES (1),(3);

EXECUTE Examples.Machine_MultiSelect @MachineList = @MachineList;
```

Beyond the ability to return a specific set of rows, passing a table of values can be used to create multiple rows in a single call. It is technically possible to do without a table, as you could either use multiple sets of parameters (@MachineId1, @MachineNumber1, @MachineId2, etc), or a complex parameter such as an XML type, but neither is as straightforward as using a table-valued parameter. As with our previous example, we start by creating a table USER DEFINED TYPE, but this time it is defined in a specific manner. We named this USER DEFINED TYPE the same as the TABLE object to reinforce that they are different name spaces, which could be something confusing in an exam question.

```
CREATE TYPE Examples.Machine AS TABLE
(
    MachineId int NOT NULL PRIMARY KEY,
    MachineNumber char(3) NOT NULL UNIQUE,
    Description varchar(50) NOT NULL
);
```

Now, create the STORED PROCEDURE to insert rows by using this table type for the parameter:

```
CREATE PROCEDURE Examples.Machine_MultiInsert
    @MachineList Examples.Machine READONLY
AS
    SET NOCOUNT ON;
    INSERT INTO Examples.Machine(MachineId, MachineNumber, Description)
    SELECT MachineId, MachineNumber, Description
    FROM    @MachineList;
```

Now you can call this STORED PROCEDURE after inserting rows into a table variable that works in a very natural manner:

```
DECLARE @NewMachineRows Examples.Machine;
INSERT INTO @NewMachineRows (MachineId, MachineNumber, Description)
VALUES (4,'004','NewThing4'), (5, '005','NewThing5');

EXECUTE Examples.Machine_MultiInsert @MachineList = @NewMachineRows;
```

## Implement return codes

When you run a STORED PROCEDURE object, there is a value returned to the caller if it requests it, and is called a return code (or sometimes, a return value). By default, the return value is 0, but you can change the value using the RETURN statement, which also ends the running of the procedure.

As an example, consider this very simple STORED PROCEDURE object that makes no mention of any return value:

```
CREATE PROCEDURE SimpleReturnValue
AS
    DECLARE @NoOp int;
```

Running this procedure, you can access the return code from the EXECUTE statement.

```
DECLARE @ReturnCode int;
EXECUTE @ReturnCode = SimpleReturnValue;
SELECT @ReturnCode as ReturnCode;
```

You see the output as:

```
-----------
0
```

You can use the RETURN statement to stop execution and send the return code to the caller to know what has occurred. Return codes can be used in addition to outputting an error (as seen in our example), or in conjunction with error handling, as you use in the final section of this section.

As an example, consider the following STORED PROCEDURE object. In the design of the procedure, the procedure creator, when needed, defines a set of return codes. A typical set of return codes that is common is to use positive vales to mean a positive outcome with some additional information. A negative value is an error, and 0 simply means the procedure ran successfully with no additional information, since that is what you get performing a procedure that has not set the value itself.

```
CREATE PROCEDURE DoOperation
(
    @Value  int
)
--Procedure returns via return code:
-- 1 - successful execution, with 0 entered
-- 0 - successful execution
-- -1 - invalid, NULL input
AS
    IF @Value = 0
        RETURN 1;
    ELSE IF @Value IS NULL
        RETURN -1;
    ElSE RETURN 0;
```

Performing this procedure always looks like a success, as there is not any code to throw an error, but the caller can check the return code to determine what has occurred. As an example, if the value is NULL:

```
DECLARE @ReturnCode int;
EXECUTE @ReturnCode = DoOperation @Value = NULL;
SELECT  @ReturnCode,
        CASE @ReturnCode WHEN 1 THEN 'Success, 0 Entered'
                         WHEN -1 THEN 'Invalid Input'
                         WHEN 0 THEN 'Success'
        END as ReturnMeaning;
```

You receive the following output:

```
            ReturnMeaning
----------- ------------------
-1          Invalid Input
```

Using the return code as the primary way to represent an error to the caller is not the typical pattern for implementation, but it is available when needed.

# Streamline existing stored procedure logic

One of the primary values of using STORED PROCEDURE objects as your interface to your data is that you can fix poorly-written code without changing compiled code of the interface. The biggest win is that often it is non-trivial code that generates the Transact-SQL in the procedural programming language.

For example, say you have the following table and seed data:

```
CREATE TABLE Examples.Player
(
    PlayerId     int NOT NULL CONSTRAINT PKPlayer PRIMARY KEY,
    TeamId       int NOT NULL, --not implemented reference to Team Table
    PlayerNumber char(2) NOT NULL,
    CONSTRAINT AKPlayer UNIQUE (TeamId, PlayerNumber)
)
INSERT INTO Examples.Player(PlayerId, TeamId, PlayerNumber)
VALUES (1,1,'18'),(2,1,'45'),(3,1,'40');
```

A programmer has written the following procedure shown in Listing 2-2 to fetch a player with a given number on any team, but did not understand how to write a set-based query.

**LISTING 2-2**  Overly complex stored procedure to fetch rows based on a simple filter

```
CREATE PROCEDURE Examples.Player_GetByPlayerNumber
(
    @PlayerNumber char(2)
) AS
    SET NOCOUNT ON;
    DECLARE @PlayerList TABLE (PlayerId int NOT NULL);

    DECLARE @Cursor cursor,
            @Loop_PlayerId int,
            @Loop_PlayerNumber char(2)

    SET @cursor = CURSOR FAST_FORWARD FOR ( SELECT PlayerId, PlayerNumber
                                            FROM   Examples.Player);

    OPEN @cursor;
    WHILE (1=1)
      BEGIN
            FETCH NEXT FROM @Cursor INTO @Loop_PlayerId, @Loop_PlayerNumber
            IF @@FETCH_STATUS <> 0
                BREAK;

            IF @PlayerNumber = @Loop_PlayerNumber
                INSERT INTO @PlayerList(PlayerId)
                VALUES (@Loop_PlayerId);

        END;

        SELECT Player.PlayerId, Player.TeamId
        FROM    Examples.Player
                JOIN @PlayerList AS PlayerList
                    on PlayerList.PlayerId = Player.PlayerId;
```

The EXECUTE statement for this STORED PROCEDURE is exactly what the requirements ask for:

```
EXECUTE  Examples.Player_Get @PlayerNumber = '18';
```

As is the output:

```
PlayerId    TeamId
----------- -----------
1           1
```

The only problem is that code is way more complex than it needs to be. Understanding the basics of writing code using proper Transact-SQL constructs, the procedure can be written far more simply:

```
ALTER PROCEDURE Examples.Player_GetByPlayerNumber
(
    @PlayerNumber char(2)
) AS
    SET NOCOUNT ON

    SELECT Player.PlayerId, Player.TeamId
    FROM   Examples.Player
    WHERE  PlayerNumber = @PlayerNumber;
```

The EXECUTE statement you use to run this STORED PROCEDURE is the same:

```
EXECUTE  Examples.Player_GetByPlayerNumber @PlayerNumber = '18';
```

As is the output:

```
PlayerId    TeamId
----------- -----------
1           1
```

Both procedures return the same amount of data, and for a development server with a few, to a few hundred, rows perform in imperceptibly similar times. However, once you get a realistic amount of data in the table, the performance for the original is very unsatisfactory.

While this is obviously an example of very egregious performance coding issues, things aren't always so obvious. There are many different ways one could create STORED PROCEDURE objects filled with Transact-SQL that is not efficient that are obvious (lots of branching, returning a variable number of result sets based on parameter values), but there are a few that are not quite so obvious with which you should be concerned:

- Parameter type mismatch with data in referenced tables
- Invalid use of functions on search arguments in queries

In the next two sections we take a look at these two considerations in a bit more detail.

## Invalid use of functions on search arguments

It is often useful to use system functions to get the current time, to format some data, etc. However, sometimes doing something in a way that seems natural can be bad for performance. For example, consider a stored procedure designed to fetch a list of the games on the current day (showing only the parts of the script that are pertinent):

```
CREATE TABLE Game
…
GameStartTime   datetime2(0)
…
CREATE PROCEDURE Game_GetForDate
(
        @SearchDate date
…

    FROM   Game
    WHERE CAST(GameTime AS DATE) = @SearchDate;
```

This is definitely the easiest way to code this, as the CAST expression strips off the time in the GameTime column values and let you compare to the @SearchDate. However, every row that is output from the FROM clause (in this case all rows in the Game table) has to have the GameTime column value converted and checked for each row. If there is an index on the GameTime column, it is not usable.

To fix this, you can change the code to something that looks more complex, such as:

```
FROM GAME
WHERE GameStartTime >= @SearchDate
    AND   GameStartTime < DATEADD(Day, 1, @SearchDate);
```

But now, the two scalar expressions of @SearchDate and DATEADD(Day, 1, @SearchDate) can be calculated once and used to probe an index to see if it matches for the GameTime column.

## Parameter type mismatch

Matching the parameter (or really any variable) to how you are using it is very important. If the sizes don't match, you can lose data. If the types don't match, queries can have to implicitly convert the data type in a query, eliminating the use of an index. The problem is very similar to the problem in the previous section on using functions on search arguments, but at its worst it happens silently in code that looks otherwise correct.

For example, say you have a STORED PROCEDURE object that includes the following (again showing only the parts of the script that are pertinent):

```
CREATE TABLE Order
…
    OrderNumber nvarchar(10)

…

CREATE PROCEDURE Order_Search
@OrderNumber int --because a "number" is an integer, one surmises
…
WHERE OrderNumber = @OrderNumber;
```

Several problems can frequently occur. First, if any order numbers have data that cannot be implicitly converted to an integer (such as 'Order#20'), when that row is reached as rows are being returned, it gives you an error and stop sending back data. It works this way because the integer data type is higher in precedence than nvarchar. In this case, had the OrderNumber column been an integer, the query processor would convert the value in the parameter variable before performing the query. In cases like the Order_Search STORED PROCEDURE object, no index would be used in the search, even if a suitable one existed.

Second, if the data types are incompatible, you can get an immediate error. For example, a datatime2 parameter and an integer column provides an operand-type clash.

> **NEED MORE REVIEW?** **DATATYPE CONVERSION AND PRECEDENCE**
>
> Datatype conversion and precedence are important topics to understand. The following two articles on MSDN cover conversion and precedence, respectively: *https://msdn.microsoft.com/en-us/library/ms191530.aspx* and *https://msdn.microsoft.com/en-us/library/ms190309.aspx.*

## Implement error handling and transaction control logic within stored procedures

Now we are going to pull the concept of creating a STORED PROCEDURE object together and look at what needs to go into a production worthy stored procedure. So far, the topics have catered to single statement procedures showing one simple concept, but now we are going to get into dealing with multiple statements that modify data. When we start to bundle together multiple modification statements, it becomes important that we are able to make sure that the first statement performed properly before continuing to the next statement.

What makes this difficult is that different types of errors behave differently when performed in different ways, from typical constraints to errors that are thrown by triggers. When an error is caused by a constraint, the batch continues, but if the transaction is rolled back in a TRIGGER object, the batch stops. By building in the proper error handling layer, all errors are treated the same way, which allows you to make sure that one statement has completed successfully.

There are several topics in the process of error handling and transaction control logic that we review in this section:

- **Throwing an error** It is often useful to be able to throw our own error messages to cause the stored procedure code (or really any code) to stop, telling the caller why.

- **Handling an error** In order to manage the code flow after an error has occurred, you need to be able to capture the error and act accordingly.

- **Transaction control logic in your error handling** Transactions are used to control grouping statements together to ensure that multiple statements complete or fail as an atomic unit.

## Throwing an error

In your stored procedure, it is often necessary to tell the caller that there is an issue. Earlier in the chapter, we had a procedure that used return codes to indicate to the caller that there was an issue with the parameter value. There are two methods of throwing an error in Transact-SQL. First is using the THROW statement. THROW lets you specify an error number (50000 or greater, as 49999 and under are system reserved values); a user defined message in plain, Unicode text; and a state value which can be used to send additional information to the client.

For example, you can perform:

```
THROW 50000, 'This is an error message',1;
```

And you get the following output:

```
Msg 50000, Level 16, State 1, Line 1115
This is an error message
```

There is another command, RAISERROR, which seemingly does the same thing, with a few subtle differences. First, when specifying an error message, you can only return error number 50000 using RAISERROR. Second, you can change the error level using RAISERROR. There are a few formatting methods you can use with RAISERROR, along with a syntax form that we won't review using custom system error messages. For more information on various forms of using RAISERROR, MSDN has an article that covers this in detail here: *https://msdn.microsoft.com/en-us/library/ms178592.aspx*.) Using typical RAISERROR usage, you can run the following statement:

```
RAISERROR ('This is an error message',16,1);
```

You get the same output as with the THROW statement. The big difference between THROW and RAISERROR is how they affect the batch you are running in. THROW stops the batch, and RAISERROR does not. For example, run the following:

```
THROW 50000, 'This is an error message',1;
SELECT 'Batch continued'
```

The output is:

```
Msg 50000, Level 16, State 1, Line 1117
This is an error message
```

But then run the following:

```
RAISERROR ('This is an error message',16,1);
SELECT 'Batch continued'
```

And the output is:

```
Msg 50000, Level 16, State 1, Line 1119
This is an error message


---------------
Batch continued
```

So, going to the simple STORED PROCEDURE we had created earlier, you might change it to include a THROW call instead of using a return code for a negative outcome, but it is important to understand what this means to the control of flow. As an example that could easily be an exam question, consider the following stored procedure:

```
CREATE PROCEDURE DoOperation
(
    @Value  int
)
AS
    SET NOCOUNT ON;
    IF @Value = 0
        RETURN 1;
    ELSE IF @Value IS NULL
      BEGIN
        THROW 50000, 'The @value parameter should not be NULL',1;
        SELECT 'Continued to here';
        RETURN -1;
      END
    ELSE RETURN 0;
```

If the following batch is run, what is the output?

```
DECLARE @ReturnCode int
EXECUTE @ReturnCode = DoOperation @Value = NULL;
SELECT  @ReturnCode AS ReturnCode;
```

The question is having choices asking if you see the @ReturnCode output, the output 'Contintued to here', or just the error message. It turns out that the output is just the error message:

```
Msg 50000, Level 16, State 1, Procedure DoOperation, Line 10
The @value parameter should not be NULL
```

If you swap out the THROW statement for the following RAISERROR statement:

```
RAISERROR ('The @value parameter should not be NULL',16,1);
```

The output changes to show all three:

```
Msg 50000, Level 16, State 1, Procedure DoOperation, Line 11
The @value parameter should not be NULL


-----------------
Continued to here


-----------
-1
```

## Handling an error

Now that we have established how to throw our own error messages, we now need to look at how to handle an error occurring. What makes this difficult is that most errors do not stop processing (an unhandled error from a TRIGGER object is an example of one that ends a batch, as does executing the statement: SET XACT_ABORT ON before your queries that may cause an error, which we discuss in the next section), so when you have a group of modification statements running in a batch without any error handling, they keep running.  For example, consider the following table set up to allow you to easily cause an error:

```
CREATE TABLE Examples.ErrorTesting
(
    ErrorTestingId int NOT NULL CONSTRAINT PKErrorTesting PRIMARY KEY,
    PositiveInteger int NOT NULL
        CONSTRAINT CHKErrorTesting_PositiveInteger CHECK PositiveInteger > 0)
);
```

Now, perform the following five statements, all as a batch:

```
INSERT INTO Examples.ErrorTesting(ErrorTestingId, PositiveInteger)
VALUES (1,1); --Succeed
INSERT INTO Examples.ErrorTesting(ErrorTestingId, PositiveInteger)
VALUES (1,1); --Fail PRIMARY KEY violation
INSERT INTO Examples.ErrorTesting(ErrorTestingId, PositiveInteger)
VALUES (2,-1); --Fail CHECK constraint violation
INSERT INTO Examples.ErrorTesting(ErrorTestingId, PositiveInteger)
VALUES (2,2); --Succeed
SELECT *
FROM   Examples.ErrorTesting;
```

This returns several error messages, and the two rows that were successfully inserted:

```
Msg 2627, Level 14, State 1, Line 1113
Violation of PRIMARY KEY constraint 'PKErrorTesting'. Cannot insert duplicate key
in object 'Examples.ErrorTesting'. The duplicate key value is (1).

Msg 547, Level 16, State 0, Line 1116
The INSERT statement conflicted with the CHECK constraint
"CHKErrorTesting_PositiveInteger". The conflict occurred in database
"ExamBook762Ch2", table "Examples.ErrorTesting", column 'PositiveInteger'.

ErrorTestingId PositiveInteger
-------------- ---------------
1              1
2              2
```

There are two prevalent methods of dealing with these errors to stop the execution. First, use the @@ERROR system function to check the error level after each statement, exiting if so. Second, use the TRY...CATCH construct. TRY...CATCH is by far the easiest and most powerful and modern method, but there are places where checking the error level is still a valid and useful thing to do.

> **NOTE   UNDOING CHANGES**
>
> **In the following section after we cover the ways to divert the code on an error, we review how the batch that we performed with errors could have all its changes undone.**

## Using @@ERROR to deal with errors

The @@ERROR system function (also referred to as a global variable, because it is prefixed with @@, though it is technically a system function), tells you the error level of the previous statement.

So, you have to either use it in a Boolean expression, or capture the value immediately after a statement that you are concerned about. You can check how the value changes when you successfully view the value the function returns.

Using the TABLE object we started with in the previous section, consider the following stored procedure. Use @@ERROR after every INSERT statement to see if the statement has completed successfully, shown in Listing 2-3.

**LISTING 2-3**   Procedure to show error checking with @@ERROR

```
CREATE PROCEDURE Examples.ErrorTesting_InsertTwo
AS
    SET NOCOUNT ON;
    INSERT INTO Examples.ErrorTesting(ErrorTestingId, PositiveInteger)
    VALUES (3,3); --Succeeds

    IF @@ERROR <> 0
        BEGIN
            THROW 50000, 'First statement failed', 1;
            RETURN -1;
        END;

    INSERT INTO Examples.ErrorTesting(ErrorTestingId, PositiveInteger)
    VALUES (4,-1); --Fail Constraint

    IF @@ERROR <> 0
        BEGIN
            THROW 50000, 'Second statement failed', 1;
            RETURN -1;
        END;

        INSERT INTO Examples.ErrorTesting(ErrorTestingId, PositiveInteger)
        VALUES (5,1); --Will succeed if statement executes
        IF @@ERROR <> 0
```

```
        BEGIN
            THROW 50000, 'Third statement failed', 1;
            RETURN -1;
        END;
```

Then run this procedure:

```
EXECUTE Examples.ErrorTesting_InsertTwo;
```

This gives you the following output (if following along, you can truncate the data if you want to run it multiple times):

```
Msg 547, Level 16, State 0, Procedure ErrorTesting_InsertTwo, Line 12
The INSERT statement conflicted with the CHECK constraint
"CHKErrorTesting_PositiveInteger". The conflict occurred in database
"ExamBook762Ch2", table "Examples.ErrorTesting", column 'PositiveInteger'.

Msg 50000, Level 16, State 1, Procedure ErrorTesting_InsertTwo, Line 17
Second statement failed
```

You get both error messages, but you are able to stop the rest of the stored procedure execution, since the error message that was thrown was for the second insert statement.

## Using TRY...CATCH

Using the TRY...CATCH construct is both far more powerful, and far easier to code with than using @@ERROR. The syntax is:

```
BEGIN TRY
    --Code you want to execute
END TRY
BEGIN CATCH
    --What to do if the code fails
END CATCH;
```

In the TRY section, you write your code as you normally would without error handling. If an error occurs, nothing is returned to the client immediately. Control is transferred to the CATCH section, and there you are able to decide what to do. You have access to information about the error through a set of system functions which are not cleared until the next error occurs, unlike @@ERROR. They are not scoped to the procedure or batch being run. If one procedure calls another, the called procedure can still see the error status information until an error occurs.

- **ERROR_NUMBER** Gives you the number of the error that caused you to be transferred to the **CATCH** section.
- **ERROR_MESSAGE** This is the text of the error message that was thrown.
- **ERROR_PROCEDURE** If the error occurred in a coded object, this contains the name of that object, otherwise it is NULL.
- **ERROR_LINE** This is the line of the batch or module where the error occurred.

- **ERROR_SEVERITY** The severity of the error. 16 is the normal error severity, higher are generally system errors.

- **ERROR_STATE** The extended error state value that an error message can include.

> **NOTE** **MORE ON ERROR STATES**
>
> For more information about error severities, the following article on MSDN has an explanation of all of them: *https://msdn.microsoft.com/en-us/library/ms164086.aspx*. For more information about error states, consult *https://msdn.microsoft.com/en-us/library/ ms180031.aspx*.

In Listing 2-4 we have written a much simpler bit of code. None of it should be too surprising, but note the THROW statement to end the CATCH section. Using THROW in this manner works in a CATCH block to send the error message to the caller that caused the CATCH to be called (typically referred to as *rethrowing* an error). This allows you to write code to deal with the error, undo changes, log the error message, etc., and then present the error message to the client as it would have looked without being caught.

**LISTING 2-4** Procedure to show error checking with TRY...CATCH

```
ALTER PROCEDURE Examples.ErrorTesting_InsertTwo
AS
    SET NOCOUNT ON;
    DECLARE @Location nvarchar(30);

    BEGIN TRY
        SET @Location = 'First statement';
        INSERT INTO Examples.ErrorTesting(ErrorTestingId, PositiveInteger)
        VALUES (6,3); --Succeeds

        SET @Location = 'Second statement';
        INSERT INTO Examples.ErrorTesting(ErrorTestingId, PositiveInteger)
        VALUES (7,-1); --Fail Constraint

        SET @Location = 'First statement';
        INSERT INTO Examples.ErrorTesting(ErrorTestingId, PositiveInteger)
        VALUES (8,1); --Will succeed if statement executes
    END TRY
    BEGIN CATCH
        SELECT ERROR_PROCEDURE() AS ErrorProcedure, @Location AS ErrorLocation
        SELECT ERROR_MESSAGE() as ErrorMessage;
        SELECT ERROR_NUMBER() AS ErrorNumber, ERROR_SEVERITY() as ErrorSeverity,
                ERROR_LINE() As ErrorLine;

            THROW;

        END CATCH;
```

The major part of the configuration is just coding the TRY...CATCH blocks. The only manual bits of code you may optionally wish to use in the TRY section is to save off the location into a variable. You can use the line number, but this is quite confusing as errors can be bubbled up from other stored procedures, triggers, etc.

Run this procedure:

```
EXECUTE Examples.ErrorTesting_InsertTwo;
```

The output tells you all of the details, including the data we selected out, and the error message that was rethrown.

```
ErrorProcedure                      ErrorLocation
-----------------------------       -----------------------------
ErrorTesting_InsertTwo              Second statement


ErrorMessage
----------------------------------------------------------------------------------
The INSERT statement conflicted with the CHECK constraint
"CHKErrorTesting_PositiveInteger". The conflict occurred in database "ExamBook762Ch2",
table "Examples.ErrorTesting", column 'PositiveInteger'.


ErrorNumber ErrorSeverity ErrorLine
----------- ------------- -----------
547         16            12


Msg 547, Level 16, State 0, Procedure ErrorTesting_InsertTwo, Line 12
The INSERT statement conflicted with the CHECK constraint
"CHKErrorTesting_PositiveInteger". The conflict occurred in database "ExamBook762Ch2",
table "Examples.ErrorTesting", column 'PositiveInteger'.
```

## Transaction Control Logic in Your Error Handling

In this final section on error handling, we combine all of the concepts we have discussed, along with an initial review of transactions (Chapter 3 will go much deeper into the various forms of transaction handling that you may need, but transactions are essential to a discussion of transactions). Every statement in SQL Server, DDL and DML alike, are performed as a transaction. By default, they are all considered *autocommit* transactions. When you want to run multiple statements together, making sure that they all complete, you use *explicit transactions*. Do this by using the BEGIN TRANSACTION statement to start a transaction, and COMMIT TRANSACTION to save the changes, or ROLLBACK TRANSACTION to undo the changes that have been made.

Transactions can be nested, as in:

```
BEGIN TRANSACTION;
BEGIN TRANSACTION;
```

You can tell how many transactions have been nested by using the @@TRANCOUNT system function.

```
SELECT @@TRANCOUNT
```

After running the two BEGIN TRANSACTION statements, the result of this query is 2. To save the changes made after the BEGIN TRANSACTION statements, you need an equal number of COMMIT TRANSACTION calls to save the changes. While syntactically there are two nested transactions, there is technically just a single transaction internally. To undo your changes, you only need a solitary ROLLBACK TRANSACTION call to undo the changes.

For example, run the following batch of statements:

```
BEGIN TRANSACTION;
INSERT INTO Examples.ErrorTesting(ErrorTestingId, PositiveInteger)
VALUES (9,1);

BEGIN TRANSACTION;
SELECT * FROM Examples.ErrorTesting WHERE ErrorTestingId = 9;
ROLLBACK TRANSACTION;
SELECT * FROM Examples.ErrorTesting WHERE ErrorTestingId = 9;
```

The statement succeeds, as no error is returned, and then the first SELECT statement returns data, but the second does not. One final system function that we need for the error handler is XACT_STATE(). You use this function to determine the current status of a transaction if one is in effect. There are three possible values: 1-There is an active transaction that can be committed; 0-There is no active transaction; -1-There is an active transaction that cannot be committed, also referred to as an *uncommitable transaction*, or a *doomed* transaction. An uncommitable transaction is caused by a few rare situations that can occur in complex code such as using XACT_ABORT with an error handler. (XACT_ABORT is a SET options that ends the batch on a transaction that we show later in this section. It is typically not used with any other error handling).

In the next three code listings, there are three possible transaction and error handling schemes that make sure that either all statements succeed, or they all fail. Our scenario uses the following two tables (note the CHECK constraint on the CompanyName column so we can force an error on the second table):

```
CREATE TABLE Examples.Worker
(
    WorkerId int NOT NULL IDENTITY(1,1) CONSTRAINT PKWorker PRIMARY KEY,
    WorkerName nvarchar(50) NOT NULL CONSTRAINT AKWorker UNIQUE
);
CREATE TABLE Examples.WorkerAssignment
(
    WorkerAssignmentId int IDENTITY(1,1) CONSTRAINT PKWorkerAssignment PRIMARY KEY,
    WorkerId int NOT NULL,
    CompanyName nvarchar(50) NOT NULL
        CONSTRAINT CHKWorkerAssignment_CompanyName
            CHECK (CompanyName <> 'Contoso, Ltd.'),
    CONSTRAINT AKWorkerAssignment UNIQUE (WorkerId, CompanyName)
);
```

To keep the processing very simple, the requirements for the STORED PROCEDURE object we are creating is to create one Worker row and one WorkerAssignment row in a single call to the STORED PROCEDURE. Hence, the basic part of the code is to perform:

```
INSERT INTO Examples.Worker...
INSERT INTO Examples.WorkerAssignment...
```

If either of the statements fails, the goal is to capture the error, return the error telling the user where in the code the error occurred, and end the batch. In Listing 2.5, we start by implementing this with a TRY...CATCH construct. The code include comments that explain anything new, and to clarify what is being accomplished.

**LISTING 2-5** Procedure to show realistic error checking with TRY...CATCH

```
CREATE PROCEDURE Examples.Worker_AddWithAssignment
    @WorkerName nvarchar(50),
    @CompanyName nvarchar(50)
AS
    SET NOCOUNT ON;
    --do any non-data testing before starting the transaction
    IF @WorkerName IS NULL or @CompanyName IS NULL
        THROW 50000,'Both parameters must be not null',1;

    DECLARE @Location nvarchar(30), @NewWorkerId int;
    BEGIN TRY
        BEGIN TRANSACTION;

        SET @Location = 'Creating Worker Row';
        INSERT INTO Examples.Worker(WorkerName)
        VALUES (@WorkerName);

        SELECT @NewWorkerId = SCOPE_IDENTITY(),
               @Location = 'Creating WorkAssignment Row';

        INSERT INTO Examples.WorkerAssignment(WorkerId, CompanyName)
        VALUES (@NewWorkerId, @CompanyName);

        COMMIT TRANSACTION;
    END TRY
    BEGIN CATCH
        --at the end of the call, we want the transaction rolled back
        --rollback the transaction first, so it definitely occurs as the THROW
        --statement would keep it from happening.
        IF XACT_STATE() <> 0 --if there is a transaction in effect
                            --commitable or not
            ROLLBACK TRANSACTION;

        --format a message that tells the error and then THROW it.
        DECLARE @ErrorMessage nvarchar(4000);
        SET @ErrorMessage = CONCAT('Error occurred during: ''',@Location,'''',
                            ' System Error: ',
                            ERROR_NUMBER(),':',ERROR_MESSAGE());
        THROW 50000, @ErrorMessage, 1;
    END CATCH;
```

Showing how the code works, first try NULL parameter values.

```
EXEC Examples.Worker_AddWithAssignment @WorkerName = NULL, @CompanyName = NULL;
```

This returns the following error, which happens even before the explicit transaction is started, which would have given an error. In some cases, it can be advantageous to check for certain types of errors before modifying data.

```
Msg 50000, Level 16, State 1, Procedure Worker_AddWithAssignment, Line 7
Both parameters must be not null
```

Next, insert a set of rows that succeed:

```
EXEC Examples.Worker_AddWithAssignment
                     @WorkerName='David So', @CompanyName='Margie''s Travel';
```

You can see what happens when there is an error by running the following statement with the same @WorkerName parameter value:

```
EXEC Examples.Worker_AddWithAssignment
                     @WorkerName='David So', @CompanyName='Margie''s Travel';
```

This results in the following error:

```
Msg 50000, Level 16, State 1, Procedure Worker_AddWithAssignment, Line 38
Error occurred during: 'Creating Worker Row' System Error: 2627:Violation of UNIQUE KEY
constraint 'AKWorker'. Cannot insert duplicate key in object 'Examples.Worker'. The
duplicate key value is (David So).
```

Now, show that a failure when an error occurs with the second table being referenced:

```
EXEC Examples.Worker_AddWithAssignment
                     @WorkerName='Ian Palangio', @CompanyName='Contoso, Ltd.';
```

This returns the following:

```
Msg 50000, Level 16, State 1, Procedure Worker_AddWithAssignment, Line 38
Error occurred during: 'Creating WorkAssignment Row' System Error: 547:The INSERT
statement conflicted with the CHECK constraint "CHKWorkerAssignment_CompanyName". The
conflict occurred in database "ExamBook762Ch2", table "Examples.WorkerAssignment",
column 'CompanyName'.
```

Then you can make sure it works by changing the @CompanyName parameter value.

```
EXEC Examples.Worker_AddWithAssignment
                     @WorkerName='Ian Palangio', @CompanyName='Humongous Insurance';
```

In Listing 2-6, we have the same goals for the stored procedure, but instead use @@error to determine if an error has occurred.

LISTING 2-6 Procedure to show realistic error checking with @@ERROR

```
ALTER PROCEDURE Examples.Worker_AddWithAssignment
    @WorkerName nvarchar(50),
    @CompanyName nvarchar(50)
AS
    SET NOCOUNT ON;
```

```
DECLARE @NewWorkerId int;
--still check the parameter values first
IF @WorkerName IS NULL or @CompanyName IS NULL
    THROW 50000,'Both parameters must be not null',1;
--Start a transaction
BEGIN TRANSACTION
INSERT INTO Examples.Worker(WorkerName)
VALUES (@WorkerName);
--check the value of the @@error system function
IF @@ERROR <> 0
  BEGIN
    --rollback the transaction before the THROW (or RETURN if using), because
    --otherwise the THROW will end the batch and transaction stay open
    ROLLBACK TRANSACTION;
    THROW 50000,'Error occurred inserting data into Examples.Worker table',1;
  END;
SELECT @NewWorkerId = SCOPE_IDENTITY()

INSERT INTO Examples.WorkerAssignment(WorkerId, CompanyName)
VALUES (@NewWorkerId, @CompanyName);
 IF @@ERROR <> 0
  BEGIN
    ROLLBACK TRANSACTION;
    THROW 50000,
      'Error occurred inserting data into Examples.WorkerAssignment table',1;
  END;
--if you get this far in the batch, you can commit the transaction
COMMIT TRANSACTION;
```

Now, run the following two commands. GO is a batch separator that splits the two executions into two independent communications with the server, so the second runs no matter what happens with the first, unless something drastic happens and the connection to the server is lost:

```
EXEC Examples.Worker_AddWithAssignment @WorkerName='Seth Grossman', @
CompanyName='Margie''s Travel';

GO
--Cause an error due to duplicating all of the data from previous call
EXEC Examples.Worker_AddWithAssignment @WorkerName='Seth Grossman', @
CompanyName='Margie''s Travel';
```

The second call returns 2 errors, the first being the error from the command, and the second coming from the THROW statement: ¡

```
Msg 2627, Level 14, State 1, Procedure Worker_AddWithAssignment, Line 14
Violation of UNIQUE KEY constraint 'AKWorker'. Cannot insert duplicate key in object
'Examples.Worker'. The duplicate key value is (Seth Grossman).

Msg 50000, Level 16, State 1, Procedure Worker_AddWithAssignment, Line 21
Error occurred inserting data into Examples.Worker table
```

Finally, in Listing 2-7, we demonstrate the final method of error-handling in a stored procedure using XACT_ABORT ON. The way this works is that when running, if an error occurs, the batch stops and the transaction is stopped. It is effective, but gives you no real control over what happens in an error. Since the batch ends immediately, to know what statement you are executing you need to print messages constantly. Hence this method is more used for system tasks, but it is an effective tool for dealing with rolling back a transaction on an error.

**LISTING 2-7** Procedure to show stopping transaction and batch using SET XACT_ABORT ON

```
ALTER PROCEDURE Examples.Worker_AddWithAssignment
    @WorkerName nvarchar(50),
    @CompanyName nvarchar(50)
AS
    SET NOCOUNT ON;
    --will cause batch to end on any error
    SET XACT_ABORT ON;

    DECLARE @NewWorkerId int;

    --Same parameter check as other cases
    IF @WorkerName IS NULL or @CompanyName IS NULL
        THROW 50000,'Both parameters must be not null',1;

    --start the transaction
    BEGIN TRANSACTION;
    --  Execute the code as normal
    INSERT INTO Examples.Worker(WorkerName)
    VALUES (@WorkerName);

    SELECT @NewWorkerId = SCOPE_IDENTITY()

    INSERT INTO Examples.WorkerAssignment(WorkerId, CompanyName)
    VALUES (@NewWorkerId, @CompanyName);

    COMMIT TRANSACTION;
```

Now all you get is just the system error message returned, as you see from the following:

```
EXEC Examples.Worker_AddWithAssignment
        @WorkerName='Stig Panduro', @CompanyName='Margie''s Travel';

GO
--Cause an error due to duplicating all of the data from previous call
EXEC Examples.Worker_AddWithAssignment
        @WorkerName='Stig Panduro', @CompanyName='Margie''s Travel';
```

This returns:

```
Msg 2627, Level 14, State 1, Procedure Worker_AddWithAssignment, Line 12
Violation of UNIQUE KEY constraint 'AKWorker'. Cannot insert duplicate key in object
'Examples.Worker'. The duplicate key value is (Stig Panduro).
```

A consideration to note when building your error handling is that a STORED PROCEDURE cannot change the transaction count from when it starts to when it finishes. For example, consider the following STORED PROCEDURE object:

```
CREATE PROCEDURE ChangeTransactionLevel
AS
    BEGIN TRANSACTION;
    ROLLBACK TRANSACTION;
```

If you perform this outside of the context of a transaction, everything works fine with no errors. But if place this in a transaction:

```
BEGIN TRANSACTION;
EXEC ChangeTransactionLevel;
ROLLBACK TRANSACTION;
```

You receive the following error messages:

```
Msg 266, Level 16, State 2, Procedure ChangeTransactionLevel, Line 0
Transaction count after EXECUTE indicates a mismatching number of BEGIN and COMMIT
statements. Previous count = 1, current count = 0.
Msg 3903, Level 16, State 1, Line 1434
The ROLLBACK TRANSACTION request has no corresponding BEGIN TRANSACTION.
```

The second message is not critical, unless you expect to be in a transaction at the time and keep modifying data or structure. There are two very standard steps to mitigate this issue. First, as we have done in the TRY...CATCH example previously, end your error handler with a THROW statement, which ends the batch:

```
ALTER PROCEDURE ChangeTransactionLevel
AS
    BEGIN TRANSACTION;
    ROLLBACK TRANSACTION;
    THROW 50000,'Error After Rollback',1;
```

Now, perform this in the same transaction:

```
BEGIN TRANSACTION;
EXEC ChangeTransactionLevel;
ROLLBACK TRANSACTION;
```

You see just the one error message:

```
Msg 50000, Level 16, State 1, Procedure ChangeTransactionLevel, Line 5
Error After Rollback
```

The alternative is to use what are called *savepoints*. Savepoints allow you to roll back part of a transaction, and is covered in Skill 3.1. Prior to THROW, savepoints were common for use in error handling, but now are used primarily for more specific purposes. Generally, using THROW after making sure that you have ended all transactions is the cleanest method of execution.

For the most part, anytime you have complex stored procedures, you should be using TRY...CATCH and THROW. These commands simplify dealing with errors. This is particularly true when you have a procedure that is called by another procedure that can cause errors (which is pretty much any statement in Transact-SQL).

For example, consider the following procedure that is used to call the example procedure we just created that changed the transaction level. Use the same error handler that we used earlier in the TRY...CATCH example, as seen in Listing 2-8.

**LISTING 2-8** Procedure to what happens when you change the transaction level in a procedure

```
ALTER PROCEDURE dbo.CallChangeTransactionLevel
AS
    BEGIN TRY
        BEGIN TRANSACTION

        DECLARE @Location nvarchar(30) = 'Execute Procedure';
        EXECUTE ChangeTransactionLevel; --This will cause an error by design

        COMMIT TRANSACTION
    END TRY
    BEGIN CATCH
        IF XACT_STATE() <> 0
            ROLLBACK;
        DECLARE @ErrorMessage nvarchar(4000)
        SET @ErrorMessage = CONCAT('Error occurred during: ''',@Location,'''',
                                ' System Error: ',ERROR_NUMBER(),':',
                                ERROR_MESSAGE());
        THROW 50000, @ErrorMessage, 1;
    END CATCH;
```

Now, perform the calling procedure:

```
EXECUTE dbo.CallChangeTransactionLevel;
```

This gives you the error from the procedure that said Error After Rollback:

```
Msg 50000, Level 16, State 1, Procedure CallChangeTransactionLevel, Line 19
Error occurred during: 'Execute Procedure' System Error: 50000:Error After Rollback
```

Now you can see the error from all of the calling procedures, in a stack as each CATCH block appends the message from the previous call. You could add an ERROR_PROCEDURE() function call to the CONCAT expression for the error message to make the entire stack more obvious, or even use RAISERROR to return a message at each level, and a THROW command to stop the batch when you have reached the top level. You can tell this using the @@nestlevel system function, but usually this is enough of error handler for the typical need, particularly keeping it simple enough for this review of error handling.

> **NEED MORE REVIEW?** **THE COMPLEXITIES OF ERROR HANDLING**
>
> To be certain, error handling is a complex topic that cannot be given a complete review in a book of this size and purpose. One of the best resources on Error and Transaction Handling is from Erland Sommarskog, here on his website: *http://sommarskog.se/error_handling/Part1.html.*

# Skill 2.3 Create triggers and user-defined functions

In this final skill of the chapter, we cover two very different, and somewhat lesser-used features of Transact-SQL, with very little overlap between them.

First we look at TRIGGER objects, which in itself is a very large topic, particularly because there are three different types of triggers that you can work with, but equally because they are quite a bit more complex than STORED PROCEDURE objects. You use them to react to some event, either a DML operation such as an INSERT, UPDATE or DELETE statement execution; someone changing a setting or object on the server; or even someone logging into a server.

Then we cover the details of User-Defined Functions (or UDFs) that allow you to create code that is called in the same way that a system function might. UDFs are very powerful tools, but are also very dangerous for performance when used poorly.

> *NOTE* **TRIGGER OBJECTS**
>
> This chapter focuses on interpreted Transact-SQL objects. You can create TRIGGER objects in managed code. Skill 3.4 highlights the differences between these solutions and the memory-optimized tables and natively-compiled modules.

**This section covers how to:**

- Design trigger logic based on business requirements
- Determine when to use Data Manipulation Language (DML) triggers, Data Definition Language (DDL) triggers, or logon triggers
- Recognize results based on execution of AFTER or INSTEAD OF triggers
- Design scalar-valued and table-valued user-defined functions based on business requirements
- Identify differences between deterministic and non-deterministic functions

## Design trigger logic based on business requirements

Triggers are coded objects, similar to stored procedures, which allow you to run code in response to events that occur in SQL Server. The most common types of triggers fire on a DML operation such as an INSERT, UPDATE or DELETE statement execution. Additionally, there are triggers that fire when someone changes something in SQL Server (DDL triggers), a setting or object on the server, or even someone logging into a server (login triggers).

In this section, we focus on DML triggers, because they are the ones that are generally used for business requirements. In the next section we review the other types of triggers, which are mostly focused on administration needs. DML TRIGGER objects are schema owned, database contained objects, like STORED PROCEDURE, VIEW, and CONSTRAINT objects, so their names must not collide with other objects in the same schema.

DML TRIGGER objects are typically used for a couple of purposes that are hard to do in the declarative configuration of tables. The logic often could be placed in a STORED PROCEDURE object, but by using a TRIGGER object, you can limit duplication of code:

- **Complex data integrity**   CHECK constraints can only see data in the same row. If you need to check data across multiple rows, only triggers can do this automatically.

- **Running code in response to some action**   For example, if an order comes in past a threshold (like a $3,000,000 order for lattes from Fourth Coffee), you could write a row to a table to have the row checked for validity.

- **Ensuring columnar data is modified**   If you want to make sure that data is modified, like a column that tells you when a row was last modified, triggers can ensure that the user does not put in invalid data.

- **Making a view editable**   If a VIEW references more than one table, it becomes complicated to modify it using simple DML operations.

There are two different types of DML Trigger objects that work for INSERT, UPDATE, and DELETE operations that you should familiarize yourself with:

- **AFTER**   These triggers perform after a DML operation. They are typically used for doing data validations, as you can see the data as it is after the operation has occurred.

- **INSTEAD OF**   These triggers perform instead of the DML operation, so if you want the operation to occur, you need repeat the DML in the code.

The following subsections contain an example of each of the scenarios that are listed, along with some commentary on the major pitfalls you encounter. This is not by any means an exhaustive list of ways that triggers can be used, but a simple overview of how they are created to implement given needs.

> ***NEED MORE REVIEW?*** **MORE ON THE CREATE TRIGGER STATEMENT**
>
> Triggers are not a simple topic that we can cover in any real depth, not even to the light depth we have reviewed other topics. If you need to study more about the many details of writing triggers, a good start is the MSDN page on CREATE TRIGGER here: *https://msdn. microsoft.com/en-us/library/ms189799.aspx*.

## Complex data integrity

The automatic data-integrity enforcement we have covered so far has been of the declarative variety. You state a predicate in the form of a column declaration/data type and possibly a constraint. A major limitation of constraints is how much they can see. For example, CHECK constraints can only see data in the same row. FOREIGN KEY constraints can only see the current row and see if another row exists.

While this covers a great percentage of needs, if you need to check data across a group of rows, triggers can do this (technically CHECK constraints can use a USER DEFINED FUNCTION, but TRIGGER objects are considered the best method). For this example, consider you have the following table (just including columns that we need for the example):

```
CREATE TABLE Examples.AccountContact
(
    AccountContactId int NOT NULL CONSTRAINT PKAccountContact PRIMARY KEY,
    AccountId        char(4) NOT NULL,
    PrimaryContactFlag bit NOT NULL
);
```

You are given the business requirement to ensure there is always one primary contact for an account, if a contact does exist. A first step is to identify the query that shows you rows that do not match this rule. In this case:

```
SELECT AccountId, SUM(CASE WHEN PrimaryContactFlag = 1 THEN 1 ELSE 0 END)
FROM    Examples.AccountContact
GROUP BY AccountId
HAVING SUM(CASE WHEN PrimaryContactFlag = 1 THEN 1 ELSE 0 END) <> 1;
```

If that query returns data, then you know something is wrong. This query is the basis of the data check. We can put this into a trigger as seen in Listing 2-9, which checks on any INSERT or UPDATE operation.

**LISTING 2-9**  Trigger to stop multiple PrimaryContacts for an Account during an UPDATE or INSERT operation

```
CREATE TRIGGER Examples.AccountContact_TriggerAfterInsertUpdate
ON Examples.AccountContact
AFTER INSERT, UPDATE AS
BEGIN
  SET NOCOUNT ON;
  SET ROWCOUNT 0; --in case the client has modified the rowcount
  BEGIN TRY
  --check to see if data is returned by the query from previously
  IF EXISTS ( SELECT AccountId
          FROM    Examples.AccountContact
                  --correlates the changed rows in inserted to the other rows
                  --for the account, so we can check if the rows have changed
          WHERE   EXISTS (SELECT *
                      FROM    inserted
                      WHERE   inserted.AccountId =
                                          AccountContact.AccountId

                      UNION ALL
                      SELECT *
                      FROM    deleted
                      WHERE   deleted.AccountId =
                                          AccountContact.AccountId)
          GROUP BY AccountId
          HAVING SUM(CASE WHEN PrimaryContactFlag = 1 then 1 ELSE 0 END) <> 1)

      THROW   50000, 'Account(s) do not have only one primary contact.', 1;
```

```
        END TRY
    BEGIN CATCH
        IF XACT_STATE() <> 0
            ROLLBACK TRANSACTION;
        THROW;
    END CATCH
END;
```

> **NOTE** **MULTIPLE** AFTER **TRIGGERS**
>
> It is possible to have multiple AFTER triggers on the same operation. However, you have minimal control over the order in which they run. For more information, see the MSDN article on sp_settriggerorder system stored procedure: *https://msdn.microsoft.com/en-us/ library/ms186762.aspx*.

For the most part, this is pretty straightforward. We give the TRIGGER a name, tell it the TABLE it is for, and then that this fires AFTER an INSERT or UPDATE operation. Then it is just like a stored procedure for the most part. There are two virtual tables inserted and deleted that instantiated when the trigger performs. Inserted shows you how the data looks after the operation, and deleted shows you how the data looks before the operation. Both tables only have data during an UPDATE operation, showing you the before and the after versions. In some cases, both tables are empty, such as an UPDATE statement where the WHERE clause matched no rows, or a MERGE statement where one of the operations had no matches.

The most important part of writing such a trigger is that you must be prepared for more than one row to be modified. In the EXISTS block, we have the query we started from, and added the WHERE EXISTS condition to limit the scope of the query to just rows that have been modified based on their AccountId. You have to use both inserted and deleted table rows because there is nothing stopping the AccountId from changing:

```
SELECT AccountId
FROM    Examples.AccountContact
--correlates the changed rows in inserted to the other rows
--for the account, so we can check if the rows have changed
----------------------------------------------------------------
WHERE   EXISTS (SELECT *
                FROM    inserted
                WHERE   inserted.AccountId = AccountContact.AccountId
                UNION ALL
                SELECT *
                FROM    deleted
                WHERE   deleted.AccountId = AccountContact.AccountId)
----------------------------------------------------------------
GROUP BY AccountId
HAVING SUM(CASE WHEN PrimaryContactFlag = 1 then 1 ELSE 0 END;
```

Many trigger writers make the mistake of writing variable declaration statements to grab values from the inserted/deleted virtual table like the following:

```
SELECT @AccountId = AccountId FROM inserted;
```

Using that AccountId to check for issues misses all but the one row. You must, though, test all of the cases with single and multiple rows. For this trigger, consider running at least the following simple tests:

```
--Success, 1 row
INSERT INTO Examples.AccountContact(AccountContactId, AccountId, PrimaryContactFlag)
VALUES (1,1,1);
--Success, two rows
INSERT INTO Examples.AccountContact(AccountContactId, AccountId, PrimaryContactFlag)
VALUES (2,2,1),(3,3,1);
--Two rows, same account
INSERT INTO Examples.AccountContact(AccountContactId, AccountId, PrimaryContactFlag)
VALUES (4,4,1),(5,4,0);
--Invalid, two accounts with primary
INSERT INTO Examples.AccountContact(AccountContactId, AccountId, PrimaryContactFlag)
VALUES (6,5,1),(7,5,1);
```

This returns:

```
Msg 50000, Level 16, State 1, Procedure AccountContact_TriggerAfterInsert, Line 29
One or more Accounts does not have one and only one primary contact.
```

Then, without showing messages:

```
--Invalid, no primary
INSERT INTO Examples.AccountContact(AccountContactId, AccountId, PrimaryContactFlag)
VALUES (8,6,0),(9,6,0);
--Won't work, because AccountId is new, and this row is not primary
UPDATE Examples.AccountContact
SET    AccountId = 6
WHERE  AccountContactId = 5;
```

Triggers can be tricky to get right, and logically tracing through the code and testing is important. On the exam, if presented with a trigger, it is important to be very careful to be able to trace through the single-row and multi-row operations that are needed.

The requirements for our problem stated that we are to make sure every account has a primary contact, if a contact exists. As it stands now, while the user can't create or modify rows to violate the requirement, a user can delete the primary row. So, creating a DELETE TRIGGER works very similar to the INSERT/UPDATE one, except now you use the deleted virtual table, as you can see in Listing 2-10.

**LISTING 2-10** Trigger to stop multiple PrimaryContacts for an Account during a DELETE operation

```
CREATE TRIGGER Examples.AccountContact_TriggerAfterDelete
ON Examples.AccountContact
AFTER DELETE AS
BEGIN
    SET NOCOUNT ON;
    SET ROWCOUNT 0; --in case the client has modified the rowcount
    BEGIN TRY
    IF EXISTS ( SELECT AccountId
                FROM    Examples.AccountContact
                WHERE   EXISTS (SELECT *
```

```
                    FROM     deleted
                    WHERE    deleted.AccountId =
                                    AccountContact.AccountId)
            GROUP BY AccountId
            HAVING SUM(CASE WHEN PrimaryContactFlag = 1 then 1 ELSE 0 END) <> 1)
    THROW  50000, 'One or more Accounts did not have one primary contact.', 1;
END TRY
BEGIN CATCH
    IF XACT_STATE() <> 0
        ROLLBACK TRANSACTION;
    THROW;
  END CATCH;
END;
```

The basic structure of the TRIGGER for data integrity is to see if there is an issue, either by checking data in the inserted/deleted tables, the primary table, or any tables, and if there is an issue, run a THROW statement and let the ROLLBACK TRANSACTION undo the statement's effect and any other activity done within the context of the transaction. If the caller has a TRY...CATCH block, they get the error captured. If not, the batch ends due to the THROW statement. If you use RAISERROR, things are trickier because the batch continues after the transaction ends.

## Running code in response to some action

There are many situations where a modification is made to a row that you want to affect a change of some sort in another table. For example, consider a table that captures promises to a charity. The table might look something like the following, including only columns pertinent to the example:

```
CREATE TABLE Examples.Promise
(
    PromiseId int NOT NULL CONSTRAINT PKPromise PRIMARY KEY,
    PromiseAmount money NOT NULL
);
```

No matter the charity, there are a few levels of promises that can be received. For simplicity, let's define two: Normal and Extranormal. A Normal promise is in a typical range that a person promises if they are normal and sincere. Extranormal promises are outside of the Normal and need verification. Extranormal promises for this scenario are those over $10,000.00. The requirements are to create a log of promises to verify when rows are created or updated.

So, you design a table that has the Promise rows to be verified, which looks like this (without the details of the row being verified):

```
CREATE TABLE Examples.VerifyPromise
(
    VerifyPromiseId int NOT NULL CONSTRAINT PKVerifyPromise PRIMARY KEY,
    PromiseId int NOT NULL CONSTRAINT AKVerifyPromise UNIQUE
                --FK not included for simplicity
);
```

In Listing 2-11 the TRIGGER object fulfills this requirement.

LISTING 2-11   Trigger to create rows in another table

```
CREATE TRIGGER Examples.Promise_TriggerInsertUpdate
ON Examples.Promise
AFTER INSERT, UPDATE AS
BEGIN
    SET NOCOUNT ON;
    SET ROWCOUNT 0; --in case the client has modified the rowcount
    BEGIN TRY
        INSERT INTO Examples.VerifyPromise(PromiseId)
        SELECT PromiseId
        FROM   inserted
        WHERE  PromiseAmount > 10000.00
          AND  NOT EXISTS (SELECT * --keep from inserting duplicates
                           FROM   VerifyPromise
                           WHERE  VerifyPromise.PromiseId = inserted.PromiseId)
    END TRY
    BEGIN CATCH
        IF XACT_STATE() <> 0
            ROLLBACK TRANSACTION;
        THROW; --will halt the batch or be caught by the caller's catch block
    END CATCH
END;
```

The biggest thing to note in this TRIGGER is how you need to do very little error handling. Just use the TRY...CATCH block to see if there is an error with the statement, and if so, run the ROLLBACK TRANSACTION statement that rethrows the error message.

> **NOTE   TRIGGERS MODIFYING DATA**
>
> When a trigger modifies data in the same or different table, there can be triggers that also get fired. Discussion of this is beyond the scope of this review, but there is an article on MSDN that covers this in detail: *https://msdn.microsoft.com/en-us/library/ms190739.aspx*.

## Ensuring columnar data is modified

In this example, we make use of INSTEAD OF TRIGGER objects, which are excellent tools for making sure some operation occurs in a statement. For example, if you want to make sure that a column tells you when a row was last modified, an INSTEAD OF TRIGGER object can be used to determine if the user inputs data that does not make sense.

Consider the following TABLE:

```
CREATE TABLE Examples.Lamp
(
    LampId          int IDENTITY(1,1) CONSTRAINT PKLamp PRIMARY KEY,
    Value           varchar(10) NOT NULL,
    RowCreatedTime  datetime2(0) NOT NULL
        CONSTRAINT DFLTLamp_RowCreatedTime DEFAULT(SYSDATETIME()),
    RowLastModifiedTime datetime2(0) NOT NULL
        CONSTRAINT DFLTLamp_RowLastModifiedTime DEFAULT(SYSDATETIME())
);
```

While we specified a DEFAULT constraint, the user can put anything at all in the table. Instead, let's use two TRIGGER objects. The first is an INSTEAD OF INSERT TRIGGER object as seen in Listing 2-12.

**LISTING 2-12** INSTEAD OF TRIGGER to automatically set RowCreated and RowLastModified time columns

```
CREATE TRIGGER Examples.Lamp_TriggerInsteadOfInsert
ON Examples.Lamp
INSTEAD OF INSERT AS
BEGIN
    SET NOCOUNT ON;
    SET ROWCOUNT 0; --in case the client has modified the rowcount
    BEGIN TRY
        --skip columns to automatically set
        INSERT INTO Examples.Lamp( Value)
        SELECT Value
        FROM   inserted
    END TRY
    BEGIN CATCH
        IF XACT_STATE() <> 0
            ROLLBACK TRANSACTION;
        THROW; --will halt the batch or be caught by the caller's catch block
    END CATCH
END;
```

> **NOTE   MORE ON INSTEAD OF TRIGGERS**
>
> You can only have one INSTEAD OF trigger per operation on a table. While you can have one INSTEAD OF TRIGGER object that does multiple operations, like INSERT, UPDATE, and DELETE, it is not typically as useful as it can be for AFTER TRIGGER objects. One use case is to make a trigger not do the actual operation.

This trigger is very similar to the one in previous sections. The biggest difference is that the INSERT statement is doing the operation that the user expected it was doing, but skipping the columns that use a defaulted value. You can use this step in the process to do any formatting that you don't want the user to have control over. After inserting a row and viewing it, you see the following:

```
INSERT INTO Examples.Lamp(Value, RowCreatedTime, RowLastModifiedTime)
VALUES ('Original','1900-01-01','1900-01-01');

SELECT *
FROM   Examples.Lamp;
```

Here are the two columns:

```
LampId      Value      RowCreatedTime               RowLastModifiedTime
----------- ---------- ---------------------------- ----------------------------
1           Original   2016-09-20 21:03:54          2016-09-20 21:03:54
```

Next, create the INSTEAD OF UPDATE TRIGGER that makes sure that the RowLastModified-Time is modified, and the RowCreatedTime is never modified.

```
CREATE TRIGGER Examples.Lamp_TriggerInsteadOfUpdate
ON Examples.Lamp
INSTEAD OF UPDATE AS
BEGIN
    SET NOCOUNT ON;
    SET ROWCOUNT 0; --in case the client has modified the rowcount
    BEGIN TRY
        UPDATE Lamp
        SET    Value = inserted.Value,
               RowLastModifiedTime = DEFAULT --use default constraint
        FROM   Examples.Lamp
                  JOIN inserted
                     ON Lamp.LampId = inserted.LampId;
    END TRY
    BEGIN CATCH
        IF XACT_STATE() <> 0
            ROLLBACK TRANSACTION;
        THROW; --will halt the batch or be caught by the caller's catch block
    END CATCH;
END;
```

This is similar to the INSERT trigger, but we do the UPDATE instead of the INSERT. This time, skip the RowCreatedTime column because the time the row was created doesn't change, but the modified time does. Update and view the row previously created:

```
UPDATE Examples.Lamp
SET    Value = 'Modified',
       RowCreatedTime = '1900-01-01',
       RowLastModifiedTime = '1900-01-01'
WHERE LampId = 1;

SELECT *
FROM   Examples.Lamp;
```

The RowLastModifiedTime is different than the first call, and different now from the Row-CreatedTime:

```
LampId      Value      RowCreatedTime              RowLastModifiedTime
----------- ---------- --------------------------- ---------------------------
1           Modified   2016-09-20 21:07:07         2016-09-20 21:10:26
```

## Making any view modifiable using INSTEAD OF triggers

A final example of DML triggers is to apply an INSTEAD OF TRIGGER to a VIEW object, making it editable. It can even be editable if the view isn't based on a table. No matter what the data that is returned from a SELECT statement on the view, as long as the INSERT statement references the columns by name, you can, using the INSERTED and/or DELETED virtual table in the INSTEAD OF trigger.

For example, create the following TABLE and VIEW objects as seen in Listing 2-13.

```
CREATE TABLE Examples.KeyTable1
(
    KeyValue int NOT NULL CONSTRAINT PKKeyTable1 PRIMARY KEY,
    Value1   varchar(10) NULL
);
CREATE TABLE Examples.KeyTable2
(
    KeyValue int NOT NULL CONSTRAINT PKKeyTable2 PRIMARY KEY,
    Value2   varchar(10) NULL
);
GO
CREATE VIEW Examples.KeyTable
AS
    SELECT COALESCE(KeyTable1.KeyValue, KeyTable2.KeyValue) as KeyValue,
           KeyTable1.Value1, KeyTable2.Value2
    FROM   Examples.KeyTable1
             FULL OUTER JOIN Examples.KeyTable2
                ON KeyTable1.KeyValue = KeyTable2.KeyValue;
```

Note that in the view, there is no way that you can insert data using this view, because the actual KeyValue columns are not exposed in the view, so the following attempt is to insert into the table:

```
INSERT INTO Examples.KeyTable (KeyValue, Value1, Value2)
VALUES (1,'Value1','Value2');
```

This gives you the following error:

```
Msg 4406, Level 16, State 1, Line 21
Update or insert of view or function 'Examples.KeyTable' failed because it contains
a derived or constant field.
```

Next, add an INSTEAD OF INSERT TRIGGER to the table. In the TRIGGER, we get the inserted and deleted virtual tables that are the shape of the VIEW objects structure, which we will use to do the INSERT operations as seen in Listing 2-14.

LISTING 2-14  INSTEAD OF TRIGGER to make view editable

```
CREATE TRIGGER Examples.KeyTable_InsteadOfInsertTrigger
ON Examples.KeyTable
INSTEAD OF INSERT
AS
BEGIN
    SET NOCOUNT ON;
    SET ROWCOUNT 0; --in case the client has modified the rowcount
    BEGIN TRY
        --Insert data into one of the tables
        INSERT INTO Examples.KeyTable1(KeyValue, Value1)
        SELECT KeyValue, Value1
        FROM   Inserted;
        --and then the other
        INSERT INTO Examples.KeyTable2(KeyValue, Value2)
        SELECT KeyValue, Value2
        FROM   Inserted;
```

```
   END TRY
  BEGIN CATCH
      IF XACT_STATE() <> 0
          ROLLBACK TRANSACTION;
      THROW; --will halt the batch or be caught by the caller's catch block
  END CATCH;
END;
```

Now, if you try to insert into the view, using the same statement as before:

```
INSERT INTO Examples.KeyTable (KeyValue, Value1, Value2)
VALUES (1,'Value1','Value2');
```

It will succeed. And to view the data:

```
SELECT *
FROM   Examples.KeyTable;
```

It looks just like any other table:

```
KeyValue    Value1     Value2
----------- ---------- ----------
1           Value1     Value2
```

This is a very simple version of what this TRIGGER may need to be for a production worthy version. When you have more than one table to be concerned with, there is a question of what happens if one row already exists, and another doesn't. If you build the UPDATE trigger, an UPDATE can either be an UPDATE or an INSERT for one of the tables. But you should make sure that one of the table's rows exists.

# Determine when to use Data Manipulation Language (DML) triggers, Data Definition Language (DDL) triggers, or logon triggers

As has been stated a few times already in this trigger skill (and in the name of this section itself) there are three types of triggers that activate upon the occurrence of a type of event. You have already seen that DML TRIGGER objects are schema bound database objects that let you react to, and even morph the results of, an INSERT, UPDATE or DELETE statement.

In this section, we review the other two types of TRIGGER objects:

- **DDL triggers**   Used to react to DDL operations at the server or database level. For example, you can capture the DDL of every CREATE TABLE and ALTER TABLE statement and log the results in a table, or even stop them from occurring.

- **Logon triggers**   Used to react to someone logging into the server. For example, you could state that login LOGIN1 (also referred to as a *server principal*) could not log in from 8PM – 7AM. These triggers just stop the login action, so if the user is already connected during this time period, it does not end their connection.

## DDL Triggers

There are two kinds of DDL Triggers that you can use to react to DDL statements. One is at the database level, where you can react to DDL only in the database where the trigger is located. For example, the trigger can fire on CREATE TABLE, DROP INDEX, ALTER VIEW, etc. The other is at the server level. Server triggers can react to actions that occur in any database, as well as things that occur strictly at the server scope, such as CREATE DATABASE, DROP LOGIN, etc.

In the next two sections, we cover examples of DDL triggers at the server, and then the database level. There is not that much difference to the syntax, but there are a few differences to understand about how they work, and where they reside.

### SERVER

For the server scoped example, a TRIGGER object logs whenever a database is created, dropped, or altered. In this example, the database location of the log table is important, because a SERVER DDL TRIGGER object is stored at the server level in the master database. So the trigger needs to address the table by three-part name.

Create the following TABLE object that contains the time, statement, and the login name of the user that made the change to the database.

```
USE ExamBook762Ch2;
GO
CREATE TABLE Examples.DDLDatabaseChangeLog
(
    DDLDatabaseChangeLogId int NOT NULL IDENTITY
        CONSTRAINT PKDDLDatabaseChangeLog PRIMARY KEY,
    LogTime datetime2(0) NOT NULL,
    DDLStatement nvarchar(max) NOT NULL,
    LoginName sysname NOT NULL
);
```

Next, since the log table is in a different database, but the trigger is not scoped to that database, we need to create security principals. Security is not on the exam, but to make the example somewhat realistic, this is needed because security chaining does not pertain to this non-schema owned object. Instead use the EXECUTE AS clause on the CREATE TRIGGER statement to dictate security principals. We start by creating a server principal, a user in the ExamBook762Ch2 database.

```
--Names used to make it clear where you have used examples from this book outside
--of primary database
CREATE LOGIN Exam762Examples_DDLTriggerLogging WITH PASSWORD = 'PASSWORD$1';
CREATE USER Exam762Examples_DDLTriggerLogging
                                    FOR LOGIN Exam762Examples_DDLTriggerLogging;
GRANT INSERT ON  Examples.DDLDatabaseChangeLog TO
                        Exam762Examples_DDLTriggerLogging;
```

We use just three events to cover the database events listed in our requirements, but there are many more. For a full list, check this link to DDL Events on Technet: *https://technet.microsoft. com/en-us/library/bb522542.aspx*.

The trigger itself is fairly simple. The interesting part is the EVENTDATA() function. It returns an XML string value that contains information about the DDL operation that caused the trigger to fire. Unlike a DML TRIGGER object, a DDL TRIGGER fires once per statement. We use just a single value from the statement, the CommandText value. Note that the DDL TRIGGER object is not a schema-owned object.

```
CREATE TRIGGER DatabaseCreations_ServerDDLTrigger
ON ALL SERVER
WITH EXECUTE AS 'Exam762Examples_DDLTriggerLogging'
FOR CREATE_DATABASE, ALTER_DATABASE, DROP_DATABASE
AS
    SET NOCOUNT ON;
    --trigger is stored in master db, so must
    INSERT INTO ExamBook762Ch2.Examples.DDLDatabaseChangeLog(LogTime, DDLStatement,
                                                            LoginName)
    SELECT SYSDATETIME(),EVENTDATA().value(
                    '(/EVENT_INSTANCE/TSQLCommand/CommandText)[1]','nvarchar(max)'),
            ORIGINAL_LOGIN(); --Original login gives you the user that is connected.
                            --Otherwise we would get the EXECUTE AS user.
```

To test this trigger, create a LOGIN and give it rights to create and alter a database, assuming your server allows SQL Standard logins. If not, the same information is captured if you use any login.

```
CREATE LOGIN Exam762Examples_DatabaseCreator WITH PASSWORD = 'PASSWORD$1';
GRANT CREATE ANY DATABASE TO Exam762Examples_DatabaseCreator;
GRANT ALTER ANY DATABASE TO Exam762Examples_DatabaseCreator;
```

Now, login as Exam762Examples_DatabaseCreator, and run the following set of batches:

```
CREATE DATABASE Example
GO
ALTER DATABASE Example SET RECOVERY SIMPLE;
GO
DROP DATABASE Example;
```

And the database owner that you have been using:

```
SELECT LogTime, DDLStatement, LoginName
FROM Examples.DDLDatabaseChangeLog;
```

You receive a log of changes:

```
LogTime                      DDLStatement                                     LoginName
--------------------------   ---------------------------------------------    -------------
2016-09-21 16:55:09          CREATE DATABASE Example                          Exam762Examp...
2016-09-21 16:55:19          ALTER DATABASE Example SET RECOVERY SIMPLE        Exam762Examp...
2016-09-21 16:55:27          DROP DATABASE Example                            Exam762Examp...
```

While mostly an administration function, this provides functionality that can be very useful. Something you can do in a DDL TRIGGER is ROLLBACK to disallow an action (no need for special security here):

```
CREATE TRIGGER DatabaseCreations_StopThemAll
ON ALL SERVER
FOR CREATE_DATABASE, ALTER_DATABASE, DROP_DATABASE
AS
    SET NOCOUNT ON;
    ROLLBACK TRANSACTION;
    THROW 50000,'No more databases created please',1;
```

Now, everyone (even system administrators), is disallowed to change a database. Something is commonly done with DDL Triggers of this type is to disable them. You can disable a TRIGGER using the DISABLE TRIGGER statement:

```
DISABLE TRIGGER DatabaseCreations_StopThemAll ON ALL SERVER;
```

It is a very good idea to clean up your objects unless you want to keep them, as they span outside of the single database:

```
DROP TRIGGER DatabaseCreations_ServerDDLTrigger ON ALL SERVER;
DROP USER Exam762Examples_DDLTriggerLogging;
DROP LOGIN Exam762Examples_DDLTriggerLogging;
DROP LOGIN Exam762Examples_DatabaseCreator;
```

### DATABASE

There is very little difference between the DDL TRIGGER objects at the database scope versus the server scope. Pretty much the exact same syntax works, but there are fewer events to react to. In this example, we demonstrate another use for DDL TRIGGERS, and that is stopping an event, while logging it.

We start with a table that is very much the same as the one for database changes:

```
CREATE TABLE Examples.DDLChangeLog
(
    DDLChangeLogId int NOT NULL IDENTITY
        CONSTRAINT PKDDLChangeLog PRIMARY KEY,
    LogTime datetime2(0) NOT NULL,
    DDLStatement nvarchar(max) NOT NULL,
    LoginName sysname NOT NULL
);
```

We again need to configure some security so the user can perform an INSERT statement into the table, but this time strictly in the context of the database:

```
CREATE USER Exam762Examples_DDLTriggerLogging WITHOUT LOGIN;
GRANT INSERT ON Examples.DDLChangeLog TO Exam762Examples_DDLTriggerLogging;
```

Now we create the DDL TRIGGER on the database scope. Just like the server version, this is not a schema-scoped object. In this version of the trigger we are going to save off the DDL into a variable, do the ROLLBACK TRANSACTION, and then log the change (note that if the DDL statement is in an externally started transaction, the change is still logged because of the ROLLBACK TRANSACTION).

```
CREATE TRIGGER DatabaseChanges_DDLTrigger
ON DATABASE
WITH EXECUTE AS 'Exam762Examples_DDLTriggerLogging'
FOR CREATE_TABLE, ALTER_TABLE, DROP_TABLE
AS
    SET NOCOUNT ON;
    DECLARE @eventdata XML = EVENTDATA();
    ROLLBACK; --Make sure the event doesn't occur
    INSERT INTO Examples.DDLChangeLog(LogTime, DDLStatement, LoginName)
    SELECT SYSDATETIME(),
           @EventData.value('(/EVENT_INSTANCE/TSQLCommand/CommandText)[1]',
                                                          'nvarchar(max)'),
           ORIGINAL_LOGIN();
    THROW 50000,'Denied!',1;
```

Now, when any user in the database (even a system administrator) tries to CREATE, ALTER, or DROP a TABLE object:

```
CREATE TABLE Examples.Test
(
    TestId int NOT NULL
);
GO
DROP TABLE Examples.DDLChangeLog;
```

You receive the following error message (or in this case, you would get two of the same error message):

```
Msg 50000, Level 16, State 1, Procedure DatabaseChanges_DDLTrigger, Line 25
Denied!
```

Then, viewing the data in the log table:

```
SELECT LogTime, DDLStatement, LoginName
FROM    Examples.DDLChangeLog;
```

You see the following statements were attempted:

| LogTime | DDLStatement | LoginName |
| --- | --- | --- |
| 2016-09-21 19:16:06 | CREATE TABLE Examples.Test<br>(<br>    TestId int NOT NULL<br>) | DomainName\louis |

Again, clean up your code or future examples do not work:

```
DROP TRIGGER DatabaseChanges_DDLTrigger ON DATABASE;
DROP USER Exam762Examples_DDLTriggerLogging;
```

## Logon Triggers

The last type of TRIGGER objects to introduce are LOGIN TRIGGER modules. A LOGIN TRIG-
GER fires whenever a server principal connects to your server. In our example, it implements
the following requirements: disallow a server principal named: Login_NotAllowed from connecting to the server, and log all other connections in a log table.

For this example, create the following table, which can capture the name of the login, the
time of login, and the application that the login comes from:

```
CREATE TABLE Examples.LoginLog
(
    LoginLogId  int NOT NULL IDENTITY(1,1)
        CONSTRAINT PKLoginLog PRIMARY KEY,
    LoginName    sysname NOT NULL,
    LoginTime    datetime2(0) NOT NULL ,
    ApplicationName sysname NOT NULL
);
```

Similar to the DDL trigger, there is very little to the LOGIN TRIGGER. The trigger fires once
per logon operation, and there is no data it provides by a function or virtual table. All data
you need comes from system functions. In order to log on to a table, just like the DDL triggers, we need to provide security information, as this is a non-schema bound object with no
database context.

```
CREATE LOGIN Exam762Examples_LogonTriggerLogging WITH PASSWORD = 'PASSWORD$1';
CREATE USER Exam762Examples_LogonTriggerLogging
                              FOR LOGIN Exam762Examples_LogonTriggerLogging;
GRANT INSERT ON Examples.LoginLog TO Exam762Examples_LogonTriggerLogging;
```

Now create the trigger. It uses the ORIGINAL_LOGIN() function to get the security context
from the principal that connected, as the EXECUTE AS clause changes the context inside the
trigger. Then, if the user is not Login_NotAllowed, it logs the data:

```
CREATE TRIGGER Exam762ExampleLogonTrigger
ON ALL SERVER
WITH EXECUTE AS 'Exam762Examples_LogonTriggerLogging'
FOR LOGON
AS
    IF ORIGINAL_LOGIN() = 'Login_NotAllowed'
        THROW 50000,'Unauthorized Access',1;
    ELSE
        INSERT INTO ExamBook762Ch2.Examples.LoginLog(LoginName, LoginTime,
                                                ApplicationName)
        VALUES (ORIGINAL_LOGIN(),SYSDATETIME(),APP_NAME());
```

To test the LOGIN TRIGGER, create the LOGIN:

```
CREATE LOGIN Login_NotAllowed WITH PASS

WORD = 'PASSWORD$1';
```

Try to log in (see Figure 2-2), using any tool, such as Management Studio.

**FIGURE 2-2** Connection dialog for SQL Server Management Studio

After clicking connect, you see the dialog in Figure 2-3.

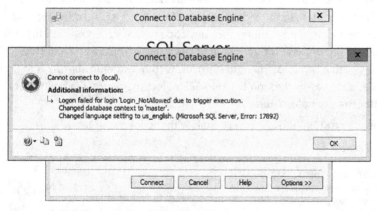

**FIGURE 2-3** Failed connection dialog from SQL Server Management Studio when LOGON TRIGGER has prevented connection

To be sure that your LOGON TRIGGER actually works before disconnecting all of your connections, connect to a new window using your typical security rights. Don't be terribly surprised when you find this log has more rows than you initially expect:

```
LoginName                LoginTime              ApplicationName
-----------------------  ---------------------  ---------------------------------------
WIN-8F59BO5AP7D\louis     2016-09-21 21:26:50   Microsoft SQL Se..IntelliSense
WIN-8F59BO5AP7D\louis     2016-09-21 21:26:50   Microsoft SQL Se..IntelliSense
WIN-8F59BO5AP7D\louis     2016-09-21 21:27:06   Microsoft SQL Se..Query
WIN-8F59BO5AP7D\louis     2016-09-21 21:27:06   Microsoft SQL Se..Query
```

As with the previous examples, be sure to clean this up if you are doing this on your server, because if the ExamBook762Ch2 database is later dropped with this trigger enabled, no one will be able to logon to the server:

```
DROP TRIGGER Exam762ExampleLogonTrigger ON ALL SERVER;
DROP USER Exam762Examples_LogonTriggerLogging;
DROP LOGIN Exam762Examples_LogonTriggerLogging;
```

> **NEED MORE REVIEW?**  **LOGON TRIGGERS**
>
> For more details on Logon Triggers, the following MSDN article covers this: *https://msdn. microsoft.com/en-us/library/bb326598.aspx.*

## Recognize results based on execution of AFTER or INSTEAD OF triggers

It is important to be able to trace through code and understand how it works and what it does based on particular inputs. Here in the trigger section of the book it is no different, except that triggers are quite a bit more complex than any code we have tried before. In the following two examples, we present you with a couple of less realistic TABLE and DML TRIGGER object combinations, with a DML statement that performs some action. Your task is to determine what occurs as data passes through the TRIGGER object (before reading on to see the solution directly after the example, naturally).

The first example, uses an AFTER TRIGGER object. Start with the following table:

```
CREATE TABLE Examples.UpdateRows
(
    UpdateRowsId int NOT NULL IDENTITY(1,1)
        CONSTRAINT PKUpdateRows PRIMARY KEY,
    Value varchar(20) NOT NULL
);
INSERT INTO Examples.UpdateRows (Value)
VALUES ('Original'),('Original'),('Original');
```

This has the following data:

```
UpdateRowsId Value
------------ --------------------
1            Original
2            Original
3            Original
```

And the AFTER UPDATE TRIGGER object in Listing 2-15 is added to the table.

**LISTING 2-15**  Trigger for the AFTER TRIGGER example

```
CREATE TRIGGER Examples.UpdateRows_TriggerInsert
ON Examples.UpdateRows
AFTER UPDATE AS
BEGIN
    SET NOCOUNT ON;
    SET ROWCOUNT 0;
    BEGIN TRY
        DECLARE @UpdateRowsId int
        SELECT @UpdateRowsId = UpdateRowsId
        FROM   inserted
        ORDER BY UpdateRowsId;

        UPDATE Examples.UpdateRows
        SET    Value = UPPER(Value)
        WHERE  UpdateRowsId = @UpdateRowsId;
    END TRY
    BEGIN CATCH
        IF XACT_STATE() <> 0
            ROLLBACK TRANSACTION;
        THROW; --will halt the batch or be caught by the caller's catch block
    END CATCH;

END;
```

Now, a user runs the following UPDATE statement:

```
UPDATE Examples.UpdateRows
SET    Value = 'Modified';
```

And receives the following output:

```
(3 row(s) affected)
```

What are the contents of the table? Either:

```
UpdateRowsId Value
------------ --------------------
1            Modified
2            Modified
3            MODIFIED
```

```
UpdateRowsId Value
------------ --------------------
1            Original
```

```
2          Original
3          Original
UpdateRowsId Value
------------ --------------------
1          MODIFIED
2          MODIFIED
3          MODIFIED


UpdateRowsId Value
------------ --------------------
1          MODIFIED
2          Modified
3          Modified
```

Or can you actually tell?

In this case, the first set of outputs match the table contents. Because of the way the TRIGGER is coded, only a single row is modified. So, it would be the first or the last set of results, or how you can't tell. You are guaranteed to get the first row in the set because of the ORDER BY clause on this statement (and it is necessary for you to realize that ORDER BY would order in ascending order by default):

```
SELECT @UpdateRowsId = UpdateRowsId
FROM   inserted
ORDER BY UpdateRowsId;
```

Without the ORDER BY clause, the order is not guaranteed, so you might get a different result (even though the fourth result would still be extremely likely).

This second example uses an INSTEAD OF TRIGGER object. Previous examples of triggers have made sure that the primary key column value was not changeable by using a column with the IDENTITY property or that it did not matter. The table we use is very simple, and the PRIMARY KEY constraint is on a column that can be changed:

```
CREATE TABLE Examples.KeyModify
(
    KeyModifyId  int CONSTRAINT PKKeyModify PRIMARY KEY,
    Value        varchar(20)
);
INSERT INTO Examples.KeyModify(KeyModifyId, Value)
VALUES (1,'Original'), (2,'Original'),(3,'Original');
```

Now, the trigger in Listing 2-16 is added to the table.

**LISTING 2-16** Trigger for the INSTEAD OF TRIGGER example

```
CREATE TRIGGER Examples.KeyModify_TriggerInsteadOfInsert
ON Examples.KeyModify
INSTEAD OF UPDATE AS
BEGIN
    SET NOCOUNT ON;
    SET ROWCOUNT 0;
    BEGIN TRY
        UPDATE Examples.KeyModify
        SET   Value = UPPER(inserted.Value)
```

```
        FROM    Examples.KeyModify
                JOIN inserted
                   ON KeyModify.KeyModifyId = inserted.KeyModifyId
   END TRY
   BEGIN CATCH
      IF XACT_STATE() <> 0
         ROLLBACK TRANSACTION;
      THROW;
   END CATCH
END;
```

Now, a user runs the following statement:

```
UPDATE Examples.KeyModify
SET     KeyModifyId = KeyModifyId + 10, --Change Primary Key Value
        Value = 'Modified';
```

After performing this statement, the user gets the following message:

```
(3 row(s) affected)
```

Did anything change in the table? Are the KeyModifyId column values 11, 12, and 13? Does the Value column say Original, ORIGINAL, Modified, or MODIFIED? The key to the answer is the JOIN on the inserted virtual table. The inserted virtual table looks like:

```
KeyModifyId Value
----------- --------------------
11          Modified
12          Modified
13          Modified
```

This is just what your statement told it to do.  However, the TABLE still has the following row values, since this is an INSTEAD OF TRIGGER object:

```
KeyModifyId Value
----------- --------------------
1           Original
2           Original
3           Original
```

At the point of the UPDATE. When you try to join these two sets together, zero rows match, so the final table looks like:

```
KeyModifyId Value
----------- --------------------
1           Original
2           Original
3           Original
```

The message from the UPDATE statement execution: (3 row(s) affected) is actually returned even if you leave off the UPDATE altogether. So nothing is changed. If it seems tricky, perhaps it is. However, they are real tables, and the code does work without error. You just have to work through the solution, regardless of whether it is realistic or not.

# Design scalar-valued and table-valued user-defined functions based on business requirements

User-defined functions are schema-owned objects (in the same name space as tables, procedures, triggers, etc.) that can be used to encapsulate code in ways that can be used very naturally in Transact-SQL calls. There are two major kinds of user defined functions:

- **Scalar**  Used to create code that returns a single value of a data type (more than just integers like STORED PROCEDURES could).
- **Table**  To the user, it appears to be essentially a view that allows you to predefine parameters that can be used to filter or alter the output.

Each function has different uses, so let's review them independently.

> **NEED MORE REVIEW?**  Beyond the review in this book, there is excellent information in the MSDN articles: User-Defined Functions (*https://msdn.microsoft.com/en-us/library/ms191007.aspx* and Create User-defined Functions (Database Engine) (*https://msdn.microsoft.com/en-us/library/ms191320.aspx*).

## Scalar-Valued user-defined functions

Scalar UDFs allow you to encapsulate small amounts of code into a module that can be called inside of other statements. As a very simple example, the following scalar function takes a single value as a parameter and returns it.

```
CREATE FUNCTION Examples.ReturnIntValue
(
    @Value int
)
RETURNS int
AS
  BEGIN
    RETURN @Value
  END;
```

This can be called in a very similar manner to any system function we have used previously, for example:

```
SELECT Examples.ReturnInValue(1) as IntValue;
```

You can access data in the function code, and they are very similar in structure to STORED PROCEDURE objects. The code in the FUNCTION has two primary limitations that make them complex to use.

First, there is no error handling that you can provide. There are runtime errors, such as those that stop a query from returning rows to occur that can't be caught during the compile process. One such example is the divide-by-zero errors. Perform the following query in the WideWorldImporters database:

```
SELECT OrderId, 1/ (4732-OrderId)
FROM   Sales.Orders;
```

You then see multiple rows returned and a divide-by-zero error. The same sort of issues occur with a scalar UDF, in that the errors come as data is being returned, not like you saw when creating STORED PROCEDURE objects. You cannot perform a THROW or RAISERROR statement to cause an error message to occur. Any error handling that you implement needs to be an understanding with the user of the function of the illegal value, like a negative, or NULL value.

Second, you may not make any side effects from the function. So you have no INSERT, UPDATE, or SELECT statements that modify tables other than a table variable (Of the form: DECLARE @table table(column datatype), which we use later in the table valued function code. They are available in scalar UDFs, but arern't typical, nor do any use of system functions change data.

Note that we did not use SET NOCOUNT ON, because that is considered a side-effecting function, even if it is simply for the scope of the object. BEGIN and END are required around the body of the code, and you must have a RETURN statement that returns a value of the data type that matches the RETURNS clause.

It is allowable to access a table in your scalar functions. For example, still in the WideWorldImporters database, if you have a business requirement to implement a scalar UDF, the user can give them the number of orders for a Customer. Optionally, for a specific OrderDate, you can write the function shown in Listing 2-17.

**LISTING 2-17** Scalar function that accesses a table

```
CREATE FUNCTION Sales.Customers_ReturnOrderCount
(
    @CustomerID int,
    @OrderDate date = NULL
)
RETURNS INT
WITH RETURNS NULL ON NULL INPUT, --if any parameter NULL, return NULL immediately
    SCHEMABINDING --make certain that the tables/columns referenced cannot change
AS
  BEGIN
      DECLARE @OutputValue int

      SELECT  @OutputValue = COUNT(*)
      FROM    Sales.Orders
      WHERE   CustomerID = @CustomerID
        AND   (OrderDate = @OrderDate
               OR @OrderDate IS NULL);

      RETURN @OutputValue
  END;
```

Using parameters of a FUNCTION object differs from using a STORED PROCEDURE, in that you can't use named parameters, and you can't skip parameters that have defaults. For example, to use this function you might code the following:

```
SELECT Sales.Customers_ReturnOrderCount(905, '2013-01-01');
```

This tells you that this customer has two orders for that day. To use the default parameter, you need to use the DEFAULT keyword:

```
SELECT Sales.Customers_ReturnOrderCount(905, DEFAULT);
```

While this can be quite useful, using functions in a query tends to cost more to perform over more direct manners. Consider the following two queries:

```
SELECT CustomerID, Sales.Customers_ReturnOrderCount(CustomerID, DEFAULT)
FROM    Sales.Customers;

SELECT CustomerID, COUNT(*)
FROM    Sales.Orders
GROUP  BY CustomerID;
```

If you compare the plans, the first plan (which looks very complex graphically) is 3 percent of the cost of the two queries. The second query's plan is very simple-looking, but at 97 percent of the cost, it seems the hands down winner is the FUNCTION. But using SET STATISTICS ON you discover why.

Query using the FUNCTION:

```
Table 'Worktable'. Scan count 0, logical reads 0, physical reads
Table 'Customers'. Scan count 1, logical reads 4, physical reads
 SQL Server Execution Times:
    CPU time = 375 ms,  elapsed time = 439 ms.
```

Query using the SELECT with the GROUP BY:

```
Table 'Orders'. Scan count 1, logical reads 191, physical reads 0
SQL Server Execution Times:
    CPU time = 16 ms,  elapsed time = 34 ms.
```

The GROUP BY query looks far worse, but performs over 10 times faster. However, we know that the function is accessing the Orders table, and that information is missing. The same is true in the plan. The code in the scalar UDF is not represented in a straightforward manner in the plan either.

The most common use case for scalar UDFs is to format some data in a common manner. For example, say you have a business need to format a value, such as the CustomerPurchase-OrderNumber in the Sales.Orders table in WideWorldImporters in a given way, and in multiple locations. In this case we just right pad the data to eight characters, and prepend 'CPO' to the number. For this you can write an expression in the SELECT clause:

```
SELECT N'CPO' + RIGHT(N'00000000' + CustomerPurchaseOrderNumber,8)
FROM WideWorldImporters.Sales.Orders;
```

Now, if you need to use this in multiple places, you can fold that expression into a scalar USER DEFINED FUNCTION object, like so:

```
CREATE FUNCTION Sales.Orders_ReturnFormattedCPO
(
    @CustomerPurchaseOrderNumber nvarchar(20)
)
RETURNS nvarchar(20)
```

```
WITH RETURNS NULL ON NULL INPUT,
    SCHEMABINDING
AS
 BEGIN
    RETURN (N'CPO' + RIGHT(N'00000000' + @CustomerPurchaseOrderNumber,8));
 END;
```

Now you can write:

```
SELECT Sales.Orders_ReturnFormattedCPO('12345') as CustomerPurchaseOrderNumber;
```

This then returns:

```
CustomerPurchaseOrderNumber
---------------------------
CPO000012345
```

Note that this, too, has performance implications that are not quite as obvious as the function that accesses a table. First, you never want to use this to format a column in a WHERE clause:

```
SELECT OrderId
FROM    Sales.Orders
WHERE   Sales.Orders_ReturnFormattedCPO(CustomerPurchaseOrderNumber) = 'CPO000019998';
```

In the best case, this scans an index that contains CustomerPurchaseOrder, but in the worst case it scans the entire base table structure. Note that this is true of any system function as well, so it is not really just a general rule of thumb that any column values that are formatted in any clause other than the SELECT clause may be cause for concern with performance.

However, even in the SELECT clause, there is some overhead with using a scalar UDF:

```
SET STATISTICS TIME ON;
SELECT Sales.Orders_ReturnFormattedCPO(CustomerPurchaseOrderNumber)
FROM    Sales.Orders;

SELECT N'CPO' + RIGHT(N'00000000' + [CustomerPurchaseOrderNumber],8)
FROM WideWorldImporters.Sales.Orders;
```

In this test, the function version took 188 ms of CPU time, and the expression only 15ms. So whether or not it is worth it to use a scalar UDF is a personal preference. So, an exam question about scalar functions can be about what you include in the function, or it can ask you to predict the better-performing statement and/or why it might be the case.

## Table-Valued user-defined functions

Table-Valued UDFs are used to present a set of data as a table, much like a view. In fact, they are generally thought of as views with parameters (or parameterized views.) There are two kinds of table-valued UDFs:

- **Simple**   Consisting of a single Transact-SQL query, simple table-valued UDFs work very much like a VIEW.

- **Multi-Statement** Consists of as many statements as you need, allowing you to build a set of data using the same logic as you had in scalar UDFs, but returning a table instead of a scalar variable.

For these examples, use the same requirements used in our scalar example, returning the number of sales for a given customer, and optionally on a given day. In addition, add a requirement to determine if they have any backorders on that day.

Starting with the simple table-valued UDF, the basics of the object is, just like a VIEW, a single SELECT query. As such, there is not a performance penalty in using a table-valued USER DEFINED FUNCTION versus a VIEW, depending on how you use it (which can also be said about how VIEW objects are used.):

```
CREATE FUNCTION Sales.Customers_ReturnOrderCountSetSimple
(
    @CustomerID int,
    @OrderDate date = NULL
)
RETURNS TABLE
AS
RETURN (SELECT COUNT(*) AS SalesCount,
               CASE WHEN MAX(BackorderOrderId) IS NOT NULL
                        THEN 1 ElSE 0 END AS HasBackorderFlag
        FROM    Sales.Orders
        WHERE   CustomerID = @CustomerID
        AND     (OrderDate = @OrderDate
                OR @OrderDate IS NULL));
```

The syntax is pretty self-explanatory, you just declare that you are returning a table, and in the RETURN clause (no BEGIN and END), you put the query with the parameters used as you desire. Usage is much like a view, only you have parameters you need to include:

```
SELECT *
FROM    Sales.Customers_ReturnOrderCountSetSimple(905,'2013-01-01');
```

This returns the following set:

```
SalesCount  HasBackorderFlag
----------- ----------------
2           1
```

And to default a parameter, you use the DEFAULT keyword as before:

```
SELECT *
FROM    Sales.Customers_ReturnOrderCountSetSimple(905,DEFAULT);
```

This returns:

```
SalesCount  HasBackorderFlag
----------- ----------------
125         1
```

Now you can use it in a query to get both calculated values by joining using the OUTER APPLY join operator, which applies column values from the left input as parameters into the right (you can also use literals):

```
SELECT CustomerId, FirstDaySales.SalesCount, FirstDaySales.HasBackorderFlag
FROM    Sales.Customers
        OUTER APPLY Sales.Customers_ReturnOrderCountSetSimple
                            (CustomerId, AcountOpenedDate) as FirstDaySales
WHERE  FirstDaySales.SalesCount > 0;
```

There are two APPLY operator versions. OUTER APPLY returns every row from the left input, while CROSS APPLY only returns rows where there is a match in the right input. Performing this query returns the following abridged output:

```
CustomerId  SalesCount  HasBackorderFlag
----------  ----------  ----------------
10          2           1
57          1           0
...         ...         ...
995         2           1
1000        2           1
```

For a multi-statement table-valued UDF, the syntax is quite different. You define the output specifically by declaring a table variable, and then by loading it. The following code in Listing 2-18 returns the exact same base query used in the simple version of the function.

LISTING 2-18  Multi-statement table-valued function that accesses a table

```
CREATE FUNCTION Sales.Customers_ReturnOrderCountSetMulti
(
    @CustomerID int,
    @OrderDate date = NULL
)
RETURNS  @OutputValue TABLE (SalesCount int NOT NULL,
                            HasBackorderFlag bit NOT NULL)
AS
 BEGIN
    INSERT INTO @OutputValue (SalesCount, HasBackorderFlag)
    SELECT COUNT(*) as SalesCount,
               CASE WHEN MAX(BackorderOrderId) IS NOT NULL
                         THEN 1 ElSE 0 END AS HasBackorderFlag
    FROM    Sales.Orders
    WHERE  CustomerID = @CustomerID
    AND    (OrderDate = @OrderDate
           OR @OrderDate IS NULL)

    RETURN;
END;
```

Multi-statement table-valued UDFs are always slower than equivalent simple ones. If you compare the plan and STATISTICS TIME output of the two queries, you see very similar issues with multi-statement table-valued UDFs, as there was with scalar UDFs that accessed tables. Compare the following two calls

```
SET STATISTICS TIME ON;
SELECT CustomerId, FirstDaySales.SalesCount, FirstDaySales.HasBackorderFlag
FROM    Sales.Customers
         OUTER APPLY Sales.Customers_ReturnOrderCountSetSimple
                           (CustomerId, AccountOpenedDate) as FirstDaySales
WHERE   FirstDaySales.SalesCount > 0;

SELECT CustomerId, FirstDaySales.SalesCount, FirstDaySales.HasBackorderFlag
FROM    Sales.Customers
         OUTER APPLY Sales.Customers_ReturnOrderCountSetMulti
                           (CustomerId, AccountOpenedDate) as FirstDaySales
WHERE   FirstDaySales.SalesCount > 0;
```

Note that the first plan that uses the simple form, is considered 89 percent of the cost. Yet when you look at the execution time, it takes twice as long. This is because the simple form is optimized like a VIEW object, incorporating the DDL of the object into the query plan, but the multi-statement form hides the costs of the coded object.

## Identify differences between deterministic and non-deterministic functions

The term deterministic is a mathematics term that indicates that a system or equation that always returns the same value. This is important when building a FUNCTION, because the query optimizer can know that if one use of FUNCTION(1) returns 2, then the second performance of FUNCTION(1) returns 2.

In the system functions, some examples of deterministic functions are ABS, which returns the absolute value of a number, and YEAR, which returns the year from a date value. Functions that are not deterministic include SYSDATETIME(), which returns the current date and time, and NEWID(), which returns a new GUID value. For more information about deterministic and non-deterministic functions, the following MSDN article provides more details and functions *https://msdn.microsoft.com/en-us/library/ms178091.aspx*. The basic criteria is that the USER DEFINED FUNCTION is declared as WITH SCHEMABINDING, accesses no external data, and uses no non-deterministic system functions.

One place this is important is when you are using a value in an index, either in a VIEW object or computed column in a TABLE object. So, when building functions, it is generally important to make your function deterministic. For example, consider the requirement you might have to build a function that proper cases a value by making the first letter in every word uppercase. Listing 2-19 includes a version of a function that does this.

**LISTING 2-19** Slightly complex scalar function to demonstrate determinism

```
CREATE FUNCTION Examples.UpperCaseFirstLetter
(
    @Value varchar(50)
)
RETURNS nvarchar(50)
WITH SCHEMABINDING
AS
```

```
BEGIN
    --start at position 2, as 1 will always be uppercase if it exists
    DECLARE @OutputValue nvarchar(50), @position int = 2, @previousPosition int
    IF LEN(@Value) = 0 RETURN @OutputValue;
                        --remove leading spaces, uppercase the first character
    SET @OutputValue = (LTRIM(CONCAT(UPPER(SUBSTRING(@Value,1,1)),
                                        LOWER(SUBSTRING(@Value,2,99)))));
    --if no space characters, exit
    IF CHARINDEX(' ',@OutputValue,1) = 0 RETURN @OutputValue;
    WHILE 1=1
      BEGIN
        SET @position = CHARINDEX(' ',@outputValue,@position) + 1
        IF @position < @previousPosition or @position = 0
            BREAK;
        SELECT @OutputValue = CONCAT(SUBSTRING(@OutputValue,1,@position - 1),
                                UPPER(SUBSTRING(@OutputValue,@position,1)),
                                SUBSTRING(@OutputValue,@position + 1,50)),
                @PreviousPosition = @Position
      END
    RETURN @OutputValue
END;
```

You can run it as:

```
SELECT Examples.UpperCaseOnlyFirstLetter(N'NO MORE YELLING') as Name;
```

This returns:

```
Name
---------------------------------------------------
No More Yelling
```

To determine if the FUNCTION is deterministic, use the OBJECTPROPERTY() function:

```
SELECT OBJECTPROPERTY(OBJECT_ID('Examples.UpperCaseFirstLetter'), 'IsDeterministic')
                                                    AS IsDeterministic
```

No matter how complex it appears, since we did not use external data or non-deterministic system functions, and used WITH SCHEMABINDING, we discover it is deterministic:

```
IsDeterministic
----------------
1
```

For a non-deterministic example, consider the following function that gives you the start of the current month. It does this by using the SYSDATETIME() system function, which is non-deterministic:

```
CREATE FUNCTION Examples.StartOfCurrentMonth
()
RETURNS date
WITH SCHEMABINDING
AS
 BEGIN
    RETURN (DATEADD(day, 0, DATEDIFF(day, 0, SYSDATETIME() ) -
                                    DATEPART(DAY,SYSDATETIME()) + 1));
```

```
END;
```

And, we test if it is deterministic:

```
SELECT OBJECTPROPERTY(OBJECT_ID('Examples.StartOfCurrentMonth'), 'IsDeterministic')
                                                        AS IsDeterministic
```

As expected, this function is not deterministic. While it might seem the case, determinism is not limited to scalar UDFs. Table-valued functions can be deterministic as well. Consider the following multi-statement table-valued UDF. It declares a table, loads it from a simple row constructor of 10 values, and returns the following:

```
CREATE FUNCTION Examples.ReturnOneToTenSet
()
RETURNS @OutputTable TABLE (I int)
WITH SCHEMABINDING
AS
  BEGIN
    INSERT INTO @OutputTable(I)
    VALUES (1),(2),(3),(4),(5),(6),(7),(8),(9),(10);

    RETURN;
  END;
```

Checking this function, you see that it is deterministic :

```
SELECT OBJECTPROPERTY(OBJECT_ID('Examples.ReturnOneToTenSet'), 'IsDeterministic')
                                                        AS IsDeterministic;
```

## Chapter summary

- There are several types of constraints that you can use to help ensure data integrity in a database:
  - **PRIMARY KEY**   Used to specify the primary uniqueness criteria for a table.
  - **UNIQUE**   Used to enforce any additional uniqueness criteria other than the PRIMARY KEY constraint
  - **FOREIGN KEY**   Enforces relationships between tables, making sure references exist. Usually references the PRIMARY KEY constraint, but can reference a UNIQUE constraint as well.
  - **CHECK**   Allows you to declaratively specify Boolean predicates that must not be FALSE.
  - **DEFAULT**   Guides the user's input when there isn't necessary a simple choice for a value.
- **NULL** values are complicated with constraints. In UNIQUE constraints, they are treated as equal to other NULL values. In CHECK constraints, they always pass the test unless explicitly tested for. For FOREIGN KEY constraints, they are always allowed, even if it is only one NULL column value in a composite key.

- There are two main ways to pick which columns to place a PRIMARY KEY constraint. Using a natural key, or a value from the logical group of attributes is one way. A very typical implementation is to use a surrogate key, usually some artificial value like an auto-generated value.

- STORED PROCEDURE objects are modules that allow you to create custom code that is performed together. A query plan is saved off with the stored procedure that is parameterized much easier than an ad-hoc batch of Transact-SQL.

- Using STORED PROCEDURE objects for building a coded interface to Transact-SQL objects allows programmers to do simple tasks in a manner similar to procedural programming languages.

- Use table-valued parameters to send a STORED PROCEDURE object many rows at a time, allowing you to create complex objects in single STORED PROCEDURE calls.

- For error handling, using the TRY...CATCH construct allows you to capture errors thrown by Transact-SQL statements. You can use THROW and RAISERROR to throw your own error messages. Unhandled THROW statements stop the batch from running, RAISERROR does not.

- TRIGGER objects can be used to react to different actions on the server. There are three kinds of triggers:

  - **DML**   Used to enhance data integrity with access to more data than CHECK constraints, cascade modifications with more control than FOREIGN KEY constraints, and manipulate the data that is being inserted and updated into a table. There are INSTEAD OF triggers where you have to redo the action, and AFTER triggers that fire after the operation.

  - **DDL**   Used to capture and react to server or database level DDL statements.

  - **Logon**   Used to take some action when a server principal accesses the server.

- USER DEFINED FUNCTION objects allow you to build modules that are used in other Transact-SQL statement in the same way a table or a system function is. There are two kinds: table-valued and scalar.

# Thought Experiment

In this thought experiment, demonstrate your skills and knowledge of the topics covered in this chapter. You can find answers in the next section. You have been assigned to implement a database for Trey Research, capturing details of the subjects they use in their research. The following list is a set of tasks that needs to be completed in the implementation. Determine what tool you can use from all of the ones we have discussed here in this chapter, and consider writing an example to make sure you understand the concepts.

- Users provide an email address when they sign up. However, sometimes the same person creates multiple accounts with the same email address, causing issues with the validity of a research results set.

- You have a stored procedure that needs to run three INSERT statements, the first two of which should all complete or all not complete. The third should run no matter what, succeeding/failing independently. How would you code this?

- In the RecipientType column in the Recipient table, there have been values entered like "Dunno" and "Whatever," which are not valid types of recipients. How can you make sure that the column does not include values that it should not?

- You need to make sure that a column that contains an offer code is always five characters long and uppercase. What tool (or tools) will you use to make sure that the string value is all uppercase letters, and how?

- You have given users rights to add indexes to a certain database, but you want to make sure that no indexes are added from 8:00AM to 10:00AM.

- You are building a complex stored procedure that can take 10-20 seconds for each execution, and much longer if the @checkAll parameter has a NULL value, a value it should never have.

## Though Experiment Answer

This section contains the solution to the thought experiment. Each answer explains why the answer choice is correct. Users provide an email address when they sign up. However, sometimes the same person creates multiple accounts with the same email address, causing issues with the validity of a research results set.

- For this need, you want to use a UNIQUE constraint on an EmailAddress column of the table where you define a participant for the survey questions. For example, the partial table was originally created:

```
CREATE TABLE Examples.Respondent
(

    RespondentId int NOT NULL CONSTRAINT PKRespondent PRIMARY KEY,
    EmailAddress  nvarchar(500) NOT NULL
);
```

- Adding the following constraint prevents the issue with duplicated data:

```
ALTER TABLE Examples.Respondent
    ADD CONSTRAINT AKRespondent UNIQUE (EmailAddress);
```

- You have a stored procedure that needs to run three INSERT statements, the first two of which should all complete or all not complete. The third INSERT should run no matter what, succeeding/failing independently. How do you code this?

Say you have the following simple table:

```
CREATE TABLE Examples.ThreeInsert
(
        ThreeInsertId int CONSTRAINT PKThreeInsert PRIMARY KEY
);
```

- You can code something like the following. In code destined for production work, you likely want to code nested TRY...CATCH blocks, and save the error messages from the first two INSERT statements in variables to throw at the end.

```
CREATE PROCEDURE Examples.ThreeInsert_Create
        @SecondValue int = 2 --Pass in 1 to and no data is inserted

AS
    SET NOCOUNT ON;
    BEGIN TRY
        BEGIN TRANSACTION;
        INSERT INTO Examples.ThreeInsert (ThreeInsertId)
        VALUES (1);
        INSERT INTO Examples.ThreeInsert (ThreeInsertId)
        VALUES (@SecondValue);
        COMMIT TRANSACTION;
    END TRY
    BEGIN CATCH
        IF XACT_STATE() <> 0
            ROLLBACK TRANSACTION;
        --No THROW will mean no reporting of message
    END CATCH;

    INSERT INTO Examples.ThreeInsert (ThreeInsertId)
    VALUES (3);
```

- In the RecipientType column in the Recipient table, there have been values entered like "Dunno" and "Whatever," which are not valid types of recipients. How can you make sure that the column does not include values that it should not?

  - This was a bit of a tricky question, but the true answer to the question as written is that you can't defend against an unknown entry, without a specific domain of legal values. It would be possible to create a CHECK constraint that has a predicate of (RecipientType NOT IN ('Dunno','Whatever')) and you have stopped two values, but not all of them.

  - After defining the legal values, say: 'Regular,' 'Special Handling;' you can then handle this in one of two ways. Consider the following partial table:

```
CREATE TABLE Examples.Recipient
(
    RecipientType varchar(30) NOT NULL
);
```

- You can add a CHECK constraint such as:

```
ALTER TABLE Examples.Recipient
    ADD CONSTRAINT CHKRecipient_RecipientType
        CHECK (RecipientType IN ('Regular','Special Handling'));
```

- An alternate solution is to use a domain TABLE object with a FOREIGN KEY constraint, such as:

```
CREATE TABLE Examples.RecipientType
(
        RecipientType varchar(30) NOT NULL CONSTRAINT PKRecipientType PRIMARY KEY
);

INSERT INTO Examples.RecipientType(RecipientType)
VALUES ('Regular'),('Special Handling');

ALTER TABLE Examples.Recipient
        ADD CONSTRAINT FKRecipient_Ref_ExamplesRecipientType
        FOREIGN KEY (RecipientType) REFERENCES Examples.
RecipientType(RecipientType);
```

- You need to make sure that the offer code column is always uppercase, what tool (or tools) would you use to make sure that the string value is all uppercase letters, and how?

    - For this question, there are two answers that would equally achieve the goal of making sure the string value is all uppercase letters. For example, consider the following table:

```
CREATE TABLE Examples.Offer
(
    OfferCode char(5) NOT NULL
);
```

    - Consider using an INSTEAD OF TRIGGER object. When you are doing the INSERT and UPDATE operations, you force the value to be uppercase; after making sure all of the characters are letters. The following is the INSERT trigger.

```
CREATE TRIGGER Examples.Offer_TriggerInsteadOfInsert
ON Examples.Offer
INSTEAD OF INSERT AS
BEGIN
    SET NOCOUNT ON;
    SET ROWCOUNT 0; --in case the client has modified the rowcount
    BEGIN TRY
        IF EXISTS (SELECT *
                    FROM   inserted
                    WHERE  OfferCode NOT LIKE '[A-Z][A-Z][A-Z][A-Z][A-Z]')
                THROW 50000,'An OfferCode is not all alpha characters',1;

            --skip columns to automatically set
            INSERT INTO Examples.Offer (OfferCode)
            SELECT UPPER(OfferCode)
```

```
        FROM    inserted
    END TRY
    BEGIN CATCH
        IF XACT_STATE() <> 0
            ROLLBACK TRANSACTION;
        THROW; --will halt the batch or be caught by the caller's catch block
    END CATCH
END;
```

- Another method is actually to use a CHECK constraint. The requirement is to make sure the string is all uppercase coming from the user. You can do this by using an expression with a case sensitive or binary collation. To determine the collation of your database, you can check sys.databases:

```
SELECT collation_name
FROM sys.databases
WHERE   database_id = DB_ID();
```

- This returns:

```
collation_name
----------------------------
Latin1_General_100_CI_AS
```

- Change it to CS for the case sensitive version of Latin1_General_100 and use this in the CHECK constraint:

```
ALTER TABLE Examples.Offer
    ADD CONSTRAINT CHKOffer_OfferCode
        CHECK (OfferCode LIKE '[A-Z][A-Z][A-Z][A-Z][A-Z]'
                            COLLATE Latin1_General_100_CS_AS);
```

- You have given user rights to add indexes to a certain database, but you want to make sure that no indexes are added from 8:00AM to 10:00AM.

  - Use a DDL Trigger, such as the following. Casting SYSDATETIME() as time gives us the time of day:

```
CREATE TRIGGER DatabaseChanges_DDLTrigger
ON DATABASE
WITH EXECUTE AS 'Exam762Examples_DDLTriggerLogging'
FOR CREATE_INDEX
AS
    SET NOCOUNT ON;
    IF CAST(SYSDATETIME() AS time) >= '08:00:00'
        AND CAST(SYSDATETIME() AS time) < '10:00:00'

    THROW 50000,'No indexes may be added between 8 and 10 AM',1;
```

- You are building a complex stored procedure that can take 10-20 seconds for each execution, and much longer if the @checkAll parameter has a NULL value, a value it should never have.

- For this, in the body of your STORED PROCEDURE, you would include a check for the parameter:

```
IF @checkAll IS NULL
        THROW 50000,'The value of @checkAll may not be NULL',1;
```

# Manage database concurrency

In a typical environment, a database receives multiple requests to perform an operation and often these requests can occur concurrently. As an administrator, you must understand how SQL Server handles these requests by default and the available options for changing this default behavior. Your overarching goal is to prevent unexpected results, while enabling as many processes as possible.

The 70-762 exam tests your skills related to this goal of managing database concurrency. Here in Skill 3.1, we review the basic properties and behaviors of transactions in SQL Server and the role of transactions in high-concurrency databases. Skill 3.2 addresses the available options for managing concurrency in SQL Server by using isolation levels and explores in detail the differences between isolation levels as well as the effect each isolation level has on concurrent transactions, system resources, and overall performance. Then in Skill 3.3 we explore the tools at your disposal to better understand locking behavior in SQL Server and the steps you can take to remediate deadlocks. Skill 3.4 introduces memory-optimized tables as another option for improving concurrency by explaining the use cases for which this approach is best, how to optimize performance when tables are held in memory instead of on disk, and considerations for using and analyzing performance of natively compiled stored procedures.

## Skills in this chapter:

- Implement transactions
- Manage isolation levels
- Optimize concurrency and locking behavior
- Implement memory-optimized tables and native stored procedures

## Skill 3.1: Implement transactions

SQL Server protects data integrity by using transactions to control how, when, or even whether data changes in a database. A *transaction* is a unit of work consisting of one or more read and write commands that SQL Server executes completely or not at all. In the exam, you must be able to recognize scenarios in which transactions can complete successfully or not, and know how to use T-SQL statements to manage transaction behavior. You must also understand potential problems with transactions executing concurrently and how SQL Server uses locks to mitigate these problems.

> **This section covers how to:**
> - Identify DML statement results based on transaction behavior
> - Recognize differences between and identify usage of explicit and implicit transactions
> - Implement savepoints within transactions
> - Determine the role of transactions in high-concurrency databases

## Identify DML statement results based on transaction behavior

The results of a DML statement depends on transaction behavior. If the transaction succeeds, then the inserts, the updates, or the deletes that SQL Server executes as part of that transaction are committed to the database and permanently change the data in the affected tables. If the transaction fails for any reason, you can cancel or rollback the transaction to reverse any changes made to the database by the transaction prior to the failure. SQL Server has various methods for managing transaction behavior, but you also have options for changing this behavior when writing code to execute transactions.

In this section, we explore the ways that SQL Server supports the following set of properties collectively known in database theory as ACID to ensure data is protected in case of system or hardware failure:

- **Atomicity**  An *atomic* transaction is a set of events that cannot be separated from one another and must be handled as a single unit of work. A common example is a bank transaction in which you transfer money from your checking account to your savings account. A successful atomic transaction not only correctly deducts the amount of the transfer from one account, but also adds it to the other account. If the transaction cannot complete all of its steps successfully, it must fail, and the database is unchanged.

- **Consistency**  When a transaction is *consistent*, any changes that it makes to the data conform to the rules defined in the database by constraints, cascades, and triggers and thereby leave the database in a valid state. To continue the previous example, the amount removed from your checking account must be the same amount added to your savings account when the transaction is consistent.

- **Isolation**  An isolated transaction behaves as if it were the only transaction interacting with the database for its duration. *Isolation* ensures that the effect on the database is the same whether two transactions run at the same time or one after the other.

Similarly, your transfer to the savings account has the same net effect on your overall bank balances whether you were the only customer performing a banking transaction at that time, or there were many other customers withdrawing, depositing, or transferring funds simultaneously.

- **Durability** A *durable* transaction is one that permanently changes the database and persists even if the database is shut down unexpectedly. Therefore, if you receive a confirmation that your transfer is complete, your bank balances remain correct even if your bank experienced a power outage immediately after the transaction completed.

> *NOTE* **ACID PROPERTY SUPPORT**
>
> By default, SQL Server guarantees all four ACID properties, although you can request an alternate isolation level if necessary. We explain isolation levels in detail in Skill 3.2.

Before we start exploring transaction behavior, let's set up a new database, add some tables, and insert some data to establish a test environment as shown in Listing 3-1.

**LISTING 3-1** Create a test environment for exploring transaction behavior

```
CREATE DATABASE ExamBook762Ch3;
GO
USE ExamBook762Ch3;
GO
CREATE SCHEMA Examples;
GO
CREATE TABLE Examples.TestParent
(
    ParentId  int NOT NULL
        CONSTRAINT PKTestParent PRIMARY KEY,
    ParentName  varchar(100) NULL
);

CREATE TABLE Examples.TestChild
(
    ChildId  int NOT NULL
        CONSTRAINT PKTestChild PRIMARY KEY,
    ParentId int NOT NULL,
    ChildName  varchar(100) NULL
);

ALTER TABLE Examples.TestChild
    ADD CONSTRAINT FKTestChild_Ref_TestParent
        FOREIGN KEY (ParentId) REFERENCES Examples.TestParent(ParentId);

INSERT INTO Examples.TestParent(ParentId, ParentName)
VALUES (1, 'Dean'),(2, 'Michael'),(3, 'Robert');

INSERT INTO Examples.TestChild (ChildId, ParentId, ChildName)
VALUES (1,1, 'Daniel'), (2, 1, 'Alex'), (3, 2, 'Matthew'), (4, 3, 'Jason');
```

Even a single statement to change data in a table is a transaction (as is each individual INSERT statement in Listing 3-1). Consider this example:

```
UPDATE Examples.TestParent
SET ParentName = 'Bob'
WHERE ParentName = 'Robert';
```

When you execute this statement, if the system doesn't crash before SQL Server lets you know that the statement completed successfully, the new value is *committed*. That is, the change to the data resulting from the UPDATE statement is permanently stored in the database. You can confirm the successful change by running the following SELECT statement.

```
SELECT ParentId, ParentName
FROM Examples.TestParent;
```

The result of the UPDATE statement properly completed as you can see in the SELECT statement results.

```
ParentId    ParentName
----------  ------------
1           Dean
2           Michael
3           Bob
```

## Atomicity

The execution of one statement at a time as a transaction does not clearly demonstrate the SQL Server support for the other ACID properties. Instead, you need a transaction with multiple statements. To do this, use the BEGIN TRANSACTION (or BEGIN TRAN) and COMMIT TRANSACTION (or COMMIT TRAN) statements (unless you implement implicit transactions as we describe in the next section).

You can test atomicity by attempting to update two different tables in the same transaction like this:

```
BEGIN TRANSACTION;
    UPDATE Examples.TestParent
    SET ParentName = 'Mike'
    WHERE ParentName = 'Michael';

    UPDATE Examples.TestChild
    SET ChildName = 'Matt'
    WHERE ChildName = 'Matthew';
COMMIT TRANSACTION;
```

When the transaction commits, the changes to both tables become permanent. Check the results with this query:

```
SELECT TestParent.ParentId, ParentName, ChildId, ChildName
FROM Examples.TestParent
    FULL OUTER JOIN Examples.TestChild ON TestParent.ParentId = TestChild.ParentId;
```

The transaction updated both tables as you can see in the query results:

```
ParentId    ParentName    ChildId    ChildName
----------  ------------  ---------  -----------
1           Dean          1          Daniel
1           Dean          2          Alex
2           Michael       3          Matt
3           Bob           4          Jason
```

On the other hand, if any one of the statements in a transaction fails, the behavior depends on the way in which you construct the transaction statements and whether you change the SQL Server default settings. A common misconception is that using BEGIN TRANSACTION and COMMIT TRANSACTION are sufficient for ensuring the atomicity of a transaction. You can test the SQL Server default behavior by adding or changing data in one statement and then trying to delete a row having a foreign key constraint in another statement like this:

```
BEGIN TRANSACTION;
    INSERT INTO Examples.TestParent(ParentId, ParentName)
    VALUES (4, 'Linda');

    DELETE Examples.TestParent
    WHERE ParentName = 'Bob';
COMMIT TRANSACTION;
```

In this case, the deletion fails, but the insertion succeeds as you can see by the messages that SQL Server returns.

```
(1 row(s) affected)
Msg 547, Level 16, State 0, Line 24
The DELETE statement conflicted with the REFERENCE constraint "FKTestChild_Ref_
TestParent". The conflict occurred in database "ExamBook762Ch3", table "Examples.
TestChild", column 'ParentId'.

The statement has been terminated.
```

When you check the data again, you see a total of four rows in the Examples.TestParent table:

```
ParentId    ParentName
----------  ------------
1           Dean
2           Michael
3           Bob
4           Linda
```

If you want SQL Server to roll back the entire transaction and thereby guarantee atomicity, one option is to use the SET XACT_ABORT option to ON prior to executing the transaction like this:

```
SET XACT_ABORT ON;
BEGIN TRANSACTION;
    INSERT INTO Examples.TestParent(ParentId, ParentName)
    VALUES (5, 'Isabelle');

    DELETE Examples.TestParent
    WHERE ParentName = 'Bob';
COMMIT TRANSACTION;
```

In this case, SQL Server rolls back all successfully completed statements in the transaction and returns the database to its state at the start of the transaction in which only four rows exist in the Examples.TestParent table as shown in the previous example. The SET XACT_ABORT option is set to OFF by default, therefore you must enable the option when you want to ensure that SQL Server rolls back a failed transaction.

What if the error raised is not a constraint violation, but a syntax error? Execute the following code that first disables the SET XACT_ABORT option (to prove the roll back works correctly with the default SQL Server setting) and then attempts an INSERT and a DELETE containing a deliberate syntax error:

```
SET XACT_ABORT OFF;
BEGIN TRANSACTION;
    INSERT INTO Examples.TestParent(ParentId, ParentName)
    VALUES (5, 'Isabelle');

  DELETE Examples.TestParent
  WHEN ParentName = 'Bob';
COMMIT TRANSACTION;
```

Although the INSERT is successful and would commit if the subsequent error were a constraint violation, SQL Server does not commit the insertion, and the database remains in its original state when it encounters a syntax error in a transaction.

Another option to consider is to explicitly include a roll back instruction in your transaction by enclosing it in a TRY block and adding a ROLLBACK TRANSACTION (or ROLLBACK TRAN) statement in a CATCH block:

```
BEGIN TRY
    BEGIN TRANSACTION;
        INSERT INTO Examples.TestParent(ParentId, ParentName)
        VALUES (5, 'Isabelle');

        DELETE Examples.TestParent
        WHERE ParentName = 'Bob';
    COMMIT TRANSACTION;
END TRY
BEGIN CATCH
    IF @@TRANCOUNT > 0 ROLLBACK TRANSACTION;
END CATCH
```

Because the transaction includes a DELETE statement that fails due to a constraint violation, the CATCH block is invoked and the transaction rolls back. Therefore, the Examples.Parent table still contains only four rows.

Notice also in the previous example that the execution of the ROLLBACK TRANSACTION requires the current status of the transaction (obtained by the @@TRANCOUNT variable) to be greater than 0, which means that a transaction is active. We explore the use of this variable in more detail in the section covering implicit and explicit transactions.

## Consistency

These last two examples not only demonstrate atomicity compliance in SQL Server, but also consistency. Another commonly used term for consistency is *data integrity*. To preserve data integrity in a database, you cannot remove a row from a table when there is an existing dependency on that row. Similarly, you cannot add a row to a table having foreign key constraints without providing a valid foreign key value in the new row. Any rule that you add to the database as we described in Chapter 2, "Implement programmability objects," is enforced by SQL Server to guarantee consistency.

## Isolation

Now let's take a look at how SQL Server handles isolation by default. We explore your options for managing isolation in detail in Skill 3.2, but for Skill 3.1 you must understand what happens if you rely on the behavior of READ COMMITTED, the SQL Server default isolation level. To observe this behavior, set up two separate sessions in SQL Server Management Studio.

In one session, execute the following statement:

```
BEGIN TRANSACTION;
    INSERT INTO Examples.TestParent(ParentId, ParentName)
    VALUES (5, 'Isabelle');
```

The omission of the COMMIT statement in this example is deliberate. At this point, the transaction is still active, but it is not yet committed. Furthermore, the uncommitted transaction continues to hold a lock on the table preventing any other access to the table as long as the transaction remains uncommitted.

In the second session, execute the following statement:

```
SELECT ParentId, ParentName
FROM Examples.TestParent;
```

When you attempt to read rows from the locked table, the query continues to execute indefinitely because it is waiting for the transaction in the first session to complete. This behavior is an example of a write operation blocking a read operation. By default, SQL Server uses the READ COMMITTED isolation level to protect the transaction by preventing other operations from returning potentially incorrect results as a result of reading uncommitted inserts that could later be rolled back. It also insulates the transaction from premature changes to the values of those inserts by another transaction's update operation.

In the first session, end the transaction like this:

```
COMMIT TRANSACTION;
```

As soon as you commit the transaction, the query in the second session returns five rows and includes the newly inserted row:

```
ParentId   ParentName
---------- -------------
1          Dean
2          Michael
3          Bob
4          Linda
5          Isabelle
```

## Durability

SQL Server guarantees full transaction durability by default. If the system crashes for some reason after SQL Server confirms a successful commit, the changes made by the transaction are visible after the system returns to an operable status even if the transaction operations had not been written to disk prior to the system failure.

To make this possible, SQL Server uses write-ahead logging to first hold data changes in a log buffer and then writes the changes to the transaction log on disk when the transaction commits or if the log buffer becomes full. The transaction log contains not only changes to data, but also page allocations and de-allocations, and changes to indexes. Each log record includes a unique log sequence number (LSN) to that every record change that belongs to the same transaction can be rolled back if necessary.

Once the transaction commits, the log buffer flushes the transaction log and writes the modifications first to the data cache, and then permanently to the database on disk. A change is never made to the database without confirming that it already exists in the transaction log. At that point, SQL Server reports a successful commit and the transaction cannot be rolled back.

What if a failure occurs after the change is written to the transaction log, but before SQL Server writes the change to the database? In this case, the data changes are uncommitted. Nonetheless, the transaction is still durable because you can recreate the change from the transaction log if necessary.

SQL Server also supports delayed durable transactions, also known as lazy commits. By using this approach, SQL Server can process more concurrent transactions with less contention for log IO, thereby increasing throughput. Once the transaction is written to the transaction log, SQL Server reports a successful transaction and any changes that it made are visible to other transactions. However, all transaction logs remain in the log buffer until the buffer is full or a buffer flush event occurs, at which point the transaction is written to disk and becomes durable. A buffer flush occurs when a fully durable transaction in the same database commits or a manual request to execute sp_flush_log is successful.

Delayed durability is useful when you are willing to trade potential data loss for reduced latency in transaction log writes and reduced contention between transactions. Such a trade-off is acceptable in a data warehouse workload that runs batches frequently enough to pick up rows lost in a previous batch. The eventual resolution of data loss is acceptable alternative to durability only because the data warehouse is not the system of record. Delayed durability is rarely acceptable in an online transaction processing (OLTP) system.

> **NEED MORE REVIEW?**    **DELAYED TRANSACTION DURABILITY**
>
> You can enable a database to support delayed transaction durability and then force or disable delayed transaction durability at the transaction level as an option of the COM-MIT statement. Although you should understand the concept and use cases for delayed durability for the exam, you do not need to identify all the possible options and interactions between database and transaction settings. However, if you would like more in-depth information about delayed transaction durability, refer to the MSDN description at *https://msdn.microsoft.com/en-us/library/ms181299.aspx*.
>
> For an in-depth assessment of the performance and data loss implications of delayed transaction durability, see "Delayed Durability in SQL Server 2014" by Aaron Bertrand at *https://sqlperformance.com/2014/04/io-subsystem/delayed-durability-in-sql-server-2014*. Although the article was written for SQL Server 2014, the principles continue to apply to SQL Server 2016.

## Recognize differences between and identify usage of explicit and implicit transactions

An important aspect of transaction management is knowing which commands are in scope. That is, you must know which commands are grouped together for execution as a single transaction. SQL Server supports the following methods for transaction control:

- **Auto-commit**   Any single statement that changes data and executes by itself is automatically an atomic transaction. Whether the change affects one row or thousands of rows, it must complete successfully for each row to be committed. You cannot manually rollback an auto-commit transaction, although SQL Server performs a rollback if a system failure occurs before the transaction completes.

- **Implicit**   An implicit transaction automatically starts when you execute certain DML statements and ends only when you use COMMIT TRANSACTION or ROLLBACK TRANSACTION. However, you must first configure a session to run in implicit transaction mode by first executing the SET IMPLICIT_TRANSACTIONS ON statement. After you do this, any of the following statements begin a new transaction: ALTER TABLE, BEGIN TRANSACTION, CREATE, DELETE, DROP, FETCH, GRANT, INSERT, OPEN, REVOKE, SELECT (only if selecting from a table), TRUNCATE TABLE, and UPDATE.

- **Explicit** An explicit transaction has a specific structure that you define by using the BEGIN TRANSACTION at the beginning of the transaction and the COMMIT TRANSACTION or ROLLBACK TRANSACTION at the end of the transaction.

> **NEED MORE REVIEW?** **BATCH-SCOPED TRANSACTIONS**
>
> SQL Server also supports batch-scoped transactions when Multiple Active Result Sets (or MARS) is enabled, but you do not need to be familiar with this topic for the exam. If you would like to learn more about batch-scoped transactions, see *https://msdn.microsoft.com/en-us/library/ms131686.aspx*.

## Implicit transactions

Let's examine the behavior of implicit transactions by executing a series of statements incrementally. First, enable the implicit transaction mode like this:

```
SET IMPLICIT_TRANSACTIONS ON;
```

Next, execute an INSERT statement and then check the status of open transactions:

```
INSERT INTO Examples.TestParent(ParentId, ParentName)
VALUES (6, 'Lukas');
SELECT @@TRANCOUNT;
```

The SELECT statement returns a 1 because SQL Server starts a new transaction when implicit transactions are enabled and the INSERT statement is executed. At this point, the transaction remains uncommitted and blocks any readers of the Examples.TestParent table.

Now you can end the transaction, check the status of open transactions, and check the change to the table by executing the following statements:

```
COMMIT TRANSACTION;
SELECT @@TRANCOUNT;
SELECT ParentId, ParentName
FROM Examples.TestParent;
```

The results of the SELECT statements show that the COMMIT statement both ended the transaction and decremented the @@TRANCOUNT variable and that a new row appears in the Examples.Parent table:

```
(No column name)
------------------
0

ParentId   ParentName
---------  ------------
1          Dean
2          Michael
3          Bob
4          Linda
5          Isabelle
6          Lukas
```

> **IMPORTANT** TRANSACTION COMMITMENT BY SQL SERVER
>
> It is important to note that the transaction commits not only because the COMMIT statement is executed, but also because the value of @@TRANCOUNT is decremented to zero. Only at that time does SQL Server write log records and commit the transaction.

Now disable the implicit transaction mode:

```
SET IMPLICIT_TRANSACTIONS OFF;
```

Just as you can see in many of the transaction examples in the previous section, an implicit transaction can contain one or more statements and ends with an explicit execution of a COMMIT TRANSACTION or ROLLBACK TRANSACTION statement. Apart from the absence of a BEGIN TRANSACTION statement, an implicit transaction resembles an explicit transaction and behaves in the same way as well.

You might use implicit transactions when migrating an application from a different database platform or when you need to run your application across multiple database platforms because fewer code changes are required. In most cases, however, best practice dictates avoiding the use of implicit transactions. When you rely on auto-commit or explicit transactions instead, changes are committed as quickly as possible and performance is less likely to be adversely affected.

**EXAM TIP**

For the exam, it is important to understand the impact of using implicit transactions. Be sure to review the remarks at "SET IMPLICIT_TRANSACTIONS (Transact-SQL)," *https://msdn. microsoft.com/en-us/library/ms187807.aspx.*

## Explicit transactions

When you want complete control over transaction behavior, use an explicit transaction. You have nothing to configure at the server or database level to enable explicit transactions. Simply enclose your transaction statements in the BEGIN TRANSACTION and COMMIT TRANSACTION statements. Furthermore, you should include logic to handle errors, such as a TRY/CATCH block, as shown in an example in the "Atomicity" section, or an IF/ELSE construct like this:

```
BEGIN TRANSACTION;
    INSERT INTO Examples.TestParent(ParentId, ParentName)
    VALUES (7, 'Mary');
    DELETE Examples.TestParent
    WHERE ParentName = 'Bob';
IF @@ERROR != 0
    BEGIN
        ROLLBACK TRANSACTION;
    RETURN
END
COMMIT TRANSACTION;
```

The following commands cannot be used in an explicit transaction:

- ALTER DATABASE
- ALTER FULLTEXT CATALOG
- ALTER FULLTEXT INDEX
- BACKUP
- CREATE DATABASE
- CREATE FULLTEXT CATALOG
- CREATE FULLTEXT INDEX
- DROP DATABASE
- DROP FULLTEXT CATALOG
- DROP FULLTEXT INDEX
- RECONFIGURE
- RESTORE

You can nest explicit transactions, although this capability is not ANSI-standard transaction behavior. As one example, consider a situation in which you have a set of statements in a transaction and one of the statements calls a stored procedure that starts its own transaction. Remember that each BEGIN TRANSACTION increments the @@TRANCOUNT variable and each COMMIT TRANSACTION decrements it. The ROLLBACK TRANSACTION resets the variable to zero and rolls back every statement to the beginning of the first transaction, but does not abort the stored procedure. When @@TRANCOUNT is zero, SQL Server writes to the transaction log. If the session ends before @@TRANCOUNT returns to zero, SQL Server automatically rolls back the transaction.

Let's test this behavior by creating a stored procedure and calling it in a transaction as shown in Listing 3-2.

**LISTING 3-2** Create and execute a stored procedure to test an explicit transaction

```
CREATE PROCEDURE Examples.DeleteParent
    @ParentId INT
AS
    BEGIN TRANSACTION;
        DELETE Examples.TestParent
        WHERE ParentId = @ParentId;
    IF @@ERROR != 0
        BEGIN
            ROLLBACK TRANSACTION;
            RETURN;
        END
    COMMIT TRANSACTION;
GO
BEGIN TRANSACTION;
    INSERT INTO Examples.TestParent(ParentId, ParentName)
```

```
       VALUES (7, 'Mary');
       EXEC Examples.DeleteParent @ParentId=3;
IF @@ERROR != 0
    BEGIN
        ROLLBACK TRANSACTION;
    RETURN
END
COMMIT TRANSACTION;
GO
```

When you execute these statements, several error messages display:

```
(1 row(s) affected)
Msg 547, Level 16, State 0, Procedure DeleteParent, Line 6 [Batch Start Line 16]
The DELETE statement conflicted with the REFERENCE constraint
"FKTestChild_Ref_TestParent". The conflict occurred in database "ExamBook762Ch3", table
"Examples.TestChild", column 'ParentId'.
The statement has been terminated.
Msg 266, Level 16, State 2, Procedure DeleteParent, Line 0 [Batch Start Line 16]
Transaction count after EXECUTE indicates a mismatching number of BEGIN and COMMIT
statements. Previous count = 1, current count = 0.
Msg 3903, Level 16, State 1, Line 25
The ROLLBACK TRANSACTION request has no corresponding BEGIN TRANSACTION.
```

The first transaction begins with an INSERT statement at which point @@TRANCOUNT
is 1. Then the call to the stored procedure results in the start of a second transaction and
increments @@TRANCOUNT to 2. The constraint violation causes an error that then calls the
ROLLBACK TRANSACTION statement, which in turn resets @@TRANCOUNT to 0 and rolls
back the INSERT. The error message regarding the mismatching transaction count occurs
because the @@TRANCOUNT value when the stored procedure ends no longer matches its
value when the stored procedure started. That error leads to the ROLLBACK TRANSACTION
statement in the first transaction. However, because @@TRANCOUNT is still 0, effectively
there is no open transaction and therefore the message about no corresponding BEGIN
TRANSACTION displays.

This situation highlights a potential problem with nested transactions in stored procedures.
If you want each stored procedure to roll back only its own work if it encounters an error, you
should test for an existing transaction, skip the step to begin a new transaction if one exists,
and use a savepoint to roll back the to the start of the current transaction if an error occurs in
the stored procedure. (We discuss savepoints in more detail in the next section.) Furthermore,
the COMMIT statement in the stored procedure should execute only if the stored procedure
starts its own transaction. By storing the @@TRANCOUNT value in a variable before you
execute the remaining stored procedure's statements, you can later test whether a transaction existed at the start. If it did not, the variable's value is 0 and you can then safely commit
the transaction that the stored procedure started. If a transaction did exist, no further action
is required in the stored procedure.

We can revise the previous example to avoid nesting transactions as shown in Listing 3-3.

**LISTING 3-3** Create a stored procedure that avoids a nested transaction

```
CREATE PROCEDURE Examples.DeleteParentNoNest
    @ParentId INT
AS
    DECLARE @CurrentTranCount INT;
    SELECT @CurrentTranCount = @@TRANCOUNT;
    IF (@CurrentTranCount = 0)
        BEGIN TRANSACTION DeleteTran;
    ELSE
        SAVE TRANSACTION DeleteTran;
    DELETE Examples.TestParent
    WHERE ParentId = @ParentId;
    IF @@ERROR != 0
        BEGIN
            ROLLBACK TRANSACTION DeleteTran;
            RETURN;
        END
    IF (@CurrentTranCount = 0)
        COMMIT TRANSACTION;
GO
BEGIN TRANSACTION;
    INSERT INTO Examples.TestParent(ParentId, ParentName)
    VALUES (7, 'Mary');
    EXEC Examples.DeleteParentNoNest @ParentId=3;
IF @@ERROR != 0
    BEGIN
        ROLLBACK TRANSACTION;
    RETURN
END
COMMIT TRANSACTION;
GO
```

When you execute the statements in Listing 3-3 and then check the table, you find that
the new row is committed in the table and the row with the ParentId value of 3 remains in the
table because the foreign key constraint caused SQL Server to roll back that transaction.

| ParentId | ParentName |
| --- | --- |
| 1 | Dean |
| 2 | Michael |
| 3 | Bob |
| 4 | Linda |
| 5 | Isabelle |
| 6 | Lukas |
| 7 | Mary |

***EXAM TIP***

**Be sure that you understand when SQL Server increments and decrements @@TRAN-
COUNT and how to implement error handling for transactions.**

The explicit transactions described to this point are all local transactions. Another option
is to execute a distributed transaction when you need to execute statements on more than

one server. To do this, start the transaction with the BEGIN DISTRIBUTED TRANSACTION and then end it with either COMMIT TRANSACTION or ROLLBACK TRANSACTION statements. The server on which you execute the distributed transaction controls the completion of the transaction.

## Implement savepoints within transactions

A *savepoint* is a named location from which a transaction can restart if part of it is conditionally canceled. That means you can rollback a transaction to a specific savepoint if a statement does not complete successfully, as shown in the previous example.

When you assign a savepoint name, you should use 32 characters or less. SQL Server allows you to assign a longer name, but the statement uses only the first 32 characters. Bear in mind that the savepoint name is case-sensitive even if SQL Server is not configured for case sensitivity. Another option is to use a variable in the SAVE TRANSACTION statement, but the data type must be char, varchar, nchar, or nvarchar. If you use the same savepoint name multiple times in the same transaction, the ROLLBACK TRANSACTION statement rolls back to the most recent savepoint.

Normally, a ROLLBACK TRANSACTION resets the value of @@TRANCOUNT to 0. However, when a transaction rolls back to a savepoint, @@TRANCOUNT is not reset. The SAVE TRANSACTION statement also has no effect on @@TRANCOUNT.

In Listing 3-4, the transaction has multiple savepoints and SELECT statements illustrate the effect of modifying data, and then rolling back to a specific savepoint.

**Listing 3-4** Create a transaction with multiple savepoints

```
BEGIN TRANSACTION;
    INSERT INTO Examples.TestParent(ParentId, ParentName)
    VALUES (8, 'Ed');
    SAVE TRANSACTION StartTran;

    SELECT 'StartTran' AS Status, ParentId, ParentName
    FROM Examples.TestParent;

    DELETE Examples.TestParent
        WHERE ParentId = 7;
    SAVE TRANSACTION DeleteTran;

    SELECT 'Delete 1' AS Status, ParentId, ParentName
    FROM Examples.TestParent;

    DELETE Examples.TestParent
        WHERE ParentId = 6;
    SELECT 'Delete 2' AS Status, ParentId, ParentName
    FROM Examples.TestParent;

    ROLLBACK TRANSACTION DeleteTran;
    SELECT 'RollbackDelete2' AS Status, ParentId, ParentName
    FROM Examples.TestParent;
```

```
        ROLLBACK TRANSACTION StartTran;
        SELECT @@TRANCOUNT AS 'TranCount';
        SELECT 'RollbackStart' AS Status, ParentId, ParentName
        FROM Examples.TestParent;
COMMIT TRANSACTION;
GO
```

The queries interspersed throughout this transaction give us visibility into the behavior of the savepoint and roll back operations:

```
Status     ParentId    ParentName
--------   ----------- --------------------------------------------------------------
StartTran 1            Dean
StartTran 2            Mike
StartTran 3            Bob
StartTran 4            Linda
StartTran 5            Isabelle
StartTran 6            Lukas
StartTran 7            Mary
StartTran 8            Ed


Status    ParentId    ParentName
--------  ----------- --------------------------------------------------------------
Delete 1 1            Dean
Delete 1 2            Mike
Delete 1 3            Bob
Delete 1 4            Linda
Delete 1 5            Isabelle
Delete 1 6            Lukas
Delete 1 8            Ed


Status    ParentId    ParentName
--------  ----------- --------------------------------------------------------------
Delete 2 1            Dean
Delete 2 2            Mike
Delete 2 3            Bob
Delete 2 4            Linda
Delete 2 5            Isabelle
Delete 2 8            Ed


Status            ParentId    ParentName
---------------   ----------- --------------------------------------------------------------
RollbackDelete2 1            Dean
RollbackDelete2 2            Mike
RollbackDelete2 3            Bob
RollbackDelete2 4            Linda
RollbackDelete2 5            Isabelle
RollbackDelete2 6            Lukas
RollbackDelete2 8            Ed


TranCount
-----------
1


Status          ParentId    ParentName
```

```
RollbackStart   1           Dean
RollbackStart   2           Mike
RollbackStart   3           Bob
RollbackStart   4           Linda
RollbackStart   5           Isabelle
RollbackStart   6           Lukas
RollbackStart   7           Mary
RollbackStart   8           Ed
```

The eight rows in the query with status StartTran show the condition of the table after the INSERT operation and reflects the state of the data for the StartTran savepoint. Next, the seven rows in the query with status *Delete 1* include one less row due to the DELETE operation. The DeleteTran savepoint includes this version of the table. After another DELETE operation executes, the query with status Delete 2 returns six rows. The first ROLLBACK TRANSACTION statement restores the version of data for the DeleteTran savepoint, and the query with status RollbackDelete2 correctly shows the seven rows prior to the second DELETE operation. Next, we can see that the @@TRANCOUNT variable at this point is still 1 because the ROLLBACK TRANSACTION statement did not reset it to 0. Last, another ROLLBACK TRANSACTION returns the table to its earlier state, which is committed at the end of the transaction.

> **NOTE**   **SAVEPOINTS IN DISTRIBUTED TRANSACTIONS**
>
> You cannot use savepoints in a distributed transaction beginning from an explicit BEGIN DISTRIBUTED TRANSACTION statement or a local transaction escalation.

# Determine the role of transactions in high-concurrency databases

A high concurrency database should support a high number of simultaneous processes that do not interfere with one another while preserving the consistency of the data affected by those processes. Processes modifying data can potentially adversely affect processes trying to read or change the same data at the same time. To prevent simultaneous attempts to change the same data, SQL Server acquires locks for the current transaction, thereby blocking all other transactions.

## Potential problems with concurrent processes

A failure to control concurrency in database can result in a variety of side effects. Typically, you want to design applications that avoid these problems. In some cases, your business requirements might allow a behavior. For now, let's focus on which potential problems might arise. In Skill 3.2, we explain how to use isolation levels to manage the behavior of concurrent transactions.

### DIRTY READS

A *dirty read*, also known as an uncommitted dependency, can occur when an uncommitted transaction updates a row at the same time that another transaction reads that row with its new value. Because the writing transaction is not committed, the row could revert to its original state and consequently the reading transaction has data that is not valid.

SQL Server does not allow dirty reads by default. However, by controlling the isolation level of the reading transaction, you can specify whether it reads both uncommitted and committed data or committed data only.

### NON-REPEATABLE READS

A *non-repeatable read* can occur when data is read more than once within the same transaction while another transaction updates the same data between read operations. Let's say that a transaction reads the current in-stock quantity of a widget from an inventory table as 5 and continues to perform other operations, which leaves the transaction in an uncommitted state. During this time, another transaction changes the in-stock quantity of the widget to 3. Then the first transaction reads the in-stock quantity of the widget again, which is now inconsistent with the initial value read.

### PHANTOM READS

Closely related to a non-repeatable read is a phantom read. This potential problem can occur when one transaction reads the same data multiple times while another transaction inserts or updates a row between read operations. As an example, consider a transaction in which a SELECT statement reads rows having in-stock quantities less than 5 from the inventory table and remains uncommitted while a second transaction inserts a row with an in-stock quantity of 1. When the first transaction reads the inventory table again, the number of rows increases by one. In this case, the additional row is considered to be a phantom row. This situation occurs only when the query uses a predicate.

### LOST UPDATES

Another potential problem can occur when two processes read the same row and then update that data with different values. This might happen if a transaction first reads a value into a variable and then uses the variable in an update statement in a later step. When this update executes, another transaction updates the same data. Whichever of these transactions is committed first becomes a *lost update* because it was replaced by the update in the other transaction. You cannot use isolation levels to change this behavior, but you can write an application that specifically allows lost updates.

## Resource locks

SQL Server locks the minimum number of resources required to complete a transaction. It uses different types of locks to support as much concurrency as possible while maintaining data consistency and transaction isolation. The SQL Server Lock Manager chooses the lock mode and resources to lock based on the operation to be performed, the amount of data to be affected by the operation, and the isolation level type (described in Skill 3.2). It also manages the compatibility of locks on the same resources, resolves deadlocks when possible, and escalates locks when necessary (as described in Skill 3.3).

SQL Server takes locks on resources at several levels to provide the necessary protection for a transaction. This group of locks at varying levels of granularity is known as a *lock hierarchy* and consists of one or more of the following lock modes:

- **Shared (S)** This lock mode, also known as a read lock, is used for SELECT, INSERT, UPDATE, and DELETE operations and is released as soon as data has been read from the locked resource. While the resource is locked, other transactions cannot change its data. However, in theory, an unlimited number of shared (s) locks can exist on a resource simultaneously. You can force SQL Server to hold the lock for the duration of the transaction by adding the HOLDLOCK table hint like this:

```
BEGIN TRANSACTION;
SELECT ParentId, ParentName
FROM Examples.TestParent WITH (HOLDLOCK);
WAITFOR DELAY '00:00:15';
ROLLBACK TRANSACTION;
```

Another way to change the lock's duration is to set the REPEATABLE_READ or SERIALIZABLE transaction isolation levels, which we explain in more detail in Skill 3.2.

- **Update (U)** SQL Server takes this lock on a resource that might be updated in order to prevent a common type of deadlocking, which we describe further in Skill 3.3. Only one update (U) lock can exist on a resource at a time. When a transaction modifies the resource, SQL Server converts the update (U) lock to an exclusive (X) lock.

- **Exclusive (X)** This lock mode protects a resource during INSERT, UPDATE, or DELETE operations to prevent that resource from multiple concurrent changes. While the lock is held, no other transaction can read or modify the data, unless a statement uses the NOLOCK hint or a transaction runs under the read uncommitted isolation level as we describe in Skill 3.2

- **Intent** An intent lock establishes a lock hierarchy to protect a resource at a lower level from getting a shared (S) lock or exclusive (X) lock. Technically speaking, intent locks are not true locks, but rather serve as an indicator that actual locks exist at a lower level. That way, another transaction cannot try to acquire a lock at the higher level that is incompatible with the existing lock at the lower level. There are six types of intent locks:

  - **Intent shared (IS)** With this lock mode, SQL Server protects requested or acquired shared (S) locks on some resources lower in the lock hierarchy.

  - **Intent exclusive (IX)** This lock mode is a superset of intent shared (IS) locks that not only protects locks on resources lower in the hierarchy, but also protects requested or acquired exclusive (X) locks on some resources lower in the hierarchy.

- **Shared with intent exclusive (SIX)** This lock mode protects requested or acquired shared (S) locks on all resources lower in the hierarchy and intent exclusive (IX) locks on some resources lower in the hierarchy. Only one shared with intent exclusive (SIX) lock can exist at a time for a resource to prevent other transactions from modifying it. However, lower level resources can have intent shared (IS) locks and can be read by other transactions.

- **Intent update (IU)** SQL Server uses this lock mode on page resources only to protect requested or acquired update (U) locks on all lower-level resources and converts it to an intent exclusive (IX) lock if a transaction performs an update operation.

- **Shared intent update (SIU)** This lock mode is a combination of shared (S) and intent update (IU) locks and occurs when a transaction acquires each lock separately but holds them at the same time.

- **Update intent exclusive (UIX)** This lock mode results from a combination of update (U) and intent exclusive (IX) locks that a transaction acquires separately but holds at the same time.

- **Schema** SQL Server acquires this lock when an operation depends the table's schema. There are two types of schema locks:

  - **Schema modification (Sch-M)** This lock mode prevents other transactions from reading from or writing to a table during a Data Definition Language (DDL) operation, such as removing a column. Some Data Manipulation Language (DML) operations, such as truncating a table, also require a schema modification (Sch-M) lock.

  - **Schema stability (Sch-S)** SQL Server uses this lock mode during query compilation and execution to block concurrent DDL operations and concurrent DML operations requiring a schema modification (Sch-M) lock from accessing a table.

- **Bulk Update (BU)** This lock mode is used for bulk copy operations to allow multiple threads to bulk load data into the same table at the same time and to prevent other transactions that are not bulk loading data from accessing the table. SQL Server acquires it when the table lock on bulk load table option is set by using sp_tableoption or when you use a TABLOCK hint like this:

```
INSERT INTO Examples.TestParent WITH (TABLOCK)
SELECT <columns> FROM <table>;
```

- **Key-range** A key-range lock is applied to a range of rows that is read by a query with the SERIALIZABLE isolation level to prevent other transactions from inserting rows that would be returned in the serializable transaction if the same query executes again. In other words, this lock mode prevents phantom reads within the set of rows that the transaction reads.

  - **RangeS-S** This lock mode is a shared range, shared resource lock used for a serializable range scan.

- **RangeS-U** This lock mode is a shared range, update resource lock used for a serializable update scan.

- **RangeI-N** This lock mode is an insert range, null resource lock that SQL Server acquires to test a range before inserting a new key into an index.

- **RangeX-X** This lock mode is an exclusive range, exclusive resource lock used when updating a key in a range.

While many locks are compatible with each other, some locks prevent other transactions from acquiring locks on the same resource, as shown in Table 3-1. Let's consider a situation in which one transaction has a shared (S) lock on a row and another transaction is requesting an exclusive (X) lock. In this case, the request is blocked until the first transaction releases its lock.

**TABLE 3-1** Lock compatibility for commonly encountered lock modes

| Requested mode | Existing granted mode | | | | | |
|---|---|---|---|---|---|---|
| | S | U | X | IS | IX | SIX |
| S | Yes | Yes | No | Yes | No | No |
| U | Yes | No | No | Yes | No | No |
| X | No | No | No | No | No | No |
| IS | Yes | Yes | No | Yes | Yes | Yes |
| IX | No | No | No | Yes | Yes | No |
| SIX | No | No | No | Yes | No | No |

*NEED MORE REVIEW?* **LOCK COMPATIBILITY**

For a complete matrix of lock compatibility, see "Lock Compatibility (Database Engine)" at *https://technet.microsoft.com/en-us/library/ms186396(v=sql.105).aspx.*

SQL Server can acquire a lock on any of the following resources to ensure that the user of that resource has a consistent view of the data throughout a transaction:

- **RID** A row identifier for the single row to lock within a heap and is acquired when possible to provide the highest possible concurrency.

- **KEY** A key or range of keys in an index for a serializable transaction can be locked in one of two ways depending on the isolation level. If a transaction runs in the READ COMMITTED or REPEATABLE READ isolation level, the index keys of the accessed rows are locked. If the table has a clustered index, SQL Server acquires key locks instead of row locks because the data rows are the leaf-level of the index. If a transaction runs in the SERIALIZABLE isolation mode, SQL Server acquires key-range locks to prevent phantom reads.

- **PAGE**  An 8-kilobyte (KB) data or index page gets locked when a transaction reads all rows on a page or when page-level maintenance, such as updating page pointers after a page-split, is performed.

- **EXTENT**  A contiguous block of eight data or index pages gets a shared (S) or exclusive (X) locks typically during space allocation and de-allocation.

- **HoBT**  A heap or B-Tree lock can be an entire index or all data pages of a heap.

- **Table**  An entire table, including both data and indexes, can be locked for SELECT, UPDATE, or DELETE operations.

- **File**  A database file can be locked individually.

- **Application**  A resource defined by your application can be locked by using sp_getapplock so that you can lock any resource you want with a specified lock mode.

- **Metadata**  Any system metadata can be locked to protect system catalog information.

- **Allocation unit**  An database allocation unit used for storage of data can be locked.

- **Database**  An entire database gets a shared (S) lock to indicate it is currently in use so that another process cannot drop it, take it offline, or restore it.

To increase concurrency, SQL Server uses dynamic lock management. That is, in a large table for which many row locks are required (as determined by the query optimizer), SQL Server might instead take a page or table lock at the beginning of a transaction. SQL Server can also escalate lock modes dynamically during a transaction. For example, if the transaction initially has a set of row locks, and later requests more row locks, SQL Server releases the row locks and takes a table lock. This behavior simplifies lock management, but reduces concurrency.

**EXAM TIP**

Locks and lock escalation in SQL Server are important concepts covered in the exam that you should understand thoroughly.

---

*NOTE*  **IMPLICIT TRANSACTION LOCKS**

Be aware that when you use implicit transactions, SQL Server holds locks until you commit the transaction. This behavior can reduce concurrency and interfere with truncation of the transaction log.

# Skill 3.2: Manage isolation levels

SQL Server uses isolation levels to manage conflict between two transactions attempting to use or change the same data at the same time. Furthermore, because the way in which you implement transactions impacts database performance, you need to understand the differences between isolation levels and be familiar with the scenarios with which each is best suited. Given a scenario in which an isolation level and a set of concurrent queries are specified, you should be able to predict the outcome of the queries. In addition, you should understand the types of locks that SQL Server acquires for each isolation level, if applicable, as well as the effect on other resources, such as *tempdb*, and the resulting potential performance impact of using a specific isolation level.

> **This section covers how to:**
> - Identify differences between isolation levels
> - Define results of concurrent queries based on isolation level
> - Identify the resource and performance impact of given isolation levels

## Identify differences between isolation levels

At one end of the spectrum, SQL Server can protect data completely to prevent one transaction from seeing the effects of another transaction, while at the other end of the spectrum, it can give all transactions full access to the data. It does this by using isolation levels to control whether a lock is acquired during a read, the type of lock, and the duration of the lock. Isolation levels also determine whether a read operation can access rows that have been changed by another transaction and whether it can access uncommitted rows. Additionally, isolation levels block transactions requiring access to a resource with an exclusive lock.

It is important to note that setting an isolation level does not change the way in which SQL Server acquires locks. If a transaction modifies data, SQL Server always acquires an exclusive (X) lock on the data to change, and holds the lock for the duration of the transaction. The purpose of the isolation levels is to specify how read operations should behave when other concurrent transactions are changing data.

If you lower the isolation level, you can increase the number of concurrent transactions that SQL Server processes, but you also increase the risk of dirty reads and other problems associated with concurrent processes as we described in Skill 3.1. If you raise the isolation level, you minimize these concurrency problems, but transactions are more likely to block one another and performance is more likely to suffer. Therefore, you must find the appropriate balance between protecting data and the effect of each isolation level.

SQL Server supports both pessimistic and optimistic isolation levels for concurrency management. Pessimistic isolation levels use blocking to avoid conflicts whereas optimistic isolation levels use snapshots of the data to enable higher concurrency. Pessimistic isolation levels rely on locks to prevent changes to data during read operations and to block read operations on data that is being changed by another operation. Optimistic isolation levels make a copy of data for read operations so that write operations can proceed unhindered. If SQL Server detects two write operations attempting to modify the same data at the same time, it returns a message to the application in which there should be appropriate logic for resolving this conflict.

**EXAM TIP**

It is important to understand the differences between SQL Server isolation levels and scenarios for which each is appropriate.

### Read Committed

READ COMMITTED is the default isolation level for SQL Server. It uses pessimistic locking to protect data. With this isolation level set, a transaction cannot read uncommitted data that is being added or changed by another transaction. A transaction attempting to read data that is currently being changed is blocked until the transaction changing the data releases the lock. A transaction running under this isolation level issues shared locks, but releases row or page locks after reading a row. If your query scans an index while another transactions changes the index key column of a row, that row could appear twice in the query results if that key change moved the row to a new position ahead of the scan. Another option is that it might not appear at all if the row moved to a position already read by the scan.

### Read Uncommitted

The READ UNCOMMITTED isolation level is the least restrictive setting. It allows a transaction to read data that has not yet been committed by other transactions. SQL Server ignores any locks and reads data from memory. Furthermore, transactions running under this isolation level do not acquire shared (S) locks to prevent other transactions from changing the data being read. Last, if a transaction is reading rows using an allocation order scan when another transaction causes a page split, your query can miss rows. For these reasons, READ UNCOMMITTED is never a good choice for line of business applications where accuracy matters most, but might be acceptable for a reporting application where the performance benefit outweighs the need for a precise value.

### Repeatable Read

When you set the REPEATABLE READ isolation level, you ensure that any data read by one transaction is not changed by another transaction. That way, the transaction can repeat a query and get identical results each time. In this case, the data is protected by shared (S) locks. It is important to note that the only data protected is the existing data that has been read. If another transaction inserts a new row, the first transaction's repeat of its query could return this row as a phantom read.

## Serializable

The most pessimistic isolation level is SERIALIZABLE, which uses range locks on the data to not only prevent changes but also insertions. Therefore, phantom reads are not possible when you set this isolation level. Each transaction is completely isolated from one another even when they execute in parallel or overlap.

## Snapshot

The SNAPSHOT isolation level is optimistic and allows read and write operations to run concurrently without blocking one another. Unlike the other isolation levels, you must first configure the database to allow it, and then you can set the isolation level for a transaction. As long as a transaction is open, SQL Server preserves the state of committed data at the start of the transaction and stores any changes to the data by other transactions in *tempdb*. It increases concurrency by eliminating the need for locks for read operations.

> **NOTE   SNAPSHOT ISOLATION AND DISTRIBUTED TRANSACTIONS**
>
> You cannot use SNAPSHOT isolation with distributed transactions. In addition, you cannot use enable it in the following databases: master, msdb, and tempdb.

## Read Committed Snapshot

The READ_COMMITTED_SNAPSHOT isolation level is an optimistic alternative to READ COMMITTED. Like the SNAPSHOT isolation level, you must first enable it at the database level before setting it for a transaction. Unlike SNAPSHOT isolation, you can use the READ_COMMITTED_SNAPSHOT isolation level with distributed transactions. The key difference between the two isolation levels is the ability with READ_COMMITTED_SNAPSHOT for a transaction to repeatedly read data as it was at the start of the read statement rather than at the start of the transaction. When each statement executes within a transaction, SQL Server takes a new snapshot that remains consistent until the next statement executes.

You use this isolation level when your application executes a long-running, multi-statement query and requires the data to be consistent to the point in time that the query starts. You should also consider using this isolation level when enough read and write blocking occurs that the resource overhead of maintaining row snapshots is preferable and there is little likelihood of a transaction rolling back due to an update conflict.

# Define results of concurrent queries based on isolation level

To better appreciate the effect of concurrent queries, let's consider a scenario that involves two users that are operating on the same data. One user starts executing a query that results in a full table scan and normally takes several minutes to complete. Meanwhile, a minute after the read operation begins, the other user updates and commits row in the same table that has not yet been read by the first user's query. The rows returned by the first user's query depend on the isolation levels set for that user.

Before we look at each isolation level's effect on this scenario, let's create a table and add some data as shown in Listing 3-5.

**LISTING 3-5** Create a test environment for testing isolation levels

```
CREATE TABLE Examples.IsolationLevels
(
    RowId   int NOT NULL
        CONSTRAINT PKRowId PRIMARY KEY,
    ColumnText  varchar(100) NOT NULL
);

INSERT INTO Examples.IsolationLevels(RowId, ColumnText)
VALUES (1, 'Row 1'), (2, 'Row 2'), (3, 'Row 3'), (4, 'Row 4');
```

You use the SET TRANSACTION ISOLATION LEVEL statement when you want to override the default isolation level and thereby change the way a SELECT statement behaves with respect to other concurrent operations. It is important to know that this statement changes the isolation level for the user session. If you want to change the isolation level for a single statement only, use a table hint instead.

## Read Committed

Because this isolation level only reads committed data, dirty reads are prevented. However, if query reads the same data multiple times, non-repeatable reads or phantom reads are possible.

Because the READ COMMITTED isolation level is the default, you do not need to explicitly set the isolation level. However, if you had previously changed the isolation level for the user session or the database, you can revert it to the default isolation level by executing the following statement:

```
SET TRANSACTION ISOLATION LEVEL READ COMMITTED;
```

To test the behavior of the READ COMMITTED isolation level, execute the following statements:

```
BEGIN TRANSACTION;
    UPDATE Examples.IsolationLevels
        SET ColumnText = 'Row 1 Updated'
        WHERE RowId = 1;
```

In a new session, read the table that you just updated:

```
SELECT RowId, ColumnText
FROM Examples.IsolationLevels;
```

In this case, the update operation blocks the read operations. Return to the first session and restore the data by rolling back the transaction:

```
ROLLBACK TRANSACTION;
```

Now the second session's read request completes successfully, and the results do not include the updated row because it was never committed.

```
RowId   ColumnText
-------  ------------
1       Row 1
2       Row 2
3       Row 3
4       Row 4
```

## Read Uncommitted

This isolation level allows dirty reads, non-repeatable reads, and phantom reads. On the other hand, a transaction set to this isolation level executes quickly because locks and validations are ignored.

Let's observe this behavior by starting a transaction without committing it:

```
BEGIN TRANSACTION;
    UPDATE Examples.IsolationLevels
        SET ColumnText = 'Row 1 Updated'
        WHERE RowId = 1;
```

Now open a new session, change the isolation level, and read the table that you just updated:

```
SET TRANSACTION ISOLATION LEVEL READ UNCOMMITTED;
SELECT RowId, ColumnText
FROM Examples.IsolationLevels;
```

The results include the updated row:

```
RowId   ColumnText
-------  ------------
1       Row 1 Updated
2       Row 2
3       Row 3
4       Row 4
```

Return to the first session and roll back the transaction:

```
ROLLBACK TRANSACTION;
```

Then in the second session, read the table again:

```
SELECT RowId, ColumnText
FROM Examples.IsolationLevels;
```

Now the results show the data in its state prior to the update that rolled back:

```
RowId   ColumnText
```

```
-------  ------------
1        Row 1
2        Row 2
3        Row 3
4        Row 4
```

Rather than change the isolation level at the session level, you can force the read uncommitted isolation level by using the NOLOCK hint. Repeat the previous example by using two new sessions to revert to the default isolation level and replacing the statements in the second session with the following statement:

```
SELECT RowId, ColumnText
FROM Examples.IsolationLevels
WITH (NOLOCK);
```

## Repeatable Read

The behavior of the REPEATABLE READ isolation level is much like that of READ COMMITTED, except that it ensures that multiple reads of the same data within a transaction are consistent. Dirty reads and non-repeatable reads are prevented, although phantom reads are a possible side effect because range locks are not used.

We can see the effects of using REPEATABLE READ by running statements in separate sessions. Start by adding the following statements in one new session:

```
SET TRANSACTION ISOLATION LEVEL REPEATABLE READ;
BEGIN TRANSACTION;
    SELECT RowId, ColumnText
    FROM Examples.IsolationLevels;
    WAITFOR DELAY '00:00:15';
    SELECT RowId, ColumnText
    FROM Examples.IsolationLevels;
ROLLBACK TRANSACTION;
```

In the second session, add the following statements and then with both sessions visible, execute both sessions:

```
UPDATE Examples.IsolationLevels
    SET ColumnText = 'Row 1 Updated'
    WHERE RowId = 1;
```

In this case, the first read operation blocks the update operation, which executes when the transaction's locks are released. The update in the second session commits the data change after the transaction. Both queries in the first session return the same results because the update occurs after the transaction ends:

```
RowId    ColumnText
-------  ------------
1        Row 1
2        Row 2
3        Row 3
4        Row 4
```

```
RowId    ColumnText
-------  ------------
1        Row 1
2        Row 2
3        Row 3
4        Row 4
```

If you check the table values again, you can see that the updated row appears in the query results:

```
RowId    ColumnText
-------  ------------
1        Row 1 Updated
2        Row 2
3        Row 3
4        Row 4
```

If you were to execute an INSERT statement in the second session instead, the first and second queries in the first session return different results by including the new rows in the second query. The isolation level prevents changes to existing data, but allows the insertion of new data.

## Serializable

The SERIALIZABLE isolation level behaves like REPEATABLE READ, but goes one step further by ensuring new rows added after the start of the transaction are not visible to the transaction's statement. Therefore, dirty reads, non-repeatable reads, and phantom reads are prevented.

Before we see how the SERIALIZABLE isolation level works, let's look at an example that produces a phantom read. In one new session, add the following statements:

```
SET TRANSACTION ISOLATION LEVEL REPEATABLE READ;
BEGIN TRANSACTION;
    SELECT RowId, ColumnText
    FROM Examples.IsolationLevels;
    WAITFOR DELAY '00:00:15';
    SELECT RowId, ColumnText
    FROM Examples.IsolationLevels;
ROLLBACK TRANSACTION;
```

As in the previous examples, start a new session to insert a row into the same table, and execute both sessions:

```
INSERT INTO Examples.IsolationLevels(RowId, ColumnText)
VALUES (5, 'Row 5');
```

In this case, the transaction starts with a read operation and returns four rows, but does not block the insert operation. The REPEATABLE READ isolation level only prevents changes to data that has been read, but does not prevent the transaction from seeing the new row, which is returned by the second query as shown here:

```
RowId   ColumnText
-------  ------------
1        Row 1 Updated
2        Row 2
3        Row 3
4        Row 4

RowId   ColumnText
-------  ------------
1        Row 1 Updated
2        Row 2
3        Row 3
4        Row 4
5        Row 5
```

Replace the isolation level statement in the first session with this statement to change the isolation level:

```
SET TRANSACTION ISOLATION LEVEL SERIALIZABLE;
```

Then create a new session to insert another row:

```
INSERT INTO Examples.IsolationLevels(RowId, ColumnText)
VALUES (6, 'Row 6');
```

This time because the INSERT operation is blocked by the transaction, both queries return the same results without the new row.

```
RowId   ColumnText
-------  ------------
1        Row 1
2        Row 2
3        Row 3
4        Row 4
5        Row 5

RowId   ColumnText
-------  ------------
1        Row 1
2        Row 2
3        Row 3
4        Row 4
5        Row 5
```

After the transaction ends, any subsequent queries to the table return six rows. The trade-off for this consistency during the transaction is the blocking of write operations.

## Snapshot

Snapshot Isolation gives you the same data for the duration of the transaction. This level of protection prevents dirty reads, non-repeatable reads, and phantom reads. As other transactions update or delete rows, a copy of the modified row is inserted into *tempdb*. This row also includes a transaction sequence number so that SQL Server can determine which version to use for a new transaction's snapshot. When the new transaction executes a read request, SQL

Server scans the version chain to find the latest committed row having a transaction sequence number lower than the current transaction. Periodically, SQL Server deletes row versions for transactions that are no longer open.

To use the SNAPSHOT isolation level, you must first enable it at the database level by using the following statement:

```
ALTER DATABASE ExamBook762Ch3
SET ALLOW_SNAPSHOT_ISOLATION ON;
```

Now set the isolation level for the session and start a transaction:

```
SET TRANSACTION ISOLATION LEVEL SNAPSHOT;
BEGIN TRANSACTION;
    SELECT RowId, ColumnText
    FROM Examples.IsolationLevels;
    WAITFOR DELAY '00:00:15';
    SELECT RowId, ColumnText
    FROM Examples.IsolationLevels;
ROLLBACK TRANSACTION;
```

Then set up a write operation in a new second session:

```
INSERT INTO Examples.IsolationLevels(RowId, ColumnText)
VALUES (7, 'Row 7');
```

The write operation runs immediately because it is no longer blocked by the read operations, yet the query results return only the six rows that existed prior to the insertion.

> **NOTE** **SNAPSHOT ISOLATION AND TEMPDB**
>
> If you access global temp tables within a transaction set to SNAPSHOT isolation, you must first enable the ALLOW_SNAPSHOT_ISOLATION database option for *tempdb*. As an alternative, you can use a hint to change the isolation level for the statement.

If you have a transaction that reads from a database that is enabled for SNAPSHOT isolation and another database that is not enabled, the transaction fails. To execute successfully, the transaction must include a table hint for the database without SNAPSHOT isolation level enabled.

Let's set up another database and a new table as shown in Listing 3-6.

**LISTING 3-6** Create a separate for testing isolation levels

```
CREATE DATABASE ExamBook762Ch3_IsolationTest;
GO
USE ExamBook762Ch3_IsolationTest;
GO
CREATE SCHEMA Examples;
GO
CREATE TABLE Examples.IsolationLevelsTest
(RowId INT NOT NULL
    CONSTRAINT PKRowId PRIMARY KEY,
    ColumnText  varchar(100) NOT NULL
);
```

```
INSERT INTO Examples.IsolationLevelsTest(RowId, ColumnText)
VALUES (1, 'Row 1'), (2, 'Row 2'), (3, 'Row 3'), (4, 'Row 4');
```

Now try to execute the following transaction that joins the data from the snapshot-enabled database with data from the other database:

```
SET TRANSACTION ISOLATION LEVEL SNAPSHOT;
BEGIN TRANSACTION;
    SELECT t1.RowId, t2.ColumnText
    FROM Examples.IsolationLevels AS t1
    INNER JOIN ExamBook762Ch3_IsolationTest.Examples.IsolationLevelsTest AS t2
    ON t1.RowId = t2.RowId;
END TRANSACTION;
```

SQL Server returns the following error:

```
Msg 3952, Level 16, State 1, Line 5
Snapshot isolation transaction failed accessing database 'ExamBook762Ch3_IsolationTest'
because snapshot isolation is not allowed in this database. Use ALTER DATABASE to allow
snapshot isolation.
```

You might not always have the option to alter the other database to enable Snapshot isolation. Instead, you can change the isolation level of the transaction's statement to READ COMMITTED, which allows the transaction to execute successfully:

```
SET TRANSACTION ISOLATION LEVEL SNAPSHOT;
BEGIN TRANSACTION;
    SELECT t1.RowId, t2.ColumnText
    FROM Examples.IsolationLevels AS t1
    INNER JOIN ExamBook762Ch3_IsolationTest.Examples.IsolationLevelsTest AS t2
    WITH (READCOMMITTED)
    ON t1.RowId = t2.RowId;
COMMIT TRANSACTION;
```

Another problem that you might encounter when using this isolation level is an update conflict, which causes the transaction to terminate and roll back. This situation can occur when one transaction using the SNAPSHOT isolation level reads data that another transaction modifies and then the first transaction attempts to update the same data. (This situation does not occur when a transaction runs using the READ_COMMITTED_SNAPSHOT isolation level.)

A problem can also arise when the state of the database changes during the transaction. As one example, a transaction set to SNAPSHOT isolation fails when the database is changed to read-only after the transaction starts, but before it accesses the database. Likewise, a failure occurs if a database recovery occurred in that same interval. A database recovery can be caused when the database is set to OFFLINE and then to ONLINE, when it auto-closes and re-opens, or when an operation detaches and attaches the database.

It is important to know that row versioning applies only to data and not to system metadata. If a statement changes metadata of an object while a transaction using the SNAPSHOT isolation level is open and the transaction subsequently references the modified object, the transaction fails. Be aware that BULK INSERT operations can change a table's metadata and cause transaction failures as a result. (This behavior does not occur when using the READ_COMMITTED_SNAPSHOT isolation level.)

One way to see this behavior is to change an index on a table while a transaction is open. Let's first add an index to a table:

```
CREATE INDEX Ix_RowId ON Examples.IsolationLevels (RowId);
```

Next set up a new transaction:

```
SET TRANSACTION ISOLATION LEVEL SNAPSHOT;
BEGIN TRANSACTION;
    SELECT RowId, ColumnText
    FROM Examples.IsolationLevels;
    WAITFOR DELAY '00:00:15';
    SELECT RowId, ColumnText
    FROM Examples.IsolationLevels;
ROLLBACK TRANSACTION;
```

Then set up a second session to change the index by using the following statement and execute both sessions:

```
ALTER INDEX Ix_RowId
    ON Examples.IsolationLevels REBUILD;
```

SQL Server returns the following error due to the metadata change:

```
Msg 3961, Level 16, State 1, Line 6
Snapshot isolation transaction failed in database 'ExamBook762Ch3' because the object
accessed by the statement has been modified by a DDL statement in another concurrent
transaction since the start of this transaction.  It is disallowed because the metadata
is not versioned. A concurrent update to metadata can lead to inconsistency if mixed
with snapshot isolation.
```

Be sure to disable snapshot isolation after completing the examples in this section:

```
ALTER DATABASE ExamBook762Ch3
SET ALLOW_SNAPSHOT_ISOLATION OFF;
```

## Read Committed snapshot

To use the READ_COMMITTED_SNAPSHOT isolation level, you need only enable it at the database level by using the following statement:

```
ALTER DATABASE ExamBook762Ch3
SET READ_COMMITTED_SNAPSHOT ON;
```

With this setting enabled, all queries that normally execute using the READ COMMITTED isolation level switch to using the READ_COMMITTED_SNAPSHOT isolation level without requiring you to change the query code. SQL Server creates a snapshot of committed data when each statement starts. Consequently, read operations at different points in a transaction might return different results.

During the transaction, SQL Server copies rows modified by other transactions into a collection of pages in tempdb known as the *version store*. When a row is updated multiple times, a copy of each change is in the version store. This set of row versions is called a version chain.

Let's see how this isolation level differs from the SNAPSHOT isolation level by setting up a new session:

```
BEGIN TRANSACTION;
    SELECT RowId, ColumnText
    FROM Examples.IsolationLevels;
    WAITFOR DELAY '00:00:15';
    SELECT RowId, ColumnText
    FROM Examples.IsolationLevels;
ROLLBACK TRANSACTION;
```

Next, set up a write operation in a new second session, and then execute both sessions:

```
INSERT INTO Examples.IsolationLevels(RowId, ColumnText)
VALUES (8, 'Row 8');
```

Just as with the SNAPSHOT isolation level, the write operation runs immediately because read operations are not blocking it. However, each query returns different results because the statements read different versions of the data.

```
RowId    ColumnText
-------  ------------
1        Row 1
2        Row 2
3        Row 3
4        Row 4
5        Row 5
6        Row 6
7        Row 7


RowId    ColumnText
-------  ------------
1        Row 1
2        Row 2
3        Row 3
4        Row 4
5        Row 5
6        Row 6
7        Row 7
8        Row 8
```

Last, disable the READ_COMMITTED_SNAPSHOT isolation level after completing this example:

```
ALTER DATABASE Examples
SET READ_COMMITTED_SNAPSHOT OFF;
```

# Identify the resource and performance impact of given isolation levels

The goal of isolation levels is to ensure that queries return complete and consistent results while other concurrent processes are running. To avoid locking contention and improve overall performance, you should keep each transaction short and concise so it can execute quickly while holding the fewest and smallest possible locks.

## Read Committed

With this isolation level, SQL Server holds two types of locks. A shared (S) lock is acquired for read operations and is held only for the duration of that single operation. On the other hand, an exclusive (X) lock is acquired for a write operation. Any changes to the data are not visible to other operations for the duration of the write operation's transaction.

## Read Uncommitted

SQL Server ignores existing locks and reads both committed and uncommitted data. Furthermore, it does not acquire shared locks for read operations. However, schema modification locks can still block reads.

## Repeatable Read

SQL Server places Shared (S) locks on the data (and up the lock hierarchy) for the duration of the transaction. Therefore, reads block write operations in other transactions. Consequently, SQL Server cannot manage as many concurrent processes and performance can be adversely impacted as deadlocks can become more frequent.

## Serializable

SQL Server locks data for a read operation and also uses key-range locks to prevent any other transactions from inserting or modifying the data for the duration of a transaction. This high level of locking reduces concurrency and potentially slows performance due to locking contention.

## Snapshot

No locks are acquired for this isolation level. Consequently, deadlocks and lock escalations occur less frequently, performance is faster, and concurrency is higher. Read operations are not blocked by write operations, and write operations are not blocked by read operations.

On the other hand, these benefits come with an overhead cost. More space is required in tempdb for row version storage and more CPU and memory is required by SQL Server to manage row versioning. Update operations might run slower as a result of the extra steps required to manage row versions. Furthermore, long running read operations can run slower if many updates or deletes are occurring and increasing the length of the version chains that SQL Server must scan. You can improve performance by placing tempdb on a dedicated, high-performance disk drive.

### Read Committed Snapshot

When a new transaction using the READ_COMMITTED_SNAPSHOT isolation level requests locked data, SQL Server provides a copy of the data. It does not acquire shared page or row locks. As a consequence, reads do not block write operations and writes do not block read operations, although writes do require exclusive locks and continue to block other writes until the end of the transaction. However, because SQL Server removes row versions from tempdb when a transaction is over, it is possible to experience some concurrency side effects.

# Skill 3.3: Optimize concurrency and locking behavior

SQL Server uses locks to control the effect of concurrent transactions on one another. Part of your job as an administrator is to improve concurrency by properly managing locking behavior. That means you need to understand how to uncover performance problems related to locks and lock escalations. Additionally, you must know how to use the tools available to you for identifying when and why deadlocks happen and the possible steps you can take to prevent deadlocks from arising.

> **This section covers how to:**
> - Troubleshoot locking issues
> - Identify lock escalation behaviors
> - Capture and analyze deadlock graphs
> - Identify ways to remediate deadlocks

# Troubleshoot locking issues

Before you can troubleshoot locking issues, you must understand how SQL Server uses locks, which we describe in detail in Skill 3.1. As part of the troubleshooting process, you need to determine which resources are locked, why they are locked, and the lock type in effect.

You can use the following dynamic management views (DMVs) to view information about locks:

- **sys.dm_tran_locks**  Use this DMV to view all current locks, the lock resources, lock mode, and other related information.

- **sys.dm_os_waiting_tasks**  Use this DMV to see which tasks are waiting for a resource.

- **sys.dm_os_wait_stats**  Use this DMV to see how often processes are waiting while locks are taken.

Before we look at these DMVs in detail, let's set up our environment as shown in Listing 3-7 so that we can establish some context for locking behavior.

**LISTING 3-7** Create a test environment for testing locking behavior

```
CREATE TABLE Examples.LockingA
(
    RowId   int NOT NULL
        CONSTRAINT PKLockingARowId PRIMARY KEY,
    ColumnText  varchar(100) NOT NULL
);

INSERT INTO Examples.LockingA(RowId, ColumnText)
VALUES (1, 'Row 1'), (2, 'Row 2'), (3, 'Row 3'), (4, 'Row 4');
CREATE TABLE Examples.LockingB
(
    RowId   int NOT NULL
        CONSTRAINT PKLockingBRowId PRIMARY KEY,
    ColumnText  varchar(100) NOT NULL
);

INSERT INTO Examples.LockingB(RowId, ColumnText)
VALUES (1, 'Row 1'), (2, 'Row 2'), (3, 'Row 3'), (4, 'Row 4');
```

## sys.dm_tran_locks

The sys.dm_tran_locks DMV provides you with information about existing locks and locks that have been requested but not yet granted in addition to details about the resource for which the lock is requested. You can use this DMV only to view information at the current point in time. It does not provide access to historical information about locks. Table 3-2 describes each column in sys.dm_tran_locks.

**TABLE 3-2** sys.dm_tran_locks

| COLUMN | DESCRIPTION |
|---|---|
| resource_type | One of the following types of resources: DATABASE, FILE, OBJECT, PAGE, KEY, EXTENT, RID, APPLICATION, METADATA, HOBT, or ALLOCATION_UNIT. |
| resource_subtype | If a resource has a subtype, this column displays it. |
| resource_database_id | The ID of the database containing the resource. |
| resource_description | Additional information, if available, about the resource not found in other resource columns. |
| resource_associated_entity_id | The ID of the entity with which the resource is associated, such as an object ID, HoBT ID, or Allocation Unit ID. |
| resource_lock_partition | The ID of the lock partition for partitioned lock resource. The value is 0 for a non-partitioned lock resource. |
| request_mode | The lock mode requested by waiting requests or granted for other requests. |
| request_type | This value is always LOCK. |
| request_status | One of the following values to reflect the current status of the request: GRANTED, CONVERT, WAIT, LOW_PRIORITY_CONVERT, LOW_PRIORITY_WAIT, or ABORT_BLOCKERS. |
| request_reference_count | The approximate number of times the requestor has requested the resource. |
| request_lifetime | This column is not supported. |
| request_session_id | The ID of the session that owns the request. An orphaned distributed transaction has a value of -2. A deferred recovery transaction has a value of -3. |
| request_exec_context_id | The ID of the execution context for the process that owns the request. |
| request_request_id | The ID of the request for the process that owns the request. This value changes when the active MARS connection for the transaction changes. |
| request_owner_type | The type of entity that owns the request: TRANSACTION, CURSOR, SESSION, SHARED_TRANSACTION_WORKSPACE, EXCLUSIVE_TRANSACTION_WORKSPACE, or NOTIFICATION_OBJECT. |
| request_owner_id | The ID of the owner of the request. |
| request_owner_guid | The GUID of the owner of the request. |
| request_owner_lockspace_id | This column is not supported. |
| lock_owner_address | The memory address of the internal data structure that is tracking the request. Join it with the resource_address column in sys.dm_os_waiting_tasks. |
| pdw_node_id | The ID for node in the Analytics Platform System (formerly known as Parallel Data Warehouse). |

> *NOTE*  **SYS.DM_TRAN_LOCKS RESOURCE TYPE SUBTYPES**
>
> For a full list of subtypes for each resource type, refer to the sys.dm_tran_locks documentation at *https://msdn.microsoft.com/en-us/library/ms190345.aspx*.

Let's start some transactions to observe the locks that SQL Server acquires. In one session, execute the following statements:

```
BEGIN TRANSACTION;
    SELECT RowId, ColumnText
    FROM Examples.LockingA
    WITH (HOLDLOCK, ROWLOCK);
```

In a separate session, start another transaction:

```
BEGIN TRANSACTION;
    UPDATE Examples.LockingA
        SET ColumnText = 'Row 2 Updated'
        WHERE RowId = 2;
```

Now let's use the sys.dm_tran_locks DMV to view some details about the current locks:

```
SELECT
    request_session_id as s_id,
    resource_type,
    resource_associated_entity_id,
    request_status,
    request_mode
FROM sys.dm_tran_locks
WHERE resource_database_id = db_id('ExamBook762Ch3');
```

Although your results might vary, especially with regard to identifiers, the DMV returns results similar to the example below. Notice the wait for the exclusive lock for session 2. It must wait until session 1 releases its shared range (RangeS-S) locks that SQL Server takes due to the HOLDLOCK table hint. This table hint is equivalent to setting the isolation level to SERIALIZABLE. SQL Server also takes intent locks on the table (which appears on the OBJECT rows of the results) and the page, with session 1 taking intent shared (IS) locks and session 2 taking intent exclusive (IX) locks.

| s_id | resource_type | resource_associated_entity_id | request_status | request_mode |
| --- | --- | --- | --- | --- |
| 1 | DATABASE | 0 | GRANT | S |
| 2 | DATABASE | 0 | GRANT | S |
| 1 | PAGE | 72057594041729024 | GRANT | IS |
| 2 | PAGE | 72057594041729024 | GRANT | IX |
| 1 | KEY | 72057594041729024 | GRANT | RangeS-S |
| 1 | KEY | 72057594041729024 | GRANT | RangeS-S |
| 1 | KEY | 72057594041729024 | GRANT | RangeS-S |
| 1 | KEY | 72057594041729024 | GRANT | RangeS-S |
| 1 | KEY | 72057594041729024 | GRANT | RangeS-S |
| 2 | KEY | 72057594041729024 | WAIT | X |
| 1 | OBJECT | 933578364 | GRANT | IS |
| 2 | OBJECT | 933578364 | GRANT | IX |

Connect to the ExamBook762Ch3 database containing the resource and use one of the resource_associated_entity_id values from the previous query in the WHERE clause to see which object is locked, like this:

```
SELECT
    object_name(object_id) as Resource,
    object_id,
    hobt_id
FROM sys.partitions
WHERE hobt_id=72057594041729024;
```

When you view the results of this latter query, you can see the name of the resource that is locked, like this:

```
Resource object_id   hobt_id
-------- ---------- -------------------
LockingA 933578364  72057594041729024
```

In the previous example, you can also see the object_id returned from sys.partitions corresponds to the resource_associated_entity_id associated with the OBJECT resource_type in the DMV.

When troubleshooting blocking situations, look for CONVERT in the request_status column in this DMV. This value indicates the request was granted a lock mode earlier, but now needs to upgrade to a different lock mode and is currently blocked.

### sys.dm_os_waiting_tasks

Another useful DMV is sys.dm_os_waiting_tasks. Whenever a user asks you why a query is taking longer to run than usual, a review of this DMV should be one of your standard trouble-shooting steps. You can find a description of each column in this DMV in Table 3-3.

**TABLE 3-3** sys.dm_os_waiting_tasks

| COLUMN | DESCRIPTION |
| --- | --- |
| waiting_task_address | The address of the waiting task. |
| session_id | The ID of the session that owns the task. |
| exec_context_id | The ID of the execution context of the task. |
| wait_duration_ms | The total wait time for this wait type in milliseconds. This value includes signal_wait_time_ms. |
| wait_type | The type of wait. |
| resource_address | The address of the resource for which the task is waiting. |
| blocking_task_address | The task that is currently holding the requested resource. |
| blocking_session_id | The ID of the session that is blocking the request. This column is NULL if the task is not blocked, -2 if the blocking resource is owned by an orphaned transaction, -3 if the blocking resource is owned by a deferred recovery transaction, and -4 if the session ID of the blocking latch owner cannot be determined due to internal latch state transitions. |
| blocking_exec_context_id | The ID of the execution context of the blocking task. |
| resource_description | The description of the resource consumed. See https://msdn.micro-soft.com/en-us/library/ms188743.aspx for more information. |
| pdw_node_id | The ID for node in the Analytics Platform System (formerly known as Parallel Data Warehouse). |

In particular, you can use the sys.dm_trans_locks DMV in conjunction with the sys.dm_os_waiting_tasks DMV to find blocked sessions, as shown in Listing 3-8.

**LISTING 3-8** Use system DMV sys.dm_tran_locks and sys.dm_os_waiting_tasks to display blocked sessions

```
SELECT
    t1.resource_type AS res_typ,
    t1.resource_database_id AS res_dbid,
    t1.resource_associated_entity_id AS res_entid,
    t1.request_mode AS mode,
    t1.request_session_id AS s_id,
    t2.blocking_session_id AS blocking_s_id
FROM sys.dm_tran_locks as t1
INNER JOIN sys.dm_os_waiting_tasks as t2
    ON t1.lock_owner_address = t2.resource_address;
```

Whereas the earlier query showing existing locks is helpful for learning how SQL Server acquires locks, the query in Listing 3-8 returns information that is more useful on a day-to-day basis for uncovering blocking chains. In the query results shown below, you can see that session 2 is blocked by session 1.

```
res_typ  res_dbid  res_entid           mode  s_id  blocking_s_id
-------  --------  ------------------  ----  ----  ----------------
KEY      27        72057594041729024   X     2     1
```

Execute the following statement in both sessions to release the locks:

```
ROLLBACK TRANSACTION;
```

## sys.dm_os_wait_stats

The sys.dm_os_wait_stats DMV is an aggregate view of all waits that occur when a requested resource is not available, a worker thread is idle typically due to background tasks, or an external event must complete first. Table 3-4 explains the columns in sys.dm_os_wait_stats.

**TABLE 3-4** sys.dm_os_wait_stats

| COLUMN | DESCRIPTION |
|---|---|
| wait_type | The type of wait. The wait types associated with locks all begin with LCK. |
| waiting_tasks_count | The number of waits having this wait type. The start of a new wait increments this value. |
| wait_time_ms | The total wait time for this wait type in milliseconds. This value includes signal_wait_time_ms. |
| max_wait_time_ms | The highest wait time for this wait type in milliseconds. |
| signal_wait_time_ms | The amount of time in milliseconds between the time the waiting thread was signaled and the time it started running. |
| pdw_node_idpdw_node_id | The ID for node in the Analytics Platform System (formerly known as Parallel Data Warehouse). |

There are many wait types unrelated to locks, so when using the sys.dm_os_wait_stats DMV, you should apply a filter to focus on lock waits only, like this:

```
SELECT
    wait_type as wait,
    waiting_tasks_count as wt_cnt,
    wait_time_ms as wt_ms,
    max_wait_time_ms as max_wt_ms,
    signal_wait_time_ms as signal_ms
FROM sys.dm_os_wait_stats
WHERE wait_type LIKE 'LCK%'
ORDER BY wait_time_ms DESC;
```

> **NOTE  WAIT TYPES**
>
> For a full list of wait types, refer to the sys.dm_os_wait_stats documentation at *https://msdn.microsoft.com/en-us/library/ms179984.aspx.*

The partial results of this query on our computer shown in the following example indicate that our SQL Server instance have the longest waits when threads are waiting for an exclusive (X) lock. On the other hand, the greatest number of waits is a result of waiting for a schema modification (SCH-M) lock. In both cases, the waits are caused because SQL Server has already granted an incompatible lock to the resource on another thread. This information is useful for identifying long-term trends, but does not show you details about the locked resources.

| wait | wt_cnt | wt_ms | max_wt_ms | signal_ms |
| --- | --- | --- | --- | --- |
| LCK_M_X | 6 | 1170670 | 712261 | 114 |
| LCK_M_S | 28 | 19398 | 2034 | 43 |
| LCK_M_SCH_M | 449 | 92 | 28 | 46 |
| LCK_M_SCH_S | 1 | 72 | 72 | 0 |

> **NOTE  WAIT TYPE TROUBLESHOOTING LIBRARY**
>
> Your SQL Server instance undoubtedly yields different results for this DMV. You can find a comprehensive library of SQL Server wait types compiled by SQLSkills available at *https://www.sqlskills.com/help/waits*. This library includes a description of wait types, general guidance for troubleshooting lock waits, and specific guidance for individual lock waits.

You can reset the cumulative values in the sys.dm_os_wait_stats DMV by executing the following statement: DBCC SQLPERF (N'sys.dm_os_wait_stats', CLEAR);. Otherwise, these values are reset each time that the SQL Server service restarts.

**EXAM TIP**

For the exam, you should know which DMVs you can reset manually as compared to the DMVs that require a SQL Server service restart to be reset.

# Identify lock escalation behaviors

Lock escalation occurs when SQL Server detects too much memory, or too many system resources are required for a query's locks. It then converts one set of locks to another set of locks applied to resources higher in the lock hierarchy. In other words, SQL Server tries to use fewer locks to cover more resources. As an example, SQL Server might choose to escalate a high number of row locks to a table lock. This capability can reduce overhead on the one hand, but can impact performance on the other hand because more data is locked. As a result, there is greater potential for blocking.

Lock escalation occurs when more than 40 percent of the available database engine memory pool is required by lock resources, or at least 5,000 locks are taken in a single T-SQL statement for a single resource. SQL Server converts an intent lock to a full lock, as long as the full lock is compatible with existing locks on the resource. It then releases system resources and locks on the lower level of the lock hierarchy. If the new lock is taken on a row or a page, SQL Server adds an intent lock on the object at the next higher level. However, if other locks prevent lock escalation, SQL Server continues attempting to perform the escalation for each new 1,250 locks it takes.

In most cases, you should let SQL Server manage the locks. If you implement a monitoring system, take note of Lock:Escalation events to establish a benchmark. When the number of Lock:Escalation events exceeds the benchmark, you can take action at the table level or at the query level.

Another option for monitoring lock escalation is to benchmark the percentage of time that intent lock waits (LCK_M_I*) occur relative to regular locks in the sys.dm_os_wait_stats DMV by using a query like this:

```
SELECT
    wait_type as wait,
    wait_time_ms as wt_ms,
    CONVERT(decimal(9,2), 100.0 * wait_time_ms /
    SUM(wait_time_ms) OVER ()) as wait_pct
FROM sys.dm_os_wait_stats
WHERE wait_type LIKE 'LCK%'
ORDER BY wait_time_ms DESC;
```

# Capture and analyze deadlock graphs

Usually the process of locking and unlocking SQL Server is fast enough to allow many users to read and write data with the appearance that it occurs simultaneously. However, sometimes two sessions block each other and neither can complete, which is a situation known as *deadlocking*. Normally, the database engine terminates a thread of a deadlocked transaction with error 1205 and suggests a remedy, such as running the transaction again.

Let's deliberately create a deadlock between two transactions. Start two sessions and add the following statements to the first session:

```
BEGIN TRANSACTION;
    UPDATE Examples.LockingA
        SET ColumnText = 'Row 1 Updated'
        WHERE RowId = 1;
    WAITFOR DELAY '00:00:05';
    UPDATE Examples.LockingB
    SET ColumnText = 'Row 1 Updated Again'
    WHERE RowId = 1;
```

Next, in the second session, add the following statements:

```
BEGIN TRANSACTION;
    UPDATE Examples.LockingB
        SET ColumnText = 'Row 1 Updated'
        WHERE RowId = 1;
    WAITFOR DELAY '00:00:05';
    UPDATE Examples.LockingA
    SET ColumnText = 'Row 1 Updated Again'
    WHERE RowId = 1;
```

Now execute the statements in the first session, and then, within five seconds, execute the second session's statements. Only one of the transaction completes and the other was terminated with a rollback by SQL Server as shown by the following message:

```
Msg 1205, Level 13, State 51, Line 6
Transaction (Process ID 70) was deadlocked on lock resources with another process and
has been chosen as the deadlock victim. Rerun the transaction.
```

In this example, both transactions need the same table resources. Both transactions can successfully update a row without conflict and have an exclusive lock on the updated data. Then they each try to update data in the table that the other transaction had updated, but each transaction is blocked while waiting for the other transaction's exclusive lock to be released. Neither transaction can ever complete and release its lock, thereby causing a deadlock. When SQL Server recognizes this condition, it terminates one of the transactions and rolls it back. It usually chooses the transaction that is least expensive to rollback based on the number of transaction log records. At that point, the aborted transaction's locks are released and the remaining open transaction can continue.

Of course, deadlocks are not typically going to happen while you watch, so how can you know when and why they occur? You can use either SQL Server Profiler or Extended Events to capture a *deadlock graph*, an XML description of a deadlock.

**EXAM TIP**

The exam also tests your knowledge about capturing deadlocks without a graph by using Trace Flags 1204 and 1222. You can enable these trace flags by using the following syntax: DBCC TRACEON(1204,1222,-1). Whenever a deadlock occurs, the deadlock victim and the other transaction involved in the deadlock appear in the SQL Server log. See "Detecting and Ending Deadlocks" at *https://technet.microsoft.com/en-us/library/ms178104.aspx* to review this topic in more depth.

## SQL Server Profiler deadlock graph

If you use SQL Server Profiler to capture a deadlock graph, you must configure the trace before deadlocks occur. Start by creating a new trace, and connect to your SQL Server instance. In the Trace Properties dialog box, select the Events Selection tab, select the Show All Events check box, expand Locks, and then select the following events:

- Deadlock graph
- Lock:Deadlock
- Lock:Deadlock Chain

On the Events Extraction Settings tab, select the Save Deadlock XML Events Separately option, navigate to a directory into which SQL Server Profiler saves deadlock graphs, and supply a name for the graph. You can choose whether to save all deadlock graphs in a single .xdl file or save multiple deadlock graphs as a separate .xdl file.

> **NOTE  VIEWING A DEADLOCK GRAPH SAVED AS AN .XDL FILE**
>
> Whenever you can save a deadlock graph as an .xdl file, you can later open that file in SQL Server Management Studio to view it.

Now set up the deadlock scenario again to generate the deadlock graph. In one session, add the following statements:

```
BEGIN TRANSACTION;
    UPDATE Examples.LockingA
        SET ColumnText = 'Row 2 Updated'
        WHERE RowId = 2;
    WAITFOR DELAY '00:00:05';
    UPDATE Examples.LockingB
    SET ColumnText = 'Row 2 Updated Again'
    WHERE RowId = 2;
```

Next, in the second session, add the following statements:

```
BEGIN TRANSACTION;
    UPDATE Examples.LockingB
        SET ColumnText = 'Row 2 Updated'
        WHERE RowId = 2;
    WAITFOR DELAY '00:00:05';
    UPDATE Examples.LockingA
    SET ColumnText = 'Row 2 Updated Again'
    WHERE RowId = 2;
```

When a deadlock occurs, you can see the deadlock graph as an event in SQL Server Profiler, as shown in Figure 3-1. In the deadlock graph, you see the tables and queries involved in the deadlock, which process was terminated, and which locks led to the deadlock. The ovals at each end of the deadlock graph contain information about the processes running the deadlocked queries. The terminated process displays in the graph with an x superimposed on it. Hover your mouse over the process to view the statement associated with it. The rectangles labeled Key Lock identify the database object and index associated with the locking. Lines in the deadlock graph show the relationship between processes and database objects. A request relationship displays when a process waits for a resource while an owner relationship displays when a resource waits for a process.

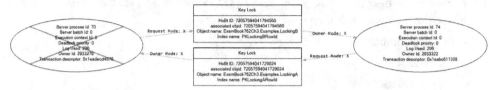

**FIGURE 3-1** A deadlock graph

## Extended Events deadlock graph

In Extended Events, you can use the continuously running system_health session to discover past deadlocks. As an alternative, you can set up a new session dedicated to capturing deadlock information. The system_health session automatically captures detected deadlocks without requiring special configuration. That means you can analyze a deadlock after it has occurred.

To find deadlock information in the Extended Events viewer, open SQL Server Management Studio, connect to the database engine, expand the Management node in Object Explorer, expand the Extended Events node, expand the Sessions node, and then expand the System_health node. Right-click Package0.event_file, and select View Target Data. In the Extended Events toolbar, click the Filters button. In the Filters dialog box, select Name in the Field drop-down list, type xml_deadlock_report in the Value text box, as shown in Figure 3-2, and then click OK. Select Xml_deadlock_report in the filtered list of events, and then click the Deadlock tab below it to view the deadlock graph.

**FIGURE 3-2** An Extended Events filter for xml_deadlock_report

# Identify ways to remediate deadlocks

Deadlocks are less likely to occur if transactions can release resources as quickly as possible. You can also lock up additional resources to avoid contention between multiple transactions. For example, you can use a hint to lock a table although this action can also cause blocking.

Usually the best way to resolve a deadlock is to rerun the transaction. For this reason, you should enclose a transaction in a TRY/CATCH block and add retry logic. Let's revise the previous example to prevent the deadlock. Start two new sessions and add the statements in Listing 3-9 to both sessions.

**LISTING 3-9** Add retry logic to avoid deadlock

```
DECLARE @Tries tinyint
SET @Tries = 1
WHILE @Tries <= 3
BEGIN

    BEGIN TRANSACTION
    BEGIN TRY
        UPDATE Examples.LockingB
            SET ColumnText = 'Row 3 Updated'
            WHERE RowId = 3;
        WAITFOR DELAY '00:00:05';
        UPDATE Examples.LockingA
        SET ColumnText = 'Row 3 Updated Again'
            WHERE RowId = 3;
        COMMIT TRANSACTION;
    END TRY
    BEGIN CATCH
        SELECT ERROR_NUMBER() AS ErrorNumber;
        ROLLBACK TRANSACTION;
        SET @Tries = @Tries + 1;
        CONTINUE;
    END CATCH
END
```

Next, execute each session. This time the deadlock occurs again, but the CATCH block captured the deadlock. SQL Server does not automatically roll back the transaction when you use this method, so you should include a ROLLBACK TRANSACTION in the CATCH block. The @@TRANCOUNT variable resets to zero in both transactions. As a result, SQL Server no longer cancels one of the transactions and you can also see the error number generated for the deadlock victim:

```
ErrorNumber
-------------
1205
```

Re-execution of the transaction might not be possible if the cause of the deadlock is still locking resources. To handle those situations, you could need to consider the following methods as alternatives for resolving deadlocks.

- Use SNAPSHOT or READ_COMMITTED_SNAPSHOT isolation levels. Either of these options avoid most blocking problems without the risk of dirty reads. However, both of these options require plenty of space in *tempdb*.

- Use the NOLOCK query hint if one of the transactions is a SELECT statement, but only use this method if the trade-off of a deadlock for dirty reads is acceptable.

- Add a new covering nonclustered index to provide another way for SQL Server to read data without requiring access to the underlying table. This approach works only if the other transaction participating in the deadlock does not use any of the covering index keys. The trade-off is the additional overhead required to maintain the index.

- Proactively prevent a transaction from locking a resource that eventually gets locked by another transaction by using the HOLDLOCK or UPDLOCK query hints.

# Skill 3.4: Implement memory-optimized tables and native stored procedures

The In-Memory OLTP feature built into SQL Server 2016 adds a new memory-optimized relational data management engine and a native stored procedure compiler to the platform that you can use to run transactional workloads with higher concurrency. A memory-optimized table is a highly optimized data structure that SQL Server uses to store data completely in memory without paging to disk. It uses hash and nonclustered ordered indexes to support faster data access from memory than traditional B-tree indexes. SQL Server maintains a copy of the data on disk to guarantee transaction durability and to reload tables during database recovery.

To further optimize query performance, you can implement natively compiled stored procedures as long as the stored procedure accesses memory-optimized tables only. A *natively compiled stored procedure* is a stored procedure compiled into machine language for faster execution, lower latency, and lower CPU utilization.

> **This section covers how to:**
> - Define use cases for memory-optimized tables
> - Optimize performance of in-memory tables
> - Determine best case usage scenarios for natively compiled stored procedures
> - Enable collection of execution statistics for natively compiled stored procedures

## Define use cases for memory-optimized tables

You use memory-optimized tables when you need to improve the performance and scalability of existing tables, or when you have frequent bottlenecks caused by locking and latching or code execution. SQL Server uses optimistic concurrency management for memory-optimized tables, which eliminates the need for locks and latches and in results in faster operations. In addition, SQL Server uses algorithms that are specifically optimized to access data from memory and natively compiled stored procedures to execute code faster. Depending on the type of workload you run, you can achieve five to 20 times performance gains with higher throughput and lower latency after migrating an existing disk-based table to a memory-optimized table.

In general, OLTP workloads with the following characteristics benefit most from migration to memory-optimized tables: short transactions with fast response times, queries accessing a limited number of tables that contain small data sets, and high concurrency requirements. This type of workload could also require high transaction throughput and low latency at scale. In the exam, you must be able to recognize the following use cases for which memory-optimized tables are best suited:

- **High data ingestion rate**   The database engine must process a high number of inserts, either as a steady stream or in bursts. Bottlenecks from locking and latching are a common problem in this scenario. Furthermore, last-page contention can occur when many threads attempt to access the same page in a standard B-tree and indexes intended to improve query performance add overhead time to insert operations. Performance is often measured in terms of throughput rate or the number of rows loaded per second. A common scenario for this workload is the Internet of Things in which multiple sensors are sending data to SQL Server. Other examples include of applications producing data at a high rate include financial trading, manufacturing, telemetry, and security monitoring. Whereas disk-based tables can have difficulty managing the rate of inserts, memory-optimized tables can eliminate resource contention and reduce logging. In some cases, requirements permitting, you can further reduce transaction execution time by implementing delayed durability, which we describe in greater detail in the next section.

- **High volume, high performance data reads**   Bottlenecks from latching and locking, or from CPU utilization can occur when there are multiple concurrent read requests competing with periodic inserts and updates, particularly when small regions of data within a large table are accessed frequently. In addition, query execution time carries overhead related to parsing, optimizing, and compiling statements. Performance in this case often requires the overall time to complete a set of steps for a business transaction to be measured in milliseconds or a smaller unit of time. Industries with these requirements include retail, online banking, and online gaming, to name a few. The use of memory-optimized tables in this scenario eliminates contention between read and write operations and retrieves data with lower latency, while the use of natively compiled stored procedures enables code to execute faster.

- **Complex business logic in stored procedures**   When an application requires intensive data processing routines and performs high volume inserts, updates, and deletes, the database can experience significant read-write contention. In some scenarios, the workload must process and transform data before writing it to a table, as is common in Extract-Transform-Load (ETL) operations, which can be a time-consuming operation.

In other scenarios, the workload must perform point lookups or minimal joins before performing update operations on a small number of rows. Industries with these types of high-volume, complex logic workloads include manufacturing supply chains and retailers maintaining online, real-time product catalogs. Memory-optimized tables can eliminate lock and latch contention and natively compiled stored procedures can reduce the execution time to enable higher throughput and lower latency. Another possibility is to use delayed durability to reduce transaction execution time, but only if the application requirements permit some potential data loss.

- **Real-time data access**  Several factors contribute to latency when accessing data in traditional disk-based tables, including the time required to parse, optimize, compile, and execute a statement, the time to write a transaction to the transaction log, and CPU utilization when the database is experiencing heavy workloads. Examples of industries requiring low latency execution include financial trading and online gaming. With memory-optimized tables, the database engine retrieves data more efficiently with reduced contention and natively compiled stored procedures execute code more efficiently and faster. In addition, point lookup queries execute faster due to the use of non-clustered hash indexes and minimal logging reduces overall transaction execution time. Altogether, these capabilities of memory-optimized tables enable significantly lower latency than disk-based tables.

- **Session state management**  Applications that require the storage of state information for stateless protocols, such as HTTP, often use a database to persist this information across multiple requests from a client. This type of workload is characterized by frequent inserts, updates, and point lookups. When running at scale with load balanced web servers, multiple servers can update data for the same session or perform point lookups, which results in increased contention for the same resources. This type of workload is characterized by frequently changes to a small amount of data and incurs a significant amount of locking and latching. Memory-optimized tables reduce contention, retrieve data effectively, and reduce or eliminate IO when using non-durable (SCHEMA_ONLY) tables, which we describe in the next section. On the other hand, the database engine does not resolve conflicts resulting from attempts by separate concurrent transactions to modify the same row, which is relatively rare in session state management. Nonetheless, the application should include logic to retry an operation if a transaction fails due to a write conflict.

- **Applications relying heavily on temporary tables, table variables, and table-valued parameters**  Many times an application needs a way to store intermediate results in a temporary location before applying additional logic to transform the data into its final state for loading into a target table. Temporary tables and table variables are different ways to fulfill this need. As an alternative, an application might use table-valued parameters to send multiple rows of data to a stored procedure or function and avoid the need for temporary tables or table variables. All three of these methods require writes to tempdb and potentially incur additional execution time due to the IO overhead. You can instead use memory-optimized temporary tables, table variables, and table-valued parameters to take advantage of the same optimizations available for memory-optimized tables. By doing so, you can eliminate both the tempdb contention and the IO overhead. You can achieve faster execution time when using these objects in a natively compiled stored procedure.

- **ETL operations**   ETL operations typically require the use of staging tables to copy data from source systems as a starting point, and might also use staging tables for intermediate steps necessary to transform data prior to loading the processed data into a target table. Although this workload does not usually suffer from bottlenecks related to concurrency problems, it can experience delays due to IO operations and the overhead associated with query processing. For applications requiring low latency in the target database, consider using memory-optimized tables for faster, more efficient access to data. To reduce or eliminate IO, use non-durable tables as we describe in the next section.

*NEED MORE REVIEW?*   **MEMORY-OPTIMIZED TABLE USE CASES AND IMPLEMENTATION STRATEGIES**

For a more in-depth review of use cases and implementation strategies for memory-optimized tables, download the "In-Memory OLTP – Common Workload Patterns and Migration Considerations" whitepaper from *https://msdn.microsoft.com/library/dn673538.aspx*. Be aware that memory-optimized tables in SQL Server 2016 support more features than described in the whitepaper, which was written about SQL Server 2014. For a complete list of the newly supported features see *https://msdn.microsoft.com/en-us/library/bb510411. aspx#InMemory*.

# Optimize performance of in-memory tables

As we described in the previous section, there are many use cases for which migrating disk-based tables to memory-optimized tables improves overall performance. However, to ensure you get optimal performance, there are several tasks that you can perform.

*IMPORTANT*   **SQL SERVER EDITIONS SUPPORTING MEMORY-OPTIMIZED TABLES**

To use memory-optimized tables, you must use the SQL Server 2016 Enterprise, Developer, or Evaluation edition. In this latest version, the maximum size of an optimized table is 2 terabytes (TB).

Before we look at these tasks, let's start by creating the data directory on the root drive to hold a new database, and then enabling in-memory OLTP in a new database as shown in Listing 3-10. Enabling a database for memory-optimized tables requires you to define the filegroup by using the CONTAINS MEMORY_OPTIMIZED_DATA option. SQL Server uses this filegroup container to store checkpoint files necessary for recovering memory-optimized tables.

**LISTING 3-10** Enable in-memory OLTP in a new database

```
CREATE DATABASE ExamBook762Ch3_IMOLTP
ON PRIMARY (
    NAME = ExamBook762Ch3_IMOLTP_data,
    FILENAME = 'C:\data\ExamBook762Ch3_IMOLTP.mdf', size=500MB
),
FILEGROUP ExamBook762Ch3_IMOLTP_FG CONTAINS MEMORY_OPTIMIZED_DATA (
    NAME = ExamBook762Ch3_IMOLTP_FG_Container,
    FILENAME = 'C:\data\ExamBook762Ch3_IMOLTP_FG_Container'
)
LOG ON (
    NAME = ExamBook762Ch3_IMOLTP_log,
    FILENAME = 'C:\data\ExamBook762Ch3_IMOLTP_log.ldf', size=500MB
);
GO
```

Now let's create the Examples schema, and then add one memory-optimized table and one disk-based table for comparison, as shown in Listing 3-11. Notice the addition of the MEMORY_OPTIMIZED = ON clause, which instructs the database engine to create a table dynamic link library (DLL) file and load the table into memory. The database engine also generates and compiles DML routines for accessing data in the table and saves the routines as DLLs, which are called when data manipulation is requested. Unless you specify otherwise, as we describe later in the "Durabiity options" section, a memory-optimized table is durable in which case it must have a primary key defined. Furthermore, it must also contain at least one index, which is satisfied below by the specification of NONCLUSTERED on the primary key column. We discuss indexing options in greater detail later in the "Indexes" section.

**LISTING 3-11** Create a new schema and add tables to the memory-optimized database

```
USE ExamBook762Ch3_IMOLTP;
GO
CREATE SCHEMA Examples;
GO
CREATE TABLE Examples.Order_Disk (
    OrderId INT NOT NULL PRIMARY KEY NONCLUSTERED,
    OrderDate DATETIME NOT NULL,
    CustomerCode NVARCHAR(10) NOT NULL
);
GO

CREATE TABLE Examples.Order_IM (
    OrderID INT NOT NULL PRIMARY KEY NONCLUSTERED,
    OrderDate DATETIME NOT NULL,
    CustomerCode NVARCHAR(10) NOT NULL
)
WITH (MEMORY_OPTIMIZED = ON);
GO
```

## Natively compiled stored procedures

The first optimization task to perform is to create a natively compile stored procedure. Natively compiled stored procedures are compiled at the time of creation, unlike interpreted stored procedures that compile at first execution. Furthermore, natively compiled stored procedures can access memory-optimized tables only. Native compilation translates the stored procedure code first into C code, and then into machine language, which enables the business logic to both execute and access data faster and more efficiently. The machine language version of the code is stored as a dynamic link library (DLL) in the default data directory for your SQL Server instance.

Many of the limitations that existed in SQL Server 2014 for natively compiled stored procedures have been removed. However, the following limitations still remain in SQL Server 2016:

- **tempdb access**   You cannot create or access temporary tables, table variables, or table-valued functions in tempdb. Instead, you can create a non-durable memory-optimized table (described later in this section) or memory-optimized table types or table variables.

***NEED MORE REVIEW?*** **MEMORY OPTIMIZATION OF TEMPORARY TABLES**

For more information about replacing temporary tables with memory-optimized objects, see "Faster temp table and table variable by using memory optimization" at *https://msdn.microsoft.com/en-us/library/mt718711.aspx*.

- **Cursors**   As an alternative, you can use set-based logic or a WHILE loop.
- **CASE statement**   To work around lack of support for the CASE statement, you can use a table variable to store the result set. The table variable includes a column to serve as a condition flag that you can then use as a filter.

***NOTE*** **WORKAROUND FOR A CASE STATEMENT IN A NATIVELY COMPILED STORED PROCEDURE**

You can see an example of code implementing a workaround for the conditional logic of a CASE statement in "Implementing a CASE Expression in a Natively Compiled Stored Procedure" at *https://msdn.microsoft.com/en-us/library/dn629453.aspx*.

- **MERGE statement**   You cannot use a memory-optimized table as the target of a MERGE statement. Therefore, you must use explicit INSERT, UPDATE, or DELETE statements instead.

- **SELECT INTO clause**   You cannot use an INTO clause with a SELECT statement. As an alternative, use INSERT INTO <table> SELECT syntax.

- **FROM clause**   You cannot use a FROM clause or subqueries in an UPDATE statement.

> *NOTE*  **WORKAROUND FOR A FROM CLAUSE IN A NATIVELY COMPILED STORED PROCEDURE.**
>
> As a workaround, you can use a memory-optimized type and a trigger as described in "Implementing UPDATE with FROM or Subqueries" at *https://msdn.microsoft.com/en-us/library/mt757375.aspx.*

- **PERCENT or WITH TIES in TOP clause**   There are no alternatives for using these options in a natively compiled stored procedure.

- **DISTINCT with aggregate functions**   There is no alternative for using this option in a natively compiled stored procedure.

- **Operators: INTERSECT, EXCEPT, APPLY, PIVOT, UNPIVOT, LIKE, CONTAINS**   There are no alternatives for using these operators in a natively compiled stored procedure.

- **Common table expressions (CTEs)**   You must rewrite your query to reproduce the functionality of a CTE in a natively compiled stored procedure.

- **Multi-row INSERT statements**   You must instead use separate INSERT statements in a natively compiled stored procedure.

- **EXECUTE WITH RECOMPILE**   There is no alternative for using this option in a natively compiled stored procedure.

- **View**   You cannot reference a view in a natively compiled stored procedure. You must define your desired SELECT statement explicitly in the procedure code.

> *NOTE*  **UNSUPPORTED T-SQL CONSTRUCTS FOR NATIVELY COMPILED STORED PROCEDURES**
>
> The list of limitations for natively compiled stored procedures highlights the main features that remain unsupported. You can find a complete list of constructs, features, operators, and so on for natively compiled stored procedures at "Transact-SQL Constructs Not Supported by In-Memory OLTP" at *https://msdn.microsoft.com/en-us/library/dn246937.aspx.*
>
> If you want to migrate an existing stored procedure to a natively compiled stored procedure, you can use the Stored Procedure Native Compilation Advisor in SQL Server Management Studio to evaluate whether your stored procedure contains elements that are not supported. You can learn more about this tool by reading "Native Compilation Advisor" at *https://msdn.microsoft.com/en-us/library/dn358355.aspx.*

To observe the performance difference between an interpreted stored procedure and a natively compiled stored procedure, create three stored procedures as shown in Listing 3-12. In this example, the following portions of the code are specific to native compilation:

- **WITH NATIVE_COMPILATION**  This clause is required to create a natively compiled stored procedure.
- **SCHEMABINDING**  This option is required to bind the natively compiled stored procedure to the object that it references. Consequently, you cannot drop tables referenced in the procedure code. Furthermore, you cannot use the wildcard (*) operator, and instead must reference column names explicitly in a SELECT statement.
- **BEGIN ATOMIC...END**  You use this option to create an atomic block, which is a block of T-SQL statements that succeed or fail together. A natively compiled stored procedure can have only one atomic block. Starting an atomic block creates a transaction if one does not yet exist or creates a savepoint if there is an existing transaction. An atomic block must include options defining the isolation level and language like this: WITH (TRANSACTION ISOLATION LEVEL = SNAPSHOT, LANGUAGE = N'English').

**LISTING 3-12** Create stored procedures to test execution performance

```
USE ExamBook762Ch3_IMOLTP;
GO

-- Create natively compiled stored procedure
CREATE PROCEDURE Examples.OrderInsert_NC
    @OrderID INT,
    @CustomerCode NVARCHAR(10)
WITH NATIVE_COMPILATION, SCHEMABINDING
AS
BEGIN ATOMIC
WITH (TRANSACTION ISOLATION LEVEL = SNAPSHOT, LANGUAGE = N'English')
    DECLARE @OrderDate DATETIME = getdate();
    INSERT INTO Examples.Order_IM (OrderId, OrderDate, CustomerCode)
    VALUES (@OrderID, @OrderDate, @CustomerCode);
END;
GO

-- Create interpreted stored procedure for Disk table
CREATE PROCEDURE Examples.OrderInsert_Interpreted_Disk
    @OrderID INT,
    @CustomerCode NVARCHAR(10)
AS
    DECLARE @OrderDate DATETIME = getdate();
    INSERT INTO Examples.Order_Disk (OrderId, OrderDate, CustomerCode)
    VALUES (@OrderID, @OrderDate, @CustomerCode);
        GO
-- Create interpreted stored procedure for In-Memory table
CREATE PROCEDURE Examples.OrderInsert_Interpreted_IM
    @OrderID INT,
    @CustomerCode NVARCHAR(10)
```

```
AS
    DECLARE @OrderDate DATETIME = getdate();
    INSERT INTO Examples.Order_IM (OrderId, OrderDate, CustomerCode)
    VALUES (@OrderID, @OrderDate, @CustomerCode);
        GO
```

Next, run the statements at least twice in Listing 3-13 to compare the performance of each type of stored procedure. Ignore the results from the first execution because the duration is skewed due to memory allocation and other operations that SQL Server performs one time only. The code in Listing 3-13 first inserts 100,000 rows into a disk-based table using an interpreted stored procedure and measures the time required to perform the INSERT operation. Then the code inserts rows into a memory-optimized table using the **corresponding** interpreted stored procedure and measures the processing time. Last, the code deletes rows from the memory-optimized table, resets the time measurement variables, and then inserts rows into the table by using a natively compiled stored procedure.

**LISTING 3-13** Execute each stored procedure to compare performance

```
SET STATISTICS TIME OFF;
SET NOCOUNT ON;

DECLARE @starttime DATETIME = sysdatetime();
DECLARE @timems INT;
DECLARE @i INT = 1;
DECLARE @rowcount INT = 100000;
DECLARE @CustomerCode NVARCHAR(10);

--Reset disk-based table
TRUNCATE TABLE Examples.Order_Disk;

-- Disk-based table and interpreted stored procedure
BEGIN TRAN;
    WHILE @i <= @rowcount
    BEGIN;
        SET @CustomerCode = 'cust' + CAST(@i as NVARCHAR(6));
        EXEC Examples.OrderInsert_Interpreted_Disk @i, @CustomerCode;
        SET @i += 1;
    END;
COMMIT;

SET @timems = datediff(ms, @starttime, sysdatetime());
SELECT 'Disk-based table and interpreted stored procedure: ' AS [Description],
    CAST(@timems AS NVARCHAR(10)) + ' ms' AS Duration;

-- Memory-based table and interpreted stored procedure
SET @i = 1;
SET @starttime = sysdatetime();

BEGIN TRAN;
    WHILE @i <= @rowcount
    BEGIN;
        SET @CustomerCode = 'cust' + CAST(@i AS NVARCHAR(6));
        EXEC Examples.OrderInsert_Interpreted_IM @i, @CustomerCode;
        SET @i += 1;
```

```
        END;
COMMIT;
SET @timems = datediff(ms, @starttime, sysdatetime());
SELECT 'Memory-optimized table and interpreted stored procedure: ' AS [Description],
    CAST(@timems AS NVARCHAR(10)) + ' ms' AS Duration;

-- Reset memory-optimized table
DELETE FROM Examples.Order_IM;
SET @i = 1;
SET @starttime = sysdatetime();

BEGIN TRAN;
    WHILE @i <= @rowcount
    BEGIN;
        SET @CustomerCode = 'cust' + CAST(@i AS NVARCHAR(6));
        EXEC Examples.OrderInsert_NC @i, @CustomerCode;
        SET @i += 1;
    END;
COMMIT;

SET @timems = datediff(ms, @starttime, sysdatetime());
SELECT 'Memory-optimized table and natively compiled stored procedure:'
    AS [Description],
    CAST(@timems AS NVARCHAR(10)) + ' ms' AS Duration;
GO
```

Your results vary from the results shown in the following example due to differences in hardware and memory configuration. However, your results should similarly reflect a variance in duration between the types of tables and stored procedures such that the memory-optimized table and natively compiled stored procedure performing inserts is considerably faster than the other two options:

```
Description                                                Duration
-------------------------------------------------- ---------
Disk-based table and interpreted stored procedure:  2882 ms

Description                                                Duration
------------------------------------------------------ ---------
Memory-optimized table and interpreted stored procedure:  2578 ms

Description                                                Duration
------------------------------------------------------------ ---------
Memory-optimized table and natively compiled stored procedure:  1969 ms
```

> **NEED MORE REVIEW?**   **NATIVELY-COMPILED USER-DEFINED FUNCTIONS AND INLINE TABLE-VALUED FUNCTIONS**
>
> You can also natively compile scalar user-defined functions (UDFs) and inline table-valued functions (TVFs) in SQL Server 2016 for more efficient data access. You can learn more by reviewing "Scalar User-Defined Functions for In-Memory OLTP" at *https://msdn.microsoft.com/en-us/library/dn935012.aspx*.

# Indexes

A memory-optimized table can have up to eight non-clustered indexes, all of which are covering indexes. That is, they include all columns in the table. Unlike a traditional B-tree index for a disk-based table, an index for a memory-optimized table exists only in memory and does not contain data. Instead, an index points to a row in memory and is recreated during database recovery. In addition, updates to an indexed memory-optimized table do not get logged.

An index for a memory-optimized table can be one of the following three types:

- **Hash** You use a nonclustered hash index when you have many queries that perform point lookups, also known as equi-joins. When you specify the index type, as shown below, you must include a bucket count. The bucket count value should be between one to two times the expected number of distinct values in the indexed column. It is better to have a bucket count that is too high rather than set it too low because it is more likely to retrieve data faster, although it consumes more memory.

```
CREATE TABLE Examples.Order_IM_Hash (
    OrderID INT NOT NULL PRIMARY KEY
        NONCLUSTERED HASH WITH (BUCKET_COUNT = 1000000),
    OrderDate DATETIME NOT NULL,
    CustomerCode NVARCHAR(5) NOT NULL
        INDEX ix_CustomerCode HASH WITH (BUCKET_COUNT = 1000000)
)
WITH (MEMORY_OPTIMIZED = ON);
```

- **Columnstore** A new feature in SQL Server 2016 is the ability to add a columnstore index to a memory-optimized table. This type of index, which we cover in greater detail in Chapter 1, "Design and implement database objects," is best when your queries perform large scans of a table because it can process data by using batch execution mode. Rather than read data row by row, it can process chunks of data in batches and thereby reduce query execution time and CPU utilization. Consider this type of index for single-threaded queries, sort operations (such as ORDER BY), and T-SQL window functions.

```
CREATE TABLE Examples.Order_IM_CCI (
    OrderID INT NOT NULL PRIMARY KEY NONCLUSTERED,
    OrderDate DATETIME NOT NULL,
    CustomerCode NVARCHAR(5) NOT NULL,
    INDEX ix_CustomerCode_cci CLUSTERED COLUMNSTORE)
WITH (MEMORY_OPTIMIZED = ON);
```

- **Nonclustered B-tree** You use a memory-optimized nonclustered B-tree index when your queries have an ORDER BY clause on an indexed column, or when your queries return a few records by performing range selections against an index column using the greater than (>) or less than (<) operators, or testing an indexed column for inequality. You also can consider using a nonclustered index in combination with a columnstore index when your queries perform point lookups or need to join together two fact tables in a data warehouse.

```
CREATE TABLE Examples.Order_IM_NC (
    OrderID INT NOT NULL PRIMARY KEY NONCLUSTERED,
    OrderDate DATETIME NOT NULL,
    CustomerCode NVARCHAR(5) NOT NULL INDEX ix_CustomerCode NONCLUSTERED
)
WITH (MEMORY_OPTIMIZED = ON);
```

A new feature in SQL Server 2016 is the ability to add or drop indexes, or change the bucket count for an index in a memory-optimized table. To do this, you use the ALTER TABLE statement only, as shown in Listing 3-14. The CREATE INDEX, DROP INDEX, and ALTER INDEX statements are invalid for memory-optimized tables.

**LISTING 3-14** Use the ALTER TABLE statement to add, modify, or drop an index

```
USE ExamBook762Ch3_IMOLTP;
GO
-- Add a column and an index
ALTER TABLE Examples.Order_IM
    ADD Quantity INT NULL,
    INDEX ix_OrderDate(OrderDate);
-- Alter an index by changing the bucket count
ALTER TABLE Examples.Order_IM_Hash
    ALTER INDEX ix_CustomerCode
        REBUILD WITH ( BUCKET_COUNT = 2000000);
-- Drop an index
ALTER TABLE Examples.Order_IM
    DROP INDEX ix_OrderDate;
```

## Offload analytics to readable secondary

The ability to use both columnstore and nonclustered indexes in memory-optimized tables makes it much easier to support both OLTP and analytics workloads in the same database. However, sometimes analytics queries require considerable CPU, IO, and memory resources that might have an adverse impact on OLTP performance. If you need to support both OLTP and analytics workloads, consider an Always On configuration to offload analytics workloads to a readable secondary.

## Durability options

When you create a memory-optimized table, you must decide how SQL Server should manage durability of the data. You can choose one of the following two types:

- **Durable**  With this type, SQL Server guarantees full durability just as if the table were disk-based. If you do not specify the durability option explicitly when you create a memory-optimized table, it is durable by default. To explicitly define a durable table, use the SCHEMA_AND_DATA durability option like this:

```
CREATE TABLE Examples.Order_IM_Durable (
    OrderID INT NOT NULL PRIMARY KEY NONCLUSTERED,
    OrderDate DATETIME NOT NULL,
    CustomerCode NVARCHAR(5) NOT NULL
)
```

```
WITH (MEMORY_OPTIMIZED = ON, DURABILITY=SCHEMA_AND_DATA);
GO
```

- **Non-durable**  By choosing this type of durability, you instruct SQL Server to persist only the table schema, but not the data. This option is most appropriate for use cases in which data is transient, such as an application's session state management, or ETL staging. SQL Server never writes a non-durable table's data changes to the transaction log. To define a non-durable table, use the SCHEMA_ONLY durability option like this:

```
CREATE TABLE Examples.Order_IM_Nondurable (
    OrderID INT NOT NULL PRIMARY KEY NONCLUSTERED,
    OrderDate DATETIME NOT NULL,
    CustomerCode NVARCHAR(5) NOT NULL
)
WITH (MEMORY_OPTIMIZED = ON, DURABILITY=SCHEMA_ONLY);
GO
```

Because non-durable memory-optimized tables do not incur logging overhead, transactions writing to them run faster than write operations on durable tables. However, to optimize performance of durable memory-optimized tables, configure delayed durability at the database or transaction level. Just as with disk-based tables, delayed durability for a memory-optimized table reduces the frequency with which SQL Server flushes log records to disk and enables SQL Server to commit transactions before writing log records to disk.

> *NOTE*  **DELAYED DURABILITY USAGE**
>
> Use delayed durability with care. You can lose some transactions if a system failure occurs.

If you set delayed durability at the database level, every transaction that commits on the database is delayed durable by default, although you can override this behavior at the transaction level. Similarly, if the database is durable, you can configure the database to allow delayed durable transactions and then explicit define a transaction as delayed durable. If you prefer, you can disable delayed durability and prevent delayed durable transactions entirely regardless of the transaction's commit level. You can also specify delayed durability for a natively compiled stored procedure. Listing 3-15 includes examples of these various settings.

**LISTING 3-15** Configure delayed durability

```
--Set at database level only, all transactions commit as delayed durable
ALTER DATABASE ExamBook762Ch3_IMOLTP
    SET DELAYED_DURABILITY = FORCED;
--Override database delayed durability at commit for durable transaction
BEGIN TRANSACTION;
    INSERT INTO Examples.Order_IM_Hash
    (OrderId, OrderDate, CustomerCode)
    VALUES (1, getdate(), 'cust1');
COMMIT TRANSACTION WITH (DELAYED_DURABILITY = OFF);
GO

--Set at transaction level only
```

```
ALTER DATABASE ExamBook762Ch3_IMOLTP
    SET DELAYED_DURABILITY = ALLOWED;
BEGIN TRANSACTION;
    INSERT INTO Examples.Order_IM_Hash
    (OrderId, OrderDate, CustomerCode)
    VALUES (2, getdate(), 'cust2');
COMMIT TRANSACTION WITH (DELAYED_DURABILITY = ON);

--Set within a natively compiled stored procedure
CREATE PROCEDURE Examples.OrderInsert_NC_DD
    @OrderID INT,
    @CustomerCode NVARCHAR(10)
WITH NATIVE_COMPILATION, SCHEMABINDING
AS
BEGIN ATOMIC
WITH (DELAYED_DURABILITY = ON,
        TRANSACTION ISOLATION LEVEL = SNAPSHOT, LANGUAGE = N'English')
    DECLARE @OrderDate DATETIME = getdate();
    INSERT INTO Examples.Order_IM (OrderId, OrderDate, CustomerCode)
    VALUES (@OrderID, @OrderDate, @CustomerCode);
END;
GO
--Disable delayed durability completely for all transactions
--    and natively compiled stored procedures
ALTER DATABASE ExamBook762Ch3_IMOLTP
    SET DELAYED_DURABILITY = DISABLED;
```

# Determine best case usage scenarios for natively compiled stored procedures

In SQL Server 2016, you can use natively compiled stored procedures to get better performance when operating on memory-optimized tables. You use them for:

- Applications for which obtaining the best possible performance is a requirement
- Queries that execute frequently
- Tasks that must perform as fast as possible

If you have a lot of rows to process and a lot of logic to apply, the natively compiled stored procedure performs faster than an interpreted stored procedure. It is also good when you need to perform any of the following tasks:

- Aggregation
- Nested loop join
- Multi-statement SELECT, INSERT, UPDATE, or DELETE operations
- Complex expressions
- Procedural logic, such as conditional statements and loops

It is not typically the best option when you need to process only a single row.

# Enable collection of execution statistics for natively compiled stored procedures

The goal of using memory-optimized tables is to execute processes as quickly as possible. Consequently, you could be surprised that some statistics, such as worker_time and elapsed_time, do not get collected by DMVs such as sys.dm_exec_query_stats and sys.dm_exec_procedure_stats. In fact, these DMVs include no information about natively compiled stored procedures.

Instead, you need to specifically enable the collection of execution statistics by using one of the following system stored procedures:

- **sys.sp_xtp_control_proc_exec_stats**   Use this system stored procedure to enable statistics collection for your SQL Server instance at the procedure level.

- **sys.sp_xtp_control_query_exec_stats**   Use this system stored procedure to enable statistics collection at the query level for selected natively compiled stored procedures.

> **NOTE   EXECUTION STATISTICS COLLECTION**
>
> Keep in mind that enabling the collection of execution statistics can have an adverse effect on the performance of natively compiled stored procedures. Rather than collect statistics globally for an instance, you should collect statistics for selected natively compiled stored procedures only to reduce this impact.

## sys.sp_xtp_control_proc_exec_stats

Use the sys.sp_xtp_control_proc_exec_stats system stored procedure to enable and disable procedure-level statistics collection on your SQL Server instance, as shown in Listing 3-16. When SQL Server or a database starts, statistics collection is automatically disabled. Note that you must be a member of the sysadmin role to execute this stored procedure.

**LISTING 3-16** Enable and disable statistics collection at the procedure level

```
--Enable statistics collection at the procedure level
EXEC sys.sp_xtp_control_proc_exec_stats @new_collection_value = 1;

--Check the current status of procedure-level statistics collection
DECLARE @c BIT;
EXEC sys.sp_xtp_control_proc_exec_stats @old_collection_value=@c output
SELECT @c AS 'Current collection status';

--Disable statistics collection at the procedure level
EXEC sys.sp_xtp_control_proc_exec_stats @new_collection_value = 0;
```

## sys.sp_xtp_control_query_exec_stats

Listing 3-17 shows an example of using the sys.sp_xtp_control_query_exec_stats system procedure to enable and disable query-level statistics collection. You can even use it to enable statistics collection for a specific natively compiled stored procedure, but it must have been executed at least once before you enable statistics collection. When SQL Server starts, query-level statistics collection is automatically disabled. Note that disabling statistics collection at the procedure level does not disable any statistics collection that you have configured at the query level. As with the previous system stored procedure, you must be a member of the sysadmin role to execute sys.sp_xtp_control_query_exec_stats.

**LISTING 3-17** Enable and disable statistics collection at the query level

```
--Enable statistics collection at the query level
EXEC sys.sp_xtp_control_query_exec_stats @new_collection_value = 1;

--Check the current status of query-level statistics collection
DECLARE @c BIT;
EXEC sys.sp_xtp_control_query_exec_stats @old_collection_value=@c output;
SELECT @c AS 'Current collection status';

--Disable statistics collection at the query level
EXEC sys.sp_xtp_control_query_exec_stats @new_collection_value = 0;

--Enable statistics collection at the query level for a specific
--natively compiled stored procedure
DECLARE @ncspid int;
DECLARE @dbid int;
SET @ncspid = OBJECT_ID(N'Examples.OrderInsert_NC');
SET @dbid = DB_ID(N'ExamBook762Ch3_IMOLTP')
EXEC [sys].[sp_xtp_control_query_exec_stats] @new_collection_value = 1,
    @database_id = @dbid, @xtp_object_id = @ncspid;

--Check the current status of query-level statistics collection for a specific
--natively compiled stored procedure
DECLARE @c bit;
DECLARE @ncspid int;
DECLARE @dbid int;
SET @ncspid = OBJECT_ID(N'Examples.OrderInsert_NC');
SET @dbid = DB_ID(N'ExamBook762Ch3_IMOLTP');
EXEC sp_xtp_control_query_exec_stats @database_id = @dbid,
    @xtp_object_id = @ncspid, @old_collection_value=@c output;
SELECT @c AS 'Current collection status';

--Disable statistics collection at the query level for a specific
--natively compiled stored procedure
DECLARE @ncspid int;
DECLARE @dbid int;
SET @ncspid = OBJECT_ID(N'Examples.OrderInsert_NC');
SET @dbid = DB_ID(N'ExamBook762Ch3_IMOLTP');
EXEC sys.sp_xtp_control_query_exec_stats @new_collection_value = 0,
    @database_id = @dbid, @xtp_object_id = @ncspid;
```

## Statistics collection queries

After enabling statistics collections at the procedure level, you can query the sys.dm_exec_procedure_stats DMV to review the results. Listing 3-19 illustrates an example query that filters for natively compiled stored procedures. This query returns results for the time during which statistics collection was enabled and remains available after you disable statistics collection at the procedure level.

> **IMPORTANT  RUN NATIVELY COMPILED STORED PROCEDURES BEFORE GETTING PROCEDURE-LEVEL STATISTICS**
>
> Be sure to execute the statements in Listing 3-13 after enabling statistics collection. Otherwise, the statement in Listing 3-18 will not return results.

**LISTING 3-18** Get procedure-level statistics

```
SELECT
    OBJECT_NAME(PS.object_id) AS obj_name,
    cached_time as cached_tm,
    last_execution_time as last_exec_tm,
    execution_count as ex_cnt,
    total_worker_time as wrkr_tm,
    total_elapsed_time as elpsd_tm
FROM sys.dm_exec_procedure_stats PS
INNER JOIN sys.all_sql_modules SM
    ON SM.object_id = PS.object_id
WHERE SM.uses_native_compilation = 1;
```

Here is an example of the results from the query in Listing 3-18:

```
obj_name        cached_tm               last_exec_tm            ex_cnt wrkr_tm  elpsd_tm
---------       ----------------------- ----------------------- ------ -------- --------
OrderInsert_NC 2016-10-15 20:44:33.917 2016-10-15 20:44:35.273 100000 376987   383365
```

You can also review the statistics collection at the query level by executing a query against the sys.dm_exec_query_stats DMV, as shown in Listing 3-19.

> **IMPORTANT  RUN NATIVELY COMPILED STORED PROCEDURES BEFORE GETTING QUERY-LEVEL STATISTICS**
>
> You must execute the statements in Listing 3-13 after enabling statistics collection to see results from executing the statement in Listing 3-19.

**LISTING 3-19** Get query-level statistics

```
SELECT
    st.objectid as obj_id,
    OBJECT_NAME(st.objectid) AS obj_nm,
    SUBSTRING(st.text,
        (QS.statement_start_offset / 2 ) + 1,
        ((QS.statement_end_offset - QS.statement_start_offset) / 2) + 1)
            AS 'Query',
```

```
    QS.last_execution_time as last_exec_tm,
    QS.execution_count as ex_cnt
FROM sys.dm_exec_query_stats QS
CROSS APPLY sys.dm_exec_sql_text(sql_handle) st
INNER JOIN sys.all_sql_modules SM
    ON SM.object_id = st.objectid
WHERE SM.uses_native_compilation = 1
```

The information available in the query results from Listing 3-19 is similar to the procedure-level statistics, but includes a row for each statement in the natively compiled stored procedure and includes the query text for each statement. Note that total_worker_time and total_elapsed_time were excluded from this example to restrict the width of the query results.

```
obj_id        obj_name        Query                   last_exec_tm            ex_cnt
-------       --------------  ----------------------  ----------------------  -------
981578535 OrderInsert_NC INSERT INTO             2016-10-15 21:09:25.877 100000
                          Examples.Order_IM
                          (OrderId, OrderDate,
                          CustomerCode)
                          VALUES (@OrderID,
                          @OrderDate,
                          @CustomerCode)
```

## Chapter summary

- Transaction management is the key to the SQL Server support of ACID. ACID properties determine whether a set of statements are handled individually or as an indivisible unit of work, whether a transaction violates database rules, whether one transaction can see the effects of other transactions, and whether a statement persists after an unexpected shutdown.

- SQL Server guarantees ACID by managing the effects of a transaction's success or failure through committing or rolling back a transaction, using a default isolation to prevent changes made by one transaction from impacting other transactions, and relying on a transaction log for durability.

- Implicit transactions start automatically for specific DML statements, but require an explicit COMMIT TRANSACTION or ROLLBACK TRANSACTION statement to end. Before using implicit transactions, you must enable the implicit transaction mode.

- Explicit transactions require a BEGIN TRANSACTION statement to start and a COMMIT TRANSACTION or ROLLBACK TRANSACTION to end. You should incorporate error handling and include logic to avoid nesting transactions for more complete control over transaction behavior.

- Savepoints allow you to partially rollback a transaction to a named location. Neither the SAVE TRANSACTION nor the ROLLBACK TRANSACTION statements have an effect on the @@TRANCOUNT variable (as long as the transaction rolls back to a specific savepoint rather than completely).

- A high concurrency database can suffer from data integrity issues when a process attempts to modify data while other simultaneous processes are trying to read or modify the data. Potential side effects include dirty reads, non-repeatable reads, phantom reads, and lost updates.

- SQL Server uses resource locks to enable high-concurrency while maintaining ACID properties for a transaction. SQL Server uses a lock hierarchy on resources to protect transactions and the types of locks that SQL Server can acquire on resources. SQL Server's response to a request for a new lock when a lock already exists depends on the compatibility between the requested and existing lock modes.

- SQL Server uses isolation levels to control the degree to which one transaction has visibility into the changes made by other transactions. Each of the following isolation levels has potential side effects on data integrity and on concurrency: READ COMMITTED, READ UNCOMMITTED, REPEATABLE READ, SERIALIZABLE, SNAPSHOT, and READ_COMMITTED_SNAPSHOT.

- You can change the isolation level at the session level by using the SET TRANSACTION ISOLATION LEVEL statement or at statement level by using a table hint to raise concurrency at the risk of introducing potential side effects.

- Because SQL Server acquires different types of locks for each isolation level, raising or lowering isolation levels have varying effects on transaction performance.

- The SNAPSHOT and READ_COMMITTED_SNAPSHOT isolation levels both create copies of data and require more CPU and memory than other isolation levels. In addition, they both require adequate space in tempdb, although of the two isolation levels, READ_COMMITTED_SNAPSHOT requires less space.

- Use the system DMVs sys.dm_tran_locks and sys.dm_os_wait_stats to find locked resources, understand why they are locked, and identify the lock mode acquired for the locked resources.

- SQL Server uses lock escalation to more effectively manage locks, but as a result can result in more blocking of transactions. Use the sys.dm_os_wait_stats DMV to monitor lock escalation events and look for ways to tune queries if performance begins to degrade due to more blocking issues.

- A deadlock graph provides you with insight into the objects involved in a deadlock and identifies the terminated process. You can capture a deadlock graph by using either SQL Server Profiler to later review deadlock events that have yet to occur or by using Extended Events to review deadlock events that have already occurred.

- Enclosing a transaction in a TRY/CATCH block to retry it is usually the best way to resolve a deadlock. Alternative methods have varying trade-offs and include using the SNAPSHOT or READ_COMMITTED_SNAPSHOT isolation levels, using the NOLOCK, HOLDLOCK, or UPDLOCK query hints, or adding a new covering nonclustered index.

- Memory-optimized tables are well-suited for specific OLTP scenarios: high data ingestion rate; high volume, high performance data reads; complex business logic in stored procedures; real-time data access; session state management; applications relying heavily on temporary tables, table variables, and table-valued parameters; and ETL operations.

- Besides implementing memory-optimized tables to improve an application's performance, you can also consider the following techniques to optimize performance even more: natively compiled stored procedures, the addition of indexes to the memory-optimized tables, the use of a readable secondary in an Always On configuration to which you can offload analytics workloads, non-durable tables, or delayed durability for transactions.

- Natively compiled stored procedures typically execute faster and are best suited for applications requiring high performance, queries that execute frequently, and tasks that must perform extremely fast. You experience better performance gains over an interpreted stored procedure when a natively compiled stored procedure must process many rows of data and apply complex logic.

- Use the system stored procedures sys.sp_xtp_control_proc_exec_stats and sys.sp_xtp_control_query_exec_stats to enable or disable the collection of execution statistics for natively compiled stored procedures at the procedure level or query level, respectively. After enabling statistics collection, use the sys.dm_exec_procedure_stats and sys.dm_exec_query_stats DMVs to review the statistics.

# Thought experiment

In this thought experiment, demonstrate your skills and knowledge of the topics covered in this chapter. You can find answers to this thought experiment in the next section.

You are a database administrator at Coho Winery. Your manager has asked you to troubleshoot and resolve a number of concurrency problems in the OLTP system running on SQL Server 2016. Your manager has presented you with the following issues that users of the system are experiencing:

1. Two users ran the same report within seconds of one another. When they meet to review the results, they notice that the totals in the reports do not match. One report has more detail rows than the other report. You examine the stored procedure code that produces the report.

```
SELECT
    so.OrderID,
    OrderDate,
    ExpectedDeliveryDate,
    CustomerID,
    CustomerPurchaseOrderNumber,
    StockItemID,
    Quantity,
    UnitPrice
FROM Sales.Orders so
    WITH (NOLOCK)
```

```
INNER JOIN Sales.OrderLines sol
    WITH (NOLOCK)
    ON so.OrderID = sol.OrderID
```

What step do you recommend to ensure greater consistency in the report and what are the ramifications of making this change?

2. Users are reporting a process to update the order system is running slowly right now. Which DMVs do you use to identify the blocking process and why?

3. A new application developer is asking for help diagnosing transaction behavior. The transaction in the following code never gets committed:

```
BEGIN TRANSACTION;
    UPDATE <do something>;
    BEGIN TRANSACTION;
        UPDATE <DO SOMETHING>;
        BEGIN TRANSACTION;
            UPDATE <DO SOMETHING>;
COMMIT TRANSACTION;
```

What recommendation can you give the developer to achieve the desired result and commit all update operations?

4. An internal application captures performance and logging data from thousands of devices through a web API. Seasonally, the incoming rate of data shifts from 3,000 transactions/sec to 30,000 transactions/sec and overwhelms the database. What implementation strategy do you recommend?

5. Which indexing strategy should be used for a memory-optimized table for which the common query pattern is shown below?

```
SELECT CustomerName FROM Customer
WHERE StartDate > DateAdd(day, -7, GetUtcDate());
```

# Thought experiment answers

This section contains the solutions to the thought experiment. Each answer explains the resolution to each of the issues identified in the OLTP system.

1. The use of the NOLOCK table hint is common in reporting applications against OLTP systems in which lack of consistency is a trade-off for faster query performance. However, when users are dissatisfied with inconsistent results, you can recommend removing this table hint and allow the default isolation in SQL Server to manage transaction isolation. Long write operations can block the report from executing. Similarly, if the report takes a long time to execute, the read operation can block write operations.

2. Start with a query that returns sys.dm_os_waiting_tasks where blocking_session_id <> 0 and session_id equals the ID for the user's session to see if anything is blocking the user's request. The following columns will give you details about the blocking situation: blocking_session_id, wait_type, and wait_duration_ms. You can join this information

to sys.dm_tran_locks to discover the current locks involved by including the request_ mode and resource_type columns. The request_status column provides information about the locks. A value of CONVERT in this column is an indicator that a request is blocked. You can also use the value in the resource_associated_entity_id column to find the associated object's name in sys.partitions.

3. In explicit transaction mode with nested transactions, each BEGIN TRANSACTION must correspond to a COMMIT TRANSACTION. As each new transaction starts with BEGIN TRANSACTION, the @@TRANCOUNT variable increments by 1 and each COMMIT TRANSACTION decrements it by 1. The complete transaction does not get written to disk and committed completely until @@TRANCOUNT is 0.

   While this solution is correct, a better solution is not to use nested transactions.

4. For this type of scenario, you recommend migrating the application to memory-optimized tables. The use of memory-optimized tables is well-suited for the ingestion of high-volume inserts because it prevents the bottlenecks commonly resulting from locking and eliminates logging. Consequently, the throughput rate (number of rows loaded per second) can substantially increase.

5. You should recommend a nonclustered B-tree index for this query pattern. It works best for range selections in contrast to a hash index which works best for point lookups or a columnstore index which works best for large table scans.

# Optimize database objects and SQL infrastructure

In the previous chapter, we considered how to optimize database performance by managing concurrency. Database optimization also requires you not only to understand how SQL Server runs queries efficiently and uses its resources effectively, but also how to recognize problems that prevent it from doing so. Given this, you must know how to use the tools that help you find those problems and the steps that you can take to tune the SQL Server infrastructure for better performance.

Often the first step you take to improve your SQL Server query performance is to add indexes to tables, as we described in Chapter 1, "Design and implement database objects." In Skill 4.1, we review the tasks you should perform periodically to ensure that the indexes you have are in fact helpful, and also to identify and resolve index issues. We then delve deeper into query performance optimization by exploring how to capture and analyze query plans in Skill 4.2. Then we shift our attention to the SQL Server infrastructure in Skill 4.3 to consider its impact on performance and understand how to use built-in tools to manage and troubleshoot the database engine's use of resources. We close the chapter with Skill 4.4 in which we review the tools at your disposal for ongoing monitoring of your database infrastructure so that you are able to recognize when performance begins to deviate from normal and can take proactive action to keep SQL Server running at its best.

## Skills in this chapter:

- Optimize statistics and indexes
- Analyze and troubleshoot query plans
- Manage performance for database instances
- Monitor and trace SQL Server baseline performance metrics

# Skill 4.1: Optimize statistics and indexes

One way to significantly improve the performance of queries is to add one or more indexes to a table. When you create an index, SQL Server creates *statistics*, a database object in which statistical information about the distribution of values in a column or index is stored. An index improves query performance only if it is up-to-date and selected by SQL Server to resolve queries. Therefore, you should periodically review and optimize indexes as part of your regular routine.

> **This section covers how to:**
> - Determine the accuracy of statistics and associated impact to query plans and performance
> - Design statistics maintenance tasks
> - Use dynamic management objects to review current index usage and identify missing indexes
> - Consolidate overlapping indexes

## Determine the accuracy of statistics and the associated impact to query plans and performance

SQL Server uses statistics to determine a column's *cardinality*, which is the number of rows containing a specific value in a column. For example, when a value is unique in a column, such as a primary key, the cardinality is 1. When a column is highly unique like this, it is commonly characterized as having high selectivity or high cardinality. Conversely, when the number of unique values in a column are fewer or non-existent, the column has low selectivity and low cardinality. This information influences the query optimizer's selection of an appropriate index as well as an efficient query plan. If the wrong index or query plan is selected, or if an index is missing, a query might not execute as optimally as possible. Therefore, the accuracy of the statistics is critical to query performance.

There are several ways that you can manage statistics. First, you can review the current statistics to determine whether the distribution of the data and the cardinality of data accessed by an index is likely to be helpful. In addition, you can control whether SQL Server updates statistics automatically. Last, you can check which objects have statistics managed by SQL Server and when they were last updated.

### Review data distribution and cardinality

To see statistics for a table, use the DBCC SHOW_STATISTICS command to return the following information:

- Metadata about the statistics including date and time of the last update of the statistics, number of rows in the table, number of rows sampled, number of steps in the histogram, index density, average key length, whether the index contains string summary statistics, filtered predicate for statistics if applicable, and number of rows before applying the filter.

- Index densities for the combination of columns in the index.

- A histogram of up to 200 sample values in the first key column in the index.

Let's create a simple index for the Purchasing.Suppliers table in the WideWorldImporters database and view its statistics, as shown in Listing 4-1, to explore the output of the DBCC SHOW_STATISTICS command.

**LISTING 4-1** Create an index and show its statistics

```
USE WideWorldImporters;
GO
CREATE NONCLUSTERED INDEX IX_Purchasing_Suppliers_ExamBook762Ch4
    ON Purchasing.Suppliers
(
    SupplierCategoryID,
    SupplierID
)
INCLUDE (SupplierName);
GO

DBCC SHOW_STATISTICS ('Purchasing.Suppliers',
    IX_Purchasing_Suppliers_ExamBook762Ch4 );

/* Output
Name              Updated        Rows     Rows Sampled    Steps  Density
Average key length   String Index    Filter Expression Unfiltered Rows
----------------------------- --------------------- ---- -------------
IX_Purchasing_Suppliers_ExamBook762Ch4 Nov  7 2016  6:40AM 13  13  5    1
8                 NO                   NULL                  13
(1 row(s) affected)


All density        Average Length Columns
-----------------  ----------- -------------------------------------------
0.125                   4                          SupplierCategoryID
0.07692308      8                      SupplierCategoryID, SupplierID
(2 row(s) affected)


RANGE_HI_KEY  RANGE_ROWS  EQ_ROWS   DISTINCT_RANGE_ROWS  AVG_RANGE_ROWS
------------------- --------------------- ---------------- ----------------
2                 0              6                 0                  1
4                 1              1                 1                  1
6                 1              1                 1                  1
8                 1              1                 1                  1
9                 0              1                 0                  1
(5 row(s) affected)
DBCC execution completed. If DBCC printed error messages, contact your system
administrator.
 */
```

The first result set is the statistics header that shows the name of the object for which statistics exist. In this case, the object is the IX_Purchasing_Suppliers_ExamBook762Ch4 index. You can see when the statistics were last updated, the number of rows in the index, the number of rows sampled for the statistics calculations, and the number of rows in the table without a filter. You also see a value for density in the statistics header. However, this density calculation is no longer used by the query optimizer in SQL Server 2016. Last, the average key length is 8 bytes, there are no string summary statistics, and no filter applied.

The second result set shows the densities of each combination of columns in the index. Density is calculated by dividing one by the count of distinct values in the column (or columns when you have a compound key). In Listing 4-1, the first row with SupplierCategoryID has higher density than the second row with SupplierCategoryID, SupplierID which means it has lower selectivity and is less helpful as an index. Conversely, the lower density of the second row indicates higher selectivity.

The last result set is the statistics histogram, which contains up to 200 sample values for the first column of the index. Each sample value is called a step and is listed in the RANGE_HI_KEY column. In Listing 4-1, there are only 5 sample values: 2, 4, 6, 8, and 9. For each step, SQL Server stores the following four values:

- **RANGE_ROWS**  The number of rows inside the range between the current step and the previous step, but does not include the step values themselves.
- **EQ_ROWS**  The number of rows having the same value as the sample value.
- **DISTINCT_RANGE_ROWS**  The number of distinct values between the current step and the previous step, but does not include the step values themselves.
- **AVG_RANGE_ROWS**  The average number of rows for each distinct value with the step range.

> *NOTE*  **DBCC SHOW_STATISTICS**
>
> For more details about the DBCC SHOW_STATISTICS output, see *https://msdn.microsoft.com/en-us/library/ms174384.aspx*.

When creating an estimated query plan (described in more detail in Skill 4.2), SQL Server looks at the histogram to estimate the number of rows that match a WHERE clause in a query as long as the condition in the clause is a single constant expression, such as WHERE SupplierCategoryID = 3. When the expression uses two columns, as in WHERE SupplierCategoryID = 3 AND SupplierID = 10, SQL Server uses the index densities to estimate rows.

Let's look at an example of how inaccurate statistics can affect a query plan. First, create a test database with automatic statistics updates disabled, load the table, add an index, and then review the statistics, as shown in Listing 4- 2.

LISTING 4-2 Create test environment with automatic statistics disabled

```
CREATE DATABASE ExamBook762Ch4_Statistics;
GO
ALTER DATABASE ExamBook762Ch4_Statistics
    SET  AUTO_CREATE_STATISTICS OFF;
ALTER DATABASE ExamBook762Ch4_Statistics
    SET AUTO_UPDATE_STATISTICS OFF;
ALTER DATABASE ExamBook762Ch4_Statistics
    SET AUTO_UPDATE_STATISTICS_ASYNC OFF;
GO
USE ExamBook762Ch4_Statistics;
GO
CREATE SCHEMA Examples;
GO
CREATE TABLE Examples.OrderLines (
    OrderLineID int NOT NULL,
    OrderID int NOT NULL,
    StockItemID int NOT NULL,
    Description nvarchar(100) NOT NULL,
    PackageTypeID int NOT NULL,
    Quantity int NOT NULL,
    UnitPrice decimal(18, 2) NULL,
    TaxRate decimal(18, 3) NOT NULL,
    PickedQuantity int NOT NULL,
    PickingCompletedWhen datetime2(7) NULL,
    LastEditedBy int NOT NULL,
    LastEditedWhen datetime2(7) NOT NULL);
GO
INSERT INTO Examples.OrderLines
SELECT *
FROM WideWorldImporters.Sales.OrderLines;
GO
CREATE INDEX ix_OrderLines_StockItemID
    ON Examples.OrderLines (StockItemID);
GO
DBCC SHOW_STATISTICS ('Examples.OrderLines',
    ix_OrderLines_StockItemID );
GO


/* Partial Output
RANGE_HI_KEY  RANGE_ROWS  EQ_ROWS  DISTINCT_RANGE_ROWS  AVG_RANGE_ROWS
------------------ --------------- ----------- ------------------------ ---
1                0            1048                0                 1
2                0            1078                0                 1
4             1022           1066                1              1022
*/
```

When the index is added to the table, its statistics are also created. However, a significant number of inserts or updates to the table can render these statistics obsolete. Execute the statements in Listing 4-3 to update rows and check the statistics afterwards to confirm there has been no change.

LISTING 4-3 Update table rows and check statistics

```
UPDATE Examples.OrderLines
    SET StockItemID = 1
    WHERE OrderLineID < 45000;
DBCC SHOW_STATISTICS ('Examples.OrderLines',
    ix_OrderLines_StockItemID );
GO
/* Partial Output
RANGE_HI_KEY  RANGE_ROWS  EQ_ROWS  DISTINCT_RANGE_ROWS  AVG_RANGE_ROWS
------------  ----------  -------  -------------------  --------------
1                     0      1048                    0               1
2                     0      1078                    0               1
4                  1022      1066                    1            1022
*/
```

Next, click the Include Actual Execution Plan button in the toolbar, and then execute the following query:

```
SELECT StockItemID

FROM Examples.OrderLines

WHERE StockItemID = 1;
```

When you hover the cursor over the Index Seek (NonClustered) in the query plan, notice the difference between Actual Number Of Rows and Estimated Number Of Rows in the tooltip, shown in Figure 4-1. Because the statistics are out-of-date, the estimated row count is 1048, which is the value currently in the histogram for rows having StockItemID = 1. Because this value is relatively low, the query optimizer generated a plan using an index seek, which could be less optimal than performing a scan when data volumes are high.

**Index Seek (NonClustered)**
Scan a particular range of rows from a nonclustered index.

| | |
|---|---|
| Physical Operation | Index Seek |
| Logical Operation | Index Seek |
| Actual Execution Mode | Row |
| Estimated Execution Mode | Row |
| Storage | RowStore |
| Number of Rows Read | 45848 |
| Actual Number of Rows | 45848 |
| Actual Number of Batches | 0 |
| Estimated I/O Cost | 0.0048197 |
| Estimated Operator Cost | 0.0061295 (100%) |
| Estimated Subtree Cost | 0.0061295 |
| Estimated CPU Cost | 0.0013098 |
| Number of Executions | 1 |
| Estimated Number of Executions | 1 |
| Estimated Number of Rows | 1048 |

FIGURE 4-1 Variance between estimated and actual rows in query plan

# Review automatic statistics updates

Statistics are generated when you add an index to a table that contains data or when you run the UPDATE STATISTICS command. In most cases, as illustrated by the previous example, you should allow SQL Server to create and update statistics automatically by setting one of the following database options - The first and third of which are enabled by default:

- **AUTO_UPDATE_STATISTICS**  SQL Server updates statistics automatically as needed. It determines an update is necessary by using a counter on modifications to column values. This counter is incremented when a row is inserted or deleted or when an indexed column is updated. The counter is reset to 0 when the statistics are generated. When it does this, it acquires compile locks and query plans might require recompilation. You can disable this option by using the sp_autostats system stored procedure.

- **AUTO_UPDATE_STATISTICS_ASYNC**  When it is enabled, SQL Server updates statistics asynchronously. That is, SQL Server uses a background thread so as not to block query execution. In this case, the query optimizer might choose a less than optimal query execution plan until the statistics are updated. Use the ALTER DATABASE T-SQL command to disable this option.

- **AUTO_CREATE_STATISTICS**  During query execution, SQL Server creates statistics on individual columns in query predicates to help the query optimizer improve query plans. Use the ALTER DATABASE T-SQL command to disable this option.

Even when statistics are set to update automatically, SQL Server does not update statistics unless one of the following thresholds is met:

- One or more rows is added to an empty table.

- More than 500 rows are added to a table having fewer than 500 rows.

- More than 500 rows are added to a table having more than 500 rows and the number of rows added is more than a dynamic percentage of total rows. With a small table under 25,000 rows, this percentage is around 20 percent. As the number of rows in the table increases, the percentage rate that triggers a statistics update is lower. For example, SQL Server updates statistics for a table with 1 billion rows when more than 1 million changes occur, or 0.1 percent. Prior to SQL Server 2016, this threshold was fixed at 20 percent of the original total number of rows in the table which means that 200 million rows were required to trigger an update of statistics.

You can check to see if SQL Server automatically created statistics in a database by checking the value of the auto_created column in the sys.stats catalog view, as shown in Listing 4-4.

LISTING 4-4 Check auto-created statistics in a database

```
Use WideWorldImporters;
GO
SELECT
    OBJECT_NAME(object_id) AS ObjectName,
    name,
    auto_created
FROM sys.stats
WHERE auto_created = 1 AND
    object_id IN
        (SELECT object_id FROM sys.objects WHERE type = 'U');

/* Partial Output
ObjectName                         name                  auto_created
-------------------------------------------    ---------------------
Colors_Archive                     _WA_Sys_00000001_04E4BC85  1
OrderLines                         _WA_Sys_00000006_05A3D694  1
OrderLines                         _WA_Sys_0000000C_05A3D694  1
plan_persist_runtime_stats         _WA_Sys_00000006_0CBAE877  1
StockGroups_Archive                _WA_Sys_00000001_10566F31  1
StateProvinces                     _WA_Sys_00000002_114A936A  1
StateProvinces                     _WA_Sys_00000009_114A936A  1
CustomerTransactions               _WA_Sys_0000000B_15DA3E5D  1
*/
```

To check the last time the statistics were updated for each statistics object in a table, you can use the STATS_DATE system function as shown in Listing 4-5. As an alternative, you can use the sys.dm_db_stats_properties DMV to get row counts and modifications occurring since the last statistics update in addition to the last update date.

**LISTING 4-5** Check last update of statistics for an object

```
SELECT
    name AS ObjectName,
    STATS_DATE(object_id, stats_id) AS UpdateDate
FROM sys.stats
WHERE object_id = OBJECT_ID('Sales.Customers');

/* Output
ObjectName                                     UpdateDate
------------------------------------    ----------------------------------------
PK_Sales_Customers                             2016-06-02 10:07:35.170
UQ_Sales_Customers_CustomerName                2016-06-02 10:07:35.240
FK_Sales_Customers_CustomerCategoryID          2016-06-02 10:08:13.080
FK_Sales_Customers_BuyingGroupID               2016-06-02 10:07:38.010
FK_Sales_Customers_PrimaryContactPersonID      2016-06-02 10:07:43.027
FK_Sales_Customers_AlternateContactPersonID    2016-06-02 10:07:48.040
FK_Sales_Customers_DeliveryMethodID            2016-06-02 10:07:53.043
FK_Sales_Customers_DeliveryCityID              2016-06-02 10:07:58.060
FK_Sales_Customers_PostalCityID                2016-06-02 10:08:03.060
IX_Sales_Customers_Perf_20160301_06            2016-06-02 10:08:08.067
_WA_Sys_00000003_2FCF1A8A                      2016-06-02 10:10:11.130
_WA_Sys_0000000B_2FCF1A8A                      2016-06-02 10:10:11.623
_WA_Sys_0000001E_2FCF1A8A                      2016-06-02 10:54:31.173
*/
```

# Design statistics maintenance tasks

SQL Server creates and updates statistics automatically for all indexes and for columns used in a WHERE or JOIN ON clause. At one extreme, the automatic statistics update process might run when the database is busy and adversely affects performance or, at the other extreme, it might not run frequently enough for a table that is subject to high-volume data changes. For these situations, you can disable the automatic statistics update options for the database and then implement a maintenance plan to update statistics on demand or on a schedule.

> **NOTE  ENABLING SQL SERVER AGENT EXTENDED STORED PROCEDURES**
>
> Before you can create a maintenance plan, you must enable SQL Server Agent extended stored procedures. You can do this by starting the SQL Server Agent service in SQL Server Management Studio or by executing the following code:

```
EXEC sp_configure 'show advanced options', 1;
GO
RECONFIGURE;
GO
EXEC sp_configure 'Agent XPs', 1;
GO
RECONFIGURE;
GO
```

To create a maintenance plan, open SQL Server Management Studio. and then, in Object Explorer, expand the Management node, right click the Maintenance Plans folder, and then select either New Maintenance Plan or Maintenance Plan Wizard. If you select New Maintenance Plan, type a name for the maintenance plan. Then drag the Update Statistics Task from the Toolbox to the plan designer surface, as shown in Figure 4-2.

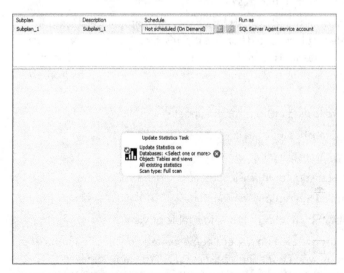

**FIGURE 4-2** The Update Statistics Task in the maintenance plan designer

Double click the task to open the Update Statistics Task dialog box, shown in Figure 4-3.

**FIGURE 4-3** The Update Statistics Task dialog box

In the Databases drop-down list, you can select one of the following options:

- **All Databases**   All SQL Server databases, except tempdb.
- **System Databases**   All SQL Server system databases, except tempdb.
- **All User Databases** (Excluding Master, Model, Msdb, Tempdb)   All user databases and none of the SQL Server system databases.
- **These Databases**   A list of user and SQL Server system databases (except tempdb) from which you must select at least one database. If you select this option, you must also specify whether to update statistics for tables, views, or both tables and views. If you select Tables or Views, you must also select one or more tables or views from the respective list.

Then you specify one of the following options for the update:

- **All Existing Statistics**   Statistics for both columns and indexes.
- **Column Statistics Only**   Statistics for columns only.
- **Index Statistics Only**   Statistics for indexes only.

Last, you select one of the following options for scan type:

- **Full Scan**   Update statistics by reading all rows in a table or view.
- **Sample By**   Update statistics based on a specified percentage or specified number of rows. This is a better option when updating statistics for a large table or view.

You can click the View T-SQL button at the bottom of the Update Statistics Task dialog box to generate the T-SQL script for the new maintenance task. Then you can use this script as a template to create additional maintenance plans for updating statistics. Listing 4-6 shows a portion of the script generated for the WideWorldImporters database:

**LISTING 4-6** Script to update statistics for a specific table

```
USE WideWorldImporters;
GO
UPDATE STATISTICS [Application].[Cities]
WITH FULLSCAN
GO
```

> **NOTE  UPDATE STATISTICS OPTIONS**
>
> You can add any of the following options when using the UPDATE STATISTICS statement.
>
> - **No FULLSCAN or SAMPLE option**  If you omit the FULLSCAN or SAMPLE option, SQL Server calculates statistics by computing an appropriate sample size and performing a sample scan.
> - **FULLSCAN**  SQL Server performs a full scan of the table data or the index to generate more accurate statistics, although this option takes more time and more IO.
> - **SAMPLE**  With this option, you specify the number or percentage of rows that SQL Server samples when generating the statistics.
> - **RESAMPLE**  SQL Server generates the statistics using the same sampling ratio that was defined during the previous statistics generation.

The maintenance task should be scheduled at a time that interferes least with regular database operations. On the Maintenance Plan designer, click the Subplan Schedule button to open the New Job Schedule dialog box. Here you can specify whether the maintenance plan is a recurring schedule, whether it runs only when SQL Server starts or when the CPU is idle, or one time only. If you choose the Recurring option, you specify a frequency, and a start and optional end date. If you instead choose the One Time option, you specify the date and time to execute the maintenance plan. When you save the schedule, a SQL Server Agent job is created and the job executes as a SQL Server Integration Services (SSIS) package.

You can also execute a maintenance plan without waiting for the scheduled SQL Server Agent job. To do this, expand the Management node, expand the Maintenance Plan node, right click the maintenance plan, and then select Execute. When you use this method, the SSIS package is launched and you can observe the execution status in the Execute Maintenance Plan dialog box.

# Use dynamic management objects to review current index usage and identify missing indexes

SQL Server uses indexes to speed up data access. In Chapter 1, we covered many of the considerations affecting the design of tables. Over time, you might find that some indexes are not as helpful as expected due to changes in the distribution of the data or in the query patterns. Furthermore, the existence of an index that SQL Server never uses adds overhead to write operations. Therefore, it's important to periodically review indexes not only to determine whether existing indexes are still useful, but also whether any are ignored or missing.

In this section, we review several dynamic management objects (DMOs) that are useful for this review process. We focus on how to perform specific review tasks that are important for index management without delving into all the possible information that you can derive from using these DMOs.

> **NEED MORE REVIEW?  RESOURCES FOR MANAGING INDEXES WITH DMOS**
>
> You can find more detail about each DMO by accessing the respective topic in Books Online. For deeper coverage of index management by using DMOs, download the free ebook "Performance Tuning with Dynamic Management Views" by Tim Ford and Louis Davidson available at *https://www.simple-talk.com/books/sql-books/performance-tuning-with-sql-server-dynamic-management-views---ebook-download.*

## Review current index usage

The following DMOs provide information about whether and how indexes are used:

- **sys.dm_db_index_usage_stats**   Use this DMV to review the use of indexes to resolve queries.
- **sys.dm_db_index_physical_stats**   Use this dynamic management function (DMF) to check the overall status of indexes in a database.

### SYS.DM_DB_INDEX_USAGE_STATS

To get a quick overview of which indexes are being used, you can use the sys.dm_db_index_usage_stats DMV as shown in Listing 4-7. To appear in this DMV's output, an index must be read or written to at least once by a user or system operation. In this example, the count of user seeks, scans, and lookups are aggregated as user_reads and sorted in descending order to make it clear which indexes are used more frequently than others. Counts in this DMV are reset when the server restarts or when an index is dropped and recreated.

LISTING 4-7 Review current index usage

```
SELECT
    OBJECT_NAME(ixu.object_id, DB_ID('WideWorldImporters')) AS [object_name] ,
    ix.[name] AS index_name ,
    ixu.user_seeks + ixu.user_scans + ixu.user_lookups AS user_reads,
    ixu.user_updates AS user_writes
FROM sys.dm_db_index_usage_stats ixu
INNER JOIN WideWorldImporters.sys.indexes ix ON
    ixu.[object_id] = ix.[object_id] AND
    ixu.index_id = ix.index_id
WHERE ixu.database_id = DB_ID('WideWorldImporters')
ORDER BY user_reads DESC;
/*Partial Output
object_name                       index_name                        user_reads user_writes
------------------------------    -----------------------------     ---------- -----------
StockGroups                       PK_Warehouse_StockGroups          19              0
Suppliers                         PK_Purchasing_Suppliers           13              0
ColdRoomTemperatures_Archive      ix_ColdRoomTemperatures_Archive   0               1959
StockItems                        FK_Warehouse_StockItems_SupplierID 0              0
*/
```

Just as important as knowing which indexes are being accessed is knowing which indexes are never used. To find these indexes, you must start by retrieving all tables and indexes in a database and then filter out those appearing in sys.dm_db_index_usage_stats as shown in Listing 4-8.

LISTING 4-8 Find unused indexes

```
USE WideWorldImporters;
GO
SELECT
    OBJECT_NAME(ix.object_id) AS ObjectName ,
    ix.name
FROM sys.indexes AS ix
INNER JOIN sys.objects AS o ON
    ix.object_id = o.object_id
WHERE ix.index_id NOT IN (
    SELECT ixu.index_id
    FROM sys.dm_db_index_usage_stats AS ixu
    WHERE
        ixu.object_id = ix.object_id AND
        ixu.index_id = ix.index_id AND
        database_id = DB_ID()
) AND
    o.[type] = 'U'
ORDER BY OBJECT_NAME(ix.object_id) ASC ;

/* Partial Output
ObjectName                      name
-----------------------------   -----------------------------------------------------
BuyingGroups                    UQ_Sales_BuyingGroups_BuyingGroupName
BuyingGroups_Archive            ix_BuyingGroups_Archive
Cities_Archive                  ix_Cities_Archive
ColdRoomTemperatures            NULL
ColdRoomTemperatures            PK_Warehouse_ColdRoomTemperatures
ColdRoomTemperatures            IX_Warehouse_ColdRoomTemperatures_ColdRoomSensorNumber
*/
```

Whereas the previous example helps you find indexes for which there is no read or write activity, Listing 4-9 helps you find indexes that SQL Server maintains but never uses to retrieve data for a query. These indexes are consuming resources without helping query performance. You should consider dropping these indexes if further investigation reveals that there is no need to continue to maintain them.

**LISTING 4-9** Find indexes that are updated but never used

```
USE WideWorldImporters;
GO
SELECT
    o.name AS ObjectName ,
    ix.name AS IndexName ,
    ixu.user_seeks + ixu.user_scans + ixu.user_lookups AS user_reads ,
    ixu.user_updates AS user_writes ,
    SUM(p.rows) AS total_rows
FROM sys.dm_db_index_usage_stats ixu
INNER JOIN sys.indexes ix ON
    ixu.object_id = ix.object_id AND
    ixu.index_id = ix.index_id
INNER JOIN sys.partitions p ON
    ixu.object_id = p.object_id AND
    ixu.index_id = p.index_id
INNER JOIN sys.objects o ON
    ixu.object_id = o.object_id
WHERE
    ixu.database_id = DB_ID() AND
    OBJECTPROPERTY(ixu.object_id, 'IsUserTable') = 1 AND
    ixu.index_id > 0
GROUP BY
    o.name ,
    ix.name ,
    ixu.user_seeks + ixu.user_scans + ixu.user_lookups ,
    ixu.user_updates
HAVING ixu.user_seeks + ixu.user_scans + ixu.user_lookups = 0
ORDER BY
    ixu.user_updates DESC,
    o.name ,
    ix.name ;


/* Output
ObjectName                 IndexName       user_reads  user_writes  total_rows
-------------------------  --------------- ----------- ------------ ------------------
ColdRoomTemperatures_Archive ix_ColdRoomTemperatures_Archive  0   2016  3654736
StockItems                 FK_Warehouse_StockItems_SupplierID 0   0     227
*/
```

## SYS.DM_DB_INDEX_PHYSICAL_STATS

In addition to reviewing usage of indexes, you should also review index health by using the sys.dm_db_index_physical_stats DMF. As inserts, updates, and deletes occur, an index becomes increasingly fragmented and IO increases as data is no longer efficiently stored on disk. Listing 4-10 shows how to review fragmentation. In general, you should focus on indexes for which fragmentation is greater than 15percent and the page count is greater than 500. When fragmentation is between 15 percent and 30 percent, you should reorganize the index, and when its greater, you should rebuild it.

**LISTING 4-10** Review index fragmentation

```
DECLARE  @db_id SMALLINT, @object_id INT;
SET @db_id = DB_ID(N'WideWorldImporters');
SET @object_id = OBJECT_ID(N'WideWorldImporters.Sales.Orders');
SELECT
    ixs.index_id AS idx_id,
    ix.name AS ObjectName,
    index_type_desc,
    page_count,
    avg_page_space_used_in_percent AS AvgPageSpacePct,
    fragment_count AS frag_ct,
    avg_fragmentation_in_percent AS AvgFragPct
FROM sys.dm_db_index_physical_stats
    (@db_id, @object_id, NULL, NULL , 'Detailed') ixs
INNER JOIN sys.indexes ix ON
    ixs.index_id = ix.index_id AND
    ixs.object_id = ix.object_id
ORDER BY avg_fragmentation_in_percent DESC;

/* Output
idx_id ObjectName    index_type_desc      pg_ct AvgPageSpacePct    frag_ct  AvgFragPct
-------- ------------------------------------ ---------- ---------------------------

4 FK_Sales_Orders_PickedByPersonID  NONCLUSTERED INDEX  237  53.6864838151717 237
                                                              99.57805907173
2 FK_Sales_Orders_CustomerID        NONCLUSTERED INDEX  189 67.3274277242402 189
                                                              97.8835978835979
5 FK_Sales_Orders_ContactPersonID   NONCLUSTERED INDEX  189 67.3274277242402 189
                                                              97.8835978835979
3 FK_Sales_Orders_SalespersonPersonID NONCLUSTERED INDEX 136 93.5749444032617 136
                                                              97.0588235294118
1 PK_Sales_Orders                   CLUSTERED INDEX    688 99.0945268099827   88
                                                              0.290697674418605
1 PK_Sales_Orders                   CLUSTERED INDEX    2   55.2260934025204  2 0
1 PK_Sales_Orders                   CLUSTERED INDEX    1 0.296515937731653  1  0
2 FK_Sales_Orders_CustomerID        NONCLUSTERED INDEX 1 39.6713615023474 1  0
3 FK_Sales_Orders_SalespersonPersonID NONCLUSTERED INDEX 1 28.5396590066716 1 0
4 FK_Sales_Orders_PickedByPersonID  NONCLUSTERED INDEX 1 58.5001235483074 1  0
5 FK_Sales_Orders_ContactPersonID   NONCLUSTERED INDEX 1 39.6713615023474 1  0
*/
```

## Identify missing indexes

When the query optimizer compiles a T-SQL statement, it also tracks up to 500 indexes that could have been used if they had existed. The following DMVs help you review these missing indexes:

- **sys.dm_db_missing_index_details**   Use this DMV to identify the columns used for equality and inequality predicates.

- **sys.dm_db_missing_index_groups**   Use this DMV as an intermediary between dm_db_missing_index_details and sys.dm_db_missing_group_stats.

- **sys.dm_db_missing_index_group_stats**   Use this DMV to retrieve metrics on a group of missing indexes.

> *NOTE*  **SQL SERVER RESTART CLEARS INFORMATION FROM DMOS**
>
> The information in these DMOs is cleared when SQL Server restarts and reflects only information accumulated since the last restart.

You use the three DMVs as a group, as shown in Listing 4-11. The output, which will vary on your computer, will list each database, schema, and table that is missing an index in descending order of the overall improvement expected by adding an index. The improvement is derived by multiplying the sum of the seeks and scans that the index helps by the average cost of the user queries that could be reduced by the index and by the average percent decrease in cost resulting from implementing the index. The equality_columns column lists one or more columns in the table that are good candidates for the new index. The inequality_columns column lists columns that are useful for queries that include the <> operator that you might consider adding to the index. Last, the included_columns column lists the columns that are suggested for addition to the index in the INCLUDE clause.

**LISTING 4-11** Review missing indexes

```
SELECT
    (user_seeks + user_scans) * avg_total_user_cost * (avg_user_impact * 0.01) AS
IndexImprovement,
    id.statement,
    id.equality_columns,
    id.inequality_columns,
    id.included_columns
FROM sys.dm_db_missing_index_group_stats AS igs
INNER JOIN sys.dm_db_missing_index_groups AS ig
    ON igs.group_handle = ig.index_group_handle
INNER JOIN sys.dm_db_missing_index_details AS id
    ON ig.index_handle = id.index_handle
ORDER BY IndexImprovement DESC;

/* Output
IndexImprovmeent  statement equality_columns   inequality_columns  included_columns
----------------------  ----------------------------- -------------------------
79.89008274829 [AdventureWorksDW].[dbo].[FactInternetSales] [ProductKey] NULL
                                                                     [CustomerKey]
*/
```

# Consolidate overlapping indexes

Consider a situation in which two indexes include similar indexes such as those shown in Listing 4-12. In this example, the two indexes are the same except one index contains an additional column. When SQL Server processes a query that needs the columns in the smaller index, it uses the smaller index. Conversely, when processing a query that uses all columns in the larger index, then SQL Server uses that index.

**LISTING 4-12** Create overlapping indexes

```
USE [WideWorldImporters];
GO
CREATE NONCLUSTERED INDEX [IX_Sales_Invoices_ExamBook762Ch4_A]
    ON [Sales].[Invoices]
(
    [CustomerID],
    [InvoiceDate]
)
INCLUDE ([TotalDryItems]);
GO
CREATE NONCLUSTERED INDEX [IX_Sales_Invoices_ExamBook762Ch4_B]
    ON [Sales].[Invoices]
(
    [CustomerID],
    [InvoiceDate],
    [CustomerPurchaseOrderNumber]
)
INCLUDE ([TotalDryItems]);
GO
```

With regard to query performance, all is well. However, SQL Server has an additional index to manage and requires more disk space for the database when similar indexes exist. This situation can occur when you create new indexes based on the DMVs for missing indexes or follow the recommendations from the Database Engine Tuning Advisor because they do not always account for existing indexes. Therefore, when using the DMVs or Database Engine Tuning Advisor to identify missing indexes, you might consider simply adding a new column to an existing index by adding it as another key or as an included column.

Meanwhile, when you encounter overlapping indexes, you should drop one of them so that database maintenance tasks run faster and less storage is required. Use the script in Listing 4-13 to find overlapping indexes.

***EXAM TIP***

**The exam has several different styles of questions to test your understanding of missing indexes and overlapping indexes. In particular, you should know how to identify overlapping indexes and what actions are necessary to consolidate and optimize them. It's also important to understand which operators can be removed with a clustered or covering index.**

**LISTING 4-13** Find overlapping indexes

```
USE [WideWorldImporters];
WITH IndexColumns AS (
    SELECT
        '[' + s.Name + '].[' + T.Name + ']' AS TableName,
        ix.name AS IndexName,
        c.name AS ColumnName,
        ix.index_id,
        ixc.index_column_id,
        COUNT(*) OVER(PARTITION BY t.OBJECT_ID, ix.index_id) AS ColumnCount
    FROM sys.schemas AS s
    INNER JOIN sys.tables AS t ON
        t.schema_id = s.schema_id
    INNER JOIN sys.indexes AS ix ON
        ix.OBJECT_ID = t.OBJECT_ID
    INNER JOIN sys.index_columns AS ixc ON
        ixc.OBJECT_ID = ix.OBJECT_ID AND
        ixc.index_id = ix.index_id
    INNER JOIN sys.columns AS c ON
        c.OBJECT_ID = ixc.OBJECT_ID AND
        c.column_id = ixc.column_id
WHERE
        ixc.is_included_column = 0 AND
        LEFT(ix.name, 2) NOT IN ('PK', 'UQ', 'FK')
)
SELECT DISTINCT
    ix1.TableName,
    ix1.IndexName AS Index1,
    ix2.IndexName AS Index2
FROM IndexColumns AS ix1
INNER JOIN IndexColumns AS ix2 ON
    ix1.TableName = ix2.TableName AND
    ix1.IndexName <> ix2.IndexName AND
    ix1.index_column_id = ix2.index_column_id AND
    ix1.ColumnName = ix2.ColumnName AND
    ix1.index_column_id < 3 AND
    ix1.index_id < ix2.index_id AND
    ix1.ColumnCount <= ix2.ColumnCount
ORDER BY ix1.TableName, ix2.IndexName;

/* Output
TableName          Index1                                          Index2
-------------------------------------------------------------------------
       [Sales].[Invoices] IX_Sales_Invoices_ExamBook762Ch4_A
                          IX_Sales_Invoices_ExamBook762Ch4_B
[Sales].[OrderLines]IX_Sales_OrderLines_AllocatedStockItems
                          IX_Sales_OrderLines_Perf_20160301_02
*/
```

# Skill 4.2: Analyze and troubleshoot query plans

One of the most important skills that you can have as a database administrator is the ability to analyze and troubleshoot query plans. In this section, we explain how to capture query plans, how certain query plan operators can indicate a potential performance problem, and how to interpret estimated versus actual query plans. We also introduce Query Store as a SQL Server 2016 feature that you can use to review SQL Server's selection of query plans for a query over time. For Azure SQL Database implementations, we show you how Azure SQL Database Performance Insight provides visibility into query performance in the cloud.

> **This section covers how to:**
> - Capture query plans using extended events and traces
> - Identify poorly performing query plan operators
> - Create efficient query plans using Query Store
> - Compare estimated and actual query plans and related metadata
> - Configure Azure SQL Database Performance Insight

## Capture query plans using extended events and traces

Before a query executes, several processes occur to manage how SQL Server performs the instructions in the T-SQL statement. The first process is *query parsing*, a step in which the database engine checks to make sure the submitted query uses valid T-SQL syntax. If query parsing is successful and if the T-SQL statement is a DML statement, the next process to run is the *algebrizer*, which verifies the existence of the referenced objects, such as tables and columns. If this process succeeds, the next process invoked is the *query optimizer*. The query optimizer checks to see if a query plan already exists for the query. If not, it generates one or more query plans based on the statistics available for the data and then selects the query plan that is good enough to perform the task at hand while minimizing the use CPU and IO when possible.

Although you can use the graphical query plan to analyze a single query, such as you might during index design as described in Chapter 1, you need an alternate approach when you need to troubleshoot many queries running on a server. In that case, you can automate the process of capturing execution plans by using extended events or SQL Trace.

> ***IMPORTANT*** **PERMISSIONS REQUIRED TO VIEW A QUERY PLAN**
>
> You must have the appropriate permissions within a database to view a query plan. If your login is assigned to the sysadmin, dbcreator, or db_owner role, you have the necessary permissions. Otherwise, you need to be granted the SHOWPLAN permission by running the following statement:

```
GRANT SHOWPLAN TO [username];
```

## Extended Events

Using Extended Events is a lightweight approach to capturing query plans. There are two Extended Events that you can use to review query plans:

- **query_pre_execution_showplan** This Extended Event captures the estimated query plan for a query. An estimated query plan is prepared without executing the query.

- **query_post_execution_showplan** This Extended Event captures the actual query plan for a query. An actual query plan is the estimated query plan that includes run-time information. For this reason, it is not available until after the query executes.

Listing 4-14 shows how to create and start an Extended Event session for actual query plans. In this example, the session definition filters the query activity on the server for a specific database and query type, ADHOC. In your own environment, you can remove filters entirely or apply more filters as needed. We describe how to work with Extended Events in greater detail in Skill 4.4.

> **NOTE  CREATE TARGET FOLDER FOR QUERY PLAN BEFORE RUNNING SAMPLE SCRIPT**
>
> The target folder for the query plan, C:\ExamBook762Ch4\, must exist before running the script shown in Listing 4-14.
>
> Also, be aware that running an Extended Event session to capture actual query plans is an expensive operation and should be used sparingly on a production server and only with highly selective filtering in place.

**LISTING 4-14**  Create and start an Extended Event session to capture an actual query plan

```
IF EXISTS(SELECT *
    FROM sys.server_event_sessions
    WHERE name='ActualQueryPlans')
    DROP EVENT SESSION ActualQueryPlans
    ON SERVER;
GO
CREATE EVENT SESSION ActualQueryPlans
ON SERVER
ADD EVENT sqlserver.query_post_execution_showplan(
    ACTION (sqlserver.database_name,
                sqlserver.client_hostname,
                sqlserver.client_app_name,
                sqlserver.plan_handle,
                sqlserver.sql_text,
                sqlserver.tsql_stack,
                package0.callstack,
                sqlserver.query_hash,
                sqlserver.session_id,
                sqlserver.request_id)
    WHERE
```

```
        sqlserver.database_name='WideWorldImporters' AND
        object_type = 'ADHOC'
)
ADD TARGET package0.event_file(SET filename=N'C:\ExamBook762Ch4\ActualQueryPlans.xel',
    max_file_size=(5),max_rollover_files=(4)),
ADD TARGET package0.ring_buffer
    WITH (MAX_DISPATCH_LATENCY=5SECONDS, TRACK_CAUSALITY=ON);
GO
ALTER EVENT SESSION ActualQueryPlans
    ON SERVER
    STATE=START;
GO
```

You can review the query plans captured by this Extended Event using the graphical interface in SQL Server Management Studio. In Object Explorer, expand the Management node, expand the Extended Events node, expand the Sessions node, right click ActualQueryPlans, and select Watch Live Data. Now that you are watching the sessions, execute a query, like this:

```
USE WideWorldImporters;
GO
SELECT *
FROM Warehouse.StockGroups;
```

In the session window, click the row in which the query event appears, and then click the Query Plan tab in the lower portion of screen, as shown in Figure 4-4.

**FIGURE 4-4** A query plan accessed from an Extended Event session

When you no longer need to capture query plans, be sure to disable or drop the Extended Event session, using the applicable statement in Listing 4-15.

**LISTING 4-15**  Disable or drop extended event sessions

```
--Disable extended event session
ALTER EVENT SESSION ActualQueryPlans
    ON SERVER
    STATE=STOP;
GO
--Drop extended event session
IF EXISTS(SELECT *
    FROM sys.server_event_sessions
    WHERE name='ActualQueryPlans')
    DROP EVENT SESSION ActualQueryPlans
    ON SERVER;
GO
```

## SQL Trace

Although SQL Trace is designated as a deprecated feature and will be removed from a future release of SQL Server, it remains an available option in SQL Server 2016. You can define server-side traces by using system stored procedures and then run these traces on demand or on a scheduled basis. As an alternative, you can use SQL Server Profiler as a client-side option. The overhead of running server-side traces is much less than the overhead of using SQL Server Profiler, but the overhead is still significant. Therefore, take care when using SQL Trace in a production environment regardless of the approach you take and disable tracing as soon as possible.

### SERVER-SIDE TRACING

To define a trace, use the following system stored procedures:

- **sp_trace_create**  This procedure creates a new trace and defines a file into which SQL Server stores trace data. It returns a trace ID that you reference in the other procedures to manage the trace.

- **sp_trace_setevent**  This procedure must be called once for each data column of the events to capture in the trace. That means you must call this procedure many times for any single trace. When you call this procedure, you pass in the following arguments, the trace identifier captured as output when you create the trace, the event identifier, the column identifier, and the status of ON (1) or OFF (0).

- **sp_trace_setfilter**  This procedure must be called once for each filter on an event data column.

- **sp_trace_setstatus**  This procedure starts, stops, or removes a trace. It must be stopped and removed before you can open the related trace file.

Listing 4-16 illustrates how to use these four system stored procedures to create a trace for a query plan. The trace data is stored in the ExamBook762Ch4 folder that must exist prior to executing the sp_trace_create system stored procedure. Next, the sp_trace_setevent system stored procedure is called multiple times to capture the query plan, the login name associated with the query, the start and end time of the query, and the text of the query, respectively.

**LISTING 4-16** Create a trace, add events and filter to a trace, and start a trace

```
USE master;
GO
DECLARE @TraceID int;
EXEC sp_trace_create
    @TraceID output,
    0,
    N'C:\ExamBook762Ch4\ActualQueryPlanTrc';

EXEC sp_trace_setevent @TraceID,
    146,    -- Showplan XML Statistics Profile
    27,     -- BinaryData column
    1;      -- Column is ON for this event

EXEC sp_trace_setevent @TraceID,
    146,
    1,      -- TextData column
    1;

EXEC sp_trace_setevent @TraceID,
    146,
    14,     -- StartTime column
    1;

EXEC sp_trace_setevent @TraceID,
    146,
    15,     -- EndTime column
    1;

-- Set filter for database
EXEC sp_trace_setfilter @TraceID,
    @ColumnID = 35, --Database Name
    @LogicalOperator = 0, -- Logical AND
    @ComparisonOperator = 6, -- Comparison LIKE
    @Value = N'WideWorldImporters' ;

-- Set filter for application name
EXEC sp_trace_setfilter @TraceID,
    @ColumnID = 10, --ApplicationName
    @LogicalOperator = 0, -- Logical AND
    @ComparisonOperator = 6, -- Comparison LIKE
    @Value = N'Microsoft SQL Server Management Studio - Query' ;

-- Start Trace (status 1 = start)
EXEC sp_trace_setstatus @TraceID, 1;
GO
```

**NOTE** **RESOURCES FOR SP_TRACE_SETEVENT AND SP_TRACE_SETFILTER**

Lists of event and column identifiers for defining the event columns are available at "sp_trace_setevent (Transact-SQL)", *https://msdn.microsoft.com/en-us/library/ms186265. aspx*. Lists of the logical and comparison operators for the trace filter are available at "sp_trace_setfilter (Transact-SQL)" at *https://msdn.microsoft.com/en-us/library/ms174404.aspx*.

Now execute a query to generate an event for the trace like this:

```
USE WideWorldImporters;
GO
SELECT *
FROM Warehouse.StockGroups;
```

To view the trace information, find the trace identifier by using the sys.fn_trace_getinfo system function and then use sp_trace_setstatus twice, as shown in Listing 4-17, replacing <traceid> with the trace identifier that you find by executing the first statement. The first time you set the status of the trace to 0 to stop it and the second time you set the status to 2 to close and delete the trace information from SQL Server.

**LISTING 4-17** Stop and delete a trace

```
----  Find the trace ID
USE master;
GO
SELECT *
FROM sys.fn_trace_getinfo(0)
WHERE value = 'C:\ExamBook762Ch4\ActualQueryPlanTrc.trc';

-- Set  the trace status to stop
EXEC sp_trace_setstatus
    @traceid = <traceid>,
    @status= 0;
GO


-- Close and Delete the trace
EXEC sp_trace_setstatus
    @traceid = <traceid>,
    @status = 2;
GO
```

The trace file remains on the file system and is available for you to view in SQL Server Profiler. Be sure to open SQL Server Profiler by using the Run As Administrator option and then open the trace file. Click the row containing the query's Showplan event to view the graphical query plan, as shown in Figure 4-5.

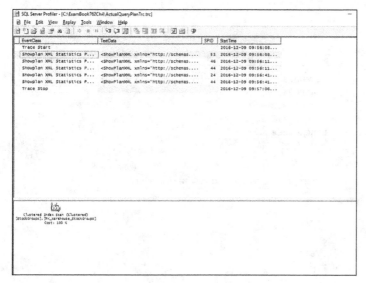

**FIGURE 4-5** A query plan accessed from a SQL trace file

Setting up traces manually by using the system stored procedures can be tedious due to the number of numeric parameters required. Rather than refer to Books Online to find the necessary values, you can take advantage of SQL Server catalog views to find the values you need, as shown in Listing 4-18.

**LISTILISTING 4-18** Get event and column identifiers for use in a trace definition

```
--Get event identifiers
SELECT
    e.trace_event_id AS EventID,
    e.name AS EventName,
    c.name AS CategoryName
FROM sys.trace_events e
JOIN sys.trace_categories c
    ON e.category_id = c.category_id
ORDER BY e.trace_event_id;

/* Partial output
EventID     EventName                         CategoryName
----------- --------------------------------- --------------------
10              RPC:Completed                       Stored Procedures
11              RPC:Starting                        Stored Procedures
12              SQL:BatchCompleted      TSQL
13              SQL:BatchStarting          TSQL
*/

--Get column identifiers for events
SELECT
    trace_column_id,
    name AS ColumnName
FROM sys.trace_columns
```

```
ORDER BY trace_column_id;

/* Partial output
trace_column_id  ColumnName
---------------------- ----------------------------
1                        TextData
2                        BinaryData
3                        DatabaseID
4                        TransactionID
5                        LineNumber
*/
```

**LISTING 4-19**  Create an indexed view to improve aggregate query performance

```
CREATE VIEW Sales.vSalesByYear
WITH SCHEMABINDING
AS
    SELECT
    YEAR(InvoiceDate) AS InvoiceYear,
    COUNT_BIG(*) AS InvoiceCount
FROM Sales.Invoices
GROUP BY YEAR(InvoiceDate);
GO
CREATE UNIQUE CLUSTERED INDEX idx_vSalesByYear
    ON Sales.vSalesByYear
    (InvoiceYear);
GO
```

### CLIENT-SIDE TRACING

You can use SQL Server Profiler instead of manually creating the many stored procedures to define a trace when you need to capture a query plan. On the File menu, click New Trace, and then connect to the server on which you want to run the trace. In the Trace Properties dialog box, click the Events Selection tab and then select the Show All Events checkbox. Expand the Performance node, and select one or more of the following checkboxes:

- **Showplan XML**  This event is raised when SQL Server selects an estimated query plan.

- **Showplan XML For Query Compile**  This event is raised when SQL Server compiles a query and produces an estimated query plan which it adds to the query plan cache. Generally, this event is raised only once for a query unless the query requires recompilation.

- **Showplan XML Statistics Profile**  This event is raised after SQL Server executes a query and has generated an actual query plan.

To minimize the performance impact of running SQL Server Profiler, you should apply as many filters as possible to capture only the query plans of interest. As an example, you might want to focus on queries in a specific database. To do this, select the Show All Columns checkbox, and then click Column Filters. In the Edit Filter dialog box, click DatabaseName, expand Like, type WideWorldImporters as shown in Figure 4-6, and then click OK. Next, click Run to start the trace.

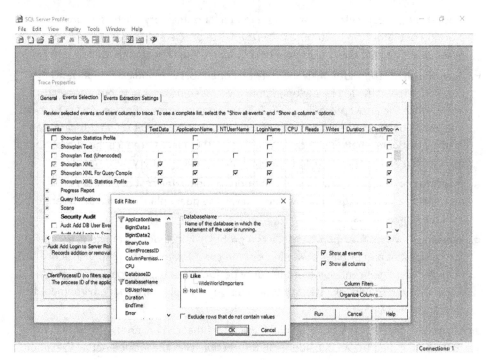

**FIGURE 4-6** Adding a filter to a trace in SQL Server Profiler

After enabling a trace, you can run a query against the WideWorldImporters database, such as the one shown in Listing 4-6. After executing the query, click the Stop Selected Trace in the SQL Server Profiler toolbar. You can click on any of the events that begin with Showplan to view the graphical estimated or actual query plan, depending on the specific event you select. To save the query plan to a separate file for later review, right click the event, and then select Extract Event Data to save the file with a SQLPlan file extension. You can then open this file in SQL Server Management Studio.

## Identify poorly performing query plan operators

Not only can a query plan tell you the specific steps performed by SQL Server during query execution, it can also help you discover which step in the sequence is performing poorly. Each step in the query plan is a separate operation performed by the database engine and is represented as an icon known as an *operator*. As you analyze a graphical query plan, you should check for the following conditions that can affect query performance:

- **Query plan optimization** You can find this property by right clicking the first operator in the plan (for example, SELECT) and selecting Properties. In the Properties window, look for the Reason For Early Termination Of Statement Optimization property. If it is Good Enough Plan Found, then proceed with further analysis of the query plan. If the value is Timeout, you should spend time tuning your query because the property indicates that the current query plan is not optimal.

- **Operators**  In particular, operators requiring a lot of memory (such as a *Sort*) or blocking operators can contribute to performance problems in a query. We describe potential issues with query plan operators in more detail later in this section.

- **Arrow width**  The width of arrows between operators is an indicator relative to the number of rows affected by the operation. If you see one operation outputs a wide arrow, while the arrow preceding a SELECT operator is narrow, the query must process many rows before returning a small number of rows in the result set. In this case, you might investigate whether you can add a filter to the query to reduce the number of rows for the earlier operation and thereby improve overall query performance.

- **Operator cost**  Each operator's contribution to the overall cost of the query is represented as a percentage value. As you analyze the query plan, look for the operators with the highest costs.

- **Warnings**  When the optimizer detects a problem, it includes a warning in an operator's properties and displays a warning icon on the operator in the graphical query plan. This is a significant clue that the query performance is likely to suffer. If you see a warning, you should take steps to tune your query or optimize your environment to eliminate the warning.

Let's consider some examples of query plan operators that can adversely affect performance. Before executing the ad hoc queries in this section, click the Include Actual Execution Plan button once to enable the graphical query plan for each query.

> **NOTE**  **UNDERSTANDING QUERY PLANS FOR QUERIES USING THE WIDEWORLDIMPORTERS DATABASE**
>
> The size of the WideWorldImporters database is too small to illustrate performance problems with the use of certain operators. Nonetheless, we use queries against this database to familiarize you with the appearance of specific poorly performing operators in a query plan, explain the conditions in which SQL Server might use them, and suggest steps you can take to improve query performance.

**EXAM TIP**

Understanding query plan operators is important both in the real world and on the exam. Be prepared for questions that present two possible query plans and ask you to choose the more optimal of the two query plans.

## Table Scan operator

As we explained in Chapter 1, SQL Server must read a heap row by row to find the rows for a query. This operation can perform slowly when run against a large table. Try this query:

```
SELECT *
FROM Warehouse.VehicleTemperatures;
```

In the Execution Plan window, as shown in Figure 4-7, you can see that SQL Server used a *Table Scan* operator that represents 100% of the query cost. Note also the size of the arrow between the SELECT and Table Scan operators to indicate a relatively large result set. In this case, the table is memory-optimized, so the performance cost of reading 659,998 rows for this query is minimal. On the other hand, if this table were not memory-optimized and you were investigating poor query performance, the presence of the Table Scan operator should lead you to consider adding a clustered index to the table or look for ways to filter the query to return fewer rows.

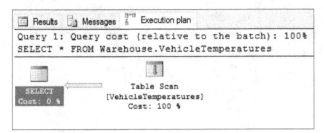

**FIGURE 4-7** Table Scan operator in a query plan

## Clustered Index Scan operator

Another potential problem for query performance is the use of the Clustered Index Scan operator. It is similar in concept to the Table Scan operator in that SQL Server must scan all the data. This might occur when the query must return so many rows that using the index to find specific rows is no longer advantageous, index selectivity is too low, or statistics are obsolete. To see this operator in action, execute the following query:

```
SELECT *
FROM Warehouse.StockGroups;
```

As you can see in Figure 4-8, SQL Server uses the Clustered Index Scan operator to process the query. You can also see which index is used, PK_Warehouse_StockGroups. This clustered index is relatively small (as you can see by the size of the arrows between operators), so performance is not an issue here. However, the presence of a Clustered Index Scan operator can indicate the source of poor query performance and merits further investigation to determine whether you can modify the query by adding a WHERE clause to return only the needed rows, as long as a proper index exists for the column used in the filter. Importantly, the WHERE clause must have a predicate that includes a column on one side of the operator and an expression on the other side with both the column and expression having the same data type. If you use the LIKE operator in the WHERE clause, you cannot use a wildcard as the first character in the search string.

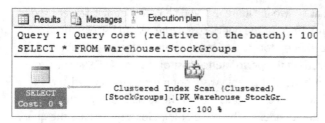

**FIGURE 4-8** Clustered Index Scan operator in a query plan

That said, an index scan is not necessarily a bad operation. It is more efficient than a table scan by comparison. Nonetheless, if you need to find a way to improve query performance, your next step is to add a filter. To see what happens when you do this, execute the following query:

```
SELECT *
FROM Warehouse.StockGroups
WHERE StockGroupID = 1;
```

Now SQL Server uses a Clustered Index Seek operator, as shown in Figure 4-9. This change to the query plan is good because a seek operator can be one of the faster data retrieval methods used by SQL Server. In particular, a Clustered Index Seek is a preferred operator because all data in the table is also included in the index and SQL Server can return results directly from the index without performing additional steps.

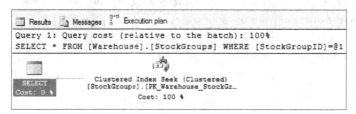

**FIGURE 4-9** Clustered Index Seek operator in a query plan

Notice also that SQL Server converted the predicate to @1 instead of using the actual value of 1 that was requested in the query. That way, SQL Server can reuse the query plan when the same query executes with a different value in the WHERE clause. This reuse is known as simple parameterization.

## Index Seek (NonClustered) and Key Lookup (Clustered) operators

Like the Clustered Index Seek operator, the Index Seek (NonClustered) operator is a much better operator to see in a query plan than a Table Scan or a Clustered Index Scan operator because it can selectively find rows in the index rather than read all the rows, although this behavior is dependent on the query. On the other hand, if the non-clustered index is not a covering index, the query plan also includes a Key Lookup (Clustered) operator, which adds a slight overhead to query performance. To see a query plan with these characteristics, as shown in Figure 4-10, execute this query:

```
SELECT
    StockGroupID,
    StockGroupName,
    ValidFrom,
    ValidTo
FROM Warehouse.StockGroups
WHERE StockGroupName = 'Novelty Items';
```

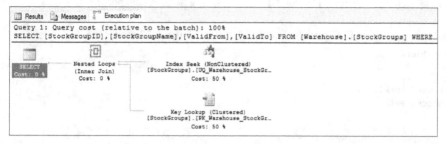

**FIGURE 4-10** Index Seek (NonClustered) and Key Lookup (Clustered) operator in a query plan.

In this case, the index used by the Index Seek (NonClustered) operator contains only the StockGroupName column, but the query references other columns in the SELECT clause, so it must use the Key Lookup (Clustered) operator to get the additional columns for each row. Incidentally, if the query references columns in JOIN conditions or the WHERE clause, SQL Server includes the Key Lookup (Clustered) operator in the query plan even if those columns are not also in the SELECT clause. Therefore, whenever you see the Key Lookup (Clustered) operator in combination with an Index Seek (NonClustered) operator, consider creating a covering index by adding the necessary columns to the index key or as included columns.

> **NOTE**  **RID LOOKUP OPERATOR VERSUS KEY LOOKUP (CLUSTERED) OPERATOR**
>
> When a query accesses a table without a clustered index, SQL Server uses the RID Lookup operator instead of the Key Lookup (Clustered) operator. The net effect of each operator type has a similar effect on query performance which can be mitigated by the addition of a covering index or a clustered index.

## Sort operator

The Sort operator can also increase the cost of a query. Consider the query plan shown in Figure 4-11 that results from executing the following query which includes an ORDER BY clause containing a column that is not used in an index:

```
SELECT *
FROM Warehouse.StockItems
ORDER BY StockItemName;
```

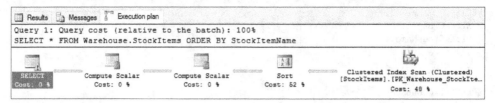

FIGURE 4-11 Sort operator in a query plan for a query sorting by a non-key column.

Contrast the query plan in Figure 4-11 with the one in Figure 4-12 that is created by executing this query:

```
SELECT *
FROM Warehouse.StockItems
ORDER BY StockItemID;
```

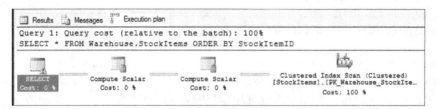

FIGURE 4-12 Sort operator in a query plan for a query sorting by a key column

Because a clustered index is already sorted, SQL Server no longer requires a Sort operator when the ORDER BY clause includes a key column from the clustered index. With this in mind, look for Sort operators with a significant query cost and consider adding the sort columns to a clustered index on the table. Another potential solution is to reduce the number of rows to sort by adding a WHERE clause to the query.

Another consideration when working with a Sort operator is the volume of data that SQL Server must sort. The query optimizer uses the estimated number of rows and the average row size to calculate the minimum amount of memory required to perform the operation and the amount of memory needed to perform the operation entirely in memory. If the actual number of rows to be sorted is larger than the estimate due to obsolete statistics, the operation spills to tempdb. You can identify this type of memory problem in the actual query plan when you see a warning symbol on the Sort, as shown in Figure 4-13, or Hash Match operators.

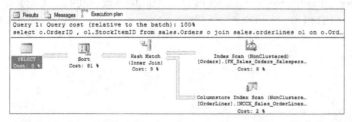

FIGURE 4-13 Sort and Hash Match operators with warning symbols in actual query plan

When you hover the cursor over the Sort operator, the tooltip includes a warning that the operator used tempdb to spill data, as shown in Figure 4-14.

**Sort**

Sort the input.

| | |
|---|---|
| Physical Operation | Sort |
| Logical Operation | Sort |
| Actual Execution Mode | Batch |
| Estimated Execution Mode | Batch |
| Actual Number of Rows | 231412 |
| Actual Number of Batches | 258 |
| Estimated Operator Cost | 1.89667 (81%) |
| Estimated I/O Cost | 0.0037538 |
| Estimated CPU Cost | 1.89292 |
| Estimated Subtree Cost | 2.33913 |
| Number of Executions | 1 |
| Estimated Number of Executions | 1 |
| Estimated Number of Rows | 231412 |
| Estimated Row Size | 15 B |
| Actual Rebinds | 0 |
| Actual Rewinds | 0 |
| Node ID | 0 |

**Output List**
[WideWorldImporters].[Sales].[Orders].OrderID,
[WideWorldImporters].[Sales].
[OrderLines].StockItemID
**Warnings**
Operator used tempdb to spill data during execution
with spill level 8 and 1 spilled thread(s)
**Order By**
[WideWorldImporters].[Sales].
[OrderLines].StockItemID Ascending

**FIGURE 4-14** Sort and Hash Match operators with warning symbols in actual query plan

The query performance will suffer when the sort must use tempdb instead of memory. Use the tooltip for the SELECT operator to check the Memory Grant property which shows how much memory that SQL Server is allocating to the query. In SQL Server 2016, you can now add a query hint to request a minimum memory grant size as a percentage of the default limit to override the minimum memory per query property that is set on the server like this:

```
OPTION(min_grant_percent = 100)
```

## Hash Match (Aggregate) operator

Aggregations in a query can have a negative effect on performance and should be reviewed carefully. Figure 4-15 shows the query plan created for the following aggregate query:

```
SELECT
    YEAR(InvoiceDate) AS InvoiceYear,
    COUNT(InvoiceID) AS InvoiceCount
FROM Sales.Invoices
GROUP BY YEAR(InvoiceDate);
```

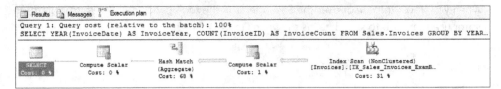

**FIGURE 4-15** Hash Match (Aggregate) operator in a query plan.

In this case, the Hash Match (Aggregate) operator to group the rows from the Index Scan (NonClustered) operator contributes a significant percentage to the query cost. To perform this aggregation, SQL Server creates a temporary hash table in memory to count the rows by invoice year. Notice the larger width of the arrow sending data into the Hash Match (Aggregate) operator as compared to the width of the arrow sending the results to the next operator as an indicator that a larger row set has been reduced to a smaller row set by the operation.

Options to consider for minimizing the impact on performance when performing aggregations is to minimize the number of rows to aggregate where possible or to use an indexed view to pre-aggregate rows. Execute the statements in Listing 4-19 to set up an indexed view to improve the previous query's performance.

```
CREATE VIEW Sales.vSalesByYear
WITH SCHEMABINDING
AS
    SELECT
    YEAR(InvoiceDate) AS InvoiceYear,
    COUNT_BIG(*) AS InvoiceCount
FROM Sales.Invoices
GROUP BY YEAR(InvoiceDate);
GO
CREATE UNIQUE CLUSTERED INDEX idx_vSalesByYear
    ON Sales.vSalesByYear
    (InvoiceYear);
GO
```

Now you can execute the earlier query again, even though it does not reference the indexed view directly, to see how the query optimizer takes advantage of the indexed view in the query plan shown in Figure 4-16.

```
SELECT
    YEAR(InvoiceDate) AS InvoiceYear,
    COUNT(InvoiceID) AS InvoiceCount
FROM Sales.Invoices
GROUP BY YEAR(InvoiceDate);
```

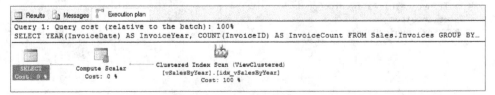

**FIGURE 4-16** Query plan using an indexed view

As a result of the addition of the indexed view, SQL Server no longer requires the Hash Match (Aggregator) operator and instead uses a Clustered Index Scan (ViewClustered) operator to retrieve data. Because the data is pre-aggregated, the index scan is much faster in this case than it would be against an index containing all rows in the table.

## Hash Match (Inner Join) operator

Thus far, the queries we have examined have been relatively simple and read data from only one table. Now let's consider a query that combines data from multiple tables to produce the query plan shown in Figure 4-17:

```
SELECT
    si.StockItemName,
    c.ColorName,
    s.SupplierName

FROM Warehouse.StockItems si
INNER JOIN Warehouse.Colors c ON
    c.ColorID = si.ColorID
INNER JOIN Purchasing.Suppliers s ON
    s.SupplierID = si.SupplierID;
```

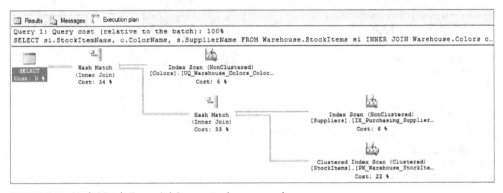

**FIGURE 4-17**  Hash Match (Inner Join) operator in a query plan

In this example, we see the addition of the Hash Match (Inner Join) operator in two places in the query plan. We also see that these two operations have the two highest costs in the plan and therefore should be the first operations we assess for possible optimization. SQL Server uses this operator when it puts data into temporary hash tables so that it can match rows in two different data sets and produce a single result set. Specifically, SQL Server converts, or *hashes*, rows from the smaller data set into a value that is more efficient for comparisons and then stores these values in a hash table in tempdb. Then it compares each row in the larger data set with the hash table to find matching rows to join. As long as the smaller data set is in fact small, this comparison operation is fast, but performance can suffer when both data sets are large. Furthermore, if a query requires many of these operations, tempdb might experience memory pressure. Last, it's important to note that the Hash Match (Inner Join) operator is a blocking operator as it requires SQL Server to gather data from each data set before it can perform the join.

In Figure 4-17, the Hash Match (Inner Join) operator combines the results of the Index Scan (NonClustered) and the Clustered Index Scan operators that gets SupplierID and SupplierName by scanning a non-clustered index on the Suppliers table and StockItemName, SupplierID, and ColorID by scanning the clustered index on the StockItems table. This result set becomes input for the second usage of the operation and is combined with ColorName set from an index scan on the Colors table.

Your options for improving the query performance based on this query plan include adding or revising indexes, filtering the data by using a WHERE clause, or fixing a WHERE clause that prevents the query optimizer from using an existing index. Let's try adding indexes to the Suppliers and StockItems tables, as shown in Listing 4-20. The index on the Suppliers table includes the SupplierID column used for the JOIN operation and the SupplierName column to return in the final query results. Similarly, the index on the StockItems table includes the ColorID and SupplierID columns used for JOIN operations and the StockItemName column to return in the final query results.

**LISTING 4-20** Add indexes to eliminate Hash Match (Inner Join) operators

```
CREATE NONCLUSTERED INDEX IX_Purchasing_Suppliers_ExamBook762Ch4_SupplierID
    ON Purchasing.Suppliers
(
    SupplierID ASC,
    SupplierName
);
GO
CREATE NONCLUSTERED INDEX IX_Warehouse_StockItems_ExamBook762Ch4_ColorID
    ON Warehouse.StockItems
(
    ColorID ASC,
    SupplierID ASC,
    StockItemName ASC
);
```

After adding the indexes, execute the following query to see the new query plan, as shown in Figure 4-18:

```
SELECT
    si.StockItemName,
    c.ColorName,
    s.SupplierName
FROM Warehouse.StockItems si
INNER JOIN Warehouse.Colors c ON
    c.ColorID = si.ColoriD
INNER JOIN Purchasing.Suppliers s ON
    s.SupplierID = si.SupplierID;
```

**FIGURE 4-18** Query plan after adding usable indexes to eliminate Hash Match (Inner Join) operators

In the new query plan, SQL Server replaces the Hash Match (Inner Join) operators with Nested Loops operators and replaces two of the index scan operations with Index Seek (NonClustered) operators which should significantly improve performance even when large tables are queried. The Nested Loops operator is an efficient operation that compares two data sets row by row. For each row output by the top operator in the query plan (known as the inner data set), which is the index scan on the small Colors table, SQL Server scans the rows output by the bottom operator (known as the outer data set), which is the index seek on the StockItems table. Then the output of this operation becomes the inner data set for the second Nested Loops operator in the query plan. For each row in this new inner data set, SQL Server scans the output from the index seek on the Suppliers table. Notice that the cost of the Nested Loops operators in the new query plan is significantly lower than the cost of the Hash Match (Inner Join) operators shown in Figure 4-17.

## Create efficient query plans using Query Store

The query plan selected by the query optimizer is not guaranteed to be the most efficient plan. When working with a version earlier than SQL Server 2016, you can capture query plans from the procedure cache periodically, but run the risk of losing access to query plans when the server comes under memory pressure and begins evicting older query plans from the cache. With Query Store in SQL Server 2016 and Azure SQL Database, you can capture and analyze information about all query plans generated over time for a query. You can then force SQL Server to use the query plan that you determine to be most efficient based on the criteria that best meets your business requirements.

## Query Store properties

By default, Query Store is not enabled. You can enable it at the database level in SQL Server Management Studio by using Object Explorer to navigate to the database for which you want to enable Query Store. Right-click the database name to open the Database Properties dialog box and click the Query Store tab. In the Operation Mode (Requested) drop-down list, select Read Write.

> **NOTE  CHANGING THE QUERY STORE BEHAVIOR**
>
> You can later change the Operation Mode (Requested) property to Read Only when you want to retain existing query plans and execution statistics information available in the query store, but no longer want to add new information. SQL Server automatically switches to this mode when the query store reaches its maximum allocated space. To disable Query Store, change this property to Off.

As shown in Figure 4-19, there are several other properties that you can configure to manage the query store:

- **Data Flush Interval (Minutes)**  The frequency in minutes at which SQL Server writes data collected by the query store to disk.

- **Statistics Collection Interval**  The granularity of time for which SQL Server aggregates runtime execution statistics for the query store. You can choose one of the following intervals: 1 minute, 5 minutes, 10 minutes, 15 minutes, 30 minutes, 1 hour, or 1 day. If you capture data at a high frequency, bear in mind that the query store requires more space to store more finely grained data.

- **Max Size (MB)**  The maximum amount of space allocated to the query store. The default value is 100 MB per database. If your database is active, this value might not be large enough to store query plans and related information.

- **Query Store Capture Mode**  The specification of the types of queries for which SQL Server captures data for the query store. You can choose one of the following options:

  - **None**  The query store stops collecting data for new queries, but continues capturing data for existing queries.

  - **All**  The query store captures data for all queries.

  - **Auto**  The query store captures data for relevant queries. It ignores infrequent queries and queries with insignificant compile and execution duration.

- **Size Based Cleanup Mode**  The specification of whether the cleanup process activates when the query store data approaches its maximum size (Auto) or never runs (OFF).

- **Stale Query Threshold (Days)**  The number of days that SQL Server keeps data in the query store.

FIGURE 4-19 Query Store properties configurable in the Database Properties dialog box

> **NOTE**  **QUERY STORE ENABLED BY DEFAULT FOR WIDEWORLDIMPORTERS DATABASE**
>
> The query store for WideWorldImporters database is already enabled when you restore it. The current disk usage that displays for you will differ from that shown in Figure 4-19 as these metrics depend on the volume of query activity that has occurred on your computer to date.

You can also use the statement shown in Listing 4-21 to enable the query store, replacing <databasename> with the name of the database that you want to configure.

Enable the query store for a database and set its properties

```
ALTER DATABASE <databasename>
    SET QUERY_STORE = ON
    (
        OPERATION_MODE = READ_WRITE ,
        CLEANUP_POLICY = ( STALE_QUERY_THRESHOLD_DAYS = 30 ),
        DATA_FLUSH_INTERVAL_SECONDS = 3000,
        MAX_STORAGE_SIZE_MB = 500,
        INTERVAL_LENGTH_MINUTES = 50
    );
```

You can clear the data from the query store by clicking Purge Query Data on the Query Store tab of the Database Properties dialog box or by executing either of the statements shown in Listing 4-22.

**LISTING 4-22** Purge data from the query store

```
--Use the ALTER DATABASE statement
ALTER DATABASE <databasename>
SET QUERY_STORE CLEAR ALL;
GO
```

## Query Store components

The query store captures information about query plans and runtime execution statistics until the maximum space allocation is reached. You can review this data in the following DMVs:

- **sys.query_store_plan** Query plan information, such as Showplan XML, the number of compilations, the date and time of the initial and last compilations, the last execution date and time, and the average and most recent duration of compilation, among other details. The query plan available in this DMV is the estimated plan only.

- **sys.query_store_query** Aggregated runtime execution statistics for a query, including CPU binding, memory, optimization, and compilation statistics. This information is stored at the statement level and not at the batch level which is different from the behavior of sys.dm_exec_query_stats.

- **sys.query_store_query_text** The text of the executed query.

- **sys.query_store_runtime_stats** Runtime execution statistics for a query, such as first and last execution date and time, the number of executions, statistics (average, last, minimum, maximum, and standard deviation) for query duration, CPU time, logical IO reads and writes, physical IO reads and writes, CLR time, DOP, maximum used memory, and row counts.

- **sys.query_store_runtime_stats_interval**  The start and end times defining the intervals during which SQL Server collects runtime execution statistics for the query store.

As an example, you can query the DMVs to find the top query with the highest average logical reads and its corresponding query plan, as shown in Listing 4-23.

**LISTING 4-23** Top query with highest average logical reads

```
USE WideWorldImporters;
GO
SELECT TOP 1
    qt.query_sql_text,
    CAST(query_plan AS XML) AS QueryPlan,
    rs.avg_logical_io_reads
FROM sys.query_store_plan qp
INNER JOIN sys.query_store_query q
  ON qp.query_id = q.query_id
INNER JOIN sys.query_store_query_text qt
    ON q.query_text_id = qt.query_text_id
INNER JOIN sys.query_store_runtime_stats rs
    ON qp.plan_id = rs.plan_id
ORDER BY rs.avg_logical_io_reads DESC;
```

You can use the following system stored procedures to manage the query store:

- **sp_query_store_flush_db**  Flush the portion of the query store currently in memory to disk. This stored procedure takes no arguments.

- **sp_query_store_force_plan**  Force SQL Server to use a specified query plan for a specified query. You provide identifiers for the query and plan as arguments for this stored procedure.

- **sp_query_store_remove_plan**  Remove a specified query plan from the query store.

- **sp_query_store_remove_query**  Remove a specified query from the query store, in addition to the query plans and runtime execution statistics related to it.

- **sp_query_store_reset_exec_stats**  Reset the runtime execution statistics for a specified plan.

- **sp_query_store_unforce_plan**  Keep a specified query plan in the query store, but no longer force SQL Server to use it for a specified query.

---

***NEED MORE REVIEW?*  MORE QUERY STORE MONITORING EXAMPLES AVAILABLE ONLINE**

See the "Key Usage Scenarios" section of the "Monitoring Performance By Using the Query Store" article at *https://msdn.microsoft.com/en-US/library/dn817826.aspx*. Here you will find several examples of using these DMVs and system stored procedures, such as showing the last n queries executed on a database, the number of executions per query, queries having the longest average execution time in the last hour, among others.

## Query Store views

An easy way to review the information available in the query store is to use Query Store views in SQL Server Management Studio. After enabling query store for a database, a Query Store node appears below the database node and contains four views, as shown in Figure 4-20.

- WideWorldImporters
  - Database Diagrams
  - Tables
  - Views
  - External Resources
  - Synonyms
  - Programmability
  - Query Store
    - Regressed Queries
    - Overall Resource Consumption
    - Top Resource Consuming Queries
    - Tracked Queries
  - Service Broker
  - Storage
  - Security

FIGURE 4-20 Query Store views for a database in SQL Server Management Studio's Object Explorer

Before we the review contents of these views, let's execute the statements in Listing 4-24 to create a test environment in which a new database and table is added. The table is populated with a random 9,999 rows of random values with an ID of 1 and one row with an ID of 2 to create a skewed distribution. A primary key clustered index and a non-clustered index on the ID column are added. Next, a parameterized stored procedure to select rows from the table is added to the database. Query Store Is enabled on the database to capture query plan changes over time using an interval length of 1 minute to capture statistics at the most granular level available for better visibility of the query examples in this section. Last, the stored procedure is called with the ID associated with a large number of rows in the table. This stored procedure is called multiple times to accumulate more statistics than other background queries in the database so that you can see it more easily in the view later.

LISTING 4-24 Create test environment for Query Store

```
CREATE DATABASE ExamBook762Ch4_QueryStore;
GO
USE ExamBook762Ch4_QueryStore;
GO
CREATE SCHEMA Examples;
GO
CREATE TABLE Examples.SimpleTable(
    Ident INT IDENTITY,
    ID INT,
    Value INT);
WITH IDs
    AS (SELECT
                TOP (9999)
                ROW_NUMBER() OVER (ORDER BY (SELECT 1)) AS n
            FROM master.sys.All_Columns ac1
            CROSS JOIN master.sys.All_Columns ac2
        )
INSERT   INTO Examples.SimpleTable(ID, Value)
SELECT
    1,
    n
FROM    IDs;
GO
INSERT Examples.SimpleTable (ID, Value)
    VALUES (2, 100);
ALTER TABLE Examples.SimpleTable
    ADD  CONSTRAINT [PK_SimpleTable_Ident]
PRIMARY KEY CLUSTERED (Ident);
CREATE NONCLUSTERED INDEX ix_SimpleTable_ID
    ON Examples.SimpleTable(ID);
GO
CREATE PROCEDURE Examples.GetValues
    @PARAMETER1 INT
AS
    SELECT
        ID,
        Value
    FROM Examples.SimpleTable
    WHERE
        ID = @PARAMETER1;
GO

ALTER DATABASE ExamBook762Ch4_QueryStore
SET QUERY_STORE = ON (
    INTERVAL_LENGTH_MINUTES = 1
);

EXEC Examples.GetValues 1;
GO 20
```

At this point, the Top Resource Consuming Queries view, shown in Figure 4-21, is the only one that contains information. The default configuration includes a column chart in the top left that displays total duration by query id, a point chart in the top right that displays duration for query plans associated with the selected query (known as a *plan summary*), and a query plan for the plan identifier currently selected in the point chart.

FIGURE 4-21 Top Resource Consuming Queries view

> **NOTE** **WORKING WITH MULTIPLE QUERIES IN THE TOP RESOURCE CONSUMING QUERIES VIEW**
>
> Depending on the activity occurring in the database, the query that you want to analyze might not be the first column in the chart as it is in Figure 4-21. You can click on each column to view the query plan associated with a query and its query text, or click the View Top Resource Consuming Queries In A Grid Format With Additional Details button in the chart's toolbar to locate your query by its query text. If you select a query in this grid and toggle back to the chart, the view retains your selection and shows the plan summary and a query plan.

Taking a closer look at the column chart, notice that each column represents a query. When multiple queries exist in the query store, the columns are sorted in descending order by the selected metric, which is currently Duration. When you hover the cursor over a column in the chart, a tooltip displays the query id, the metric and its selected statistic, and the query text. If the query includes a WHERE clause, the query text is parameterized. You can find similar information by using the sys.query_store_query, sys.query_store_query_text, and sys.

query_store_runtime_stats DMVs. By using the Query Store view in SQL Server Management Studio, you can quickly visualize and access key metrics about your queries without writing any code.

The plan summary chart displays one point per query plan for the query selected in the column chart. When you hover the cursor over a point on this chart, as shown in Figure 4-22, a tooltip displays some of the information related to the selected metric that is available in the sys.query_store_runtime_stats DMV. Last, notice the graphical query plan shows that SQL Server used a Clustered Index Scan operator to retrieve rows for the SELECT statement in the stored procedure. An index scan is used instead of a seek because the number of rows for the parameter value of 1 is high relative to the size of the table.

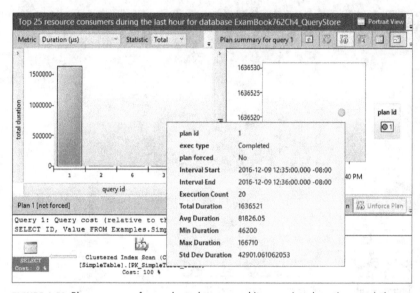

**FIGURE 4-22** Plan summary for a selected query and its associated runtime statistics

You can change the configuration of the charts by changing the y-axis of the column chart and by selecting new metric and statistic values in the respective drop-down lists above the column chart. For example, select Logical Reads in the Metric drop-down list, and Avg in the Statistic drop down list, and point to your query's column in the chart to view the corresponding metric value, execution count, and number of query plans for the selected query.

Now let's modify the query slightly by changing the parameter to the other possible ID value in the table, and execute it by using the code shown in Listing 4-25.

**LISTING 4-25** Execute stored procedure with new parameter value

```
EXEC Examples.GetValues 2;
GO
```

Return to the Top Resource Consuming Queries dashboard and click the Refresh button above the column chart to update it. When you click the query's column in the column chart, the plan summary chart now has two points that are associated with the same query plan, as shown in Figure 4-23. That means the index scan for the query executed to get rows with ID 1 was also used to get the one row with ID 2. This is condition is a result of *parameter sniffing* in which the query optimizer uses the estimated rows from the first execution of the stored procedure to select a query plan and then uses it for all subsequent executions without considering the estimated rows for the new parameter values. In the current example, an index seek is a more efficient operator for retrieving the one row for ID 2, but it is not considered due to the parameter sniffing behavior.

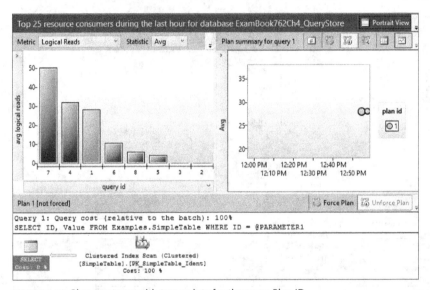

**FIGURE 4-23** Plan summary with two points for the same Plan ID

Let's clear the procedure cache and see what happens when SQL Server must generate a new query plan rather than use the one created previously. To do this, execute the statements shown in Listing 4-26. Click the Refresh button in the Query Store view to see the effect of the last query execution. When you click the Plan ID with the higher identifier in the legend, you can see its new query plan, as shown in Figure 4-24. Notice the disparity between the points in the point chart which indicates the new query plan has a lower average logical read value than the first query plan and is therefore more efficient. As you can see in the graphical query plan at the bottom of the view, SQL Server used an index seek operation to retrieve a single row from the table.

**LISTING 4-26** Execute stored procedure after clearing procedure cache

```
DBCC FREEPROCCACHE();
GO
EXEC Examples.GetValues 2;
GO
```

**FIGURE 4-24** An improved query plan in the Plan Summary after clearing the procedure cache

Another way to compare the differences between the query plans is to view their respective metrics. To do this, click the View Plan Summary In A Grid Format button in the toolbar to switch the plan summary from a chart to a grid, as shown in Figure 4-25.

| | plan id | plan forced | exec type | exec count | min logical reads | max logical reads | avg logical reads |
|---|---|---|---|---|---|---|---|
| 1 | 10 | 0 | 0 | 1 | 4 | 4 | 4 |
| 2 | 1 | 0 | 0 | 21 | 28 | 28 | 28 |

Plan summary for query 1

**FIGURE 4-25** Plan Summary metrics in a grid format

When you click a row in the grid, you can see the associated graphical query plan, but you can only view one graphical query plan at a time this way. If you want to compare query plans, click the View Plan Summary In A Chart Format button in the toolbar to switch back to the point chart, click one plan identifier in the legend and then, while holding the Shift key, click the other plan identifier. Next, click the Compare The Plans For The Selected Query In A Separate Window button in the toolbar. In the Showplan Comparison window that opens, shown in Figure 4-26, you can more easily compare the differences between the two plans. The top query plan (which was the last to execute) uses an index seek to retrieve one row, whereas the bottom query plan uses an index scan to retrieve many rows and performs less efficiently for small rowsets.

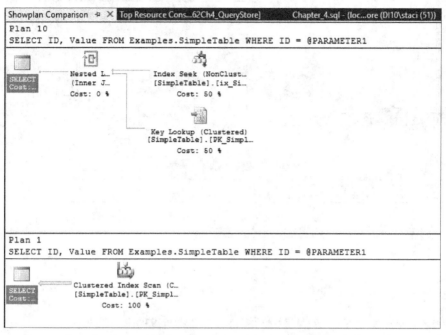

**FIGURE 4-26** Showplan Comparison between query plans captured by Query Store

Let's say that the normal query pattern for this particular stored procedure is to retrieve a limited number of rows. In that case, the use of the query plan that uses the index seek is preferable. An advantage of using Query Store is the ability to force this plan to be used for all executions of the same query. Returning to the Top Resource Consuming Queries view, click the plan identifier for the last query plan (with the lower average logical reads) and then click the Force Plan button to require SQL Server to use this query plan for all future queries. You must confirm that you want to force the selected plan before SQL Server accepts the change.

Run the query shown in Listing 4-27 to retrieve most of the rows from the table, and then refresh the Top Resource Consuming Queries view to check the results, as shown in Figure 4-27. Although there is a forced plan for the query that should be reused, the Plan Summary chart now shows a third plan identifier, Plan ID 15, for which the average logical reads is significantly higher than it was for Plan ID 10, the forced plan. (You can identify the forced plan id by the check mark on the point in the chart.)

**LISTING 4-27** Execute stored procedure with new parameter value and forced query plan

```
EXEC Examples.GetValues 1;
GO
```

FIGURE 4-27 A new query plan in the Query Store view based on the forced plan

If you check the graphical query plan for Plan ID 10 and Plan ID 15, you find that both query plans use an index seek operation to retrieve rows. SQL Server generated a new query plan for the stored procedure due to the difference in estimated rows, but the same operations are used. Although this is not the most efficient operation when retrieving a relatively high number of rows, as we discussed previously, it might be a reasonable trade-off when the majority of executions retrieves a small number of rows. If you execute the stored procedure again using a parameter value of 2 and refresh the view, another point associated with Plan ID 10 appears on the Plan Summary chart with a lower value for average logical reads.

Of course, this approach is not a suitable solution for all performance problems. Furthermore, forcing a query plan does not guarantee that SQL Server always uses that query plan. As an example, if a forced query plan is dependent on an index that is subsequently dropped, the plan forcing will fail. For this reason, you should periodically review the status of forced plans and reasons for failure by running the query shown in Listing 4-28. You can also use the query_store_plan_forcing_failed Extended Event to monitor failed plan forcing.

LISTING 4-28 Check status of forced plans

```
SELECT
    p.plan_id,
    p.query_id,
    q.object_id,
    force_failure_count,
    last_force_failure_reason_desc
FROM sys.query_store_plan AS p
INNER JOIN sys.query_store_query AS q
    ON p.query_id = q.query_id
WHERE is_forced_plan = 1;
```

The following three Query Store views behave much like the view we explored in detail in this section, but focus on different types of queries:

- **Regressed Queries** Displays a column chart of metrics by query, a plan summary, and query plan for *regressed queries* executed in the previous hour. A regressed query is one for which a new query plan generated for a particular query is less optimal than a query plan that was previously used for the same query. Regression can happen due to changes in statistics, structural changes to the data, addition or removal or indexes, and so on. Use this view to find regressed queries and determine whether to force an earlier query plan.

- **Overall Resource Consumption** Displays overall resource consumption during the last month in separate charts: duration, execution count, CPU time, and logical reads. You can toggle between the chart view and grid view. This view does not provide access to the query plan details.

- **Tracked Queries** Displays tracked queries. You add a query to this dashboard view by selecting it in the metric chart and then clicking the Track The Selected Query In A New Tracked Queries Window. That way, you can focus on the metrics for a single query rather than try to find it among the changing set of Query IDs on the Top Resource Consuming Queries view.

## Compare estimated and actual query plans and related metadata

After the query optimizer generates a query plan or uses a query plan existing in the plan cache, the storage engine is responsible for executing the query according to that plan. However, the plan that it starts with is an *estimated query plan*. That is, it is the plan determined by the query optimizer to be the most efficient query plan based on the calculations performed by the query optimizer. At runtime, SQL Server reports an *actual query plan* to add runtime information to the estimated query plan. When you compare an estimated and actual query plan for the same query, you can see differences when either of the following situations occur:

- **Inaccurate statistics** As data is inserted into or deleted from a table, both the indexes and the distribution of data in each column change. The automatic statistics update uses a data sample rather than the entire table to reduce the overhead of the process, Therefore, statistics can become less accurate over time.

- **Structural changes** Changing the schema of a table or changing its structure also affects indexes and data distribution and causes a recompilation as does changing or dropping an index used by the query or updating statistics.

A common reason to work with estimated query plans is to evaluate performance of a query in development, particularly when the query execution time is long or when restoring the database to its state prior to query execution is challenging. You can add or change indexes or modify the query structure and then analyze changes to the estimated query plan after making these changes.

To set up an environment to compare estimated and actual query plans that differ, execute the code in Listing 4-29.

**LISTING 4-29** Create test environment for comparing estimated and actual query plans

```
CREATE DATABASE ExamBook762Ch4_QueryPlans;
GO
USE ExamBook762Ch4_QueryPlans;
GO
CREATE SCHEMA Examples;
GO
CREATE TABLE Examples.OrderLines (
    OrderLineID int NOT NULL,
    OrderID int NOT NULL,
    StockItemID int NOT NULL,
    Description nvarchar(100) NOT NULL,
    PackageTypeID int NOT NULL,
    Quantity int NOT NULL,
    UnitPrice decimal(18, 2) NULL,
    TaxRate decimal(18, 3) NOT NULL,
    PickedQuantity int NOT NULL,
    PickingCompletedWhen datetime2(7) NULL,
    LastEditedBy int NOT NULL,
    LastEditedWhen datetime2(7) NOT NULL);
GO
INSERT INTO Examples.OrderLines
SELECT *
FROM WideWorldImporters.Sales.OrderLines;
GO
CREATE INDEX ix_OrderLines_StockItemID
ON Examples.OrderLines (StockItemID);
GO
```

Next, execute the code in Listing 4-30 to generate an estimated query plan. The inclusion of the SET SHOWPLAN_XML ON statement instructs SQL Server to generate the estimated plan without executing the query. As an alternative, you can use the following statements:

- **SET SHOWPLAN_TEXT ON** Returns a single column containing a hierarchical tree that describes the operations and includes the physical operator and optionally the logical operator.

- **SET SHOWPLAN_ALL ON** Returns the same information as SET SHOWPLAN_TEXT except the information is spread across a set of columns in which you can more easily see property values for each operator.

**LISTING 4-30** Generate estimated query plan

```
SET SHOWPLAN_XML ON;
GO
BEGIN TRANSACTION;
    UPDATE Examples.OrderLines
        SET StockItemID = 300
        WHERE StockItemID < 100;
    SELECT
        OrderID,
        Description,
        UnitPrice
    FROM Examples.OrderLines
    WHERE StockItemID = 300;
ROLLBACK TRANSACTION;
GO
SET SHOWPLAN_XML OFF;
GO
```

Click the result row to view the graphical query plan in its own window, as shown in Figure 4-28. Query 3 shows the use of an index seek operation in the SELECT statement.

> **NOTE  SQL SERVER 2016 SERVICE PACK 1 (SP1) BEHAVIOR**
>
> If you are using SQL Server 2016 SP1 and have not applied any subsequent cumulative updates or service packs, the query plan is displayed as XML text instead of the graphical query plan.

**FIGURE 4-28** Estimated query plan

Let's take a closer look at the SELECT statement operations. Because this is an estimated plan, the UPDATE operation has not yet occurred. Therefore, there are no rows with StockItemID equal to 300 in the statistics. By hovering the cursor over the Index Seek (NonClustered) operator, you can display the tooltip that shows the Estimated Number of Rows is 1, as shown in Figure 4-29. It does not yet factor in the effect of the UPDATE operation. Consequently, the query optimizer selects an index seek an operation because it is efficient for a single row. However, if you check the Estimated Row Size for the UPDATE operator for Query 2 in the estimated query plan, the value is 104391, which is a significant discrepancy from the estimate for the index seek operation in Query 3.

**Index Seek (NonClustered)**
Scan a particular range of rows from a nonclustered index.

| | |
|---|---|
| **Physical Operation** | Index Seek |
| **Logical Operation** | Index Seek |
| **Estimated Execution Mode** | Row |
| **Storage** | RowStore |
| **Estimated Operator Cost** | 0.0032831 (50%) |
| **Estimated I/O Cost** | 0.003125 |
| **Estimated Subtree Cost** | 0.0032831 |
| **Estimated CPU Cost** | 0.0001581 |
| **Estimated Number of Executions** | 1 |
| **Estimated Number of Rows** | 1 |
| **Estimated Row Size** | 15 B |
| **Ordered** | True |
| **Node ID** | 1 |

**Object**
[ExamBook762Ch4_QueryPlans].[Examples].
[OrderLines].[ix_OrderLines_StockItemID]
**Output List**
Bmk1000
**Seek Predicates**
Seek Keys[1]: Prefix: [ExamBook762Ch4_QueryPlans].
[Examples].[OrderLines].StockItemID = Scalar Operator
((300))

**FIGURE 4-29** Estimated Row Size in estimated query plan for Index Seek (NonClustered) operator

To generate an actual query plan, execute the statements in Listing 4-31, which uses the SET STATISTICS XML ON statement to have SQL Server generate a graphical actual query plan. As an alternative, you can use the SET STATISTICS PROFILE ON statement to get the query plan information in a hierarchical tree with profile information available across columns in the result set. Figure 4-30 shows that SQL Server recognized the change of greater than 20% in the table's statistics and performed an automatic update which in turn forced a recompilation of the SELECT statement's query plan. This time the query optimizer chose a Table Scan operator because the number of rows to retrieve is nearly half the number of rows in the table.

> *NOTE* **SQL SERVER 2016 SP1 BEHAVIOR**
>
> If you are using SQL Server 2016 SP1 and have not applied any subsequent cumulative updates or service packs, the query plan is displayed as XML text instead of the graphical query plan.

LISTING 4-31 Generate actual query plan

```
SET STATISTICS XML ON;
GO
BEGIN TRANSACTION;
    UPDATE Examples.OrderLines
        SET StockItemID = 300
        WHERE StockItemID < 100;
    SELECT
        OrderID,
        Description,
        UnitPrice
    FROM Examples.OrderLines
    WHERE StockItemID = 300;
ROLLBACK TRANSACTION;
GO
SET STATISTICS XML OFF;
GO
```

FIGURE 4-30 Actual query plan

Checking the tooltip for the Table Scan operation, shown in Figure 4-31, notice the Estimated Number of Rows is 104066 to reflect the updated statistics and the Actual Number of Rows is 104391.

**Table Scan**
Scan rows from a table.

| | |
|---|---|
| Physical Operation | Table Scan |
| Logical Operation | Table Scan |
| Actual Execution Mode | Row |
| Estimated Execution Mode | Row |
| Storage | RowStore |
| Number of Rows Read | 231412 |
| Actual Number of Rows | 104391 |
| Actual Number of Batches | 0 |
| Estimated Operator Cost | 3.67413 (100%) |
| Estimated I/O Cost | 3.41942 |
| Estimated CPU Cost | 0.25471 |
| Estimated Subtree Cost | 3.67413 |
| Number of Executions | 1 |
| Estimated Number of Executions | 1 |
| Estimated Number of Rows | 104066 |
| Estimated Row Size | 128 B |
| Actual Rebinds | 0 |
| Actual Rewinds | 0 |
| Ordered | False |
| Node ID | 0 |

FIGURE 4-31 Estimated Number of Rows and Actual Number of Rows in actual query plan for Table Scan operator.

**NEED MORE REVIEW?** **ADDITIONAL RESOURCE FOR QUERY PLANS**

For a deep dive into query plans, also known as execution plans, download Grant Fritchey's *SQL Server Execution Plans, Second Edition*, a free e-book available at *https://www.simple-talk.com/books/sql-books/sql-server-execution-plans-second-edition-by-grant-fritchey/*.

# Configure Azure SQL Database Performance Insight

Query Performance Insight is the name of a feature available in Azure SQL Database that allows you to review the effect of queries on database resources, identify long-running queries, or create custom settings to review query workloads. This feature available only with Azure SQL Database V12 and requires you to enable Query Store on your database before you can analyze queries. Because Query Store is enabled by default for a V12 database, you do not need to perform this extra step unless you previously disabled it.

**NOTE** **CREATING A SQL DATABASE IN THE AZURE PORTAL**

To work with the monitoring tools in SQL Database, you must have an Azure account and description. You must then create a SQL Database and associate it with a new or existing server. Last, you must configure the firewall settings to enable your IP address to access the database.

If you do not currently have an account, you can set up a free trial at *https://azure.micro-soft.com/en-us/free/*. Then connect to the Azure portal at *https://portal.azure.com*. Next, to create a new sample database, click SQL Databases in the navigation pane on the left side of the screen, and then click Add to open the SQL Database blade. Here you provide a name for your database, select a subscription, select Create New in the Resource Group section, and provide a name for the resource group. In the Select Source dropdown list, select Sample, and then in the Select Sample dropdown list, select AdventureWorksLT [V12]. Click Server, click Create A New Server, provide a server name, a server admin login, password and password confirmation, and location. Be sure to keep the default selection of Yes for Create V12 Server (Lastest Update) as Query Performance Insight works only with SQL Database V12. Click Select to create the server. In the SQL Database blade, click Pricing Tier, select the Basic tier, and then click the Select button. For the sample database, you can use the lowest service tier level to minimize charges associated with this service. When you no longer need to work with the database, be sure to delete it in the Azure portal to avoid incurring ongoing charges. In the SQL Database blade, click Create to finalize the creation of the sample database. When the database is ready, it appears in the list of SQL Databases. You might need to click Refresh several times to see it appear.

When the SQL Database is available, click the dataset to open its blade, and then click the server name to open the server's blade. Click Show Firewall Settings, click Add Client IP, and then click Save to enable your connection to the SQL Database. You can manually add client IPs to open the firewall to allow other users to access the database also.

Although you use the Azure portal to view the information available from Query Performance Insight, you must use SQL Server Management Studio to first enable Query Store on a SQL Database. To do this, click Connect in Object Explorer, type the full name of the server (such as mysampleserver2016.database.windows.net), select SQL Server Authentication in the Authentication drop-down list, type the admin login and password that you created for the database, and then click Connect.

Of course, before you can analyze queries, you must first execute several queries. Execute the query shown in Listing 4-32 which runs 20 times to create a workload on SQL Database. You must wait at least a couple of hours before you can view the corresponding workload analysis in Azure SQL Database Performance Insight.

**LISTING 4-32** Execute SQL Database query multiple times after enabling Query Store

```
SELECT
    c.LastName,
    c.FirstName,
    c.CompanyName,
    year(OrderDate) AS OrderYear,
    sum(OrderQty) AS OrderQty,
    p.Name AS ProductName,
    sum(LineTotal) AS SalesTotal
FROM SalesLT.SalesOrderHeader soh
JOIN SalesLT.SalesOrderDetail sod ON
    soh.SalesOrderID = sod.SalesOrderID
JOIN SalesLT.Customer c ON
    soh.CustomerID = c.CustomerID
JOIN SalesLT.Product p ON
    sod.ProductID = p.ProductID
GROUP BY
    c.LastName,
    c.FirstName,
    c.CompanyName,
    year(OrderDate),
    p.Name
ORDER BY
    c.CompanyName,
    c.LastName,
    c.FirstName,
    p.Name;
GO 20
```

When Query Store is unable to collect new data, you might see the following messages:

- "Query Store is not properly configured on this database. Click here to learn more."
- "Query Store is not properly configured on this database. Click here to change settings."

There are two ways to clear these messages. First, you can increase the Query Store size or clear Query Store. Second, you can change the Retention and Capture policy and enable Query Store by executing the ALTER DATABASE commands described in the "Create efficient query plans using Query Store" section earlier in this chapter.

When enough time has passed after queries have executed, open the Azure portal, select SQL databases in the navigation pane, click the database to analyze, and then select Query Performance Insight in the Support + Troubleshooting category. The Query Performance Insight blade includes the following three tabs:

- Resource consuming queries
- Long running queries
- Custom

## Resource consuming queries

The Resource Consuming Queries tab lists the queries consuming the most resources for the last 24 hours. The top of this section shows a line chart that by default shows the percentage of CPU over time consumed by various queries, as shown in Figure 4-32, although the values for the individual queries are too low to see clearly on the chart. You can click Data IO or Log IO in the top left section to review the relative resource consumption for these resources instead of CPU.

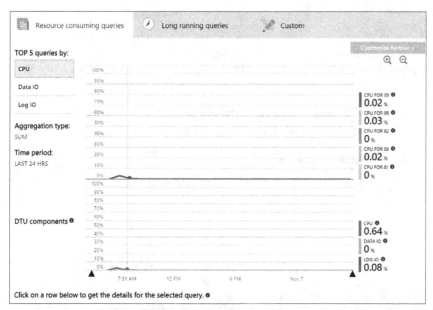

**FIGURE 4-32** Resource Consuming Queries chart showing CPU and DTU components consumption for top resource consuming queries

This chart has many interactive features. For example, you can click on the red line on the chart to show the overall *Database Throughput Unit (DTU)* values, as shown in Figure 4-33. A DTU is a single metric to represent CPU, memory, and IO thresholds. You can also change the basis for determining the top five queries from CPU as shown to Data IO or Log IO by clicking the respective filter labels in the top left of the chart. Another option is to zoom in on a period of time by using the sliders (as indicated by the triangles along the horizontal axis of the chart) to increase or decrease the period of time to view in the chart.

**FIGURE 4-33** Resource Consuming Queries chart showing Overall DTU and DTU components consumption

When you scroll down this page, you can view the average CPU, Data IO, Log IO, duration, and execution count for the top 5 queries for a table, as shown in Figure 4-34.

Click on a row below to get the details for the selected query. ⓘ

| QUERY ID | CPU[%] | ^ | DATA IO[%] | ^ | LOG IO[%] | ^ | DURATION[HH:MM:SS] | ^ | EXECUTIONS COUNT | ^ | # |
|---|---|---|---|---|---|---|---|---|---|---|---|
| 99 | 0 | | 0 | | 0 | | 00:00:00.070 | | 6 | | ✓ |
| 38 | 0 | | 0 | | 0 | | 00:00:00.060 | | 6 | | ✓ |
| 82 | 0 | | 0 | | 0 | | 00:00:00.060 | | 46 | | ✓ |
| 88 | 0 | | 0 | | 0 | | 00:00:00.080 | | 29 | | ✓ |
| 81 | 0 | | 0 | | 0 | | 00:00:00.030 | | 279 | | ✓ |

**FIGURE 4-34** Query Performance Insight table listing average metrics for individual queries

When you click a query in this list, you can view its related details in a set of charts, as shown in Figure 4-35.

Details of Query ID 99 (Aggregation type: sum) Last 24 hrs

CPU FOR 99 ❶
**0.02** %

DATA IO FOR 99 ❶
**0** %

LOG IO FOR 99 ❶
**0** %

DURATION FOR 99 ❶
**70** ms

EXECUTION COUNT F... ❶
**6**

7:30 AM     12 PM     6 PM     Nov 7

**FIGURE 4-35** Query Performance Insight chart showing metrics for a selected query

Below the charts, a table of time intervals displays the metrics, duration, and execution count for the selected query, as shown in Figure 4-36.

| INTERVAL | CPU[%] | DATA IO[%] | LOG IO[%] | DURATION[HH:MM:SS] | EXECUTIONS C... |
|---|---|---|---|---|---|
| 11/6: 05 AM - 06 AM | 0 | 0 | 0 | | 0 |
| 11/6: 06 AM - 07 AM | 0 | 0 | 0 | | 0 |
| 11/6: 07 AM - 08 AM | 0.02 | 0 | 0 | 00:00:00.070 | 6 |

**FIGURE 4-36** Query Performance Insight table showing metrics for a selected query at different time intervals

## Long running queries

The Long Running Queries tab, shown in Figure 4-37, shows the top queries based on duration that have executed on the SQL Database during the past 24 hours. The top of the page shows a chart of each query's duration by execution time and the bottom of the page shows a table of the key performance metrics for each query. You can use this information to find queries that might require tuning.

**FIGURE 4-37** Query Performance Insight chart showing durations of the top 5 long running queries

## Custom

You can also optionally configure a custom view by selecting the Custom tab and then select-ing values in each of the following drop-down lists:

- **Metric type**   Select one of the following metrics by which to determine top queries: CPU, Data IO, Log IO, Duration, or Execution Count.

- **Time interval**   Select one of the following time intervals to set as boundaries for se-lecting top queries: last 6 hours, 24 hours, past week, past month, and a custom range.

- **Number of queries**   Select one of the following numbers to use when selecting top queries: 5, 10, or 20.

- **Aggregate function**   Select one of the following aggregate functions to use when aggregating metric values: Sum, Max, or Avg.

# Skill 4.3: Manage performance for database instances

SQL Server 2016 and Azure SQL Database include many features that help you monitor and manage the performance of database instances. In this section, we review your options for allocating and optimizing server resources. In addition, we introduce DMVs and SQL Server performance counters that you can use to monitor and troubleshoot database performance over time.

# Manage database workload in SQL Server

The SQL Server Resource Governor helps you manage database workloads by setting limits for the amount of CPU, IO, and memory that incoming requests can consume. Within Resource Governor, a workload is a set of queries or requests for which SQL Server should consistently allocate a specific set of resources. This capability is useful when you are managing multiple tenants on the same server and need to minimize the impact of one tenant's workload on the other tenants' workloads or when you need to track resource consumption by workload for chargeback purposes, just to name two examples.

> **IMPORTANT   EDITIONS SUPPORTING RESOURCE GOVERNOR**
>
> Resource Governor is supported only in the Enterprise, Developer, or Evaluation editions of SQL Server.

Figure 4-38 shows the relationship between several components managed by Resource Governor. A *resource pool* defines the physical resources of the server and behaves much like a virtual server. SQL Server creates an internal pool and a default pool during installation, and you can add user-defined resource pools. You associate one or more *workload groups*, a set of requests having common characteristics, to a resource pool. As SQL Server receives a request from a session, the *classification* process assigns it to the workload group having matching characteristics. You can fine-tune the results of this process by creating classifier user-defined functions.

**FIGURE 4-38** Resource Governor components

You must enable Resource Governor to start using it. You can do this in SQL Server Management Studio by expanding the Management node in Object Explorer, right-clicking Resource Governor, and selecting Enable. As an alternative, you can execute the following T-SQL statement:

```
ALTER RESOURCE GOVERNOR RECONFIGURE;
GO
```

**EXAM TIP**

For the exam, you should be able to review a Resource Governor configuration and identify which workload group will execute a specified T-SQL statement. To correctly answer this type of question, you should have a thorough understanding of Resource Governor's architecture and configuration.

## Resource pools

You distribute the amount of memory, CPU, and IO available to SQL Server among resource pools as a means of reducing contention between workloads. Each resource pool is configured with the following settings (except the external resource pool as described later in this section): Minimum CPU%, Maximum CPU%, Minimum Memory %, and Maximum Memory %. The sum of Minimum CPU% and of Minimum Memory % for all resources pools cannot be more than 100. These values represent the guaranteed average amount of that resource that each resource pool can use to respond to requests. The Maximum CPU% and Maximum Memory % reflect the maximum average amount for the respective resources. SQL Server can use more than the maximum percentage defined for a resource if it is available. To prevent this behavior, you can configure a hard cap on the resource available to the resource pool.

After you enable Resource Governor, SQL Server has the following types of resource pools:

- **Internal**   SQL Server uses the internal resource pool for resources required to run the database engine. You cannot change the resource configuration for the internal resource pool. SQL Server creates one when you enable the Resource Governor.

- **Default**   In SQL Server 2016, there is one resource pool for standard database operations and a separate resource pool for external processes such as R script execution. These two resource pools are created when you enable the Resource Governor.

- **External**   An external resource pool is a new type for SQL Server 2016 that was added to support R Services. Because the execution of R scripts can be resource-intensive, the ability to manage resource consumption by using the Resource Governor is necessary to protect normal database operations. In addition, you can add an external resource pool to allocate resources for other external processes. The configuration for an external resource pool differs from the other resource pool types and includes only the following settings: Maximum CPU%, Maximum Memory %, and Maximum Processes.

- **User-defined resource pool**   You can add a resource pool to allocate resources for database operations related to a specific workload.

---

*NOTE*   **MAXIMUM NUMBER OF SUPPORTED RESOURCE POOLS PER INSTANCE**

SQL Server supports a maximum of 64 resource pools per instance.

---

You can use the Resource Governor node in Object Explorer to open a dialog box and add or configure resource pools as needed, although this interface does not include all settings available to configure by using T-SQL. When you create a resource pool by using T-SQL, as shown in Listing 4-33, you specify any or all arguments for CPU, the scheduler, memory, and I/O operations per second (IOPS).

**Listing 4-33** Create user-defined resource pools

```
CREATE RESOURCE POOL poolExamBookDaytime
WITH (
    MIN_CPU_PERCENT = 50,
    MAX_CPU_PERCENT = 80,
    CAP_CPU_PERCENT = 90,
    AFFINITY SCHEDULER = (0 TO 3),
    MIN_MEMORY_PERCENT = 50,
    MAX_MEMORY_PERCENT = 100,
    MIN_IOPS_PER_VOLUME = 20,
    MAX_IOPS_PER_VOLUME = 100
);
GO
CREATE RESOURCE POOL poolExamBookNighttime
WITH (
    MIN_CPU_PERCENT =      0,
    MAX_CPU_PERCENT = 50,
    CAP_CPU_PERCENT = 50,
    AFFINITY SCHEDULER = (0 TO 3),
    MIN_MEMORY_PERCENT = 5,
    MAX_MEMORY_PERCENT = 15,
```

```
        MIN_IOPS_PER_VOLUME = 45,
        MAX_IOPS_PER_VOLUME = 100
);
GO
ALTER RESOURCE GOVERNOR RECONFIGURE;
GO
```

> **NEED MORE REVIEW?**   **ADDITIONAL INFORMATION REGARDING RESOURCE POOLCREATION**
>
> For more information about using T-SQL to create a resource pool, see "CREATE RESOURCE
> POOL (Transact-SQL")" at *https://msdn.microsoft.com/en-us/library/bb895329.aspx.*

## Workload groups

Resource Governor monitors the resources consumed in aggregate by the sessions in a
workload group to ensure consumption does not exceed the thresholds defined for both
the workload group and the resource pool to which it is assigned. The predefined resource
pools each have a predefined workload group, but you can also add workload groups to the
default, external, and user-defined resource pools.

When you configure a workload group, as shown in Listing 4-34, you can specify the
relative importance of a workload group as compared to other workload groups in the same
resource pool only. You can also specify the maximum amount of memory or CPU time that a
request in the workload group can acquire from the resource pool, the maximum degree of
parallelism (DOP) for parallel requests, or the maximum number of concurrent requests.

**Listing 4-34** Create workload groups

```
CREATE WORKLOAD GROUP apps
WITH (
    IMPORTANCE = HIGH,
    REQUEST_MAX_MEMORY_GRANT_PERCENT = 35,
    REQUEST_MAX_CPU_TIME_SEC = 0, --0 = unlimited
    REQUEST_MEMORY_GRANT_TIMEOUT_SEC = 60, --seconds
    MAX_DOP = 0, -- uses global setting
    GROUP_MAX_REQUESTS = 1000 --0 = unlimited
)
USING "poolExamBookDaytime";
GO
CREATE WORKLOAD GROUP reports
WITH (
    IMPORTANCE = LOW,
    REQUEST_MAX_MEMORY_GRANT_PERCENT = 25,
    REQUEST_MAX_CPU_TIME_SEC = 0, --0 = unlimited
    REQUEST_MEMORY_GRANT_TIMEOUT_SEC = 60, --seconds
    MAX_DOP = 0, -- uses global setting
    GROUP_MAX_REQUESTS = 100 --0 = unlimited
)
USING "poolExamBookNighttime";
GO
ALTER RESOURCE GOVERNOR RECONFIGURE;
GO
```

## Classifier user-defined functions

Resource Governor assigns a request to the default group if there is no criteria that matches the request to a workload group. You must create a user-defined function to provide the criteria necessary to assign a request to a specific workload group. If the user-defined function assigns the request to a non-existent workload group, or if the classification process fails for any reason, Resource Governor assigns the request to the default group.

Let's say that you want to establish a classification function to assign a request to a workload group based on the time of day. Furthermore, you want to use a lookup table for the start and end times applicable to a workload group. Let's start by creating and adding a row to the lookup table, as shown in Listing 4-35. Note that you must create this table in the *master* database because Resource Governor uses schema bindings for classifier functions.

**Listing 4-35** Create lookup table

```
USE master
GO
CREATE TABLE tblClassificationTime  (
    TimeOfDay SYSNAME NOT NULL,
    TimeStart TIME NOT NULL,
    TimeEnd   TIME NOT NULL
) ;
GO
INSERT INTO tblClassificationTime
VALUES('apps', '8:00 AM', '6:00 PM');
GO
INSERT INTO tblClassificationTime
VALUES('reports', '6:00 PM', '8:00 AM');
GO
```

Next, you create the classifier function that uses the lookup table to instruct the Resource Governor which workload group to use when classifying an incoming request. An example of such a classifier function is shown in Listing 4-36.

**Listing 4-36** Create and register classifier function

```
USE master;
GO
CREATE FUNCTION fnTimeOfDayClassifier()
RETURNS sysname
WITH SCHEMABINDING  AS
BEGIN
    DECLARE @TimeOfDay sysname
    DECLARE @loginTime time
    SET @loginTime = CONVERT(time,GETDATE())
    SELECT
        TOP 1 @TimeOfDay = TimeOfDay
    FROM dbo.tblClassificationTime
    WHERE
      -- Interval does not overlap midnight
      TimeStart <= @loginTime and TimeEnd > @loginTime
      -- Interval overlaps midnight and session starts before midnight and within the
interval
```

```
        OR (TimeStart <= @loginTime and TimeEnd < TimeStart)
        -- Interval overlaps midnight and session starts after midnight and within the
interval
        OR (TimeEnd > @loginTime and TimeEnd < TimeStart)
    IF(@TimeOfDay IS NOT NULL)
        BEGIN
            RETURN @TimeOfDay
        END
    RETURN N'default'
END;
GO
ALTER RESOURCE GOVERNOR with (CLASSIFIER_FUNCTION = dbo.fnTimeOfDayClassifier);
ALTER RESOURCE GOVERNOR RECONFIGURE;
GO
```

> **NOTE** **RESOURCES FOR CHECKING CONFIGURATION OF RESOURCE GOVERNOR COMPONENTS**
>
> You can confirm the configuration of resource pools, workload groups, and user-defined classifier functions by querying the sys.resource_governor_resource_pools, sys.resource_governor_workload_groups, and sys.resource_governor_configuration system tables respectively. For more information, see "Create and Test a Classifier User-Defined Function" at *https://msdn.microsoft.com/en-us/library/cc645892.aspx*.

## Resource Governor management queries

After you configure all the components necessary for Resource Governor, you can monitor resource consumption by using any of the queries shown in Listing 4-37.

**Listing 4-37** Monitor resource consumption

```
--Current runtime data
SELECT * FROM sys.dm_resource_governor_resource_pools;
GO

SELECT * FROM sys.dm_resource_governor_workload_groups;
GO

--Determine the workload group for each session
SELECT
    s.group_id,
    CAST(g.name as nvarchar(20)) AS WkGrp,
    s.session_id,
    s.login_time,
    CAST(s.host_name as nvarchar(20)) AS Host,
    CAST(s.program_name AS nvarchar(20))  AS Program
FROM sys.dm_exec_sessions s
INNER JOIN sys.dm_resource_governor_workload_groups g
    ON g.group_id = s.group_id
ORDER BY g.name ;
GO

SELECT
```

```
        r.group_id,
        g.name,
        r.status,
        r.session_id,
        r.request_id,
        r.start_time,
        r.command,
        r.sql_handle,
        t.text
FROM sys.dm_exec_requests r
INNER JOIN sys.dm_resource_governor_workload_groups g
    ON g.group_id = r.group_id
CROSS APPLY sys.dm_exec_sql_text(r.sql_handle) AS t
    ORDER BY g.name
GO

-- Determine the classifier running the request
SELECT
    s.group_id,
    g.name,
    s.session_id,
    s.login_time,
    s.host_name,
    s.program_name
FROM sys.dm_exec_sessions s
INNER JOIN sys.dm_resource_governor_workload_groups g
    ON g.group_id = s.group_id   AND
        s.status = 'preconnect'
ORDER BY g.name;
GO

SELECT
    r.group_id,
    g.name,
    r.status,
    r.session_id,
    r.request_id,
    r.start_time,
    r.command,
    r.sql_handle,
    t.text
FROM sys.dm_exec_requests r
INNER JOIN sys.dm_resource_governor_workload_groups g
    ON g.group_id = r.group_id
        AND r.status = 'preconnect'
CROSS APPLY sys.dm_exec_sql_text(r.sql_handle) AS t
ORDER BY g.name;
GO
```

# Design and implement Elastic Scale for Azure SQL Database

*Elastic Scale* is a feature in SQL Database that you use to adjust the database capacity to match the scalability requirements for different applications. In other words, you can grow or shrink the database by using a technique known as *sharding*, which partitions your data across identically structured database. Sharding is useful when the application data in aggregate exceeds the maximum size supported by SQL Database or when you need to separate data by geography for compliance, latency, or geopolitical reasons.

Although sharding is not a new concept, it requires the use of custom code to create and manage sharded applications and adds complexity to your solution architecture. Elastic Scale provides an elastic database client library and a Split-Merge service that help simplify the management of your applications. That way you can adapt the capacity of SQL Database to support varying workloads and ensure consistent performance without manual intervention.

## Elastic database client library

You must use the elastic database client library to implement standard sharding patterns in a SQL Database by calling its features in your elastic scale application. You use it to perform operations across the all shards as a unit or to perform operations on individual shards, as shown in Figure 4-39. The elastic database client library provides the following features:

- **Shard map management**  You first register each database as a shard, and then define a shard map manager that directs connection requests to the correct shard by using a *sharding key* or a key range. A sharding key is data such as a customer ID number that the database engine uses to keep related transactions in one database.

- **Data-dependent routing**  Rather than define a connection in your application, you can use this feature to automatically assign a connection to the correct shard.

- **Multishard querying**  The database engine uses this feature to process queries in parallel across separate shards and then combine the results into a single result set.

- **Shard elasticity**  This feature monitors resource consumption for the current workload and dynamically allocates more resource as necessary and shrinks the database to its normal state when those resources are no longer required.

**FIGURE 4-39**  Sharding management with elastic database client library

---

*NOTE*  **LEARNING MORE ABOUT WORKING WITH THE ELASTIC DATABASE CLIENT LIBRARY**

To use the elastic database client library, you must use Visual Studio 2012 (or higher), C#, and Nuget 2.7 (or higher). You can learn more about working with this client library at "Get started with Elastic Database tools" at *https://azure.microsoft.com/en-us/documentation/articles/sql-database-elastic-scale-get-started/.*

---

## Split-Merge service

You use the Split-Merge service to add or remove databases as shards from the shard set and redistribute the data across more or fewer shards, as shown in Figure 4-40. As demand increases, you can split the data out across a greater number of shards. Conversely, you can merge the data into fewer shards as demand lowers.

FIGURE 4-40 Examples of splitting and merging shards

---

*NOTE* **A TUTORIAL FOR USING THE SPLIT-MERGE SERVICE**

A tutorial that includes a link for the split-merge tool and instructions for using it is available at "Deploy a split-merge service," *https://docs.microsoft.com/en-us/azure/sql-data-base/sql-database-elastic-scale-configure-deploy-split-and-merge*.

---

*NEED MORE REVIEW?* **ELASTIC SCALE RESOURCES ONLINE**

For the exam, you should be familiar with the architecture, features, and tools of Elastic Scale and understand use cases. For more details about Elastic Scale, refer to "Scaling out with Azure SQL Database" at *https://docs.microsoft.com/en-us/azure/sql-database/sql-database-elastic-scale-introduction*.

# Select an appropriate service tier or edition

Microsoft uses editions for SQL Server 2016 and service tiers for Azure SQL Database to provide combinations of product features, performance, and price levels so that you can select one that best meets your application's requirements. You should be familiar with the general features and limitations of each edition and understand the differences between each edition for the exam.

SQL Server 2016 is available in the following editions:

- **Express** This edition is a free version of SQL Server with limited features that you can use for small applications and Web sites. The maximum database size supported by this edition is 10 GB. It uses up to 1 GB memory and to the lesser of 1 physical processor or 4 cores. There are three types of SQL Server 2016 Express from which to choose:

  - **LocalDB** You use *LocalDB* for a simple application with a local embedded database that runs in single-user mode.

  - **Express** You use Express when your application requires a small database only and does not require any other components packaged with SQL Server in the Standard edition. You can install this edition on a server and then enable remote connections to support multiple users.

  - **Express with Advanced Services** This edition includes the database engine as well as Full Text Search and Reporting Services.

- **Web** This edition is scalable up to 64 GB of memory and the lesser of 4 physical processors or 16 cores with a maximum database size of 524 PB. It includes the database engine, but without support for availability groups and other high-availability features. It also does not include many of the advanced security and replication features available in Standard or Enterprise edition, nor does it include the business intelligence components such as Analysis Services and Reporting Services, among others. Web edition is intended for use only by Web hosters and third-party software service providers.

- **Standard** This edition scales to 128 GB of memory and the lesser of 4 physical processors or 24 cores. The maximum database size with Standard edition is 524 PB. This edition includes core database and business intelligence functionality and includes basic high-availability and disaster recovery features, new security features such as row-level security and dynamic data masking, and access to non-relational data sources by using JSON and PolyBase.

- **Enterprise** This edition includes all features available in the SQL Server platform and provides the highest scalability, greatest number of security features, and the most advanced business intelligence and analytics features. Like Standard edition, Enterprise edition supports a database size up to 524 PB, but its only limits on memory and processor sizes are the maximums set by your operating system.

  To support higher availability, this edition supports up to 8 secondary replicas, with up to two synchronous secondary replicas, in an availability group, online page and file restore, online indexing, fast recovery, mirrored backups, and the ability to hot add memory and CPU.

For greater performance, Enterprise edition supports in-memory OLTP, table and index partitioning, data compression, Resource Governor, parallelism for partitioned tables, multiple file stream containers, and delayed durability, among other features.

Enterprise edition includes many security features not found in Standard edition. In particular, Always Encrypted protects data at rest and in motion. Additional security features exclusive to Enterprise edition include more finely-grained auditing, transparent data encryption, and extensible key management.

Features supporting data warehouse operations found only in Enterprise edition include change data capture, star join query optimizations, and parallel query processing on partitioned indexes and tables.

- **Developer**   This edition is for developers that create, test, and demonstrate applications using any of the data platform components available in Enterprise edition. However, the Developer edition cannot be used in a production environment.

- **Evaluation**   This edition is a free trial version of SQL Server 2016. You can use this for up to 180 days that you can use to explore all of the features available in Enterprise Edition before making a purchasing decision.

---

*NEED MORE REVIEW?*   **FEATURES AND LIMITATIONS OF SQL SERVER EDITIONS**

A complete list of the features and limitations of each edition is available at *https://technet. microsoft.com/en-us/windows/cc645993(v=sql.90)*.

---

When you select the type of SQL Database to implement, you choose a service tier along with a performance level. The service tier sets the maximum database size while the performance level determines the amount of CPU, memory, and IO thresholds which collectively are measured as a DTU. When you create a new SQL Database, you can choose from the following service tiers:

- **Basic**   This service tier has a maximum database size of 2 GB and performance level of 5 DTUs. You use this option when you need a small database for an application or website with relatively few concurrent requests. The benchmark transaction rate is 16,600 transactions per hour.

- **Standard**   This service tier has a maximum database size of 250 GB and performance levels ranging from 10 to 100 DTUs. You can use this option when a database needs to support multiple applications and multiple concurrent requests for workgroup and web applications. With 50 DTUs, the benchmark transaction rate is 2,570 transactions per minute.

- **Premium**   This service tier has a maximum database size of 1 TB and performance levels ranging from 125 to 4,000 DTUs. You use this option for enterprise-level database requirements. With 1,000 DTUs, the benchmark transaction rate is 735 transactions per second.

# Optimize database file and tempdb configuration

One option that you have for improving the performance of read and write operations is to optimize the configuration of files that SQL Server uses to store data and log files. Your optimization goal is to reduce contention for storage and IO of files used not only by your database, but also by tempdb.

## Database file optimization

When your application must support a high volume of read/write operations, you should consider taking the following steps to mitigate disk contention:

- **File placement** Data and log files should be placed on separate physical disks for better performance. Remember from the explanation of transactions that we described in Chapter 3, "Managing database concurrency," that SQL Server writes each transaction to the log before updating the data file. By separating the two file types, the read/write head for the disk with the log file can work more efficiently without frequent interruptions by the writes to the data file. Furthermore, consider using a disk with high write performance for the log file. This recommendation is less applicable when the bulk of SQL Server activity is read operations.

  By default, the data and log files for a new database are placed on the same drive, and normally in the same directory as the system databases: \Program Files\Microsoft SQL Server\MSSQL13.MSSQLSERVER\MSSQL\DATA. You can move the data and log files to a new location by using the ALTER DATABASE command as shown in Listing 4-38, replacing <databasename> and <drive:\filepath> with the appropriate names for your database and folder structures.

LISTING 4-38 Relocate data and log files

```
ALTER DATABASE <databasename>
SET OFFLINE;
GO
ALTER DATABASE <databasename>
MODIFY FILE (NAME = <databasename>_Data, FILENAME = "<drive:\filepath>\
Data\<databasename>_Data.mdf");
GO
ALTER DATABASE <databasename>
MODIFY FILE (NAME = <databasename>_Log, FILENAME = "drive:filepath>\
Log\<databasename>_Log.mdf");
ALTER DATABASE <databasename>
SET ONLINE;
```

Another benefit of separating data and log files on separate drives is mitigating a potential failure. If the drive containing the data files fails, you can still access the log file from the other disk and recover data up to the point of failure.

- **File groups and secondary data files** By default, each database has a primary filegroup that contains the primary data file containing system tables and database files created without a filegroup specification. SQL Server uses the primary filegroup as the default for new indexes and tables that you create without placing them in a specific filegroup, but you can create a new filegroup and designate it as the default. There can only be one default filegroup, but you can create as many additional file groups as you need as containers for one or more data and log files. Files within a single filegroup can be spread across multiple disks to increase the parallelism of data access. Furthermore, you can separate tables or indexes that are heavily accessed from lesser used tables or indexes by assigning them to different filegroups, which in turn are each placed on separate disks. Listing 4-39 shows how to create a database with multiple filegroups and how to add a filegroup to an existing database to isolate an index on its own disk:

**Listing 4-39 Create and alter database with multiple file groups**

```
--Create a database on 4 drives
CREATE DATABASE DB1 ON
PRIMARY
    (Name = <databasename>, FILENAME = '<drive1:filepath>\<databasename>.mdf'),
    FILEGROUP FGHeavyAccess1
    (Name = <databasename>_1, FILENAME = '<drive3:filepath>\<databasename>_1.ndf')
LOG ON
    (Name = <databasename>_1_Log, FILENAME = '<drive3:filepath>\<databasename>_1_
log.ldf'),
    (Name = <databasename>_1, FILENAME = '<drive4:filepath>\<databasename>_1_
log_2.ldf');
-- Add filegroup for index
ALTER DATABASE <databasename>
    ADD FILEGROUP FGIndex;
--  Add data file to the new filegroup
ALTER DATABASE <databasename>
ADD FILE (
    NAME = <databasename>,
    FILENAME = '<drive1:filepath>\<databasename>.ndf',
    SIZE=1024MB,
    MAXSIZE=10GB,
    FILEGROWTH=10%)
TO FILEGROUP FGIndex;
-- Add index to filegroup
CREATE NONCLUSTERED INDEX ix_Example
    ON Examples.BusyTable(TableColumn)
    ON FGIndex;
```

- **Partitioning** You can use partitioning to place a table across multiple filegroups. Each partition should be in its own filegroup to improve performance. To map a value in a partition function to a specific filegroup, you use a partition scheme. Let's say you have four filegroups—FGYear1, FGYear2, FGYear3, and FGYear4—and a partition function PFYearRange that defines four partitions for a table. You can create a partition schema to apply the partition function to these filegroups as shown in Listing 4-40.

```
CREATE PARTITION SCHEME PSYear
   AS PARTITION PFYearRange
   TO (FGYear1, FGYear2, FGYear3, FGYear4);
```

## tempdb optimization

Because so many operations, such as cursors, temp tables, and sorts, to name a few, rely on tempdb, configuring tempdb properly is critical to the performance of the database engine. Consider performing the following steps to optimize tempdb configuration:

- **SIMPLE recovery model**   By using the SIMPLE recovery model, which is the default, SQL Server reclaims log space automatically so that the space required for the database is kept as low as possible.

- **Autogrowth**   You should keep the default setting which allows tempdb files to automatically grow as needed.

- **File placement**   The tempdb data and log files should be placed on different disks than your production database data and log files. Do not place the tempdb data files on the C drive to prevent the server from failing to start after running out of hard drive space. In addition, be sure to place the tempdb log file on its own disk. Regardless, put tempdb files on fast drives.

- **Files per core**   In general, the number of data files for tempdb should be a 1:1 ratio of data files to CPU cores. In fact, in SQL Server 2016, the setup wizard now assigns the correct number based on the number of logical processors that it detects on your server, up to a maximum of 8, as shown in Figure 4-41.

- **File size**   When you configure the database engine at setup, the default file size recommended by the setup wizard of 8 MB for an initial size with an autogrowth setting of 64MB is conservative and too small for most implementations. Instead, consider starting with an initial size of 4,096 MB with an autogrowth setting of 512 MB to reduce contention and minimize the impact of uncontrolled tempdb growth on performance. If you dedicate a drive to tempdb, you can set up the log files evenly on the drive to avoid performance issues caused by SQL Server pausing user activity as it grows the log files.

**FIGURE 4-41** TempDB configuration in SQL Server 2016 Setup wizard

---

**NEED MORE REVIEW?** **OPTIMIZATION AND CAPACITY PLANNING FOR TEMPDB**

For specific size and placement recommendations, see "Optimizing tempdb Performance" at *https://technet.microsoft.com/en-us/library/ms175527.aspx* and "Capacity Planning for tempdb" at *https://technet.microsoft.com/en-us/library/ms345368.aspx*.

---

## Optimize memory configuration

SQL Server's memory manager dynamically allocates memory according to the workloads on the host computer and in the database engine. However, you can use the following server configuration options to optimize SQL Server memory:

- **min server memory**   Use this option to prevent SQL Server from releasing memory to the operating system when the server memory drops to this threshold.

- **max server memory**   Use this option to ensure that other applications running on the same computer as SQL Server have adequate memory. When an application requests memory only as needed, you do not need to configure this option. It applies only when an application uses the memory available when it starts and does not later request more memory when necessary. You should configure this option to prevent SQL Server from taking the memory that the application might need.

- **max worker threads**   Use this configuration to define the number of threads available to user operations. If you keep the default value of 0, SQL Server configures the number of worker threads each time the service restarts.

- **index create memory**   Use this option to set the maximum amount of memory that SQL Server initially allocates for index creation. SQL Server will allocate more memory later if necessary, but only if it is available. Typically, you do not need to configure this option, but if SQL Server is experiencing performance delays related to indexing, you can increase the value of this option.

- **min memory per query**   Use this option to improve performance of memory-intensive queries by establishing the minimum amount of memory allocated for query execution. SQL Server can use more memory than the configured minimum if it is available.

To configure memory, right-click the server instance in Object Explorer and select Properties. Click the Memory page, and then in the Server Memory Options, type the appropriate values for any property except *max worker threads*. You can also use T-SQL to adjust a property value like this:

```
EXEC sp_configure 'show advanced options', 1;
GO
RECONFIGURE;
GO
EXEC sp_configure 'min memory per query', 512 ;
GO
RECONFIGURE;
GO
```

# Monitor and diagnose schedule and wait statistics using dynamic management objects

One of the best ways to determine which SQL Server resource is a bottleneck on performance is to review wait statistics. To better understand why waits, it is helpful first to understand how SQL Server manages incoming requests. Each authenticated connection is assigned to a session by SQL Server which then uses a pseudo-operating system called the SQL Operating System (SQLOS) Scheduler to schedule CPU time for each session's requests. There is one SQLOS Scheduler per logical CPU core on the server to manage the worker threads performing operations necessary to complete a request. These worker threads must work cooperatively by running only for 4-milliseconds, known as a *quantum*, before yielding the CPU to another worker thread and waiting in a runnable queue for another turn. It might voluntarily yield the CPU if its quantum has not yet expired and it cannot complete its task, because a resource it needs is unavailable. In this case, the worker thread is moved to a waiter list and then later moves back to the runnable queue when the needed resource becomes available.

Wait statistics allow you to analyze the time a worker thread spends in various states before it completes a request by providing the following key pieces of information:

- **Wait type**   The cause of the wait. For example, the disk IO is slow, resources are locked, CPU is under pressure, an index is missing, or many other reasons. There are hundreds of wait types that SQL Server tracks.

- **Service time**   The amount of time that a thread runs on the CPU.

- **Wait time**   The amount of time that a thread is not running because it is in the waiter list.

- **Signal wait time**   The amount of time that a thread is in the runnable queue ready to run, but waiting for CPU time.

- **Total wait time**   The sum of wait time and signal wait time.

You can access wait statistics through the following DMVS:

- **sys.dm_os_wait_stats**   View information about completed waits at the instance level.

- **sys.dm_exec_session_wait_stats**   View information about waits at the session level.

- **sys.dm_os_waiting_tasks**   View information about requests in the waiter list.

## sys.dm_os_wait_stats

In Chapter 3 we explored how to use this DMV for troubleshooting lock issues, but it is also useful for discovering the most frequently occurring waits since the last reset of the cumulative values. The cumulative wait time in this DMV includes the cumulative signal wait time, so subtract signal wait time from wait time when you want to determine the cumulative time threads spend in the waiter list.

> **NOTE   ISOLATING TOP WAITS**
>
> You can find a useful query for isolating top waits to help focus your troubleshooting efforts in Paul Randal's blog post, "Wait statistics, or please tell me where it hurts" at *http://www.sqlskills.com/blogs/paul/wait-statistics-or-please-tell-me-where-it-hurts/.*

By reviewing this DMV for specific characteristics, you can uncover some of the following potential issues on your server:

- **CPU pressure**   Compare the signal wait time to the total wait time to determine the relative percentage of time that a thread has to wait for its turn to run on the CPU. When this value is relatively high, it can be an indicator that the CPU is overwhelmed by queries that require tuning or your server needs more CPU. You can confirm whether the issue is related to CPU by checking the runnable_tasks_count column in the sys.dm_os_schedulers DMV to see if there is a high number of tasks in the runnable queue. You might also see a higher occurrence of the SOS_SCHEDULER_YIELD wait type if the CPU is under pressure. In addition, you can monitor CPU-related performance counters as described in Skill 4.4.

- **IO issues**   If tasks are waiting for the IO subsystem, you will see waits that contain *IO* in the name. In particular, monitor the trend in average wait time which is calculated by dividing wait_time_ms by waiting_tasks_count. If it starts trending upward, investigate IO using performance counters.

Two wait types that will appear frequently in this DMV when IO issues exist are ASYNC_IO_COMPLETION and IO_COMPLETION. Check physical disk performance counters to confirm this diagnosis, which we describe in the next section, "Troubleshoot and analyze storage, IO, and cache issues." Consider adding indexes to reduce IO contention.

You might also see PAGEIOLATCH waits when a thread is waiting for latches to release after writing a data page in memory to disk or WRITELOG waits when the log management system is waiting to flush to disk. These wait types can indicate either an IO subsystem problem or a memory problem. To narrow down the possibilities, you need to check IO statistics by using sys.dm_io_virtual_file_stats and by reviewing IO-related performance counters.

- **Memory pressure**  The PAGEIOLATCH wait might also indicate memory pressure instead of an IO subsystem problem. It appears when SQL Server does not have enough free memory available for the buffer pool. Check the Page Life Expectancy performance counter to see if it is dropping as compared to a baseline value to confirm whether memory is the reason for this wait type. If you see an increase in CXPACKET waits in conjunction with PAGEIOLATCH waits, the culprit could be a query plan using large table or index scans.

  Another indicator of a memory pressure issue is the RESOURCE_SEMAPHORE wait. It occurs when a query requests more memory than is currently available. You can check the sys.dm_exec_query_memory_grants DMV and combine it with sys.dm_exec_sql_text and sys.dm_exec_sql_plan DMVs to find the memory-intensive queries and review their query plans.

### sys.dm_exec_session_wait_stats

This DMV is new in SQL Server 2016 and is identical in structure to sys.dm_os_wait_stats, but has an additional column for session ID. However, it is important to note that this new DMV only includes information for sessions that are currently connected. When a session disconnects, its wait statistics are cleared from the DMV. Nonetheless, it can be helpful when you need to diagnose the workload for a specific session.

### sys.dm_os_waiting_tasks

We introduced this DMV in Chapter 3 as a tool for finding blocked sessions, but you can also use it to find the requests currently waiting for a resource and why. As one example, you might filter the DMV by using the wait_duration_ms column to find tasks that have been waiting longer than a threshold that you specify.

# Troubleshoot and analyze storage, IO, and cache issues

Troubleshooting and analyzing storage, IO, and cache issues is a huge topic to which many
books, blog posts, and workshops are dedicated because there are many different ways to
configure the disk and IO subsystem and many different issues that can arise. For the exam,
you should understand how to get information about storage, IO, and cache performance
from SQL Server and the Microsoft Windows operating system.

## Storage and IO

Storage bottlenecks occur when your data or log files are stored on slow disks or when the
RAID is not configured appropriately for your workload. Unless your application is using
memory-optimized tables, SQL Server is frequently reading data from disk in response to
queries or writing new or changed data to disk. Meanwhile, tempdb is disk-based and uses
a lot of IO for grouping and sorting operations. Conditions within SQL Server that create
IO bottlenecks include frequent index scans, inefficient queries, and outdated statistics.
Although SQL Server is requesting the reads and writes, the operating system controls the
system bus, disk controller cards, disks, and other IO devices to physically perform the disk IO.
Another factor to consider is the demand that other applications running on the server can
place on the IO subsystem.

Your first indication that you might have an IO problem might come from an analysis
of waits as we described in the previous section. Your next step is to use the sys.dm_io_vir-
tual_file_stats DMV in combination with sys.master_files to analyze cumulative metrics related
to each database including its data and log files. These DMVs help you find the busiest files
and provides IO stall information that tells you how long users had to wait for IO operations
to finish.

Another way to find these issues is to use the sys.dm_os_performance_counters DMV. The availability of the DMV means you can easily get SQL Server-related performance counter information without first setting up Windows Performance Monitor.

The following performance counters, accessible by executing the statements shown in Listing 4-41, provide insight into the amount of IO that SQL Server is directly contributing to the server:

- **SQLServer:Buffer Manager: Page lookups/sec** Average requests per second at which SQL Server finds a page in the buffer pool. This value should be lower than *SQLServer:SQL Statistics: Batch Requests/sec* multiplied by 100.

- **SQLServer:Buffer Manager: Page reads/sec** Average rate at which SQL Server reads from disk. This value should be lower than the hardware specifications for the IO subsystem's read operations.

- **SQLServer:Buffer Manager: Page writes/sec** Average rate at which SQL Server writes to disk. This value should be lower than the hardware specifications for the IO subsystem's write operations.

**Listing 4-41** Review SQL Server:Buffer Manager performance counters

```
SELECT
    object_name,
    counter_name,
    instance_name,
    cntr_value,
    cntr_type
FROM sys.dm_os_performance_counters
WHERE object_name = 'SQLServer:Buffer Manager' AND
    counter_name IN
        ('Page lookups/sec', 'Page reads/sec', 'Page writes/sec')
```

If these performance counters are too high, consider one or more of the following solutions:

- Tune database performance by adding new indexes, improving existing indexes, or normalizing tables, or partitioning tables.
- Replace the IO subsystem hardware with faster components.

## Cache issues

SQL Server is self-tuning and manages memory dynamically. It will use as much memory as you can give it, and it will not release memory until the operating system sets the low memory resource notification flag. Cache bottlenecks occur when SQL Server does not have enough memory to manage. To diagnose cache issues, start by checking the physical memory of the server and identifying how other applications on the server are using memory. You might need to analyze and tune specific queries as well. For example, if an index is missing on a large table, SQL Server must perform a table scan which reads a significant amount of data into memory.

The following DMVs are useful for understanding memory usage on your server:

- **sys.dm_os_memory_cache_counters**   View the current state of the cache.
- **sys.dm_os_sys_memory**   View resource usage information for the server, including total physical and available memory and high or low memory state.
- **sys.dm_os_memory_clerks**   View usage information by memory clerk processes that manage memory for SQL Server.

> *NOTE*  **LEARNING MORE ABOUT USING DMVS TO TUNE PERFORMANCE**
>
> You can learn more about using these and related DMVs to investigate memory usage in Louis Davidson and Tim Ford's free book, *Performance Tuning with SQL Server Dynamic Management Views*, which you can download from *https://assets.red-gate.com/community/books/performance-tuning-with-dmvs.pdf*.

You should also use the following performance counters to monitor whether SQL Server has adequate memory:

- **SQLServer:Buffer Manager: Free List Stalls/Sec**   Number of requests per second that SQL Server waits for a free page in the buffer cache. If this value is greater than zero on a frequent basis, the server is experiencing memory pressure.
- **SQLServer:Buffer Manager: Lazy Writes/Sec**   Number of times per second that SQL Server flushes pages to disk. If this number is rising over time, and Free List Stalls/Sec is also greater than zero, you likely need more memory on the server.
- **SQLServer:Memory Manager: Memory Grants Outstanding**   Number of processes that have acquired a memory grant successfully. A low value might signify memory pressure.

- **SQLServer:Memory Manager: Memory Grants Pending**   Number of processes that are waiting for a memory grant. If this value is greater than zero, consider turning queries or adding memory to the server.

## Monitor Azure SQL Database query plans

To monitor Azure SQL Database query plans, you use many of the same techniques that you use to monitor SQL Server query plans. Specifically, you can choose any of the following methods:

- **T-SQL statements**   You can use the Showplan SET options in SQL Server Management Studio to capture query plans, just as you can for SQL Server.  You can also use the Display Estimated Execution Plan and Include Actual Execution Plan buttons in the toolbar to generate the respective graphical query plan.
- **Extended Events**   You can use Extended Events to capture query plans, much like you can for SQL Server. There are some slight differences, however. Instead of using the ON SERVER clause in the CREATE EVENT SESSION, ALTER EVENT SESSION, and DROP EVENT SESSION commands, you must use ON DATABASE instead. If you want to save a query plan to a file, you must write the file to an Azure Storage container. In addition, there are also several DMVS for Extended Events that are unique to SQL Database.

> *NOTE*   **UNDERSTANDING DIFFERENCES IN EXTENDED EVENTS BETWEEN SQL SERVER AND SQL DATABASE**
>
> For more information about the differences in usage of Extended Events between SQL Server and SQL Database, see "Extended events in SQL Database" at *https://docs.microsoft. com/en-us/azure/sql-database/sql-database-xevent-db-diff-from-svr.*

- **Query Store**   Query Store is enabled by default for V12 databases. You can access the Query Store views in SQL Server Management Studio in the same way that you do for SQL Server. Also, you can use the same Query Store DMVs.

> *IMPORTANT*   **SQL DATABASE LACKS SUPPORT FOR SQL TRACE**
>
> The use of SQL Trace is not supported in SQL Database.

# Skill 4.4: Monitor and trace SQL Server baseline performance metrics

One of the most important responsibilities of a DBA is to ensure that SQL Server runs smooth-ly and performs optimally. To fulfill this responsibility, you should be familiar with the array of tools available to help you uncover and diagnose problems occurring on the server. We have introduced several of these tools in the preceding pages of this chapter, but we did so with specific contexts in mind. Now let's step back and survey the tools again in terms of how you can use them to baseline server performance at the operating system and SQL Server instance levels. In addition, we introduce some new tools that you can use towards this same goal.

**This section covers how to:**

- Monitor operating system and SQL Server performance metrics
- Compare baseline metrics to observed metrics while troubleshooting performance issues
- Identify differences between performance monitoring and logging tools
- Monitor Azure SQL Database performance
- Determine best practice use cases for Extended Events
- Distinguish between Extended Events targets
- Compare the impact of Extended Events and SQL Trace
- Define differences between Extended Events Packages, Targets, Actions, and Sessions

## Monitor operating system and SQL Server performance metrics

At any time, without any elaborate setup requirements, you can access the following tools to check performance metrics for the operating system and SQL Server:

- **Dynamic management objects (DMOs)**   DMVs and DMFs provide insight into the historical and current state of SQL Server. You can query DMOs on an ad hoc basis, or you can create export the data into tables for long-term storage and trend analysis.

- **Performance Monitor**   Operating system and SQL Server performance counters provide useful information to corroborate metrics obtained from other sources and to help narrow down the range of possible causes when investigating specific problems.

- **SQL Trace**   You can set up server-side or SQL Server Profiler tracing for a variety of events as a method of investigating problematic workloads and poorly performing queries.

- **Extended Events** You can create Extended Events sessions as a more lightweight approach to server-side tracing.

## Dynamic management objects

In Chapter 3 and earlier in this chapter, we explored a wide variety of DMOs that you can use to troubleshoot locking and blocking issues, collect execution statistics on natively compiled stored procedures, review index usage, access Query Store information, review wait statistics, and troubleshoot storage, IO, and cache issues. Did you happen to notice any patterns in the naming of these DMOs? By understanding the naming conventions, you can get a high-level view of the range of information that DMOs supply. For the exam, you do not need to be familiar with the complete list of DMO categories supported in SQL Server. However, given the name of a specific DMO, you should be able to identify the type of information it provides at a general level by its association with one of the following categories:

- **sys.dm_exec_*** Connections, sessions, requests, and query execution
- **sys.dm_os_*** Information for the operating system on which SQL Server runs
- **sys.dm_tran_*** Details about transactions
- **sys.dm_io_*** IO processes
- **sys.dm_db_*** Database-scoped information

> *NOTE* **ADDITIONAL INFORMATION ABOUT DMOS**
>
> For more in-depth information about dynamic management objects, refer to "Dynamic Management Views and Functions (Transact-SQL)" at *https://msdn.microsoft.com/en-us/library/ms188754.aspx*.

Most DMOs provide information about the current state, such as currently blocked sessions in sys.dm_os_waiting_tasks, or information accumulated since SQL Server last restarted, such as sys.dm_os_wait_stats. SQL Server retains the information accessible through DMOs in memory only and does not persist it to disk. Therefore, the information is reset when SQL Server restarts.

## Performance Monitor

Performance Monitor, also known as PerfMon, is a tool provided with the Windows operating system that you can use to monitor operating system, application, and hardware performance in real time. You can even establish thresholds and receive alerts when thresholds are crossed. As an alternative, you can capture performance data in logs that you can review in the graphical interface or save to SQL Server tables for trend analysis.

Typically, you use performance counters to confirm suspicions of a problem that you uncover by using wait statistics rather than as a starting point. Like DMOs,

For real-time analysis, open Performance Monitor, and click the Add button in the toolbar. In the Add Counters dialog box, select the server to monitor in the Select Counters From

Computer drop-down list (or use the Browse button to locate a server on your network), and then scroll through the Available Counters list to locate the set of counters to monitor, such as PhysicalDisk. When you monitor PhysicalDisk counters, you can select a specific disk to monitor or all disks. Select a specific counter, such as % Disk Time, and click the Add button. Continue adding counters as needed. When finished, click OK. You can then view real-time metrics for the selected counters. If you are monitoring multiple counters at the same time, right-click a counter and select Properties to change Color, Width, Style values to more easily distinguish between counters, as shown in Figure 4-42. You might also need to reset the scale for a counter.

**FIGURE 4-42** Real-time monitoring of performance counters in Performance Monitor

To identify issues in disk IO activity, start by reviewing the following performance counters (replacing PhysicalDisk with the LogicalDisk if you have multiple logical partitions on the same disk):

- **PhysicalDisk: % Disk Time**   Percentage of time the disk is active with reads and writes. If this percentage is greater than 90 percent, review the *Physical Disk: Current Disk Queue Length* counter.

- **PhysicalDisk: Avg. Disk sec/Read**   Average read latency in seconds. This value should be less than 0.020.

- **PhysicalDisk: Avg. Disk sec/Transfer**   Average latency of IO requests to the disk in seconds. This value should be less than .020.

- **PhysicalDisk: Avg. Disk sec/Write**   Average write latency of IO requests to the disk in seconds. This value should be less than .020.

- **PhysicalDisk: Current Disk Queue Length**   Number of IO requests waiting for access to the disk. This value should be no more than two times the number of spindles for the disk. Most disks have a single spindle, but a redundant array of independent disks (RAID) typically have more than one spindle, even though the RAID device appears as a single physical disk in System Monitor.

- **Memory: Page Faults/sec**   This performance counter increases when processes on the server are consuming too much memory and SQL Server must page to disk. Paging itself is not necessarily a cause of an I/O bottleneck, but can slow the performance of the IO subsystem.

Another important resource to monitor is CPU usage, which you can watch by using the following performance counters:

- **Processor: % Privileged Time**   Percentage of time that the operating system spends processes SQL Server I/O requests. If this value is high at the same time that the disk-related performance counters described in the "Troubleshoot and analyze storage, IO, and cache issues" section are also high, your server likely needs a faster disk.

- **Processor: % Processor Time**   Percentage of time that each processor spends executing a thread that is not idle. If this value is consistently between 80 and 90 percent, you should upgrade the CPU or add more processors.

- **Processor: % User Time**   Percentage of time that the operating system executes user processes, including IO requests from SQL Server. If this value approaches 100%, it might indicate that the CPU is under pressure.

- **System: Processor Queue Length**   Number of threads waiting for processor time. An increase in this counter means the CPU is not keeping up with demand and a faster processor is necessary.

To monitor memory, use the following performance counters:

- **Memory: Available Bytes**   Amount of memory available for processes on the server. If this value is too low, check to see if another application on the server is failing to release memory or if memory on the server is adequate for your requirements.

- **Memory: Pages/sec**   Frequency with which pages are retrieved from or written to disk due to hard page faults. When this value is consistently high, the server might be paging excessively. If it is, the Memory: Page Faults/sec performance counter will also be high.

- **Process: Working Set**   Amount of memory used by a process. If this number is consistently lower than the minimum server memory option, SQL Server is configured to use too much memory.

## SQL Trace

As we described in Skill 4.2, "Analyze and troubleshoot query plans," SQL Trace is useful for server-side or client-side tracing when you want to capture query plans. However, you can use tracing to monitor other aspects of SQL Server performance. Unlike DMOs that allow you to capture activity as it occurs, SQL Trace requires that a monitored event is completed before its data is added to the trace.

Besides using SQL Trace to get query plans, consider using it as a diagnostic tool when you need to monitor SQL Server's behavior during query processing. For example, you might use SQL Trace in the following situations:

- **Lock escalation**   You can find correlations between lock escalation events and queries running when lock escalation occurs by creating a trace that includes the Lock:Escalation, SP:Started, T-SQL:StmtStarted, SP:Completed, and T-SQL:StmtCompleted.

- **Deadlocks**   As we described in Chapter 3, you can capture a deadlock graph by creating a trace that includes the Deadlock Graph, Lock:Deadlock, and Lock:Deadlock Chain events.

- **Slow queries**   You can identify and capture information about slow queries in a trace containing the RPC:Completed, SP:StmtCompleted, SQL:BatchStarting, SQL:BatchCompleted, and Showplan XML events.

## Extended Events

We introduced Extended Events in Chapter 3 as a method for finding deadlocks after they occur and explored this feature again as lightweight alternative to SQL Trace for capturing query plans. The Extended Events feature in SQL Server provides even more functionality than deadlock and query plan monitoring.

As the replacement for SQL Trace, which is slated for deprecation in a future version of SQL Server, Extended Events not only allow you to perform the same tasks with greater flexibility and better performance, but also allow you to monitor more events. In SQL Server 2016, you can monitor 180 events by using SQL Trace, whereas you can monitor 1209 events by using Extended Events. Later in this chapter, we provide specific examples of how you might use Extended Events, we compare the performance impact between Extended Events and SQL Trace, and explain its architecture of this event-handling infrastructure.

# Compare baseline metrics to observed metrics while troubleshooting performance issues

When using dynamic management objects to gain insight into SQL Server performance, you can only see current or recent historical information. Some problems become apparent only when you view how this information changes over time. Rather than wait for users to complain about application or query performance, you can proactively monitor the health of SQL Server by collecting baseline metrics and then periodically comparing current system behavior. That way you can identify negative trends as early as possible.

SQL Server includes a data collector to help you gather data and store it in the management data warehouse. This is a database that you use as centralized storage for many types of data, not just performance data. When you set up the management data warehouse, you specify which DMOs to query, which performance counters from the operating system and SQL Server to collect, and which SQL Trace events to capture. You can also use this infrastructure to capture other types of data that you might want to store centrally.

To set up management data warehouse in SQL Server Management Studio, expand the Management node in Object Explorer, right-click Data Collection, point to Tasks, and select Configure Management Data Warehouse. In the Configure Management Data Warehouse Wizard, click Next, and click New to open the New Database dialog box. Type a name for the database, click OK, and then click Next. On the Map Logins And Users page of the wizard, select the login for your SQL Server service account, select mdw_admin, and then click OK. Next click Finish, and then click Close.

To set up data collection, right-click Data Collection again, point to Tasks, and select Configure Data Collection. In the Configure Data Collection Wizard, click Next, and then select the server and database hosting the management data warehouse. Select the System Data Collection Sets checkbox, click Next, click Finish, and then click Close.

To view information collected in the management data warehouse, right-click Data Collection once more, point to Reports, point to Management Data Warehouse, and select one of the following reports:

- **Server Activity History** This report, a portion of which is shown in Figure 4-43, displays data collected from DMVs and performance counters, such as waits, locks, latches, among other SQL Server statistics, and CPU, memory, disk, and network usage. By default, this information is gathered every 60 seconds, uploaded into the Management Data Warehouse every 15 minutes, and retained for 14 days. The report is interactive. When you click on a chart, a new report page displays. For example, when you click the SQL Server Waits report, you can view a table and chart containing wait statistics for the selected period of time.

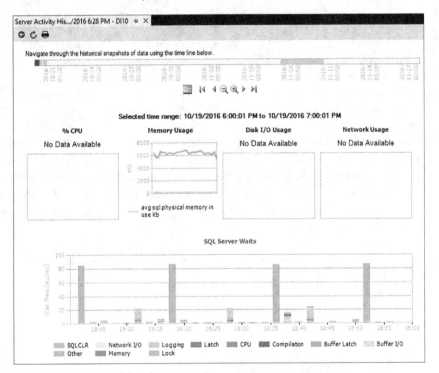

**FIGURE 4-43** Server Activity History report

- **Disk Usage Summary** This report displays a table of databases listing the starting and current size of the database and log files, the average growth measured as megabytes per day, and a sparkline chart to show the growth trend over time. You can click on a database name to view disk usage details for the database and log files as pie charts or click on the sparkline to view the disk space growth trends and collection details for each size metric, as shown in Figure 4-44.

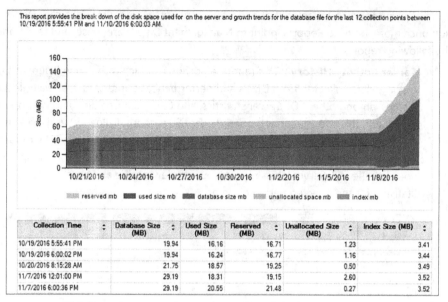

This report provides the break down of the disk space used for on the server and growth trends for the database file for the last 12 collection points between 10/19/2016 5:55:41 PM and 11/10/2016 6:00:03 AM.

| Collection Time | Database Size (MB) | Used Size (MB) | Reserved (MB) | Unallocated Size (MB) | Index Size (MB) |
|---|---|---|---|---|---|
| 10/19/2016 5:55:41 PM | 19.94 | 16.16 | 16.71 | 1.23 | 3.41 |
| 10/19/2016 6:00:02 PM | 19.94 | 16.24 | 16.77 | 1.16 | 3.44 |
| 10/20/2016 8:15:28 AM | 21.75 | 18.57 | 19.25 | 0.50 | 3.49 |
| 11/7/2016 12:01:00 PM | 29.19 | 18.31 | 19.15 | 2.60 | 3.52 |
| 11/7/2016 6:00:36 PM | 29.19 | 20.55 | 21.48 | 0.27 | 3.52 |

**FIGURE 4-44** Disk Usage Summary subreport for a selected database

- **Query Statistics History** This report displays a column chart the top 10 queries within a specified interval by CPU usage, duration, total IO, physical reads, or logical writes and a table that includes the following query executions statistics: Executions/min, CPU ms/sec, Total Duration (sec), Physical Reads/sec, and Logical Writes/sec. The data is cached on the local file system and then uploaded to the Management Data Warehouse every 15 minutes.

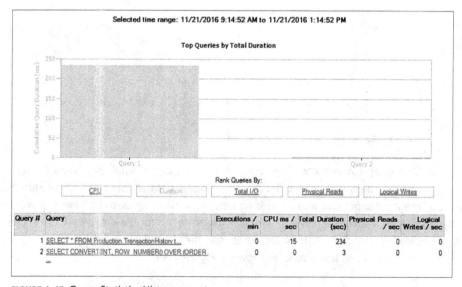

**FIGURE 4-45** Query Statistics History report

You can click on one of these queries to view its details in a subreport, such as the query text, and more detailed execution statistics such as Average Duration (ms) per Execution or Average Executions Per Min. The subreport also displays a column chart of query plans that you can rank by CPU, duration, physical reads, or logical writes. Statistics by query plan are also available. Click on a query plan to view the query plan details much like the details for a query. Other links on this page allow you to view sampled waits or the graphical query plan.

## Identify differences between performance monitoring and logging tools

Now that we have reviewed the various tools available for performance monitoring and logging, let's compare and contrast them to better understand their differences. That way, you can select the right tool for the particular task and objectives at hand. Table 4-1 provides a comparison of the tools by capability.

**TABLE 4-1** Comparison of performance monitoring and logging tools

| Capability | DMOs | Performance Monitor | SQL Trace | Extended Events | Management Data Warehouse |
|---|---|---|---|---|---|
| Requires coding | Yes | No | Yes, if using stored procedures | Yes, if using T-SQL statements | No |
| Graphical interface | No | Yes | Yes | Yes | Yes |
| Templates available | No | Yes | Yes | Yes | No |
| SQL performance monitoring | Yes | Yes | Yes | Yes | Yes |
| Operating system monitoring | Limited | Yes | No | Limited | Limited |
| Query plans | Yes | No | Yes | Yes | Yes |
| Deadlock graphs | Yes | No | Yes | Yes | No |
| Performance impact | Light | Light | Varies | Light | Light |
| Real-time activity | Yes | Yes | Yes | Yes | No |
| Historical activity | Only if saved to table | Yes | Yes | Yes | Yes |
| Save results to table | Yes | Yes | Yes | Yes | Yes |
| Alerting | No | Yes | No | No | No |
| Schedule at startup | No | Yes | No | Yes | No (data collection is scheduled at intervals) |

# Monitor Azure SQL Database performance

There are several diagnostic tools available to you for monitoring SQL Database performance. For a quick view of performance metrics, use the Azure portal. For more targeted analysis, you can use DMVs, Query Store, or Extended Events to monitor SQL Database performance just as you do for SQL Server.

## Azure Portal

In the Azure portal, you can select the metrics that you want to monitor and display a chart that shows average utilization for selected metrics. To configure the chart, open the blade for your database in the Azure portal, and then click Edit inside the Monitoring chart. In the Edit Chart blade, select one of the following time ranges: Past Hour, Today, Past Week, or Custom. If you select Custom, you can type in a data range or use calendar controls to set a beginning and end date for the range. Next, select one of the following chart types: Bar or Line. Then select one or more of the following metrics:

- Blocked by firewall
- CPU percentage
- DTU limit
- DTU percentage
- DTU used
- Data IO percentage
- Database size percentage
- Deadlocks
- Failed connections
- In-memory OLTP storage percent
- Log IO percentage
- Sessions percentage
- Successful connections
- Total database size
- Workers percentage

After you add the metrics to monitor, you can view the results in the Monitoring chart in addition to details in the Metric window. When you select metrics, you can select compatible metrics only. For example, you can select metrics that count connections, as shown in Figure 4-46, or you can select metrics that measure the percentage of resources consumed, but you cannot mix those two types of metrics in the same chart.

Monitoring

FIGURE 4-46 Monitoring chart for SQL Database in the Azure portal

You can also use the Azure portal to configure an email alert when a performance metric exceeds or drops below a specified threshold. Click the Monitoring chart to open the Metric blade. Then click Add Alert and follow the instructions in the Add Alert Rule blade. For example, you can add an alert to send an email when the number of connections blocked by the firewall exceeds 1, as shown in Figure 4-47. Not shown in this figure is the name of the resource, the name of the alert rule, and whether to email the alert to owners, contributors, and readers and optionally additional administrators.

FIGURE 4-47 Add An Alert Rule blade for SQL Database

## DMVs for SQL Database

Use the following DMVs to monitor SQL Database performance:

- **sys.database_connection_stats**  Count successful and failed connections. The count of failed connections is the sum of login failures, terminated connections, and throttled connections.

- **sys.dm_db_resource_stats**  Get the resource consumption percentages for CPU, data IO, and log IO. It returns one row for every 15 seconds, even when there is no activity in the database. For less granular data, you can use sys.resource_stats in the logical master database for your server.

- **sys.dm_exec_query_stats**  In combination with sys.dm_exec_sql_text, find queries that use a lot of resources, such as CPU time or IO.

- **sys.dm_tran_locks**  Discover blocked queries.

- **sys.event_log**  Find issues such as deadlocking and throttling over the last 30 days. You must have permission to read the *master* database on the Azure server. As an example, you can search for specific types of events, such as deadlocks or throttle events, and when they occurred, as shown in Listing 4-42.

**LISTING 4-42 Review SQL Server:Buffer Manager performance counters**

```
SELECT
    Event_Category,
    Event_Type,
    Event_Subtype_Desc,
    Event_Count,
    Description,
    Start_Time
FROM sys.event_log
WHERE Event_Type = 'deadlock' OR
    Event_Type like 'throttling%'
```

> *NOTE*  **PERMISSION REQUIRED FOR USING DMVS IN SQL DATABASE**
>
> To use a DMV in SQL Database, you must be granted the VIEW DATABASE STATE permission.

## Extended Events in SQL Database

You can use Extended Events to troubleshoot performance in SQL Database. It is similar to using Extended Events in SQL Server, although the set of extended events in SQL Database is smaller than the set available for SQL Server. In addition, there are some slight syntax differences when creating, altering, or dropping an event session as we noted in the "Monitor Azure SQL Database query plans" section earlier in this chapter.

# Determine best practice use cases for extended events

Extended Events is a robust, yet lightweight tracing infrastructure that you can use to monitor and analyze SQL Server activity by collecting as much or as little information as you need. At minimum, you can use Extended Events for any diagnostic task that you can perform by using SQL Trace, but it can do so much more. In particular, Extended Events offers greater flexibility because you can filter events with more granularity. For this exam, you should be familiar with the following types of use cases that Extended Events supports:

- **System health**  By default, an Extended Events session dedicated to system health information starts automatically when SQL Server starts. System health information includes session_id and sql_text for sessions with a severity greater than or equal to 20 or experiencing a memory-related error, non-yielding scheduler problems, deadlocks, long latch and lock waits, connectivity and security errors, and more. For complete details, see *https://msdn.microsoft.com/en-us/library/ff877955.aspx*.

- **Query performance diagnostics**  Find historical deadlocks or queries that did not end, troubleshoot waits for a particular session or query, capture queries that match a specific pattern, and get query plans, to name a few. You can count the number of occurrences of a specific event to determine if a problem is recurring frequently.

- **Resource utilization monitoring and troubleshooting**  You can create a session to capture information about server resources, such as CPU, IO or memory utilization. You can filter events for specific utilization thresholds to fine-tune the diagnostic process. Furthermore, you can correlate SQL Server events with Windows Event Tracing for Windows (ETW) logs that capture details about operating system activities.

- **Security audits**  Capture login failures by filtering events with Severity 14 and Error 18456 with client application name to find malicious login attempts.

# Distinguish between Extended Events targets

An Extended Event *target* receives information about an event. For example, in the "Capture query plans using extended events and traces" section earlier in this chapter, the target for the example Extended Events session is a file in which the session stores a query plan. In the last section of this chapter, we explain targets in greater detail. For now, be sure you understand the difference between the following targets for an Extended Events session:

- **etw_classic_sync_target**  Unlike the other targets that receive data asynchronously, this is an ETW target that receives data synchronously. You use it to monitor system activity.

- **event_counter**  This target counts the number of times that a specific event occurred.

- **event_file**  This target writes the event session output to a file on disk in binary format. You use the sys.fn_xe_file_target_read_file function to read the contents of the file.

- **histogram**  Like the event_counter target, the histogram target counts the occurrences of an event, but can count occurrences for multiple items separately and for both event fields or actions.

- **pair_matching**  This target helps you find start events that do not have a corresponding end event. For example, you can discover when a lock_acquired event occurred without a matching lock_released event within a reasonable time.

- **ring_buffer**  This target holds data in memory using an first-in, first-out method in which the oldest data is removed when the memory allocation is reached.

## Compare the impact of Extended Events and SQL Trace

As we have explained throughout this chapter, you can use Extended Events and SQL Trace interchangeably to provide many similar diagnostic functions. However, it is important to note that there is considerable difference between them when considering their respective impact on the observed server. Both tools by necessity add overhead to the server, which is measurable by observing performance counters for monitoring CPU processor time and batch requests per second. The use of SQL Server Profiler for client-side tracing is the most intrusive option whereas using SQL Trace stored procedures for server-side tracing is less intrusive. With this in mind, you should try to limit the number of events and number of columns captured to minimize the overhead as much as possible.

The least intrusive option is Extended Events, which was developed as a lightweight replacement for SQL Trace. Nonetheless, because it does incur overhead, you should take care to create events that collect the minimum amount of data necessary for troubleshooting. In particular, be aware that the query_post_execution_showplan event is expensive and should be avoided on a production server. If you must use it to troubleshoot a specific issue, take care to restrict its use to a limited time only.

## Define differences between Extended Events Packages, Targets, Actions, and Sessions

Throughout this chapter, we have discussed specific capabilities of Extended Events as well as the benefits of this feature, but we have yet to explore its components in detail. In this final section of the chapter, we review Extended Events concepts and objects that you should understand.

Events in Extended Events correspond to events in SQL Trace, but many more are supported in Extended Events to give you better diagnostic capabilities. An example of an event is sp_statement_starting.

### Packages

A package is the top-level container for the various types of Extended Events objects: events, targets, actions, types, predicates, and maps. Of all the available packages, you can only use the following three packages in an event session:

- **package0**   Contains Extended Events system objects
- **sqlserver**   Contains objects related to SQL Server
- **sqlos**   Contains SQLOS objects

## Targets

A target is the destination for the data collected about an event. For short-term diagnostics, you can use a memory-resident target. To persist the data, you can use the event_file target. Review the section "Distinguish between Extended Events targets" earlier in this chapter to see the full list of available targets. After you create an Extended Event session, you can add one or more targets, like this:

```
ADD TARGET package0.event_file(SET filename=N'C:\ExamBook762Ch4\query.xel',
    max_file_size=(5),max_rollover_files=(4)),
ADD TARGET package0.ring_buffer
```

## Actions

An action is a response or series of responses that you bind to an event. For example, you can use an action to detect an execution plan or calculate run-time statistics. Or you can add information from the global state, such as session_id, to the firing event to aid in troubleshooting, like this:

```
ADD EVENT sqlserver.sql_statement_completed(
    ACTION (sqlserver.session_id,
        sqlserver.sql_text))
```

## Sessions

An Extended Events session is the equivalent of a trace. When you create a session, you add an event and actions to fire with that event, define one or more targets for the data collected about the event, and optionally create predicates that define filters for the event. Listing 4-43 provides an example of an event session that captures session_id and sql_text when a stored procedure executes on the server and sends the data to a file on the local drive and to the ring buffer.

**LISTING 4-43** Create event session

```
CREATE EVENT SESSION [stored_proc]
ON SERVER
ADD EVENT sqlserver.sp_statement_completed(
    ACTION (sqlserver.session_id,
        sqlserver.sql_text))
ADD TARGET package0.event_file(SET filename=N'C:\ExamBook762Ch4\query.xel',
    max_file_size=(5),max_rollover_files=(4)),
ADD TARGET package0.ring_buffer;
```

## Chapter summary

- SQL Server relies on statistics to select an optimal query plan. For this reason, it's important to keep statistics current. Statistics can become obsolete when a table is the target of high volume inserts or deletions because the data distribution can change significantly. You can use the DBCC SHOW_STATISTICS command to check the histogram and index densities for an index.

- SQL Server updates statistics automatically by default, but you can disable the automatic update and instead rely on a maintenance plan to update statistics when you need greater control over the timing of the update. When you create a maintenance plan, SQL Server creates a SQL Server Agent job that you can schedule to run at a convenient time.

- There are several DMOs available to help you manage indexes. Use sys.dm_db_index_usage_stats to review current index usage or, in combination with sys.indexes and sys.objects, to find indexes that are never used. Use sys.dm_db_index_physical_stats to find fragmented indexes. To find missing indexes, use sys.dm_db_missing_index_details, sys.dm_db_missing_index_groups, and sys.dm_db_missing_index_group_stats.

- The existence of overlapping indexes adds unnecessary overhead to SQL Server. You should periodically review index columns to ensure an index was not inadvertently added that overlaps with a similar index.

- Use the query_pre_execution_showplan or query_post_execution_showplan Extended Events as a lightweight method to capture the estimated or actual query plans, respectively. As an alternative, you can use SQL Trace system stored procedures for server-side tracing or use SQL Server Profiler to capture the Showplan XML or Showplan XML For Query Compile events for an estimated query plan or the Showplan XML Statistics Profile event for an actual query plan.

- When reviewing a query plan, you should review whether the following operators exist in the plan: Table Scan, Clustered Index Scan, Key Lookup (Clustered) or RID Lookup (Clustered) in conjunction with Index Seek (NonClustered), Sort, or Hash Match. Although the presence of these operators is not bad in all cases, you might consider options for tuning your query such as adding indexes to tables or adding filters to the query if operations are performed on large tables and your goal is to improve query performance.

- Query Store is a new feature in SQL Server 2016 and SQL Database that you can use to capture query plans and associated runtime execution statistics over time. Several built-in views are available to help you find queries that consume a lot of resources or have regressed from a previous point in time. You can also force a query plan when necessary.

- Usually an estimated query plan and an actual query plan are the same plan except that an actual query plan includes calculations and information that is available only after the query executes. You can create an estimated query plan to assess the impact of potential changes to a query or to table structures without executing the query. The actual query plan can vary from the estimated query plan if statistics are out-of-date or if the data structures changes after the estimated query plan is generated.

- Query Performance Insight is an Azure SQL Database features that graphically shows you which queries are consuming the most CPU, memory, IO, and DTU resources over time.

- The Resource Governor (available only in Enterprise, Developer, or Evaluation editions) allows you to define how SQL Server allocates CPU, memory, and IOPS resources on the server. You specify this allocation by creating one or more resource pools and then create workload groups that you assign to a resource pool. A workload group can have further resource consumption limits imposed and can be configured with relative importance within a resource pool to prioritize access to server resources when workload groups run concurrently. SQL Server assigns a session to a workload group by using criteria that you define in a classifier function. It if cannot match the session to a workload group, Resource Governor assigns the session to the default workload group assigned to the default resource pool.

- By using Elastic Scale for Azure SQL Database, you can manage your data in separate shards for which resource requirements can dynamically grow or shrink as needed to match the current workload. To use this feature, you must use the elastic database client library in your application to perform operations across all shards or in individual shards. You can also use the Split-Merge service to separate data in one shard into multiple shards or to combine data from multiple shards into a single shard.

- When choosing one of the following SQL Server 2016 editions, you must consider the scalability and features each supports: Express, Web, Standard, Enterprise, Developer, and Evaluation. For SQL Database, you choose the Basic, Standard, or Premium service level based on the maximum size of your database and the range of performance levels required. Performance levels are measured as DTUs which represent CPU, memory, and IO thresholds.

- One aspect of query performance is the efficiency of your storage and IO subsystems which you can optimize by managing file placement for system, data, and log files. Use filegroups as separate containers that can be spread across separate disks and optionally use secondary data files and partitioning to improve data access.

- The setup wizard for SQL Server 2016 makes it easier than in previous versions to optimize the configuration of tempdb by allowing you to define its file placement, the number of files to create, the initial file size, and autogrowth settings.

- As long as SQL Server is the only application running on a server, it can manage memory dynamically without intervention. When you must run other applications on the server, you can optimize SQL Server's memory configuration by specifying minimum and maximum memory thresholds, maximum worker threads, maximum memory for index creation, and minimum memory for query execution.

- You use the sys.dm_os_wait_stats, sys.dm_exec_session_wait_stats, or sys.dm_os_waiting_tasks DMVs to gather information about the amount of time that threads must wait on resources, determine whether the server is experiencing CPU, memory, or IO pressure, or find out which resources are causing excessive waits.

- You can troubleshoot IO issues by analyzing IO subsystem latencies captured in the sys.dm_io_virtual_file_stats and sys.master_files DMVs or by reviewing performance counters for SQL Server's buffer manager in the sys.dm_os_performance_counters DMV.

- You can troubleshoot cache issues by using the following DMVs: sys.dm_os_memory_cache_counters, sys.dm_os_sys_memory, or sys.dm_os_memory_clerks. You can also use performance counters for SQL Server's buffer manager and memory manager in the sys.dm_os_performance_counters DMV.

- SQL Database query plans are accessible by using Showplan SET options, Extended Events, or Query Store, but not by using SQL Trace.

- You have a variety of tools that you can use to monitor operating system and SQL Server performance metrics: DMOs, Performance Monitor, SQL Trace, and Extended Events. In many cases, you are likely to use a combination of tools to diagnose SQL Server behavior.

- Management Data Warehouse is a SQL Server feature that allows you to capture performance-related information over time in contrast to other available monitoring tools which primarily provide point-in-time or cumulative information. Management Data Warehouse provides the following reports for your review: Server Activity History, Disk Usage Summary, and Query Statistics History.

- To monitor SQL Database performance, you can monitor specific metrics in the Azure portal. In addition, you can use the following DMVs with SQL Database for monitoring: sys.database_connection_stats, sys.dm_db_resource_stats, sys.dm_exec_query_stats, sys.dm_tran_locks, and sys.event_log. Extended Events are also available for SQL Database, although the set of supported events is smaller than the set that supports SQL Server.

- You should be familiar with the following best practice use cases for extend events: system health, query performance diagnostics, resource utilization monitoring and troubleshooting, and security audits.

- You should also understand how Extended Events uses the following targets to store information about an event: etw_classic_sync_target, event_counter, event_file ,histogram, pair_matching, and ring_buffer.

- Although Extended Events and SQL Trace can often be used interchangeably, Extended Events has a much lower impact on performance. You can measure the difference in impact by observing CPU processor time and batch requests per second.

- The Extended Events architecture is comprised of several components. A package is the top-level container for the other objects. As data is collected about an event, it is sent to a target. In addition, you can configure an action to occur in response to an event. A session is a set of events, actions, and targets that you configure and enable or disable as a group.

# Thought experiment

In this thought experiment, demonstrate your skills and knowledge of the topics covered in this chapter. You can find answer to this thought experiment in the next section.

You recently started as a new database administrator at Consolidated Messenger. Because you are unfamiliar with this SQL Server environment as a new employee, you decide to perform some analysis to determine if there are any significant problems to fix.

1.  Which query or command do you use to find the most recent update for statistics on tables or indexed views?

    A.  DBCC SHOW_STATISTICS('ConsolidatedMessengerDB',All Indexes);

    B.  SELECT name, STATS_DATE(object_id, stats_id) FROM sys.stats WHERE object_id IN (SELECT object_id FROM sys.objects WHERE type = 'U');

    C.  SELECT name, auto_created (object_id, stats_id) FROM sys.stats WHERE object_id IN (SELECT object_id FROM sys.objects WHERE type = 'U');

    D.  SELECT name, auto_created (object_id, stats_id) FROM sys.stats WHERE object_id IN (SELECT object_id FROM sys.objects WHERE type = 'U');

2.  When you query the sys.dm_db_index_physical_stats DMV, you see the output shown below. What problem do you see and what step should you take to resolve it?

```
idx_id ObjectName                            index_type_desc                 pg_ct
AvgPageSpacePct     frag_ct AvgFragPct
-------- ------------------------------------ ------------------------------- -------------------------------
-------- ------------------------------ ---------- --------------------------
1           PK_SalesOrders_OrderD     CLUSTERED INDEX              2037
54.9851742031134 237         34.02189781021898
2           IX_SalesOrders_CustomerID NONCLUSTERED INDEX    685    98.4313442055844
2           0
```

3.  You enabled Query Store on the main corporate database several weeks ago. Which DMV do you use to locate the top 5 queries with the longest duration?

A. sys.query_store_plan

B. sys.query_store_query

C. sys.query_store_query_text

D. sys.query_store_runtime_stats

E. sys.query_store_runtime_stats_interval

4. When you use Query Store to examine the query plans for a frequently executed query, you notice that for one plan uses an Index Scan operator and a second plan uses and Index Seek operator. If the normal query pattern is to retrieve a small number of rows, which is the more optimal query plan and how can you require SQL Server to use it?

5. You have been monitoring wait statistics in the sys.dm_os_wait_stats DMV for several weeks and notice that the ratio of signal_wait_time_ms to wait_time_ms has been increased from 10% to 30%. What type of problem is this likely to indicate?

A. CPU pressure

B. Memory pressure

C. Network bandwidth issues

D. IO subsystem failures

6. As another method to confirm your diagnosis for the scenario in the previous question, which performance counters should you check?

A. Physical disk counters: % Disk Time, Avg. Disk sec/Read, Avg. Disk sec/Transfer, Avg. Disk sec/Write, Current Disk Queue Length.

B. Processor counters: % Privileged Time, % Processor Time, % User Time, Processor Queue Length.

C. Memory counters: Available bytes, Pages/sec, Working set.

D. SQL Server counters: Page lookups/sec, Page reads/sec, Page writes/sec, Free List Stalls/Sec, Lazy Writes/Sec, Memory Grants Outstanding, Memory Grants Pending.

7. Which tool monitoring tools can you use to get information about SQL Server memory usage without writing any code?

A. DMVs or SQL Profiler

B. Server-side SQL Trace or Extended Events

C. Performance Monitor or Management Data Warehouse

D. Client-side SQL Trace or Resource Governor

# Thought experiment answer

This section contains the solution to the thought experiment.

1. **The answer is B**. The sys.stats catalog view contains both the stats_id and object_id columns necessary to use the STATS_DATE system function that returns the most recent update date for an object's statistics. The DBCC SHOW_STATISTICS command requires you to include a specific index name as the second argument, therefore A is incorrect due to the syntax. Similarly, C and D are examples of incorrect syntax because T-SQL does not include an auto_created function.

2. The clustered index has a page count greater than 500 and fragmentation is 34%. In this case, you should rebuild the index.

3. **The answer is D**. You can order by the avg_duration column in descending order in the sys.query_store_runtime_stats DMV to find the queries that run the longest. The sys.query_store_plan in A is incorrect because this DMV includes only information about estimated query plans. Sys.query_store_query is incorrect in B because this DMV collects aggregated information for a query's compilation, but does not collect execution statistics. On its own the sys.query_store_query_text DMV in C is not a correct answer because it includes the query text without duration information, although you can join it to sys.query_store_runtime_stats to get more complete information about long-running queries. Sys.query_store_runtime_stats_interval is stores information about the intervals of time during which statistics are captured, but does not report duration information.

4. When multiple query plans exist for a selected query, Query Store allows you to select a query plan and then force that plan for all subsequent executions of the same query. In this example, the more optimal query plan is the one that includes the Index Seek because it incurs a lower cost by selecting specific rows from the index rather than scanning the entire index to find the rows to select.

5. **The answer is A**. The signal wait time is the amount of time that a thread is able to run a task, but is waiting its turn on the CPU. To confirm this diagnosis, check for an increasing number of SOS_SCHEDULER_YIELD wait types in the sys.dm_os_wait_stats DMV and check the sys.dm_os_schedulers DMV for a high value in the runnable_tasks_count column. Answer B is incorrect because memory pressure is indicated by PAGE-IOLATCH waits in combination with a Page Life Expectancy performance counter value dropping over time. Answer C is incorrect because you generally use network-related wait types and performance counters to confirm your diagnosis of network bandwidth issues. Answer D is incorrect because a failure in the IO subsystem will become evident when there are many waits containing IO in the name and average wait time begins to increase.

6. **The answer is B**. You can monitor CPU usage by using the Processor performance counters. In particular, if % Processor Time is between 80 and 90 percent consistently, % User Time nears 100% consistently, and the Processor Queue Length value is increasing over time, the CPU is experiencing pressure. You should consider upgrading the CPU or adding more processors. The counters listed for Answers A, C, and D are useful performance counters. However, they do not provide any confirmation of whether the observations in Question 5 are related to CPU pressure.

7. **The answer is C**. Both Performance Monitor and Management Data Warehouse provide graphical interfaces that you can use to monitor SQL Server's memory usage. In Performance Monitor, you can set up the data collection of performance counters for the SQL Server Memory Manager, such as Memory Grants Outstanding or Memory Grants Pending, among others. In Management Data Warehouse, you can use the Server Activity History report to drill into Memory Usage details for the server. To access information from DMVs, you must write a T-SQL query; therefore, A is incorrect. Similarly, B is incorrect because a server-side SQL Trace requires you to write code. Answer D is incorrect because Resource Governor is not a performance monitoring tool.

# Index

## A

## B

# C

CREATE TABLE statement 12–15
CTEs. *See* common table expressions (CTEs)

# D

DAC. *See* Datacenter Activation Coordination
DAGs. *See* Database Availability Groups
DAS. *See* Direct-Attached Storage
data
    binary 17
    character (string) 17
    hiding 53
    limiting, through DDL 61–62
    modifying in views, with multiple tables 62–64
    redundant 8, 9
    reformatting 53, 54–55
    view structure design to select 53–57
data access
    real-time 244
database concurrency 195–264
    isolation levels and 216–229
    locking behavior and 230–241
    memory-optimized tables and 242–255
    natively compiled stored procedures and 242,
        255–258
    transactions and 195–216
DATABASE DDL triggers 172–174
database design
    adding indexes during 26–32
    based on business requirements 2–4
    denormalization 11
    determining data types 15–24
    using normalization 4–11
    writing table create statements 11–15
Database Engine Tuning Advisor 281
database file optimization 336–337
database instances
    performance management for 324–346
        database file optimization 336–337
        database workload 325–331
        Elastic Scale 331–333
        memory optimization 339–340
        query plans 346
        storage, IO, and cache troubleshooting 343–346
        wait statistics 340–343
    tempdb optimization 338–339
Database Manipulation Language (DML)
    statements 196–203

database objects 1–100
    changing definition of 61
    columnstore indexes 70–93
    dropping 61
    indexes 24–50
    naming 11–12, 12–13
    relational database schema 2–24
    views 52–69
databases. *See* mailbox databases
    columnar 70–71
    logical database model 4
    tuning 32
database scalability 331–333
Database Throughput Unit (DTU) 321–322
database workload
    managing, in SQL Server 325–331
    Resource Governor management queries 330–331
    resource pools 326–328
    user-defined functions 328–329
    workload groups 328
Databse Definition Language (DDL) triggers 159
Data Definition Language (DDL) 123
Data Definition Language (DDL) triggers 169–174
data distribution 266–270
data files 336
data format 107, 109–110
data input
    CHECK constraints on 107–111
    coordinating multiple values 110–111
data integrity
    complex 160–164
    constraints for 102–129
data loading
    into columnstore index 89–95
Data Manipulation Language (DML) 123–125
Data Manipulation Language (DML) triggers 159–160,
    169. *See also* triggers
data storage. *See also* storage architectures; *See
    also* storage requirements
datatype
    choosing 108–109
    conversion 144
    int 107
    precedence 144
data types 15–24
    approximate numeric 16
    binary data 17
    character (string) data 17

# Q

# R

# About the authors

**LOUIS DAVIDSON** is a Microsoft MVP (Data Platform), and a Senior Data Architect for CBN. He has Over 20 years of experience with SQL Server as an architect, developer, and writer. Follow him on Twitter at @drsql.

**STACIA VARGA**, Microsoft MVP (Data Platform) is a consultant, educator, mentor, and author specializing in data solutions since 1999. She provides consulting and custom education services through her company, Data Inspirations, writes about her experiences with data at blog.datainspirations. com, and tweets as @_StaciaV_.

Free ebooks

From technical overviews to drilldowns on special topics, get *free* ebooks from Microsoft Press at:

**www.microsoftvirtualacademy.com/ebooks**

Download your free ebooks in PDF, EPUB, and/or Mobi for Kindle formats.

Look for other great resources at Microsoft Virtual Academy, where you can learn new skills and help advance your career with free Microsoft training delivered by experts.

# Microsoft Press

# Now that you've read the book...

## Tell us what you think!

Was it useful?
Did it teach you what you wanted to learn?
Was there room for improvement?

**Let us know at https://aka.ms/tellpress**

Your feedback goes directly to the staff at Microsoft Press,
and we read every one of your responses. Thanks in advance!

# Exam Ref 70-761
# Querying Data with
# Transact-SQL

Itzik Ben-Gan

**Exam Ref 70-761 Querying Data with Transact-SQL**

**Published with the authorization of Microsoft Corporation by:**
**Pearson Education, Inc.**

**Copyright © 2017 by Itzik Ben-Gan**

ISBN-13: 978-1-5093-0433-2
ISBN-10: 1-5093-0433-9

Library of Congress Control Number: 2017935711

32 2019

**Trademarks**

Microsoft and the trademarks listed at https://www.microsoft.com on the "Trademarks" webpage are trademarks of the Microsoft group of companies. All other marks are property of their respective owners.

**Warning and Disclaimer**

Every effort has been made to make this book as complete and as accurate as possible, but no warranty or fitness is implied. The information provided is on an "as is" basis. The authors, the publisher, and Microsoft Corporation shall have neither liability nor responsibility to any person or entity with respect to any loss or damages arising from the information contained in this book or programs accompanying it.

**Special Sales**

For information about buying this title in bulk quantities, or for special sales opportunities (which may include electronic versions; custom cover designs; and content particular to your business, training goals, marketing focus, or branding interests), please contact our corporate sales department at corpsales@pearsoned.com or (800) 382-3419.

For government sales inquiries, please contact governmentsales@pearsoned.com.

For questions about sales outside the U.S., please contact intlcs@pearson.com.

| | |
|---|---|
| **Editor-in-Chief** | Greg Wiegand |
| **Acquisitions Editor** | Trina MacDonald |
| **Development Editor** | Troy Mott |
| **Managing Editor** | Sandra Schroeder |
| **Senior Project Editor** | Tracey Croom |
| **Editorial Production** | Backstop Media |
| **Copy Editor** | Christina Rudloff |
| **Indexer** | Julie Grady |
| **Proofreader** | Christina Rudloff |
| **Technical Editor** | Dejan Sarka |
| **Cover Designer** | Twist Creative, Seattle |

*In memory of my dad, Gabriel Ben-Gan, who appreciated the beauty of numbers, logic and puzzles.*

*—Itzik*

# Contents at a glance

# Contents

---

**What do you think of this book? We want to hear from you!**

Microsoft is interested in hearing your feedback so we can continually improve our
books and learning resources for you. To participate in a brief online survey, please visit:

**https://aka.ms/tellpress**

# Introduction

The 70-761 exam focuses on T-SQL querying and programming constructs. Whether you're taking it as part of a Microsoft data platform related certification path, or to assess your T-SQL skills for any other reason, this is a crucial exam, since it covers the essential language constructs. If you need to do work with any of the Microsoft data platform technologies, a good grasp of T-SQL is vital.

The exam covers query constructs like filtering, grouping and sorting, combining data from multiple tables using joins, subqueries, set operators, modifying data, as well as some aspects of data definition like choosing data types and enforcing data integrity. The exam also covers more advanced query constructs like pivoting and unpivoting data, using window functions, grouping sets, using the APPLY operator, the complexities of NULLs, as well as implicit conversions. The exam covers querying system-versioned temporal tables, as well as XML and JSON data. The exam also covers T-SQL modules and programmatic constructs like views, user-defined functions, and stored procedures, as well as working with transactions and error handling.

This exam is intended for SQL Server database administrators, system engineers, and developers with two or more years of experience who are seeking to validate their skills and knowledge in writing queries.

This book covers every major topic area found on the exam, but it does not cover every exam question. Only the Microsoft exam team has access to the exam questions, and Microsoft regularly adds new questions to the exam, making it impossible to cover specific questions. You should consider this book a supplement to your relevant real-world experience and other study materials. If you encounter a topic in this book that you do not feel completely comfortable with, use the "Need more review?" links you'll find in the text to find more information and take the time to research and study the topic. Great information is available on MSDN, TechNet, and in blogs and forums.

## Organization of this book

This book is organized by the "Skills measured" list published for the exam. The "Skills measured" list is available for each exam on the Microsoft Learning website: *https://aka.ms/examlist*. Each chapter in this book corresponds to a major topic area in the list, and the technical tasks in each topic area determine a chapter's organization. If an exam covers six major topic areas, for example, the book will contain six chapters.

# Microsoft certifications

Microsoft certifications distinguish you by proving your command of a broad set of skills and experience with current Microsoft products and technologies. The exams and corresponding certifications are developed to validate your mastery of critical competencies as you design and develop, or implement and support, solutions with Microsoft products and technologies both on-premises and in the cloud. Certification brings a variety of benefits to the individual and to employers and organizations.

> **MORE INFO** **ALL MICROSOFT CERTIFICATIONS**
>
> For information about Microsoft certifications, including a full list of available certifications, go to *https://www.microsoft.com/learning*.

# Acknowledgments

**Itzik Ben-Gan** Writing a book is a demanding yet rewarding project. A big part of what makes it rewarding is that you get to work with other people, and together create something that will hopefully contribute to increase technological and scientific knowledge out there. I'd like to recognize those who were involved in this book for their contributions. Special thanks to Trina MacDonald, my editor, for your outstanding handling of the project. Many thanks to Dejan Sarka who tech edited the book, as well as wrote the section about querying XML and JSON data. I know I can always count on you both in terms of your depth of knowledge and ethics. Thanks, are also due to Troy Mott, the book's Development Editor, Christina Rudloff, the Copy Editor, Ellie Volckhausen who handled the book's layout, and Julie Grady, the book's Indexer. Lastly, to Lilach, my wife, for helping with the first reviews, and for giving reason to what I do.

# Free ebooks from Microsoft Press

From technical overviews to in-depth information on special topics, the free ebooks from Microsoft Press cover a wide range of topics. These ebooks are available in PDF, EPUB, and Mobi for Kindle formats, ready for you to download at:

*https://aka.ms/mspressfree*

Check back often to see what is new!

# Microsoft Virtual Academy

Build your knowledge of Microsoft technologies with free expert-led online training from Microsoft Virtual Academy (MVA). MVA offers a comprehensive library of videos, live events, and more to help you learn the latest technologies and prepare for certification exams. You'll find what you need here:

*https://www.microsoftvirtualacademy.com*

# Quick access to online references

Throughout this book are addresses to webpages that the author has recommended you visit for more information. Some of these addresses (also known as URLs) can be painstaking to type into a web browser, so we've compiled all of them into a single list that readers of the print edition can refer to while they read.

Download the list at *https://aka.ms/exam761transactsql/downloads*.

The URLs are organized by chapter and heading. Every time you come across a URL in the book, find the hyperlink in the list to go directly to the webpage.

# Errata, updates, & book support

We've made every effort to ensure the accuracy of this book and its companion content. You can access updates to this book—in the form of a list of submitted errata and their related corrections—at:

*https://aka.ms/exam761transactsql/errata*

If you discover an error that is not already listed, please submit it to us at the same page.

If you need additional support, email Microsoft Press Book Support at *mspinput@microsoft.com*.

Please note that product support for Microsoft software and hardware is not offered through the previous addresses. For help with Microsoft software or hardware, go to *https://support.microsoft.com*.

Download the source code and sample database from the book's website

*https://aka.ms/exam761transactsql/detail*

The author also created a personal companion website for the book, which you can find at *http://tsql.solidq.com/books/er70761*.

In order to run the code samples from the book, you will need access to SQL Server 2016 with Service Pack1 or later, or Azure SQL Database.

## We want to hear from you

At Microsoft Press, your satisfaction is our top priority, and your feedback our most valuable asset. Please tell us what you think of this book at:

*https://aka.ms/tellpress*

We know you're busy, so we've kept it short with just a few questions. Your answers go directly to the editors at Microsoft Press. (No personal information will be requested.) Thanks in advance for your input!

## Stay in touch

Let's keep the conversation going! We're on Twitter: *http://twitter.com/MicrosoftPress*.

# Important: How to use this book to study for the exam

Certification exams validate your on-the-job experience and product knowledge. To gauge your readiness to take an exam, use this Exam Ref to help you check your understanding of the skills tested by the exam. Determine the topics you know well and the areas in which you need more experience. To help you refresh your skills in specific areas, we have also provided "Need more review?" pointers, which direct you to more in-depth information outside the book.

The Exam Ref is not a substitute for hands-on experience. This book is not designed to teach you new skills.

We recommend that you round out your exam preparation by using a combination of available study materials and courses. Learn more about available classroom training at *https://www.microsoft.com/learning*. Microsoft Official Practice Tests are available for many exams at *https://aka.ms/practicetests*. You can also find free online courses and live events from Microsoft Virtual Academy at *https://www.microsoftvirtualacademy.com*.

This book is organized by the "Skills measured" list published for the exam. The "Skills measured" list for each exam is available on the Microsoft Learning website: *https://aka.ms/examlist*.

Note that this Exam Ref is based on publicly available information and the author's experience. To safeguard the integrity of the exam, authors do not have access to the exam questions.

# Manage data with Transact-SQL

Transact-SQL (T-SQL) is the main language used to manage and manipulate data in Microsoft SQL Server and Azure SQL Database. If you work with any of the Microsoft SQL products—as a developer, DBA, BI professional, data analyst, data scientist, or in any other capacity—you need to know your T-SQL. Exam 70-761 is a foundational exam that tests your T-SQL querying knowledge, and is a required part of several of the Microsoft SQL certification paths.

This chapter focuses on managing data with T-SQL. It covers the elements of the SELECT statement, how to combine data from multiple tables with set operators and joins, use of built-in functions, and how to modify data.

> **IMPORTANT**
>
> **Have you read page xv?**
>
> It contains valuable information regarding the skills you need to pass the exam.

## Skills in this chapter:

- Create Transact-SQL SELECT queries
- Query multiple tables by using joins
- Implement functions and aggregate data
- Modify data

## Skill 1.1: Create Transact-SQL SELECT queries

To write correct and robust T-SQL code, it's important to first understand the roots of the language, as well as a concept called logical query processing. You also need to understand the structure of the SELECT statement and how to use its clauses to perform data manipulation tasks like filtering and sorting. You often need to combine data from different sources, and one of the ways to achieve this in T-SQL is using set operators.

**This section covers how to:**

- Identify proper SELECT query structure
- Write specific queries to satisfy business requirements
- Construct results from multiple queries using set operators
- Distinguish between UNION and UNION ALL behavior
- Identify the query that would return expected results based on provided table structure and/or data

# Understanding the foundations of T-SQL

Many aspects of computing, like programming languages, evolve based on intuition and the current trend. Without strong foundations, their lifespan can be very short, and if they do survive, often the changes are very rapid due to changes in trends. T-SQL is different, mainly because it has strong foundations—mathematics. You don't need to be a mathematician to write SQL well (though it certainly doesn't hurt), but as long as you understand what those foundations are, and some of their key principles, you will better understand the language you are dealing with. Without those foundations, you can still write T-SQL code—even code that runs successfully—but it will be like eating soup with a fork!

## Evolution of T-SQL

As mentioned, unlike many other aspects of computing, T-SQL is based on strong mathematical foundations. Understanding some of the key principles from those foundations can help you better understand the language you are dealing with. Then you will think in T-SQL terms when coding in T-SQL, as opposed to coding with T-SQL while thinking in procedural terms.

Figure 1-1 illustrates the evolution of T-SQL from its core mathematical foundations.

**FIGURE 1-1** Evolution of T-SQL

T-SQL is the main language used to manage and manipulate data in the Microsoft relational database management systems (RDBMSs) SQL Server (the box product), and Azure SQL Database (the cloud platform). The code base for both the cloud platform and the box product is one unified code base. For simplicity I will use the term *SQL Server* in reference to both, as far as T-SQL is concerned. SQL Server also supports other languages, like Microsoft Visual C# and Microsoft Visual Basic, but T-SQL is usually the preferred language for data management and manipulation.

T-SQL is a dialect of standard SQL. SQL is a standard of both the International Organization for Standards (ISO) and the American National Standards Institute (ANSI). The two standards for SQL are basically the same. The SQL standard keeps evolving with time. Following is a list of the major revisions of the standard so far:

- SQL-86
- SQL-89
- SQL-92
- SQL:1999
- SQL:2003
- SQL:2006
- SQL:2008
- SQL:2011

All leading database vendors, including Microsoft, implement a dialect of SQL as the main language to manage and manipulate data in their database platforms. Therefore, the core language elements look the same. However, each vendor decides which features to implement, and which features to not implement. Also, the standard sometimes leaves some aspects as an implementation choice. Each vendor also usually implements extensions to the standard in cases where the vendor feels that an important feature isn't covered by the standard.

Writing in a standard way is considered a best practice. When you do so, your code is more portable. Your knowledge is more portable, too, because it is easy for you to start working with new platforms. When the dialect you're working with supports both a standard and a nonstandard way to do something, you should always prefer the standard form as your default choice. You should consider a nonstandard option only when it has some important benefit to you that is not covered by the standard alternative.

As an example of when to choose the standard form, T-SQL supports two "not equal to" operators: <> and !=. The former is standard and the latter is not. In this case, the choice should be obvious: go for the standard one!

As an example of when the choice of standard or nonstandard depends on the circumstances, consider the following: T-SQL supports multiple functions that convert a source expression to a target type. Among them are the CAST and CONVERT functions. The former is standard and the latter isn't. The nonstandard CONVERT function has a style argument that CAST doesn't support. Because CAST is standard, you should consider it your default choice for conversions. You should consider using CONVERT only when you need to rely on the style argument.

Yet another example of choosing the standard form is in the termination of T-SQL statements. According to standard SQL, you should terminate your statements with a semicolon.

The T-SQL documentation specifies that not terminating all statements with a semicolon is a deprecated feature, but T-SQL currently doesn't enforce this for all statements, rather only in cases where there would otherwise be ambiguity of code elements. For example, a statement preceding the WITH clause of a common table expression (CTE) has to be terminated because this clause can also be used to define a table hint in the preceding statement. As another example, the MERGE statement has to be terminated due to possible ambiguity of the MERGE keyword. You should still follow the standard and terminate all of your statements even where it is currently not required.

Standard SQL is based on the relational model, which is a mathematical model for data management and manipulation. The relational model was initially created and proposed by Edgar F. Codd in 1969. After its creation, it has been explained and further developed by Codd, Chris Date, Hugh Darwen, and others.

A common misconception is that the name "relational" has to do with relationships between tables (that is, foreign keys). Actually, the true source for the model's name is the mathematical concept relation.

A relation in the relational model is what SQL represents with a table. The two are not synonymous. You could say that a table is an attempt by SQL to represent a relation (in addition to a relation variable, but that's not necessary to get into here). Some say that it is not a very successful attempt. Even though SQL is based on the relational model, it deviates from it in a number of ways. But it's important to note that as you understand the model's principles, you can use SQL—or more precisely, the dialect you are using—in a relational way. More on this, including a further reading recommendation, is in the next section, "Using T-SQL in a relational way."

Getting back to a relation, which is what SQL attempts to represent with a table: a relation has a heading and a body. The heading is a set of attributes (what SQL attempts to represent with columns), each of a given type. An attribute is identified by name and type name. The body is a set of tuples (what SQL attempts to represent with rows). Each tuple's heading is the heading of the relation. Each value of each tuple's attribute is of its respective type.

Some of the most important aspects to understand about T-SQL stem from the relational model's core foundations: set theory and predicate logic.

Remember that the heading of a relation is a set of attributes, and the body is a set of tuples. So what is a set? According to the creator of mathematical set theory, Georg Cantor, a set is described as follows:

> By a "set" we mean any collection M into a whole of definite, distinct objects m (which are called the "elements" of M) of our perception or of our thought.
>
> —GEORGE CANTOR, IN
> "GEORG CANTOR" BY JOSEPH
> W. DAUBEN (PRINCETON
> UNIVERSITY PRESS, 1990)

There are a number of very important elements in this definition that, if understood, should have direct implications on your T-SQL coding practices. One element that requires notice is the term *whole*. A set should be considered as a whole. This means that you do not interact with the individual elements of the set, rather with the set as a whole.

Notice the term *distinct*; a set has no duplicates. Codd once remarked on the no duplicates aspect: "If something is true, then saying it twice won't make it any truer." For example, the set {a, b, c} is considered equal to the set {a, a, b, c, c, c}.

Another critical aspect of a set doesn't explicitly appear in the aforementioned definition by Cantor, but rather is implied; there's no relevance to the order of elements in a set. In contrast, a sequence (which is an ordered set), does have an order to its elements. Combining the no duplicates and no relevance to order aspects means that the collection {a, b, c} is a set, but the collection {b, a, c, c, a, c} isn't.

The other branch of mathematics that the relational model is based on is called *predicate logic*. A predicate is an expression that when attributed to some object, makes a proposition either true or false. For example, "salary greater than $50,000" is a predicate. You can evaluate this predicate for a specific employee, in which case you have a proposition. For example, suppose that for a particular employee, the salary is $60,000. When you evaluate the proposition for that employee, you get a true proposition. In other words, a predicate is a parameterized proposition.

The relational model uses predicates as one of its core elements. You can enforce data integrity by using predicates. You can filter data by using predicates. You can even use predicates to define the data model itself. You first identify propositions that need to be stored in the database. Here's an example proposition: an order with order ID 10248 was placed on February 12, 2017 by the customer with ID 7, and handled by the employee with ID 3. You then create predicates from the propositions by removing the data and keeping the heading. Remember, the heading is a set of attributes, each identified by name and type name. In this example, you have orderid INT, orderdate DATE, custid INT, and empid INT.

## Using T-SQL in a relational way

As mentioned, T-SQL is based on SQL, which in turn is based on the relational model. However, there are a number of ways in which SQL, and therefore T-SQL, deviates from the relational model. But T-SQL gives you enough tools so that if you understand the relational model, you can use the language in a relational manner, and thus write more correct code.

> **MORE INFO** **SQL AND RELATIONAL THEORY**
>
> For detailed information about the differences between SQL and the relational model, and how to use SQL in a relational way, see *SQL and Relational Theory*, 3rd Edition by C. J. Date (O'Reilly Media, 2015). It's an excellent book that all database practitioners should read.

Remember that a relation has a heading and a body. The heading is a set of attributes and the body is a set of tuples. Remember that a set is supposed to be considered as a whole.

What this translates to in T-SQL is that you're supposed to write queries that interact with the tables as a whole. You should try to avoid using iterative constructs like cursors and loops that iterate through the rows one at a time. You should also try to avoid thinking in iterative terms because this kind of thinking is what leads to iterative solutions.

For people with a procedural programming background, the natural way to interact with data (in a file, record set, or data reader) is with iterations. So using cursors and other iterative constructs in T-SQL is, in a way, an extension to what they already know. However, the correct way from the relational model's perspective is not to interact with the rows one at a time, rather, use relational operations and return a relational result. This, in T-SQL, translates to writing queries.

Remember also that a set has no duplicates. In other words, it has unique members. T-SQL doesn't always enforce this rule. For example, you can create a table without a key. In such a case, you are allowed to have duplicate rows in the table. To follow relational theory, you need to enforce uniqueness in your tables. For example, you can enforce uniqueness in your tables by using a primary key, or a unique constraint.

Even when the table doesn't allow duplicate rows, a query against the table can still return duplicate rows in its result. Consider the following query:

```
USE TSQLV4;

SELECT country
FROM HR.Employees;
```

The query is issued against the TSQLV4 sample database. It returns the country attribute of the employees stored in the HR.Employees table. According to the relational model, a relational operation against a relation is supposed to return a relation. In this case, this should translate to returning the *set* of countries where there are employees, with an emphasis on set, as in no duplicates. However, T-SQL doesn't attempt to remove duplicates by default.

Here's the output of this query:

```
country
---------------
USA
USA
USA
USA
UK
UK
UK
USA
UK
```

In fact, T-SQL is based more on multiset theory than on set theory. A *multiset* (also known as a bag or a superset) in many respects is similar to a set, but can have duplicates. As mentioned, T-SQL does give you enough tools so that if you want to follow relational theory, you can do so. For example, the language provides you with a DISTINCT clause to remove duplicates. Here's the revised query:

```
SELECT DISTINCT country
FROM HR.Employees;
```

Here's the revised query's output:

```
Country
---------------
UK
USA
```

Another fundamental aspect of a set is that there's no relevance to the order of the ele-ments. For this reason, rows in a table have no particular order, conceptually. So when you issue a query against a table and don't indicate explicitly that you want to return the rows in particular presentation order, the result is supposed to be relational. Therefore, you shouldn't assume any specific order to the rows in the result; never mind what you know about the physical representation of the data, for example, when the data is indexed.

As an example, consider the following query:

```
SELECT empid, lastname
FROM HR.Employees;
```

When this query was run on one system, it returned the following output, which looks like it is sorted by the column lastname:

```
empid       lastname
----------- --------------------
8           Cameron
1           Davis
9           Doyle
2           Funk
7           King
3           Lew
5           Mortensen
4           Peled
6           Suurs
```

Even if the rows were returned in a different order, the result would have still been con-sidered correct. SQL Server can choose between different physical access methods to process the query, knowing that it doesn't need to guarantee the order in the result. For example, SQL Server could decide to parallelize the query or scan the data in file order (as opposed to index order).

If you do need to guarantee a specific presentation order to the rows in the result, you need to add an ORDER BY clause to the query, as follows:

```
SELECT empid, lastname
FROM HR.Employees
ORDER BY empid;
```

This time, the result isn't relational, it's what standard SQL calls a *cursor*. The order of the rows in the output is guaranteed based on the empid attribute. Here's the output of this query:

```
empid        lastname
-----------  --------------------
1            Davis
2            Funk
3            Lew
4            Peled
5            Mortensen
6            Suurs
7            King
8            Cameron
9            Doyle
```

The heading of a relation is a set of attributes; as such, the attributes are unordered and unique. This means that you are supposed to identify an attribute by name and type name. Conversely, T-SQL does keep track of ordinal positions of columns based on their order of appearance in the table definition. When you issue a query with SELECT *, you are guaranteed to get the columns in the result based on definition order. Also, T-SQL allows referring to ordinal positions of columns from the result in the ORDER BY clause, as follows:

```
SELECT empid, lastname
FROM HR.Employees
ORDER BY 1;
```

Beyond the fact that this practice is not relational, think about the potential for error if at some point you change the SELECT list and forget to change the ORDER BY list accordingly. Therefore, the recommendation is to always indicate the names of the attributes that you need to order by.

T-SQL has another deviation from the relational model in that it allows defining result columns based on an expression without assigning a name to the target column. For example, the following query is valid in T-SQL:

```
SELECT empid, firstname + ' ' + lastname
FROM HR.Employees;
```

This query generates the following output:

```
empid
-----------  -----------------------------
1            Sara Davis
2            Don Funk
3            Judy Lew
4            Yael Peled
5            Sven Mortensen
6            Paul Suurs
7            Russell King
8            Maria Cameron
9            Patricia Doyle
```

But according to the relational model, all attributes must have names. In order for the query to be relational, you need to assign an alias to the target attribute. You can do so by using the AS clause, as follows:

```
SELECT empid, firstname + ' ' + lastname AS fullname
FROM HR.Employees;
```

Also, with T-SQL a query can return multiple result columns with the same name. For example, consider a join between two tables, T1 and T2, both with a column called keycol. With T-SQL, a SELECT list can look like the following:

```
SELECT T1.keycol, T2.keycol ...
```

For the result to be relational, all attributes must have unique names, so you would need to use different aliases for the result attributes as follows:

```
SELECT T1.keycol AS key1, T2.keycol AS key2 ...
```

As for predicates, following the law of excluded middle in mathematical logic, a predicate can evaluate to true or false. In other words, predicates are supposed to use two-valued logic. However, Codd wanted to reflect the possibility for values to be missing in his model. He referred to two kinds of missing values: missing but applicable (A-Values marker) and missing but inapplicable (I-Values marker). As an example for a missing but applicable case, consider a mobilephone attribute of an employee. Suppose that an employee has a mobile phone, but did not want to provide this information, for example, for privacy reasons. As an example for a missing but inapplicable case, consider a salescommission attribute of an employee. This attribute is applicable only to sales people, but not to other kinds of employees. According to Codd, a language based on his model should provide two different markers for the two cases. T-SQL—again, based on standard SQL—implements only one general-purpose marker called NULL for any kind of missing value. This leads to three-valued predicate logic. Namely, when a predicate compares two values, for example, mobilephone = '(425) 555-0136', if both are present, the result evaluates to either true or false. But if at least one of them is NULL, the result evaluates to a third logical value—unknown. That's the case both when you use the equality operator = and when you use an inequality operator such as: <>, >, >=, <, <=.

Note that some believe that a valid relational model should follow two-valued logic, and strongly object to the concept of NULLs in SQL. But as mentioned, the creator of the relational model believed in the idea of supporting missing values, and predicates that extend beyond two-valued logic. What's important from a perspective of coding with T-SQL is to realize that if the database you are querying supports NULLs, their treatment is far from being trivial. That is, you need to carefully understand what happens when NULLs are involved in the data you're manipulating with various query constructs, like filtering, sorting, grouping, joining, or intersecting. Hence, with every piece of code you write with T-SQL, you want to ask yourself whether NULLs are possible in the data you're interacting with. If the answer is yes, you want to make sure that you understand the treatment of NULLs in your query, and ensure that your tests address treatment of NULLs specifically.

## Using correct terminology

Your use of terminology reflects on your knowledge. Therefore, you should make an effort to understand and use correct terminology. When discussing T-SQL–related topics, people often use incorrect terms. And if that's not enough, even when you do realize what the correct terms are, you also need to understand the differences between the terms in T-SQL and those in the relational model.

As an example of incorrect terms in T-SQL, people often use the terms "field" and "record" to refer to what T-SQL calls "column" and "row," respectively. Fields and records are physical. Fields are what you have in user interfaces in client applications, and records are what you have in files and cursors. Tables are logical, and they have logical rows and columns.

Another example of an incorrect term is referring to "NULL values." A NULL is a marker for a missing value—not a value itself. Hence, the correct usage of the term is either just "NULL" or "NULL marker." Personally, I prefer the former.

Besides using correct T-SQL terminology, it's also important to understand the differences between T-SQL terms and their relational counterparts. Remember from the previous section that T-SQL attempts to represent a relation with a table, a tuple with a row, and an attribute with a column; but the T-SQL concepts and their relational counterparts differ in a number of ways. As long as you are conscious of those differences, you can, and should, strive to use T-SQL in a relational way.

# Understanding logical query processing

T-SQL has both logical and physical sides to it. The logical side is the conceptual interpretation of the query that explains what the correct result of the query is. The physical side is the processing of the query by the database engine. Physical processing must produce the result defined by logical query processing. To achieve this goal, the database engine can apply optimization. Optimization can rearrange steps from logical query processing or remove steps altogether, but only as long as the result remains the one defined by logical query processing. The focus of this section is logical query processing—the conceptual interpretation of the query that guarantees returning what I defined as the correct result.

## T-SQL as a declarative English-like language

T-SQL, being based on standard SQL, is a declarative English-like language. In this language, declarative means you define what you want, as opposed to imperative languages that define also how to achieve what you want. Standard SQL describes the logical interpretation of the declarative request (the "what" part), but it's the database engine's responsibility to figure out how to physically process the request (the "how" part).

For this reason, it is important not to draw any performance-related conclusions from what you are reviewing about logical query processing. That's because logical query processing only defines the correctness of the query. When addressing performance aspects of the query, you need to understand how optimization works. As mentioned, optimization can be quite different from logical query processing because it's allowed to change things as long as the result achieved is the one defined by logical query processing.

It's interesting to note that the standard language SQL wasn't originally called so; rather, it was called SEQUEL; an acronym for "structured English query language." But then due to a trademark dispute with an airline company, the language was renamed to SQL, for "structured query language." Still, the point is that you provide your instructions in an English-like manner. For example, consider the instruction, "Bring me a soda from the refrigerator." Observe that in the English instruction, the object comes before the location. Consider the following request in T-SQL:

```
SELECT shipperid, phone, companyname
FROM Sales.Shippers;
```

Observe the similarity of the query's keyed-in order to English. The query first indicates the SELECT list with the attributes you want to return, and then the FROM clause with the table you want to query.

Now try to think of the order in which the request needs to be logically interpreted. For example, how would you define the instructions to a robot instead of a human? The original English instruction to get a soda from the refrigerator would probably need to be revised to something like, "Go to the refrigerator; open the door; get a soda; bring it to me."

Similarly, the logical processing of a query must first know which table is being queried before it can know which attributes can be returned from that table. Therefore, contrary to the keyed-in order of the previous query, the logical query processing has to be as follows:

```
FROM Sales.Shippers
SELECT shipperid, phone, companyname
```

This is a basic example with just two query clauses. Of course, things can get more complex. If you understand the concept of logical query processing well, you will be able to explain many things about the way the language behaves—things that are very hard to explain otherwise.

## Logical query processing phases

This section covers logical query processing and the phases involved. The main statement used to retrieve data in T-SQL is the SELECT statement. Following are the main query clauses specified in the order that you are supposed to type them (known as "keyed-in order"):

1. SELECT
2. FROM
3. WHERE
4. GROUP BY
5. HAVING
6. ORDER BY

But as mentioned, the logical query processing order, which is the conceptual interpretation order, is different. It starts with the FROM clause. Here is the logical query processing order of the six main query clauses:

1. FROM
2. WHERE
3. GROUP BY
4. HAVING
5. SELECT
6. ORDER BY

Each phase operates on one or more tables as inputs and returns a virtual table as output. The output table of one phase is considered the input to the next phase. This is in accord with operations on relations that yield a relation. Note that if an ORDER BY is specified, the result isn't relational. This means that you can't operate on such result with an outer query because an outer query expects a relation as input.

Consider the following query as an example:

```
SELECT country, YEAR(hiredate) AS yearhired, COUNT(*) AS numemployees
FROM HR.Employees
WHERE hiredate >= '20140101'
GROUP BY country, YEAR(hiredate)
HAVING COUNT(*) > 1
ORDER BY country, yearhired DESC;
```

This query is issued against the HR.Employees table. It filters only employees that were hired in or after the year 2014. It groups the remaining employees by country and the hire year. It keeps only groups with more than one employee. For each qualifying group, the query returns the hire year and count of employees, sorted by country and hire year, in descending order.

The following sections provide a brief description of what happens in each phase according to logical query processing.

### 1. EVALUATE THE FROM CLAUSE

In the first phase, the FROM clause is evaluated. That's where you indicate the tables you want to query and table operators like joins if applicable. If you need to query just one table, you indicate the table name as the input table in this clause. Then, the output of this phase is a table result with all rows from the input table. That's the case in the following query: the input is the HR.Employees table (nine rows), and the output is a table result with all nine rows (only a subset of the attributes are shown):

```
empid   country   hiredate
------  --------  ----------
1       USA       2013-05-01
2       USA       2013-08-14
3       USA       2013-04-01
```

```
4       USA       2014-05-03
5       UK        2014-10-17
6       UK        2014-10-17
7       UK        2015-01-02
8       USA       2015-03-05
9       UK        2015-11-15
```

## 2. FILTER ROWS BASED ON THE WHERE CLAUSE

The second phase filters rows based on the predicate in the WHERE clause. Only rows for which the predicate evaluates to true are returned.

In this query, the WHERE filtering phase filters only rows for employees hired on or after January 1, 2014. Six rows are returned from this phase and are provided as input to the next one. Here's the result of this phase:

```
empid  country  hiredate
------ -------- ----------
4      USA      2014-05-03
5      UK       2014-10-17
6      UK       2014-10-17
7      UK       2015-01-02
8      USA      2015-03-05
9      UK       2015-11-15
```

A typical mistake made by people who don't understand logical query processing is attempting to refer in the WHERE clause to a column alias defined in the SELECT clause. You can't do this because the WHERE clause is evaluated before the SELECT clause. As an example, consider the following query:

```
SELECT country, YEAR(hiredate) AS yearhired
FROM HR.Employees
WHERE yearhired >= 2014;
```

This query fails with the following error:

```
Msg 207, Level 16, State 1, Line 114
Invalid column name 'yearhired'.
```

If you understand that the WHERE clause is evaluated before the SELECT clause, you realize that this attempt is wrong because at this phase, the attribute yearhired doesn't yet exist. You can indicate the expression YEAR(hiredate) >= 2014 in the WHERE clause. Better yet, for optimization reasons that are discussed later in Skill 1.3 in the section "Search arguments," use the form hiredate >= '20140101' as done in the original query.

## 3. GROUP ROWS BASED ON THE GROUP BY CLAUSE

This phase defines a group for each distinct combination of values in the grouped elements from the input virtual table. It then associates each input row to its respective group. The query you've been working with groups the rows by country and YEAR(hiredate). Within the six rows in the input table, this step identifies four groups. Here are the groups and the detail rows that are associated with them (redundant information removed for purposes of illustration).

| group country | group year(hiredate) | detail empid | detail country | detail hiredate |
|---------|---------------|-------|---------|------------|
| UK | 2014 | 5 | UK | 2014-10-17 |
| | | 6 | UK | 2014-10-17 |
| UK | 2015 | 7 | UK | 2015-01-02 |
| | | 9 | UK | 2015-11-15 |
| USA | 2014 | 4 | USA | 2014-05-03 |
| USA | 2015 | 8 | USA | 2015-03-05 |

As you can see, the group UK, 2014 has two associated detail rows with employees 5 and 6; the group for UK, 2015 also has two associated detail rows with employees 7 and 9; the group for USA, 2014 has one associated detail row with employee 4; the group for USA, 2015 also has one associated detail row with employee 8.

The final result of this query has one row representing each group (unless filtered out). Therefore, expressions in all phases that take place after the current grouping phase are somewhat limited. All expressions processed in subsequent phases must guarantee a single value per group. If you refer to an element from the GROUP BY list (for example, country), you already have such a guarantee, so such a reference is allowed. However, if you want to refer to an element that is not part of your GROUP BY list (for example, empid), it must be contained within an aggregate function like MAX. That's because multiple values are possible in the element within a single group, and the only way to guarantee that just one will be returned is to aggregate the values.

### 4. FILTER GROUPS BASED ON THE HAVING CLAUSE

This phase is also responsible for filtering data based on a predicate, but it is evaluated after the data has been grouped; hence, it is evaluated per group and filters groups as a whole. As is usual in T-SQL, the filtering predicate can evaluate to true, false, or unknown. Only groups for which the predicate evaluates to true are returned from this phase. In this case, the HAVING clause uses the predicate COUNT(*) > 1, meaning filter only country and hire year groups that have more than one employee. If you look at the number of rows that were associated with each group in the previous step, you will notice that only the groups UK, 2014 and UK, 2015 qualify. Hence, the result of this phase has the following remaining groups, shown here with their associated detail rows.

| group country | group year(hiredate) | detail empid | detail country | detail hiredate |
|---------|---------------|-------|---------|------------|
| UK | 2014 | 5 | UK | 2014-10-17 |
| | | 6 | UK | 2014-10-17 |
| UK | 2015 | 7 | UK | 2015-01-02 |
| | | 9 | UK | 2015-11-15 |

It's important to understand the difference between WHERE and HAVING. The WHERE clause is evaluated before rows are grouped, and therefore is evaluated per row. The HAVING clause is evaluated after rows are grouped, and therefore is evaluated per group.

## 5. PROCESS THE SELECT CLAUSE

The fifth phase is the one responsible for processing the SELECT clause. What's interesting about it is the point in logical query processing where it gets evaluated—almost last. That's interesting considering the fact that the SELECT clause appears first in the query.

This phase includes two main steps. The first step is evaluating the expressions in the SELECT list and producing the result attributes. This includes assigning attributes with names if they are derived from expressions. Remember that if a query is a grouped query, each group is represented by a single row in the result. In the query, two groups remain after the processing of the HAVING filter. Therefore, this step generates two rows. In this case, the SELECT list returns for each country and order year group a row with the following attributes: country, YEAR(hiredate) aliased as yearhired, and COUNT(*) aliased as numemployees.

The second step in this phase is applicable if you indicate the DISTINCT clause, in which case this step removes duplicates. Remember that T-SQL is based on multiset theory more than it is on set theory, and therefore, if duplicates are possible in the result, it's your responsibility to remove those with the DISTINCT clause. In this query's case, this step is inapplicable. Here's the result of this phase in the query:

```
country          yearhired    numemployees
---------------  -----------  ------------
UK               2014         2
UK               2015         2
```

The fifth phase returns a relational result. Therefore, the order of the rows isn't guaranteed. In this query's case, there is an ORDER BY clause that guarantees the order in the result, but this will be discussed when the next phase is described. What's important to note is that the outcome of the phase that processes the SELECT clause is still relational.

Also, remember that this phase assigns column aliases, like yearhired and numemployees. This means that newly created column aliases are not visible to clauses processed in previous phases, like FROM, WHERE, GROUP BY, and HAVING.

Note that an alias created by the SELECT phase isn't even visible to other expressions that appear in the same SELECT list. For example, the following query isn't valid:

```
SELECT empid, country, YEAR(hiredate) AS yearhired, yearhired - 1 AS prevyear
FROM HR.Employees;
```

This query generates the following error:

```
Msg 207, Level 16, State 1, Line 117
Invalid column name 'yearhired'.
```

The reason that this isn't allowed is that all expressions that appear in the same logical query-processing step are treated as a set, and a set has no order. In other words, conceptually, T-SQL evaluates all expressions that appear in the same phase in an all-at-once manner. Note the use of the word conceptually. SQL Server won't necessarily physically process all expressions at the same point in time, but it has to produce a result as if it did. This behavior is different than many other programming languages where expressions usually get evaluated in a left-to-right order, making a result produced in one expression visible to the one that appears to its right. But T-SQL is different.

### 6. HANDLE PRESENTATION ORDERING

The sixth phase is applicable if the query has an ORDER BY clause. This phase is responsible for returning the result in a specific presentation order according to the expressions that appear in the ORDER BY list. The query indicates that the result rows should be ordered first by country (in ascending order by default), and then by yearhired, descending, yielding the following output:

```
country          yearhired   numemployees
---------------  ----------- ------------
UK               2015        2
UK               2014        2
```

Notice that the ORDER BY clause is the first and only clause that is allowed to refer to column aliases defined in the SELECT clause. That's because the ORDER BY clause is the only one to be evaluated after the SELECT clause.

Unlike in previous phases where the result was relational, the output of this phase isn't relational because it has a guaranteed order. The result of this phase is what standard SQL calls a cursor. Note that the use of the term cursor here is conceptual. T-SQL also supports an object called a cursor that is defined based on a result of a query, and that allows fetching rows one at a time in a specified order.

You might care about returning the result of a query in a specific order for presentation purposes or if the caller needs to consume the result in that manner through some cursor mechanism that fetches the rows one at a time. But remember that such processing isn't relational. If you need to process the query result in a relational manner—for example, define a table expression like a view based on the query—the result will need to be relational. Also, sorting data can add cost to the query processing. If you don't care about the order in which the result rows are returned, you can avoid this unnecessary cost by not adding an ORDER BY clause.

A query can specify the TOP or OFFSET-FETCH filtering options. If it does, the same ORDER BY clause that is normally used to define presentation ordering also defines which rows to filter for these options. It's important to note that such a filter is processed after the SELECT phase evaluates all expressions and removes duplicates (in case a DISTINCT clause was specified). You might even consider the TOP and OFFSET-FETCH filters as being processed in their own phase number 7. The query doesn't indicate such a filter, and therefore, this phase is inapplicable in this case.

For more information about logical query processing, see the following article series on the topic in SQL Server Pro magazine:

- Part 1 at *http://sqlmag.com/sql-server/logical-query-processing-what-it-and-what-it-means-you*
- Part 2 at *http://sqlmag.com/sql-server/logical-query-processing-clause-and-joins*

- Part 3 at *http://sqlmag.com/sql-server/logical-query-processing-clause-and-apply*
- Part 4: *http://sqlmag.com/sql-server/logical-query-processing-clause-and-pivot*
- Part 5 at *http://sqlmag.com/sql-server/logical-query-processing-part-5-clause-and-unpivot*
- Part 6 at *http://sqlmag.com/sql-server-2016/logical-query-processing-part-6-where-clause*
- Part 7 at *http://sqlmag.com/sql-server/logical-query-processing-part-7-group-and-having*
- Part 8 at *http://sqlmag.com/sql-server/logical-query-processing-part-8-select-and-order*

# Getting started with the SELECT statement

The FROM and SELECT clauses are two principal clauses that appear in almost every query that retrieves data. This section explains the purpose of these clauses, how to use them, and best practices associated with them. It also explains what regular and irregular identifiers are, and how to delimit identifiers.

## The FROM clause

According to logical query processing, the FROM clause is the first clause to be evaluated logically in a SELECT query. The FROM clause has two main roles:

- It's the clause where you indicate the tables that you want to query.
- It's the clause where you can apply table operators like joins to input tables.

This section focuses on the first role.

As a basic example, assuming you are connected to the sample database TSQLV4, the following query uses the FROM clause to specify that HR.Employees is the table being queried:

```
SELECT empid, firstname, lastname, country
FROM HR.Employees;
```

Observe the use of the two-part name to refer to the table. The first part (HR) is the schema name and the second part (Employees) is the table name. In some cases, T-SQL supports omitting the schema name, as in FROM Employees, in which case it uses an implicit schema name resolution process. It is considered a best practice to always explicitly indicate the schema name. This practice can prevent you from ending up with a schema name that you did not intend to use, and can also remove the cost involved in the implicit resolution process, although this cost is minor.

In the FROM clause, you can alias the queried tables with your chosen names. You can use the form <table> <alias>, as in HR.Employees E, or <table> AS <alias>, as in HR.Employees AS E. The latter form is more readable. When using aliases, the convention is to use short names, typically one letter that is somehow indicative of the queried table, like E for Employees. Then, when referring to an ambiguous column name in a multi-table query (same column name appears in multiple queried tables), to avoid ambiguity, you add the table alias as a column prefix.

Note that if you assign an alias to a table, you basically rename the table for the duration of the query. The original table name isn't visible anymore; only the alias is. Normally, you can prefix a column name you refer to in a query with the table name, as in Employees.empid. However, if you aliased the Employees table as E, the reference Employees.empid is invalid; you have to use E.empid, as the following example demonstrates:

```
SELECT E.empid, firstname, lastname, country
FROM HR.Employees AS E;
```

If you try running this code by using the full table name as the column prefix, the code will fail.

## The SELECT clause

The SELECT clause of a query has two main roles:

- It evaluates expressions that define the attributes in the query's result, assigning them with aliases if needed.
- Using a DISTINCT clause, you can eliminate duplicate rows in the result if needed.

Let's start with the first role. Take the following query as an example:

```
SELECT empid, firstname, lastname
FROM HR.Employees;
```

The FROM clause indicates that the HR.Employees table is the input table of the query. The SELECT clause then projects only three of the attributes from the input as the returned attributes in the result of the query.

T-SQL supports using an asterisk (*) as an alternative to listing all attributes from the input tables, but this is considered a bad practice for a number of reasons. Often, you need to return only a subset of the input attributes, and using an * is just a matter of laziness. By returning more attributes than you really need, you can prevent SQL Server from using what would normally be considered covering indexes with respect to the interesting set of attributes. You also send more data than is needed over the network, and this can have a negative impact on the system's performance. In addition, the underlying table definition could change over time; even if, when the query was initially authored, * really represented all attributes you needed; it might not be the case anymore at a later point in time. For these reasons and others, it is considered a best practice to always explicitly list the attributes that you need.

In the SELECT clause, you can assign your own aliases to the expressions that define the result attributes. There are a number of supported forms of aliasing: <expression> AS <alias> as in empid AS employeeid, <expression> <alias> as in empid employeeid, and <alias> = <expression> as in employeeid = empid.

Consider the following query:

```
SELECT empid, firstname lastname
FROM HR.Employees;
```

The developer who authored the query intended to return the attributes empid, firstname, and lastname but missed indicating the comma between firstname and lastname. The query doesn't fail; instead, it returns the following result:

```
empid       lastname
----------- ----------
1           Sara
2           Don
3           Judy
...
```

Although not the author's intention, SQL Server interprets the request as assigning the alias lastname to the attribute firstname instead of returning both. If you're used to aliasing expressions with the space form as a common practice, it will be harder for you to spot such bugs.

There are two main uses for intentional attribute aliasing. One is renaming—when you need the result attribute to be named differently than the source attribute—for example, if you need to name the result attribute employeeid instead of empid, as follows:

```
SELECT empid AS employeeid, firstname, lastname
FROM HR.Employees;
```

Another use is to assign a name to an attribute that results from an expression that would otherwise be unnamed. For example, suppose you need to generate a result attribute from an expression that concatenates the firstname attribute, a space, and the lastname attribute. You use the following query:

```
SELECT empid, firstname + N' ' + lastname
FROM HR.Employees;
```

You get a nonrelational result because the result attribute has no name:

```
empid
----------- ------------------------------
1           Sara Davis
2           Don Funk
3           Judy Lew
...
```

By aliasing the expression, you assign a name to the result attribute, making the result of the query relational, as follows.

```
SELECT empid, firstname + N' ' + lastname AS fullname
FROM HR.Employees;
```

Here's an abbreviated form of the result of this query:

```
empid       fulllname
----------- ------------------------------
1           Sara Davis
2           Don Funk
3           Judy Lew
...
```

Remember that if duplicates are possible in the result, T-SQL won't try to eliminate those unless instructed. A result with duplicates is considered nonrelational because relations—being sets—are not supposed to have duplicates. Therefore, if duplicates are possible in the result, and you want to eliminate them in order to return a relational result, you can do so by adding a DISTINCT clause, as in the following query:

```
SELECT DISTINCT country, region, city
FROM HR.Employees;
```

The HR.Employees table has nine rows but five distinct locations; hence, the output of this query has five rows:

```
country         region          city
--------------- --------------- ---------------
UK              NULL            London
USA             WA              Kirkland
USA             WA              Redmond
USA             WA              Seattle
USA             WA              Tacoma
```

There's an interesting difference between standard SQL and T-SQL in terms of minimal SELECT query requirements. According to standard SQL, a SELECT query must have at minimum FROM and SELECT clauses. Conversely, T-SQL supports a SELECT query with only a SELECT clause and without a FROM clause. Such a query is as if issued against an imaginary table that has only one row. For example, the following query is invalid according to standard SQL, but is valid according to T-SQL:

```
SELECT 10 AS col1, 'ABC' AS col2;
```

The output of this query is a single row with attributes resulting from the expressions with names assigned using the aliases:

```
col1        col2
----------- ----
10          ABC
```

## Delimiting identifiers

When referring to identifiers of attributes, schemas, tables, and other objects, there are cases in which you are required to use delimiters versus cases in which the use of delimiters is optional. T-SQL supports both a standard form to delimit identifiers using double quotation marks, as in "Sales"."Orders", as well as a proprietary form using square brackets, as in [Sales]. [Orders]. The latter is the more commonly used, and recommended, form in T-SQL.

When the identifier is *regular*, delimiting it is optional. In a regular identifier, the identifier complies with the rules for formatting identifiers. The rules say that the first character must be a letter defined by the Unicode Standard 3.2 (a-z, A-Z, and letters from other Unicode languages), underscore (_), at sign (@), or number sign (#). Subsequent characters can include letters, decimal numbers, at sign, dollar sign ($), number sign, or underscore. The identifier cannot be a reserved keyword in T-SQL, cannot have embedded spaces, and must not include supplementary characters.

An identifier that doesn't comply with these rules must be delimited. For example, an attribute called 2017 is considered an irregular identifier because it starts with a digit, and therefore must be delimited as "2017" or [2017]. A regular identifier such as y2017 can be referenced without delimiters simply as y2017, or optionally it can be delimited. You might prefer not to delimit regular identifiers because the delimiters tend to clutter the code.

# Filtering data with predicates

Filtering data is one of the most fundamental aspects of T-SQL querying. Almost every query that you write involves some form of filtering. This section covers filtering data with predicates. Later sections in this skill cover filtering data with the TOP and OFFSET-FETCH options.

## Predicates and three-valued-logic

Let's use the HR.Employees table to demonstrate a few filtering examples. Run the following code to show the contents of this table:

```
SELECT empid, firstname, lastname, country, region, city
FROM HR.Employees;
```

This query generates the following output:

```
empid firstname  lastname    country  region  city
----- ---------- ----------  -------- ------- ---------
1     Sara       Davis       USA      WA      Seattle
2     Don        Funk        USA      WA      Tacoma
3     Judy       Lew         USA      WA      Kirkland
4     Yael       Peled       USA      WA      Redmond
5     Sven       Mortensen   UK       NULL    London
6     Paul       Suurs       UK       NULL    London
7     Russell    King        UK       NULL    London
8     Maria      Cameron     USA      WA      Seattle
9     Patricia   Doyle       UK       NULL    London
```

Consider the following query, which filters only employees from the US:

```
SELECT empid, firstname, lastname, country, region, city
FROM HR.Employees
WHERE country = N'USA';
```

In case you're wondering why the literal 'USA' is preceded with the letter N as a prefix, that's to denote a Unicode character string literal, because the country column is of the data type NVARCHAR. Had the country column been of a regular character string data type, such as VARCHAR, the literal should have been just 'USA'.

When NULLs are not possible in the data that you're filtering, such as in the above example, T-SQL uses two-valued logic; namely, for any given row the predicate can evaluate to either true or false. The filter returns only the rows for which the predicate evaluates to true and discards the ones for which the predicate evaluates to false. Therefore, this query returns the following output:

```
empid firstname  lastname   country  region  city
----- ---------- ---------- -------- ------- ----------
1     Sara       Davis      USA      WA      Seattle
2     Don        Funk       USA      WA      Tacoma
3     Judy       Lew        USA      WA      Kirkland
4     Yael       Peled      USA      WA      Redmond
8     Maria      Cameron    USA      WA      Seattle
```

However, when NULLs are possible in the data, things get trickier. For instance, consider the following query:

```
SELECT empid, firstname, lastname, country, region, city
FROM HR.Employees
WHERE region = N'WA';
```

Here you're looking for only those employees who are from Washington (have WA in the region attribute). It's clear that the predicate evaluates to true for rows that have WA in the region attribute and that those rows are returned. It's also clear that the predicate would have evaluated to false had there been any rows with a present region other than WA, for example CA, and that those rows would have been discarded. However, remember that the predicate evaluates to unknown for rows that have a NULL in the region attribute, and that the WHERE clause discards such rows. This happens to be the desired behavior in our case because you know that when the region is NULL, it can't be Washington. However, remember that even when you use the inequality operator <> a comparison with a NULL yields unknown. For instance, suppose that you wanted to return only employees with a region other than Washington, and that you used the following query in attempt to achieve this:

```
SELECT empid, firstname, lastname, country, region, city
FROM HR.Employees
WHERE region <> N'WA';
```

The predicate evaluates to false for rows with WA in the region attribute and those rows are discarded. The predicate would have evaluated to true had there been rows with a present region other than WA, and those rows would have been returned. However, the predicate evaluates to unknown for rows with NULL in the region attribute, and those rows get discarded, even though you know that if region is NULL, it cannot be Washington. This query returns an empty set because our sample data contains only rows with either WA or NULL in the region attribute:

```
empid firstname  lastname   country  region  city
----- ---------- ---------- -------- ------- ---------
```

This is an example where you need to intervene and add some logic to your query to also return the rows where the region attribute is NULL. Be careful though not to use an equality operator when looking for a NULL because remember that nothing is considered equal to a NULL—not even another NULL. The following query still returns an empty set:

```
SELECT empid, firstname, lastname, country, region, city
FROM HR.Employees
WHERE region <> N'WA'
   OR region = NULL;
```

T-SQL supports the IS NULL and IS NOT NULL operators to check if a NULL is or isn't present, respectively. Here's the solution query that correctly handles NULLs:

```
SELECT empid, firstname, lastname, country, region, city
FROM HR.Employees
WHERE region <> N'WA'
   OR region IS NULL;
```

This query generates the following output:

```
empid firstname  lastname   country  region  city
----- ---------- ---------- -------- ------- ---------
5     Sven       Mortensen  UK       NULL    London
6     Paul       Suurs      UK       NULL    London
7     Russell    King       UK       NULL    London
9     Patricia   Doyle      UK       NULL    London
```

## Combining predicates

You can combine predicates in the WHERE clause by using the logical operators AND and OR. You can also negate predicates by using the NOT logical operator. This section starts by describing important aspects of negation and then discusses combining predicates.

Negation of true and false is straightforward—NOT true is false, and NOT false is true.

What can be surprising to some is what happens when you negate unknown—NOT unknown is still unknown. Recall from the previous section the query that returned all employees from Washington; the query used the predicate region = N'WA' in the WHERE clause. Suppose that you want to return the employees that are not from WA, and for this you use the predicate NOT region = N'WA'. It's clear that cases that return false from the positive predicate (say the region is NY) return true from the negated predicate. It's also clear that cases that return true from the positive predicate (say the region is WA) return false from the negated predicate. However, when the region is NULL, both the positive predicate and the negated one return unknown and the row is discarded. So the right way for you to include NULL cases in the result—if that's what you know that you need to do—is to use the IS NULL operator, as in NOT region = N'WA' OR region IS NULL.

As for combining predicates, there are several interesting things to note. Some precedence rules determine the logical evaluation order of the different predicates. The NOT operator precedes AND and OR, and AND precedes OR. For example, suppose that the WHERE filter in your query had the following combination of predicates:

```
WHERE col1 = 'w' AND col2 = 'x' OR col3 = 'y' AND col4 = 'z'
```

Because AND precedes OR, you get the equivalent of the following:

```
WHERE (col1 = 'w' AND col2 = 'x') OR (col3 = 'y' AND col4 = 'z')
```

Trying to express the operators as pseudo functions, this combination of operators is equivalent to OR( AND( col1 = 'w', col2 = 'x' ), AND( col3 = 'y', col4 = 'z' ) ).

Because parentheses have the highest precedence among all operators, you can always use those to fully control the logical evaluation order that you need, as the following example shows:

```
WHERE col1 = 'w' AND (col2 = 'x' OR col3 = 'y') AND col4 = 'z'
```

Again, using pseudo functions, this combination of operators and use of parentheses is equivalent to AND( col1 = 'w', OR( col2 = 'x', col3 = 'y' ), col4 = 'z' ).

Recall that all expressions that appear in the same logical query-processing phase—for example, the WHERE phase—are conceptually evaluated at the same point in time. For example, consider the following filter predicate:

```
WHERE propertytype = 'INT' AND CAST(propertyval AS INT) > 10
```

Suppose that the table being queried holds different property values. The propertytype column represents the type of the property (an INT, a DATE, and so on), and the propertyval column holds the value in a character string. When propertytype is 'INT', the value in propertyval is convertible to INT; otherwise, not necessarily.

Some assume that unless precedence rules dictate otherwise, predicates will be evaluated from left to right, and that short-circuiting will take place when possible. In other words, if the first predicate propertytype = 'INT' evaluates to false, SQL Server won't evaluate the second predicate CAST(propertyval AS INT) > 10 because the result is already known. Based on this assumption, the expectation is that the query should never fail trying to convert something that isn't convertible.

The reality, though, is different. SQL Server does internally support a short-circuit concept; however, due to the all-at-once concept in the language, it is not necessarily going to evaluate the expressions in left-to-right order. It could decide, based on cost-related reasons, to start with the second expression, and then if the second expression evaluates to true, to evaluate the first expression as well. This means that if there are rows in the table where propertytype is different than 'INT', and in those rows propertyval isn't convertible to INT, the query can fail due to a conversion error.

You can deal with this problem in a number of ways. A simple option is to use the TRY_CAST function instead of CAST. When the input expression isn't convertible to the target type, TRY_CAST returns a NULL instead of failing. And comparing a NULL to anything yields unknown. Eventually, you will get the correct result, without allowing the query to fail. So your WHERE clause should be revised as follows:

```
WHERE propertytype = 'INT' AND TRY_CAST(propertyval AS INT) > 10
```

## Filtering character data

In many respects, filtering character data is the same as filtering other types of data. This section covers a couple of items that are specific to character data: proper form of literals and the LIKE predicate.

A literal has a type. If you write an expression that involves operands of different types, SQL Server will have to apply implicit conversion to align the types. Depending on the circumstances, implicit conversions can sometimes hurt performance. It is important to know the proper form of literals of different types and make sure you use the right ones. A classic example for using incorrect literal types is with Unicode character strings (NVARCHAR and NCHAR types). The right form for a Unicode character string literal is to prefix the literal with a capital N and delimit the literal with single quotation marks, for example, N'literal'. For a regular character string literal, you just delimit the literal with single quotation marks, for example, 'literal'. It's a typical bad habit to specify a regular character string literal when the filtered column is of a Unicode type, as in the following example:

```
SELECT empid, firstname, lastname
FROM HR.Employees
WHERE lastname = 'Davis';
```

Because the column and the literal have different types, SQL Server implicitly converts one operand's type to the other. In this example, fortunately, SQL Server converts the literal's type to the column's type, so it can still efficiently rely on indexing. However, there can be cases where implicit conversion hurts performance. It is a best practice to use the proper form as follows:

```
SELECT empid, firstname, lastname
FROM HR.Employees
WHERE lastname = N'Davis';
```

T-SQL provides the LIKE predicate, which you can use to filter character string data (regular and Unicode) based on pattern matching. The form of a predicate using LIKE is as follows:

```
<column> LIKE <pattern>
```

The LIKE predicate supports wildcards that you can use in your patterns. Table 1-1 describes the available wildcards, their meaning, and an example demonstrating their use.

**TABLE 1-1** Wildcards used in LIKE patterns

| Wildcard | Meaning | Example |
|---|---|---|
| % (percent sign) | Any string including an empty one | 'D%': string starting with D |
| _ (underscore) | A single character | '_D%': string where second character is D |
| [<character list>] | A single character from a list | '[AC]%': string where first character is A or C |
| [<character range>] | A single character from a range | '[0-9]%': string where first character is a digit |
| [^<character list or range>] | A single character that is not in the list or range | '[^0-9]%': string where first character is not a digit |

As an example, suppose you want to return all employees whose last name starts with the letter D. You would use the following query:

```
SELECT empid, firstname, lastname
FROM HR.Employees
WHERE lastname LIKE N'D%';
```

This query returns the following output:

```
empid       firstname  lastname
----------- ---------- --------------------
1           Sara       Davis
9           Patricia   Doyle
```

If you want to look for a character that is considered a wildcard, you can indicate it after a character that you designate as an escape character by using the ESCAPE keyword. For example, the expression col1 LIKE '!_%' ESCAPE '!' looks for strings that start with an underscore (_) by using an exclamation point (!) as the escape character. Alternatively, you can place the wildcard in square brackets, as in col1 LIKE '[_]%'.

## Filtering date and time data

There are several important considerations when filtering date and time data. You want to think of things like how to express literals and how to filter ranges. Suppose that you need to query the Sales.Orders table and return only orders placed on February 12, 2016. You use the following query:

```
SELECT orderid, orderdate, empid, custid
FROM Sales.Orders
WHERE orderdate = '02/12/16';
```

If you're an American, this form probably means February 12, 2016, to you. However, if you're British, this form probably means December 2, 2016. If you're Japanese, it probably means December 16, 2002. The question is, when SQL Server converts this character string to a date and time type to align it with the filtered column's type, how does it interpret the value? As it turns out, it depends on the language of the login that runs the code. Each login has a default language associated with it, and the default language sets various session options on the login's behalf, including one called DATEFORMAT. A login with us_english will have the DATEFORMAT setting set to mdy, British to dmy, and Japanese to ymd. The problem is, how do you as a developer express a date if you want it to be interpreted the way you intended, regardless of who runs your code?

There are two main approaches. One is to use a form that is considered language-neutral. For example, the form '20160212' is always interpreted as ymd, regardless of your language. Note that the form '2016-02-12' is considered language-neutral only for the data types DATE, DATETIME2, and DATETIMEOFFSET. Unfortunately, due to historic reasons, this form is considered language-dependent for the types DATETIME and SMALLDATETIME. The advantage of the form without the separators is that it is language-neutral for all date and time types. So the recommendation is to write the query as follows:

```
SELECT orderid, orderdate, empid, custid
FROM Sales.Orders
WHERE orderdate = '20160212';
```

Another approach is to explicitly convert the string to the target type using the CONVERT function, and indicating the style number that represents the style that you used. You can find the documentation of the CONVERT function with the different style numbers that it supports at *https://msdn.microsoft.com/en-GB/library/ms187928.aspx*. For instance, to use the U.S. style, specify style number 101, as CONVERT(DATE, '02/12/2016', 101).

When filtering data stored in a DATETIME data type, you need to be very careful with ranges. To demonstrate why, first run the following code to create a table called Sales.Orders2 and populate it with a copy of the data from Sales.Orders, using the DATETIME data type for the orderdate attribute:

```
DROP TABLE IF EXISTS Sales.Orders2;

SELECT orderid, CAST(orderdate AS DATETIME) AS orderdate, empid, custid
INTO Sales.Orders2
FROM Sales.Orders;
```

Suppose you need to filter only the orders that were placed in April 2016. You use the following query in attempt to achieve this, thinking that the DATETIME type supports a three-digit precision as the fraction of the second:

```
SELECT orderid, orderdate, empid, custid
FROM Sales.Orders2
WHERE orderdate BETWEEN '20160401' AND '20160430 23:59:59.999';
```

In practice, though, the precision of DATETIME is three and a third milliseconds. Because 999 is not a multiplication of this precision, the value is rounded up to the next millisecond, which happens to be the midnight of the next day. To make matters worse, when people want to store only a date in a DATETIME type, they store the date with midnight in the time, so besides returning orders placed in April 2016, this query also returns all orders placed in May 1, 2016. Here's the output of this query, shown here in abbreviated format:

```
orderid     orderdate                empid    custid
----------- ------------------------ -------- -----------
10990       2016-04-01 00:00:00.000 2         20
...
11063       2016-04-30 00:00:00.000 3         37
11064       2016-05-01 00:00:00.000 1         71
11065       2016-05-01 00:00:00.000 8         46
11066       2016-05-01 00:00:00.000 7         89

(77 row(s) affected)
```

The recommended way to express a date and time range is with a closed-open interval as follows:

```
SELECT orderid, orderdate, empid, custid
FROM Sales.Orders2
WHERE orderdate >= '20160401' AND orderdate < '20160501';
```

This time the output contains only the orders placed in April 2016.

## Sorting data

One of the most confusing aspects of working with T-SQL is understanding when a query result is guaranteed to be ordered versus when it isn't. Correct understanding of this aspect of the language ties directly to the foundations of T-SQL—particularly mathematical set theory. If you understand this from the very early stages of writing T-SQL code, you will have a much easier time than many who simply have incorrect assumptions and expectations from the language.

Consider the following query as an example:

```
SELECT empid, firstname, lastname, city, MONTH(birthdate) AS birthmonth
FROM HR.Employees
WHERE country = N'USA' AND region = N'WA';
```

Is there a guarantee that the rows will be returned in particular order, and if so, what is that order? Some make an intuitive assumption that the rows will be returned in insertion order; some assume primary key order; some assume clustered index order; others know that there's no guarantee for any kind of order.

Remember that a table in T-SQL is supposed to represent a relation; a relation is a set, and a set has no order to its elements. With this in mind, unless you explicitly instruct the query otherwise, the result of a query has no guaranteed order. For example, this query gave the following output when run on one system:

```
empid       firstname  lastname             city             birthmonth
----------- ---------- -------------------- ---------------- -----------
1           Sara       Davis                Seattle          12
2           Don        Funk                 Tacoma           2
3           Judy       Lew                  Kirkland         8
4           Yael       Peled                Redmond          9
8           Maria      Cameron              Seattle          1
```

It might seem like the output is sorted by empid, but that's not guaranteed. What could be more confusing is that if you run the query repeatedly, it seems like the result keeps being returned in the same order; but again, that's not guaranteed. When the database engine (SQL Server in this case) processes this query, it knows that it can return the data in any order because there is no explicit instruction to return the data in a specific order. It could be that, due to optimization and other reasons, the SQL Server database engine chose to process the data in a particular way this time. There's even some likelihood that such choices will be repeated if the physical circumstances remain the same. But there's a big difference between what's likely to happen due to optimization and other reasons, and what's actually guaranteed.

The database engine can—and sometimes does—change choices that can affect the order in which rows are returned, knowing that it is free to do so. Examples for such changes in choices include changes in data distribution, availability of physical structures such as indexes, and availability of resources like CPU and memory. Also, with changes in the engine after an upgrade to a newer version of the product, or even after application of a service pack, optimization aspects can change. In turn, such changes could affect, among other things, the order of the rows in the result.

In short, this cannot be stressed enough: A query that doesn't have an explicit instruction to return the rows in a particular order doesn't guarantee the order of rows in the result. When you do need such a guarantee, the only way to provide it is by adding an ORDER BY clause to the query.

For example, if you want to return information about employees from Washington in the US, sorted by city, you specify the city column in the ORDER BY clause as follows:

```
SELECT empid, firstname, lastname, city, MONTH(birthdate) AS birthmonth
FROM HR.Employees
WHERE country = N'USA' AND region = N'WA'
ORDER BY city;
```

Here's the output of this query:

```
empid       firstname  lastname             city             birthmonth
----------- ---------- -------------------- ---------------- -----------
3           Judy       Lew                  Kirkland         8
4           Yael       Peled                Redmond          9
8           Maria      Cameron              Seattle          1
1           Sara       Davis                Seattle          12
2           Don        Funk                 Tacoma           2
```

If you don't indicate a direction for sorting, ascending order is assumed by default. You can be explicit and specify city ASC, but it means the same thing as not indicating the direction. For descending ordering, you need to explicitly specify DESC, as follows:

```
SELECT empid, firstname, lastname, city, MONTH(birthdate) AS birthmonth
FROM HR.Employees
WHERE country = N'USA' AND region = N'WA'
ORDER BY city DESC;
```

This time, the output shows the rows in city order, descending direction:

| empid | firstname | lastname | city | birthmonth |
| --- | --- | --- | --- | --- |
| 2 | Don | Funk | Tacoma | 2 |
| 1 | Sara | Davis | Seattle | 12 |
| 8 | Maria | Cameron | Seattle | 1 |
| 4 | Yael | Peled | Redmond | 9 |
| 3 | Judy | Lew | Kirkland | 8 |

The city column isn't unique within the filtered country and region, and therefore, the ordering of rows with the same city (see Seattle, for example) isn't guaranteed. In such a case, it is said that the ordering isn't deterministic. Just like a query without an ORDER BY clause doesn't guarantee order among result rows in general, a query with ORDER BY city, when city isn't unique, doesn't guarantee order among rows with the same city. Fortunately, you can specify multiple expressions in the ORDER BY list, separated by commas. One use case of this capability is to apply a tiebreaker for ordering. For example, you could define empid as the secondary sort column, as follows:

```
SELECT empid, firstname, lastname, city, MONTH(birthdate) AS birthmonth
FROM HR.Employees
WHERE country = N'USA' AND region = N'WA'
ORDER BY city, empid;
```

Here's the output of this query:

| empid | firstname | lastname | city | birthmonth |
| --- | --- | --- | --- | --- |
| 3 | Judy | Lew | Kirkland | 8 |
| 4 | Yael | Peled | Redmond | 9 |
| 1 | Sara | Davis | Seattle | 12 |
| 8 | Maria | Cameron | Seattle | 1 |
| 2 | Don | Funk | Tacoma | 2 |

The ORDER BY list is now unique; hence, the ordering is deterministic. As long as the underlying data doesn't change, the results are guaranteed to be repeatable, in addition to their presentation ordering. You can indicate the ordering direction on an expression-by-expression basis, as in ORDER BY col1 DESC, col2, col3 DESC (col1 descending, then col2 ascending, then col3 descending).

With T-SQL, you can sort by ordinal positions of columns in the SELECT list, but it is considered a bad practice. Consider the following query as an example:

```
SELECT empid, firstname, lastname, city, MONTH(birthdate) AS birthmonth
FROM HR.Employees
WHERE country = N'USA' AND region = N'WA'
ORDER BY 4, 1;
```

In this query, you're asking to order the rows by the fourth expression in the SELECT list (city), and then by the first (empid). In this particular query, it is equivalent to using ORDER BY city, empid. However, this practice is considered a bad one for a number of reasons. For one, T-SQL does keep track of ordinal positions of columns in a table, in addition to in a query result, but this is nonrelational. Recall that the heading of a relation is a set of attributes, and a set has no order. Also, when you are using ordinal positions, it is very easy after making changes to the SELECT list to miss changing the ordinals accordingly. For example, suppose that you decide to apply changes to your previous query, returning city right after empid in the SELECT list. You apply the change to the SELECT list but forget to change the ORDER BY list accordingly, and end up with the following query:

```
SELECT empid, city, firstname, lastname, MONTH(birthdate) AS birthmonth
FROM HR.Employees
WHERE country = N'USA' AND region = N'WA'
ORDER BY 4, 1;
```

Now the query is ordering the data by lastname and empid instead of by city and empid. In short, it's a best practice to refer to column names, or expressions based on column names, and not to ordinal positions.

Note that you can order the result rows by elements that you're not returning. For example, the following query returns, for each qualifying employee, the employee ID and city, ordering the result rows by the employee birth date:

```
SELECT empid, city
FROM HR.Employees
WHERE country = N'USA' AND region = N'WA'
ORDER BY birthdate;
```

Here's the output of this query:

```
empid       city
----------- ----------------
4           Redmond
1           Seattle
2           Tacoma
8           Seattle
3           Kirkland
```

Of course, the result would appear much more meaningful if you included the birthdate attribute, but if it makes sense for you not to, it's perfectly valid. The rule is that you can order the result rows by elements that are not part of the SELECT list, as long as those elements would have normally been allowed there. This rule changes when the DISTINCT clause is also specified, and for a good reason. When DISTINCT is used, duplicates are removed; then the result rows don't necessarily map to source rows in a one-to-one manner, rather than one-to-many. For example, try to reason why the following query isn't valid:

```
SELECT DISTINCT city
FROM HR.Employees
WHERE country = N'USA' AND region = N'WA'
ORDER BY birthdate;
```

You can have multiple employees—each with a different birth date—from the same city. But you're returning only one row for each distinct city in the result. So given one city (say, Seattle) with multiple employees, which of the employee birth dates should apply as the ordering value? The query won't just pick one; rather, it simply fails.

So, in case the DISTINCT clause is used, you are limited in the ORDER BY list to only elements that appear in the SELECT list, as in the following query:

```
SELECT DISTINCT city
FROM HR.Employees
WHERE country = N'USA' AND region = N'WA'
ORDER BY city;
```

Now the query is perfectly sensible, returning the following output:

```
city
---------------
Kirkland
Redmond
Seattle
Tacoma
```

What's also interesting to note about the ORDER BY clause is that it gets evaluated conceptually after the SELECT clause—unlike most other query clauses. This means that column aliases assigned in the SELECT clause are actually visible to the ORDER BY clause. As an example, the following query uses the MONTH function to return the birth month, assigning the expression with the column alias birthmonth. The query then refers to the column alias birthmonth directly in the ORDER BY clause:

```
SELECT empid, firstname, lastname, city, MONTH(birthdate) AS birthmonth
FROM HR.Employees
WHERE country = N'USA' AND region = N'WA'
ORDER BY birthmonth;
```

This query returns the following output:

```
empid       firstname  lastname              city             birthmonth
----------- ---------- -------------------- ---------------- -----------
8           Maria      Cameron               Seattle          1
2           Don        Funk                  Tacoma           2
3           Judy       Lew                   Kirkland         8
4           Yael       Peled                 Redmond          9
1           Sara       Davis                 Seattle          12
```

Another tricky aspect of ordering is treatment of NULLs. Recall that a NULL represents a missing value, so when comparing a NULL to anything, you get the logical result unknown. That's the case even when comparing two NULLs. So it's not that trivial to ask how NULLs should behave in terms of sorting. Should they all sort together? If so, should they sort before or after non-NULL values? Standard SQL says that NULLs should sort together, but leaves it to the implementation to decide whether to sort them before or after non-NULL values. In SQL Server the decision was to sort them before non-NULLs (when using an ascending direction). As an example, the following query returns for each order the order ID and shipped date, ordered by the latter:

```
SELECT orderid, shippeddate
FROM Sales.Orders
WHERE custid = 20
ORDER BY shippeddate;
```

Remember that unshipped orders have a NULL in the shippeddate column; hence, they sort before shipped orders, as the query output shows:

```
orderid     shippeddate
----------- -----------
11008       NULL
11072       NULL
10258       2014-07-23
10263       2014-07-31
...
```

Standard SQL supports the options NULLS FIRST and NULLS LAST to control how NULLs sort, but T-SQL doesn't support this option. As an interesting challenge, see if you can figure out how to sort the orders by shipped date ascending, but have NULLs sort last. (Hint: You can specify expressions in the ORDER BY clause; think of how to use the CASE expression to achieve this task.)

So remember, a query without an ORDER BY clause returns a relational result (at least from an ordering perspective), and hence doesn't guarantee any order. The only way to guarantee order is with an ORDER BY clause. According to standard SQL, a query with an ORDER BY clause conceptually returns a cursor and not a relation.

Creating the right indexes can help SQL Server avoid the need to actually sort the data to address an ORDER BY request. Without good indexes, SQL Server needs to sort the data, and sorting can be expensive, especially when a large set is involved. If you don't need to return the data sorted, make sure you do not specify an ORDER BY clause, to avoid unnecessary costs.

# Filtering data with TOP and OFFSET-FETCH

Besides supporting filters that are based on predicates, like the WHERE filter, T-SQL also supports filters that are based on a number, or percent of rows and ordering. Those are the TOP and OFFSET-FETCH filters. The former is used in a lot of common filtering tasks, and the latter is typically used in more specialized paging-related tasks.

## Filtering data with TOP

With the TOP option, you can filter a requested number or percent of rows from the query result based on indicated ordering. You specify the TOP option in the SELECT clause followed by the requested number of rows in parentheses (as a BIGINT typed value). The ordering specification of the TOP filter is based on the same ORDER BY clause that is normally used for presentation ordering.

As an example, the following query returns the three most recent orders:

```
SELECT TOP (3) orderid, orderdate, custid, empid
FROM Sales.Orders
ORDER BY orderdate DESC;
```

You specify 3 as the number of rows you want to filter, and orderdate DESC as the ordering specification. So you get the three rows with the most recent order dates. Here's the output of this query:

```
orderid     orderdate   custid      empid
----------- ----------- ----------- -----------
11077       2016-05-06  65          1
11076       2016-05-06  9           4
11075       2016-05-06  68          8
```

**EXAM TIP**

T-SQL supports specifying the number of rows to filter using the TOP option in SELECT queries without parentheses, but that's only for backward-compatibility reasons. The correct syntax is with parentheses.

You can also specify a percent of rows to filter instead of a number. To do so, specify a FLOAT value in the range 0 through 100 in the parentheses, and the keyword PERCENT after the parentheses, as follows:

```
SELECT TOP (1) PERCENT orderid, orderdate, custid, empid
FROM Sales.Orders
ORDER BY orderdate DESC;
```

The PERCENT option computes the ceiling of the resulting number of rows if it's not whole. In this example, without the TOP option, the number of rows in the result is 830. Filtering 1 percent gives you 8.3, and then the ceiling of this value gives you 9; hence, the query returns 9 rows:

```
orderid     orderdate   custid      empid
----------- ----------- ----------- -----------
11074       2016-05-06  73          7
11075       2016-05-06  68          8
11076       2016-05-06  9           4
11077       2016-05-06  65          1
11070       2016-05-05  44          2
11071       2016-05-05  46          1
11072       2016-05-05  20          4
11073       2016-05-05  58          2
11067       2016-05-04  17          1
```

The TOP option isn't limited to a constant input; instead, it allows you to specify a self-contained expression. From a practical perspective, this capability is especially important when you need to pass a parameter or a variable as input, as the following code demonstrates:

```
DECLARE @n AS BIGINT = 5;

SELECT TOP (@n) orderid, orderdate, custid, empid
FROM Sales.Orders
ORDER BY orderdate DESC;
```

This query generates the following output:

```
orderid     orderdate   custid     empid
----------- ----------- ---------- -----------
11074       2016-05-06  73         7
11075       2016-05-06  68         8
11076       2016-05-06  9          4
11077       2016-05-06  65         1
11070       2016-05-05  44         2
```

In most cases, you need your TOP option to rely on some ordering specification, but as it turns out, an ORDER BY clause isn't mandatory. For example, the following query is technically valid:

```
SELECT TOP (3) orderid, orderdate, custid, empid
FROM Sales.Orders;
```

However, the query isn't deterministic. The query filters three rows, but you have no guarantee which three rows will be returned. You end up getting whichever three rows SQL Server happened to access first, and that's dependent on physical data layout and optimization choices, none of which is guaranteed to be repeatable. For example, this query gave the following output on one system:

```
orderid     orderdate   custid     empid
----------- ----------- ---------- -----------
10248       2014-07-04  85         5
10249       2014-07-05  79         6
10250       2014-07-08  34         4
```

But there's no guarantee that the same rows will be returned if you run the query again. If you are really after three arbitrary rows, it might be a good idea to add an ORDER BY clause with the expression (SELECT NULL) to let people know that your choice is intentional and not an oversight. Here's how your query would look:

```
SELECT TOP (3) orderid, orderdate, custid, empid
FROM Sales.Orders
ORDER BY (SELECT NULL);
```

Note that even when you do have an ORDER BY clause, in order for the query to be completely deterministic, the ordering must be unique. For example, consider again the first query from this section:

```
SELECT TOP (3) orderid, orderdate, custid, empid
FROM Sales.Orders
ORDER BY orderdate DESC;
```

The orderdate column isn't unique, so the ordering in case of ties is arbitrary. When I ran this query on my system, I received the following output.

```
orderid      orderdate   custid       empid
-----------  ----------  -----------  -----------
11077        2016-05-06  65           1
11076        2016-05-06  9            4
11075        2016-05-06  68           8
```

But what if there are other rows in the result without TOP that have the same order date as in the last row here? You don't always care about guaranteeing deterministic or repeatable results; but if you do, two options are available to you. One option is to ask to include all ties with the last row by adding the WITH TIES option, as follows:

```
SELECT TOP (3) WITH TIES orderid, orderdate, custid, empid
FROM Sales.Orders
ORDER BY orderdate DESC;
```

Of course, this could result in returning more rows than you asked for, as the output of this query shows:

```
orderid      orderdate   custid       empid
-----------  ----------  -----------  -----------
11074        2016-05-06  73           7
11075        2016-05-06  68           8
11076        2016-05-06  9            4
11077        2016-05-06  65           1
```

Now the selection of rows is deterministic, but still the presentation order between rows with the same order date isn't.

The other option to guarantee determinism is to break the ties by adding a tiebreaker that makes the ordering unique. For example, in case of ties in the order date, suppose you wanted to use the order ID, descending, as the tiebreaker. To do so, add orderid DESC to your ORDER BY clause, as follows:

```
SELECT TOP (3) orderid, orderdate, custid, empid
FROM Sales.Orders
ORDER BY orderdate DESC, orderid DESC;
```

Now both the selection of rows and presentation order are deterministic. This query generates the following output:

```
orderid      orderdate   custid       empid
-----------  ----------  -----------  -----------
11077        2016-05-06  65           1
11076        2016-05-06  9            4
11075        2016-05-06  68           8
```

## Filtering data with OFFSET-FETCH

The OFFSET-FETCH option is a filtering option that, like TOP, you can use to filter data based on a specified number of rows and ordering. But unlike TOP, it is standard, and also has a skipping capability, making it useful for ad-hoc paging purposes.

The OFFSET and FETCH clauses appear right after the ORDER BY clause, and in fact, in T-SQL, they require an ORDER BY clause to be present. You first specify the OFFSET clause indicating how many rows you want to skip (0 if you don't want to skip any); you then optionally specify the FETCH clause indicating how many rows you want to filter. For example, the following query defines ordering based on order date descending, followed by order ID descending; it then skips the first 50 rows and fetches the next 25 rows:

```
SELECT orderid, orderdate, custid, empid
FROM Sales.Orders
ORDER BY orderdate DESC, orderid DESC
OFFSET 50 ROWS FETCH NEXT 25 ROWS ONLY;
```

Here's an abbreviated form of the output:

```
orderid     orderdate   custid      empid
----------- ----------- ----------- -----------
11027       2016-04-16  10          1
11026       2016-04-15  27          4
...
11004       2016-04-07  50          3
11003       2016-04-06  78          3
```

The ORDER BY clause now plays two roles: One role is telling the OFFSET-FETCH option which rows it needs to filter. Another role is determining presentation ordering in the query.

As mentioned, in T-SQL, the OFFSET-FETCH option requires an ORDER BY clause to be present. Also, in T-SQL—contrary to standard SQL—a FETCH clause requires an OFFSET clause to be present. So if you do want to filter some rows but skip none, you still need to specify the OFFSET clause with 0 ROWS.

In order to make the syntax intuitive, you can use the keywords NEXT or FIRST interchangeably. When skipping some rows, it might be more intuitive to you to use the keywords FETCH NEXT to indicate how many rows to filter; but when not skipping any rows, it might be more intuitive to you to use the keywords FETCH FIRST, as follows:

```
SELECT orderid, orderdate, custid, empid
FROM Sales.Orders
ORDER BY orderdate DESC, orderid DESC
OFFSET 0 ROWS FETCH FIRST 25 ROWS ONLY;
```

For similar reasons, you can use the singular form ROW or the plural form ROWS interchangeably, both for the number of rows to skip and for the number of rows to filter. But it's not like you will get an error if you say FETCH NEXT 1 ROWS or FETCH NEXT 25 ROW. It's up to you to use a proper form, just like with English.

In T-SQL, a FETCH clause requires an OFFSET clause, but the OFFSET clause doesn't require a FETCH clause. In other words, by indicating an OFFSET clause, you're requesting to skip some rows; then by not indicating a FETCH clause, you're requesting to return all remaining rows. For example, the following query requests to skip 50 rows, returning all the rest.

```
SELECT orderid, orderdate, custid, empid
FROM Sales.Orders
ORDER BY orderdate DESC, orderid DESC
OFFSET 50 ROWS;
```

This query generates the following output, shown here in abbreviated form:

```
orderid     orderdate  custid      empid
----------- ---------- ----------- -----------
11027       2016-04-16 10          1
11026       2016-04-15 27          4
...
10249       2014-07-05 79          6
10248       2014-07-04 85          5

(780 row(s) affected)
```

As mentioned earlier, the OFFSET-FETCH option requires an ORDER BY clause. But what if you need to filter a certain number of rows based on arbitrary order? To do so, you can specify the expression (SELECT NULL) in the ORDER BY clause, as follows:

```
SELECT orderid, orderdate, custid, empid
FROM Sales.Orders
ORDER BY (SELECT NULL)
OFFSET 0 ROWS FETCH FIRST 3 ROWS ONLY;
```

This code simply filters three arbitrary rows. Here's the output that I got when running this query on our system:

```
orderid     orderdate  custid      empid
----------- ---------- ----------- -----------
10248       2014-07-04 85          5
10249       2014-07-05 79          6
10250       2014-07-08 34          4
```

With both the OFFSET and the FETCH clauses, you can use expressions as inputs. This is very handy when you need to compute the input values dynamically. For example, suppose that you're implementing a paging solution where you return to the user one page of rows at a time. The user passes as input parameters to your procedure or function the page number they are after (@pagenum parameter) and page size (@pagesize parameter). This means that you need to skip as many rows as @pagenum minus one times @pagesize, and fetch the next @pagesize rows. This can be implemented using the following code (using local variables for simplicity):

```
DECLARE @pagesize AS BIGINT = 25, @pagenum AS BIGINT = 3;

SELECT orderid, orderdate, custid, empid
FROM Sales.Orders
ORDER BY orderdate DESC, orderid DESC
OFFSET (@pagenum - 1) * @pagesize ROWS FETCH NEXT @pagesize ROWS ONLY;
```

With these inputs, the code returns the following output:

| orderid | orderdate  | custid | empid |
|---------|------------|--------|-------|
| 11027   | 2016-04-16 | 10     | 1     |
| 11026   | 2016-04-15 | 27     | 4     |
| ...     |            |        |       |
| 11004   | 2016-04-07 | 50     | 3     |
| 11003   | 2016-04-06 | 78     | 3     |

You can feel free to change the input values and see how the result changes accordingly.

**EXAM TIP**

In terms of logical query processing, the TOP and OFFSET-FETCH filters are processed after the FROM, WHERE, GROUP, HAVING and SELECT phases. You can consider these filters as being an extension to the ORDER BY clause. So, for example, if the query is a grouped query, and also involves a TOP or OFFSET-FETCH filter, the filter is applied after grouping. The same applies if the query has a DISTINCT clause and/or ROW_NUMBER calculation as part of the SELECT clause, as well as a TOP or OFFSET-FETCH filter. The filter is applied after the DISTINCT clause and/or ROW_NUMBER calculation.

Because the OFFSET-FETCH option is standard and TOP isn't, in cases where they are logically equivalent, it's recommended to stick to the former. Remember that OFFSET-FETCH also has an advantage over TOP in the sense that it supports a skipping capability. However, for now, OFFSET-FETCH does not support options similar to TOP's PERCENT and WITH TIES, even though the standard does define them.

From a performance standpoint, you should consider indexing the ORDER BY columns to support the TOP and OFFSET-FETCH options. Such indexing serves a similar purpose to indexing filtered columns and can help avoid scanning unnecessary data as well as sorting.

**MORE INFO**  **ON TOP AND OFFSET-FETCH**

For more information on the TOP and OFFSET-FETCH filters, see the free sample chapter of the book, "T-SQL Querying: Chapter 5 - TOP and OFFSET-FETCH." This book is more advanced, and includes detailed coverage of optimization aspects. You can find the online version of this chapter at *https://www.microsoftpressstore.com/articles/article. aspx?p=2314819*. You can download the PDF version of this chapter at *https://ptgmedia. pearsoncmg.com/images/9780735685048/samplepages/9780735685048.pdf*.

# Combining sets with set operators

Set operators operate on two result sets of queries, comparing complete rows between the results. Depending on the result of the comparison and the operator used, the operator determines whether to return the row or not. T-SQL supports the operators: UNION, UNION ALL, INTERSECT, and EXCEPT.

The general form of code using these operators is as follows:

```
<query 1>
<operator>
<query 2>
[ORDER BY <order_by_list>];
```

When working with these operators you need to remember the following guidelines:

- Because complete rows are matched between the result sets, the number of columns in the queries has to be the same and the column types of corresponding columns need to be compatible (implicitly convertible).

- These operators use distinctness-based comparison and not equality based. Consequently, a comparison between two NULLs yields true, and a comparison between a NULL and a non-NULL value yields a false. This is in contrast to filtering clauses like WHERE, ON, and HAVING, which yield unknown when comparing a NULL with anything using both equality and inequality operators.

- Because these operators are set operators and not cursor operators, the individual queries are not allowed to have ORDER BY clauses.

- You can optionally add an ORDER BY clause that determines presentation ordering of the result of the set operator.

- The column names of result columns are determined by the first query.

**EXAM TIP**

The term *set operator* is not a precise term to describe the UNION, INERSECT, and EXCEPT operators, rather *relational operator* is a better term. Whereas in mathematical set theory you can unify a set of teachers with a set of prime numbers, in relational theory, you can't. You can only unify two relations that share the same attributes. This is explained in Dejan Sarka's blog post on the topic at *http://sqlblog.com/blogs/dejan_sarka/archive/2014/01/10/ sql-set-operators-set-really.aspx*. However, both the SQL community and the official T-SQL documentation use the term set operator. Also, chances are that the same terminology will be used in the exam. Therefore, I am using this terminology in this book.

## UNION and UNION ALL

The UNION operator unifies the results of the two input queries. As a set operator, UNION has an implied DISTINCT property, meaning that it does not return duplicate rows. Figure 1-2 shows an illustration of the UNION operator.

**FIGURE 1-2**  The UNION operator

As an example for using the UNION operator, the following query returns locations that are employee locations, or customer locations, or both:

```
SELECT country, region, city
FROM HR.Employees

UNION

SELECT country, region, city
FROM Sales.Customers;
```

This query generates the following output, shown here in abbreviated form:

```
country           region            city
--------------- --------------- ---------------
Argentina         NULL              Buenos Aires
Austria           NULL              Graz
Austria           NULL              Salzburg
...

(71 row(s) affected)
```

The HR.Employees table has nine rows, and the Sales.Customers table has 91 rows, but there are 71 distinct locations in the unified results; hence, the UNION operator returns 71 rows.

If you want to keep the duplicates—for example, to later group the rows and count occurrences—you need to use the UNION ALL operator instead of UNION. The UNION ALL operator unifies the results of the two input queries, but doesn't try to eliminate duplicates.

As an example, the following query unifies employee locations and customer locations using the UNION ALL operator:

```
SELECT country, region, city
FROM HR.Employees

UNION ALL

SELECT country, region, city
FROM Sales.Customers;
```

Because UNION ALL doesn't attempt to remove duplicates, the result has 100 rows (nine employees and 91 customers):

```
country          region           city
---------------- ---------------- ----------------
USA              WA               Seattle
USA              WA               Tacoma
USA              WA               Kirkland
USA              WA               Redmond
UK               NULL             London
UK               NULL             London
UK               NULL             London
USA              WA               Seattle
UK               NULL             London
Germany          NULL             Berlin
...

(100 row(s) affected)
```

If the sets you're unifying are disjoint and there's no potential for duplicates, UNION and UNION ALL return the same result. However, it's important to use UNION ALL in such a case from a performance standpoint because with UNION, SQL Server can try to eliminate duplicates, incurring unnecessary cost. Figure 1-3 shows the query execution plans for both the UNION (top plan) and UNION ALL (bottom) queries.

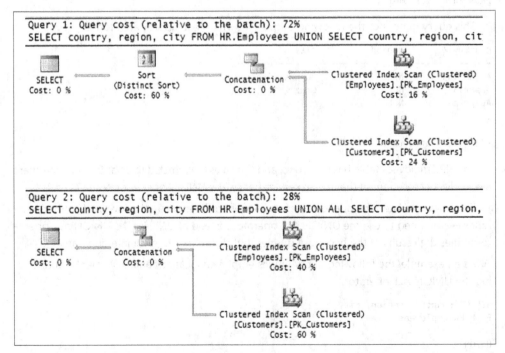

FIGURE 1-3   Query plan for UNION and UNION ALL operators

> **NOTE** **DISPLAYING AN ACTUAL EXECUTION PLAN**
>
> To see graphical execution plans in SQL Server Management Studio (SSMS) click the Include Actual Execution Plan button, or press Ctrl+M, and run the code. The plans appear in the Execution Plan tab. You can find tips about analyzing query plans efficiently at *http://sqlmag.com/t-sql/understanding-query-plans*.

Observe that both plans start the same by scanning the two input tables and then concatenating (unifying) the results. But only the UNION operator includes an extra step with the Sort (Distinct Sort) operator to eliminate duplicates.

## INTERSECT

The INTERSECT operator returns only distinct rows that are common to both sets. In other words, if a row appears at least once in the first set and at least once in the second set, it appears once in the result of the INTERSECT operator.

Figure 1-4 shows an illustration of the INTERSECT operator.

**FIGURE 1-4**   The INTERSECT operator

As an example, the following code uses the INTERSECT operator to return distinct locations that are both employee and customer locations (locations where there's at least one employee and at least one customer):

```
SELECT country, region, city
FROM HR.Employees

INTERSECT

SELECT country, region, city
FROM Sales.Customers;
```

This query generates the following output:

```
country          region            city
---------------  ----------------  ----------------
UK               NULL              London
USA              WA                Kirkland
USA              WA                Seattle
```

Observe that the location (UK, NULL, London) was returned because it appears in both sides. When comparing the NULLs in the region column in the rows from the two sides, the INTERSECT operator considered them as not distinct from each other. Also note that never mind how many times the same location appears in each side, as long as it appears at least once in both sides, it's returned only once in the output.

## EXCEPT

The EXCEPT operator performs set difference. It returns distinct rows that appear in the result of the first query but not the second. In other words, if a row appears at least once in the first query result and zero times in the second, it's returned once in the output.

Figure 1-5 shows an illustration of the EXCEPT operator.

**FIGURE 1-5**  The EXCEPT operator

As an example for using EXCEPT, the following query returns locations that are employee locations but not customer locations:

```
SELECT country, region, city
FROM HR.Employees

EXCEPT

SELECT country, region, city
FROM Sales.Customers;
```

This query generates the following output:

```
country           region            city
---------------   ---------------   ---------------
USA               WA                Redmond
USA               WA                Tacoma
```

With UNION and INTERSECT, the order of the input queries doesn't matter. However, with EXCEPT, there's different meaning to:

```
<query 1> EXCEPT <query 2>
```

Versus:

```
<query 2> EXCEPT <query 1>
```

Finally, set operators have precedence: INTERSECT precedes UNION and EXCEPT, and UNION and EXCEPT are evaluated from left to right based on their position in the expression. Consider the following set operators:

```
<query 1> UNION <query 2> INTERSECT <query 3>;
```

First, the intersection between query 2 and query 3 takes place, and then a union between the result of the intersection and query 1. You can always force precedence by using parentheses. So, if you want the union to take place first, you use the following form:

```
(<query 1> UNION <query 2>) INTERSECT <query 3>;
```

When you're done, run the following code for cleanup:

```
DROP TABLE IF EXISTS Sales.Orders2;
```

# Skill 1.2: Query multiple tables by using joins

Often, data that you need to query is spread across multiple tables. The tables are usually related through keys, such as a foreign key in one side and a primary key in the other. Then you can use joins to query the data from the different tables and match the rows that need to be related. This section covers the different types of joins that T-SQL supports: cross, inner, and outer.

---

**This section covers how to:**

- Write queries with join statements based on provided tables, data, and requirements
- Determine proper usage of INNER JOIN, LEFT/RIGHT/FULL OUTER JOIN, and CROSS JOIN
- Construct multiple JOIN operators using AND and OR
- Determine the correct results when presented with multi-table SELECT statements and source data
- Write queries with NULLs on joins

---

Before running the code samples in this skill, add a row to the Suppliers table by running the following code:

```
USE TSQLV4;

INSERT INTO Production.Suppliers
  (companyname, contactname, contacttitle, address, city, postalcode, country, phone)
  VALUES(N'Supplier XYZ', N'Jiru', N'Head of Security', N'42 Sekimai Musashino-shi',
    N'Tokyo', N'01759', N'Japan', N'(02) 4311-2609');
```

# Cross joins

A cross join is the simplest type of join, though not the most commonly used one. This join performs what's known as a Cartesian product of the two input tables. In other words, it performs a multiplication between the tables, yielding a row for each combination of rows from both sides. If you have m rows in table T1 and n rows in table T2, the result of a cross join between T1 and T2 is a virtual table with m × n rows. Figure 1-6 provides an illustration of a cross join.

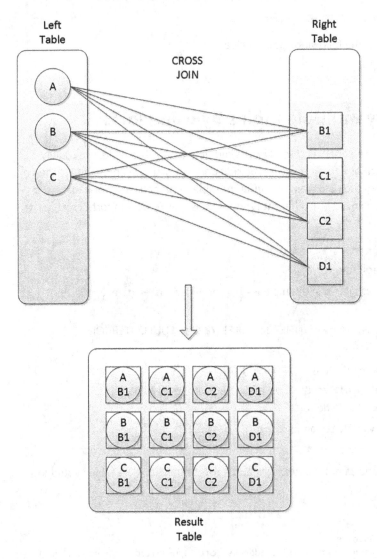

**FIGURE 1-6** Cross join

The left table has three rows with the key values A, B, and C. The right table has four rows with the key values B1, C1, C2, and D1. The result is a table with 12 rows containing all possible combinations of rows from the two input tables.

Consider an example from the TSQLV4 sample database. This database contains a table called dbo.Nums that has a column called n with a sequence of integers from 1 and on. Your task is to use the Nums table to generate a result with a row for each weekday (1 through 7) and shift number (1 through 3), assuming there are three shifts a day. The result can later be used as the basis for building information about activities in the different shifts in the different days. With seven days in the week, and three shifts every day, the result should have 21 rows.

Here's a query that achieves the task by performing a cross join between two instances of the Nums table—one representing the days (aliased as D), and the other representing the shifts (aliased as S):

```
USE TSQLV4;

SELECT D.n AS theday, S.n AS shiftno
FROM dbo.Nums AS D
  CROSS JOIN dbo.Nums AS S
WHERE D.n <= 7
  AND S.N <= 3
ORDER BY theday, shiftno;
```

Here's the output of this query:

```
theday      shiftno
----------- -----------
1           1
1           2
1           3
2           1
2           2
2           3
3           1
3           2
3           3
4           1
4           2
4           3
5           1
5           2
5           3
6           1
6           2
6           3
7           1
7           2
7           3
```

The Nums table has 100,000 rows. According to logical query processing, the first step in the processing of the query is evaluating the FROM clause. The cross join operates in the FROM clause, performing a Cartesian product between the two instances of Nums, yielding a table with 10,000,000,000 rows (not to worry, that's only conceptually). Then the WHERE clause filters only the rows where the column D.n is less than or equal to 7, and the column S.n is less than or equal to 3. After applying the filter, the result has 21 qualifying rows. The SELECT clause then returns D.n aliasing it theday, and S.n aliasing it shiftno.

Fortunately, SQL Server doesn't have to follow logical query processing literally as long as it can return the correct result. That's what optimization is all about—returning the result as fast as possible. SQL Server knows that with a cross join followed by a filter it can evaluate the filters first (which is especially efficient when there are indexes to support the filters), and then match the remaining rows. This optimization technique is called *predicate pushdown*.

Note the importance of aliasing the tables in the join. For one, it's convenient to refer to a table by using a shorter name. But in a self-join like ours, table aliasing is mandatory. If you don't assign different aliases to the two instances of the table, you end up with an invalid result because there are duplicate column names even when including the table name as a prefix. By aliasing the tables differently, you can refer to columns in an unambiguous way using the form table_alias.column_name, as in D.n versus S.n.

Also, note that in addition to supporting the syntax for cross joins with the CROSS JOIN keywords, both standard SQL and T-SQL support an older syntax where you specify a comma between the table names, as in FROM T1, T2. However, for a number of reasons, it is recommended to stick to the newer syntax; it is less prone to errors and allows for more consistent code.

## Inner joins

With an inner join, you can match rows from two tables based on a predicate—usually one that compares a primary key value in one side to a foreign key value in another side. Figure 1-7 illustrates an inner join.

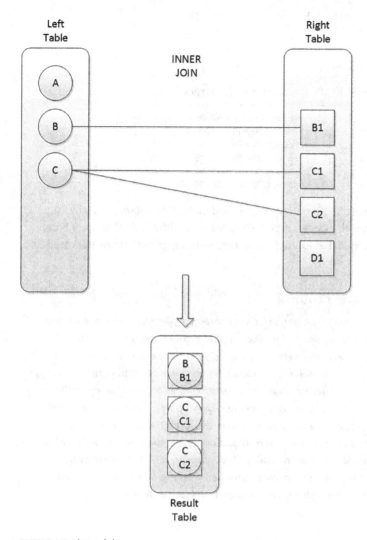

**FIGURE 1-7** Inner join

The letters represent primary key values in the left table and foreign key values in the right table. Assuming the join is an equijoin (using a predicate with an equality operator such as lefttable.keycol = righttable.keycol), the inner join returns only matching rows for which the predicate evaluates to true. Rows for which the predicate evaluates to false or unknown are discarded.

As an example, the following query returns suppliers from Japan and the products they supply:

```
SELECT
  S.companyname AS supplier, S.country,
  P.productid, P.productname, P.unitprice
FROM Production.Suppliers AS S
```

```
    INNER JOIN Production.Products AS P
      ON S.supplierid = P.supplierid
WHERE S.country = N'Japan';
```

Here's the output of this query:

```
supplier         country  productid  productname     unitprice
---------------  -------  ---------  --------------  ----------
Supplier QOVFD   Japan    9          Product AOZBW   97.00
Supplier QOVFD   Japan    10         Product YHXGE   31.00
Supplier QWUSF   Japan    13         Product POXFU   6.00
Supplier QWUSF   Japan    14         Product PWCJB   23.25
Supplier QWUSF   Japan    15         Product KSZOI   15.50
Supplier QOVFD   Japan    74         Product BKAZJ   10.00
```

Observe that the join's matching predicate is specified in the ON clause. It matches suppliers and products that share the same supplier ID. Rows from either side that don't find a match in the other are discarded. For example, suppliers from Japan with no related products aren't returned.

> **NOTE  INDEXING FOREIGN KEY COLUMNS**
>
> Often, when joining tables, you join them based on a foreign key–unique key relationship. For example, there's a foreign key defined on the supplierid column in the Production. Products table (the referencing table), referencing the primary key column supplierid in the Production.Suppliers table (the referenced table). It's also important to note that when you define a primary key or unique constraint, SQL Server creates a unique index on the constraint columns to enforce the constraint's uniqueness property. But when you define a foreign key, SQL Server doesn't create any indexes on the foreign key columns. Such indexes could improve the performance of joins based on those relationships. Because SQL Server doesn't create such indexes automatically, it's your responsibility to identify the cases where they can be useful and create them. So when working on index tuning, one interesting area to examine is foreign key columns, and evaluating the benefits of creating indexes on those.

Regarding the last query, again, notice the convenience of using short table aliases when needing to refer to ambiguous column names like supplierid. Observe that the query uses table aliases to prefix even nonambiguous column names such as s.country. This practice isn't mandatory as long as the column name is not ambiguous, but it is still considered a best practice for clarity.

A very common question is, "What's the difference between the ON and the WHERE clauses, and does it matter if you specify your predicate in one or the other?" The answer is that for inner joins it doesn't matter. Both clauses serve the same filtering purpose. Both filter only rows for which the predicate evaluates to true and discard rows for which the predicate evaluates to false or unknown. In terms of logical query processing, the WHERE is evaluated right after the FROM, so conceptually it is equivalent to concatenating the predicates with an AND operator, forming a conjunction of predicates. SQL Server knows this, and therefore can internally rearrange the order in which it evaluates the predicates in practice, and it does so based on cost estimates.

For these reasons, if you wanted, you could rearrange the placement of the predicates from the previous query, specifying both in the ON clause, and still retain the original meaning, as follows:

```
SELECT
  S.companyname AS supplier, S.country,
  P.productid, P.productname, P.unitprice
FROM Production.Suppliers AS S
  INNER JOIN Production.Products AS P
    ON S.supplierid = P.supplierid
    AND S.country = N'Japan';
```

For many people, though, it's intuitive to specify the predicate that matches columns from both sides in the ON clause, and predicates that filter columns from only one side in the WHERE clause. Also think about the potential that in the future you will need to change an inner join to an outer join, where there's a difference between the roles that the ON and WHERE clauses play, as I describe in the next section. But again, with inner joins it doesn't matter. In the discussion of outer joins in the next section, you will see that, with those, ON and WHERE play different roles; you need to figure out, according to your needs, which is the appropriate clause for each of your predicates.

As another example for an inner join, the following query joins two instances of the HR.Employees table to match employees with their managers (a manager is also an employee, hence the self-join):

```
SELECT E.empid,
  E.firstname + N' ' + E.lastname AS emp,
  M.firstname + N' ' + M.lastname AS mgr
FROM HR.Employees AS E
  INNER JOIN HR.Employees AS M
    ON E.mgrid = M.empid;
```

This query generates the following output:

```
empid       emp                             mgr
----------- ------------------------------- -------------------------------
2           Don Funk                        Sara Davis
3           Judy Lew                        Don Funk
4           Yael Peled                      Judy Lew
5           Sven Mortensen                  Don Funk
6           Paul Suurs                      Sven Mortensen
7           Russell King                    Sven Mortensen
8           Maria Cameron                   Judy Lew
9           Patricia Doyle                  Sven Mortensen
```

Observe the join predicate: ON E.mgrid = M.empid. The employee instance is aliased as E and the manager instance as M. To find the right matches, the employee's manager ID needs to be equal to the manager's employee ID.

Note that only eight rows were returned even though there are nine rows in the table. The reason is that the CEO (Sara Davis, employee ID 1) has no manager, and therefore, her mgrid column is NULL. Remember that an inner join does not return rows that don't find matches.

As with cross joins, both standard SQL and T-SQL support an older syntax for inner joins where you specify a comma between the table names, and then all predicates in the WHERE clause. But as mentioned, it is considered best practice to stick to the newer syntax with the JOIN keyword. When using the older syntax, if you forget to indicate the join predicate, you end up with an unintentional cross join. When using the newer syntax, an inner join isn't valid syntactically without an ON clause, so if you forget to indicate the join predicate, the parser will generate an error.

Because an inner join is the most commonly used type of join, the standard decided to make it the default in case you specify just the JOIN keyword. So T1 JOIN T2 is equivalent to T1 INNER JOIN T2.

## Outer joins

With outer joins, you can request to preserve all rows from one or both sides of the join, never mind if there are matching rows in the other side based on the ON predicate.

By using the keywords LEFT OUTER JOIN (or LEFT JOIN for short), you ask to preserve the left table. The join returns what an inner join normally would—that is, matches (call those inner rows). In addition, the join also returns rows from the left table that have no matches in the right table (call those outer rows), with NULLs used as placeholders in the right side. Figure 1-8 shows an illustration of a left outer join.

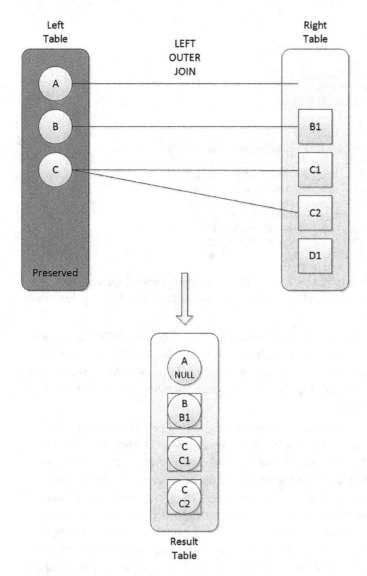

**FIGURE 1-8**  Left outer join

Unlike in the inner join, the left row with the key A is returned even though it has no match in the right side. It's returned with NULLs as placeholders in the right side.

As an example, the following query returns suppliers from Japan and the products they supply, including suppliers from Japan that don't have related products.

```
SELECT
  S.companyname AS supplier, S.country,
  P.productid, P.productname, P.unitprice
FROM Production.Suppliers AS S
  LEFT OUTER JOIN Production.Products AS P
    ON S.supplierid = P.supplierid
WHERE S.country = N'Japan';
```

This query generates the following output:

```
supplier        country  productid  productname      unitprice
--------------- -------- ---------- ---------------- ----------
Supplier QOVFD  Japan    9          Product AOZBW    97.00
Supplier QOVFD  Japan    10         Product YHXGE    31.00
Supplier QOVFD  Japan    74         Product BKAZJ    10.00
Supplier QWUSF  Japan    13         Product POXFU    6.00
Supplier QWUSF  Japan    14         Product PWCJB    23.25
Supplier QWUSF  Japan    15         Product KSZOI    15.50
Supplier XYZ    Japan    NULL       NULL             NULL
```

Because the Production.Suppliers table is the preserved side of the join, Supplier XYZ is returned even though it has no matching products. As you recall, an inner join did not return this supplier.

It is very important to understand that, with outer joins, the ON and WHERE clauses play very different roles, and therefore, they aren't interchangeable. The WHERE clause still plays a simple filtering role—namely, it keeps true cases and discards false and unknown cases. In our query, the WHERE clause filters only suppliers from Japan, so suppliers that aren't from Japan simply don't show up in the output.

However, the ON clause doesn't play a simple filtering role; rather, it's a more sophisticated matching role. In other words, a row in the preserved side will be returned whether the ON predicate finds a match for it or not. So the ON predicate only determines which rows from the nonpreserved side get matched to rows from the preserved side—not whether to return the rows from the preserved side. In our query, the ON clause matches rows from both sides by comparing their supplier ID values. Because it's a matching predicate (as opposed to a filter), the join won't discard suppliers; instead, it only determines which products get matched to each supplier. But even if a supplier has no matches based on the ON predicate, the supplier is still returned. In other words, ON is not final with respect to the preserved side of the join. WHERE is final. So when in doubt, whether to specify the predicate in the ON or WHERE clauses, ask yourself: Is the predicate used to filter or match? Is it supposed to be final or nonfinal?

With this in mind, guess what happens if you specify both the predicate that compares the supplier IDs from both sides, and the one comparing the supplier country to Japan in the ON clause? Try it.

```
SELECT
  S.companyname AS supplier, S.country,
  P.productid, P.productname, P.unitprice
FROM Production.Suppliers AS S
  LEFT OUTER JOIN Production.Products AS P
    ON S.supplierid = P.supplierid
  AND S.country = N'Japan';
```

Observe what's different in the result (shown here in abbreviated form) and see if you can explain in your own words what the query returns now:

```
supplier          country   productid  productname      unitprice
----------------  --------  ---------  ---------------  ----------
Supplier SWRXU    UK        NULL       NULL             NULL
Supplier VHQZD    USA       NULL       NULL             NULL
Supplier STUAZ    USA       NULL       NULL             NULL
Supplier QOVFD    Japan     9          Product AOZBW    97.00
Supplier QOVFD    Japan     10         Product YHXGE    31.00
Supplier QOVFD    Japan     74         Product BKAZJ    10.00
Supplier EQPNC    Spain     NULL       NULL             NULL
Supplier QWUSF    Japan     13         Product POXFU    6.00
Supplier QWUSF    Japan     14         Product PWCJB    23.25
Supplier QWUSF    Japan     15         Product KSZOI    15.50
...
```

```
(34 row(s) affected)
```

Now that both predicates appear in the ON clause, both serve a matching purpose. What this means is that all suppliers are returned—even those that aren't from Japan. But in order to match a product to a supplier, the supplier IDs in both sides need to match, and the supplier country needs to be Japan.

Just like you can use a left outer join to preserve the left side, you can use a right outer join to preserve the right side. Use the keywords RIGHT OUTER JOIN (or RIGHT JOIN in short). Figure 1-9 shows an illustration of a right outer join.

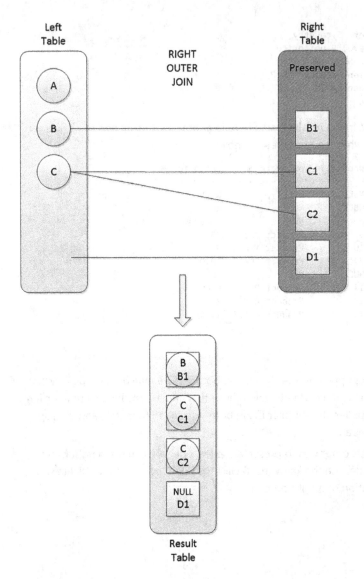

**FIGURE 1-9** Right outer join

T-SQL also supports a full outer join (FULL OUTER JOIN, or FULL JOIN in short) that pre-serves both sides. Figure 1-10 shows an illustration of this type of join.

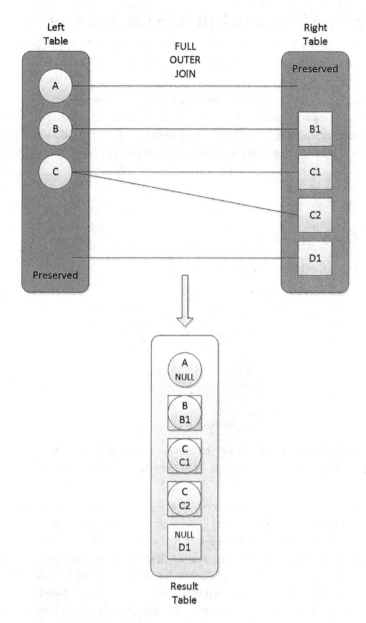

**FIGURE 1-10** Full outer join

A full outer join returns the matched rows, which are normally returned from an inner join; plus rows from the left that don't have matches in the right, with NULLs used as placeholders in the right side; plus rows from the right that don't have matches in the left, with NULLs used as placeholders in the left side. It's not common to need a full outer join because most relationships between tables allow only one of the sides to have rows that don't have matches in the other, in which case, a one-sided outer join is needed.

# Queries with composite joins and NULLs in join columns

Some joins can be a bit tricky to handle, for instance when the join columns can have NULLs, or when you have multiple join columns—what's known as a composite join. This section focuses on such cases.

Earlier in the inner joins section is a query that matched employees and their managers. Remember that the inner join eliminated the CEO's row because the mgrid is NULL in that row, and therefore the join found no matching manager. If you want to include the CEO's row, you need to use an outer join to preserve the side representing the employees (E) as follows:

```
SELECT E.empid,
  E.firstname + N' ' + E.lastname AS emp,
  M.firstname + N' ' + M.lastname AS mgr
FROM HR.Employees AS E
  LEFT OUTER JOIN HR.Employees AS M
    ON E.mgrid = M.empid;
```

Here's the output of this query, this time including the CEO's row:

| empid | emp | mgr |
| --- | --- | --- |
| 1 | Sara Davis | NULL |
| 2 | Don Funk | Sara Davis |
| 3 | Judy Lew | Don Funk |
| 4 | Yael Peled | Judy Lew |
| 5 | Sven Mortensen | Don Funk |
| 6 | Paul Suurs | Sven Mortensen |
| 7 | Russell King | Sven Mortensen |
| 8 | Maria Cameron | Judy Lew |
| 9 | Patricia Doyle | Sven Mortensen |

As a reminder, the order of the output is not guaranteed unless you add an ORDER BY clause to the query. This means that theoretically you can have the results returned in a different order than mine.

When you need to join tables that are related based on multiple columns, the join is called a *composite join* and the ON clause typically consists of a conjunction of predicates (predicates separated by AND operators) that match the corresponding columns from the two sides. Sometimes you need more complex predicates, especially when NULLs are involved. I'll demonstrate this by using a pair of tables. One table is called EmpLocations and it holds employee locations and the number of employees in each location. Another table is called CustLocations and it holds customer locations and the number of customers in each location. Run the following code to create these tables and populate them with sample data:

```
DROP TABLE IF EXISTS dbo.EmpLocations;

SELECT country, region, city, COUNT(*) AS numemps
INTO dbo.EmpLocations
FROM HR.Employees
GROUP BY country, region, city;

ALTER TABLE dbo.EmpLocations ADD CONSTRAINT UNQ_EmpLocations
  UNIQUE CLUSTERED(country, region, city);
```

```
DROP TABLE IF EXISTS dbo.CustLocations;

SELECT country, region, city, COUNT(*) AS numcusts
INTO dbo.CustLocations
FROM Sales.Customers
GROUP BY country, region, city;

ALTER TABLE dbo.CustLocations ADD CONSTRAINT UNQ_CustLocations
  UNIQUE CLUSTERED(country, region, city);
```

There's a key defined in both tables on the location attributes: country, region, and city. Instead of using a primary key constraint I used a unique constraint to enforce the key because the region attribute allows NULLs, and between the two types of constraints, only the latter allows NULLs. I also specified the CLUSTERED keyword in the unique constraint definitions to have SQL Server create a clustered index type to enforce the constraint's uniqueness property. This index will be beneficial in supporting joins between the tables based on the location attributes as well filters based on those attributes.

Query the EmpLocations table to see its contents:

```
SELECT country, region, city, numemps
FROM dbo.EmpLocations;
```

This query generates the following output:

```
country           region            city              numemps
---------------   ---------------   ---------------   -----------
UK                NULL              London            4
USA               WA                Kirkland          1
USA               WA                Redmond           1
USA               WA                Seattle           2
USA               WA                Tacoma            1
```

Query the CustLocations table:

```
SELECT country, region, city, numcusts
FROM dbo.CustLocations;
```

This query generates the following output, shown here in abbreviated form:

```
country           region            city              numcusts
---------------   ---------------   ---------------   -----------
Argentina         NULL              Buenos Aires      3
Austria           NULL              Graz              1
Austria           NULL              Salzburg          1
Belgium           NULL              Bruxelles         1
Belgium           NULL              Charleroi         1
Brazil            RJ                Rio de Janeiro    3
Brazil            SP                Campinas          1
Brazil            SP                Resende           1
Brazil            SP                Sao Paulo         4
Canada            BC                Tsawassen         1
...

(69 row(s) affected)
```

Suppose that you needed to join the two tables returning only matched locations, with both the employee and customer counts returned along with the location attributes. Your first attempt might be to write a composite join with an ON clause that has a conjunction of simple equality predicates as follows:

```
SELECT EL.country, EL.region, EL.city, EL.numemps, CL.numcusts
FROM dbo.EmpLocations AS EL
  INNER JOIN dbo.CustLocations AS CL
    ON EL.country = CL.country
    AND EL.region = CL.region
    AND EL.city = CL.city;
```

This query generates the following output:

```
country           region            city              numemps     numcusts
---------------   ---------------   ---------------   -----------  -----------
USA               WA                Kirkland          1            1
USA               WA                Seattle           2            1
```

The problem is that the region column supports NULLs representing cases where the region is irrelevant (missing but inapplicable) and when you compare NULLs with an equality-based predicate the result is the logical value unknown, in which case the row is discarded. For instance, the location UK, NULL, London appears in both tables, and therefore you expect to see it in the result of the join, but you don't. A common way for people to resolve this problem is to use the ISNULL or COALESCE functions to substitute a NULL in both sides with a value that can't normally appear in the data, and this way when both sides are NULL you get a true back from the comparison. Here's an example for implementing this solution using the ISNULL function:

```
SELECT EL.country, EL.region, EL.city, EL.numemps, CL.numcusts
FROM dbo.EmpLocations AS EL
  INNER JOIN dbo.CustLocations AS CL
    ON EL.country = CL.country
    AND ISNULL(EL.region, N'<N/A>') = ISNULL(CL.region, N'<N/A>')
    AND EL.city = CL.city;
```

This time the query generates the correct result:

```
country           region            city              numemps     numcusts
---------------   ---------------   ---------------   -----------  -----------
UK                NULL              London            4            6
USA               WA                Kirkland          1            1
USA               WA                Seattle           2            1
```

The problem with this approach is that once you apply manipulation to a column, SQL Server cannot trust that the result values preserve the same ordering behavior as the original values. This can negatively affect the ability of SQL Server to rely on index ordering when it optimizes the query. Our query gets the plan shown in Figure 1-11.

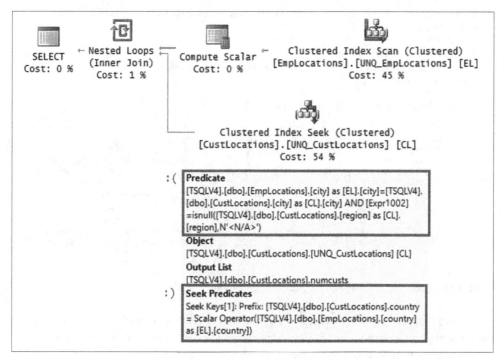

**FIGURE 1-11** Plan for query with ISNULL

The plan scans the clustered index on EmpLocations, and for each row (employee location) performs a seek in the clustered index on CustLocations. However, notice that the seek relies on only the country attribute in the seek predicate. It cannot rely on the region and city attributes because of the manipulation that you applied to the region attribute. The predicates involving the region and city attributes appear as residual predicates (under the Predicate property). This means that for each employee location row, the Clustered Index Seek operator that is applied to the CustLocations index performs a range scan of the entire customer location's country that is equal to the current employee location's country. The residual predicates that are based on region and city then determine whether to keep or discard each row. That's a lot of unnecessary effort.

The optimizer picked the nested loops strategy in the plan shown in Figure 1-11 because the sample tables that we used are so tiny. With bigger, more realistic, table sizes, the optimizer typically chooses a merge join algorithm when the data is preordered by the join columns in both sides. This algorithm processes both sides of the join based on join column order, and in a way, zips matching rows together. The data can either be pulled preordered from an index, or explicitly sorted. As mentioned, applying manipulation to join columns breaks the ordering property of the data, and therefore even if it's preordered in an index, the optimizer cannot trust this order. To illustrate how this can affect the merge algorithm, force it in our query by adding the MERGE join hint as follows.

```
SELECT EL.country, EL.region, EL.city, EL.numemps, CL.numcusts
FROM dbo.EmpLocations AS EL
  INNER MERGE JOIN dbo.CustLocations AS CL
    ON EL.country = CL.country
    AND ISNULL(EL.region, N'<N/A>') = ISNULL(CL.region, N'<N/A>')
    AND EL.city = CL.city;
```

The plan for this query is shown in Figure 1-12.

**FIGURE 1-12**  Plan for query with ISNULL and MERGE algorithm

Observe that the clustered indexes on both tables are scanned in an Orderd: False fashion, meaning that the scan is not requested to return the data in index order. Then the join columns sort both sides explicitly before being merged.

You can handle NULLs in a manner that gives you the desired logical meaning and that at the same time is considered order preserving by the optimizer using the predicate: (EL.region = CL.region OR (EL.region IS NULL AND CL.region IS NULL)). Here's the complete solution query:

```
SELECT EL.country, EL.region, EL.city, EL.numemps, CL.numcusts
FROM dbo.EmpLocations AS EL
  INNER JOIN dbo.CustLocations AS CL
    ON EL.country = CL.country
    AND (EL.region = CL.region OR (EL.region IS NULL AND CL.region IS NULL))
    AND EL.city = CL.city;
```

The plan for this query is shown in Figure 1-13.

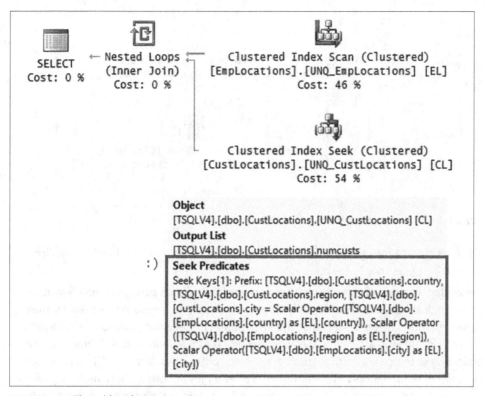

**FIGURE 1-13** Plan with order preservation

Notice that this time all predicates show up as seek predicates.

Similarly, with the new predicate, the optimizer can rely on index order when using the merge join algorithm. To demonstrate this, again, force this algorithm by adding the MERGE join hint as follows:

```
SELECT EL.country, EL.region, EL.city, EL.numemps, CL.numcusts
FROM dbo.EmpLocations AS EL
  INNER MERGE JOIN dbo.CustLocations AS CL
    ON EL.country = CL.country
    AND (EL.region = CL.region OR (EL.region IS NULL AND CL.region IS NULL))
    AND EL.city = CL.city;
```

The plan for this query is shown in Figure 1-14.

**FIGURE 1-14** Plan with order preservation and MERGE algorithm

Observe that the plan scans both clustered indexes in order, and that there's no explicit sorting taking place prior to the merge join.

Recall that when set operators combine query results they compare corresponding attributes using distinctness and not equality, producing true when comparing two NULLs. However, one drawback that set operators have is that they compare complete rows. Unlike joins, which allow comparing a subset of the attributes and return additional ones in the result, set operators must compare all attributes from the two input queries. But in T-SQL, you can combine joins and set operators to benefit from the advantages of both tools. Namely, rely on the distinctness-based comparison of set operators and the ability of joins to return additional attributes beyond what you compare. In our querying task, the solution looks like this:

```
SELECT EL.country, EL.region, EL.city, EL.numemps, CL.numcusts
FROM dbo.EmpLocations AS EL
  INNER JOIN dbo.CustLocations AS CL
    ON EXISTS (SELECT EL.country, EL.region, EL.city
               INTERSECT
               SELECT CL.country, CL.region, CL.city);
```

For each row that is evaluated by the join, the set operator performs an intersection of the employee location attributes and customer location attributes using FROM-less SELECT statements, each producing one row. If the locations intersect, the result is one row, in which case the EXISTS predicate returns true, and the evaluated row is considered a match. If the locations don't intersect, the result is an empty set, in which case the EXISTS predicate returns false, and the evaluated row is not considered a match. Remarkably, Microsoft added logic to the optimizer to consider this form order-preserving. The plan for this query is the same as the one shown earlier in Figure 1-13.

Use the following code to force the merge algorithm in the query:

```
SELECT EL.country, EL.region, EL.city, EL.numemps, CL.numcusts
FROM dbo.EmpLocations AS EL
  INNER MERGE JOIN dbo.CustLocations AS CL
    ON EXISTS (SELECT EL.country, EL.region, EL.city
```

```
                    INTERSECT
                    SELECT CL.country, CL.region, CL.city);
```

Also here the ordering property of the data is preserved and you get the plan shown earlier in Figure 1-14, where the clustered indexes of both sides are scanned in order and there's no need for explicit sorting prior to performing the merge join.

When you're done, run the following code for cleanup:

```
DROP TABLE IF EXISTS dbo.CustLocations;
DROP TABLE IF EXISTS dbo.EmpLocations;
```

# Multi-join queries

It's important to remember that a join in T-SQL takes place conceptually between two tables at a time. A multi-join query evaluates the joins conceptually from left to right. So the result of one join is used as the left input to the next join. If you don't understand this, you can end up with logical bugs, especially when outer joins are involved. (With inner and cross-joins, the order cannot affect the meaning.)

As an example, suppose that you wanted to return all suppliers from Japan, and matching products where relevant. For this, you need an outer join between Production.Suppliers and Production.Products, preserving Suppliers. But you also want to include product category information, so you add an inner join to Production.Categories, as follows:

```
SELECT
  S.companyname AS supplier, S.country,
  P.productid, P.productname, P.unitprice,
  C.categoryname
FROM Production.Suppliers AS S
  LEFT OUTER JOIN Production.Products AS P
    ON S.supplierid = P.supplierid
  INNER JOIN Production.Categories AS C
    ON C.categoryid = P.categoryid
WHERE S.country = N'Japan';
```

This query generates the following output:

```
supplier        country productid productname      unitprice categoryname
--------------- ------- --------- --------------- --------- -------------
Supplier QOVFD  Japan   9         Product AOZBW   97.00     Meat/Poultry
Supplier QOVFD  Japan   10        Product YHXGE   31.00     Seafood
Supplier QWUSF  Japan   13        Product POXFU   6.00      Seafood
Supplier QWUSF  Japan   14        Product PWCJB   23.25     Produce
Supplier QWUSF  Japan   15        Product KSZOI   15.50     Condiments
Supplier QOVFD  Japan   74        Product BKAZJ   10.00     Produce
```

Supplier XYZ from Japan was discarded. Can you explain why?

Conceptually, the first join included outer rows (suppliers with no products) but produced NULLs as placeholders in the product attributes in those rows. Then the join to Production.Categories compared the NULLs in the categoryid column in the outer rows to categoryid values in Production.Categories, and discarded those rows. In short, the inner join that followed the outer join nullified the outer part of the join. In fact, if you look at the query plan for this query, you will find that the optimizer didn't even bother to process the join between Production.Suppliers and Production.Products as an outer join. It detected the contradiction between the outer join and the subsequent inner join, and converted the first join to an inner join too.

There are a number of ways to address this problem. One is to use a LEFT OUTER in both joins, like so:

```
SELECT
  S.companyname AS supplier, S.country,
  P.productid, P.productname, P.unitprice,
  C.categoryname
FROM Production.Suppliers AS S
  LEFT OUTER JOIN Production.Products AS P
    ON S.supplierid = P.supplierid
  LEFT OUTER JOIN Production.Categories AS C
    ON C.categoryid = P.categoryid
WHERE S.country = N'Japan';
```

Another option is to use an interesting capability in the language—separate some of the joins to their own independent logical phase. What you're after is a left outer join between Production.Suppliers and the result of the inner join between Production.Products and Production.Categories. You can phrase your query exactly like this:

```
SELECT
  S.companyname AS supplier, S.country,
  P.productid, P.productname, P.unitprice,
  C.categoryname
FROM Production.Suppliers AS S
  LEFT OUTER JOIN
    (Production.Products AS P
      INNER JOIN Production.Categories AS C
        ON C.categoryid = P.categoryid)
    ON S.supplierid = P.supplierid
WHERE S.country = N'Japan';
```

With both fixes, the query generates the correct result, including suppliers who currently don't have related products:

| supplier | country | productid | productname | unitprice | categoryname |
| --- | --- | --- | --- | --- | --- |
| Supplier QOVFD | Japan | 9 | Product AOZBW | 97.00 | Meat/Poultry |
| Supplier QOVFD | Japan | 10 | Product YHXGE | 31.00 | Seafood |
| Supplier QOVFD | Japan | 74 | Product BKAZJ | 10.00 | Produce |
| Supplier QWUSF | Japan | 13 | Product POXFU | 6.00 | Seafood |
| Supplier QWUSF | Japan | 14 | Product PWCJB | 23.25 | Produce |
| Supplier QWUSF | Japan | 15 | Product KSZOI | 15.50 | Condiments |
| Supplier XYZ | Japan | NULL | NULL | NULL | NULL |

Note that the important change that made the difference is the arrangement of the ON clauses with respect to the joined tables. The ON clause ordering is what defines the logical join ordering. Each ON clause must appear right below the two units that it joins. By specifying the ON clause that matches attributes from Production.Products and Production. Categories first, you set this inner join to be logically evaluated first. Then the second ON clause handles the left outer join by matching an attribute from Production.Suppliers with an attribute from the result of the inner join. Curiously, T-SQL doesn't really require the parentheses that I added to the query; remove those and rerun the query, and you will see that it runs successfully. However, it's recommended to use those for clarity.

---

**EXAM TIP**

Multi join queries that mix different join types are very common in practice and therefore there's a high likelihood that questions about those will show up in the exam. Make sure that you understand the pitfalls in mixing join types, especially when an outer join is subsequently followed by an inner join, which discards the outer rows that were produced by the outer join.

---

When you're done, run the following code to delete the supplier row that you added at the beginning of this skill:

```
DELETE FROM Production.Suppliers WHERE supplierid > 29;
```

# Skill 1.3: Implement functions and aggregate data

T-SQL supports many built-in functions that you can use to manipulate data. Scalar-valued functions return a single value and table-valued functions return a table result. Use of built-in functions can improve developer productivity, but you also need to understand cases where their use in certain context can end up negatively affecting query performance. It's also important to understand the concept of function determinism and its effects on your queries.

Note that this skill is not meant to be an exhaustive coverage of all functions that T-SQL supports—this would require a whole book in its own right. Instead, this chapter explains key aspects of working with functions, usually in the context of certain types of data, like date and time data, or character data. For more details about built-in functions, see the topic "Built-in Functions (Transact-SQL)" at *http://msdn.microsoft.com/en-us/library/ms174318(v=SQL.110).aspx.*

---

**This section covers how to:**

- Construct queries using scalar-valued and table-valued functions
- Identify the impact of function usage to query performance and WHERE clause sargability
- Identify the differences between deterministic and non-deterministic functions
- Use built-in aggregate functions
- Use arithmetic functions, date-related functions, and system functions

# Type conversion functions

T-SQL supports a number of functions that can convert a source expression to a target data type. In my examples I use constants as the source values to demonstrate the use of the functions, but typically you apply such functions to columns or expressions based on columns as part of a query.

The two fundamental functions that T-SQL supports for conversion purposes are CAST and CONVERT. The former is standard whereas the latter is proprietary in T-SQL. The CAST function's syntax is CAST(source_expression AS target_type. For example, CAST('100' AS INT) converts the source character string constant to the target integer value 100. The CONVERT function is handy when you need to specify a style for the conversion. Its syntax is CONVERT(target_type, source_expression [, style_number]). You can find the supported style numbers and their meaning at *https://msdn.microsoft.com/en-us/library/ms187928.aspx*. For instance, when converting a character string to a date and time type or the other way around, you can specify the style number to avoid ambiguity in case the form you use is considered language dependent. As an example, the expression CONVERT(DATE, '01/02/2017', 101) converts the input string to a date using the U.S. style, meaning January 2, 2017. The expression CONVERT(DATE, '01/02/2017', 103) uses the British/French style, meaning February 1, 2017.

The PARSE function is an alternative to CONVERT when you want to parse a character string input to a target type, but instead of using cryptic style numbers, it uses a more user-friendly .NET culture name. For instance, the expression PARSE('01/02/2017' AS DATE USING 'en-US') uses the English US culture, parsing the input as a date meaning January 2, 2017. The expression PARSE('01/02/2017' AS DATE USING 'en-GB') uses the English Great Britain culture, parsing the input as a date meaning February 1, 2017. Note though that this function is significantly slower than CONVERT, so I personally stay away from using it.

One of the problems with CAST, CONVERT, and PARSE is that if the function fails to convert a value within a query, the whole query fails and stops processing. As an alternative to these functions, T-SQL supports the TRY_CAST, TRY_CONVERT, and TRY_PARSE functions, which behave the same as their counterparts when the conversion is valid, but return a NULL instead of failing when the conversion isn't valid. As an example, run the following code to try and convert two strings to dates using the CONVERT function:

```
SELECT CONVERT(DATE, '14/02/2017', 101) AS col1,
   CONVERT(DATE, '02/14/2017', 101) AS col2;
```

The first value doesn't convert successfully and therefore this code fails with the following error:

```
Msg 241, Level 16, State 1, Line 26
Conversion failed when converting date and/or time from character string.
```

Use the TRY_CONVERT function instead of CONVERT, like so:

```
SELECT TRY_CONVERT(DATE, '14/02/2017', 101) AS col1,
   TRY_CONVERT(DATE, '02/14/2017', 101) AS col2;
```

This time the code doesn't fail, but the first expression returns a NULL, as the following output shows:

```
col1        col2
----------  ----------
NULL        2017-02-14
```

Lastly, the FORMAT function is an alternative to the CONVERT function when you want to format an input expression of some type as a character string, but instead of using cryptic style numbers, you specify a .NET format string and culture, if relevant. For instance, to format an input date and time value, such as now, as a character string using the form 'yyyy-MM-dd', use the expression: FORMAT(SYSDATETIME(), 'yyyy-MM-dd'). You can use any format string supported by the .NET Framework. (For details, see the topics "FORMAT (Transact-SQL)" and "Formatting Types in the .NET Framework" at *https://msdn.microsoft.com/en-us/library/hh213505.aspx* and *http://msdn.microsoft.com/en-us/library/26etazsy.aspx*.). Note that like PARSE, the FORMAT function is also quite slow, so when you need to format a large number of values in a query, you typically get much better performance with alternative built-in functions.

# Date and time functions

T-SQL supports a number of date and time functions that allow you to manipulate your date and time data. This section covers some of the important functions supported by T-SQL and provides some examples. For the full list, as well as the technical details and syntax, see the T-SQL documentation for the topic at *https://msdn.microsoft.com/en-us/library/ms186724.aspx*.

## Current date and time

One important category of functions is the category that returns the current date and time.

The functions in this category are GETDATE, CURRENT_TIMESTAMP, GETUTCDATE, SYSDATE-TIME, SYSUTCDATETIME, and SYSDATETIMEOFFSET. GETDATE is T-SQL–specific, returning the current date and time in the SQL Server instance you're connected to as a DATETIME data type. CURRENT_TIMESTAMP is the same, only it's standard, and hence the recommended one to use. SYSDATETIME and SYSDATETIMEOFFSET are similar, only returning the values as the more precise DATETIME2 and DATETIMEOFFSET types (including the time zone offset from UTC), respectively. Note that there are no built-in functions to return the current date and the current time. To get such information, simply cast the SYSDATETIME function to DATE or TIME, respectively. For example, to get the current date, use CAST(SYSDATETIME() AS DATE). The GETUTCDATE function returns the current date and time in UTC terms as a DATETIME type, and SYSUTCDATETIME does the same, only returning the result as the more precise DATETIME2 type.

## Date and time parts

This section covers date and time functions that either extract a part from a date and time value (like DATEPART) or construct a date and time value from parts (like DATEFROMPARTS).

Using the DATEPART function, you can extract from an input date and time value a desired part, such as a year, minute, or nanosecond, and return the extracted part as an integer. For example, the expression DATEPART(month, '20170212') returns 2. T-SQL provides the functions YEAR, MONTH, and DAY as abbreviations to DATEPART, not requiring you to specify the part. The DATENAME function is similar to DATEPART, only it returns the name of the part as a character string, as opposed to the integer value. Note that the function is language dependent. That is, if the effective language in your session is us_english, the expression DATENAME(month, '20170212') returns 'February', but for Italian, it returns 'febbraio.'

T-SQL provides a set of functions that construct a desired date and time value from its numeric parts. You have such a function for each of the six available date and time types: DATE-FROMPARTS, DATETIME2FROMPARTS, DATETIMEFROMPARTS, DATETIMEOFFSETFROMPARTS, SMALLDATETIMEFROMPARTS, and TIMEFROMPARTS. For example, to build a DATE value from its parts, you would use an expression such as DATEFROMPARTS(2017, 02, 12).

Finally, the EOMONTH function computes the respective end of month date for the input date and time value. For example, suppose that today was February 12, 2017. The expression EOMONTH(SYSDATETIME()) would then return the date '2017-02-29'. This function supports a second optional input indicating how many months to add to the result (or subtract if negative).

## Add and diff functions

T-SQL supports addition and difference date and time functions called DATEADD and DATE-DIFF.

DATEADD is a very commonly used function. With it, you can add a requested number of units of a specified part to a specified date and time value. For example, the expression DATEADD(year, 1, '20170212') adds one year to the input date February 12, 2017.

DATEDIFF is another commonly used function; it returns the difference in terms of a requested part between two date and time values. For example, the expression DATEDIFF(day, '20160212', '20170212') computes the difference in days between February 12, 2016 and February 12, 2017, returning the value 366. Note that this function looks only at the parts from the requested one and above in the date and time hierarchy—not below. For example, the expression DATEDIFF(year, '20161231', '20170101') looks only at the year part, and hence returns 1. It doesn't look at the month and day parts of the values.

The DATEDIFF function returns a value of an INT type. If the difference doesn't fit in a four-byte integer, use the DATEDIFF_BIG function instead. This function returns the result as a BIGINT type.

# Offset

T-SQL supports three functions related to date and time values with an offset: SWITCHOFF-SET, TODATETIMEOFFSET, and AT TIME ZONE.

The SWITCHOFFSET function returns an input DATETIMEOFFSET value adjusted to a requested target offset (from the UTC time zone). For example, consider the expression SWITC HOFFSET(SYSDATETIMEOFFSET(), '-08:00'). Regardless of the offset of the SQL Server instance you are connected to, you request to present the current date and time value in terms of offset '-08:00'. If the system's offset is, say, '-05:00', the function will compensate for this by subtracting three hours from the input value.

The TODATETIMEOFFSET function is used for a different purpose. You use it to construct a DATETIMEOFFSET value from two inputs: the first is a date and time value that is not offset-aware, and the second is the offset. You can use this function to convert a value that is not offset aware to a target offset typed value without the need to manually convert the value and the offset to character strings with the right style and then to DATETIMEOFFSET. You can also use this function when migrating from data that is not offset-aware, where you keep the local date and time value in one attribute, and the offset in another, to offset-aware data. Say you have the local date and time in an attribute called mydatetime, and the offset in an attribute called theoffset. You add an attribute called mydatetimeoffset of a DATETIMEOFFSET type to the table. You then update the new attribute to the expression TODATETIMEOFFSET(mydatetime, theoffset), and then drop the original attributes mydate-time and theoffset from the table.

The following code demonstrates using both functions:

```
SELECT
  SWITCHOFFSET('20170212 14:00:00.0000000 -05:00', '-08:00') AS [SWITCHOFFSET],
  TODATETIMEOFFSET('20170212 14:00:00.0000000', '-08:00') AS [TODATETIMEOFFSET];
```

This code generates the following output:

```
SWITCHOFFSET                      TODATETIMEOFFSET
--------------------------------- ---------------------------------
2017-02-12 11:00:00.0000000 -08:00 2017-02-12 14:00:00.0000000 -08:00
```

What's tricky about both functions is that many time zones support a daylight savings concept where twice a year you move the clock by an hour. So when you capture the date and time value, you need to make sure that you also capture the right offset depending on whether it's currently daylight savings or not. For instance, in the time zone Pacific Standard Time the offset from UTC is '-07:00' when it's daylight savings time and '-08:00' when it isn't.

T-SQL supports a function called AT TIME ZONE that can be used instead of both the SWITCHOFFSET and the TODATETIMEOFFSET functions, and that uses named time zones instead of offsets. This way you don't need to worry about capturing the right offset and whether it's daylight savings time or not, you just capture the time zone name. When the input value is of a DATETIMEOFFSET type, the function assumes that you want to treat the conversion similar to SWITCHOFFSET. For instance, never mind what's the current time zone setting in the current instance, suppose that you want to return now as a DATETIMEOFFSET value in the time zone Pacific Standard Time. You use the expression: SYSDATETIMEOFFSET() AT TIME ZONE 'Pacific Standard Time'. If when you're running this code it's currently daylight savings, the function will switch the input value to offset '-07:00', otherwise to '-08:00'.

When the input value is not an offset-aware value, the AT TIME ZONE function assumes that you want to treat the conversion similar to TODATETIMEOFFSET and that the source value is already of the target time zone. Again, you don't need to worry about daylight savings considerations. Based on the point in the year, the function will know whether to apply daylight savings time. Here's an example demonstrating the use of the function with an input that is not offset-aware:

```
DECLARE @dt AS DATETIME2 = '20170212 14:00:00.0000000';
SELECT @dt AT TIME ZONE 'Pacific Standard Time';
```

This code generates the following output:

```
----------------------------------
2017-02-12 14:00:00.0000000 -08:00
```

The get the set of supported time zones query the view sys.time_zone_info.

When you store date and time values as a type that is not offset aware and you can present them as DATETIMEOFFSET values of a different target time zone, you need to apply the AT TIME ZONE function twice—once to convert the value to DATETIMEOFFSET with the source time zone and another to switch the now DATETIMEOFFSET value from its current time zone to the target one. For instance, suppose that you have a column called lastmodified that is typed as DATETIME2 and holds the value in UTC terms. You want to present it in the time zone Pacific Standard Time. You use the following expression: lastmodified AT TIME ZONE 'UTC' AT TIME ZONE 'Pacific Standard Time.'

# Character functions

T-SQL was not really designed to support very sophisticated character string manipulation functions, so you won't find a very large set of such functions. This section describes the character string functions that T-SQL does support, arranged in categories.

## Concatenation

Character string concatenation is a very common need. T-SQL supports two ways to concatenate strings—one with the plus (+) operator, and another with the CONCAT function.

Here's an example for concatenating strings in a query by using the + operator:

```
SELECT empid, country, region, city,
  country + N', ' + region + N', ' + city AS location
FROM HR.Employees;
```

This query generates the following output:

| empid | country | region | city | location |
|-------|---------|--------|---------|------------------|
| 1 | USA | WA | Seattle | USA, WA, Seattle |
| 2 | USA | WA | Tacoma | USA, WA, Tacoma |
| 3 | USA | WA | Kirkland | USA, WA, Kirkland |
| 4 | USA | WA | Redmond | USA, WA, Redmond |
| 5 | UK | NULL | London | NULL |
| 6 | UK | NULL | London | NULL |
| 7 | UK | NULL | London | NULL |
| 8 | USA | WA | Seattle | USA, WA, Seattle |
| 9 | UK | NULL | London | NULL |

Observe that when any of the inputs is NULL, the + operator returns a NULL. That's standard behavior that can be changed by turning off a session option called CONCAT_NULL_YIELDS_NULL, though it's not recommended to rely on such nonstandard behavior. If you want to substitute a NULL with an empty string, there are a number of ways for you to do this programmatically. One option is to use ISNULL or COALESCE functions to replace a NULL with an empty string. For example, in this data, only region can be NULL, so you can use the following query to replace a comma plus region with an empty string when region is NULL:

```
SELECT empid, country, region, city,
  country + ISNULL(N', ' + region, N'') + N', ' + city AS location
FROM HR.Employees;
```

Another option is to use the CONCAT function which, unlike the + operator, substitutes a NULL input with an empty string. Here's how the query looks:

```
SELECT empid, country, region, city,
  CONCAT(country, N', ' + region, N', ' + city) AS location
FROM HR.Employees;
```

Here's the output of this query:

| empid | country | region | city | location |
|-------|---------|--------|---------|------------------|
| 1 | USA | WA | Seattle | USA, WA, Seattle |
| 2 | USA | WA | Tacoma | USA, WA, Tacoma |
| 3 | USA | WA | Kirkland | USA, WA, Kirkland |
| 4 | USA | WA | Redmond | USA, WA, Redmond |
| 5 | UK | NULL | London | UK, London |
| 6 | UK | NULL | London | UK, London |
| 7 | UK | NULL | London | UK, London |
| 8 | USA | WA | Seattle | USA, WA, Seattle |
| 9 | UK | NULL | London | UK, London |

Observe that this time, when region was NULL, it was replaced with an empty string.

## Substring extraction and position

This section covers functions that you can use to extract a substring from a string, and identify the position of a substring within a string.

With the SUBSTRING function, you can extract a substring from a string given as the first argument, starting with the position given as the second argument, and a length given as the third argument. For example, the expression SUBSTRING('abcde', 1, 3) returns 'abc'. If the third argument is greater than what would get you to the end of the string, the function doesn't fail; instead, it just extracts the substring until the end of the string.

The LEFT and RIGHT functions extract a requested number of characters from the left and right ends of the input string, respectively. For example, LEFT('abcde', 3) returns 'abc' and RIGHT('abcde', 3) returns 'cde'.

The CHARINDEX function returns the position of the first occurrence of the string provided as the first argument within the string provided as the second argument. For example, the expression CHARINDEX(' ','Inigo Montoya') looks for the first occurrence of a space in the second input, returning 6 in this example. Note that you can provide a third argument indicating to the function the position where to start looking.

You can combine, or nest, functions in the same expression. For example, suppose you query a table with an attribute called fullname formatted as '<first> <last>', and you need to write an expression that extracts the first name part. You can use the following expression:

```
LEFT(fullname, CHARINDEX(' ', fullname) - 1)
```

T-SQL also supports a function called PATINDEX that, like CHARINDEX, you can use to locate the first position of a string within another string. But whereas with CHARINDEX you're looking for a constant string, with PATINDEX you're looking for a pattern. The pattern is formed very similar to the LIKE patterns that you're probably familiar with, where you use wildcards like % for any string, _ for a single character, and square brackets ([]) representing a single character from a certain list or range. If you're not familiar with such pattern construction, see the topics "PATINDEX (Transact-SQL)" and "LIKE (Transact-SQL)" in the T-SQL documentation at *https://msdn.microsoft.com/en-us/library/ms188395.aspx* and *https://msdn.microsoft.com/en-us/library/ms179859.aspx*. As an example, the expression PATINDEX('%[0-9]%', 'abcd123efgh') looks for the first occurrence of a digit (a character in the range 0–9) in the second input, returning the position 5 in this case.

## String length

T-SQL provides two functions that you can use to measure the length of an input value—LEN and DATALENGTH.

The LEN function returns the length of an input string in terms of the number of characters. Note that it returns the number of characters, not bytes, whether the input is a regular character or Unicode character string. For example, the expression LEN(N'xyz') returns 3. If there are any trailing spaces, LEN removes them.

The DATALENGTH function returns the length of the input in terms of number of bytes. This means, for example, that if the input is a Unicode character string, it will count 2 bytes per character. For example, the expression DATALENGTH(N'xyz') returns 6. Note also that, unlike LEN, the DATALENGTH function doesn't remove trailing spaces.

## String alteration

T-SQL supports a number of functions that you can use to apply alterations to an input string. Those are REPLACE, REPLICATE, and STUFF.

With the REPLACE function, you can replace in an input string provided as the first argument all occurrences of the string provided as the second argument, with the string provided as the third argument. For example, the expression REPLACE('.1.2.3.', '.', '/') substitutes all occurrences of a dot (.) with a slash (/), returning the string '/1/2/3/'.

The REPLICATE function allows you to replicate an input string a requested number of times. For example, the expression REPLICATE('0', 10) replicates the string '0' ten times, returning '0000000000'.

The STUFF function operates on an input string provided as the first argument; then, from the character position indicated as the second argument, deletes the number of characters indicated by the third argument. Then it inserts in that position the string specified as the fourth argument. For example, the expression STUFF(',x,y,z', 1, 1, '') removes the first character from the input string, returning 'x,y,z'.

## Formatting

This section covers functions that you can use to apply formatting options to an input string. Those are the UPPER, LOWER, LTRIM, RTRIM, and FORMAT functions.

The first four functions are self-explanatory (uppercase form of the input, lowercase form of the input, input after removal of leading spaces, and input after removal of trailing spaces). Note that there's no TRIM function that removes both leading and trailing spaces; to achieve this, you need to nest one function call within another, as in RTRIM(LTRIM(<input>)).

As mentioned earlier, with the FORMAT function, you can format an input value based on a .NET format string. I demonstrated an example with date and time values. As another example, this time with numeric values, the expression FORMAT(1759, '0000000000') formats the input number as a character string with a fixed size of 10 characters with leading zeros, returning '0000001759'. The same thing can be achieved with the format string 'd10', meaning decimal value with 10 digits, with the expression FORMAT(1759, 'd10').

## String splitting

T-SQL supports a table-valued function called STRING_SPLIT that accepts a charter string with a separated list of values provided as the first input, and a character string with the separator as the second input, and returns a result set with a column called value holding the individual split strings. The function supports all character string types for both inputs—regular and

Unicode. The type of the result value column, which is actually named *value*, is NVARCHAR if the first input is of a Unicode character string type, and VARCHAR otherwise.

As an example, the following code splits an input string that holds a separated list of order IDs:

```
DECLARE @orderids AS VARCHAR(MAX) = N'10248,10542,10731,10765,10812';

SELECT value
FROM STRING_SPLIT(@orderids, ',');
```

This code generates the following output:

```
Value
------
10248
10542
10731
10765
10812
```

Suppose that @orderids is a parameter provided to a stored procedure or a function, and that routine is supposed to split those IDs, and join the result with the Sales.Orders table to return information about the input orders. You achieve this with the following query, using a local variable here for simplicity:

```
DECLARE @orderids AS VARCHAR(MAX) = N'10248,10542,10731,10765,10812';

SELECT O.orderid, O.orderdate, O.custid, O.empid
FROM STRING_SPLIT(@orderids, ',') AS K
  INNER JOIN Sales.Orders AS O
    ON O.orderid = CAST(K.value AS INT);
```

This query generates the following output:

```
orderid     orderdate  custid      empid
----------- ---------- ----------- -----------
10248       2014-07-04 85          5
10542       2015-05-20 39          1
10812       2016-01-02 66          5
10765       2015-12-04 63          3
10731       2015-11-06 14          7
```

## CASE expressions and related functions

T-SQL supports an expression called CASE and a number of related functions that you can use to apply conditional logic to determine the returned value. Many people incorrectly refer to CASE as a statement. A statement performs some kind of an action or controls the flow of the code, and that's not what CASE does; CASE returns a value, and hence is an expression.

The CASE expression has two forms—the simple form and the searched form. Here's an example of the simple CASE form issued against the sample database TSQLV4.

```
SELECT productid, productname, unitprice, discontinued,
  CASE discontinued
    WHEN 0 THEN 'No'
    WHEN 1 THEN 'Yes'
    ELSE 'Unknown'
  END AS discontinued_desc
FROM Production.Products;
```

The simple form compares an input expression (in this case the attribute discontinued) to multiple possible scalar when expressions (in this case, 0 and 1), and returns the result expression (in this case, 'No' and 'Yes', respectively) associated with the first match. If there's no match and an ELSE clause is specified, the else expression (in this case, 'Unknown') is returned. If there's no ELSE clause, the default is ELSE NULL. Here's an abbreviated form of the output of this query:

```
productid    productname      unitprice              discontinued discontinued_desc
-----------  --------------   --------------------   ------------ -----------------
1            Product HHYDP    18.00                  0            No
2            Product RECZE    19.00                  0            No
3            Product IMEHJ    10.00                  0            No
4            Product KSBRM    22.00                  0            No
5            Product EPEIM    21.35                  1            Yes
6            Product VAIIV    25.00                  0            No
...
```

The searched form of the CASE expression is more flexible. Instead of comparing an input expression to multiple possible expressions, it uses predicates in the WHEN clauses, and the first predicate that evaluates to true determines which when expression is returned. If none is true, the CASE expression returns the else expression. Here's an example:

```
SELECT productid, productname, unitprice,
  CASE
    WHEN unitprice < 20.00 THEN 'Low'
    WHEN unitprice < 40.00 THEN 'Medium'
    WHEN unitprice >= 40.00 THEN 'High'
    ELSE 'Unknown'
  END AS pricerange
FROM Production.Products;
```

In this example, the CASE expression returns a description of the product's unit price range. When the unit price is below $20.00, it returns 'Low', when it's $20.00 or more and below $40.00, it returns 'Medium', and when it's $40.00 or more, it returns 'High'. There's an ELSE clause for safety; if the input is NULL, the else expression returned is 'Unknown'. Notice that the second when predicate didn't need to check whether the value is $20.00 or more explicitly. That's because the when predicates are evaluated in order and the first when predicate did not evaluate to true. Here's an abbreviated form of the output of this query.

```
productid    productname    unitprice              pricerange
-----------  -------------  ---------------------  ----------
1            Product HHYDP  18.00                  Low
2            Product RECZE  19.00                  Low
3            Product IMEHJ  10.00                  Low
4            Product KSBRM  22.00                  Medium
5            Product EPEIM  21.35                  Medium
...
```

T-SQL supports a number of functions that can be considered as abbreviates of the CASE expression. Those are the standard COALESCE and NULLIF functions, and the nonstandard ISNULL, IIF, and CHOOSE.

The COALESCE function accepts a list of expressions as input and returns the first that is not NULL, or NULL if all are NULLs. If all inputs are the untyped NULL constant, as in COALESCE(NULL, NULL, NULL), SQL Server generates an error. For example, the expression COALESCE(NULL, 'x', 'y') returns 'x'. More generally, the expression:

```
COALESCE(<exp1>, <exp2>, ..., <expn>)
```

is similar to the following:

```
CASE
  WHEN <exp1> IS NOT NULL THEN <exp1>
  WHEN <exp2> IS NOT NULL THEN <exp2>
  ...
  WHEN <expn> IS NOT NULL THEN <expn>
  ELSE NULL
END
```

A typical use of COALESCE is to substitute a NULL with something else. For example, the expression COALESCE(region, '') returns region if it's not NULL and returns an empty string if it is NULL.

T-SQL supports a nonstandard function called ISNULL that is similar to the standard COALESCE, but it's a bit more limited in the sense that it supports only two inputs. Like COALESCE, it returns the first input that is not NULL. So, instead of COALESCE(region, ''), you could use ISNULL(region, ''). If there's a requirement to use standard code in the application when possible, you should prefer COALESCE in such a case.

There are a few interesting differences between COALESCE and ISNULL that you should be aware of when working with these functions. One is which input determines the type of the output. Consider the following code:

```
DECLARE
  @x AS VARCHAR(3) = NULL,
  @y AS VARCHAR(10) = '1234567890';

SELECT COALESCE(@x, @y) AS [COALESCE], ISNULL(@x, @y) AS [ISNULL];
```

Here's the output of this code:

```
COALESCE    ISNULL
----------  ------
1234567890  123
```

Observe that the type of the COALESCE expression is determined by the returned element, whereas the type of the ISNULL expression is determined by the first input.

The other difference is when you use the SELECT INTO statement, which writes a query result into a target table, including creating the table. Suppose the SELECT list of a SELECT INTO statement contains the expressions COALESCE(col1, 0) AS newcol1 versus ISNULL(col1, 0) AS newcol1. If the source attribute col1 is defined as NOT NULL, both expressions will produce an attribute in the result table defined as NOT NULL. However, if the source attribute col1 is defined as allowing NULLs, COALESCE will create a result attribute allowing NULLs, whereas ISNULL will create one that disallows NULLs.

T-SQL also supports the standard NULLIF function. This function accepts two input expressions, returns NULL if they are equal, and returns the first input if they are not. For example, consider the expression NULLIF(col1, col2). If col1 is equal to col2, the function returns a NULL; otherwise, it returns the col1 value.

As for IIF and CHOOSE, these are nonstandard T-SQL functions that were added to simplify migrations from Microsoft Access platforms. Because these functions aren't standard and there are simple standard alternatives with CASE expressions, it is not usually recommended that you use them. However, when you are migrating from Access to SQL Server, these functions can help with smoother migration, and then gradually you can refactor your code to use the available standard functions. With the IIF function, you can return one value if an input predicate is true and another value otherwise. The function has the following form:

```
IIF(<predicate>, <true_result>, <false_or_unknown_result>)
```

This expression is equivalent to the following:

```
CASE WHEN <predicate> THEN <true_result> ELSE <false_or_unknown_result> END
```

For example, the expression IIF(orderyear = 2017, qty, 0) returns the value in the qty attribute when the orderyear attribute is equal to 2017, and zero otherwise.

The CHOOSE function allows you to provide a position and a list of expressions, and returns the expression in the indicated position. The function takes the following form:

```
CHOOSE(<pos>, <exp1>, <exp2>, …, <expn>)
```

For example, the expression CHOOSE(2, 'x', 'y', 'z') returns 'y'. Again, it's straightforward to replace a CHOOSE expression with a logically equivalent CASE expression; but the point in supporting CHOOSE, as well as IIF, is to simplify migrations from Access to SQL Server as a temporary solution.

# System functions

System functions return information about various aspects of the system. Here I highlight a few of the functions. You can find the full list in the Transact-SQL documentation at *https://msdn.microsoft.com/en-us/library/ms187786.aspx.*

## The @@ROWCOUNT and ROWCOUNT_BIG functions

The @@ROWCOUNT function is a very popular function that returns the number of rows affected by the last statement that you executed. It's very common to use it to check if the previous statement affected any rows by checking that the function's result is zero or greater than zero. For example, the following code queries the input employee row, and prints a message if the requested employee was not found:

```
DECLARE @empid AS INT = 10;

SELECT empid, firstname, lastname
FROM HR.Employees
WHERE empid = @empid;

IF @@ROWCOUNT = 0
  PRINT CONCAT('Employee ', CAST(@empid AS VARCHAR(10)), ' was not found.');
```

This code generates the following output:

```
empid       firstname  lastname
----------- ---------- --------------------

(0 row(s) affected)

Employee 10 was not found.
```

The @@ROWCOUNT function returns an INT typed value. If the row count can exceed the maximum INT value (2,147,483,647), use the ROWCOUNT_BIG function, which returns a BIGINT typed value.

## Compression functions

T-SQL supports a function called COMPRESS that enables you to compress an input character or binary string using the GZIP algorithm into a result binary string. It also supports a function called DECOMPRESS that allows you to decompress a previously compressed string.

Note that you need to explicitly invoke the COMPRESS function to compress the input string before you store the result compressed binary string in a table. For example, supposed that you have a stored procedure parameter called @notes of the type NVARCHAR(MAX) that you need to compress and store the result in a table, in a column called notes. As part of your INSERT statement against the target table, the VALUES clause includes the expression COM-PRESS(@notes) as the target value for the target column. Your code might look like this:

```
INSERT INTO dbo.MyNotes(notes)
  VALUES(COMPRESS(@notes));
```

When you later query the table, you use the expression DECOMPRESS(notes) to decompress the column value. However, because the result is a binary string, you need to convert it to the target type using the expression CAST(DECOMPRESS(notes) AS NVARCHAR(MAX)). Your code might look like this.

```
SELECT keycol,
  CAST(DECOMPRESS(notes) AS NVARCHAR(MAX)) AS notes
FROM dbo.MyNotes;
```

## Context info and session context

When you need to pass information from one level in the call stack to another, you usually use parameters. For instance, if you want to pass something to a procedure, you use an input parameter, and if you want to return something back, you use an output parameter. However, certain modules in T-SQL, for example, triggers, are by design *niladic*, meaning they don't support parameters. One technique to pass information between an outer level and a niladic module is to use either context info or session context.

*Context info* is a binary string of up to 128 bytes that is associated with your session. You write to it using the SET CONTEXT_INFO command and read it using the CONTEXT_INFO function. For example, the following code writes the value 'us_english,' after converting it to a binary string, as the current session's context info:

```
DECLARE @mycontextinfo AS VARBINARY(128) = CAST('us_english' AS VARBINARY(128));
SET CONTEXT_INFO @mycontextinfo;
```

You can read the context info from anywhere in your session, including triggers as follows:

```
SELECT CAST(CONTEXT_INFO() AS VARCHAR(128)) AS mycontextinfo;
```

This code generates the following output:

```
Mycontextinfo
--------------
us_english
```

The tricky thing about context info is that there's only one such binary string for the session. If you need to use it to store multiple values from different places in the code, you need to designate different parts of it for the different values. Every time you need to store a value, you need to read the current contents, and reconstruct it with the new value planted in the right section, being careful not to overwrite existing used parts. The potential to corrupt meaningful information is high.

T-SQL provides a tool called *session context* as a more convenient and robust alternative to context info. With session context, you store key-value pairs, where the key is a name of a sysname type (internally mapped to NVARCHAR(128)) that you assign to your session's variable, and the value is a SQL_VARIANT typed value that is associated with the key. You can also mark the pair as read only, and then until the session resets, no one will be able to overwrite the value associated with that key. You create the key and set its associated value using the sp_set_session_context stored procedure and read it using the SESSION_CONTEXT function.

As an example, the following code creates a key called language and associates with it the value 'us_english', marking it as read only.

```
EXEC sys.sp_set_session_context
  @key = N'language', @value = 'us_english', @read_only = 1;
```

Then when you need to read the value from anywhere in your session, you use the following code:

```
SELECT SESSION_CONTEXT(N'language') AS [language];
```

This code generates the following output:

```
Language
-----------
us_english
```

## GUID and identity functions

T-SQL provides a number of solutions for generating values that you can use as keys for your rows. T-SQL also provides system functions to generate and query the newly generated keys.

If you need to generate a key that is globally unique, even across systems, you use the NEWID function to generate it as a UNIQUEIDENTIFER typed value. As an example, run the following code:

```
SELECT NEWID() AS myguid;
```

You can run this code several times and see that every time you get a different globally unique identifier (GUID). For instance, in one of my executions of this code I got the following output:

```
Myguid
------------------------------------
203B8382-77E4-4B7E-B6B9-260CC7A9CB8C
```

If you want the GUIDs to always increase within the machine, use the NEWSEQUENTIALID system function instead. Note that you cannot invoke this function independently, rather only as an expression in a default constraint that is associated with a column.

If you need a numeric key generator, you use either a sequence object or the identity column property. The former is an independent object in the database that you create using the CREATE SEQUENCE command. Once created, every time you need a new value, you invoke the function NEXT VALUE FOR <sequence_name>. The latter is a property of a column in a table. SQL Server generates a new key only as part of an INSERT statement that you submit against the target table, where you ignore the column with the identity property. After adding the row, you query the system function SCOPE_IDENTITY to get the last identity value that was generated in the same session and scope. In *the same scope* I mean that if a trigger was fired and also added a row to a table with an identity property, this will not affect the value that the function will return. If you want to get the last identity value generated in your session, irrespective of scope, you query the system function @@IDENTITY. You can find examples for using both the identity property and the sequence object later in this chapter in Skill 1.4.

# Arithmetic operators and aggregate functions

T-SQL supports the four classic arithmetic operators + (add), - (subtract), * (multiply), / (divide), as well as the fifth operator % (modulo). The last computes the remainder of an integer division. T-SQL also supports aggregate functions, which you apply to a set of rows, and get a single value back.

## Arithmetic operators

For the most part, work with these arithmetic operators is intuitive. They follow classic arithmetic operator precedence rules, which say that multiplication, division and modulo precede addition and subtraction. To change precedence of operations, use parentheses because they precede arithmetic operators. For example, consider the following expression:

```
SELECT 2 + 3 * 2 + 10 / 2;
```

It is equivalent to the following expression:

```
SELECT 2 + (3 * 2) + (10 / 2);
```

The result of this expression is 13.

If you want to evaluate the operations from left to right, you need to use parentheses as follows:

```
SELECT ((2 + 3) * 2 + 10) / 2;
```

This expression evaluates to 10.

The data types of the operands in an arithmetic computation determine the data type of the result. If the operands are integers, the result of arithmetic operations is an integer. With this in mind, consider the following expression:

```
SELECT 9 / 2;
```

With integer division, the result of this expression is 4 and not 4.5. Obviously, when using constants, you can simply specify numeric values instead of integer values to get numeric division; however, when the operands are integer columns or parameters, but you need numeric division, you have two options. One option is to explicitly cast the operands to a numeric type with the appropriate precision and scale as follows:

```
DECLARE @p1 AS INT = 9, @p2 AS INT = 2;
SELECT CAST(@p1 AS NUMERIC(12, 2)) / CAST(@p2 AS NUMERIC(12, 2));
```

The rules for determining the precision and scale of the result of the computation can be found at *https://msdn.microsoft.com/en-us/library/ms190476.aspx*. The result of this expression is 4.500000000000000. The operation here is division. The applicable formula to calculate the precision here is p1 - s1 + s2 + max(6, s1 + p2 + 1), which when applied to our inputs results in 27. The formula for the scale is max(6, s1 + p2 + 1), which in this case results in 15.

Another option is to multiply the first operand by a numeric constant, and this way force implicit conversion of both the first and the second operands to a numeric type as follows:

```
DECLARE @p1 AS INT = 9, @p2 AS INT = 2;
SELECT 1.0 * @p1 / @p2;
```

## Aggregate functions

An aggregate function is a function that you apply to a set of rows and get a single value back. T-SQL supports aggregate functions such as SUM, COUNT, MIN, MAX, AVG and others. You can find the full list at *https://msdn.microsoft.com/en-us/library/ms173454.aspx*.

Aggregate functions ignore NULL inputs when applied to an expression. The COUNT(*) aggregate just counts rows, and returns the result as an INT value. Use COUNT_BIG to return the row count as a BIGINT value. If you want to apply an aggregate function to distinct values, add the DISTINCT clause, as in COUNT(DISTINCT custid).

You can apply aggregate functions in explicit grouped queries as the following example shows:

```
SELECT empid, SUM(qty) AS totalqty
FROM Sales.OrderValues
GROUP BY empid;
```

In a grouped query the aggregate is applied per group, and returns a single value per group, as part of the single result row that represents the group. This query generates the following output:

```
empid        totalqty
-----------  -----------
9            2670
3            7852
6            3527
7            4654
1            7812
4            9798
5            3036
2            6055
8            5913
```

An aggregate function can also be applied as a scalar aggregate in an implied grouped query. The presence of the aggregate function causes the query to be considered a grouped one, as in the following example:

```
SELECT SUM(qty) AS totalqty FROM Sales.OrderValues;
```

This query returns the grand total quantity 51,317.

Like with arithmetic operators, also with aggregate functions like AVG, the data type of the input determines the data type of the result. For instance, the following query produces an integer average:

```
SELECT AVG(qty) AS avgqty FROM Sales.OrderValues;
```

The result of this average is the integer 61.

You can use the two aforementioned options that I described for arithmetic operations to get a numeric average. Either explicitly cast the input to a numeric type as follows:

```
SELECT AVG(CAST(qty AS NUMERIC(12, 2))) AS avgqty FROM Sales.OrderValues;
```

Or implicitly as follows:

```
SELECT AVG(1.0 * qty) AS avgqty FROM Sales.OrderValues;
```

This time you get the result 61.827710.

If you're wondering why the scale of the result value here is 6 digits, the AVG function is handled internally as a sum divided by a count. The scale of the input expression (1.0 * qty) is the sum of the scales of the operands (1 for 1.0 and 0 for the integer qty), which in our case is 1. The sum aggregate's scale is the maximum scale among the input values, which in our case is 1. Then the scale of the result of the division between the sum and the count is based on the formula max(6, s1 + p2 + 1), which in our case is 6.

As an alternative to grouping, aggregate functions can be applied in windowed queries, as window aggregates. This, as well as further aspects of grouping and aggregation are covered in Chapter 2, Skill 2.3.

## Example involving arithmetic operators and aggregate functions

As mentioned, the % (modulo) operator computes the remainder of an integer division. Suppose that you were tasked with computing the median quantity (qty column) from the Sales. OrderValues view using a continuous distribution model. This means that if there are an odd number of rows you need to return the middle quantity, and if there are an even number of rows, you need to return the average of the two middle quantities. Using the COUNT aggregate, you can first count how many rows there are and store in a variable called @cnt. Then you can compute parameters for the OFFSET-FETCH filter to specify, based on qty ordering, how many rows to skip (offset value) and how many to filter (fetch value). The number of rows to skip is (@cnt - 1) / 2. It's clear that for an odd count this calculation is correct because you first subtract 1 for the single middle value, before you divide by 2.

This also works correctly for an even count because the division used in the expression is integer division; so, when subtracting 1 from an even count, you're left with an odd value. When dividing that odd value by 2, the fraction part of the result (.5) is truncated. The number of rows to fetch is 2 - (@cnt % 2). The idea is that when the count is odd the result of the modulo operation is 1, and you need to fetch 1 row. When the count is even the result of the modulo operation is 0, and you need to fetch 2 rows. By subtracting the 1 or 0 result of the modulo operation from 2, you get the desired 1 or 2, respectively. Finally, to compute the median quantity, take the one or two result quantities, and apply an average after converting the input integer value to a numeric one as follows:

```
DECLARE @cnt AS INT = (SELECT COUNT(*) FROM Sales.OrderValues);

SELECT AVG(1.0 * qty) AS median
```

```
FROM ( SELECT qty
       FROM Sales.OrderValues
       ORDER BY qty
       OFFSET (@cnt - 1) / 2 ROWS FETCH NEXT 2 - @cnt % 2 ROWS ONLY ) AS D;
```

You cannot apply the AVG aggregate directly in the query with the OFFSET-FETCH filter. That's because if you did, there would have been implied grouping, which happens in the third step of logical query processing. Then the reference to the detail qty column in the OR-DER BY clause, which is processed in the sixth logical query processing step, would have been invalid. Therefore, the solution defines a derived table (a table subquery in the FROM clause) called D that represents the one or two quantities that need to participate in the median calculation, and then the outer query handles the average calculation. This query returns the median quantity 50.000000.

## Search arguments

One of the most important aspects of query tuning to know is what a search argument is. A *search argument*, or *SARG* in short, is a filter predicate that enables the optimizer to rely on index order. The filter predicate uses the following form (or a variant with two delimiters of a range, or with the operand positions flipped):

```
WHERE <column> <operator> <expression>
```

Such a filter is sargable if:

1. You don't apply manipulation to the filtered column.

2. The operator identifies a consecutive range of qualifying rows in the index. That's the case with operators like =, >, >=, <, <=, BETWEEN, LIKE with a known prefix, and so on. That's not the case with operators like <>, LIKE with a wildcard as a prefix.

In most cases, when you apply manipulation to the filtered column, the optimizer doesn't try to be too smart and understand the meaning of the calculation, and if index ordering can still be relied. It simply assumes that the result values might sort differently than the source values, and therefore index ordering can't be trusted. This, for example, can prevent the ability to rely on the index to filter the data by applying a seek and range scan.

As an example, consider the following query:

```
SELECT orderid, orderdate
FROM Sales.Orders
WHERE YEAR(orderdate) = 2015;
```

The plan for this query is shown in Figure 1-15.

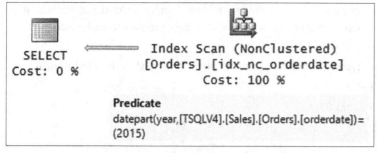

**FIGURE 1-15**   Plan with an index scan for example with date range

There is a nonclustered covering index defined on the orderdate column as the leading key, with orderid being implicitly part of the index because it's the clustered index key. Clearly, the qualifying rows appear in a consecutive range in the index. However, the manipulation applied to the orderdate column with the YEAR function prevents the filter's sargability, and causes the optimizer to scan the whole index. The predicate is applied as a residual predicate, and shows up under the scan's Predicate property.

The alternative that is considered a search argument expresses the predicate as a range, without applying manipulation to the filtered column as follows:

```
SELECT orderid, orderdate
FROM Sales.Orders
WHERE orderdate >= '20150101'
  AND orderdate < '20160101';
```

The plan for this query is shown in Figure 1-16.

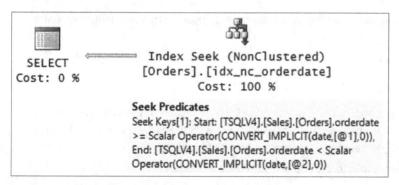

**FIGURE 1-16**   Plan with an index seek for example with date range

This time the plan applies a seek in the index and a range scan in the index leaf, physically touching only qualifying rows. The predicate appears under the Seek Predicates property.

Note that in some rare cases, Microsoft added logic to the optimizer to convert a nonsar-gable predicate to a sargable one. For instance, when using the predicate CAST(dt AS DATE) = '20170212', where dt is an indexed date and time typed column, SQL Server can compute two delimiters in an open-open interval, and then process the filter with a sargable predicate where the column is greater than the first delimiter and less than the second. But because it's so uncommon for SQL Server to do such conversions, it's a best practice to make sure that you write in a sargable way to begin with.

There are plenty more typical examples where people fall into such traps. For instance, consider the following query:

```
DECLARE @todt AS DATE = '20151231';

SELECT orderid, orderdate
FROM Sales.Orders
WHERE DATEADD(day, -1, orderdate) < @todt;
```

This query resides in a stored procedure or user defined function that accepts a parameter called @todt (emulated here with an ad-hoc batch with a local variable), and is supposed to return all orders that were placed prior to the day after the input parameter. As written, the query isn't sargable due to the manipulated filtered column. The plan for this query is similar to the one shown earlier in Figure 1-15, only with the current query's filter predicate.

A simple mathematical transformation, applying a plus one day to the parameter instead of a minus one day to the column enables sargability as follows:

```
DECLARE @todt AS DATE = '20151231';

SELECT orderid, orderdate
FROM Sales.Orders
WHERE orderdate < DATEADD(day, 1, @todt);
```

The plan for this query is similar to the one shown earlier in Figure 1-16, only with the current query's filter predicate.

As another example, the following query returns employees with a last name that starts with the letter D:

```
SELECT empid, lastname
FROM HR.Employees
WHERE LEFT(lastname, 1) = N'D';
```

This filter isn't sargable due to the function LEFT that is applied to the lastname column, and therefore the plan for this query is similar to the one shown earlier in Figure 1-15, only with the index idx_nc_lastname and the current query's filter predicate.

The sargable alternative is to use the LIKE predicate as follows:

```
SELECT empid, lastname
FROM HR.Employees
WHERE lastname LIKE N'D%';
```

When using the LIKE predicate with a known prefix SQL Server internally translates the pattern to a closed-open interval, and process the filter as a range that is greater than or equal to the first delimiter and less than the second delimiter. The plan for this query is similar to the one shown earlier in Figure 1-16.

Yet another common example is when filtering a NULLable column. Consider the following query:

```
DECLARE @dt AS DATE = '20150212';

SELECT orderid, shippeddate
FROM Sales.Orders
WHERE shippeddate = @dt;
```

There's an index defined on the shippeddate column, with the orderid column implicitly included. Clearly, this filter is sargable, but there is a bug in this query. Unshipped orders are marked with a NULL in the shippeddate column, so when you want to see unshipped orders you pass a NULL as input as follows:

```
DECLARE @dt AS DATE = NULL;

SELECT orderid, shippeddate
FROM Sales.Orders
WHERE shippeddate = @dt;
```

This query uses an equality-based comparison, where a comparison between anything and a NULL, including between two NULLs, yields unknown, and therefore the result is an empty set.

One of the common techniques that people use to cope with such cases is to use the COALESCE or ISNULL function to replace a NULL in both sides with a value that can't normally appear in the data as follows:

```
DECLARE @dt AS DATE = NULL;

SELECT orderid, shippeddate
FROM Sales.Orders
WHERE ISNULL(shippeddate, '99991231') = ISNULL(@dt, '99991231');
```

You do get the correct result, but the filter isn't sargable, so the plan for this query is similar to the one shown earlier in Figure 1-15, only with the current index and query filter predicate.

One recommended solution that is considered sargable is to use the IS NULL predicate to check for NULLs as follows:

```
DECLARE @dt AS DATE = NULL;

SELECT orderid, shippeddate
FROM Sales.Orders
WHERE shippeddate = @dt
    OR (shippeddate IS NULL AND @dt IS NULL);
```

The plan for this query is similar to the one shown earlier in Figure 1-16.

This solution is correct, but if you have a conjunction of multiple predicates based on NULLable columns that you need to filter by, your WHERE clause will end up being long and convoluted. Recall the trick you used in the joins section when comparing NULLable columns using the EXISTS predicate and the INTERSECT set operator. You can apply the same trick here as follows:

```
DECLARE @dt AS DATE = NULL;

SELECT orderid, shippeddate
FROM Sales.Orders
WHERE EXISTS (SELECT shippeddate INTERSECT SELECT @dt);
```

With multiple columns you simply extend the SELECT lists in both sides. Set operators use a distinctness-based comparison and not an equality-based one, giving you the desired meaning without the need for special handling of NULLs. What's more, remarkably this form is sargable and therefore the plan for this query is also similar to the one shown earlier in Figure 1-16.

In the same way that manipulation of a filtered column prevents the sargability of a filter, such manipulation breaks the ordering property of the data. This means that even if there's an index on a column, SQL Server cannot rely on the index order to support an order-based algorithm for presentation ordering, window-function ordering, joining, grouping, distinctness, and so on.

## Function determinism

Function determinism is a characteristic that indicates whether the function is guaranteed to return the same result given the same set of input values (including an empty set) in different invocations. If the function provides such a guarantee, it is said to be *deterministic*; otherwise, it is said to be *nondeterministic*. I am not going to go over the full list of functions and their determinism quality here. You can find the details at *https://msdn.microsoft.com/en-us/ library/ms178091.aspx*. Here I am going to describe the different categories of determinism and illustrate each with a couple of examples. I also describe the limitations that nondeterministic functions impose.

There are three main categories of function determinism. There are functions that are always deterministic, those that are deterministic when invoked in a certain way, and those that are always nondeterministic.

Examples for functions that are always deterministic: all string functions, COALESCE, ISNULL, ABS, SQRT and many others. For instance, the expression ABS(-1759) always returns 1759.

Certain functions are either deterministic or not depending on how they're used. For example, the CAST function is not deterministic when converting from a character string to a date and time type or the other way around because the interpretation of the value might depend on the login's language. For instance, the expression CAST('02/12/17' AS DATE) converts to February 12, 2017 under us_english, December 2, 2017 under British, and December 17, 2002 under Swedish and Japanese. The same applies to CONVERT when using certain styles. Another example is the RAND function. This function returns a float in the range 0 through 1. When using it with a seed, it is deterministic. For instance, run the following code several times:

```
SELECT RAND(1759);
```

You keep getting the same result, 0.746348756684839.

When you invoke the function without a seed, SQL Server computes a new seed based on the previous invocation and you get a pseudo random value. Run the following code several times and notice that you keep getting different results:

```
SELECT RAND();
```

In *pseudo*, I mean that even though technically without a seed the function is considered nondeterministic, if invoked right after an invocation with a seed, the result is repeatable. Run the following code several times:

```
SELECT RAND(1759);
SELECT RAND();
```

You repeatedly get the following output:

```
---------------------
0.746348756684839


---------------------
0.201391138037653
```

Certain functions are always nondeterministic, for example SYSDATETIME and NEWID. The former returns the current date and time value as a DATETIME2 typed value, and the latter returns a globally unique identifier as a UNIQUEIDENTIFIER typed value. NEWID returns a fairly random value, but its type is awkward to work with. To get a random integer value in a certain range, for instance, 1 through 10, use the following expression:

```
SELECT 1 + ABS(CHECKSUM(NEWID())) % 10;
```

By applying CHECKSUM to the result of NEWID you get a random integer. The absolute value modulo 10 gives you a random value in the range 0 through 9. Adding the result to 1 gives you a random value in the range 1 through 10.

Most nondeterministic functions are invoked once per query. That's the case for instance with SYSDATETIME and RAND (when invoked without a seed). The NEWID function is an exception in the sense that it gets invoked per row. Consider the following query:

```
SELECT empid, SYSDATETIME() AS dtnow, RAND() AS rnd, NEWID() AS newguid
FROM HR.Employees;
```

In one of the executions of this query on my system I got the following result (formatted as two outputs to fit on the page).

```
empid   dtnow                         rnd
------  ----------------------------  ------------------
2       2016-10-02 09:35:46.8024874   0.980769010450262
7       2016-10-02 09:35:46.8024874   0.980769010450262
1       2016-10-02 09:35:46.8024874   0.980769010450262
5       2016-10-02 09:35:46.8024874   0.980769010450262
6       2016-10-02 09:35:46.8024874   0.980769010450262
8       2016-10-02 09:35:46.8024874   0.980769010450262
3       2016-10-02 09:35:46.8024874   0.980769010450262
9       2016-10-02 09:35:46.8024874   0.980769010450262
4       2016-10-02 09:35:46.8024874   0.980769010450262

empid   newguid
------  ------------------------------------
2       F2EC6CC7-E986-4A43-9ED9-1A08C56600D2
7       74A018CF-5E95-4C7F-BA8F-D707A3DD5177
1       B894EAAF-07C8-4CC1-AD20-4CE7DA4AFB81
5       10B86C1F-BD18-4E7E-8A70-195A239B54EA
6       20514C7A-4F3C-4C3F-BFBB-014E5FAC6B85
8       86C29355-16B2-4A48-9068-039ABBD56B85
3       D923AEBB-0FD7-424D-93C2-E68E199A24C1
9       E2940155-3C66-4F1A-BBF9-0D001AF9A4AB
4       2B3BE2DD-00CE-494E-B52C-989CA71A36E9
```

Keep this in mind, for instance, if you want to return the results ordered randomly, or select a random set of rows. For instance, suppose that you need to return a random set of three employees, and you use the following query in attempt to achieve this:

```
SELECT TOP (3) empid, firstname, lastname
FROM HR.Employees
ORDER BY RAND();
```

Run this code repeatedly and you probably keep getting the same result. Because the RAND function returns the same value in all rows, the ORDER BY is meaningless here. To get different random values in the different rows, order by NEWID, or for even better random distribution, apply CHECKSUM to NEWID as follows:

```
SELECT TOP (3) empid, firstname, lastname
FROM HR.Employees
ORDER BY CHECKSUM(NEWID());
```

Note that the use of a nondeterministic function in a computed column prevents the ability to create an index on the column. Similarly, the use of a nondeterministic function in a view prevents the ability to create a clustered index on the view. That's the case whether the function is always nondeterministic, or nondeterministic in certain cases.

# Skill 1.4: Modify data

The T-SQL support for data manipulation language (DML) includes both statements that retrieve data (SELECT) and statements that modify data (INSERT, UPDATE, DELETE, TRUNCATE TABLE, and MERGE). The previous skills focused on data retrieval; this skill focuses on data modification.

> **This section covers how to:**
> - Write INSERT, UPDATE, and DELETE statements
> - Determine which statements can be used to load data to a table based on its structure and constraints
> - Construct Data Manipulation Language (DML) statements using the OUTPUT statement
> - Determine the results of Data Definition Language (DDL) statements on supplied tables and data

## Inserting data

T-SQL supports a number of different methods that you can use to insert data into your tables. Those include statements like INSERT VALUES, INSERT SELECT, INSERT EXEC, and SE-LECT INTO. This section covers these statements and demonstrates how to use them through examples.

Some of the code examples in this section use a table called Sales.MyOrders. Use the following code to create such a table in the sample database TSQLV4:

```
USE TSQLV4;
DROP TABLE IF EXISTS Sales.MyOrders;
GO

CREATE TABLE Sales.MyOrders
(
  orderid INT NOT NULL IDENTITY(1, 1)
    CONSTRAINT PK_MyOrders_orderid PRIMARY KEY,
  custid  INT NOT NULL,
  empid   INT NOT NULL,
  orderdate DATE NOT NULL
    CONSTRAINT DFT_MyOrders_orderdate DEFAULT (CAST(SYSDATETIME() AS DATE)),
  shipcountry NVARCHAR(15) NOT NULL,
  freight MONEY NOT NULL
);
```

Observe that the orderid column has an identity property defined with a seed 1 and an increment 1. This property generates the values in this column automatically when rows are inserted. As an alternative to the identity property you can use a sequence object to generate surrogate keys. For details about the sequence object and a comparison between the two options, see the following articles:

- Sequences part 1 at *http://sqlmag.com/sql-server/sequences-part-1*
- Sequences part 2 at *http://sqlmag.com/sql-server/sequences-part-2*
- Sequence and identity performance at *http://sqlmag.com/sql-server/sequence-and-identity-performance*

Also observe that the orderdate column has a default constraint with an expression that returns the current system's date.

## INSERT VALUES

With the INSERT VALUES statement, you can insert one or more rows into a target table based on value expressions. Here's an example for a statement inserting one row into the Sales.MyOrderValues table:

```
INSERT INTO Sales.MyOrders(custid, empid, orderdate, shipcountry, freight)
  VALUES(2, 19, '20170620', N'USA', 30.00);
```

Specifying the target column names after the table name is optional but considered a best practice. That's because it enables you to control the source value to target column association, irrespective of the order in which the columns were defined in the table.

Without the target column list, you must specify the values in column definition order. If the underlying table definition changes but the INSERT statements aren't modified accordingly, this can result in either errors, or worse, values written to the wrong columns.

The INSERT VALUES statement does not specify a value for a column with an identity property because the property generates the value for the column automatically. Observe that the previous statement doesn't specify the orderid column. If you do want to provide your own value instead of letting the identity property do it for you, you need to first turn on a session option called IDENTITY_INSERT, as follows:

```
SET IDENTITY_INSERT <table> ON;
```

When you're done, you need to remember to turn it off.

Note that in order to use this option, you need quite strong permissions; you need to be the owner of the table or have ALTER permissions on the table.

Besides using the identity property, there are other ways for a column to get its value automatically in an INSERT statement. A column can have a default constraint associated with it like the orderdate column in the Sales.MyOrders table. If the INSERT statement doesn't specify a value for the column explicitly, SQL Server will use the default expression to generate that value. For example, the following statement doesn't specify a value for orderdate, and therefore SQL Server uses the default expression:

```
INSERT INTO Sales.MyOrders(custid, empid, shipcountry, freight)
  VALUES(3, 11, N'USA', 10.00);
```

Another way to achieve the same behavior is to specify the column name in the names list and the keyword DEFAULT in the respective element in the VALUES list. Here's an INSERT example demonstrating this:

```
INSERT INTO Sales.MyOrders(custid, empid, orderdate, shipcountry, freight)
  VALUES(3, 17, DEFAULT, N'USA', 30.00);
```

If you don't specify a value for a column, SQL Server first checks whether the column gets its value automatically—for example, from an identity property or a default constraint. If that's not the case, SQL Server checks whether the column allows NULLs, in which case it assumes a NULL. If that's not the case, SQL Server generates an error.

The INSERT VALUES statement doesn't limit you to inserting only one row; rather, it enables you to insert multiple rows. Simply separate the rows with commas, as follows:

```
INSERT INTO Sales.MyOrders(custid, empid, orderdate, shipcountry, freight) VALUES
  (2, 11, '20170620', N'USA', 50.00),
  (5, 13, '20170620', N'USA', 40.00),
  (7, 17, '20170620', N'USA', 45.00);
```

Note that the entire statement is considered one transaction, meaning that if any row fails to enter the target table, the entire statement fails and no row is inserted.

To see the result of running all INSERT examples in this section, query the table by using the following query:

```
SELECT * FROM Sales.MyOrders;
```

> **NOTE  SELECT \***
>
> As explained earlier, using SELECT * in production code is considered a bad practice. Here, SELECT * is used only for ad hoc querying purposes to examine the contents of tables after applying changes.

When I ran this code on my system, it returned the following output:

```
orderid  custid  empid  orderdate   shipcountry   freight
-------- ------- ------ ----------- ------------  --------
1        2       19     2017-06-20  USA           30.00
2        3       11     2017-02-12  USA           10.00
3        3       17     2017-02-12  USA           30.00
4        2       11     2017-06-20  USA           50.00
5        5       13     2017-06-20  USA           40.00
6        7       17     2017-06-20  USA           45.00
```

Remember that some of the INSERT examples relied on the default expression associated with the orderdate column, so naturally the dates you get reflect the date when you ran those examples.

## INSERT SELECT

The INSERT SELECT statement inserts the result set returned by a query into the specified target table. As with INSERT VALUES, the INSERT SELECT statement supports optionally specifying the target column names. Also, you can omit columns that get their values automatically from an identity property, default constraint, or when allowing NULLs.

As an example, the following code inserts into the Sales.MyOrders table the result of a query against Sales.Orders returning orders shipped to customers in Norway:

```
SET IDENTITY_INSERT Sales.MyOrders ON;

INSERT INTO Sales.MyOrders(orderid, custid, empid, orderdate, shipcountry, freight)
  SELECT orderid, custid, empid, orderdate, shipcountry, freight
  FROM Sales.Orders
  WHERE shipcountry = N'Norway';

SET IDENTITY_INSERT Sales.MyOrders OFF;
```

The code turns on the IDENTITY_INSERT option against Sales.MyOrders in order to use the original order IDs and not let the identity property generate those.

Query the table after running this code:

```
SELECT * FROM Sales.MyOrders;
```

This query generates the following output (mostly new rows shown for brevity):

```
orderid   custid   empid   orderdate    shipcountry   freight
--------  -------  ------  -----------  ------------  --------
1         2        19      2017-06-20   USA           30.00
2         3        11      2017-02-12   USA           10.00
3         3        17      2017-02-12   USA           30.00
...
10387     70       1       2014-12-18   Norway        93.63
10520     70       7       2015-04-29   Norway        13.37
10639     70       7       2015-08-20   Norway        38.64
10831     70       3       2016-01-14   Norway        72.19
10909     70       1       2016-02-26   Norway        53.05
11015     70       2       2016-04-10   Norway        4.62
```

Setting IDENTITY_INSERT to OFF causes the current identity value of the table to be set to the current maximum value in the identity column. In our example, the current identity value was set to 11015. If you now add another row to the table, the order ID will be set to 11016.

## INSERT EXEC

With the INSERT EXEC statement, you can insert the result set (or sets) returned by a dynamic batch or a stored procedure into the specified target table. Much like the INSERT VALUES and INSERT SELECT statements, INSERT EXEC supports specifying an optional target column list, and allows omitting columns that accept their values automatically.

To demonstrate the INSERT EXEC statement, the following example uses a procedure called Sales.OrdersForCountry, which accepts a ship country as input and returns orders shipped to the input country. Run the following code to create the Sales.OrdersForCountry procedure:

```
DROP PROC IF EXISTS Sales.OrdersForCountry;
GO

CREATE PROC Sales.OrdersForCountry
  @country AS NVARCHAR(15)
AS

SELECT orderid, custid, empid, orderdate, shipcountry, freight
FROM Sales.Orders
WHERE shipcountry = @country;
GO
```

Run the following code to invoke the stored procedure with Portugal as the input country, and insert the result of the procedure into the Sales.MyOrders table:

```
SET IDENTITY_INSERT Sales.MyOrders ON;

INSERT INTO Sales.MyOrders(orderid, custid, empid, orderdate, shipcountry, freight)
  EXEC Sales.OrdersForCountry
    @country = N'Portugal';

SET IDENTITY_INSERT Sales.MyOrders OFF;
```

Here as well, the code turns on the IDENTITY_INSERT option against the target table so that the INSERT statement can specify the values for the identity column instead of letting the property assign those.

Query the table after running the INSERT statement and notice the new additions of the orders that were shipped to Portugal:

```
SELECT * FROM Sales.MyOrders;
```

INSERT EXEC works even when the source dynamic batch or stored procedure has more than one query. But that's as long as all queries return result sets that are compatible with the target table definition.

## SELECT INTO

The SELECT INTO statement involves a query (the SELECT part) and a target table (the INTO part). The statement creates the target table based on the definition of the source and inserts the result rows from the query into that table. The statement copies from the source some aspects of the data definition like the column names, types, nullability, and identity property, in addition to the data itself. Certain aspects of the data definition aren't copied like indexes, constraints, triggers, permissions, and others. If you want to include these aspects, you need to script them from the source and apply them to the target.

The following code shows an example for a SELECT INTO statement that queries the Sales. Orders table returning orders shipped to Norway, creates a target table called Sales.MyOrders, and stores the query's result in the target table:

```
DROP TABLE IF EXISTS Sales.MyOrders;

SELECT orderid, custid, orderdate, shipcountry, freight
INTO Sales.MyOrders
FROM Sales.Orders
WHERE shipcountry = N'Norway';
```

As mentioned, the SELECT INTO statement creates the target table based on the definition of the source. You don't have direct control over the definition of the target. If you want target columns to be defined different than the source, you need to apply some manipulation.

For example, the source orderid column has an identity property, and hence the target column is defined with an identity property as well. If you want the target column not to have the property, you need to apply some kind of manipulation, like orderid + 0 AS orderid. Note that after you apply manipulation, the target column definition allows NULLs. If you want the target column to be defined as not allowing NULLs, you need to use the ISNULL function, returning a non-NULL value in case the source is a NULL. This is just an artificial expression that lets SQL Server know that the outcome cannot be NULL and, hence, the column can be defined as not enabling NULLs. For example, you could use an expression such as this one: ISNULL(orderid + 0, -1) AS orderid.

Similarly, the source custid column is defined in the source as allowing NULLs. To make the target column be defined as NOT NULL, use the expression ISNULL(custid, -1) AS custid.

If you want the target column's type to be different than the source, you can use the CAST or CONVERT functions. But remember that in such a case, the target column definition enables NULLs even if the source column disallowed NULLs, because you applied manipulation to the source column. As with the previous examples, you can use the ISNULL function to make SQL Server define the target column as not enabling NULLs. For example, to convert the orderdate column from its source type DATETIME to DATE in the target, and disallow NULLs, use the expression ISNULL(CAST(orderdate AS DATE), '19000101') AS orderdate.

To put it all together, the following code uses a query similar to the previous example, only defining the orderid column without the identity property as NOT NULL, the custid column as NOT NULL, and the orderdate column as DATE NOT NULL:

```
DROP TABLE IF EXISTS Sales.MyOrders;

SELECT
  ISNULL(orderid + 0, -1) AS orderid, -- get rid of identity property
                                      -- make column NOT NULL
  ISNULL(custid, -1) AS custid, -- make column NOT NULL
  empid,
  ISNULL(CAST(orderdate AS DATE), '19000101') AS orderdate,
  shipcountry, freight
INTO Sales.MyOrders
FROM Sales.Orders
WHERE shipcountry = N'Norway';
```

Remember that SELECT INTO does not copy constraints from the source table, so if you need those, it's your responsibility to define them in the target. For example, the following code defines a primary key constraint in the target table:

```
ALTER TABLE Sales.MyOrders
  ADD CONSTRAINT PK_MyOrders PRIMARY KEY(orderid);
```

Query the table to see the result of the SELECT INTO statement:

```
SELECT * FROM Sales.MyOrders;
```

You get the following output:

```
orderid  custid  empid  orderdate   shipcountry  freight
-------- ------- ------ ----------  ------------ --------
10387    70      1      2014-12-18  Norway       93.63
10520    70      7      2015-04-29  Norway       13.37
10639    70      7      2015-08-20  Norway       38.64
10831    70      3      2016-01-14  Norway       72.19
10909    70      1      2016-02-26  Norway       53.05
11015    70      2      2016-04-10  Norway       4.62
```

One of the benefits of using SELECT INTO is that when the database's recovery model is not set to full, but instead to either simple or bulk logged, the statement uses an optimized logging mode. This can potentially result in a faster insert compared to when full logging is used. You can find details about recovery models at *https://msdn.microsoft.com/en-us/library/ms189275.aspx*. You can find further details on data loading performance at *https://msdn.microsoft.com/en-us/library/dd425070.aspx*.

The SELECT INTO statement also has drawbacks. One of them is that you have only limited control over the definition of the target table. Earlier in this lesson, you reviewed how to control the definition of the target columns indirectly. But some things you simply cannot control—for example the filegroup of the target table.

Also, remember that SELECT INTO involves both creating a table and populating it with data. This means that both the metadata related to the target table and the data are exclusively locked until the SELECT INTO transaction finishes. As a result, you can run into blocking situations due to conflicts related to both data and metadata access.

When you are done, run the following code for cleanup:

```
DROP TABLE IF EXISTS Sales.MyOrders;
```

# Updating data

T-SQL supports the UPDATE statement to enable you to update existing data in your tables. In this section, you review both the standard UPDATE statement and also about a few T-SQL extensions to the standard. You also review modifying data by using joins. You also review nondeterministic updates. Finally, you review how to update with variables, and how all-at-once operations affect updates.

Both the current section, which covers updating data, and the next one, which covers deleting data, use sample data involving tables called Sales.MyCustomers with customer data, Sales.MyOrders with order data, and Sales.MyOrderDetails with order lines data. These tables are made as initial copies of the tables Sales.Customers, Sales.Orders, and Sales.OrderDetails from the TSQLV4 sample database. By working with copies of the original tables, you can safely run code samples that update and delete rows without worrying about making changes to the original tables. Use the following code to create and populate the sample tables:

```
DROP TABLE IF EXISTS Sales.MyOrderDetails, Sales.MyOrders, Sales.MyCustomers;

SELECT * INTO Sales.MyCustomers FROM Sales.Customers;
ALTER TABLE Sales.MyCustomers
  ADD CONSTRAINT PK_MyCustomers PRIMARY KEY(custid);

SELECT * INTO Sales.MyOrders FROM Sales.Orders;
ALTER TABLE Sales.MyOrders
  ADD CONSTRAINT PK_MyOrders PRIMARY KEY(orderid);

SELECT * INTO Sales.MyOrderDetails FROM Sales.OrderDetails;
ALTER TABLE Sales.MyOrderDetails
  ADD CONSTRAINT PK_MyOrderDetails PRIMARY KEY(orderid, productid);
```

## UPDATE statement

T-SQL supports the standard UPDATE statement, which enables you to update existing rows in a table. The standard UPDATE statement has the following form:

```
UPDATE <target table>
  SET <col 1> = <expression 1>,
      ...,
      <col n> = <expression n>
WHERE <predicate>;
```

You specify the target table name in the UPDATE clause. If you want to filter a subset of rows, you indicate a WHERE clause with a predicate. Only rows for which the predicate evaluates to true are updated. Rows for which the predicate evaluates to false or unknown are not affected. An UPDATE statement without a WHERE clause affects all rows. You assign values to target columns in the SET clause. The source expressions can involve columns from the table, in which case their values before the update are used.

As an example, you modify rows in the Sales.MyOrderDetails table representing order lines associated with order 10251. First, query those rows to examine their state prior to the update:

```
SELECT *
FROM Sales.MyOrderDetails
WHERE orderid = 10251;
```

You get the following output:

| orderid | productid | unitprice | qty | discount |
|---------|-----------|-----------|-----|----------|
| 10251   | 22        | 16.80     | 6   | 0.050    |
| 10251   | 57        | 15.60     | 15  | 0.050    |
| 10251   | 65        | 16.80     | 20  | 0.000    |

The following code demonstrates an UPDATE statement that adds a five percent discount to these order lines:

```
UPDATE Sales.MyOrderDetails
   SET discount += 0.05
WHERE orderid = 10251;
```

Notice the use of the compound assignment operator discount += 0.05. This assignment is equivalent to discount = discount + 0.05. T-SQL supports such enhanced operators for all binary assignment operators: += (add), -= (subtract), *= (multiply), /= (divide), %= (modulo), &= (bitwise and), |= (bitwise or), ^= (bitwise xor), += (concatenate).

Query again the order lines associated with order 10251 to see their state after the update:

```
SELECT *
FROM Sales.MyOrderDetails
WHERE orderid = 10251;
```

You get the following output showing an increase of five percent in the discount:

| orderid | productid | unitprice | qty | discount |
|---------|-----------|-----------|-----|----------|
| 10251   | 22        | 16.80     | 6   | 0.100    |
| 10251   | 57        | 15.60     | 15  | 0.100    |
| 10251   | 65        | 16.80     | 20  | 0.050    |

Use the following code to reduce the discount in the aforementioned order lines by five percent:

```
UPDATE Sales.MyOrderDetails
   SET discount -= 0.05
WHERE orderid = 10251;
```

These rows should now be back to their original state before the first update.

## UPDATE based on join

Standard SQL doesn't support using joins in UPDATE statements, but T-SQL does. The idea is that you might want to update rows in a table, and refer to related rows in other tables for filtering and assignment purposes.

As an example, suppose that you want to add a five percent discount to order lines associated with orders placed by customers from Norway. The rows you need to modify are in the Sales.MyOrderDetails table. But the information you need to examine for filtering purposes is in rows in the Sales.MyCustomers table. In order to match a customer with its related order lines, you need to join Sales.MyCustomers with Sales.MyOrders, and then join the result with Sales.MyOrderDetails. Note that it's not sufficient to examine the shipcountry column in Sales.MyOrders; instead, you must check the country column in Sales.MyCustomers.

Based on your knowledge of joins, if you wanted to write a SELECT statement returning the order lines that are the target for the update, you would write a query like the following one:

```
SELECT OD.*
FROM Sales.MyCustomers AS C
  INNER JOIN Sales.MyOrders AS O
    ON C.custid = O.custid
  INNER JOIN Sales.MyOrderDetails AS OD
    ON O.orderid = OD.orderid
WHERE C.country = N'Norway';
```

This query identifies 16 order lines, all currently with a discount value of 0.000.

In order to perform the desired update, simply replace the SELECT clause from the last query with an UPDATE clause, indicating the alias of the table that is the target for the UPDATE (OD in this case), and the assignment in the SET clause, as follows:

```
UPDATE OD
  SET OD.discount += 0.05
FROM Sales.MyCustomers AS C
  INNER JOIN Sales.MyOrders AS O
    ON C.custid = O.custid
  INNER JOIN Sales.MyOrderDetails AS OD
    ON O.orderid = OD.orderid
WHERE C.country = N'Norway';
```

Note that you can refer to elements from all tables involved in the statement in the source expressions, but you're allowed to modify only one target table at a time. Rerun the SELECT query to examine the affected order lines, and you find that they now have a discount value of 0.050.

To get the previous order lines back to their original state, run an UPDATE statement that reduces the discount by five percent:

```
UPDATE OD
  SET OD.discount -= 0.05
FROM Sales.MyCustomers AS C
  INNER JOIN Sales.MyOrders AS O
    ON C.custid = O.custid
  INNER JOIN Sales.MyOrderDetails AS OD
    ON O.orderid = OD.orderid
WHERE C.country = N'Norway';
```

## Nondeterministic UPDATE

You should be aware that the proprietary T-SQL UPDATE syntax based on joins could be non-deterministic. The statement is nondeterministic when multiple source rows match one target row. Unfortunately, in such a case, SQL Server doesn't generate an error or even a warning. Instead, SQL Server silently performs a nondeterministic UPDATE where it arbitrarily chooses one of the source rows.

As an example, the following query matches customers with their related orders, returning the customers' postal codes, as well as shipping postal codes from related orders:

```
SELECT C.custid, C.postalcode, O.shippostalcode
FROM Sales.MyCustomers AS C
  INNER JOIN Sales.MyOrders AS O
    ON C.custid = O.custid
ORDER BY C.custid;
```

This query generates the following output:

```
custid       postalcode shippostalcode
-----------  ---------- --------------
1            10092      10154
1            10092      10156
1            10092      10155
1            10092      10154
1            10092      10154
1            10092      10154
2            10077      10182
2            10077      10181
...
```

Each customer row is repeated in the output for each matching order. This means that each customer's only postal code is repeated in the output as many times as the number of matching orders. It's important for the purposes of this example to remember that there is only one postal code per customer. The shipping postal code is associated with an order, so as you can realize, there can be multiple distinct shipping postal codes per customer. With this in mind, consider the following UPDATE statement:

```
UPDATE C
  SET C.postalcode = O.shippostalcode
FROM Sales.MyCustomers AS C
  INNER JOIN Sales.MyOrders AS O
    ON C.custid = O.custid;
```

There are 89 customers that have matching orders—some with multiple matches. SQL Server doesn't generate an error though; instead it arbitrarily chooses for each target row which source row is to be considered for the update, returning the following message:

```
(89 row(s) affected)
```

Query the rows from the Sales.Customers table after the update:

```
SELECT custid, postalcode
FROM Sales.MyCustomers
ORDER BY custid;
```

This generated the following output on one system, but your results could be different:

```
custid       postalcode
-----------  ----------
1            10154
2            10182
...
```

```
(91 row(s) affected)
```

Note that the table has 91 rows, but because only 89 of those customers have related orders, the previous UPDATE statement affected 89 rows.

As to which source row gets chosen for each target row, the choice isn't exactly random, but arbitrary; in other words, it's optimization-dependent. At any rate, you do not have any logical elements in the language to control this choice. The recommended approach is simply not to use such nondeterministic UPDATE statements, rather have logic in your solution to break ties.

For example, suppose that you want to update the customer's postal code with the shipping postal code from the customer's first order (based on the sort order of orderdate, orderid). You can achieve this using the following code:

```
UPDATE C
  SET C.postalcode = A.shippostalcode
FROM Sales.MyCustomers AS C
  CROSS APPLY (SELECT TOP (1) O.shippostalcode
               FROM Sales.MyOrders AS O
               WHERE O.custid = C.custid
               ORDER BY orderdate, orderid) AS A;
```

The book covers the APPLY operator and correlated subqueries in Chapter 2. For now, suffice to say that for each customer, the operator applies a subquery that identifies its most recent order. Customers who don't have orders aren't affected. Can't wait till Chapter 2 and feel like watching a movie? Grab some popcorn and watch the following video seminar about the APPLY operator at *http://aka.ms/BoostTSQL*.

SQL Server generates the following message:

```
(89 row(s) affected)
```

Query the Sales.MyCustomers table after the update:

```
SELECT custid, postalcode
FROM Sales.MyCustomers
ORDER BY custid;
```

You get the following output:

```
custid      postalcode
----------- ----------
1           10154
2           10180
...

(91 row(s) affected)
```

If you want to use the most-recent order as the source for the update, simply use descending sort order in both columns: ORDER BY orderdate DESC, orderid DESC.

## UPDATE with a variable

Sometimes you need to modify a row and also collect the result of the modified columns into variables. You can handle such a need with a combination of UPDATE and SELECT statements, but this would require two visits to the row. T-SQL supports a specialized UPDATE syntax that allows achieving the task by using one statement and one visit to the row.

As an example, run the following query to examine the current state of the order line associated with order 10250 and product 51:

```
SELECT *
FROM Sales.MyOrderDetails
WHERE orderid = 10250
  AND productid = 51;
```

This code generates the following output:

```
orderid     productid   unitprice             qty    discount
----------- ----------- --------------------- ------ ---------
10250       51          42.40                 35     0.150
```

Suppose that you need to modify the row, increasing the discount by five percent, and collect the new discount into a variable called @newdiscount. You can achieve this using a single UPDATE statement, as follows.

```
DECLARE @newdiscount AS NUMERIC(4, 3) = NULL;

UPDATE Sales.MyOrderDetails
  SET @newdiscount = discount += 0.05
WHERE orderid = 10250
  AND productid = 51;

SELECT @newdiscount;
```

As you can see, the UPDATE and WHERE clauses are similar to those you use in normal UPDATE statements. But the SET clause uses the assignment @newdiscount = discount += 0.05, which is equivalent to using @newdiscount = discount = discount + 0.05. The statement assigns the result of discount + 0.05 to discount, and then assigns the result to the variable @newdiscount. The last SELECT statement in the code returns the new discount 0.200.

When you're done, issue the following code to undo the last change:

```
UPDATE Sales.MyOrderDetails
  SET discount -= 0.05
WHERE orderid = 10250
  AND productid = 51;
```

## UPDATE all-at-once

Earlier in the book as part of the discussion about logical query processing I explained that expressions that appear in the same logical phase are treated as a set, in an *all-at-once* manner. The all-at-once concept also has implications on UPDATE statements. To demonstrate those implications, this section uses a table called T1. Use the following code to create the table T1 and insert a row into it:

```
DROP TABLE IF EXISTS dbo.T1;

CREATE TABLE dbo.T1
(
  keycol INT NOT NULL
    CONSTRAINT PK_T1 PRIMARY KEY,
  col1 INT NOT NULL,
  col2 INT NOT NULL
);

INSERT INTO dbo.T1(keycol, col1, col2) VALUES(1, 100, 0);
```

Next, examine the following code but don't run it yet:

```
DECLARE @add AS INT = 10;

UPDATE dbo.T1
  SET col1 += @add, col2 = col1
WHERE keycol = 1;

SELECT * FROM dbo.T1;
```

Can you guess what should be the value of col2 in the modified row after the update? If you guessed 110, you were not thinking of the assignments as a set, all-at-once. All assignments use the original values of the row as the source values, irrespective of their order of appearance. So the assignment col2 = col1 doesn't get the col1 value after the change, but rather before the change—namely 100. To verify this, run the previous code.

You get the following output:

```
keycol      col1        col2
----------- ----------- -----------
1           110         100
```

When you're done, run the following code for cleanup:

```
DROP TABLE IF EXISTS dbo.T1;
```

# Deleting data

T-SQL supports two statements that you can use to delete rows from a table: DELETE and TRUNCATE TABLE. This section describes these statements, the differences between them, and different aspects of working with them.

This section uses the same sample data that was used in the previous section. As a reminder, the sample data involves the tables Sales.MyCustomers, Sales.MyOrders, and Sales.MyOrderDetails, which are initially created as copies of the tables Sales.Customers, Sales.Orders, and Sales.OrderDetails, respectively. Use the following code to recreate tables and repopulate them with sample data:

```
DROP TABLE IF EXISTS Sales.MyOrderDetails, Sales.MyOrders, Sales.MyCustomers;

SELECT * INTO Sales.MyCustomers FROM Sales.Customers;
ALTER TABLE Sales.MyCustomers
  ADD CONSTRAINT PK_MyCustomers PRIMARY KEY(custid);

SELECT * INTO Sales.MyOrders FROM Sales.Orders;
ALTER TABLE Sales.MyOrders
  ADD CONSTRAINT PK_MyOrders PRIMARY KEY(orderid);

SELECT * INTO Sales.MyOrderDetails FROM Sales.OrderDetails;
ALTER TABLE Sales.MyOrderDetails
  ADD CONSTRAINT PK_MyOrderDetails PRIMARY KEY(orderid, productid);
```

## DELETE statement

With the DELETE statement, you can delete rows from a table. You can optionally specify a predicate to restrict the rows to be deleted. The general form of a DELETE statement looks like the following:

```
DELETE FROM <table>
WHERE <predicate>;
```

If you don't specify a predicate, all rows from the target table are deleted. As with un-qualified updates, you need to be especially careful about accidentally deleting all rows by highlighting only the DELETE part of the statement, missing the WHERE part.

The following example deletes all order lines containing product ID 11 from the Sales.MyOrderDetails table:

```
DELETE FROM Sales.MyOrderDetails
WHERE productid = 11;
```

You get a message indicating that 38 rows were affected.

The tables used by the examples in this chapter are very small, but in a more realistic pro-duction environment, the volumes of data are likely to be much bigger. A DELETE statement is fully logged (you can find details on the transaction log at *https://msdn.microsoft.com/en-us/library/ms190925.aspx*) and as a result, large deletes can take a long time to complete, and much longer to roll back if you need to terminate them. Such large deletes can cause the transaction log to increase in size dramatically during the process. They can also result in lock escalation, meaning that SQL Server escalates fine-grained locks like row or page locks to a full-blown table lock. Such escalation can result in blocking access to all table data by other processes. You can find details on locking at *https://technet.microsoft.com/en-us/library/ms190615(v=sql.105).aspx*.

To prevent the aforementioned problems from happening, you can split your large delete into smaller chunks. You can achieve this by using a DELETE statement with a TOP option that limits the number of affected rows in a loop. Here's an example for implementing such a solu-tion:

```
WHILE 1 = 1
BEGIN
  DELETE TOP (1000) FROM Sales.MyOrderDetails
  WHERE productid = 12;

  IF @@rowcount < 1000 BREAK;
END
```

As you can see, the code uses an infinite loop (WHILE 1 = 1 is always true). In each itera-tion, a DELETE statement with a TOP option limits the number of affected rows to no more than 1,000 at a time. Then the IF statement checks if the number of affected rows is less than 1,000; in such a case, the last iteration deleted the last chunk of qualifying rows. After the last chunk of rows has been deleted, the code breaks from the loop. With this sample data, there are only 14 qualifying rows in total. So if you run this code, it is done after one round, break from the loop, and return. But with a large number of qualifying rows, say, millions, you'd very likely be better off with such a solution.

**EXAM TIP**

Similar to the UPDATE WHERE CURRENT OF syntax, if you're using a cursor to iterate through rows of a table, you can delete the table row that the cursor is currently positioned on by using the syntax DELETE WHERE CURRENT OF. For example, suppose that you iterate through rows of a table called MyTable using a cursor called MyCursor. Based on some condition that is met, you want to delete the current row. You achieve this using the statement:

```
DELETE FROM dbo.MyTable WHERE CURRENT OF MyCursor;
```

## TRUNCATE TABLE statement

TRUNCATE TABLE is an optimized statement that deletes all rows from the target table or partition. Unlike the DELETE statement, the TRUNCATE TABLE statement doesn't support a filter. Also, whereas the DELETE statement is fully logged and therefore tends to be quite slow, the TRUNCATE table statement uses an optimized logging mode and therefore is significantly faster.

For example, the following statement truncates the table Sales.MyOrderDetails:

```
TRUNCATE TABLE Sales.MyOrderDetails;
```

Suppose that you had a partitioned table called MyTable and you wanted to truncate partitions 1, 2 and 11 to 20. You would achieve this with the following code:

```
TRUNCATE TABLE MyTable WITH ( PARTITIONS(1, 2, 11 TO 20) );
```

Besides the performance difference and the fact that TRUNCATE TABLE doesn't support a filter, there are a few additional differences compared to the DELETE statement:

- You cannot assign direct TRUNCATE TABLE permissions, rather at minimum you need ALTER permission on the target table. A common workaround is to place the TRUNCATE TABLE statement in a module, like a stored procedure, and assign the required permission to the module using the EXECUTE AS clause.

- If there's a column with an identity property in the target table, DELETE doesn't reset the property whereas TRUNCATE TABLE does.

- If there are any foreign keys pointing to the target table, a DELETE statement is supported as long as there are no related rows in the referencing table, but a TRUNCATE TABLE statement isn't. You need to first drop the foreign keys, truncate the table, and then recreate the foreign keys.

- If there are any indexed views based on the table, a DELETE statement is supported whereas a TRUNCATE TABLE statement isn't.

Clearly, if you need to delete all rows from a table or a partition but leave the table definition in place, the recommended tool to use is the TRUNCATE TABLE statement.

### DELETE based on a join

Much like the proprietary syntax that T-SQL supports for an UPDATE statement based on a join, T-SQL supports similar syntax for a DELETE statement based on a join. The idea is to allow you to delete rows from one table based on the presence of related rows in other tables, with the ability to apply a filter predicate that is based on attributes in the related tables.

As an example, the following statement deletes orders placed by customers from the US:

```
DELETE FROM O
FROM Sales.MyOrders AS O
  INNER JOIN Sales.MyCustomers AS C
    ON O.custid = C.custid
WHERE C.country = N'USA';
```

Notice that there are two FROM clauses. The second is mandatory and is similar to the FROM clause in a SELECT statement. That's where you apply table operators like joins. The first FROM clause appears right after the DELETE clause and is optional. That's where you specify the target for the delete. In our case it's the alias O representing the Sales.MyOrders table.

When you're done, run the following code for cleanup:

```
DROP TABLE IF EXISTS Sales.MyOrderDetails, Sales.MyOrders, Sales.MyCustomers;
```

## Merging data

With the MERGE statement, you can merge data from a source table into a target table. The statement has many practical uses in both online transaction processing (OLTP) scenarios and in data warehousing ones. As an example of an OLTP use case, suppose that you have a table that isn't updated directly by your application; instead, you get the delta of changes periodically from an external system. You first load the delta of changes into a staging table, and then use the staging table as the source for the merge operation into the target.

As an example for a data warehousing scenario, suppose that you maintain aggregated views of the data in your data warehouse. Using the MERGE statement, you can apply changes that were applied to detail rows into the aggregated form.

These are just a couple of typical use cases; there are many more. This lesson describes the MERGE statement and its different options, and demonstrates its use through examples.

### Using the MERGE statement

With the MERGE statement, you can merge data from a source table or table expression into a target table. This statement is mostly standard, with one proprietary extension by Microsoft of a clause called WHEN NOT MATCHED BY SOURCE. The general form of the MERGE statement is as follows:

```
MERGE INTO <target table> AS TGT
USING <SOURCE TABLE> AS SRC
  ON <merge predicate>
WHEN MATCHED [AND <predicate>] -- two clauses allowed:
  THEN <action> -- one with UPDATE one with DELETE
WHEN NOT MATCHED [BY TARGET] [AND <predicate>] -- one clause allowed:
  THEN INSERT... -- if indicated, action must be INSERT
WHEN NOT MATCHED BY SOURCE [AND <predicate>] -- two clauses allowed:
  THEN <action>; -- one with UPDATE one with DELETE
```

The following are the clauses of the statement and their roles:

- **MERGE INTO <target table>**   This clause defines the target table for the operation. You can alias the table in this clause if you want.

- **USING <source table>**   This clause defines the source table for the operation. You can alias the table in this clause if you want. Note that the USING clause is designed similar to a FROM clause in a SELECT query, meaning that in this clause you can define table operators like joins, refer to a table expression like a derived table or a common table expression (CTE), or even refer to a table function like OPENROWSET. The outcome of the USING clause is eventually a table result, and that table is considered the source of the merge operation.

- **ON <merge predicate>**   In this clause, you specify a predicate that matches rows between the source and the target and defines whether a source row is or isn't matched by a target row. Note that this clause isn't a filter like the ON clause in a join.

- **WHEN MATCHED [AND <predicate>] THEN <action>**   This clause defines an action to take when a source row is matched by a target row. Because a target row exists, an INSERT action isn't allowed in this clause. The two actions that are enabled are UPDATE and DELETE. If you want to apply different actions in different conditions, you can specify two WHEN MATCHED clauses, each with a different additional predicate to determine when to apply an UPDATE and when to apply a DELETE.

- **WHEN NOT MATCHED [BY TARGET] [AND <predicate>] THEN <action>**
  This clause defines what action to take when a source row is not matched by a target row. Because a target row does not exist, the only action allowed in this clause (if you choose to include this clause in the statement) is INSERT. Using UPDATE or DELETE holds no meaning when a target row doesn't exist. You can still add an additional predicate that must be true in order to perform the action.

- **WHEN NOT MATCHED BY SOURCE [AND <predicate>] THEN <action>**
  This clause is a proprietary extension by Microsoft to the standard MERGE statement syntax. It defines an action to take when a target row exists, but it is not matched by a source row. Because a target row exists, you can apply either an UPDATE or a DELETE, but not an INSERT. If you want, you can have two such clauses with different additional predicates that define when to use an UPDATE and when to use a DELETE.

To demonstrate examples of the MERGE statement, this section uses the Sales.MyOrders table and the Sales.SeqOrderIDs sequence. Use the following code to create these objects.

```
DROP TABLE IF EXISTS Sales.MyOrders;
DROP SEQUENCE IF EXISTS Sales.SeqOrderIDs;

CREATE SEQUENCE Sales.SeqOrderIDs AS INT
  MINVALUE 1
  CACHE 10000;

CREATE TABLE Sales.MyOrders
(
  orderid INT NOT NULL
    CONSTRAINT PK_MyOrders_orderid PRIMARY KEY
    CONSTRAINT DFT_MyOrders_orderid
      DEFAULT(NEXT VALUE FOR Sales.SeqOrderIDs),
  custid   INT NOT NULL
    CONSTRAINT CHK_MyOrders_custid CHECK(custid > 0),
  empid    INT NOT NULL
    CONSTRAINT CHK_MyOrders_empid CHECK(empid > 0),
  orderdate DATE NOT NULL
);
```

Notice that the sequence is defined to start with the value 1, and uses a cache size of 10,000 for performance reasons. The cache size defines how frequently to write a recoverable value to disk. To request a new key from the sequence, you use the function NEXT VALUE FOR <sequence_name>. Our code defines a default constraint with the function call for the orderid column to automate the creation of keys when new rows are inserted.

Suppose that you need to define a stored procedure that accepts as input parameters attributes of an order. If an order with the input order ID already exists in the Sales.MyOrders table, you need to update the row, setting the values of the nonkey columns to the new ones. If the order ID doesn't exist in the target table, you need to insert a new row. Because this book doesn't cover stored procedures until Chapter 3, the examples in this section use local variables for now. A MERGE statement in a stored procedure simply refers to the procedure's input parameters instead of the local variables.

The first things to identify in a MERGE statement are the target and the source tables. The target is easy—it's the Sales.MyOrders table. The source is supposed to be a table or table expression, but in this case, it's just a set of input parameters making an order. To turn the inputs into a table expression, you can define a derived table based on the VALUES clause, which is also known as a table value constructor. The following MERGE statement updates the target row if the source key exists in the target, and inserts a new row if it doesn't:

```
DECLARE
  @orderid   AS INT  = 1, @custid    AS INT  = 1,
  @empid     AS INT  = 2, @orderdate AS DATE = '20170212';

MERGE INTO Sales.MyOrders WITH (SERIALIZABLE) AS TGT
USING (VALUES(@orderid, @custid, @empid, @orderdate))
      AS SRC( orderid,  custid,  empid,  orderdate)
  ON SRC.orderid = TGT.orderid
WHEN MATCHED THEN
  UPDATE
    SET TGT.custid   = SRC.custid,
```

```
        TGT.empid       = SRC.empid,
        TGT.orderdate = SRC.orderdate
WHEN NOT MATCHED THEN
    INSERT VALUES(SRC.orderid, SRC.custid, SRC.empid, SRC.orderdate);
```

Observe that the MERGE predicate compares the source order ID with the target order ID. When a match is found (the source order ID is matched by a target order ID), the MERGE statement performs an UPDATE action that updates the values of the nonkey columns in the target to those from the respective source row.

When a match isn't found (the source order ID is not matched by a target order ID), the MERGE statement inserts a new row with the source order information into the target.

> **IMPORTANT  MERGE CONFLICTS**
>
> Suppose that a certain key K doesn't yet exist in the target table. Two processes, P1 and P2, run a MERGE statement such as the previous one at the same time with the same source key K. It is normally possible for the MERGE statement issued by P1 to insert a new row with the key K between the points in time when the MERGE statement issued by P2 checks whether the target already has that key and inserts rows. In such a case, the MERGE statement issued by P2 fails due to a primary key violation. To prevent such a failure, use the hint SERIALIZABLE or HOLDLOCK (both have equivalent meanings) against the target as shown in the previous statement. This hint means that the statement uses a serializable isolation level to serialize access to the data, meaning that once you get access to the data, it's as if you're the only one interacting with it.

Remember that you cleared the Sales.MyOrders table at the beginning of this section. So if you run the previous code for the first time, it performs an INSERT action against the target. If you run it a second time, it performs an UPDATE action.

Regarding the second run of the code, notice that it's a waste to issue an UPDATE action when the source and target rows are completely identical. An update costs you resources and time, and furthermore, if there are any triggers or auditing activity taking place, they consider the target row as updated. There is a way to avoid such an update when there's no real value change. Remember that each WHEN clause in the MERGE statement allows an additional predicate that must be true in order for the respective action to be applied. You can add a predicate that says that at least one of the nonkey column values in the source and the target must be different in order to apply the UPDATE action. Your code would look like the following:

```
DECLARE
    @orderid    AS INT  = 1, @custid    AS INT  = 1,
    @empid      AS INT  = 2, @orderdate AS DATE = '20170212';

MERGE INTO Sales.MyOrders WITH (SERIALIZABLE) AS TGT
USING (VALUES(@orderid, @custid, @empid, @orderdate))
        AS SRC( orderid,  custid,  empid,  orderdate)
    ON SRC.orderid = TGT.orderid
```

```
WHEN MATCHED AND (    TGT.custid      <> SRC.custid
                  OR TGT.empid       <> SRC.empid
                  OR TGT.orderdate <> SRC.orderdate) THEN
  UPDATE
    SET TGT.custid      = SRC.custid,
        TGT.empid       = SRC.empid,
        TGT.orderdate = SRC.orderdate
WHEN NOT MATCHED THEN
  INSERT VALUES(SRC.orderid, SRC.custid, SRC.empid, SRC.orderdate);
```

Note that if any of the nonkey columns use NULLs, you need to add extra logic for correct NULL treatment. For instance, suppose that the custid column used NULLs. The predicates for this column would be:

```
   TGT.custid <> SRC.custid
OR (TGT.custid IS NULL AND SRC.custid IS NOT NULL)
OR (TGT.custid IS NOT NULL AND SRC.custid IS NULL)
```

Alternatively, similar to the way you matched rows in a join using a set operator, you can identify a difference here between the source and target rows as follows:

```
WHEN MATCHED AND EXISTS( SELECT SRC.* EXCEPT SELECT TGT.* ) THEN UPDATE
```

Remember that a set operator uses distinctness in the comparison, and one NULL is distinct from a non-NULL value, but not distinct from another NULL. When there is a difference between the source and target rows, the EXCEPT operator returns one row, the EXISTS predicate returns true, and the MERGE statement applies the update. When the source and target rows are the same, the set operator yields an empty set, EXISTS returns false, and the MERGE statement doesn't proceed with the update.

What's interesting about the USING clause where you define the source for the MERGE operation is that it's designed like the FROM clause in a SELECT statement. This means that you can define table operators like JOIN, APPLY, PIVOT, and UNPIVOT; and use table expressions like derived tables, CTEs, views, inline table functions, and even table functions like OPENROWSET and OPENXML. You can refer to real tables, temporary tables, or table variables as the source. Ultimately, the USING clause returns a table result, and that table result is used as the source for the MERGE statement.

T-SQL extends standard SQL by supporting a third clause called WHEN NOT MATCHED BY SOURCE. With this clause, you can define an action to take against the target row when the target row exists but is not matched by a source row. The allowed actions are UPDATE and DELETE. For example, suppose that you want to add such a clause to the last example to indicate that if a target row exists and it is not matched by a source row, you want to delete the target row. Here's how your MERGE statement would look (this time using a table variable with multiple orders as the source):

```
DECLARE @Orders AS TABLE
(
  orderid   INT  NOT NULL PRIMARY KEY,
  custid    INT  NOT NULL,
  empid     INT  NOT NULL,
```

```
    orderdate DATE NOT NULL
);

INSERT INTO @Orders(orderid, custid, empid, orderdate)
    VALUES (2, 1, 3, '20170212'),
           (3, 2, 2, '20170212'),
           (4, 3, 5, '20170212');

-- update where exists (only if different), insert where not exists,
-- delete when exists in target but not in source
MERGE INTO Sales.MyOrders AS TGT
USING @Orders AS SRC
    ON SRC.orderid = TGT.orderid
WHEN MATCHED AND EXISTS( SELECT SRC.* EXCEPT SELECT TGT.* ) THEN
    UPDATE
      SET TGT.custid    = SRC.custid,
          TGT.empid     = SRC.empid,
          TGT.orderdate = SRC.orderdate
WHEN NOT MATCHED THEN
    INSERT VALUES(SRC.orderid, SRC.custid, SRC.empid, SRC.orderdate)
WHEN NOT MATCHED BY SOURCE THEN
    DELETE;
```

Before you ran this statement, only one row in the table had order ID 1. So the statement inserted the three rows with order IDs 2, 3, and 4, and deleted the row that had order ID 1. Query the current state of the table:

```
SELECT * FROM Sales.MyOrders;
```

You get the following output with the three remaining rows:

| orderid | custid | empid | orderdate |
| --- | --- | --- | --- |
| 2 | 1 | 3 | 2017-02-12 |
| 3 | 2 | 2 | 2017-02-12 |
| 4 | 3 | 5 | 2017-02-12 |

You can find more information about the MERGE statement at *http://sqlmag.com/sql-server/merge-statement-tips*.

## Using the OUTPUT option

T-SQL supports an OUTPUT clause for modification statements, which you can use to return information from modified rows. You can use the output for purposes like auditing, archiving and others. This section covers the OUTPUT clause with the different types of modification statements and demonstrates using the clause through examples. I use the same Sales.MyOrders table and Sales.SeqOrderIDs sequence from the Merging data section in my examples, so make sure you still have them around. Run the following code to clear the table and reset the sequence start value to 1:

```
TRUNCATE TABLE Sales.MyOrders;
ALTER SEQUENCE Sales.SeqOrderIDs RESTART WITH 1;
```

The design of the OUTPUT clause is very similar to that of the SELECT clause in the sense that you can specify expressions and assign them with result column aliases. One difference from the SELECT clause is that, in the OUTPUT clause, when you refer to columns from the modified rows, you need to prefix the column names with the keywords *inserted* or *deleted*. Use the prefix inserted when the rows are inserted rows and the prefix deleted when they are deleted rows. In an UPDATE statement, inserted represents the state of the rows after the update and deleted represents the state before the update.

You can have the OUTPUT clause return a result set back to the caller much like a SELECT does. Or you can add an INTO clause to direct the output rows into a target table. In fact, you can have two OUTPUT clauses if you like—the first with INTO directing the rows into a table, and the second without INTO, returning a result set from the query. If you do use the INTO clause, the target table cannot participate in either side of a foreign key relationship and cannot have triggers defined on it.

## INSERT with OUTPUT

The OUTPUT clause can be used in an INSERT statement to return information from the inserted rows. An example for a practical use case is when you have a multi-row INSERT statement that generates new keys by using the identity property or a sequence, and you need to know which new keys were generated.

For example, suppose that you need to query the Sales.Orders table and insert orders shipped to Norway to the Sales.MyOrders table. You are not going to use the original order IDs in the target rows; instead, let the sequence object generate those for you. But you need to get back information from the INSERT statement about which order IDs were generated, plus additional columns from the inserted rows. To achieve this, simply add an OUTPUT clause to the INSERT statement right before the query. List the columns that you need to return from the inserted rows and prefix them with the keyword inserted, as follows:

```
INSERT INTO Sales.MyOrders(custid, empid, orderdate)
  OUTPUT
    inserted.orderid, inserted.custid, inserted.empid, inserted.orderdate
  SELECT custid, empid, orderdate
  FROM Sales.Orders
  WHERE shipcountry = N'Norway';
```

This code generates the following output:

| orderid | custid | empid | orderdate |
|---------|--------|-------|-----------|
| 1 | 70 | 1 | 2014-12-18 |
| 2 | 70 | 7 | 2015-04-29 |
| 3 | 70 | 7 | 2015-08-20 |
| 4 | 70 | 3 | 2016-01-14 |
| 5 | 70 | 1 | 2016-02-26 |
| 6 | 70 | 2 | 2016-04-10 |

You can see that the sequence object generated the order IDs 1 through 6 for the new rows. If you need to store the result in a table instead of returning it back to the caller, add an INTO clause with an existing target table name as follows:

```
OUTPUT
  inserted.orderid, inserted.custid, inserted.empid, inserted.orderdate
  INTO SomeTable(orderid, custid, empid, orderdate)
```

In an INSERT statement you're not allowed to use the deleted prefix given how there are no deleted rows.

## DELETE with OUTPUT

You can use the OUTPUT clause to return information from deleted rows in a DELETE statement. You need to prefix the columns that you refer to with the keyword deleted. In a DELETE statement you're not allowed to use the inserted prefix given that there are no inserted rows.

The following example deletes the rows from the Sales.MyOrders table where the employee ID is equal to 1. Using the OUTPUT clause, the code returns the order IDs of the deleted orders:

```
DELETE FROM Sales.MyOrders
  OUTPUT deleted.orderid
WHERE empid = 1;
```

This code generates the following output:

```
orderid
-----------
1
5
```

Remember that if you need to persist the output rows in a table—for example, for archiving purposes—you can add an INTO clause with the target table name.

## UPDATE with OUTPUT

You can use the OUTPUT clause to return information from modified rows in an UPDATE statement. With updated rows, you have access to both the old and the new images of the modified rows. To refer to columns from the original state of the row before the update, prefix the column names with the keyword deleted. To refer to columns from the new state of the row after the update, prefix the column names with the keyword inserted.

As an example, the following UPDATE statement adds a day to the order date of all orders that were handled by employee 7:

```
UPDATE Sales.MyOrders
  SET orderdate = DATEADD(day, 1, orderdate)
  OUTPUT
    inserted.orderid,
    deleted.orderdate AS old_orderdate,
    inserted.orderdate AS neworderdate
WHERE empid = 7;
```

The code uses the OUTPUT clause to return the order IDs of the modified rows, in addition to the order dates—both before and after the update. This code generates the following output:

```
orderid    old_orderdate neworderdate
---------- ------------- ------------
2          2015-04-29    2015-04-30
3          2015-08-20    2015-08-21
```

## MERGE with OUTPUT

You can use the OUTPUT clause with the MERGE statement, but there are special considerations with this statement. Remember that one MERGE statement can apply different actions against the target table. And suppose that when returning output rows, you need to know which action (INSERT, UPDATE, or DELETE) affected the output row. For this purpose, SQL Server provides you with the $action function. This function returns a string ('INSERT', 'UPDATE', or 'DELETE') indicating the action.

As explained before, you can refer to columns from the deleted rows with the deleted prefix and to columns from the inserted rows with the inserted prefix. Rows affected by an INSERT action have values in the inserted row and NULLs in the deleted row. Rows affected by a DELETE action have NULLs in the inserted row and values in the deleted row. Rows affected by an UPDATE action have values in both. So, for example, if you want to return the key of the affected row (assuming the key itself wasn't modified), you can use the expression COALESCE(inserted.orderid, deleted.orderid).

The following example demonstrates the use of the MERGE statement with the OUTPUT clause, returning the output of the $action function to indicate which action affected the row, and the key of the modified row:

```
MERGE INTO Sales.MyOrders AS TGT
USING (VALUES(1, 70, 1, '20151218'), (2, 70, 7, '20160429'), (3, 70, 7, '20160820'),
             (4, 70, 3, '20170114'), (5, 70, 1, '20170226'), (6, 70, 2, '20170410'))
      AS SRC(orderid, custid, empid, orderdate)
  ON SRC.orderid = TGT.orderid
WHEN MATCHED AND EXISTS( SELECT SRC.* EXCEPT SELECT TGT.* ) THEN
    UPDATE SET TGT.custid    = SRC.custid,
               TGT.empid     = SRC.empid,
               TGT.orderdate = SRC.orderdate
WHEN NOT MATCHED THEN
    INSERT VALUES(SRC.orderid, SRC.custid, SRC.empid, SRC.orderdate)
WHEN NOT MATCHED BY SOURCE THEN
    DELETE
OUTPUT
    $action AS the_action,
    COALESCE(inserted.orderid, deleted.orderid) AS orderid;
```

This code generates the following output:

```
the_action orderid
---------- -----------
INSERT     1
```

```
UPDATE    2
UPDATE    3
UPDATE    4
INSERT    5
UPDATE    6
```

The output shows that two rows were inserted and two were updated.

---

**EXAM TIP**

In INSERT, UPDATE, and DELETE statements, you can only refer to columns from the target table in the OUTPUT clause. In a MERGE statement you can refer to columns from both the target and the source. For example, suppose that in the multi-row INSERT example from the INSERT with OUTPUT section you wanted the OUTPUT clause to return both the source key and the target key. This cannot be done directly in the INSERT statement because you don't have access to the source table. You can achieve this with the MERGE statement instead. Because an INSERT action is only allowed when the merge predicate is false, simply use a condition that is always false, such as 1 = 2. The revised example would be as follows:

```
MERGE INTO Sales.MyOrders AS TGT
USING ( SELECT orderid, custid, empid, orderdate
        FROM Sales.Orders
        WHERE shipcountry = N'Norway' ) AS SRC
  ON 1 = 2
WHEN NOT MATCHED THEN
  INSERT(custid, empid, orderdate) VALUES(custid, empid, orderdate)
OUTPUT
  SRC.orderid AS srcorderid, inserted.orderid AS tgtorderid,
  inserted.custid, inserted.empid, inserted.orderdate;
```

---

At this point, run the following code to clear the table and reset the sequence start value to 1:

```
TRUNCATE TABLE Sales.MyOrders;
ALTER SEQUENCE Sales.SeqOrderIDs RESTART WITH 1;
```

## Nested DML

Suppose you need to capture output from a modification statement, but you are interested only in a subset of the output rows and not all of them. T-SQL has a solution for this in the form of *nested DML* (data manipulation language).

With T-SQL, you can define something that looks like a derived table based on a modification with an OUTPUT clause. Then you can have an outer INSERT SELECT statement against a target table, with the source table being this special derived table. The outer INSERT SELECT can have a WHERE clause that filters the output rows from the derived table, inserting only the rows that satisfy the search condition into the target. The outer INSERT SELECT statement cannot have other elements besides WHERE like table operators, GROUP BY, HAVING, and so on.

As an example of nested DML, consider the previous MERGE statement. Suppose that you need to capture only the rows affected by an INSERT action in a table variable for further processing. You can achieve this by using the following code:

```
DECLARE @InsertedOrders AS TABLE
(
  orderid   INT  NOT NULL PRIMARY KEY,
  custid    INT  NOT NULL,
  empid     INT  NOT NULL,
  orderdate DATE NOT NULL
);

INSERT INTO @InsertedOrders(orderid, custid, empid, orderdate)
  SELECT orderid, custid, empid, orderdate
  FROM (MERGE INTO Sales.MyOrders AS TGT
    USING (VALUES(1, 70, 1, '20151218'), (2, 70, 7, '20160429'), (3, 70, 7, '20160820'),
               (4, 70, 3, '20170114'), (5, 70, 1, '20170226'), (6, 70, 2, '20170410'))
           AS SRC(orderid, custid, empid, orderdate)
       ON SRC.orderid = TGT.orderid
      WHEN MATCHED AND EXISTS( SELECT SRC.* EXCEPT SELECT TGT.* ) THEN
        UPDATE SET TGT.custid    = SRC.custid,
                   TGT.empid     = SRC.empid,
                   TGT.orderdate = SRC.orderdate
      WHEN NOT MATCHED THEN
        INSERT VALUES(SRC.orderid, SRC.custid, SRC.empid, SRC.orderdate)
      WHEN NOT MATCHED BY SOURCE THEN
        DELETE
      OUTPUT
        $action AS the_action, inserted.*) AS D
  WHERE the_action = 'INSERT';

SELECT * FROM @InsertedOrders;
```

Notice the derived table D that is defined based on the MERGE statement with the OUTPUT clause. The OUTPUT clause returns, among other things, the result of the $action function, naming the target column the_action. The code uses an INSERT SELECT statement with the source being the derived table D and the target table being the table variable @InsertedOrders. The WHERE clause in the outer query filters only the rows that have the INSERT action.

When you run the previous code for the first time, you get the following output:

```
orderid     custid      empid       orderdate
----------- ----------- ----------- ----------
1           70          1           2015-12-18
2           70          7           2016-04-29
3           70          7           2016-08-20
4           70          3           2017-01-14
5           70          1           2017-02-26
6           70          2           2017-04-10
```

Run it for the second time. It should return an empty set this time.

# Impact of structural changes on data

This section describes the impact of structural changes like adding, dropping, and altering columns on data. In the examples in this section I use the Sales.MyOrders table and Sales. SeqOrderIDs sequence from the Merging data section. Run the following code to populate the table with initial sample data:

```
TRUNCATE TABLE Sales.MyOrders;
ALTER SEQUENCE Sales.SeqOrderIDs RESTART WITH 1;
INSERT INTO Sales.MyOrders(custid, empid, orderdate)
  VALUES(70, 1, '20151218'), (70, 7, '20160429'), (70, 7, '20160820'),
        (70, 3, '20170114'), (70, 1, '20170226'), (70, 2, '20170410');
```

## Adding a column

In order to add a column to a table, you use the following syntax:

```
ALTER TABLE < table_name > ADD <column_definition> [<column_constraint>] [WITH VALUES];
```

If the table is empty, you can add a column that doesn't allow NULLs and also doesn't get its values somehow automatically. If the table isn't empty, such an attempt fails. To demonstrate this, run the following code:

```
ALTER TABLE Sales.MyOrders ADD requireddate DATE NOT NULL;
```

This attempt fails with the following error:

```
Msg 4901, Level 16, State 1, Line 608
ALTER TABLE only allows columns to be added that can contain nulls, or have a DEFAULT
definition specified, or the column being added is an identity or timestamp column, or
alternatively if none of the previous conditions are satisfied the table must be empty
to allow addition of this column. Column 'requireddate' cannot be added to non-empty
table 'MyOrders' because it does not satisfy these conditions.
```

Read the error message carefully. Observe that in order to add a column to a nonempty table, the column either needs to allow NULLs, or somehow get its values automatically. For instance, you can associate a default constraint with the column when you add it. You can also indicate that you want the default expression to be applied to the existing rows by adding the WITH VALUES clause as follows:

```
ALTER TABLE Sales.MyOrders
  ADD requireddate DATE NOT NULL
  CONSTRAINT DFT_MyOrders_requireddate DEFAULT ('19000101') WITH VALUES;
```

Note that if the column is defined as NOT NULL as in our case, the default expression is applied with or without this clause. If the column allows NULLs, without the clause a NULL is used and with the clause the default expression is used.

Query the table after adding this column and notice that the requireddate is January 1, 1900 in all rows.

## Dropping a column

In order to drop a column from a table, you use the following syntax:

```
ALTER TABLE <table_name> DROP COLUMN <column_name>;
```

The attempt to drop the column fails when the column:

- Is used in an index.
- Is used in a default, check, foreign key, unique, or primary key constraint.
- Is bound to a default object or a rule.

For example, try to drop the requireddate column by running the following code:

```
ALTER TABLE Sales.MyOrders DROP COLUMN requireddate;
```

This attempt fails because there's a default constraint associated with the column. You get the following error:

```
Msg 5074, Level 16, State 1, Line 631
The object 'DFT_MyOrders_requireddate' is dependent on column 'requireddate'.
Msg 4922, Level 16, State 9, Line 631
ALTER TABLE DROP COLUMN requireddate failed because one or more objects access this
column.
```

In order to drop the column, you need to drop the constraint first.

## Altering a column

In order to alter a column, you use the following syntax:

```
ALTER TABLE <table_name> ALTER COLUMN <column_definition> WITH ( ONLINE = ON | OFF );
```

There are a number of cases where the attempt to alter the column fails (partial list):

- When used in a primary key or foreign key constraint.
- When used in a check or unique constraint, unless you're just keeping or increasing the length of a variable-length column.
- When used in a default constraint, unless you're changing the length, precision, or scale of a column as long as the data type is not changed.

As an example, run the following code in attempt to change the data type of the requireddate column from DATE to DATETIME:

```
ALTER TABLE Sales.MyOrders ALTER COLUMN requireddate DATETIME NOT NULL;
```

This attempts fails with the following error because there's a default constraint associated with the column.

```
Msg 5074, Level 16, State 1, Line 649
The object 'DFT_MyOrders_requireddate' is dependent on column 'requireddate'.
Msg 4922, Level 16, State 9, Line 649
ALTER TABLE ALTER COLUMN requireddate failed because one or more objects access this
column.
```

In terms of nullability, if a column is included in a primary key constraint you cannot alter it from NOT NULL to NULL, otherwise you can. For example, run the following code:

```
ALTER TABLE Sales.MyOrders ALTER COLUMN requireddate DATE NULL;
```

This code completes successfully.

As for altering a column that allows NULLs to not allowing NULLs, this is allowed as long as there are no NULLs present in the data. Run the following code:

```
ALTER TABLE Sales.MyOrders ALTER COLUMN requireddate DATE NOT NULL;
```

This code completes successfully.

If there are NULLs present in the data, an attempt to add the NOT NULL constraint fails. In a similar way, attempting to add a primary key or unique constraint fails if duplicates exist in the data. With check and foreign key constraints you do have control over whether existing data is verified or not. By default SQL Server uses a WITH CHECK mode that verifies that the existing data meets the constraint's requirements, and fails the attempt to add the constraint if the data is invalid. However, you can specify the WITH NOCHECK option to ask SQL Server not to verify existing data.

For many column alteration operations, SQL Server supports indicating the option ONLINE = ON (it is OFF by default). With this option set to ON, the table is available while the alter operation is in progress. Examples for operations that can be done online include a change in the data type, nullability, precision, length and others.

If you need to alter a column to start or stop getting its values from a sequence object you can achieve this easily by either adding or dropping a default constraint with the NEXT VALUE FOR function call. For instance, the orderid column in the Sales.MyOrders table gets its values from the Sales.SeqOrderIDs sequence using a default constraint. To drop the default constraint from the existing table, use the following code:

```
ALTER TABLE Sales.MyOrders DROP CONSTRAINT DFT_MyOrders_orderid;
```

To add the constraint, use the following code:

```
ALTER TABLE Sales.MyOrders ADD CONSTRAINT DFT_MyOrders_orderid
  DEFAULT(NEXT VALUE FOR Sales.SeqOrderIDs) FOR orderid;
```

With identity, it's not that simple. You're not allowed to alter a column to add or remove the identity property. So if you need to apply such a change, it's a very expensive offline operation that involves creating another table, copying the data, dropping the original table, and renaming the new table to the original table name.

**EXAM TIP**

Despite the fact that the exam tries to measure your real life knowledge and proficiency with the subject matter, keep in mind that the exam puts you in different conditions than in real life. For example, when you take the exam you don't have access to any online or offline resources, unlike in life. This means that you need to memorize the syntax of the different T-SQL statements that are covered by the exam. Also, try to focus on what the question is asking exactly, and what seems to be the most correct answer to the question, as opposed to what is considered the best practice or how you would have done things.

For more information about altering tables see the official documentation on the topic at *https://msdn.microsoft.com/en-us/library/ms190273.aspx.*

When you're done, run the following code for cleanup:

```
DROP TABLE IF EXISTS Sales.MyOrders;
DROP SEQUENCE IF EXISTS Sales.SeqOrderIDs;
```

# Chapter summary

- Understanding the foundations of T-SQL is key to writing correct and robust code.
- Logical query processing describes the conceptual interpretation of a query, and evaluates the major query clauses in the following order: FROM, WHERE, GROUP BY, HAVING, SELECT, ORDER BY.
- Use the WHERE clause to filter data based on predicates and always remember to think of NULLs and the three-valued-logic (true, false and unknown).
- Use the ORDER BY clause in the outer query to apply presentation ordering to the query result, and remember that a query without an order by clause does not guarantee presentation order, despite any observed behavior.
- Use the UNION, UNION ALL, INTERSECT and EXCEPT operators to combine query results. These operators use distinctness-based comparison unlike the WHERE, ON and HAVING clauses, which use equality-based comparison.
- Joins allow you to combine rows from tables and return both matched attributes and additional attributes from both sides.
- Cross joins return a Cartesian product of the two inputs.
- Inner joins return only matching rows from the two sides.
- Outer joins return both matching rows and rows without matches from the nonpreserved side or sides.
- In an outer join the ON clauses serves a matching purpose and the WHERE clause a filtering purpose.

- If NULLs are present in the join columns you need to add special handling. Avoid applying manipulation on the join columns to preserve the data's ordering property and allow efficient use of indexing.

- T-SQL provides you with built-in functions of various categories such as string, date and time, conversion, system, and others.

- Scalar-valued functions return a single value; table-valued functions return a table result and are used in the FROM clause of a query. Aggregate functions are applied to a set and return a single value, and can be used in grouped queries and windowed queries.

- When at all possible, try to avoid applying manipulation to filtered columns to enable filter sargability and efficient use of indexes.

- Function determinism determines whether the function is guaranteed to return the same output given the same set of inputs.

- T-SQL supports the following statements to modify data: INSERT, SELECT INTO, UPDATE, DELETE, TRUNCATE TABLE, and MERGE.

- Use the OUTPUT clause in a modification statement to return data from the modified rows for purposes like auditing, archiving, and others. You can either return the result set to the caller, or write it to a table using the INTO clause.

- Make sure you understand the impact that structural changes to a table like adding, altering and dropping columns have on existing data.

# Thought experiment

In this thought experiment, demonstrate your skills and knowledge of the topics covered in this chapter. You can find the answer to this thought experiment in the next section.

You're being interviewed for a T-SQL developer role in the IT department of a large technology company. Answer the following questions to the best of your knowledge:

1. How come you cannot use an alias you define in the SELECT list in the WHERE clause, or even the same SELECT clause? Where can you use such an alias?

2. What are the differences between joins and set operators?

3. What could prevent SQL Server from treating a query filter optimally, meaning, from using an index efficiently to support the filter? What other query elements could also be affected in a similar manner and what can you do to get optimal treatment?

4. What is the difference between the ON and WHERE clauses?

5. Explain what function determinism means and what are the implications of using non-deterministic functions?

6. What are the differences between DELETE and TRUNCATE TABLE?

7. You need to perform a multi-row insert into a target table that has a column with an identity property. You need to capture the newly generated identity values for further processing. How can you achieve this?

8. When should you use the WITH VALUES clause explicitly as part of adding a column to a table?

# Thought experiment answer

This section contains the solution to the thought experiment.

1. According to logical query processing, which describes the conceptual interpretation of a query, the order in which the major query clauses are interpreted is: FROM, WHERE, GROUP BY, HAVING, SELECT, ORDER BY. You cannot use an alias that is created in the SELECT clause in clauses that are processed in an earlier step. This explains why you cannot use such an alias in the FROM, WHERE, GROUP BY and HAVING clauses. As for why you cannot use such an alias in other expressions in the same SELECT clause, that's because all expressions that appear in the same logical query-processing step are treated as a set, and a set has no order. The only clause that can refer to aliases that are created in the SELECT clause is the ORDER BY clause, because that's the only clause that is evaluated after the SELECT clause.

2. A join can compare a subset of the elements from the input tables while returning elements that it doesn't compare. Also, a join uses equality (or inequality) based comparison as the join predicate, whereas a comparison between two NULLs or between a NULL and anything yields unknown. A set operator implicitly compares all expressions in corresponding positions in the two input queries. Also, a set operator uses distinctness-based comparison, whereas a comparison between two NULLs yields true, and a comparison between a NULL and a non-NULL value yields false.

3. Manipulation of the filtered column in most cases prevents the filter's sargability. This means that the optimizer cannot rely on index order, for instance, to perform a seek within the index. In a similar way, manipulation of a column can prevent the optimizer from relying on index order for purposes of joining, grouping, and ordering.

4. In an outer join the ON clause serves a matching purpose. It determines which rows from the preserved side get matched with which rows from the non-preserved side. It cannot determine which rows from the preserved side of the join are returned—it's predetermined that all of them are returned. The WHERE clause serves a simpler filtering meaning. It determines which rows from the result of the FROM clause to keep and which to discard. In an inner join both ON and WHERE serve the same simple filtering meaning.

5. A function is said to be deterministic if given the same set of input values it is guaranteed to return repeatable results, otherwise it is said to be nondeterministic. If you use a nondeterministic function in a computed column, you cannot create an index on that

column. Similarly, if you use a nondeterministic function in a view, you cannot create a clustered index on the view.

6. DELETE supports a filter, is fully logged, and does not reset the current identity value. TRUNCATE TABLE has no filter, is minimally logged and therefore much faster than DELETE, and does reset the current identity value. Unlike DELETE, TRUNCATE TABLE is disallowed if there's an indexed view based on the table, or a foreign key pointing to the table, even if there are no related rows in the referencing table.

7. Use the OUTPUT clause and write the newly generated identity values along with any other data that you need from the inserted rows aside, for example into a table variable. You can then use the data from the table variable in the next step where you apply further processing.

8. When the column is defined as a nullable one, and you want to apply the default expression that is associated with the column in the new rows, you need to specify the WITH VALUES clause explicitly. If the column is defined as NOT NULL, and you associate a default expression with it, the default expression is applied even when not specifying the WITH VALUES clause explicitly.

# Query data with advanced Transact-SQL components

This chapter covers a number of T-SQL components that allow you to manipulate and analyze data, some of which might be considered more advanced than the ones covered in Chapter 1, "Manage data with Transact-SQL." You will learn how to nest queries and use the APPLY operator, work with table expressions, apply data analysis calculations with grouping, pivoting, and windowing, query historical data from temporal tables, and query and output XML and JSON data.

## Skills in this chapter:

- Query data by using subqueries and APPLY
- Query data by using table expressions
- Group and pivot data by using queries
- Query temporal data and non-relational data

## Skill 2.1: Query data by using subqueries and APPLY

This skill focuses on the nesting of queries, known as subqueries, and the APPLY operator, which allows you to apply a table subquery to each row from some table.

> **This section covers how to:**
> - Determine the results of queries using subqueries and table joins
> - Evaluate performance differences between table joins and correlated subqueries based on provided data and query plans
> - Distinguish between the use of CROSS APPLY and OUTER APPLY
> - Write APPLY statements that return a given data set based on supplied data

# Subqueries

Subqueries can be self-contained—independent of the outer query; or they can be corre-lated—namely, having a reference to a column from the table in the outer query. In terms of the result of the subquery, it can be scalar, multi-valued (table with a single column), or multi-column table-valued (table with multiple columns).

This section starts by covering the simpler self-contained subqueries, and then continues to correlated subqueries.

## Self-contained subqueries

*Self-contained subqueries* are subqueries that have no dependency on the outer query. If you want, you can highlight the inner query in SSMS and run it independently. This makes the troubleshooting of problems with self-contained subqueries easier compared to correlated subqueries.

As mentioned, a subquery can return different forms of results. It can return a single value, table with multiple values in a single column, or even a multi-column table result. Table-val-ued subqueries, or table expressions, are discussed in Skill 2.2 later in this chapter.

Subqueries that return a single value, or scalar subqueries, can be used where a single-val-ued expression is expected, like in one side of a comparison. For example, the following query uses a self-contained subquery to return the products with the minimum unit price:

```
USE TSQLV4;

SELECT productid, productname, unitprice
FROM Production.Products
WHERE unitprice =
  (SELECT MIN(unitprice)
   FROM Production.Products);
```

Here's the output of this query.

```
productid   productname      unitprice
----------  ---------------  ----------
33          Product ASTMN    2.50
```

As you can see, the subquery returns the minimum unit price from the Production. Products table. The outer query then returns information about products with the minimum unit price. Try highlighting only the inner query and executing it, and you will find that this is possible.

Note that if what's supposed to be a scalar subquery returns in practice more than one value, the code fails at run time. If the scalar subquery returns an empty set, it is converted to a NULL.

A subquery can also return multiple values in the form of a single column and multiple rows. Such a subquery can be used where a multi-valued result is expected—for example, when using the IN predicate. As an example, the following query uses a multi-valued sub-query to return products supplied by suppliers from Japan.

```
SELECT productid, productname, unitprice
FROM Production.Products
WHERE supplierid IN
  (SELECT supplierid
   FROM Production.Suppliers
   WHERE country = N'Japan');
```

This query generates the following output.

```
productid   productname      unitprice
----------  --------------   ----------
9           Product AOZBW    97.00
10          Product YHXGE    31.00
13          Product POXFU    6.00
14          Product PWCJB    23.25
15          Product KSZOI    15.50
74          Product BKAZJ    10.00
```

The inner query returns supplier IDs of suppliers from Japan. The outer query then returns information about products whose supplier ID is in the set returned by the subquery. As with predicates in general, you can negate an IN predicate, so if you wanted to return products supplied by suppliers that are not from Japan, simply change IN to NOT IN.

T-SQL supports a few esoteric predicates that operate on subqueries. Those are ALL, ANY and SOME. They are rarely used because there are usually simpler and more intuitive alternatives, but since there's a chance that they will be mentioned in the exam, you want to make sure that you are familiar with them. Following is the form for using these elements:

```
SELECT <select_list>
FROM <table>
WHERE <expression> <operator> {ALL | ANY | SOME} (<subquery>);
```

The ALL predicate returns true only if when applying the operator to the input expression and all values returned by the subquery, you get a true in all cases. For example, the following query is an alternative solution to the one shown earlier for returning the product with the minimum unit price:

```
SELECT productid, productname, unitprice
FROM Production.Products
WHERE unitprice <= ALL (SELECT unitprice FROM Production.Products);
```

The way the query is phrased is "return the products where the unit price is less than or equal to all product unit prices."

The ANY and SOME predicates have identical meaning. Suffice that you get a true for at least one of the values returned by the subquery for the whole predicate to return true. As an example, the following query returns all products with a unit price that is greater than the minimum.

```
SELECT productid, productname, unitprice
FROM Production.Products
WHERE unitprice > ANY (SELECT unitprice FROM Production.Products);
```

The way the query is phrased is "return the products where the unit price is greater than any product unit prices." This will be false only for the product with the minimum price.

## Correlated subqueries

*Correlated subqueries* are subqueries where the inner query has a reference to a column from the table in the outer query. They are trickier to work with compared to self-contained subqueries because you can't just highlight the inner portion and run it independently.

As an example, suppose that you need to return products with the minimum unit price per category. You can use a correlated subquery to return the minimum unit price out of the products where the category ID is equal to the one in the outer row (the correlation), as follows:

```
SELECT categoryid, productid, productname, unitprice
FROM Production.Products AS P1
WHERE unitprice =
  (SELECT MIN(unitprice)
   FROM Production.Products AS P2
   WHERE P2.categoryid = P1.categoryid);
```

This query generates the following output:

| categoryid | productid | productname | unitprice |
| --- | --- | --- | --- |
| 1 | 24 | Product QOGNU | 4.50 |
| 2 | 3 | Product IMEHJ | 10.00 |
| 3 | 19 | Product XKXDO | 9.20 |
| 4 | 33 | Product ASTMN | 2.50 |
| 5 | 52 | Product QSRXF | 7.00 |
| 6 | 54 | Product QAQRL | 7.45 |
| 7 | 74 | Product BKAZJ | 10.00 |
| 8 | 13 | Product POXFU | 6.00 |

Notice that the outer query and the inner query refer to different instances of the same table, Production.Products. In order for the subquery to be able to distinguish between the two, you must assign different aliases to the different instances. The query assigns the alias P1 to the outer instance and P2 to the inner instance, and by using the table alias as a prefix, you can refer to columns in an unambiguous way. The subquery uses a correlation in the predicate P2.categoryid = P1.categoryid, meaning that it filters only the products where the category ID is equal to the one in the outer row. So, when the outer row has category ID 1, the inner query returns the minimum unit price out of all products where the category ID is 1. And when the outer row has category ID 2, the inner query returns the minimum unit price out of all the products where the category ID is 2; and so on.

As another example of a correlated subquery, the following query returns customers who placed orders on February 12, 2016:

```
SELECT custid, companyname
FROM Sales.Customers AS C
WHERE EXISTS
  (SELECT *
  FROM Sales.Orders AS O
  WHERE O.custid = C.custid
    AND O.orderdate = '20070212');
```

This query generates the following output:

```
custid  companyname
-------  ---------------
45      Customer QXPPT
48      Customer DVFMB
76      Customer SFOGW
```

The EXISTS predicate accepts a subquery as input and returns true when the subquery returns at least one row and false otherwise. In this case, the subquery returns orders placed by the customer whose ID is equal to the customer ID in the outer row (the correlation) and where the order date is February 12, 2016. So the outer query returns a customer only if there's at least one order placed by that customer on the date in question.

As a predicate, EXISTS doesn't need to return the result set of the subquery; rather, it returns only true or false, depending on whether the subquery returns any rows. For this reason, the query optimizer ignores the SELECT list of the subquery, and therefore, whatever you specify there will not affect optimization choices like index selection.

As with other predicates, you can negate the EXISTS predicate as well. The following query negates the previous query's predicate, returning customers who did not place orders on February 12, 2016:

```
SELECT custid, companyname
FROM Sales.Customers AS C
WHERE NOT EXISTS
  (SELECT *
  FROM Sales.Orders AS O
  WHERE O.custid = C.custid
    AND O.orderdate = '20160212');
```

This query generates the following output, shown here in abbreviated form:

```
custid  companyname
-------  ---------------
72      Customer AHPOP
58      Customer AHXHT
25      Customer AZJED
18      Customer BSVAR
91      Customer CCFIZ
...
```

## Optimization of subqueries versus joins

When comparing the performance of solutions using subqueries versus solutions using joins, you will find that it's not like one tool always performs better than the other. There are cases where you will get the same query execution plans for both, cases where subqueries perform better, and cases where joins perform better. Ultimately, in performance critical cases you will want to test solutions based on both tools. However, there are specific aspects of these tools where SQL Server is known to handle one better than the other that you want to make sure that you're aware of.

I'll start with an example where subqueries are optimized less efficiently than joins. If you have multiple subqueries that need to apply computations such as aggregates based on the same set of rows, SQL Server will perform a separate access to the data for each subquery. With a join, you can apply multiple aggregate calculations based on the same access to the data. For example, suppose that you need to query the Sales.Orders table and compute for each order the percent of the current freight value out of the customer total, as well as the difference from the customer average. You create the following covering index to support your solutions:

```
CREATE INDEX idx_cid_i_frt_oid
  ON Sales.Orders(custid) INCLUDE(freight, orderid);
```

Here's the solution for the task using correlated subqueries:

```
SELECT orderid, custid, freight,
  freight / ( SELECT SUM(O2.freight)
              FROM Sales.Orders AS O2
              WHERE O2.custid = O1.custid ) AS pctcust,
  freight - ( SELECT AVG(O3.freight)
              FROM Sales.Orders AS O3
              WHERE O3.custid = O1.custid ) AS diffavgcust
FROM Sales.Orders AS O1;
```

Here's the solution for the task using a derived table and a join:

```
SELECT O.orderid, O.custid, O.freight,
  freight / totalfreight AS pctcust,
  freight - avgfreight AS diffavgcust
FROM Sales.Orders AS O
  INNER JOIN ( SELECT custid, SUM(freight) AS totalfreight, AVG(freight) AS avgfreight
               FROM Sales.Orders
               GROUP BY custid ) AS A
    ON O.custid = A.custid;
```

The query in the derived table A (more on derived tables in Skill 2.2) computes the customer aggregates, and the outer query joins the detail and the aggregates based on a match between the customer IDs and computes the percent and difference from the average.

Figure 2-1 shows the execution plans for both solutions. Query 1 represents the solution with the subqueries and Query 2 represents the solution with the join.

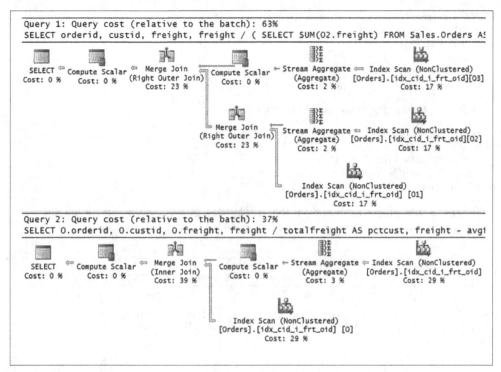

```
Query 1: Query cost (relative to the batch): 63%
SELECT orderid, custid, freight, freight / ( SELECT SUM(O2.freight) FROM Sales.Orders AS
```
SELECT    Compute Scalar    Merge Join    Compute Scalar  ← Stream Aggregate ⇐ Index Scan (NonClustered)
Cost: 0 %   Cost: 0 %   (Right Outer Join)   Cost: 0 %       (Aggregate)      [Orders].[idx_cid_i_frt_oid][O3]
                           Cost: 23 %                          Cost: 2 %             Cost: 17 %

                                    Merge Join   ← Stream Aggregate ⇐ Index Scan (NonClustered)
                                  (Right Outer Join)   (Aggregate)    [Orders].[idx_cid_i_frt_oid][O2]
                                     Cost: 23 %         Cost: 2 %           Cost: 17 %

                                              Index Scan (NonClustered)
                                            [Orders].[idx_cid_i_frt_oid] [O1]
                                                     Cost: 17 %

```
Query 2: Query cost (relative to the batch): 37%
SELECT O.orderid, O.custid, O.freight, freight / totalfreight AS pctcust, freight - avg1
```
SELECT    Compute Scalar    Merge Join    Compute Scalar  ← Stream Aggregate ⇐ Index Scan (NonClustered)
Cost: 0 %   Cost: 0 %    (Inner Join)    Cost: 0 %         (Aggregate)     [Orders].[idx_cid_i_frt_oid]
                          Cost: 39 %                          Cost: 3 %           Cost: 29 %

                                              Index Scan (NonClustered)
                                            [Orders].[idx_cid_i_frt_oid] [O]
                                                     Cost: 29 %

**FIGURE 2-1** Query plans for solutions that compute percent of total and difference from the average

Observe in the first plan that the index is accessed three times; once for the detail reference to the table (instance O1) and two additional times for the two subqueries (instances
O2 and O3). In the second plan the index is accessed only twice; once for the detail reference
(instance O), and only one more time for the computation of both aggregates. Also notice the
relative cost of each query plan out of the entire batch; the first plan costs twice as much as
the second.

When you're done, run the following code for cleanup:

```
DROP INDEX idx_cid_i_frt_oid ON Sales.Orders;
```

In the second example, consider a case where SQL Server optimizes subqueries better than
joins. For this example, first run the following code to add a shipper row into the Sales.Ship-
pers table:

```
INSERT INTO Sales.Shippers(companyname, phone)
  VALUES('Shipper XYZ', '(123) 456-7890');
```

Your task is to write a solution that returns shippers who didn't handle any orders yet. The
important index for this task is a nonclustered index on the shipperid column in the Sales.
Orders table, which already exists.

Here's a solution to the task based on a subquery.

```
SELECT S.shipperid
FROM Sales.Shippers AS S
WHERE NOT EXISTS
  (SELECT *
   FROM Sales.Orders AS O
   WHERE O.shipperid = S.shipperid);
```

Here's a solution to the task based on a join:

```
SELECT S.shipperid
FROM Sales.Shippers AS S
  LEFT OUTER JOIN Sales.Orders AS O
    ON S.shipperid = O.shipperid
WHERE O.orderid IS NULL;
```

Figure 2-2 shows the execution plans for both queries. Query 1 represents the solution based on the subquery and Query 2 represents the solution based on the join.

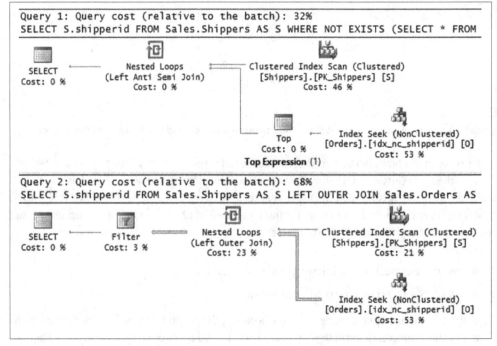

**FIGURE 2-2** Query plans for solutions that identify shippers without orders

Both plans use a Nested Loops algorithm to process the join. In this algorithm the outer input of the loop scans shipper rows from the Sales.Shippers table. For each shipper row, the inner input of the loop looks for matching orders in the nonclustered index on Sales.Orders. The key difference between the plans is that with the subquery-based solution the optimizer is capable of using a specialized optimization called Anti Semi Join. With this optimization, as soon as a match is found, the execution short circuits (notice the Top operator with the Top Expression property set to 1). With the join-based solution a shipper row is matched with all of its corresponding orders, and later the plan filters only the shippers that didn't have any matches. Observe the relative cost of each query plan out of the entire batch. The plan for the subquery-based solution costs less than half of the plan for the join-based solution. At the time of writing, SQL Server does not use the Anti Semi Join optimization for queries based on an actual join, but does so for queries based on subqueries and set operators.

When you're done, run the following code to delete the new shipper row:

```
DELETE FROM Sales.Shippers WHERE shipperid > 3;
```

In short, when optimizing your solutions, it's important to be informed about cases where one tool does better than another. Also, make sure to keep an open mind, test different solutions, compare their run times and query plans, and eventually choose the optimal one.

## The APPLY operator

The APPLY operator is a powerful operator that you can use to apply some query logic to each row from a table. The operator evaluates the left input first, and for each of its rows, applies a derived table query or table function that you provide as the right input. Let's refer to the right input in short as a table expression (more on table expressions in Skill 2.2). What's interesting about the APPLY operator as compared to a join is that a join treats its two inputs as a set of inputs, and recall that a set has no order. This means that if any of the join inputs is a query, you cannot refer in that query to elements from the other side. In other words—correlations aren't allowed. Conversely, the APPLY operator evaluates the left side first, and for each of the left rows, applies the table expression that you provide as the right input. As a result, the query in the right side can have references to elements from the left side. If this sounds similar to a correlated subquery, that's for a good reason. The references from the right side to elements from the left are correlations. However, with normal subqueries you're generally limited to returning only one column, whereas with an applied table expression you can return a whole table result with multiple columns and multiple rows. This means that you can replace the use of cursors in some cases with the APPLY operator.

For example, suppose that you have a query that performs some logic for a particular supplier. And let's also suppose that you need to apply this query logic to each supplier from the Production.Suppliers table. You could use a cursor to iterate through the suppliers, and in each iteration invoke the query for the current supplier. Instead, you can use the APPLY operator, providing the Production.Suppliers table as the left input, and a table expression based on your query as the right input. You can correlate the supplier ID in the inner query of the right table expression to the supplier ID from the left table.

The two forms of the APPLY operator—CROSS and OUTER—are described in the next sections.

Before running the code samples in these sections, add a row to the Suppliers table by running the following code:

```
INSERT INTO Production.Suppliers
```

```
(companyname, contactname, contacttitle, address, city, postalcode, country, phone)
VALUES(N'Supplier XYZ', N'Jiru', N'Head of Security', N'42 Sekimai Musashino-shi',
    N'Tokyo', N'01759', N'Japan', N'(02) 4311-2609');
```

## CROSS APPLY

The CROSS APPLY operator operates on left and right inputs. The right table expression can have a correlation to elements from the left table. The right table expression is applied to each row from the left input. What's special about the CROSS APPLY operator as compared to OUTER APPLY is that if the right table expression returns an empty set for a left row, the left row isn't returned. The reason that this operator is called *CROSS* APPLY is that per the left row, the operator behaves like a cross join between that row and the result set returned for it from the right input. Figure 2-3 shows an illustration of the CROSS APPLY operator.

**FIGURE 2-3** The CROSS APPLY operator

The letters X, Y, and Z represent key values from the left table. F represents the table expression provided as the right input, and in parentheses, you can see the key value from the left row passed as the correlated element. On the right side of the illustration, you can see the result returned from the right table expression for each left row. Then at the bottom, you can see the result of the CROSS APPLY operator, where left rows are matched with the respective right rows that were returned for them. Notice that a left row that gets an empty set back from the right table expression isn't returned. That's just like with a cross join between one row and zero rows; the result is an empty set. Such is the case with the row with the key value Z.

As an example, consider the following query, which returns the two products with the lowest unit prices for supplier 1:

```
SELECT TOP (2) productid, productname, unitprice
FROM Production.Products
WHERE supplierid = 1
ORDER BY unitprice, productid;
```

This query generates the following output.

```
productid   productname     unitprice
----------  --------------  ----------
3           Product IMEHJ   10.00
1           Product HHYDP   18.00
```

Suppose that you need to apply this logic to each of the suppliers from Japan that you have in the Production.Suppliers table. You don't want to use a cursor to iterate through the suppliers one at a time and invoke a separate query for each. Instead, you can use the CROSS APPLY operator, like so:

```
SELECT S.supplierid, S.companyname AS supplier, A.*
FROM Production.Suppliers AS S
  CROSS APPLY (SELECT TOP (2) productid, productname, unitprice
               FROM Production.Products AS P
               WHERE P.supplierid = S.supplierid
               ORDER BY unitprice, productid) AS A
WHERE S.country = N'Japan';
```

This query generates the following output.

```
supplierid   supplier          productid   productname     unitprice
-----------  ----------------  ----------  --------------  ----------
4            Supplier QOVFD    74          Product BKAZJ   10.00
4            Supplier QOVFD    10          Product YHXGE   31.00
6            Supplier QWUSF    13          Product POXFU   6.00
6            Supplier QWUSF    15          Product KSZOI   15.50
```

As you can see in the query, the left input to the APPLY operator is the Production.Suppliers table, with only suppliers from Japan filtered. The right table expression is a correlated derived table returning the two products with the lowest prices for the left supplier. Because the APPLY operator applies the right table expression to each supplier from the left, you get the two products with the lowest prices for each supplier from Japan. Because the CROSS

APPLY operator doesn't return left rows for which the right table expression returns an empty set, suppliers from Japan who don't have any related products aren't returned.

## OUTER APPLY

The OUTER APPLY operator extends what the CROSS APPLY operator does by also including in the result rows from the left side that get an empty set back from the right side. NULLs are used as placeholders for the result columns from the right side. In other words, the OUTER APPLY operator preserves the left side. In a sense, for each single left row, the difference between OUTER APPLY and CROSS APPLY is similar to the difference between a LEFT OUTER JOIN and a CROSS JOIN. Figure 2-4 shows an illustration of the OUTER APPLY operator:

**FIGURE 2-4** The OUTER APPLY operator

Observe that this time the left row with the key value Z is preserved.

Let's re-examine the example returning the two products with the lowest prices per supplier from Japan: If you use the OUTER APPLY operator instead of CROSS APPLY, you will preserve the left side. Here's the revised query.

```
SELECT S.supplierid, S.companyname AS supplier, A.*
FROM Production.Suppliers AS S
  OUTER APPLY (SELECT TOP (2) productid, productname, unitprice
               FROM Production.Products AS P
               WHERE P.supplierid = S.supplierid
               ORDER BY unitprice, productid) AS A
WHERE S.country = N'Japan';
```

Here's the output of this query.

```
supplierid  supplier          productid  productname      unitprice
----------  ---------------   ---------- --------------   ----------
4           Supplier QOVFD    74         Product BKAZJ    10.00
4           Supplier QOVFD    10         Product YHXGE    31.00
6           Supplier QWUSF    13         Product POXFU    6.00
6           Supplier QWUSF    15         Product KSZOI    15.50
30          Supplier XYZ      NULL       NULL             NULL
```

Observe that supplier 30 was preserved this time even though it has no related products.

When you're done, run the following code to delete the supplier row that you added earlier:

```
DELETE FROM Production.Suppliers WHERE supplierid > 29;
```

---

***MORE INFO*** **ON APPLY**

For more information and examples of creative uses of the APPLY operator, make sure to watch the Microsoft Virtual Academy video seminar "Boost your T-SQL with the APPLY operator" at *http://aka.ms/BoostTSQL* or at *https://channel9.msdn.com/Series/Boost-Your-T-SQL-With-the-APPLY-Operator*.

---

***MORE INFO*** **ON LOGICAL ASPECTS OF APPLY**

For details about the logical aspects of APPLY, see "Logical Query Processing: The FROM Clause and APPLY" at *http://sqlmag.com/sql-server/logical-query-processing-clause-and-apply*.

---

# Skill 2.2: Query data by using table expressions

This skill focuses on querying data by using table expressions. It starts with a description of what table expressions are, compares them to temporary tables, and then provides the details about the different kinds of table expressions.

## Table expressions, described

Table expressions are named queries. You write an inner query that returns a relational result set, name it, and query it from an outer query. T-SQL supports four forms of table expressions: derived tables, common table expressions (CTEs), views and inline table-valued functions.

The first two forms are visible only to the statement that defines them. As for the last two forms, you preserve the definition of the table expression in the database as an object; therefore, it's reusable, and you can also control access to the object with permissions.

Note that because a table expression is supposed to represent a relation, the inner query defining it needs to be relational. This means that all columns returned by the inner query must have names (use aliases if the column is a result of an expression), and all column names must be unique. Also, the inner query is not allowed to have an ORDER BY clause. (Remember, a set has no order.) There's an exception to the last rule: If you use the TOP or OFFSET-FETCH option in the inner query, the ORDER BY serves a meaning that is not related to presentation ordering; rather, it's part of the filter's specification. So if the inner query uses the TOP or OFFSET-FETCH option, it's allowed to have an ORDER BY clause as well. But then the outer query has no presentation ordering guarantees if it doesn't have its own ORDER BY clause.

## Table expressions or temporary tables?

It's important to note that, from a performance standpoint, when SQL Server optimizes queries involving table expressions, it first unnests, or inlines, the table expression's logic, and therefore interacts with the underlying tables directly. It does not somehow persist the table expression's result in an internal work table and then interact with that work table. If for optimization reasons you do need to persist the result of a query for further processing, you should be using a temporary table or table variable.

There are cases where the use of table expressions is more optimal than temporary tables. For instance, imagine that you need to query some table T1 only once, then interact with the result of that query from some outer query, and finally interact with the result of that outer query from yet another outer query. You do not want to pay the penalty of writing the intermediate results physically to some temporary table, rather, you want the physical processing to interact directly with the underlying table. To achieve this, define a table expression based on the query against T1, give it a name, say D1, and then write an outer query against D1. Behind the scenes, SQL Server will unnest, or inline, the logic of the inner queries, like pealing the layers of an onion, and the query plan will interact directly with T1.

There are cases where you will get more optimal treatment when using temporary tables (which you create like regular tables, and name with a # sign as a prefix, such as #T1) or table variables (which you declare, and name with the @ sign as a prefix, such as @T1). That's typically the case when you have some expensive query, like one that scans large tables, joins them, and groups and aggregates the data. You need to interact with that query result multiple times—whether with a single query that joins multiple instances of the result or with multiple separate queries. If you use a table expression, the physical treatment repeats the work for each reference. In such cases you want to persist the result of the expensive work in a temporary table or table variable, and then interact with that temporary object a number of times. Between table variables and temporary tables, the main difference from an optimization perspective is that SQL Server maintains full blown statistics on temporary tables but very minimal statistics on table variables. Therefore, cardinality estimates (estimates for row counts during optimization) tend to be more accurate with temporary tables. So, when dealing with very small amounts of data like just a few rows, typically it's recommended to use table variables since that's the assumption that the optimizer makes any way. With larger table sizes, the recommendation is to use temporary tables, to allow better estimates, that will hopefully result in more optimal plans.

The following sections describe the different forms of table expressions that T-SQL supports.

## Derived tables

A derived table is a named table subquery. You define the derived table's inner query in parentheses in the FROM clause of the outer query, and specify the name of the derived table after the parentheses.

Before demonstrating the use of derived tables, this section describes a query that returns a certain desired result. Then it explains a need that cannot be addressed directly in the query, and shows how you can address that need by using a derived table (or any other table expression type for that matter).

Consider the following query, which computes row numbers for products, partitioned by categoryid, and ordered by unitprice and productid:

```
USE TSQLV4;

SELECT
  ROW_NUMBER() OVER(PARTITION BY categoryid
                 ORDER BY unitprice, productid) AS rownum,
  categoryid, productid, productname, unitprice
FROM Production.Products;
```

This query generates the following output, shown here in abbreviated form:

```
rownum  categoryid  productid  productname    unitprice
-------  ----------  ---------  -------------  ----------
1        1           24         Product QOGNU  4.50
2        1           75         Product BWRLG  7.75
```

```
3        1              34      Product SWNJY  14.00
4        1              67      Product XLXQF  14.00
5        1              70      Product TOONT  15.00
...
1        2              3       Product IMEHJ  10.00
2        2              77      Product LUNZZ  13.00
3        2              15      Product KSZOI  15.50
4        2              66      Product LQMGN  17.00
5        2              44      Product VJIEO  19.45
...
```

You learn about the ROW_NUMBER function, as well as other window functions, in Skill 2.3; but for now, suffice it to say that the ROW_NUMBER function computes unique incrementing integers from 1 and is based on indicated ordering, possibly within partitions of rows. As you can see in the query's result, the ROW_NUMBER function generates unique incrementing integers starting with 1 based on unitprice and productid ordering, within each partition defined by categoryid.

The thing with the ROW_NUMBER function—and window functions in general—is that they are only allowed in the SELECT and ORDER BY clauses of a query. So, what if you want to filter rows based on such a function's result? For example, suppose you want to return only the rows where the row number is less than or equal to 2; namely, in each category you want to return the two products with the lowest unit prices, with the product ID used as a tiebreaker. You are not allowed to refer to the ROW_NUMBER function in the query's WHERE clause. Remember also that according to logical query processing, you're not allowed to refer to a column alias that was assigned in the SELECT list in the WHERE clause, because the WHERE clause is conceptually evaluated before the SELECT clause.

You can circumvent the restriction by using a table expression. You write a query such as the previous query that computes the window function in the SELECT clause, and assign a column alias to the result column. You then define a table expression based on that query, and refer to the column alias in the outer query's WHERE clause, like so:

```
SELECT categoryid, productid, productname, unitprice
FROM (SELECT
        ROW_NUMBER() OVER(PARTITION BY categoryid
                          ORDER BY unitprice, productid) AS rownum,
        categoryid, productid, productname, unitprice
      FROM Production.Products) AS D
WHERE rownum <= 2;
```

This query generates the following output, shown here in abbreviated form:

```
categoryid  productid  productname     unitprice
----------- ---------- --------------- ----------
1           24         Product QOGNU   4.50
1           75         Product BWRLG   7.75
2           3          Product IMEHJ   10.00
2           77         Product LUNZZ   13.00
3           19         Product XKXDO   9.20
3           47         Product EZZPR   9.50
...
```

As you can see, the derived table is defined in the FROM clause of the outer query in parentheses, followed by the derived table name. Then the outer query is allowed to refer to column aliases that were assigned by the inner query. That's a classic use of table expressions.

### EXAM TIP

During the exam pay attention to multi-choice questions where some of the suggested answers include invalid code. For instance, code that defines an alias in the SELECT list and refers to that alias in clauses that are evaluated before the SELECT, like the WHERE clause, or even the same SELECT clause itself. Make sure that you identify the answer with the valid syntax after eliminating the ones that are invalid.

Two column aliasing options are available to you when working with derived tables: both inline and external. With the inline form, you specify the column alias as part of the expression, as in <expression> AS alias. The last query used the inline form to assign the alias rownum to the expression with the ROW_NUMBER function. With the external aliasing form, you don't specify result column aliases as part of the column expressions; instead, you name all target columns right after the derived table's name, as in FROM (...) AS D(rownum, categoryid, productid, productname, unitprice). With the external form, you must specify all target column names and not just those that are results of computations. If you use both inline and external aliases, the external ones prevail as far as the outer query is concerned.

There are a couple of problematic aspects to working with derived tables that stem from the fact that a derived table is defined in the FROM clause of the outer query. One problem has to do with cases where you want to refer to one derived table from another. In such a case, you end up nesting derived tables, and nesting often complicates the logic, making it hard to follow and increasing the likelihood for errors. Consider the following general form of nesting of derived tables:

```
SELECT ...
FROM (SELECT
      FROM (SELECT ...
            FROM T1
            WHERE ...) AS D1
      WHERE ...) AS D2
WHERE ...;
```

The other problem with derived tables has to do with the fact that a join treats its two inputs as a set, meaning no order; the two inputs are evaluated in an *all-at-once* manner. As a result, if you define a derived table as the left input of the join, that derived table is not visible to the right input of the join. This means that if you want to join multiple instances of the same derived table, you can't. You have no choice but to duplicate the code, defining multiple derived tables based on the same query. The general form of such a query looks like this:

```
SELECT ...
FROM (SELECT ...
      FROM T1) AS D1
  INNER JOIN
```

```
            (SELECT ...
              FROM T1) AS D2
          ON ...;
```

The derived tables D1 and D2 are based on the same query. This repetition of code in-creases the likelihood for errors when you need to make revisions to the inner queries.

## Common table expressions

A common table expression (CTE) is a similar concept to a derived table in the sense that it's a named table expression that is visible only to the statement that defines it. Like a query against a derived table, a query against a CTE involves three main parts:

- The inner query

- The name you assign to the query and its columns

- The outer query

However, with CTEs, the arrangement of the three parts is different. Recall that with de-rived tables the inner query appears in the FROM clause of the outer query—in the middle of things. With CTEs, you first name the CTE, then specify the inner query, and then the outer query—a much more modular approach:

```
WITH <CTE_name>
AS
(
  <inner_query>
)
<outer_query>;
```

Recall the example from the section about derived tables where you returned for each product category the two products with the lowest unit prices. Here's how you can imple-ment the same task with a CTE:

```
WITH C AS
(
  SELECT
    ROW_NUMBER() OVER(PARTITION BY categoryid
                        ORDER BY unitprice, productid) AS rownum,
      categoryid, productid, productname, unitprice
  FROM Production.Products
)
SELECT categoryid, productid, productname, unitprice
FROM C
WHERE rownum <= 2;
```

As you can see, it's a similar concept to derived tables, except the inner query is not defined in the middle of the outer query. Instead, first you name the table expression, then define the inner query—from start to end—and then the outer query—from start to end. This design leads to much clearer code that is easier to understand.

You don't nest CTEs like you do derived tables. If you need to define multiple CTEs, you simply separate them by commas. Each can refer to the previously defined CTEs, and the outer query can refer to all of them. After the outer query terminates, all CTEs defined in that WITH statement are gone. The fact that you don't nest CTEs makes it easier to follow the logic and therefore reduces the chances for errors. For example, if you want to refer to one CTE from another, you can use the following general form:

```
WITH C1 AS
(
  SELECT ...
  FROM T1
  WHERE ...
),
C2 AS
(
  SELECT
  FROM  C1
  WHERE ...
)
SELECT ...
FROM C2
WHERE ...;
```

Because the CTE name is assigned before the start of the outer query, you can refer to multiple instances of the same CTE name, unlike with derived tables. The general form looks like the following.

```
WITH C AS
(
  SELECT ...
  FROM T1
)
SELECT ...
FROM C AS C1
  INNER JOIN C AS C2
    ON ...;
```

**EXAM TIP**

Since in the last example the outer query has multiple reference to the same CTE name, the underlying work is going to be repeated. If the inner query performs expensive work, and generates a fairly small result set, a table expression might not be the best choice. In such a case you should consider persisting the inner query's result in a temporary table first, and then joining two instances of that temporary table.

CTEs also have a recursive form. The body of the recursive query has two or more queries, usually separated by a UNION ALL operator. At least one of the queries in the CTE body, known as the anchor member, is a query that returns a valid relational result. The anchor query is invoked only once. In addition, at least one of the queries in the CTE body, known as the recursive member, has a reference to the CTE name. This query is invoked repeatedly until it returns an empty result set. In each iteration, the reference to the CTE name from the recursive member represents the previous result set. Then the reference to the CTE name from the outer query represents the unified results of the invocation of the anchor member and all invocations of the recursive member.

As an example, the following code uses a recursive CTE to return the management chain, leading all the way up to the CEO for a specified employee:

```
WITH EmpsCTE AS
(
  SELECT empid, mgrid, firstname, lastname, 0 AS distance
  FROM HR.Employees
  WHERE empid = 9

  UNION ALL

  SELECT M.empid, M.mgrid, M.firstname, M.lastname, S.distance + 1 AS distance
  FROM EmpsCTE AS S
    JOIN HR.Employees AS M
      ON S.mgrid = M.empid
)
SELECT empid, mgrid, firstname, lastname, distance
FROM EmpsCTE;
```

This code returns the following output.

| empid | mgrid | firstname | lastname | distance |
| --- | --- | --- | --- | --- |
| 9 | 5 | Patricia | Doyle | 0 |
| 5 | 2 | Sven | Mortensen | 1 |
| 2 | 1 | Don | Funk | 2 |
| 1 | NULL | Sara | Davis | 3 |

As you can see, the anchor member returns the row for employee 9. Then the recursive member is invoked repeatedly, and in each round joins the previous result set with the HR.Employees table to return the direct manager of the employee from the previous round. The recursive query stops as soon as it returns an empty set—in this case, after not finding a manager of the CEO. Then the outer query returns the unified results of the invocation of the anchor member (the row for employee 9) and all invocations of the recursive member (all managers above employee 9).

## Views and inline table-valued functions

As you learned in the previous sections, derived tables and CTEs are table expressions that are visible only in the scope of the statement that defines them. After that statement terminates, the table expression is gone. Hence, derived tables and CTEs are not reusable. For reusability, you need to store the definition of the table expression as an object in the database, and for this you can use either views or inline table-valued functions. Because these are objects in the database, you can control access by assigning permissions.

The main difference between views and inline table-valued functions is that the former doesn't accept input parameters and the latter does. As an example, suppose you need to persist the definition of the query with the row number computation from the examples in the previous sections. To achieve this, you create the following view:

```
DROP VIEW IF EXISTS Sales.RankedProducts;
GO
CREATE VIEW Sales.RankedProducts
AS

SELECT
  ROW_NUMBER() OVER(PARTITION BY categoryid
                    ORDER BY unitprice, productid) AS rownum,
  categoryid, productid, productname, unitprice
FROM Production.Products;
GO
```

Note that it's not the result set of the view that is stored in the database; rather, only its definition is stored. Now that the definition is stored, the object is reusable. Whenever you need to query the view, it's available to you, assuming you have the permissions to query it:

```
SELECT categoryid, productid, productname, unitprice
FROM Sales.RankedProducts
WHERE rownum <= 2;
```

As for inline table-valued functions, they are very similar to views in concept; however, as mentioned, they do support input parameters. So if you want to define something like a view with parameters, the closest you have is an inline table-valued function. As an example, consider the recursive CTE from the section about CTEs that retuned the management chain leading all the way up to the CEO for a specified employee. Suppose that you wanted to encapsulate the logic in a table expression for reusability, but also wanted to parameterize the input employee instead of using the constant 9. You can achieve this by using an inline table-valued function with the following definition:

```
DROP FUNCTION IF EXISTS HR.GetManagers;
GO
CREATE FUNCTION HR.GetManagers(@empid AS INT) RETURNS TABLE
AS

RETURN
  WITH EmpsCTE AS
  (
    SELECT empid, mgrid, firstname, lastname, 0 AS distance
    FROM HR.Employees
    WHERE empid = @empid

    UNION ALL

    SELECT M.empid, M.mgrid, M.firstname, M.lastname, S.distance + 1 AS distance
    FROM EmpsCTE AS S
      JOIN HR.Employees AS M
        ON S.mgrid = M.empid
  )
  SELECT empid, mgrid, firstname, lastname, distance
  FROM EmpsCTE;
GO
```

Observe that the header assigns the function with a name (HR.GetManagers), defines the input parameter (@empid AS INT), and indicates that the function returns a table result (defined by the returned query). Then the function has a RETURN clause returning the result of the recursive query, and the anchor member of the recursive CTE filters the employee whose ID is equal to the input employee ID. When querying the function, you pass a specific input employee ID as the following example shows:

```
SELECT *
FROM HR.GetManagers(9) AS M;
```

**EXAM TIP**

You're not limited to only issuing SELECT statements against table expressions, rather you can also modify data through them. The outer statement could be INSERT, UPDATE, DELETE and MERGE. Since the table expression is merely a reflection of data from some underlying table, it's the underlying table that is actually modified.

When you're done, run the following code for cleanup:

```
DROP VIEW IF EXISTS Sales.RankedProducts;
DROP FUNCTION IF EXISTS HR.GetManagers;
```

# Skill 2.3: Group and pivot data by using queries

This skill covers various data analysis tools that T-SQL supports. It covers aggregating data with both grouped queries and windowed queries. It covers the ability to group the data in multiple different ways by defining what's called grouping sets. It also covers data rotation with pivoting and unpivoting techniques.

> **This section covers how to:**
> - Use windowing functions to group and rank the results of a query
> - Distinguish between using windowing functions and GROUP BY
> - Construct complex GROUP BY clauses using GROUPING SETS, and CUBE
> - Construct PIVOT and UNPIVOT statements to return desired results based on supplied data
> - Determine the impact of NULL values in PIVOT and UNPIVOT queries

# Writing grouped queries

You can use grouped queries to define groups in your data, and then you can perform data analysis computations per group. You group the data by a set of expressions known as a grouping set. Traditional T-SQL queries define a single grouping set; namely, they group the data in only one way. T-SQL also supports defining multiple grouping sets in one query.

## Working with a single grouping set

With grouped queries, you can arrange the rows you're querying in groups and apply data analysis computations like aggregate functions against those groups. A query becomes a grouped query when you use a group function, a GROUP BY clause, or both.

A query that invokes a group aggregate function but doesn't have an explicit GROUP BY clause arranges all rows in one group. Such an aggregate is referred to as a *scalar aggregate*. Consider the following query as an example:

```
USE TSQLV4;

SELECT COUNT(*) AS numorders
FROM Sales.Orders;
```

This query generates the following output.

```
numorders
-----------
830
```

Because there's no explicit GROUP BY clause, all rows queried from the Sales.Orders table are arranged in one group, and then the COUNT(*) function counts the number of rows in that group. Grouped queries return one result row per group, and because the query defines only one group, it returns only one row in the result set.

Using an explicit GROUP BY clause, you can group the rows based on a specified grouping set of expressions. For example, the following query groups the rows by shipper ID and counts the number of rows (orders, in this case) per distinct group:

```
SELECT shipperid, COUNT(*) AS numorders
FROM Sales.Orders
GROUP BY shipperid;
```

This query generates the following output:

```
shipperid   numorders
----------- -----------
1           249
2           326
3           255
```

The query identifies three groups because there are three distinct shipper IDs.

The grouping set can be made of multiple elements. For example, the following query groups the rows by shipper ID and shipped year:

```
SELECT shipperid, YEAR(shippeddate) AS shippedyear,
    COUNT(*) AS numorders
FROM Sales.Orders
GROUP BY shipperid, YEAR(shippeddate);
```

This query generates the following output:

```
shipperid    shippedyear numorders
-----------  ----------- -----------
1            2014         36
2            2015         143
1            NULL         4
3            2016         73
3            NULL         6
3            2014         51
2            2016         116
2            NULL         11
1            2015         130
3            2015         125
1            2016         79
2            2014         56
```

Notice that you get a group for each distinct shipper ID and shipped year combination that exists in the data, even when the shipped year is NULL. Remember that a NULL in the shippeddate column represents unshipped orders, so a NULL in the shippedyear column represents the group of unshipped orders for the respective shipper.

If you need to filter entire groups, you need a filtering option that is evaluated at the group level—unlike the WHERE clause, which is evaluated at the row level. For this, T-SQL provides the HAVING clause. Like the WHERE clause, the HAVING clause uses a predicate but evaluates the predicate per group as opposed to per row. This means that you can refer to aggregate computations because the data has already been grouped.

For example, suppose that you need to group only shipped orders by shipper ID and shipping year, and filter only groups having fewer than 100 orders. You can use the following query to achieve this task:

```
SELECT shipperid, YEAR(shippeddate) AS shippedyear,
    COUNT(*) AS numorders
FROM Sales.Orders
WHERE shippeddate IS NOT NULL
GROUP BY shipperid, YEAR(shippeddate)
HAVING COUNT(*) < 100;
```

This query generates the following output.

```
shipperid    shippedyear numorders
-----------  ----------- -----------
1            2014        36
3            2016        73
3            2014        51
1            2016        79
2            2014        56
```

Notice that the query filters only shipped orders in the WHERE clause. This filter is applied at the row level conceptually before the data is grouped. Next the query groups the data by shipper ID and shipped year. Then the HAVING clause filters only groups that have a count of rows (orders) that is less than 100. Finally, the SELECT clause returns the shipper ID, shipped year, and count of orders per remaining group.

T-SQL supports a number of aggregate functions. Those include COUNT(*) and a few general set functions (as they are categorized by standard SQL) like COUNT, SUM, AVG, MIN, and MAX. General set functions are applied to an expression and ignore NULLs.

The following query invokes the COUNT(*) function, in addition to a number of general set functions, including COUNT:

```
SELECT shipperid,
  COUNT(*) AS numorders,
  COUNT(shippeddate) AS shippedorders,
  MIN(shippeddate) AS firstshipdate,
  MAX(shippeddate) AS lastshipdate,
  SUM(val) AS totalvalue
FROM Sales.OrderValues
GROUP BY shipperid;
```

This query generates the following output:

```
shipperid    numorders    shippedorders firstshipdate lastshipdate totalvalue
-----------  -----------  ------------- ------------- ------------ ----------
3            255          249           2014-07-15    2016-05-01   383405.53
1            249          245           2014-07-10    2016-05-04   348840.00
2            326          315           2014-07-11    2016-05-06   533547.69
```

Notice the difference between the results of COUNT(shippeddate) and COUNT(*). The former ignores NULLs in the shippeddate column, and therefore the counts are less than or equal to those produced by the latter.

With aggregate functions, you can work with distinct occurrences by specifying a DISTINCT clause before the expression, as follows:

```
SELECT shipperid, COUNT(DISTINCT shippeddate) AS numshippingdates
FROM Sales.Orders
GROUP BY shipperid;
```

This query generates the following output.

```
shipperid    numshippingdates
-----------  -----------------
1            188
2            215
3            198
```

Note that the DISTINCT option is available not only to the COUNT function, but also to other general set functions. However, it's more common to use it with COUNT.

From a logical query processing perspective, the GROUP BY clause is evaluated after the FROM and WHERE clauses, and before the HAVING, SELECT, and ORDER BY clauses. So the last three clauses already work with a grouped table, and therefore the expressions that they support are limited. Each group is represented by only one result row; therefore, all expressions that appear in those clauses must guarantee a single result value per group. There's no problem referring directly to elements that appear in the GROUP BY clause because each of those returns only one distinct value per group. But if you want to refer to elements from the underlying tables that don't appear in the GROUP BY list, you must apply an aggregate function to them. That's how you can be sure that the expression returns only one value per group. As an example, the following query isn't valid:

```
SELECT S.shipperid, S.companyname, COUNT(*) AS numorders
FROM Sales.Shippers AS S
  INNER JOIN Sales.Orders AS O
    ON S.shipperid = O.shipperid
GROUP BY S.shipperid;
```

This query generates the following error:

```
Msg 8120, Level 16, State 1, Line 58
Column 'Sales.Shippers.companyname' is invalid in the select list because it is not
contained in either an aggregate function or the GROUP BY clause.
```

Even though you know that there can't be more than one distinct company name per distinct shipper ID, T-SQL doesn't know this. Because the S.companyname column neither appears in the GROUP BY list nor is it contained in an aggregate function, it's not allowed in the HAVING, SELECT, and ORDER BY clauses.

You can use a number of workarounds. One solution is to add the S.companyname column to the GROUP BY list, as follows:

```
SELECT S.shipperid, S.companyname,
  COUNT(*) AS numorders
FROM Sales.Shippers AS S
  INNER JOIN Sales.Orders AS O
    ON S.shipperid = O.shipperid
GROUP BY S.shipperid, S.companyname;
```

This query generates the following output.

```
shipperid    companyname      numorders
-----------  --------------   -----------
1            Shipper GVSUA    249
2            Shipper ETYNR    326
3            Shipper ZHISN    255
```

Another workaround is to apply an aggregate function like MAX to the column, as follows:

```
SELECT S.shipperid,
  MAX(S.companyname) AS companyname,
  COUNT(*) AS numorders
FROM Sales.Shippers AS S
  INNER JOIN Sales.Orders AS O
    ON S.shipperid = O.shipperid
GROUP BY S.shipperid;
```

In this case, the aggregate function is an artificial one because there can't be more than one distinct company name per distinct shipper ID. The first workaround, though, tends to produce more optimal plans, and also seems to be the more natural solution.

The third workaround is to group and aggregate the rows from the Orders table first, define a table expression based on the grouped query, and then join the table expression with the Shippers table to get the shipper company names. Here's the solution's code:

```
WITH C AS
(
  SELECT shipperid, COUNT(*) AS numorders
  FROM Sales.Orders
  GROUP BY shipperid
)
SELECT S.shipperid, S.companyname, numorders
FROM Sales.Shippers AS S
  INNER JOIN C
    ON S.shipperid = C.shipperid;
```

SQL Server usually optimizes the third solution like it does the first. The first solution might be preferable because it involves much less code.

> **MORE INFO**   **ON USER DEFINED AGGREGATES**
>
> SQL Server also allows you to create user defined aggregates (UDA) using .NET code based on the Common Language Runtime (CLR). It provides some built-in CLR UDAs for the spatial data types GEOMETRY and GEOGRAPHY and also allows you to create new UDAs operating on spatial types as inputs. For more details see the topic "CLR User-Defined Aggregates" in books online at *https://msdn.microsoft.com/en-us/library/ms131057.aspx.*

## Working with multiple grouping sets

With T-SQL, you can define multiple grouping sets in the same query. In other words, you can use one query to group the data in more than one way. T-SQL supports three clauses that allow defined multiple grouping sets: GROUPING SETS, CUBE, and ROLLUP. You use these in the GROUP BY clause.

You can use the GROUPING SETS clause to list all grouping sets that you want to define in the query. As an example, the following query defines four grouping sets:

```
SELECT shipperid, YEAR(shippeddate) AS shipyear, COUNT(*) AS numorders
FROM Sales.Orders
WHERE shippeddate IS NOT NULL -- exclude unshipped orders
GROUP BY GROUPING SETS
(
  ( shipperid, YEAR(shippeddate) ),
  ( shipperid                    ),
  ( YEAR(shippeddate)            ),
  (                              )
);
```

You list the grouping sets separated by commas within the outer pair of parentheses, which belongs to the GROUPING SETS clause. You use an inner pair of parentheses to enclose each grouping set. If you don't indicate an inner pair of parentheses, each individual element is considered a separate grouping set.

This query defines four grouping sets. One of them is the empty grouping set, which defines one group with all rows for computation of grand aggregates. The query generates the following output:

```
shipperid   shipyear    numorders
----------- ----------- -----------
1           2014        36
2           2014        56
3           2014        51
NULL        2014        143
1           2015        130
2           2015        143
3           2015        125
NULL        2015        398
1           2016        79
2           2016        116
3           2016        73
NULL        2016        268
NULL        NULL        809
3           NULL        249
1           NULL        245
2           NULL        315
```

The output combines the results of grouping and aggregating the data of four different grouping sets. As you can see in the output, NULLs are used as placeholders in rows where an element isn't part of the grouping set. For example, in result rows that are associated with the grouping set (shipperid), the `shipyear` result column is set to NULL. Similarly, in rows that are associated with the grouping set (YEAR(shippeddate)), the `shipperid` column is set to NULL.

You can achieve the same result by writing four separate grouped queries—each defining only a single grouping set—and unifying their results with a UNION ALL operator. However, such a solution would involve much more code and won't get optimized as efficiently as the query with the GROUPING SETS clause.

T-SQL supports two additional clauses called CUBE and ROLLUP, which you can consider as abbreviations of the GROUPING SETS clause. The CUBE clause accepts a list of expressions as inputs and defines all possible grouping sets that can be generated from the inputs—including the empty grouping set. For example, the following query is a logical equivalent of the previous query that used the GROUPING SETS clause:

```
SELECT shipperid, YEAR(shippeddate) AS shipyear, COUNT(*) AS numorders
FROM Sales.Orders
WHERE shippeddate IS NOT NULL
GROUP BY CUBE( shipperid, YEAR(shippeddate) );
```

The CUBE clause defines all four possible grouping sets from the two inputs:

- ( shipperid, YEAR(shippeddate) )
- ( shipperid )
- ( YEAR(shippeddate) )
- ( )

The ROLLUP clause is also an abbreviation of the GROUPING SETS clause, but you use it when there's a natural hierarchy formed by the input elements. In such a case, only a subset of the possible grouping sets is really interesting. Consider, for example, a location hierarchy made of the elements `shipcountry`, `shipregion`, and `shipcity`, in this order. It's only interesting to roll up the data in one direction, computing aggregates for the following grouping sets:

- ( shipcountry, shipregion, shipcity )
- ( shipcountry, shipregion )
- ( shipcountry )
- ( )

The other grouping sets are simply not interesting. For example, even though the same city name can appear in different places in the world, it's not interesting to aggregate all of the occurrences—irrespective of region and country.

So, when the elements form a hierarchy, you use the ROLLUP clause and this way avoid computing unnecessary aggregates. Here's an example of a query using the ROLLUP clause based on the aforementioned hierarchy:

```
SELECT shipcountry, shipregion, shipcity, COUNT(*) AS numorders
FROM Sales.Orders
GROUP BY ROLLUP( shipcountry, shipregion, shipcity );
```

This query generates the following output (shown here in abbreviated form):

```
shipcountry       shipregion        shipcity          numorders
---------------   ---------------   ---------------   -----------
Argentina         NULL              Buenos Aires      16
Argentina         NULL              NULL              16
Argentina         NULL              NULL              16
...
USA               AK                Anchorage         10
USA               AK                NULL              10
USA               CA                San Francisco     4
USA               CA                NULL              4
USA               ID                Boise             31
USA               ID                NULL              31
...
USA               NULL              NULL              122
...
NULL              NULL              NULL              830
```

As mentioned, NULLs are used as placeholders when an element isn't part of the grouping set. If all grouped columns disallow NULLs in the underlying table, you can identify the rows that are associated with a single grouping set based on a unique combination of NULLs and non-NULLs in those columns. A problem arises in identifying the rows that are associated with a single grouping set when a grouped column allows NULLs—as is the case with the shipregion column. How do you tell whether a NULL in the result represents a placeholder (meaning "all regions") or an original NULL from the table (meaning "missing region")? T-SQL provides two functions to help address this problem: GROUPING and GROUPING_ID.

The GROUPING function accepts a single element as input and returns 0 when the element is part of the grouping set and 1 when it isn't. In other words, 0 defines a detail element and 1 defines a hyperaggregate. The following query demonstrates using the GROUPING function:

```
SELECT
  shipcountry, GROUPING(shipcountry) AS grpcountry,
  shipregion , GROUPING(shipregion)  AS grpregion,
  shipcity   , GROUPING(shipcity)    AS grpcity,
  COUNT(*) AS numorders
FROM Sales.Orders
GROUP BY ROLLUP( shipcountry, shipregion, shipcity );
```

This query generates the following output (shown here in abbreviated form):

| shipcountry | grpcountry | shipregion | grpregion | shipcity | grpcitry | numorders |
|-------------|------------|------------|-----------|----------|----------|-----------|
| Argentina | 0 | NULL | 0 | Buenos Aires | 0 | 16 |
| Argentina | 0 | NULL | 0 | NULL | 1 | 16 |
| Argentina | 0 | NULL | 1 | NULL | 1 | 16 |
| ... | | | | | | |
| USA | 0 | AK | 0 | Anchorage | 0 | 10 |
| USA | 0 | AK | 0 | NULL | 1 | 10 |
| USA | 0 | CA | 0 | San Francisco | 0 | 4 |

| USA | 0 | CA | 0 | NULL | 1 | 4 |
|-----|---|----|----|------|---|---|
| USA | 0 | ID | 0 | Boise | 0 | 31 |
| USA | 0 | ID | 0 | NULL | 1 | 31 |
| ... | | | | | | |
| USA | 0 | NULL | 1 | NULL | 1 | 122 |
| ... | | | | | | |
| NULL | 1 | NULL | 1 | NULL | 1 | 830 |

Now you can identify a grouping set by looking for 0s in the elements that are part of the grouping set (detail elements) and 1s in the rest (aggregate elements).

Another function that you can use to identify the grouping sets is GROUPING_ID. This function accepts the list of grouped columns as inputs and returns an integer representing a bitmap. The rightmost bit represents the rightmost input. The bit is 0 when the respective element is part of the grouping set and 1 when it isn't. Each bit represents 2 raised to the power of the bit position minus 1; so, the rightmost bit represents 1, the one to the left of it 2, then 4, then 8, and so on. The result integer is the sum of the values representing elements that are not part of the grouping set because their bits are turned on. Here's a query demonstrating the use of this function:

```
SELECT GROUPING_ID( shipcountry, shipregion, shipcity ) AS grp_id,
  shipcountry, shipregion, shipcity,
  COUNT(*) AS numorders
FROM Sales.Orders
GROUP BY ROLLUP( shipcountry, shipregion, shipcity );
```

This query generates the following output (shown here in abbreviated form):

| grp_id | shipcountry | shipregion | shipcity | numorders |
|--------|-------------|------------|----------|-----------|
| 0 | Argentina | NULL | Buenos Aires | 16 |
| 1 | Argentina | NULL | NULL | 16 |
| 3 | Argentina | NULL | NULL | 16 |
| ... | | | | |
| 0 | USA | AK | Anchorage | 10 |
| 1 | USA | AK | NULL | 10 |
| 0 | USA | CA | San Francisco | 4 |
| 1 | USA | CA | NULL | 4 |
| 0 | USA | ID | Boise | 31 |
| 1 | USA | ID | NULL | 31 |
| ... | | | | |
| 3 | USA | NULL | NULL | 122 |
| ... | | | | |
| 7 | NULL | NULL | NULL | 830 |

The last row in this output represents the empty grouping set—none of the three elements is part of the grouping set. Therefore, the respective bits (values 1, 2, and 4) are turned on. The sum of the values that those bits represent is 7.

# Pivoting and Unpivoting Data

Pivoting is a specialized case of grouping and aggregating of data. Unpivoting is, in a sense, the inverse of pivoting. T-SQL supports native operators for both. Let's first describe the PIVOT operator and then the UNPIVOT operator.

## Pivoting Data

Pivoting is a technique that groups and aggregates data, transitioning it from a state of rows to a state of columns. In all pivot queries, you need to identify three elements:

1. What do you want to see on rows? This element is known as the *on rows*, or *grouping* element.

2. What do you want to see on columns? This element is known as the *on cols*, or *spreading* element.

3. What do you want to see in the intersection of each distinct row and column value? This element is known as the *data*, or *aggregation* element.

As an example of a pivot request, suppose that you want to query the Sales.Orders table. You want to return a row for each distinct customer ID (the grouping element), a column for each distinct shipper ID (the spreading element), and in the intersection of each customer and shipper you want to see the sum of freight values (the aggregation element). With T-SQL, you can achieve such a pivoting task by using the PIVOT table operator. The recommended form for a pivot query (more on why it's the recommended form later) is generally like the following.

```
WITH PivotData AS
(
  SELECT
    < grouping column >,
    < spreading column >,
    < aggregation column >
  FROM < source table >
)
SELECT < select list >
FROM PivotData
  PIVOT( < aggregate function >(< aggregation column >)
    FOR < spreading column > IN (< distinct spreading values >) ) AS P;
```

This recommended general form is made of the following elements:

- You define a table expression (like the one named PivotData) that returns the three elements that are involved in pivoting, which in this example are custid, shipperid and freight from Sales.Orders. It is not recommended to query the underlying source table directly; the reason for this is explained shortly.

- You issue the outer query against the table expression and apply the PIVOT operator to that table expression. The PIVOT operator returns a table result. You need to assign an alias to that table, for example, P.

- The specification for the PIVOT operator starts by indicating an aggregate function applied to the aggregation element—in this example, SUM(freight).

- Then you specify the FOR clause followed by the spreading column, which in this example is shipperid.

- Then you specify the IN clause followed by the list of distinct values that appear in the spreading element, separated by commas. What used to be values in the spreading column (in this example, shipper IDs) become column names in the result table. Therefore, the items in the list should be expressed as column identifiers. Remember that if a column identifier is irregular, it has to be delimited. Because shipper IDs are integers, they have to be delimited: [1],[2],[3].

Following this recommended syntax for pivot queries, the following query addresses our task (return customer IDs on rows, shipper IDs on columns, and the total freight in the intersections):

```
WITH PivotData AS
(
  SELECT
    custid,     -- grouping column
    shipperid, -- spreading column
    freight    -- aggregation column
  FROM Sales.Orders
)
SELECT custid, [1], [2], [3]
FROM PivotData
  PIVOT(SUM(freight) FOR shipperid IN ([1],[2],[3]) ) AS P;
```

This query generates the following output (shown here in abbreviated form):

```
custid  1         2         3
------- --------- --------- --------
1        95.03     61.02     69.53
2        43.90     NULL      53.52
3        63.09     116.56    88.87
4        41.95     358.54    71.46
5        189.44    1074.51   295.57
6        0.15      126.19    41.92
7        217.96    215.70    190.00
8        16.16     175.01    NULL
9        341.16    419.57    597.14
10       129.42    162.17    502.36
...

(89 row(s) affected)
```

**EXAM TIP**

As you can see in the output, in cases where a shipper hasn't shipped any orders for a customer, the result of the aggregate is NULL. If you need to return something else instead of a NULL in such cases, say, zero, apply the ISNULL or COALESCE function to the result columns in the outer query's SELECT list. For example ISNULL([1], 0.00). Your revised query would look like this:

```
WITH PivotData AS
(
  SELECT
    custid,
    shipperid,
    freight
  FROM Sales.Orders
)
SELECT custid,
  ISNULL([1], 0.00) AS [1],
  ISNULL([2], 0.00) AS [2],
  ISNULL([3], 0.00) AS [3]
FROM PivotData
  PIVOT(SUM(freight) FOR shipperid IN ([1],[2],[3]) ) AS P;
```

This code generates the following output:

```
custid  1         2         3
------- --------- --------- --------
1        95.03     61.02     69.53
2        43.90     0.00      53.52
3        63.09     116.56    88.87
4        41.95     358.54    71.46
5        189.44    1074.51   295.57
6        0.15      126.19    41.92
7        217.96    215.70    190.00
8        16.16     175.01    0.00
9        341.16    419.57    597.14
10       129.42    162.17    502.36
...
```

Make sure that whenever you write T-SQL code you always think about NULLs and how you want to handle them.

If you look carefully at the specification of the PIVOT operator, you will notice that you indicate the aggregation and spreading elements, but not the grouping element. The grouping element is identified by elimination—it's what's left from the queried table besides the aggregation and spreading elements. This is why it is recommended to prepare a table expression for the pivot operator returning only the three elements that should be involved in the pivoting task. If you query the underlying table directly (Sales.Orders in this case), all columns from the table besides the aggregation (freight) and spreading (shipperid) columns will implicitly become your grouping elements. This includes even the primary key column orderid. So instead of getting a row per customer, you end up getting a row per order. You can see it for yourself by running the following code:

```
SELECT custid, [1], [2], [3]
FROM Sales.Orders
  PIVOT(SUM(freight) FOR shipperid IN ([1],[2],[3]) ) AS P;
```

This query generates the following output (shown here in abbreviated form):

```
custid  1        2        3
------- -------  -------  -------
85      NULL     NULL     32.38
79      11.61    NULL     NULL
34      NULL     65.83    NULL
84      41.34    NULL     NULL
76      NULL     51.30    NULL
34      NULL     58.17    NULL
14      NULL     22.98    NULL
68      NULL     NULL     148.33
88      NULL     13.97    NULL
35      NULL     NULL     81.91
...

(830 row(s) affected)
```

You get 830 rows back because there are 830 rows in the Sales.Orders table. By defining a table expression as was shown in the recommended solution, you control which columns will be used as the grouping columns. If you return custid, shipperid, and freight in the table expression, and use the last two as the spreading and aggregation elements, respectively, the PIVOT operator implicitly assumes that custid is the grouping element. Therefore, it groups the data by custid, and as a result, returns a single row per customer.

You should be aware of a few limitations of the PIVOT operator.

- The aggregation and spreading elements cannot directly be results of expressions; instead, they must be column names from the queried table. You can, however, apply expressions in the query defining the table expression, assign aliases to those expressions, and then use the aliases in the PIVOT operator.

- The COUNT(*) function isn't allowed as the aggregate function used by the PIVOT operator. If you need a count, you have to use the general COUNT(<col name>) aggregate function. A simple workaround is to define a dummy column in the table expression made of a constant, as in 1 AS agg_col, and then in the PIVOT operator apply the aggregate function to that column: COUNT(agg_col). In this case you can also use SUM(agg_col) as an alternative.

- A PIVOT operator is limited to using only one aggregate function.

- The IN clause of the PIVOT operator accepts a static list of spreading values. It doesn't support a subquery as input. You need to know ahead what the distinct values are in the spreading column and specify those in the IN clause. When the list isn't known ahead, you can use dynamic SQL to construct and execute the query string after querying the distinct values from the data. You can find an example for building and executing a pivot query dynamically at *http://sqlmag.com/sql-server/logical-query-processing-clause-and-pivot*.

## Unpivoting Data

Unpivoting data can be considered the inverse of pivoting. The starting point is some pivoted data. When unpivoting data, you rotate the input data from a state of columns to a state of rows. Just like T-SQL supports the native PIVOT table operator to perform pivoting, it supports a native UNPIVOT operator to perform unpivoting. Like PIVOT, UNPIVOT is implemented as a table operator that you use in the FROM clause. The operator operates on the input table that is provided to its left, which could be the result of other table operators, like joins. The outcome of the UNPIVOT operator is a table result that can be used as the input to other table operators that appear to its right.

To demonstrate unpivoting, use as an example a sample table called Sales.FreightTotals. The following code creates the sample data and queries it to show its contents:

```
USE TSQLV4;
DROP TABLE IF EXISTS Sales.FreightTotals;
GO

WITH PivotData AS
(
  SELECT
    custid,    -- grouping column
    shipperid, -- spreading column
    freight    -- aggregation column
  FROM Sales.Orders
)
SELECT *
INTO Sales.FreightTotals
```

```
FROM PivotData
  PIVOT( SUM(freight) FOR shipperid IN ([1],[2],[3]) ) AS P;

SELECT * FROM Sales.FreightTotals;
```

This code generates the following output, shown here in abbreviated form:

```
custid  1         2         3
-------  --------  --------  --------
1        95.03     61.02     69.53
2        43.90     NULL      53.52
3        63.09     116.56    88.87
4        41.95     358.54    71.46
5        189.44    1074.51   295.57
6        0.15      126.19    41.92
7        217.96    215.70    190.00
8        16.16     175.01    NULL
9        341.16    419.57    597.14
10        129.42    162.17    502.36
...
```

As you can see, the source table has a row for each customer and a column for each shipper (shippers 1, 2, and 3). The intersection of each customer and shipper has the total freight values. The unpivoting task at hand is to return a row for each customer and shipper holding the customer ID in one column, the shipper ID in a second column, and the freight value in a third column.

Unpivoting always takes a set of source columns and rotates those to multiple rows, generating two target columns: one to hold the source column values and another to hold the source column names. The source columns already exist, so their names should be known to you. But the two target columns are created by the unpivoting solution, so you need to choose names for those. In our example, the source columns are [1], [2], and [3]. As for names for the target columns, you need to decide on those. In this case, it might be suitable to call the values column freight and the names column shipperid. So remember, in every unpivoting task, you need to identify the three elements involved:

1. The name you want to assign to the target values column (in this case, freight).

2. The name you want to assign to the target names column (in this case, shipperid).

3. The set of source columns that you're unpivoting (in this case, [1],[2],[3]).

After you identify these three elements, you use the following query form to handle the unpivoting task:

```
SELECT < column list >, < names column >, < values column >
FROM < source table >
  UNPIVOT( < values column > FOR < names column > IN( <source columns> ) ) AS U;
```

Based on this syntax, the following query addresses the current task:

```
SELECT custid, shipperid, freight
FROM Sales.FreightTotals
  UNPIVOT( freight FOR shipperid IN([1],[2],[3]) ) AS U;
```

This query generates the following output (shown here in abbreviated form).

```
custid   shipperid   freight
-------  ----------  --------
1        1            95.03
1        2            61.02
1        3            69.53
2        1            43.90
2        3            53.52
3        1            63.09
3        2           116.56
3        3            88.87
4        1            41.95
4        2           358.54
4        3            71.46
...
```

> **NOTE** **UNPIVOT AND NULLS**
>
> Besides unpivoting the data, the UNPIVOT operator filters out rows with NULLs in the value column (freight in this case). The assumption is that those represent inapplicable cases. There was no escape from keeping NULLs in the source if the column was applicable to at least one other customer. But after unpivoting the data, there's no reason to keep a row for a certain customer-shipper pair if it's inapplicable—if that shipper did not ship orders to that customer. However, if you want to return rows for cases that were NULL originally, you need to prepare a table expression where you replace the NULLs with some other value using the ISNULL or COALESCE function, and then in the outer query replace that value back with a NULL using the NULLIF function. Here's how you apply this technique to our example:

```
WITH C AS
(
  SELECT custid,
    ISNULL([1], 0.00) AS [1],
    ISNULL([2], 0.00) AS [2],
    ISNULL([3], 0.00) AS [3]
  FROM Sales.FreightTotals
)
SELECT custid, shipperid, NULLIF(freight, 0.00) AS freight
FROM C
  UNPIVOT( freight FOR shipperid IN([1],[2],[3]) ) AS U;
```

This time the output includes rows with NULLs:

```
custid   shipperid   freight
-------  ----------  --------
1        1            95.03
1        2            61.02
1        3            69.53
2        1            43.90
2        2           NULL
2        3            53.52
3        1            63.09
3        2           116.56
```

```
3       3       88.87
4       1       41.95
4       2       358.54
4       3       71.46
...
```

Naturally you need to replace the NULL with a value that normally can't appear in your data.

In terms of data types, the names column is defined as a Unicode character string (NVAR-CHAR(128)). The values column is defined with the same type as the type of the source columns that were unpivoted. For this reason, the types of all columns that you're unpivoting must be the same.

Just like with the PIVOT operator, in a static query the UNPIVOT operator requires you to hard code the columns that you want to unpivot. If you don't want to hard code those, you can query the column names from the sys.columns view, construct the UNPIVOT query string, and execute it with dynamic SQL. Also, the UNPIVOT operator is limited to unpivoting only one measure (one values column). If you need to unpivot multiple measures, you need to use an alternative solution that is based on the APPLY operator. The below resources provide further reading material with examples for constructing and executing dynamic queries as well as unpivoting multiple measures.

When you're done, run the following code for cleanup:

```
DROP TABLE IF EXISTS Sales.FreightTotals;
```

> **MORE INFO**  **ON PIVOT AND UNPIVOT**
>
> For more information about the logical query processing aspects of the PIVOT and UNPIVOT operators, see "Logical Query Processing: The FROM Clause and PIVOT" at *https://sqlmag.com/sql-server/logical-query-processing-clause-and-pivot* and "Logical Query Processing Part 5: The FROM Clause and UNPIVOT" at *https://sqlmag.com/sql-server/logical-query-processing-part-5-clause-and-unpivot*.

## Using Window Functions

Like group functions, window functions also enable you to perform data analysis computations. The difference between the two is in how you define the set of rows for the function to work with. With group functions, you use grouped queries to arrange the queried rows in groups, and then the group functions are applied to each group. You get one result row per group—not per underlying row. With window functions, you define the set of rows per function—and then return one result value per underlying row and function. You define the set of rows for the function to work with using a clause called OVER.

This section covers three types of window functions: aggregate, ranking, and offset.

## Window aggregate functions

Window aggregate functions are the same as the group aggregate functions (for example, SUM, COUNT, AVG, MIN, and MAX), except window aggregate functions are applied to a window of rows defined by the OVER clause.

One of the benefits of using window functions is that unlike grouped queries, windowed queries do not hide the detail—they return a row for every underlying query's row. This means that you can mix detail and aggregated elements in the same query, and even in the same expression. Using the OVER clause, you define a set of rows for the function to work with per underlying row. In other words, a windowed query defines a window of rows per function and row in the underlying query.

As mentioned, you use an OVER clause to define a window of rows for the function. The window is defined with respect to the current row. When using empty parentheses, the OVER clause represents the entire underlying query's result set. For example, the expression SUM(val) OVER() represents the grand total of all rows in the underlying query. You can use a window partition clause to restrict the window. For example, the expression SUM(val) OVER(PARTITION BY custid) represents the current customer's total. As an example, if the current row has customer ID 1, the OVER clause filters only those rows from the underlying query's result set where the customer ID is 1; hence, the expression returns the total for customer 1.

Here's an example of a query against the Sales.OrderValues view returning for each order the customer ID, order ID, and order value; using window functions, the query also returns the grand total of all values and the customer total:

```
SELECT custid, orderid, val,
  SUM(val) OVER(PARTITION BY custid) AS custtotal,
  SUM(val) OVER() AS grandtotal
FROM Sales.OrderValues;
```

This query generates the following output (shown here in abbreviated form):

```
custid  orderid  val      custtotal  grandtotal
------- -------- -------  ---------- -----------
1       10643    814.50   4273.00    1265793.22
1       10692    878.00   4273.00    1265793.22
1       10702    330.00   4273.00    1265793.22
1       10835    845.80   4273.00    1265793.22
1       10952    471.20   4273.00    1265793.22
1       11011    933.50   4273.00    1265793.22
2       10926    514.40   1402.95    1265793.22
2       10759    320.00   1402.95    1265793.22
2       10625    479.75   1402.95    1265793.22
2       10308    88.80    1402.95    1265793.22
...
```

The grand total is of course the same for all rows. The customer total is the same for all rows with the same customer ID.

You can mix detail elements and windowed aggregates in the same expression. For example, the following query computes for each order the percent of the current order value out of the customer total, and also the percent of the grand total:

```
SELECT custid, orderid, val,
  CAST(100.0 * val / SUM(val) OVER(PARTITION BY custid) AS NUMERIC(5, 2)) AS pctcust,
  CAST(100.0 * val / SUM(val) OVER()                   AS NUMERIC(5, 2)) AS pcttotal
FROM Sales.OrderValues;
```

This query generates the following output (shown here in abbreviated form):

```
custid  orderid  val     pctcust  pcttotal
------  -------  ------  -------  ---------
1       10643    814.50  19.06    0.06
1       10692    878.00  20.55    0.07
1       10702    330.00  7.72     0.03
1       10835    845.80  19.79    0.07
1       10952    471.20  11.03    0.04
1       11011    933.50  21.85    0.07
2       10926    514.40  36.67    0.04
2       10759    320.00  22.81    0.03
2       10625    479.75  34.20    0.04
2       10308    88.80   6.33     0.01
...
```

The sum of all percentages out of the grand total is 100. The sum of all percentages out of the customer total is 100 for each partition of rows with the same customer.

Window aggregate functions support another filtering option called *window frame*. The idea is that you define ordering within the partition by using a window order clause, and then based on that order, you can confine a frame of rows between two delimiters. You define the delimiters by using a window frame clause. The window frame clause requires a window order clause to be present because a set has no order, and without order, limiting rows between two delimiters would have no meaning.

In the window frame clause, you indicate the *window frame unit* (ROWS or RANGE) and the *window frame extent* (the delimiters). With the ROWS window frame unit, you can indicate the delimiters as one of three options:

- UNBOUNDED PRECEDING or FOLLOWING, meaning the beginning or end of the partition, respectively.
- CURRENT ROW, obviously representing the current row.
- <n> ROWS PRECEDING or FOLLOWING, meaning n rows before or after the current, respectively.

As an example, suppose that you wanted to query the Sales.OrderValues view and compute the running total values from the beginning of the current customer's activity until the current order, assuming a sort based on orderdate and orderid as a tiebreaker. You need to use the SUM aggregate. You partition the window by custid. You order the window by orderdate, orderid. You then frame the rows from the beginning of the partition (UNBOUNDED PRECEDING) until the current row. Your query should look like the following.

```
SELECT custid, orderid, orderdate, val,
  SUM(val) OVER(PARTITION BY custid
                ORDER BY orderdate, orderid
                ROWS BETWEEN UNBOUNDED PRECEDING
                        AND CURRENT ROW) AS runningtotal
FROM Sales.OrderValues;
```

This query generates the following output (shown here in abbreviated form):

```
custid       orderid     orderdate    val      runningtotal
-----------  ----------- -----------  -------  -------------
1            10643       2015-08-25  814.50   814.50
1            10692       2015-10-03  878.00   1692.50
1            10702       2015-10-13  330.00   2022.50
1            10835       2016-01-15  845.80   2868.30
1            10952       2016-03-16  471.20   3339.50
1            11011       2016-04-09  933.50   4273.00
2            10308       2014-09-18  88.80    88.80
2            10625       2015-08-08  479.75   568.55
2            10759       2015-11-28  320.00   888.55
2            10926       2016-03-04  514.40   1402.95
...
```

Observe how the values keep accumulating from the beginning of the customer partition until the current row. By the way, instead of the verbose form of the frame extent ROWS BE-TWEEN UNBOUNDED PRECEDING AND CURRENT ROW, you can use the shorter form ROWS UNBOUNDED PRECEDING, and retain the same meaning.

Using window aggregate functions to perform computations such as running totals, you typically get much better performance compared to using joins or subqueries and group aggregate functions. Window functions lend themselves to good optimization—especially when using UNBOUNDED PRECEDING as the first delimiter.

From an indexing standpoint, an optimal index to support window functions is one created on the partitioning and ordering elements as the key list, and includes the rest of the elements from the query for coverage. I like to think of this index as a *POC index* as an acronym for partitioning, ordering and covering. With such an index in place SQL Server won't need to explicitly sort the data, rather pull it preordered from the index.

---

**EXAM TIP**

In terms of logical query processing, a query's result is established when you get to the SELECT phase—after the FROM, WHERE, GROUP BY, and HAVING phases have been processed. Because window functions are supposed to operate on the underlying query's result set, they are allowed only in the SELECT and ORDER BY clauses. If you need to refer to the result of a window function in any clause that is evaluated before the SELECT clause, you need to use a table expression. You invoke the window function in the SELECT clause of the inner query, assigning the expression with a column alias. Then you can refer to that column alias in the outer query in all clauses.

---

Suppose that you need to filter the result of the last query, returning only those rows where the running total is less than 1,000.00. The following code achieves this by defining a common table expression (CTE) based on the previous query and then doing the filtering in the outer query:

```
WITH RunningTotals AS
(
```

```
SELECT custid, orderid, orderdate, val,
    SUM(val) OVER(PARTITION BY custid
                  ORDER BY orderdate, orderid
                  ROWS BETWEEN UNBOUNDED PRECEDING
                             AND CURRENT ROW) AS runningtotal
  FROM Sales.OrderValues
)
SELECT *
FROM RunningTotals
WHERE runningtotal < 1000.00;
```

This query generates the following output (shown here in abbreviated form):

```
custid      orderid     orderdate   val      runningtotal
----------- ----------- ----------- -------- -------------
1           10643       2015-08-25  814.50   814.50
2           10308       2014-09-18  88.80    88.80
2           10625       2015-08-08  479.75   568.55
2           10759       2015-11-28  320.00   888.55
3           10365       2014-11-27  403.20   403.20
...
```

As another example for a window frame extent, if you wanted the frame to include only the last three rows, you would use the form ROWS BETWEEN 2 PRECEDING AND CURRENT ROW.

As for the RANGE window frame extent, according to standard SQL, it allows you to define delimiters based on an offset from the current row's ordering value, as opposed to an offset in terms of a number of rows. However, T-SQL has a limited implementation of the RANGE option, supporting only UNBOUNDED (PRECEDING and FOLLOWING) and CURRENT ROW as delimiters. One subtle difference between ROWS and RANGE when using the same delimiters is that the former doesn't include peers (tied rows in terms of the ordering values) and the latter does.

> **IMPORTANT   IMPLICIT RANGE**
>
> The ROWS option usually gets optimized much better than RANGE when using the same delimiters. If you define a window with a window order clause but without a window frame clause, the default is RANGE BETWEEN UNBOUNDED PRECEDING AND CURRENT ROW. Therefore, unless you are after the special behavior you get from RANGE that includes peers, make sure you explicitly use the ROWS option. Even if you do need RANGE, it might be a good idea to mention it explicitly to let everyone know that your choice was intentional and not an oversight. SQL Server 2016 eliminates this performance problem when using columnstore technology and the batch mode Window Aggregate operator. For details, see "What You Need to Know about the Batch Mode Window Aggregate Operator in SQL Server 2016: Part 3" at *http://sqlmag.com/sql-server/what-you-need-know-about-batch-mode-window-aggregate-operator-sql-server-2016-part-3*.

## Window Ranking Functions

With window ranking functions, you can rank rows within a partition based on specified ordering. As with the other window functions, if you don't indicate a window partition clause, the entire underlying query result is considered one partition. The window order clause is mandatory. Window ranking functions do not support a window frame clause. T-SQL supports four window ranking functions: ROW_NUMBER, RANK, DENSE_RANK, and NTILE.

The following query demonstrates the use of these functions:

```
SELECT custid, orderid, val,
  ROW_NUMBER() OVER(ORDER BY val) AS rownum,
  RANK()       OVER(ORDER BY val) AS rnk,
  DENSE_RANK() OVER(ORDER BY val) AS densernk,
  NTILE(100)   OVER(ORDER BY val) AS ntile100
FROM Sales.OrderValues;
```

This query generates the following output (shown here in abbreviated form):

```
custid  orderid  val     rownum  rnk  densernk  ntile100
------  -------  ------  ------  ---  --------  --------
12      10782    12.50   1       1    1         1
27      10807    18.40   2       2    2         1
66      10586    23.80   3       3    3         1
76      10767    28.00   4       4    4         1
54      10898    30.00   5       5    5         1
88      10900    33.75   6       6    6         1
48      10883    36.00   7       7    7         1
41      11051    36.00   8       7    7         1
71      10815    40.00   9       9    8         1
38      10674    45.00   10      10   9         2
53      11057    45.00   11      10   9         2
75      10271    48.00   12      12   10        2
...
```

> **IMPORTANT**   **ORDERING OF RESULT**
>
> The sample query doesn't have a presentation ORDER BY clause, and therefore, there's no assurance that the rows will be presented in any particular order. The window order clause only determines ordering for the window function's computation. If you invoke a window function in your query but don't specify a presentation ORDER BY clause, there's no guarantee that the rows will be presented in the same order as the window function's ordering. If you need such a guarantee, you need to add a presentation ORDER BY clause.

The ROW_NUMBER function computes unique incrementing integers starting with 1 within the window partition based on the window ordering. Because the example query doesn't have a window partition clause, the function considers the entire query's result set as one partition; hence, the function assigns unique row numbers across the entire query's result set.

Note that if the ordering isn't unique, the ROW_NUMBER function is not deterministic. For example, notice in the result that two rows have the same ordering value of 36.00, but the two rows were assigned with different row numbers. That's because the function must generate unique integers in the partition. Currently, there's no explicit tiebreaker, and therefore the choice of which row gets the higher row number is arbitrary (optimization dependent). If you need a deterministic computation (guaranteed repeatable results), you need to add a tiebreaker. For example, you can add the primary key to make the ordering unique, as in ORDER BY val, orderid.

RANK and DENSE_RANK differ from ROW_NUMBER in the sense that they assign the same ranking value to all rows that share the same ordering value. The RANK function returns the number of rows in the partition that have a lower ordering value than the current, plus 1. For example, consider the rows in the sample query's result that have an ordering value of 45.00. Nine rows have ordering values that are lower than 45.00; hence, these rows got the rank 10 (9 + 1).

The DENSE_RANK function returns the number of distinct ordering values that are lower than the current, plus 1. For example, the same rows that got the rank 10 got the dense rank 9. That's because these rows have an ordering value 45.00, and there are eight distinct ordering values that are lower than 45.00. Because RANK considers the count of rows and DENSE_RANK considers the count of distinct values, the former can have gaps between result ranking values, and the latter cannot have gaps. Because the RANK and DENSE_RANK functions compute the same ranking value to rows with the same ordering value, both functions are deterministic even when the ordering isn't unique. In fact, if you use unique ordering, both functions return the same result as the ROW_NUMBER function. So usually these functions are interesting to use when the ordering isn't unique.

> **NOTE    FUNCTION DETERMINISM**
>
> The official T-SQL documentation has a section describing function determinism at *https:// msdn.microsoft.com/en-us/library/ms178091.aspx*. You will notice that this article considers all window ranking functions as nondeterministic. That's because it seems that SQL Server doesn't consider the partitioning and ordering values technically as the function's inputs. With all window ranking functions, two different rows can get two different rank values, and therefore are considered nondeterministic. This means you can't create indexes on computed columns and indexed views when using such functions. The aspect of determinism that I described is a bit different and not related to restrictions on indexing. In my use of the concept of determinism I was referring to whether two rows with the same partitioning and ordering values are guaranteed to get the same rank value or not.

With the NTILE function, you can arrange the rows within the partition in a requested number of equally sized tiles, based on the specified ordering. You specify the desired number of tiles as input to the function. In the sample query, you requested 100 tiles. There are 830 rows in the result set, so the base tile size is 830 / 100 = 8 with a remainder of 30. Because there is a remainder of 30, the first 30 tiles are assigned with an additional row. Namely, tiles 1 through 30 will have nine rows each, and all remaining tiles (31 through 100) will have eight rows each. Observe in the result of this sample query that the first nine rows (according to val ordering) are assigned with tile number 1, then the next nine rows are assigned with tile number 2, and so on. Like ROW_NUMBER, the NTILE function isn't deterministic when the ordering isn't unique. If you need to guarantee determinism, you need to define unique ordering.

**EXAM TIP**

As explained in the discussion of window aggregate functions, window functions are allowed only in the SELECT and ORDER BY clauses of the query. If you need to refer to those in other clauses—for example, in the WHERE clause—you need to use a table expression such as a CTE. You invoke the window function in the inner query's SELECT clause, and assign the expression with a column alias. Then you refer to that column alias in the outer query's WHERE clause. That's a common need with ranking calculations. I demonstrated this earlier in Skill 2.2 when discussing table expressions.

## Window Offset Functions

Window offset functions return an element from a single row that is in a given offset from the current row in the window partition, or from the first or last row in the window frame. T-SQL supports the following window offset functions: LAG, LEAD, FIRST_VALUE, and LAST_VALUE. The LAG and LEAD functions rely on an offset with respect to the current row, and the FIRST_VALUE and LAST_VALUE functions operate on the first or last row in the frame, respectively.

The LAG and LEAD functions support window partition and ordering clauses. They don't support a window frame clause. The LAG function returns an element from the row in the current partition that is a requested number of rows before the current row (based on the window ordering), with 1 assumed as the default offset. The LEAD function returns an element from the row that is in the requested offset after the current row.

As an example, the following query uses the LAG and LEAD functions to return along with each order the value of the previous customer's order, in addition to the value from the next customer's order:

```
SELECT custid, orderid, orderdate, val,
  LAG(val)  OVER(PARTITION BY custid
              ORDER BY orderdate, orderid) AS prev_val,
  LEAD(val) OVER(PARTITION BY custid
              ORDER BY orderdate, orderid) AS next_val
FROM Sales.OrderValues;
```

This query generates the following output (shown here in abbreviated form, with presentation ordering not guaranteed):

```
custid      orderid      orderdate   val     prev_val  next_val
----------- ------------ ----------- ------- --------- ---------
1           10643        2015-08-25  814.50  NULL      878.00
1           10692        2015-10-03  878.00  814.50    330.00
1           10702        2015-10-13  330.00  878.00    845.80
1           10835        2016-01-15  845.80  330.00    471.20
1           10952        2016-03-16  471.20  845.80    933.50
1           11011        2016-04-09  933.50  471.20    NULL
2           10308        2014-09-18  88.80   NULL      479.75
2           10625        2015-08-08  479.75  88.80     320.00
2           10759        2015-11-28  320.00  479.75    514.40
2           10926        2016-03-04  514.40  320.00    NULL
...
```

Because an explicit offset wasn't specified, both functions relied on the default offset of 1. If you want a different offset than 1, you specify it as the second argument, as in LAG(val, 3). Notice that if a row does not exist in the requested offset, the function returns a NULL by default. If you want to return a different value in such a case, specify it as the third argument, as in LAG(val, 3, 0).

The FIRST_VALUE and LAST_VALUE functions return a value expression from the first or last rows in the window frame, respectively. Naturally, the functions support window partition, order, and frame clauses. As an example, the following query returns along with each order the values of the customer's first and last orders:

```
SELECT custid, orderid, orderdate, val,
  FIRST_VALUE(val)  OVER(PARTITION BY custid
                   ORDER BY orderdate, orderid
                   ROWS BETWEEN UNBOUNDED PRECEDING
                               AND CURRENT ROW) AS first_val,
  LAST_VALUE(val) OVER(PARTITION BY custid
                   ORDER BY orderdate, orderid
                   ROWS BETWEEN CURRENT ROW
                               AND UNBOUNDED FOLLOWING) AS last_val
FROM Sales.OrderValues
ORDER BY custid, orderdate, orderid;
```

This query generates the following output (shown here in abbreviated form):

```
custid  orderid  orderdate   val      first_val  last_val
------- -------- ----------- -------  ---------- ---------
1       10643    2015-08-25  814.50   814.50     933.50
1       10692    2015-10-03  878.00   814.50     933.50
1       10702    2015-10-13  330.00   814.50     933.50
1       10835    2016-01-15  845.80   814.50     933.50
1       10952    2016-03-16  471.20   814.50     933.50
1       11011    2016-04-09  933.50   814.50     933.50
2       10308    2014-09-18  88.80    88.80      514.40
2       10625    2015-08-08  479.75   88.80      514.40
2       10759    2015-11-28  320.00   88.80      514.40
2       10926    2016-03-04  514.40   88.80      514.40
...
```

# Skill 2.4: Query temporal data and non-relational data

This skill covers querying temporal data using system-versioned temporal tables. It also covers using T-SQL to query and output JSON data as well as to query and output XML data.

The sections about XML and JSON were written by Data Platform MVP, Dejan Sarka.

# System-versioned temporal tables

Companies often need to be able to track changes to their data. That's for purposes like auditing, point in time analysis, comparing current with older states, slowly-changing dimensions, restoring older state of rows due to an error, and others. Normally, you can only access the current state of the data in your tables. If you need to be able to access older states, you need a solution that tracks changes to the data. One of the solutions that companies used in the past was to create a history table that keeps older states of modified rows and triggers that automatically write history data to that table whenever the current table is modified. In SQL Server 2016 and Azure SQL Database there's no need for this anymore thanks to the support for a feature called *system-versioned temporal tables*. I'll just use the term *temporal tables* in short.

SQL Server supports marking a table as a temporal table using an option called SYSTEM_VERSIONING and connecting it to a history table. When you modify data, you interact only with the current table, and SQL Server behind the scenes writes historical states of modified rows to the history table. Also when you read data, you query only the current table. You use a clause called FOR SYSTEM_TIME that allows you to request earlier states of the data at a previous point or period of time.

At the date of writing SQL Server currently supports only system-versioned temporal tables, meaning that the system transaction time determines the effective time of the change. The SQL Standard also supports what's called *application-time period tables* where the application defines the validity period of a row. With this feature, you can set a change to be effective in a future period. For example, suppose that there's a planned price change of a product during an upcoming holiday period. Then bi-temporal tables combine system versioning and application versioning.

The following sections cover creating, modifying and querying temporal tables.

## Creating tables

You can mark a table as a temporal table when you create it, or alter an existing table to become a temporal table. Also, you can have SQL Server create the related history table for you, or provide an already existing history table.

There are certain elements that are required in the table definition in order to mark it as a temporal one:

- A primary key constraint.

- Two DATETIME2 columns with your chosen precision to store the start and end of the validity period of the row (stored in the UTC time zone). The period is expressed as a closed-open interval, meaning that the start is inclusive and the end is exclusive.

- The start column needs to be marked with the clause GENERATED ALWAYS AS ROW START.

- The end column needs to be marked with the clause GENERATED ALWAYS AS ROW END.

- The designation of the pair of columns that store the row's validity period with the clause PERIOD FOR SYSTEM_TIME (<startcol>, <endcol>).

- The table option SYSTEM_VERSIONING needs to be set to ON.

- A linked history table, which SQL Server can create for you.

As an example, run the following code to create a table called dbo.Products in the TSQLV4 database as a temporal table (not to be confused with the already existing Production.Products table):

```
USE TSQLV4;

CREATE TABLE dbo.Products
(
  productid   INT         NOT NULL
    CONSTRAINT PK_dboProducts PRIMARY KEY(productid),
  productname NVARCHAR(40) NOT NULL,
  supplierid  INT         NOT NULL,
  categoryid  INT         NOT NULL,
  unitprice   MONEY       NOT NULL,
-- below are additions related to temporal table
  validfrom   DATETIME2(3)
    GENERATED ALWAYS AS ROW START HIDDEN NOT NULL,
  validto     DATETIME2(3)
    GENERATED ALWAYS AS ROW END   HIDDEN NOT NULL,
  PERIOD FOR SYSTEM_TIME (validfrom, validto)
)
WITH ( SYSTEM_VERSIONING = ON ( HISTORY_TABLE = dbo.ProductsHistory ) );
```

Observe the use of the optional HIDDEN property for the period columns. With this property, the period columns are not returned when using SELECT * rather only when referring to them explicitly.

Regarding the history table, if you don't specify one at all, SQL Server creates it for you with the naming convention: MSSQL_TemporalHistoryFor_<object_id>. If you do specify a history table as in the above example, SQL Server first checks if it already exists. If it does, SQL Server by default applies a consistency check to verify that there are no overlapping periods. You can opt not to perform the consistency check by specifying DATA_CONSISTENCY_CHECK = OFF. If the specified history table doesn't exist, SQL Server will create it for you using your chosen name. SQL Server creates the history table with the following characteristics:

- No primary key.

- A clustered index on (<endcol>, <startcol>), with page compression.

- The period columns are not marked with GENERATED ALWAYS AS ROW START/END or HIDDEN.

- There's no designation of period columns with the clause PERIOD FOR SYSTEM_TIME.

- The table is not marked with the option SYSTEM_VERSIONING.

You can see that a table is a temporal table in SQL Server Management Studio (SSMS). In Object Explorer, expand the Tables folder under the TSQLV4 database, and then the dbo. Products table, as shown in Figure 2-5.

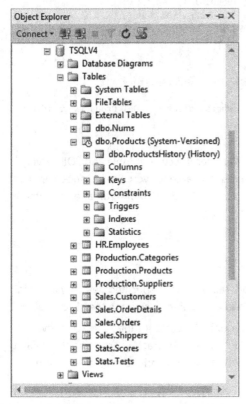

**FIGURE 2-5** Object Explorer

Observe the table with the clock icon to the left of the current table name and the fact that it says System-Versioned in parentheses after the table name. Also, observe the con-nected history table below the current table, and the fact that it says History in parentheses after the history table name.

If you need to turn an existing table to become a temporal table, you do so by first alter-ing the table and adding the period columns with the aforementioned designations, and then altering the table to mark it as system-versioned and connecting it to a history table. You will need to add default constraints to the period columns to set initial values in the existing rows. The end column in the current table has to store the maximum possible value in the data type with the select precision. Once the table is marked as a temporal table, you can drop the default constraints if you wish since SQL Server will automatically set the period column values moving forward. For example, if the dbo.Products wasn't already a temporal table, you would have turned it to become one by using the following code (don't actually run this code since our table is already temporal):

```
BEGIN TRAN;

ALTER TABLE dbo.Products ADD
  validfrom DATETIME2(3) GENERATED ALWAYS AS ROW START HIDDEN NOT NULL
    CONSTRAINT DFT_Products_validfrom DEFAULT('19000101'),
  validto DATETIME2(3) GENERATED ALWAYS AS ROW END HIDDEN NOT NULL
    CONSTRAINT DFT_Products_validto DEFAULT('99991231 23:59:59.999'),
  PERIOD FOR SYSTEM_TIME (validfrom, validto);

ALTER TABLE dbo.Products
  SET ( SYSTEM_VERSIONING = ON ( HISTORY_TABLE = dbo.ProductsHistory ) );

ALTER TABLE dbo.Products DROP CONSTRAINT DFT_Products_validfrom, DFT_Products_validto;

COMMIT TRAN;
```

SQL Server supports altering temporal tables. You alter the current table and SQL Server takes care of applying the relevant changes to the history table for you. For instance, suppose that you want to add a column called discontinued to the Products table. You alter the current table by running the following code:

```
ALTER TABLE dbo.Products
  ADD discontinued BIT NOT NULL
    CONSTRAINT DFT_Products_discontinued DEFAULT(0);
```

SQL Server adds the same column to the history table with the specified default value 0 in existing rows, if such were present, but does not add a default constraint in the history table.

Similarly, if you want to drop a column, you alter only the current table, and SQL Server takes care of dropping it from the history table. You will want to start by dropping the default constraint, and then the column. For example, run the following code to drop the column discontinued from the Products table:

```
ALTER TABLE dbo.Products
  DROP CONSTRAINT DFT_Products_discontinued;

ALTER TABLE dbo.Products
  DROP COLUMN discontinued;
```

SQL Server also drops the column discontinued from the history table for you.

## Modifying data

When you modify data in a temporal table, you do so just like with a normal table. You submit your changes to the current table, and SQL Server takes care of writing history rows to the history table when relevant. A couple of things to remember:

1.  SQL Server records the change times in the UTC time zone.

2.  If you apply multiple changes in a transaction, the transaction start time is considered the effective change time for all changes in the transaction.

When you insert rows into the current table, SQL Server sets the start column to the transaction's start time and the end time to the maximum possible point in time in the data type. No rows need to be written to the history table. I ran the examples in this section on November 11th, 2016, so all of the period columns will have this date in the examples. Suppose that at 14:07:26.263 (UTC) you run the following code:

```
INSERT INTO dbo.Products(productid, productname, supplierid, categoryid, unitprice)
  SELECT productid, productname, supplierid, categoryid, unitprice
  FROM Production.Products
  WHERE productid <= 10;
```

Query the current table after inserting the data:

```
SELECT productid, supplierid, unitprice, validfrom, validto
FROM dbo.Products;
```

Notice that in order to return the period columns, the query refers to them explicitly since these columns are marked as hidden in our table. This query generates the following output (of course, in this case the validfrom column will reflect the time I ran the insert):

```
productid  supplierid  unitprice  validfrom                validto
---------- ----------- ---------- ------------------------ ------------------------
1          1           18.00      2016-11-01 14:07:26.263  9999-12-31 23:59:59.999
2          1           19.00      2016-11-01 14:07:26.263  9999-12-31 23:59:59.999
3          1           10.00      2016-11-01 14:07:26.263  9999-12-31 23:59:59.999
4          2           22.00      2016-11-01 14:07:26.263  9999-12-31 23:59:59.999
5          2           21.35      2016-11-01 14:07:26.263  9999-12-31 23:59:59.999
6          3           25.00      2016-11-01 14:07:26.263  9999-12-31 23:59:59.999
7          3           30.00      2016-11-01 14:07:26.263  9999-12-31 23:59:59.999
8          3           40.00      2016-11-01 14:07:26.263  9999-12-31 23:59:59.999
9          4           97.00      2016-11-01 14:07:26.263  9999-12-31 23:59:59.999
10         4           31.00      2016-11-01 14:07:26.263  9999-12-31 23:59:59.999
```

As mentioned, when you insert data, only the current table is affected. Query the history table:

```
SELECT productid, unitprice, validfrom, validto
FROM dbo.ProductsHistory;
```

This query generates an empty set:

```
productid  supplierid  unitprice  validfrom                validto
----------  -----------  ----------  ------------------------  ------------------------
```

When you delete rows, SQL Server moves the affected rows to the history table, and sets the end column to the start time of the transaction that applied the change. Suppose that you run the following code to delete the row for product 10 at 14:08:41.758:

```
DELETE FROM dbo.Products
WHERE productid = 10;
```

An update is handled as a delete plus insert. In other words, the current table will have the new state of the modified rows, with the start column set to the change time, and the history table will have the old state of the modified rows, with the end column set to the change time. For example, suppose that you run the following code at 14:09:18.584:

```
UPDATE dbo.Products
  SET unitprice *= 1.05
WHERE supplierid = 3;
```

Products 6, 7 and 8 are affected.

Run the following code to query the current table after these changes:

```
SELECT productid, supplierid, unitprice, validfrom, validto
FROM dbo.Products;
```

This query generates the following output:

```
productid  supplierid  unitprice  validfrom                validto
----------  -----------  ----------  ------------------------  ------------------------
1          1            18.00      2016-11-01 14:07:26.263  9999-12-31 23:59:59.999
2          1            19.00      2016-11-01 14:07:26.263  9999-12-31 23:59:59.999
3          1            10.00      2016-11-01 14:07:26.263  9999-12-31 23:59:59.999
4          2            22.00      2016-11-01 14:07:26.263  9999-12-31 23:59:59.999
5          2            21.35      2016-11-01 14:07:26.263  9999-12-31 23:59:59.999
6          3            26.25      2016-11-01 14:09:18.584  9999-12-31 23:59:59.999
7          3            31.50      2016-11-01 14:09:18.584  9999-12-31 23:59:59.999
8          3            42.00      2016-11-01 14:09:18.584  9999-12-31 23:59:59.999
9          4            97.00      2016-11-01 14:07:26.263  9999-12-31 23:59:59.999
```

Observe that product 10 isn't present in the table, and products 6, 7 and 8, which are supplied by supplier 3, show the new prices, and a validity period starting at 2016-11-01 14:09:18.584.

Query the history table:

```
SELECT productid, supplierid, unitprice, validfrom, validto
FROM dbo.ProductsHistory;
```

This query generates the following output:

```
productid   supplierid   unitprice   validfrom                 validto
----------  -----------  ----------  ------------------------  ------------------------
10          4            31.00       2016-11-01 14:07:26.263   2016-11-01 14:08:41.758
6           3            25.00       2016-11-01 14:07:26.263   2016-11-01 14:09:18.584
7           3            30.00       2016-11-01 14:07:26.263   2016-11-01 14:09:18.584
8           3            40.00       2016-11-01 14:07:26.263   2016-11-01 14:09:18.584
```

Observe that the old states of both deleted and updated rows are recorded in the history table, and notice their validity periods start with the insert time and end with the delete/update time.

As mentioned, when you modify data in a temporal table, the transaction start time is considered the effective time of the change. If you have multiple modifications within the same user transaction, they will all have the same effective modification time. For example, consider the following code, which modifies three different rows within a single transaction, with five second intervals between the modifications:

```
BEGIN TRAN;

PRINT CAST(SYSUTCDATETIME() AS DATETIME2(3));

UPDATE dbo.Products
  SET unitprice *= 0.95
WHERE productid = 1;

WAITFOR DELAY '00:00:05.000';

UPDATE dbo.Products
  SET unitprice *= 0.90
WHERE productid = 2;

WAITFOR DELAY '00:00:05.000';

UPDATE dbo.Products
  SET unitprice *= 0.85
WHERE productid = 3;

COMMIT TRAN;
```

The PRINT statement reported the following time as the transaction start time when running this code on my system:

```
2016-11-01 14:10:43.470
```

Run the following code to query the modified rows from the current table:

```
SELECT productid, supplierid, unitprice, validfrom, validto
FROM dbo.Products
WHERE productid IN (1, 2, 3);
```

This query generates the following output:

```
productid   supplierid   unitprice   validfrom                 validto
----------  -----------  ----------  ------------------------  ------------------------
1           1            17.10       2016-11-01 14:10:43.470   9999-12-31 23:59:59.999
2           1            17.10       2016-11-01 14:10:43.470   9999-12-31 23:59:59.999
3           1            8.50        2016-11-01 14:10:43.470   9999-12-31 23:59:59.999
```

Notice that all three rows show the same validfrom value, which is the transaction start time reported earlier. The older state of the modified rows was written to the history table with the validto value set to the transaction start time.

If you update the same row multiple times in the same transaction, a curious thing happens. The original and last states of the row will naturally have nonzero length intervals as the validity period; however, the in-between states will have *degenerate intervals* as the validity period where the validfrom value will be equal to the validto value. That's the result of using the transaction start time as the effective time of all changes in the transaction. Since the validity period is a closed-open interval, conceptually, it's as if those states lasted zero time. If you query the history table directly, you will see those rows that have a degenerate interval as the validity period. If you query the temporal table using the FOR SYSTEM_TIME clause to ask for a previous point or period of time, SQL Server will discard those rows.

As an example, run the following code to update the same row multiple times in the same transaction:

```
BEGIN TRAN;

PRINT CAST(SYSUTCDATETIME() AS DATETIME2(3));

UPDATE dbo.Products
  SET unitprice = 1.0
WHERE productid = 9;

WAITFOR DELAY '00:00:05.000';

UPDATE dbo.Products
  SET unitprice = 2.0
WHERE productid = 9;

WAITFOR DELAY '00:00:05.000';

UPDATE dbo.Products
  SET unitprice = 3.0
WHERE productid = 9;

COMMIT TRAN;
```

The PRINT statement reported the following transaction start time when I ran this code on my system:

```
2016-11-01 14:11:38.113
```

Query the current table:

```
SELECT productid, unitprice, validfrom, validto
FROM dbo.Products
WHERE productid = 9;
```

This query generates the following output, showing the current state:

```
productid   unitprice   validfrom                 validto
----------  ----------  ------------------------  ------------------------
9           3.00        2016-11-01 14:11:38.113   9999-12-31 23:59:59.999
```

Query history table:

```
SELECT productid, unitprice, validfrom, validto
FROM dbo.ProductsHistory
WHERE productid = 9;
```

This query generates the following output, showing that two of the states have a degenerate interval as the validity period:

```
productid   unitprice   validfrom                 validto
----------  ----------  ------------------------  ------------------------
9           97.00       2016-11-01 14:07:26.263   2016-11-01 14:11:38.113
9           1.00        2016-11-01 14:11:38.113   2016-11-01 14:11:38.113
9           2.00        2016-11-01 14:11:38.113   2016-11-01 14:11:38.113
```

## Querying data

You can directly query the current and history tables, and get current and historical states of the rows. However, to simplify the code, SQL Server enables you to ask for the state of the data at a previous point or period of time by querying only the current table and specifying a clause called FOR SYSTEM_TIME. Using different subclauses you can specify either a point or a period during which the rows were valid. Behind the scenes, SQL Server will retrieve the data from both the current and history tables as needed, and return a single unified set of rows as the result set of the query. You can also query views with the FOR SYSTEM_TIME clause, provided that there's at least one underlying table that is a temporal table. SQL Server will propagate the clause to the underlying temporal tables.

If you want to run the code samples in this section and get the same results as the ones I'll provide, you need to populate the tables with the same data as in mine. Run the following code to achieve this:

```
USE TSQLV4;

-- drop tables if exist
IF OBJECT_ID(N'dbo.Products', N'U') IS NOT NULL
BEGIN
  IF OBJECTPROPERTY(OBJECT_ID(N'dbo.Products', N'U'), N'TableTemporalType') = 2
    ALTER TABLE dbo.Products SET ( SYSTEM_VERSIONING = OFF );
  DROP TABLE IF EXISTS dbo.ProductsHistory, dbo.Products;
END;
GO
```

```
-- create and populate Products table
CREATE TABLE dbo.Products
(
  productid   INT         NOT NULL
    CONSTRAINT PK_dboProducts PRIMARY KEY(productid),
  productname NVARCHAR(40) NOT NULL,
  supplierid  INT         NOT NULL,
  categoryid  INT         NOT NULL,
  unitprice   MONEY       NOT NULL,
  validfrom   DATETIME2(3) NOT NULL,
  validto     DATETIME2(3) NOT NULL
);

INSERT INTO dbo.Products
  (productid, productname, supplierid, categoryid, unitprice, validfrom, validto)
VALUES
  (1, 'Product HHYDP', 1, 1, 17.10, '20161101 14:10:43.470', '99991231 23:59:59.999'),
  (2, 'Product RECZE', 1, 1, 17.10, '20161101 14:10:43.470', '99991231 23:59:59.999'),
  (3, 'Product IMEHJ', 1, 2,  8.50, '20161101 14:10:43.470', '99991231 23:59:59.999'),
  (4, 'Product KSBRM', 2, 2, 22.00, '20161101 14:07:26.263', '99991231 23:59:59.999'),
  (5, 'Product EPEIM', 2, 2, 21.35, '20161101 14:07:26.263', '99991231 23:59:59.999'),
  (6, 'Product VAIIV', 3, 2, 26.25, '20161101 14:09:18.584', '99991231 23:59:59.999'),
  (7, 'Product HMLNI', 3, 7, 31.50, '20161101 14:09:18.584', '99991231 23:59:59.999'),
  (8, 'Product WVJFP', 3, 2, 42.00, '20161101 14:09:18.584', '99991231 23:59:59.999'),
  (9, 'Product AOZBW', 4, 6,  3.00, '20161101 14:11:38.113', '99991231 23:59:59.999');

-- create and populate ProductsHistory table
CREATE TABLE dbo.ProductsHistory
(
  productid   INT         NOT NULL,
  productname NVARCHAR(40) NOT NULL,
  supplierid  INT         NOT NULL,
  categoryid  INT         NOT NULL,
  unitprice   MONEY       NOT NULL,
  validfrom   DATETIME2(3) NOT NULL,
  validto     DATETIME2(3) NOT NULL,
  INDEX ix_ProductsHistory CLUSTERED(validto, validfrom)
    WITH (DATA_COMPRESSION = PAGE)
);

INSERT INTO dbo.ProductsHistory
  (productid, productname, supplierid, categoryid, unitprice, validfrom, validto)
VALUES
  ( 1, 'Product HHYDP', 1, 1, 18.00, '20161101 14:07:26.263', '20161101 14:10:43.470'),
  ( 2, 'Product RECZE', 1, 1, 19.00, '20161101 14:07:26.263', '20161101 14:10:43.470'),
  ( 3, 'Product IMEHJ', 1, 2, 10.00, '20161101 14:07:26.263', '20161101 14:10:43.470'),
  ( 6, 'Product VAIIV', 3, 2, 25.00, '20161101 14:07:26.263', '20161101 14:09:18.584'),
  ( 7, 'Product HMLNI', 3, 7, 30.00, '20161101 14:07:26.263', '20161101 14:09:18.584'),
  ( 8, 'Product WVJFP', 3, 2, 40.00, '20161101 14:07:26.263', '20161101 14:09:18.584'),
  ( 9, 'Product AOZBW', 4, 6, 97.00, '20161101 14:07:26.263', '20161101 14:11:38.113'),
  ( 9, 'Product AOZBW', 4, 6,  1.00, '20161101 14:11:38.113', '20161101 14:11:38.113'),
  ( 9, 'Product AOZBW', 4, 6,  2.00, '20161101 14:11:38.113', '20161101 14:11:38.113'),
  (10, 'Product YHXGE', 4, 8, 31.00, '20161101 14:07:26.263', '20161101 14:08:41.758');

-- enable system versioning
```

```
ALTER TABLE dbo.Products ADD PERIOD FOR SYSTEM_TIME (validfrom, validto);

ALTER TABLE dbo.Products ALTER COLUMN validfrom ADD HIDDEN;
ALTER TABLE dbo.Products ALTER COLUMN validto ADD HIDDEN;

ALTER TABLE dbo.Products
  SET ( SYSTEM_VERSIONING = ON ( HISTORY_TABLE = dbo.ProductsHistory ) );
```

Query the current table to see its contents:

```
SELECT productid, supplierid, unitprice, validfrom, validto
FROM dbo.Products;
```

This query generates the following output:

```
productid  supplierid  unitprice  validfrom                validto
---------  ----------  ---------  -----------------------  -----------------------
1          1           17.10      2016-11-01 14:10:43.470  9999-12-31 23:59:59.999
2          1           17.10      2016-11-01 14:10:43.470  9999-12-31 23:59:59.999
3          1           8.50       2016-11-01 14:10:43.470  9999-12-31 23:59:59.999
4          2           22.00      2016-11-01 14:07:26.263  9999-12-31 23:59:59.999
5          2           21.35      2016-11-01 14:07:26.263  9999-12-31 23:59:59.999
6          3           26.25      2016-11-01 14:09:18.584  9999-12-31 23:59:59.999
7          3           31.50      2016-11-01 14:09:18.584  9999-12-31 23:59:59.999
8          3           42.00      2016-11-01 14:09:18.584  9999-12-31 23:59:59.999
9          4           3.00       2016-11-01 14:11:38.113  9999-12-31 23:59:59.999
```

Query the history table to see its contents:

```
SELECT productid, supplierid, unitprice, validfrom, validto
FROM dbo.ProductsHistory;
```

This query generates the following output:

```
productid  supplierid  unitprice  validfrom                validto
---------  ----------  ---------  -----------------------  -----------------------
10         4           31.00      2016-11-01 14:07:26.263  2016-11-01 14:08:41.758
6          3           25.00      2016-11-01 14:07:26.263  2016-11-01 14:09:18.584
7          3           30.00      2016-11-01 14:07:26.263  2016-11-01 14:09:18.584
8          3           40.00      2016-11-01 14:07:26.263  2016-11-01 14:09:18.584
1          1           18.00      2016-11-01 14:07:26.263  2016-11-01 14:10:43.470
2          1           19.00      2016-11-01 14:07:26.263  2016-11-01 14:10:43.470
3          1           10.00      2016-11-01 14:07:26.263  2016-11-01 14:10:43.470
9          4           97.00      2016-11-01 14:07:26.263  2016-11-01 14:11:38.113
9          4           1.00       2016-11-01 14:11:38.113  2016-11-01 14:11:38.113
9          4           2.00       2016-11-01 14:11:38.113  2016-11-01 14:11:38.113
```

A commonly used subclause of the FOR SYSTEM_TIME clause is AS OF @dt. It returns the rows that were valid during the input point in time @dt. Since the validity period is a closed-open interval, you get the rows where @dt >= validfrom AND @dt < validto (@dt is on or after validfrom and before validto). In other words, the validity period starts on or before @dt and ends after @dt.

Recall that I issued the first insertion into the Products table at 14:07:26.263. Run the following code to query the state of the data at a point in time prior to the first insertion:

```
SELECT productid, supplierid, unitprice
FROM dbo.Products FOR SYSTEM_TIME AS OF '20161101 14:06:00.000';
```

You get an empty set back.

Run the following code to query the state of the data after the first insertion and before any other modification:

```
SELECT productid, supplierid, unitprice
FROM dbo.Products FOR SYSTEM_TIME AS OF '20161101 14:07:55.000';
```

This query generates the following output:

```
productid   supplierid   unitprice
----------  -----------  ----------
4           2            22.00
5           2            21.35
10          4            31.00
6           3            25.00
7           3            30.00
8           3            40.00
1           1            18.00
2           1            19.00
3           1            10.00
9           4            97.00
```

You can also query multiple instances of the table, each with a different point in time as input to the AS OF clause, and this way compare different states of the data at different points in time. For example, the following query identifies products that experienced an increase in the unit price between the points 14:08:55 and 14:10:55, and returns the percent of increase in the price:

```
SELECT T1.productid, T1.productname,
  CAST( (T2.unitprice / T1.unitprice - 1.0) * 100.0 AS NUMERIC(10, 2) ) AS pct
FROM dbo.Products FOR SYSTEM_TIME AS OF '20161101 14:08:55.000' AS T1
  INNER JOIN dbo.Products FOR SYSTEM_TIME AS OF '20161101 14:10:55.000' AS T2
    ON T1.productid = T2.productid
    AND T2.unitprice > T1.unitprice;
```

This query generates the following output:

```
productid   productname     pct
----------  --------------  -----
6           Product VAIIV   5.00
7           Product HMLNI   5.00
8           Product WVJFP   5.00
```

It would appear that three products experience a five percent increase in their price.

The second subclause of the FOR SYSTEM_TIME clause is FROM @start TO @end. It returns all rows that have a validity period that intersects with the input period, exclusive of the two input delimiters. You get the rows where validfrom < @end AND validto > @start. Namely the validity interval starts before the input interval ends and ends after the input interval starts. As mentioned, the FOR SYSTEM_TIME clause discards degenerate intervals with all subclauses.

As an example, the following query returns the versions of product 9 that were valid during a period that ended after 2016-11-01 14:00:00.000 and started before 2016-11-01 14:11:38.113 (intersection excluding the edges):

```
SELECT productid, supplierid, unitprice, validfrom, validto
FROM dbo.Products
   FOR SYSTEM_TIME FROM '20161101 14:00:00.000' TO '20161101 14:11:38.113'
WHERE productid = 9;
```

This query generates the following output:

```
productid   supplierid   unitprice   validfrom                 validto
----------  -----------  ----------  ------------------------  ------------------------
9           4            97.00       2016-11-01 14:07:26.263   2016-11-01 14:11:38.113
```

The output shows that there's only one version that qualifies. The product row experienced a change at 2016-11-01 14:11:38.113, but since both input delimiters are excluded, that version isn't returned. In order to include the input end time, use the subclause BETWEEN @start AND @end instead. You get the rows where validfrom <= @end AND validto > @start. Namely, the validity interval starts *on or* before the input interval ends and ends after the input interval starts.

Here's the same query as the last, only this time using BETWEEN instead of FROM:

```
SELECT productid, supplierid, unitprice, validfrom, validto
FROM dbo.Products
   FOR SYSTEM_TIME BETWEEN '20161101 14:00:00.000' AND '20161101 14:11:38.113'
WHERE productid = 9;
```

This time the query returns two versions of the row for product 9:

```
productid   supplierid   unitprice   validfrom                 validto
----------  -----------  ----------  ------------------------  ------------------------
9           4            3.00        2016-11-01 14:11:38.113   9999-12-31 23:59:59.999
9           4            97.00       2016-11-01 14:07:26.263   2016-11-01 14:11:38.113
```

The CONTAINED IN(@start, @end) subclause returns rows with a validity period that is entirely contained within the input period, inclusive of both input delimiters. You get the rows where validfrom >= @start AND validto <= @end. Meaning, that the validity interval starts on or after the input interval starts and ends on or before the input interval ends.

As an example, the following code returns the rows with a validity that is contained in the period that starts with 2016-11-01 14:07:00.000 and ends with 2016-11-01 14:10:00.000:

```
SELECT productid, supplierid, unitprice, validfrom, validto
FROM dbo.Products
   FOR SYSTEM_TIME CONTAINED IN('20161101 14:07:00.000', '20161101 14:10:00.000');
```

This query generates the following output:

```
productid   supplierid   unitprice   validfrom                 validto
----------  -----------  ----------  ------------------------  ------------------------
10          4            31.00       2016-11-01 14:07:26.263   2016-11-01 14:08:41.758
6           3            25.00       2016-11-01 14:07:26.263   2016-11-01 14:09:18.584
7           3            30.00       2016-11-01 14:07:26.263   2016-11-01 14:09:18.584
8           3            40.00       2016-11-01 14:07:26.263   2016-11-01 14:09:18.584
```

What's interesting is that you would expect the SQL Server optimizer to realize that since all rows in the current table have a validity period that ends with the maximum value in the type, there's no need to internally access the current table at all. But that's not the case. Examine the execution plan that SQL Server creates for this query as shown in Figure 2-6.

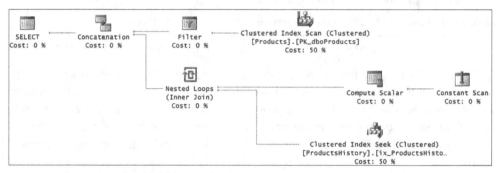

**FIGURE 2-6** Query plan when CHECK constraint doesn't exist

Notice that both tables are accessed.

What you can do to help the optimizer figure out it doesn't need to access the current table is to add a CHECK constraint that verifies that the validto column value is indeed the maximum possible value in the type, like so:

```
ALTER TABLE dbo.Products
  ADD CONSTRAINT CHK_Products_validto
    CHECK (validto = '99991231 23:59:59.999');
```

Rerun the CONTAINED IN query after adding the constraint and examine the plan for this query as shown in Figure 2-7.

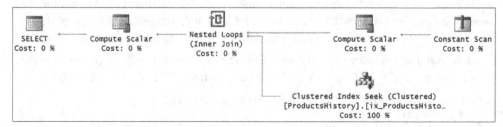

**FIGURE 2-7** Query plan when CHECK constraint exists

This time based on a contradiction detection the optimizer realizes that it doesn't need to access the current table.

The ALL subclause simply returns all versions, from both the current and history table, excluding degenerate intervals. As an example, the following query returns all versions of all rows from the Products table:

```
SELECT productid, supplierid, unitprice, validfrom, validto
FROM dbo.Products FOR SYSTEM_TIME ALL
ORDER BY productid, validfrom, validto;
```

This query generates the following output:

```
productid  supplierid  unitprice  validfrom                validto
---------- ----------- ---------- ------------------------ ------------------------
1          1           18.00      2016-11-01 14:07:26.263  2016-11-01 14:10:43.470
1          1           17.10      2016-11-01 14:10:43.470  9999-12-31 23:59:59.999
2          1           19.00      2016-11-01 14:07:26.263  2016-11-01 14:10:43.470
2          1           17.10      2016-11-01 14:10:43.470  9999-12-31 23:59:59.999
3          1           10.00      2016-11-01 14:07:26.263  2016-11-01 14:10:43.470
3          1           8.50       2016-11-01 14:10:43.470  9999-12-31 23:59:59.999
4          2           22.00      2016-11-01 14:07:26.263  9999-12-31 23:59:59.999
5          2           21.35      2016-11-01 14:07:26.263  9999-12-31 23:59:59.999
6          3           25.00      2016-11-01 14:07:26.263  2016-11-01 14:09:18.584
6          3           26.25      2016-11-01 14:09:18.584  9999-12-31 23:59:59.999
7          3           30.00      2016-11-01 14:07:26.263  2016-11-01 14:09:18.584
7          3           31.50      2016-11-01 14:09:18.584  9999-12-31 23:59:59.999
8          3           40.00      2016-11-01 14:07:26.263  2016-11-01 14:09:18.584
8          3           42.00      2016-11-01 14:09:18.584  9999-12-31 23:59:59.999
9          4           97.00      2016-11-01 14:07:26.263  2016-11-01 14:11:38.113
9          4           3.00       2016-11-01 14:11:38.113  9999-12-31 23:59:59.999
10         4           31.00      2016-11-01 14:07:26.263  2016-11-01 14:08:41.758
```

Remember that the period columns store the time in the UTC time zone. If you want to present the values in a desired target time zone, you can use the AT TIME ZONE function to achieve this. There are a couple of things to think about, though. One is that you need one conversion from a non-offset type to an offset type using <period_column> AT TIME ZONE 'UTC', and another conversion to switch the UTC value to the target time zone. Another is that when the validto value is the maximum in the type, you don't want to switch its offset, but rather keep it as UTC. You can use a CASE expression to achieve this. As an example, the following query returns all versions of rows from the Products table and presents the period column values in the time zone Pacific Standard Time:

```
SELECT productid, unitprice,
  validfrom AT TIME ZONE 'UTC' AT TIME ZONE 'Pacific Standard Time' AS validfrom,
  CASE
    WHEN validto = '99991231 23:59:59.999'
      THEN validto AT TIME ZONE 'UTC'
    ELSE validto AT TIME ZONE 'UTC' AT TIME ZONE 'Pacific Standard Time'
  END AS validto
FROM dbo.Products FOR SYSTEM_TIME ALL
ORDER BY productid, validfrom, validto;
```

This query generates the following output:

```
productid  unitprice  validfrom                        validto
---------- ---------- -------------------------------- --------------------------------
1          18.00      2016-11-01 07:07:26.263 -07:00   2016-11-01 07:10:43.470 -07:00
1          17.10      2016-11-01 07:10:43.470 -07:00   9999-12-31 23:59:59.999 +00:00
2          19.00      2016-11-01 07:07:26.263 -07:00   2016-11-01 07:10:43.470 -07:00
2          17.10      2016-11-01 07:10:43.470 -07:00   9999-12-31 23:59:59.999 +00:00
3          10.00      2016-11-01 07:07:26.263 -07:00   2016-11-01 07:10:43.470 -07:00
3          8.50       2016-11-01 07:10:43.470 -07:00   9999-12-31 23:59:59.999 +00:00
4          22.00      2016-11-01 07:07:26.263 -07:00   9999-12-31 23:59:59.999 +00:00
5          21.35      2016-11-01 07:07:26.263 -07:00   9999-12-31 23:59:59.999 +00:00
6          25.00      2016-11-01 07:07:26.263 -07:00   2016-11-01 07:09:18.584 -07:00
6          26.25      2016-11-01 07:09:18.584 -07:00   9999-12-31 23:59:59.999 +00:00
7          30.00      2016-11-01 07:07:26.263 -07:00   2016-11-01 07:09:18.584 -07:00
7          31.50      2016-11-01 07:09:18.584 -07:00   9999-12-31 23:59:59.999 +00:00
8          40.00      2016-11-01 07:07:26.263 -07:00   2016-11-01 07:09:18.584 -07:00
8          42.00      2016-11-01 07:09:18.584 -07:00   9999-12-31 23:59:59.999 +00:00
9          97.00      2016-11-01 07:07:26.263 -07:00   2016-11-01 07:11:38.113 -07:00
9          3.00       2016-11-01 07:11:38.113 -07:00   9999-12-31 23:59:59.999 +00:00
10         31.00      2016-11-01 07:07:26.263 -07:00   2016-11-01 07:08:41.758 -07:00
```

When you're done, run the following code for cleanup:

```
IF OBJECT_ID(N'dbo.Products', N'U') IS NOT NULL
BEGIN
  IF OBJECTPROPERTY(OBJECT_ID(N'dbo.Products', N'U'), N'TableTemporalType') = 2
    ALTER TABLE dbo.Products SET ( SYSTEM_VERSIONING = OFF );
  DROP TABLE IF EXISTS dbo.ProductsHistory, dbo.Products;
END;
```

# Query and output XML data

XML is a widely used standard for data exchange, that calls Web services methods, configuration files, and more. This section starts with a short introduction to XML. After that, you learn how to create XML as a result of a query by using different flavors of the FOR XML clause. The section finishes with information on shredding XML to relational tables by using the OPENXML rowset function.

The following is an example of an XML document, created with the FOR XML clause of the SELECT statement:

```
<CustomersOrders>
  <Customer custid="1" companyname="Customer NRZBB">
    <Order orderid="10692" orderdate="2007-10-03T00:00:00" />
    <Order orderid="10702" orderdate="2007-10-13T00:00:00" />
    <Order orderid="10952" orderdate="2008-03-16T00:00:00" />
  </Customer>
  <Customer custid="2" companyname="Customer MLTDN">
    <Order orderid="10308" orderdate="2006-09-18T00:00:00" />
    <Order orderid="10926" orderdate="2008-03-04T00:00:00" />
  </Customer>
</CustomersOrders>
```

As you can see, XML uses *tags* to name parts of an *XML document*. These parts are called *elements*. Every begin tag, such as <Customer>, must have a corresponding end tag, in this case </Customer>. If an element has no nested elements, the notation can be abbreviated to a single tag that denotes the beginning and end of an element, such as <Order ... />. Elements can be nested, and tags cannot be interleaved; the end tag of a parent element must be after the end tag of the last nested element. If every begin tag has a corresponding end tag, and if tags are nested properly, the XML document is *well-formed*.

XML documents are *ordered*. This does not mean they are ordered by any specific element value; it means that the position of elements matters. For example, the element with orderid equal to 10702 in the preceding example is the second Order element under the first Customer element.

XML is *case-sensitive Unicode text*. You should never forget that XML is case sensitive. In addition, some characters in XML, such as <, which introduces a tag, are processed as *markup* and have special meanings. If you want to include these characters in the values of your XML document, they must be escaped using an ampersand (&), followed by a special code, followed by a semicolon (;), as shown in Table 2-1.

**TABLE 2-1** Characters with special values in XML documents

| Character | Replacement text |
| --- | --- |
| & (ampersand) | & |
| " (quotation mark) | " |
| < (less than) | &lt; |
| > (greater than) | &gt; |
| ' (apostrophe) | ' |

Alternatively, you can use the special XML CDATA section written as <![CDATA[...]]>. You can replace the three dots with any character string that does not include the string literal "]]>"; this will prevent special characters in the string from being parsed as XML markup.

XML can have a prolog at the beginning of the document, denoting the XML version and encoding of the document, such as <?xml version="1.0" encoding="ISO-8859-15"?>.

In addition to XML documents, you can also have *XML fragments*. The only difference between a document and a fragment is that a document has a single *root node*, like <CustomersOrders> in the preceding example. If you delete this node, you get an XML fragment.

As you can see from the example, elements can have *attributes*. Attributes have their own names, and their values are enclosed in quotes. This is *attribute-centric* presentation. However, you can write XML differently; every attribute can be a nested element of the original element. This is *element-centric* presentation.

Element names do not have to be unique, because they can be referred to by their position; however, to distinguish between elements from different business areas, different departments, or different companies, you can add *namespaces*. You declare namespaces used in the root element of an XML document. You can also use an alias for every single namespace. Then you prefix element names with a namespace *alias*.

XML is very flexible. There are very few rules for creating a well-formed XML document. In an XML document, the actual data is mixed with *metadata*, such as element and attribute names. Because XML is text, it is very convenient for exchanging data between different systems and even between different platforms. However, when exchanging data, it becomes important to have metadata fixed. If you had to import a document with customers' orders, as in the preceding examples, every couple of minutes, you'd definitely want to automate the import process. Imagine how hard you'd have to work if the metadata changed with every new import.

Many different standards have evolved to describe the metadata of XML documents. Currently, the most widely used metadata description is with *XML Schema Description* (XSD) documents. XSD documents are XML documents that describe the metadata of other XML documents. The schema of an XSD document is predefined. With the XSD standard, you can specify element names, data types, and number of occurrences of an element, constraints, and more.

> **MORE INFO   ON XML SCHEMAS**
>
> For details about XML schemas, see the MSDN article "Understanding XML Schema" at *https://msdn.microsoft.com/en-us/library/aa468557.aspx.*

When you check whether an XML document complies with a schema, you *validate* the document. A document with a predefined schema is said to be a *typed* XML document.

## Producing and using XML in queries

With the T-SQL SELECT statement, you can create all of the XML outputs that are shown in this section. This section explains how you can convert a query result set to XML by using the FOR XML clause of the SELECT statement. Here you will learn about the most useful options and directives of this clause.

> **MORE INFO   ON THE FOR XML CLAUSE**
>
> For additional information about the FOR XML clause, please refer to the Books Online for SQL Server 2016 article "FOR XML (SQL Server)" at *https://msdn.microsoft.com/en-us/library/ms178107.aspx.*

The first option for creating XML from a query result is the RAW option. The XML created is quite close to the relational (tabular) presentation of the data. In RAW mode, every row from the returned result set converts to a single element named row, and columns translate to the attributes of this element. Here is an example of a query that creates the RAW version of the FOR XML output:

```
SELECT Customer.custid, Customer.companyname,
```

```
   [Order].orderid, [Order].orderdate
FROM Sales.Customers AS Customer
  INNER JOIN Sales.Orders AS [Order]
    ON Customer.custid = [Order].custid
WHERE Customer.custid <= 2
  AND [Order].orderid %2 = 0
ORDER BY Customer.custid, [Order].orderid
FOR XML RAW;
```

This query generates the following output:

```
<row custid="1" companyname="Customer NRZBB" orderid="10692" orderdate="2015-10-03" />
<row custid="1" companyname="Customer NRZBB" orderid="10702" orderdate="2015-10-13" />
<row custid="1" companyname="Customer NRZBB" orderid="10952" orderdate="2016-03-16" />
<row custid="2" companyname="Customer MLTDN" orderid="10308" orderdate="2014-09-18" />
<row custid="2" companyname="Customer MLTDN" orderid="10926" orderdate="2016-03-04" />
```

You can notice that the result is actually an XML fragment and not an XML document, because the root node is missing. You can enhance the RAW mode by renaming the row element, adding a root element, including namespaces, and making the XML returned element-centric.

The FOR XML AUTO option gives you nice XML documents with nested elements, and it is not complicated to use. In AUTO and RAW modes, you can use the keyword ELEMENTS to produce element-centric XML. The WITH NAMESPACES clause, preceding the SELECT part of the query, defines namespaces and aliases in the returned XML. Here is an example of a query with the FOR XML AUTO option used, element-centric, with a namespace defined:

```
WITH XMLNAMESPACES('ER70761-CustomersOrders' AS co)
SELECT [co:Customer].custid AS [co:custid],
  [co:Customer].companyname AS [co:companyname],
  [co:Order].orderid AS [co:orderid],
  [co:Order].orderdate AS [co:orderdate]
FROM Sales.Customers AS [co:Customer]
  INNER JOIN Sales.Orders AS [co:Order]
    ON [co:Customer].custid = [co:Order].custid
WHERE [co:Customer].custid <= 2
  AND [co:Order].orderid %2 = 0
ORDER BY [co:Customer].custid, [co:Order].orderid
FOR XML AUTO, ELEMENTS, ROOT('CustomersOrders');
```

The T-SQL table and column aliases in the query are used to produce element names, prefixed with a namespace. A colon is used in XML to separate the namespace from the element name. The WHERE clause of the query limits the output to two customers, with only every second order for each customer retrieved. The output is quite a nice element-centric XML document. This query produces the following result (shown here in abbreviated form):

```
<CustomersOrders xmlns:co="ER70761-CustomersOrders">
  <co:Customer>
    <co:custid>1</co:custid>
    <co:companyname>Customer NRZBB</co:companyname>
    <co:Order>
      <co:orderid>10692</co:orderid>
```

```
        <co:orderdate>2015-10-03</co:orderdate>
    </co:Order>
...
    <co:custid>2</co:custid>
    <co:companyname>Customer MLTDN</co:companyname>
    <co:Order>
...
    </co:Order>
  </co:Customer>
</CustomersOrders>
```

Note that a proper ORDER BY clause is very important. With the SELECT statement, you are actually formatting the returned XML. Without the ORDER BY clause, the order of rows returned is unpredictable, and you can get a weird XML document with an element repeated multiple times with just part of nested elements every time.

It is not only the ORDER BY clause that is important; the order of columns in the SELECT clause also influences the XML returned. SQL Server uses column order to determine the nesting of elements. The order of the columns should follow one-to-many relationships. A customer can have many orders; therefore, you should have customer columns before order columns in your query.

You might be vexed by the fact that you have to take care of column order; in a relation, the order of columns and rows is not important. Nevertheless, you have to realize that the result of your query is not a relation; it is text in XML format, and parts of your query are used for formatting the text.

There are additional more detailed options for formatting the returned XML document by using the FOR XML PATH option. In addition, besides the XML document, you can also return the XSD schema of the document with the XMLSCHEMA directive.

Besides generating XML from a query, you can also do the opposite: convert XML to tables. Converting XML to relational tables is known as *shredding* XML. You shred XML with the OPENXML `rowset` function.

The OPENXML function provides a rowset over in-memory XML documents by using the *Document Object Model* (DOM) presentation. Before parsing the DOM, you need to prepare it. To prepare the DOM presentation of XML, you need to call the system stored procedure sys.sp_xml_preparedocument. After you shred the document, you must remove the DOM presentation by using the system procedure sys.sp_xml_removedocument.

The OPENXML function uses the following parameters:

- An XML DOM document handle, returned by sp_xml_preparedocument
- An XPath expression to find the nodes you want to map to rows of a rowset returned
- A description of the rowset returned
- Mapping between XML nodes and rowset columns

The document handle is an integer. This is the simplest parameter. The XPath expression is specified as *rowpattern*, which defines how XML nodes translate to rows. The path to a node is used as a pattern; nodes below the selected node define rows of the returned rowset.

You can map XML elements or attributes to rows and columns by using the WITH clause of the OPENXML function. In this clause, you can specify an existing table, which is used as a template for the rowset returned, or you can define a table with syntax similar to the CREATE TABLE statement syntax.

The OPENXML function accepts an optional third parameter, called flags, which allows you to specify the mapping used between the XML data and the relational rowset. The value 1 means attribute-centric mapping, and 2 means element-centric. Flag value 8 can be combined with values 1 and 2 with a bitwise OR (|) operator to get both attribute and element-centric mapping. The XML used for the following OPENXML examples uses attributes and elements; for example, `custid` is the attribute and `companyname` is the element. The intention of this slightly overcomplicated XML is to show you the difference between attribute-centric and element-centric mappings. The following code shreds an XML by using 11 for the flag parameter (8 | 1 | 2).

```
DECLARE @DocHandle AS INT;
DECLARE @XmlDocument AS NVARCHAR(1000);
SET @XmlDocument = N'
<CustomersOrders>
  <Customer custid="1">
    <companyname>Customer NRZBB</companyname>
    <Order orderid="10692">
      <orderdate>2015-10-03T00:00:00</orderdate>
    </Order>
    <Order orderid="10702">
      <orderdate>2015-10-13T00:00:00</orderdate>
    </Order>
    <Order orderid="10952">
      <orderdate>2016-03-16T00:00:00</orderdate>
    </Order>
  </Customer>
  <Customer custid="2">
    <companyname>Customer MLTDN</companyname>
    <Order orderid="10308">
      <orderdate>2014-09-18T00:00:00</orderdate>
    </Order>
    <Order orderid="10926">
      <orderdate>2016-03-04T00:00:00</orderdate>
    </Order>
  </Customer>
</CustomersOrders>';
-- Create an internal representation
EXEC sys.sp_xml_preparedocument @DocHandle OUTPUT, @XmlDocument;
-- Attribute- and element-centric mapping
-- Combining flag 8 with flags 1 and 2
SELECT *
FROM OPENXML (@DocHandle, '/CustomersOrders/Customer', 11)
    WITH (custid INT,
          companyname NVARCHAR(40));
-- Remove the DOM
EXEC sys.sp_xml_removedocument @DocHandle;
```

This query produces the following result:

```
custid      companyname
----------- ----------------------------------------
1           Customer NRZBB
2           Customer MLTDN
```

> **MORE INFO** **ON OPENXML**
>
> For more details about the OPENXML function, please refer to the "OPENXML (Transact-SQL)" topic at *https://msdn.microsoft.com/en-us/library/ms186918.aspx*.

## Querying XML data with XQuery

*XQuery* is a standard language for browsing XML instances and returning XML output. It is much richer than *XPath* expressions—an older standard, which you can use for simple navigation only. With XQuery, you can navigate as with XPath; however, you can also loop over nodes, shape the returned XML instance, and much more.

XQuery, like XML, is case sensitive. For example, if you write Data() instead of data(), you will get an error stating that there is no Data() function. XQuery returns sequences. Sequences can include *atomic* values or *complex* values (XML nodes). Any node, such as an element, attribute, text, processing instruction, comment, or document, can be included in the sequence. Of course, you can format the sequences to get well-formed XML.

Every identifier in XQuery is a qualified name, or a *QName*. A QName consists of a local name and, optionally, a namespace prefix. You define namespaces in the *prolog*, which appears at the beginning of your XQuery expression. You separate the prolog from the query body with a semicolon. In addition, in T-SQL, you can declare namespaces used in XQuery expressions in advance in the WITH clause of the SELECT statement. If your XML uses a single namespace, you can also declare it as the default namespace for all elements in the XQuery prolog.

XQuery uses about 50 predefined data types. Do not worry too much about XQuery types; you'll never use most of them. This paragraph lists only the most important ones, without going into details about them. XQuery data types are divided into node types and atomic types. The node types include attribute, comment, element, namespace, text, processing-instruction, and document-node. The most important atomic types you might use in queries are xs:boolean, xs:string, xs:QName, xs:date, xs:time, xs:datetime, xs:float, xs:double, xs:decimal and xs:integer. Just as there are many data types, there are dozens of functions in XQuery as well.

A basic way to navigate in the XML document using XQuery is with XPath expressions. With XQuery, you can specify a path absolutely or relatively from the current node. XQuery takes care of the current position in the document; it means you can refer to a path relatively, starting from current node, where you navigated through a previous path expression. Every path consists of a sequence of steps, listed from left to right. A complete path might take the following form: `Node-name/child::element-name[@attribute-name=value]`.

The real power of XQuery lies in the so-called *FLWOR* expressions. FLWOR is the acronym for `for`, `let`, `where`, `order by`, and `return`. A FLWOR expression is actually a `for` each loop. You can use it to iterate through a sequence returned by an XPath expression. Although you typically iterate through a sequence of nodes, you can use FLWOR expressions to iterate through any sequence. You can limit the nodes to be processed with a predicate, sort the nodes, and format the returned XML. The parts of a FLWOR statement are:

- **For**   With a `for` clause, you bind iterator variables to input sequences. Input sequences are either sequences of nodes or sequences of atomic values. You create atomic value sequences using literals or functions.

- **Let**   With the optional `let` clause, you assign a value to a variable for a specific iteration. The expression used for an assignment can return a sequence of nodes or a sequence of atomic values.

- **Where**   With the optional `where` clause, you filter the iteration.

- **Order by**   Using the `order by` clause, you can control the order in which the elements of the input sequence are processed. You control the order based on atomic values.

- **Return**   The `return` clause is evaluated once per iteration, and the results are returned to the client in the iteration order. With this clause, you format the resulting XML.

Here is an example of a SELECT statement with a complex XQuery expression that uses all of the five FLWOR expressions:

```
DECLARE @x AS XML = N'
<CustomersOrders>
  <Customer custid="1">
    <!-- Comment 111 -->
    <companyname>Customer NRZBB</companyname>
    <Order orderid="10692">
      <orderdate>2015-10-03T00:00:00</orderdate>
    </Order>
    <Order orderid="10702">
      <orderdate>2015-10-13T00:00:00</orderdate>
    </Order>
    <Order orderid="10952">
      <orderdate>2016-03-16T00:00:00</orderdate>
    </Order>
  </Customer>
  <Customer custid="2">
    <!-- Comment 222 -->
    <companyname>Customer MLTDN</companyname>
    <Order orderid="10308">
      <orderdate>2014-09-18T00:00:00</orderdate>
    </Order>
    <Order orderid="10952">
      <orderdate>2016-03-04T00:00:00</orderdate>
    </Order>
```

```
          </Customer>
</CustomersOrders>';
SELECT @x.query('for $i in CustomersOrders/Customer/Order
                 let $j := $i/orderdate
                 where $i/@orderid < 10900
                 order by ($j)[1]
                 return
                 <Order-orderid-element>
                  <orderid>{data($i/@orderid)}</orderid>
                  {$j}
                 </Order-orderid-element>')
      AS [Filtered, sorted and reformatted orders with let clause];
```

This query produces the following XML fragment:

```
<Order-orderid-element>
  <orderid>10308</orderid>
  <orderdate>2014-09-18T00:00:00</orderdate>
</Order-orderid-element>
<Order-orderid-element>
  <orderid>10692</orderid>
  <orderdate>2015-10-03T00:00:00</orderdate>
</Order-orderid-element>
<Order-orderid-element>
  <orderid>10702</orderid>
  <orderdate>2015-10-13T00:00:00</orderdate>
</Order-orderid-element>
```

> **MORE INFO**  **ON XQUERY**
>
> For more details on XQuery, please refer to the MSDN topic "XQuery Language Reference
> (SQL Server)" at *https://msdn.microsoft.com/en-us/library/ms189075.aspx.*

## The XML data type

In SQL Server, you can store XML as simple text. However, plain text representation means
having no knowledge of the structure built into an XML document. You can decompose the
text, store it in multiple relational tables, and use relational technologies to manipulate the
data. Relational structures are quite static and not so easy to change. Think of dynamic or
volatile XML structures. Storing XML data in a native XML data type solves these problems,
enabling functionality attached to the type that can accommodate support for a wide variety
of XML technologies. SQL Server supports a native XML data type.

In the XQuery introduction in this chapter, you saw the XML data type. The XQuery expression was a parameter for the query() method of this type. The XML data type supports five
methods that accept an XQuery expression as a parameter. Those methods enable querying
(the query() method), retrieving atomic values (the value() method), existence checks (the
exist() method), modifying sections within the XML data (the modify() method) as opposed
to overwriting the whole thing, and shredding XML data into multiple rows in a result set (the
nodes() method).

The value() method of the XML data type returns a scalar value, so it can be specified anywhere where scalar values are allowed, for example in the SELECT list of a query. Note that the value() method accepts an XQuery expression as the first input parameter. The second parameter is the SQL Server data type returned. The value() method must return a scalar value; therefore, you have to specify the position of the element in the sequence you are browsing, even if you know that there is only one.

You can use the exist() method to test if a specific node exists in an XML instance. Typical usage of this clause is in the WHERE clause of T-SQL queries. The exist() method returns a bit, a flag that represents true or false. It can return the following:

- 1, representing true, if the XQuery expression in a query returns a nonempty result. That means that the node searched for exists in the XML instance.

- 0, representing false, if the XQuery expression returns an empty result.

- NULL, if the XML instance is NULL.

The query() method, as the name implies, is used to query XML data. You already know this method from an earlier example. It returns an instance of an untyped XML value.

The XML data type is a large object type. The amount of data stored in a column of this type can be very large. It would not be very practical to replace the complete value when all you need is just to change a small portion of it, for example, a scalar value of some subelement. The SQL Server XML data type provides you with the modify() method, similar in concept to the WRITE method that can be used in a T-SQL UPDATE statement for VARCHAR(MAX) and the other MAX types. You invoke the modify() method in an UPDATE T-SQL statement.

The W3C standard doesn't support data modification with XQuery. However, SQL Server provides its own language extensions to support data modification with XQuery. SQL Server XQuery supports three data modification language (DML) keywords for data modification: insert, delete, and replace value of.

The nodes() method is useful when you want to shred an XML value into relational data. Its purpose is therefore the same as the purpose of the OPENXML rowset function introduced earlier. However, using the nodes() method is usually much faster than preparing the DOM with a call to sp_xml_preparedocument, executing a SELECT ... FROM OPENXML statement, and calling sp_xml_removedocument. The nodes() method prepares DOM internally, during the execution of the SELECT statement. The OPENXML approach could be faster if you prepared the DOM once and then shredded it multiple times in the same batch.

The result of the nodes() method is a result set that contains logical copies of the original XML instances. In those logical copies, the context node of every row instance is set to one of the nodes identified by the XQuery expression, meaning that you get a row for every single node from the starting point defined by the XQuery expression. The nodes() method returns copies of the XML values, so you have to use additional methods to extract the scalar values out of them. The nodes() method has to be invoked for every row in the table. With the T-SQL APPLY operator, you can invoke a right table expression for every row of a left table expression in the FROM part.

You will learn how to use an XML data type inside your database through an example. This example shows how you can make a relational database schema dynamic. The example extends the Products table from the TSQLV4 database.

Suppose that you need to store some specific attributes only for beverages and other attributes only for condiments. For example, you need to store the percentage of recommended daily allowance (RDA) of vitamins only for beverages, and a short description only for condiments to indicate the condiment's general character (such as sweet, spicy, or salty). You could add an XML data type column to the Production.Products table; for this example, call it additionalattributes. Because the other product categories have no additional attributes, this column has to be nullable. The following code alters the Production.Products table to add this column:

```
ALTER TABLE Production.Products
 ADD additionalattributes XML NULL;
```

Before inserting data in the new column, you might want to constrain the values of this column. You should use a typed XML, which is an XML validated against a schema. With an XML schema, you constrain the possible nodes, the data type of those nodes, and more. In SQL Server, you can validate XML data against an XML schema collection. This is exactly what you need for a dynamic schema; if you could validate XML data against a single schema only, you could not use an XML data type for a dynamic schema solution, because XML instances would be limited to a single schema. Validation against a collection of schemas enables support of different schemas for beverages and condiments. If you wanted to validate XML values only against a single schema, you would define only a single schema in the collection.

You create the schema collection by using the CREATE XML SCHEMA COLLECTION T-SQL statement. You have to supply the XML schema, an XSD document, as input. Creating the schema is a task that should not be taken lightly. If you make an error in the schema, some invalid data might be accepted and some valid data might be rejected.

The easiest way to create XML schemas is to create relational tables first, and then use the XMLSCHEMA option of the FOR XML clause. Store the resulting XML value (the schema) in a variable, and provide the variable as input to the CREATE XML SCHEMA COLLECTION statement. The following code creates two auxiliary empty tables for beverages and condiments, and then uses a SELECT statement with the FOR XML clause to create an XML schema from those tables. Then it stores the schemas in a variable, and creates a schema collection from that variable. Finally, after the schema collection is created, the code drops the auxiliary tables.

```
-- Auxiliary tables
CREATE TABLE dbo.Beverages(percentvitaminsRDA INT);
CREATE TABLE dbo.Condiments(shortdescription NVARCHAR(50));
GO
-- Store the schemas in a variable and create the collection
DECLARE @mySchema AS NVARCHAR(MAX) = N'';
SET @mySchema +=
  (SELECT *
   FROM Beverages
```

```
    FOR XML AUTO, ELEMENTS, XMLSCHEMA('Beverages'));
SET @mySchema +=
  (SELECT *
   FROM Condiments
   FOR XML AUTO, ELEMENTS, XMLSCHEMA('Condiments'));
SELECT CAST(@mySchema AS XML);
CREATE XML SCHEMA COLLECTION dbo.ProductsAdditionalAttributes AS @mySchema;
GO
-- Drop auxiliary tables
DROP TABLE dbo.Beverages, dbo.Condiments;
GO
```

The next step is to alter the XML column from a well-formed state to a schema-validated one:

```
ALTER TABLE Production.Products
  ALTER COLUMN additionalattributes
  XML(dbo.ProductsAdditionalAttributes);
```

Before using the new data type, you have to take care of one more issue. How do you prevent binding the wrong schema to a product of a specific category? For example, how do you prevent binding a condiments schema to a beverage? You could solve this issue with a trigger; however, having a declarative constraint—a check constraint—is preferable. This is why the code added namespaces to the schemas. You need to check whether the namespace is the same as the product category name. You cannot use XML data type methods inside constraints. You have to create two additional functions: one retrieves the XML namespace of the additionalattributes XML column, and the other retrieves the category name of a product. In the check constraint, you can check whether the return values of both functions are equal. Here is the code that creates both functions and adds a check constraint to the Production. Products table:

```
-- Function to retrieve the namespace
CREATE FUNCTION dbo.GetNamespace(@chkcol AS XML)
 RETURNS NVARCHAR(15)
AS
BEGIN
 RETURN @chkcol.value('namespace-uri((/*)[1])','NVARCHAR(15)');
END;
GO
-- Function to retrieve the category name
CREATE FUNCTION dbo.GetCategoryName(@catid AS INT)
 RETURNS NVARCHAR(15)
AS
BEGIN
 RETURN
  (SELECT categoryname
   FROM Production.Categories
   WHERE categoryid = @catid);
END;
GO
-- Add the constraint
ALTER TABLE Production.Products ADD CONSTRAINT ck_Namespace
```

```
       CHECK (dbo.GetNamespace(additionalattributes) =
            dbo.GetCategoryName(categoryid));
GO
```

The infrastructure is prepared. Run the following code to try and insert some valid XML data into your new column:

```
-- Beverage
UPDATE Production.Products
    SET additionalattributes = N'
<Beverages xmlns="Beverages">
  <percentvitaminsRDA>27</percentvitaminsRDA>
</Beverages>'
WHERE productid = 1;
-- Condiment
UPDATE Production.Products
    SET additionalattributes = N'
<Condiments xmlns="Condiments">
  <shortdescription>very sweet</shortdescription>
</Condiments>'
WHERE productid = 3;
```

To test whether the schema validation and check constraint work, you should try to insert some invalid data as well:

```
-- String instead of int
UPDATE Production.Products
    SET additionalattributes = N'
<Beverages xmlns="Beverages">
  <percentvitaminsRDA>twenty seven</percentvitaminsRDA>
</Beverages>'
WHERE productid = 1;
-- Wrong namespace
UPDATE Production.Products
    SET additionalattributes = N'
<Condiments xmlns="Condiments">
  <shortdescription>very sweet</shortdescription>
</Condiments>'
WHERE productid = 2;
-- Wrong element
UPDATE Production.Products
    SET additionalattributes = N'
<Condiments xmlns="Condiments">
  <unknownelement>very sweet</unknownelement>
</Condiments>'
WHERE productid = 3;
```

You should get errors for all three UPDATE statements. You can check the data with the SELECT statement.

When you are done, run the following code for cleanup:

```
ALTER TABLE Production.Products
 DROP CONSTRAINT ck_Namespace;
ALTER TABLE Production.Products
 DROP COLUMN additionalattributes;
```

```
DROP XML SCHEMA COLLECTION dbo.ProductsAdditionalAttributes;
DROP FUNCTION dbo.GetNamespace;
DROP FUNCTION dbo.GetCategoryName;
```

> **MORE INFO**   **ON THE XML DATA TYPE**
>
> For more information on the XML data type, please refer to the MSDN topic "XML Data Type
> and Columns (SQL Server)" at *https://msdn.microsoft.com/en-us/library/hh403385.aspx*.

The XML data type is actually a large object type. There can be up to 2 gigabytes (GB) of data in every single column value. Scanning through the XML data sequentially is not a very efficient way of retrieving a simple scalar value. With relational data, you can create an index on a filtered column, allowing an index seek operation instead of a table scan. Similarly, you can index XML columns with specialized *XML indexes*. The first index you create on an XML column is the *primary XML index*. This index contains a shredded persisted representation of the XML values. For each XML value in the column, the index creates several rows of data. The number of rows in the index is approximately the number of nodes in the XML value. Such an index alone can speed up searches for a specific element by using the `exist()` method. After creating the primary XML index, you can create up to three other types of *secondary XML indexes*:

- **PATH**   This secondary XML index is especially useful if your queries specify path expressions. It speeds up the `exist()` method better than the primary XML index. Such an index also speeds up queries that use the `value()` method for a fully specified path.

- **VALUE**   This secondary XML index is useful if queries are value-based and the path is not fully specified or it includes a wildcard.

- **PROPERTY**   This secondary XML index is very useful for queries that retrieve one or more values from individual XML instances using the `value()` method.

The primary XML index has to be created first. It can be created only on tables with a clustered primary key.

> **MORE INFO**   **ON XML INDEXES**
>
> For details on how to create, use and maintain XML indexes, please refer to the MSDN topic
> "XML Indexes (SQL Server)" at *https://msdn.microsoft.com/en-us/library/ms191497.aspx*.

# Query and output JSON data

Although XML is a standard for many years, many developers do not like it because it is somehow too verbose.  Especially when you use element-centric XML, you have each element name for every value listed twice in your XML document. In addition, XML is not very clear for reading. Don't understand this incorrectly: XML is here to stay. It is the standard for many things, for example for calling Web services, for storing configurations, for exchanging data, and more. Nevertheless, a new simplified standard called JSON evolved in the last decade. JSON is simpler, easier to read than XML, focused on data exchange.

> **NOTE**  **JSON SPECIFICATION**
>
> You can read the full JSON specification in "The JSON Data Interchange Format" document at *http://www.ecma-international.org/publications/files/ECMA-ST/ECMA-404.pdf*.

Let's start with a simple example again. The following document is showing the same data that was used for the first XML example earlier in this chapter, just this time in JSON format, produced with the FOR JSON clause of the T-SQL SELECT statement:

```
[
    {
        "custid":1,
        "companyname":"Customer NRZBB",
        "Order":[
            {
                "orderid":10692,
                "orderdate":"2015-10-03"
            },
            {
                "orderid":10702,
                "orderdate":"2015-10-13"
            },
            {
                "orderid":10952,
                "orderdate":"2016-03-16"
            }
        ]
    },
    {
        "custid":2,
        "companyname":"Customer MLTDN",
        "Order":[
            {
                "orderid":10308,
                "orderdate":"2014-09-18"
            },
            {
                "orderid":10926,
                "orderdate":"2016-03-04"
            }
        ]
    }
]
```

At first glance, you might think that JSON is even more verbose than XML. However, the number of characters is approximately the same as in the first XML example, which is attribute-centric, and is approximately 40% lower than it would be in an element-centric XML. In addition, the JSON data is formatted in a very extensive way, using as many lines as possible. SQL Server Management Studio (SSMS) does not format JSON in such a nice way as it does

XML. It returns JSON as a character string, which you can find at *https://jsonformatter.curious-concept.com/.*

You can also see from the previous example that JSON is readable and simple. A JSON object (or document) consists of *collections* of *name – value pairs* known as object *members*. The name and the value are separated by a *colon*. Object member separator is a *comma*. *Curly brackets* are wrapping collections. Name is always a string, while JSON supports only four *primitive data types* for values: string, number, Boolean, and null. In addition, a value can be of one of two *complex data types*: an array or a nested JSON object. Arrays are enclosed in brackets. Names don't need to be unique.

Like XML documents, JSON objects also use special characters, and you need to escape them using a backslash (\), followed by a special code, as shown in Table 2-2.

**TABLE 2-2** Characters with special values in JSON objects

| Character | Replacement text |
| --- | --- |
| " (quotation mark) | \" |
| \ (backslash) | \\ |
| / (slash) | \/ |
| Backspace | \b |
| form feed | \f |
| new line | \l |
| carriage return | \r |
| horizontal tab | \t |

In addition, the FOR JSON clause returns control characters (characters with ASCII code 00 to 31) in the JSON output in \u<code> format, where <code> is in hexadecimal format, for example CHAR(0) as \u0000 and CHAR(31) as u\001f.

## Producing JSON output from queries

The first, simple option to generate JSON objects from T-SQL query results, is the FOR JSON AUTO clause. With this option, SQL Server formats the JSON output automatically, based on the order of columns in the SELECT list and on the order of tables in the FROM list. You can't change this format. The following query was used to produce the JSON output shown at the beginning of this section:

```
SELECT Customer.custid, Customer.companyname,
  [Order].orderid, [Order].orderdate
FROM Sales.Customers AS Customer
  INNER JOIN Sales.Orders AS [Order]
    ON Customer.custid = [Order].custid
WHERE Customer.custid <= 2
  AND [Order].orderid %2 = 0
ORDER BY Customer.custid, [Order].orderid
FOR JSON AUTO;
```

If you noticed, JSON does not support even date and time data types. Of course, the natural question is how SQL Server data types are converted to JSON data types. Table 2-3 shows the conversion rules.

TABLE 2-3 SQL Server to JSON data type conversion rules

| Category | SQL Server type | JSON type |
| --- | --- | --- |
| String | char, varchar, nchar, nvarchar | string |
| Numeric | tinyint, smallint, int, bigint, real, float, decimal, numeric | number |
| Boolean | Bit | Boolean – true or false |
| date & time | date, time, datetime, datetime2, datetimeoffset | string |
| Binary | BASE64-encoded string | BASE64-encoded string |
| CLR | user-defined CLR types, geometry, geography | not supported |
| Other | uniqueidentifier, money | string |

You have much more influence on the format of the JSON returned with the FOR JSON PATH clause. In the PATH mode, you can wrap and nest objects using multiple levels of hierarchy. The following query is very simple, showing the basic usage of the PATH mode:

```
SELECT TOP (2) custid, companyname, contactname
FROM Sales.Customers
ORDER BY custid
FOR JSON PATH;
```

The formatted result is:

```
[
    {
        "custid":1,
        "companyname":"Customer NRZBB",
        "contactname":"Allen, Michael"
    },
    {
        "custid":2,
        "companyname":"Customer MLTDN",
        "contactname":"Hassall, Mark"
    }
]
```

Your first formatting option is to use dot-separated alias names for the column names. The dot-separated aliases produce nested objects. The following query shows the usage of dot separated alias; for the sake of brevity, it limits the result set to a single customer:

```
SELECT custid AS [CustomerId],
    companyname AS [Company],
    contactname AS [Contact.Name]
FROM Sales.Customers
WHERE custid = 1
FOR JSON PATH;
```

The formatted result is:

```
[
    {
        "CustomerId":1,
        "Company":"Customer NRZBB",
        "Contact":{
            "Name":"Allen, Michael"
        }
    }
]
```

Of course, you can combine data from multiple tables. Just take care to use the same first part of the member name (or the column alias) for the data you want to nest together, as shown in the following example:

```
SELECT c.custid AS [Customer.Id],
  c.companyname AS [Customer.Name],
  o.orderid AS [Order.Id],
  o.orderdate AS [Order.Date]
FROM Sales.Customers AS c
  INNER JOIN Sales.Orders AS o
    ON c.custid = o.custid
WHERE c.custid = 1
  AND o.orderid = 10692
ORDER BY c.custid, o.orderid
FOR JSON PATH;
```

Here is the result:

```
[
    {
        "Customer":{
            "Id":1,
            "Name":"Customer NRZBB"
        },
        "Order":{ '
            "Id":10692,
            "Date":"2015-10-03"
        }
    }
]
```

Of course, the next question is whether you could nest orders inside customers. You can use more than one dot in column aliases, like you would nest namespaces in a .NET application. The following query shows how to produce multiple nesting levels:

```
SELECT c.custid AS [Customer.Id],
  c.companyname AS [Customer.Name],
  o.orderid AS [Customer.Order.Id],
  o.orderdate AS [Customer.Order.Date]
FROM Sales.Customers AS c
  INNER JOIN Sales.Orders AS o
    ON c.custid = o.custid
WHERE c.custid = 1
```

```
      AND o.orderid = 10692
ORDER BY c.custid, o.orderid
FOR JSON PATH;
```

And here is the formatted result:

```
[
    {
        "Customer":{
            "Id":1,
            "Name":"Customer NRZBB",
            "Order":{
                "Id":10692,
                "Date":"2015-10-03"
            }
        }
    }
]
```

In the FOR JSON clause, in both AUTO and PATH modes, you can specify three additional clauses:

- **ROOT**    Adds a single, top level member.

- **INCLUDE_NULL_VALUES**    Include nulls in the output. Nulls are by default excluded from the JSON output.

- **WITHOUT_ARRAY_WRAPPER**    Removes square brackets around the output.

The following query removes the array wrapper from the result:

```
SELECT c.custid AS [Customer.Id],
    c.companyname AS [Customer.Name],
    o.orderid AS [Customer.Order.Id],
    o.orderdate AS [Customer.Order.Date]
FROM Sales.Customers AS c
    INNER JOIN Sales.Orders AS o
        ON c.custid = o.custid
WHERE c.custid = 1
    AND o.orderid = 10692
ORDER BY c.custid, o.orderid
FOR JSON PATH,
        WITHOUT_ARRAY_WRAPPER;
```

The query returns the following result:

```
{
    "Customer":{
        "Id":1,
        "Name":"Customer NRZBB",
        "Order":{
            "Id":10692,
            "Date":"2015-10-03"
        }
    }
}
```

You cannot remove the array wrapper brackets and have a root element at the same time. The following query adds a root element instead of the brackets:

```
SELECT c.custid AS [Customer.Id],
  c.companyname AS [Customer.Name],
  o.orderid AS [Customer.Order.Id],
  o.orderdate AS [Customer.Order.Date]
FROM Sales.Customers AS c
  INNER JOIN Sales.Orders AS o
    ON c.custid = o.custid
WHERE c.custid = 1
  AND o.orderid = 10692
ORDER BY c.custid, o.orderid
FOR JSON PATH,
    ROOT('Customer 1');
```

Here's the result of this query:

```
{
    "Customer 1":[
      {
        "Customer":{
          "Id":1,
          "Name":"Customer NRZBB",
          "Order":{
            "Id":10692,
            "Date":"2015-10-03"
          }
        }
      }
    ]
}
```

Notice that the elements inside the root element are still treated as an array, and hence are enclosed in brackets.

Finally, the following query removes the array wrapper and includes nulls in the output:

```
SELECT c.custid AS [Customer.Id],
  c.companyname AS [Customer.Name],
  o.orderid AS [Customer.Order.Id],
  o.orderdate AS [Customer.Order.Date],
  NULL AS [Customer.Order.Delivery]
FROM Sales.Customers AS c
  INNER JOIN Sales.Orders AS o
    ON c.custid = o.custid
WHERE c.custid = 1
  AND o.orderid = 10692
ORDER BY c.custid, o.orderid
FOR JSON PATH,
    WITHOUT_ARRAY_WRAPPER,
    INCLUDE_NULL_VALUES;
```

Here's the result of this query:

```
{
```

```
    "Customer":{
        "Id":1,
        "Name":"Customer NRZBB",
        "Order":{
            "Id":10692,
            "Date":"2015-10-03",
            "Delivery":null
        }
    }
}
```

This should be enough to give you an idea how to format JSON output using the SELECT
statement.

> **MORE INFO**  **ON FOR JSON CLAUSE**
>
> For more information about the FOR JSON clause, please read the MSDN article "Format
> Query Results as JSON with FOR JSON (SQL Server)" at *https://msdn.microsoft.com/en-us/
> library/dn921882.aspx*.

## Convert JSON data to tabular format

Of course, you don't just produce JSON from T-SQL queries, you can also read JSON data and
present it in tabular format. Just like you shred XML with the OPENXML function, you shred
JSON with the OPENJSON function. The function accepts two parameters: the JSON expression and the path where to start processing the JSON fragment. The second argument is
optional; if you don't provide it, the whole JSON object is processed. The returned table can
have an implicit schema, or you define an explicit schema in the WITH clause.

When you don't define an explicit schema, the OPENJSON function returns a table with
three columns:

- **key**   The name of the JSON property.
- **value**   The actual value of the JSON property.
- **type**   JSON data type of the value as a tiny integer. Table 2-4 shows the possible values of this column and their meaning.

**TABLE 2-4** Characters with special values in JSON objects

| Type value | JSON data type |
|------------|----------------|
| 0 | null |
| 1 | string |
| 2 | number |
| 3 | true/false |
| 4 | array |
| 5 | object |

Since the OPENJSON function can return only one table, it converts only the first level of JSON object properties as rows. Remember, a JSON object can have nested objects. The following code shows the simplest usage of the OPENJSON function:

```
DECLARE @json AS NVARCHAR(MAX) = N'
{
    "Customer":{
        "Id":1,
        "Name":"Customer NRZBB",
        "Order":{
            "Id":10692,
            "Date":"2015-10-03",
            "Delivery":null
        }
    }
}';
SELECT *
FROM OPENJSON(@json);
```

The result of this code is a single row for the Customer element (abbreviated):

| key | value | type |
| --- | --- | --- |
| Customer | {        "Id":1,       "Name":"Custom... | 5 |

As you can see, only the first level property is converted to a single row. To return properties of nested objects, you need to use the path parameter, like so:

```
DECLARE @json AS NVARCHAR(MAX) = N'
{
    "Customer":{
        "Id":1,
        "Name":"Customer NRZBB",
        "Order":{
            "Id":10692,
            "Date":"2015-10-03",
            "Delivery":null
        }
    }
}';
SELECT *
FROM OPENJSON(@json,'$.Customer');
```

This query returns all properties of the customer element, generating the following output:

| key | value | type |
| --- | --- | --- |
| Id | 1 | 2 |
| Name | Customer NRZBB | 1 |
| Order | {        "Id":10692,      "Dat... | 5 |

In the path property, you can specify either *lax* or *strict* mode of checking for the JSON elements. Lax is the default and it means relaxed mode. If a property does not exist, you get an empty table. In strict mode, if you refer to a non-existing property, you get an error. The following code shows this on a simple example:

```
DECLARE @json AS NVARCHAR(MAX) = N'
{
  "Customer":{
      "Name":"Customer NRZBB"
      }
}';
SELECT *
FROM OPENJSON(@json,'lax $.Buyer');
SELECT *
FROM OPENJSON(@json,'strict $.Buyer');
```

The first query returns an empty table, whereas the second query returns an empty table and an error.

Finally, I'll show how you can define an explicit schema in the WITH clause. The following query extracts customer id as integer, customer name as string, and customer orders as a nested JSON object of type NVARCHAR(MAX) from the JSON input:

```
DECLARE @json AS NVARCHAR(MAX) = N'
{
    "Customer":{
        "Id":1,
        "Name":"Customer NRZBB",
        "Order":{
            "Id":10692,
            "Date":"2015-10-03",
            "Delivery":null
        }
    }
}';
SELECT *
FROM OPENJSON(@json)
WITH
 (
 CustomerId    INT            '$.Customer.Id',
 CustomerName  NVARCHAR(20)   '$.Customer.Name',
 Orders        NVARCHAR(MAX)  '$.Customer.Order' AS JSON
);
```

Here is the result:

```
CustomerId CustomerName   Orders
---------- -------------- -------------------------------------------------------------
1          Customer NRZBB {           "Id":10692,          "Date":"2015-10-03",
```

> **MORE INFO** **ON THE OPENJSON FUNCTION**
>
> For more details on the OPENJSON function, please refer to the "OPENJSON (Transact-SQL)" MSDN topic at *https://msdn.microsoft.com/en-us/library/dn921885.aspx*.

In addition to shredding JSON data to rows with the OPENJSON rowset function, you can also extract a scalar value from JSON text with the JSON_VALUE function or an object or an array with the JSON_QUERY function. The following code shows how to use these two functions:

```
DECLARE @json AS NVARCHAR(MAX) = N'
{
    "Customer":{
        "Id":1,
        "Name":"Customer NRZBB",
        "Order":{
            "Id":10692,
            "Date":"2015-10-03",
            "Delivery":null
        }
    }
}';
SELECT JSON_VALUE(@json, '$.Customer.Id') AS CustomerId,
 JSON_VALUE(@json, '$.Customer.Name') AS CustomerName,
 JSON_QUERY(@json, '$.Customer.Order') AS Orders;
```

The query returns the same result as the previous query that used the OPENJSON function:

```
CustomerId CustomerName    Orders
---------- --------------- -----------------------------------------------------------
1          Customer NRZBB {     "Id":10692,           "Date":"2015-10-03",...
```

You can also update JSON text with the JSON_MODIFY function. You can update a scalar value of a property, add a new property and its value, add an element to an array, delete a property, and more. The function returns the modified JSON text. Here is an example of usage of this function:

```
DECLARE @json AS NVARCHAR(MAX) = N'
{
    "Customer":{
        "Id":1,
        "Name":"Customer NRZBB",
        "Order":{
            "Id":10692,
            "Date":"2015-10-03",
            "Delivery":null
        }
    }
}';
-- Update name
SET @json = JSON_MODIFY(@json, '$.Customer.Name', 'Modified first name');

-- Delete Id
SET @json = JSON_MODIFY(@json, '$.Customer.Id', NULL)

-- Insert last name
SET @json = JSON_MODIFY(@json, '$.Customer.LastName', 'Added last name')

PRINT @json;
```

The modified JSON document is shown below.

```
{
    "Customer":{

        "Name":"Modified first name",
        "Order":{
            "Id":10692,
            "Date":"2015-10-03",
            "Delivery":null
        }
    ,"LastName":"Added last name"}
}
```

For storing XML, SQL Server provides native XML data type. There is no native JSON data type. You can store JSON in a NVARCHAR(MAX) column. You can test the validity of the JSON document with the ISJSON function. The following example shows how to use this function:

```
SELECT ISJSON ('str') AS s1,  ISJSON ('') AS s2,
  ISJSON ('{}') AS s3,  ISJSON ('{"a"}') AS s4,
  ISJSON ('{"a":1}') AS s5;
```

And here is the result:

```
s1           s2            s3            s4            s5
-----------  ------------  -----------   -----------   -----------
0            0             1             0             1
```

As you can see, JSON support in SQL Server is not yet a first-class citizen like XML, but you do have the means to both produce JSON data as a character string output from queries, as well as shred JSON data to tabular form.

## Chapter summary

- Self-contained subqueries are independent of the outer query. They are convenient to troubleshoot since you can always highlight the inner query and execute it independently.

- Correlated subqueries have references to columns from the tables in the outer query and are generally more complex to work with.

- There are cases where SQL Server handles subqueries more efficiently then joins, and cases where the opposite is true. It's important to understand those cases, and also make sure that when performance is critical, you test both options and compare their performance.

- Using the APPLY operator you can apply a table expression to each row from some table. The CROSS APPLY operator doesn't return the left row if the right side is an empty set, whereas the OUTER APPLY operator does.

- Table expressions are named queries that help you simplify and reuse code. T-SQL supports four kinds of table expressions: derived tables, CTEs, views and inline table-valued functions.

- Use derived tables and CTEs when you need to use the table expression only in one statement. Use views and inline table-valued functions when you need to reuse the table expression. If there are no parameters involved, use views, otherwise use inline table-valued functions.

- Use table expressions when you don't want to persist the inner query's result in a work table, and temporary tables or table variables when you do.

- T-SQL supports both traditional grouped queries that define one grouping set, and grouped queries that define multiple grouping sets using the clauses GROUPING SETS, CUBE and ROLLUP. Use the GROUPING_ID function to compute a grouping set identifier.

- Use the PIVOT operator to pivot data from a state of rows to columns, and the UN-PIVOT operator to unpivot data from a state of columns to rows. With PIVOT, make sure to use a table expression that project the elements involved to avoid grouping implicitly by undesired columns. With UNPIVOT, remember that the operator removes rows with NULLs.

- Window functions allow you to perform data analysis calculations against the underlying query result without hiding the detail. T-SQL supports aggregate, ranking, offset and statistical window functions.

- System-versioned temporal tables allow you to keep track of the history of changes to your data for long periods of time. You enable system versioning on a table, and connect it to a corresponding history table. Temporal tables use a pair of DATETIME2 columns to represent the start and end of the validity period of the row.

- You modify the current table as usual, and SQL Server keeps track of historical states of rows in the history table automatically.

- To read data, you query the current table with the FOR SYSTEM_TIME clause. Using the AT subclause you request to return the state of the data at a specified point in time. Using the FROM, BETWEEN and CONTAINED IN subclauses, you request to return the states of the data that were valid during a specified period of time. Using the ALL subclause, you request to see all states of the rows, both current and historical.

- You create XML documents as output of a SELECT statement with the FOR XML clause. You can read XML data and shred it to tabular format with the OPENXML function. You can store XML data in SQL Server in a column of the XML data type. You can use methods of this column to extract scalar values, XML fragments, modify XML data, and more. You use XQuery expressions as parameters to the XML data type methods to navigate to the appropriate element or attribute.

- There is no native JSON data type in SQL Server. However, you can create JSON documents from queries with the FOR JSON clause, shred JSON documents to tabular format with the OPENJSON function, extract scalar values and JSON fragments with the JSON_VALUE and JSON_QUERY functions, modify JSON data with the JSON_MODIFY function, and test validity with the ISJSON function.

# Thought experiment

In this thought experiment, demonstrate your skills and knowledge of the topics covered in this chapter. You can find the answer to this thought experiment in the next section.

You're hired as a consultant to serve as a subject matter expert in a large database migration project. In one of the preliminary stages of the project you have a meeting with the company's DBAs, who pose a few questions. Demonstrate your expertise by answering the following questions:

1. Generally, when solving tasks with T-SQL, is it more efficient to use joins or subqueries?
2. What is the difference between a self-contained subquery and a correlated one?
3. In what way is the APPLY operator different than joins and subqueries? Can you provide an example when it should be used?
4. From a performance perspective, is it better to use table expressions or temporary tables?
5. What are the limitations of the PIVOT operator in T-SQL?
6. What are the limitations of the UNPIVOT operator in T-SQL?
7. What is the best way in T-SQL to compute running totals, and what are the performance considerations that you need to be aware of when using such computations?
8. Why can't you place a row number calculation in the WHERE clause if you want to filter a range of row numbers?
9. How would you quickly create, with minimal effort, an element-centric XML document from a T-SQL SELECT result set?
10. What is the difference between the JSON_VALUE and JSON_QUERY functions?

# Thought experiment answer

This section contains the solution to the thought experiment.

1. You're not going to be perceived as a proper consultant unless you start your answer with "it depends." The answer to this question is no different. It's very rare in T-SQL that one tool is always better than another. But it is important to know what are the cases when each tool does better, and also how to tell which is better when you're not sure. Joins tend to do better when you need to apply multiple calculations, like aggregates, based on the same set of rows. With subqueries you access the data separately for each aggregate and with joins you access the data once for all aggregates. However, when looking for nonmatches, joins currently aren't optimized with the Anti Semi Join optimization, whereas subqueries are. With this optimization SQL Server short circuits the work as soon as a match is found, resulting typically in less effort.

When you're not certain which solution is better, test your solutions. The run time is ultimately what the user cares about. If there's a significant performance difference, you want to try and identify what SQL Server does differently by comparing the query execution plans.

2. When the inner query is completely independent of the outer query, it's a self-contained subquery. It can be highlighted and executed independently. A correlated subquery has references to columns from tables in the outer query. It cannot be run independently, making it harder to troubleshoot.

3. A join treats its two inputs as a set, therefore if a join input is a query (table expression), the query cannot refer to elements from the other input; in other words, a join doesn't support correlations. A subqueries can be correlated, but normally subqueries are limited to returning only one column. The APPLY operator combines the advantages of both joins and subqueries. Like in a join, if an input is a table expression, it can return multiple columns and multiple rows. Like a subquery, the right side can have correlations to elements from the left side. An example for a case where APPLY is handy is when you need to return the three most recent orders for each employee. You use the CROSS APPLY operator where the left input is the HR.Employees table and the right input is a correlated derived table where you use a TOP query against the Sales. Orders table, correlating the order's employee ID with the employee's employee ID.

4. Table expressions don't persist the result of the inner query physically anywhere. When you're querying a table expression, SQL Server inlines the inner query logic, and the physical processing interacts directly with the underlying table's data. Temporary tables and table variables do persist the result set that you store in them. So usually you want to use temporary tables when you have a result set that is expensive to create, and you need to interact with it multiple times. If you need to interact with the result only once, and the use of the temporary object is more about simplifying your solution or circumventing language limitations such as ones related to reuse of column aliases, you typically want to use table expressions in such cases.

5. The PIVOT operator is limited to only one aggregate. If you use the COUNT aggregate, you're limited to COUNT(*). In a static query, you have to hard code the spreading values. If you don't want to hard code those, you have to construct and execute the query string with dynamic SQL.

6. The UNPIVOT operator removes rows with NULLs in the value column. It doesn't make this step optional. It requires all columns that you're unpivoting to have exactly the same data type. It supports only one measure (values column). Like with PIVOT, in a static query you have to hard code the columns that you're unpivoting, or otherwise build and execute the query string with dynamic SQL.

7. The best way is with a window aggregate function with the frame ROWS UNBOUNDED PRECEDING. This is much more efficient than doing this with joins or subqueries. You can support the calculation with a POC index (partitioning, ordering, covering) to avoid the need for explicit sorting. You want to be careful not to use the RANGE option,

which is much more expensive. You want to remember that if you specify a window order clause but don't specify the window frame unit (ROWS or RANGE), you get RANGE by default. So, you need to make sure to explicitly use ROWS. If you use columnstore technology, the running total calculation can be optimized with a highly efficient batch mode Window Aggregate operator.

8. That's because as a window function, the ROW_NUMBER function is supposed to be applied to the underlying query result. In logical query processing terms, the underlying query result is established only when you get to the SELECT phase (step 5), after FROM, WHERE, GROUP BY and HAVING. For this reason, you can only use window functions in the SELECT and ORDER BY clauses of a query. If you need to refer to them in clauses that are processed before the SELECT clause, like the WHERE clause, write a query where you invoke the window function in the SELECT and assign it with an alias, and then have the outer query refer to that alias in the WHERE clause.

9. You should use the FOR XML AUTO, ELEMENTS, ROOT('Root Name') clause. You could use also FOR XML PATH, but this would not be with minimal effort. You need the ELEMENTS sub-clause to generate an element-centric XML. Finally, you need the ROOT sub-clause because without root you get an XML fragment and not an XML document.

10. You extract a scalar value from JSON text with the JSON_VALUE function and an object or an array with the JSON_QUERY function.

# Program databases by using Transact-SQL

This chapter covers programmability features in T-SQL. It starts with programmability objects like views, user-defined functions, and stored procedures. It then covers handling errors with the TRY-CATCH construct, and working with transactions. The chapter completes with coverage of handling of data types and treatment of NULLs.

## Skills in this chapter:

- Create database programmability objects by using Transact-SQL
- Implement error handling and transactions
- Implement data types and NULLs

## Skill 3.1: Create database programmability objects by using Transact-SQL

This skill focuses on working with programmability objects using T-SQL. It covers simplifying and reusing query logic using views; encapsulating single expressions, queries, and multiple statements in user-defined functions; and lastly, working with stored procedures.

> ***NOTE*** **CREATE OR ALTER**
>
> SQL Server 2016 starting with Service Pack 1 and Azure SQL Database support the CREATE OR ALTER command for views, user-defined functions, stored procedures, and triggers. This command creates the object if it doesn't exist and alters it if it already exists. Prior to the introduction of this command, it was up to you to handle logic, such as checking if the object already existed before dropping it with the DROP command, or using the DROP IF EXISTS command (introduced in SQL Server 2016 RTM), creating it with the CREATE command, or altering it with the ALTER command. Many examples in this skill use the CREATE OR ALTER command. If you're running this book's code samples on SQL Server 2016, make sure that you have at minimum Service Pack 1 installed because that's when this command was introduced. If you're using Azure SQL Database, there's nothing special that you need to do because the CREATE OR ALTER command is supported there.

# Views

A view is a reusable named query, or *table expression*, whose definition is stored as an object in the database. It is accessible to users who were granted with permissions to query it. You can also modify data in underlying tables through it.

Views enable you to simplify the database's data model for users by presenting them with customized views of the data. For example, views can join underlying tables to simplify reporting queries. Instead of repeating complex queries in multiple places in the code, they can achieve reusability by querying the view. If you need to alter the structure of tables, you can use views to provide the application with backward compatible representation of the data. Views can also be used as a security layer, by granting users with access to the view but not to the underlying tables. This way, users can see only the customized representation of the data that you want them to see.

## Working with views

There's probably no better way to start the discussion about working with views than by jumping straight to an example. The following code creates a view called Sales.OrderTotals in the TSQLV4 database:

```
USE TSQLV4;
GO
CREATE OR ALTER VIEW Sales.OrderTotals
  WITH SCHEMABINDING
AS

SELECT
  O.orderid, O.custid, O.empid, O.shipperid,  O.orderdate,
  O.requireddate, O.shippeddate,
  SUM(OD.qty) AS qty,
  CAST(SUM(OD.qty * OD.unitprice * (1 - OD.discount))
      AS NUMERIC(12, 2)) AS val
FROM Sales.Orders AS O
  INNER JOIN Sales.OrderDetails AS OD
    ON O.orderid = OD.orderid
GROUP BY
  O.orderid, O.custid, O.empid, O.shipperid, O.orderdate,
  O.requireddate, O.shippeddate;
GO
```

This view computes total order quantities and net values by joining the Sales.Orders and Sales.OrderDetails tables, grouping the data by the order elements, and aggregating the quantities and net values.

Notice the GO batch separator after the USE TSQLV4 statement. The CREATE OR ALTER VIEW statement must be the first statement in the batch. The same applies to the CREATE VIEW and ALTER VIEW statements.

Also, notice the use of the SCHEMABINDING option in the view's header. This option prevents structural changes to dependent tables and columns while the view exists. This option is not set by default, but there are situations where it's mandatory, such as if you want to create an index on the view. Some, including myself, see this option as a best practice that increases system stability since it helps you avoid having objects in the database that depend on nonexistent or altered objects. However, you do need to be aware that the use of SCHEMABINDING does increase the complexity of handling structural changes, such as ones done as part of application upgrades. Such changes require dropping and recreating schema-bound objects before and after the change, respectively.

Recall the discussion about table expressions in Chapter 2, Skill 2.2. I explained that a view is one of the kinds of table expressions that T-SQL supports in addition to derived tables, CTEs, and inline table-valued functions. I also explained that the inner query has to follow three requirements:

- All columns must have names. This means that if the column is a result of a computation, you must assign it with an alias.

- All column names must be unique. This means that if you join tables and you want to return columns with the same name from the different tables, you have to assign the columns with different aliases.

- The inner query is not allowed to have an ORDER BY clause, unless this clause supports a TOP or OFFSET-FETCH filter. Either way, unless the outer query against the view has its own ORDER BY clause, presentation ordering for the rows in the result is not guaranteed.

If you need to assign aliases to target columns, you can use an inline aliasing form where you assign the alias as part of the expression, such as in the example above for the result columns qty and val. As an alternative, you could use an external aliasing form where you specify the target column names right after the view name in parentheses, like so:

```
CREATE OR ALTER VIEW Sales.OrderTotals
  (orderid, custid, empid, shipperid,  orderdate, requireddate, shippeddate,
  qty, val)...
```

Run the following code to query the view that you just created:

```
SELECT orderid, orderdate, custid, empid, val
FROM Sales.OrderTotals;
```

You get the following output, shown here in abbreviated form:

```
orderid   orderdate   custid  empid  val
--------  ----------  ------  -----  --------
10248     2014-07-04  85      5      440.00
10249     2014-07-05  79      6      1863.40
10250     2014-07-08  34      4      1552.60
10251     2014-07-08  84      3      654.06
10252     2014-07-09  76      4      3597.90
10253     2014-07-10  34      3      1444.80
10254     2014-07-11  14      5      556.62
10255     2014-07-12  68      9      2490.50
10256     2014-07-15  88      3      517.80
10257     2014-07-16  35      4      1119.90
...
```

SQL Server typically doesn't persist the view's result anywhere; rather it internally keeps the query text and some additional metadata information about the view and its columns in catalog objects. When you query the view, SQL Server expands the view definition and queries the underlying tables. This can be seen in the execution plan of the last query in Figure 3-1.

**FIGURE 3-1** Execution plan for query against Sales.OrderTotals view

Observe that the plan has no mention of the view; rather it shows that the clustered indexes of the Orders and OrderDetails tables are scanned. You would get the same plan if you issued the following query straight against the underlying tables:

```
SELECT
  O.orderid, O.orderdate, O.custid, O.empid,
  CAST(SUM(OD.qty * OD.unitprice * (1 - OD.discount))
      AS NUMERIC(12, 2)) AS val
FROM Sales.Orders AS O
  INNER JOIN Sales.OrderDetails AS OD
    ON O.orderid = OD.orderid
GROUP BY
  O.orderid, O.custid, O.empid, O.shipperid, O.orderdate,
  O.requireddate, O.shippeddate;
```

If you want to get the definition of an existing view (or other module), use the OBJECT_DEFINITION function, like so:

```
PRINT OBJECT_DEFINITION(OBJECT_ID(N'Sales.OrderTotals'));
```

T-SQL supports defining views based on a query against a CTE. As an example, the following code defines a view called Sales.CustLast5OrderDates based on a query that for each customer, returns the last five distinct order dates:

```
CREATE OR ALTER VIEW Sales.CustLast5OrderDates
  WITH SCHEMABINDING
AS

WITH C AS
(
  SELECT
    custid, orderdate,
    DENSE_RANK() OVER(PARTITION BY custid ORDER BY orderdate DESC) AS pos
  FROM Sales.Orders
)
SELECT custid, [1], [2], [3], [4], [5]
FROM C
  PIVOT(MAX(orderdate) FOR pos IN ([1], [2], [3], [4], [5])) AS P;
GO
```

If you need a refresher of the meaning and syntax of the DENSE_RANK function and PIVOT operator, those were covered in Chapter 2, Skill 2.3. Examine the code and make sure you understand it well. The query that defines the CTE named C returns for each order the customer ID, order date, and dense rank of the order date (descending) for the customer. The outer query against C groups the data implicitly by the customer ID, and pivots the five most recent distinct order dates using the artificial MAX aggregate. The aggregate is artificial in the sense that for each customer and position there's only one distinct order date, but the PIVOT syntax requires you to use an aggregate function to return it.

Notice the use of square brackets to delimit the target column names representing the positions of the order dates. In T-SQL, irregular identifiers such as ones that start with a digit must be delimited. If you remove the delimiters from the columns in the IN clause, you get a syntax error. If you remove them from the columns in the SELECT list, instead of getting the values of the columns [1], [2] and on, which represent order dates, you get back the constants 1, 2, and on. Try it.

Query the view:

```
SELECT custid, [1], [2], [3], [4], [5]
FROM Sales.CustLast5OrderDates;
```

This code generates the following output, shown here in abbreviated form:

```
custid      1          2          3          4          5
----------- ---------- ---------- ---------- ---------- ----------
1           2016-04-09 2016-03-16 2016-01-15 2015-10-13 2015-10-03
2           2016-03-04 2015-11-28 2015-08-08 2014-09-18 NULL
3           2016-01-28 2015-09-25 2015-09-22 2015-06-19 2015-05-13
4           2016-04-10 2016-03-16 2016-03-03 2016-02-02 2015-12-24
5           2016-03-04 2016-02-06 2016-02-03 2016-01-28 2016-01-16
6           2016-04-29 2016-03-17 2016-01-27 2015-07-29 2015-06-27
7           2016-01-12 2015-09-23 2015-08-12 2015-06-30 2015-06-12
8           2016-03-24 2015-12-29 2014-10-10 NULL       NULL
9           2016-05-06 2016-03-11 2016-03-06 2016-02-09 2016-02-05
10          2016-04-24 2016-04-23 2016-04-16 2016-03-27 2016-03-25
...
```

A view can even be defined based on multiple CTEs. Consider the following example, which defines a view called CustTop5OrderValues:

```
CREATE OR ALTER VIEW Sales.CustTop5OrderValues
  WITH SCHEMABINDING
AS

WITH C1 AS
(
  SELECT
    O.orderid, O.custid,
    CAST(SUM(OD.qty * OD.unitprice * (1 - OD.discount))
        AS NUMERIC(12, 2)) AS val
  FROM Sales.Orders AS O
    INNER JOIN Sales.OrderDetails AS OD
      ON O.orderid = OD.orderid
  GROUP BY
    O.orderid, O.custid
),
C2 AS
(
  SELECT
    custid, val,
    ROW_NUMBER() OVER(PARTITION BY custid ORDER BY val DESC, orderid DESC) AS pos
  FROM C1
)
SELECT custid, [1], [2], [3], [4], [5]
FROM C2
  PIVOT(MAX(val) FOR pos IN ([1], [2], [3], [4], [5])) AS P;
GO
```

The code defines a CTE called C1, which computes net order values. The code then defines a CTE called C2, which queries the CTE called C1. It computes row numbers that position orders within each customer partition, ordered by value, descending, and then order ID, descending, as a tiebreaker. The last step is a query against C2 that pivots the five highest order values for each customer to five separate columns named [1], [2], [3], [4] and [5].

Run the following code to query the view:

```
SELECT custid, [1], [2], [3], [4], [5]
FROM Sales.CustTop5OrderValues;
```

This code generates the following output, shown here in abbreviated form:

```
custid  1         2         3         4         5
------  --------  --------  --------  --------  --------
1        933.50    878.00    845.80    814.50    471.20
2        514.40    479.75    320.00    88.80     NULL
3        2082.00   1940.85   813.37    749.06    660.00
4        4441.25   2142.90   1641.00   1477.00   899.00
5        3815.25   3192.65   2222.40   2048.21   1835.70
6        858.00    677.00    625.00    464.00    330.00
7        7390.20   1994.52   1838.20   1761.00   1420.00
8        3026.85   982.00    224.00    NULL      NULL
9        2550.00   2436.18   1979.23   1948.50   1930.40
10       4422.00   3118.00   1892.25   1832.80   1447.50
...
```

As another example for a view that is based on multiple CTEs, the following code creates a view called Sales.OrderValuePcts:

```
CREATE OR ALTER VIEW Sales.OrderValuePcts
  WITH SCHEMABINDING
AS

WITH OrderTotals AS
(
  SELECT
    O.orderid, O.custid,
    SUM(OD.qty * OD.unitprice * (1 - OD.discount)) AS val
  FROM Sales.Orders AS O
    INNER JOIN Sales.OrderDetails AS OD
      ON O.orderid = OD.orderid
  GROUP BY
    O.orderid, O.custid
),
GrandTotal AS
(
  SELECT SUM(val) AS grandtotalval FROM OrderTotals
),
CustomerTotals AS
(
  SELECT custid, SUM(val) AS custtotalval
  FROM OrderTotals
  GROUP BY custid
)
SELECT
  O.orderid, O.custid,
  CAST(O.val AS NUMERIC(12, 2)) AS val,
  CAST(O.val / G.grandtotalval * 100.0 AS NUMERIC(5, 2)) AS pctall,
  CAST(O.val / C.custtotalval * 100.0 AS NUMERIC(5, 2)) AS pctcust
FROM OrderTotals AS O
  CROSS JOIN GrandTotal AS G
  INNER JOIN CustomerTotals AS C
    ON O.custid = C.custid;
GO
```

The OrderTotals CTE computes net order values; the CTE GrandTotal computes the grand total value, and the CTE CustomerTotals computes customer total values. The outer query joins all three CTEs and computes percentages of the order value out of both the grand total and the customer total.

Run the following code to query the view:

```
SELECT orderid, custid, val, pctall, pctcust
FROM Sales.OrderValuePcts;
```

This code generates the following output, shown here in abbreviated form:

```
orderid  custid  val     pctall  pctcust
--------  ------  ------  ------  --------
10835    1       845.80  0.07    19.79
10952    1       471.20  0.04    11.03
10643    1       814.50  0.06    19.06
10692    1       878.00  0.07    20.55
11011    1       933.50  0.07    21.85
10702    1       330.00  0.03    7.72
10625    2       479.75  0.04    34.20
10759    2       320.00  0.03    22.81
10308    2       88.80   0.01    6.33
10926    2       514.40  0.04    36.67
...
```

As a reminder, in Chapter 2 you learned about window functions, which could be used as an alternative to grouping and joining. The same task can be achieved with much less code with window functions, like so:

```
CREATE OR ALTER VIEW Sales.OrderValuePcts
  WITH SCHEMABINDING
AS

WITH OrderTotals AS
(
  SELECT
    O.orderid, O.custid,
    CAST(SUM(OD.qty * OD.unitprice * (1 - OD.discount)) AS NUMERIC(12, 2)) AS val
  FROM Sales.Orders AS O
    INNER JOIN Sales.OrderDetails AS OD
      ON O.orderid = OD.orderid
  GROUP BY
    O.orderid, O.custid
)
SELECT
  orderid, custid, val,
  CAST(val / SUM(val) OVER() * 100.0 AS NUMERIC(5, 2)) AS pctall,
  CAST(val / SUM(val) OVER(PARTITION BY custid) * 100.0 AS NUMERIC(5, 2)) AS pctcust
FROM OrderTotals;
GO
```

Views can also be used to restrict access to only filtered representation of the data. For instance, suppose that you want to grant users from the US branch access to only customers from the US. You can achieve this by creating a view that filters only customers from the US, like so:

```
CREATE OR ALTER VIEW Sales.USACusts
  WITH SCHEMABINDING
AS

SELECT
  custid, companyname, contactname, contacttitle, address,
  city, region, postalcode, country, phone, fax
FROM Sales.Customers
WHERE country = N'USA';
GO
```

You then grant users from the US branch permissions to query the view, and do not grant permissions to access the underlying table directly.

## View attributes

As you have noticed, all view definitions in my examples specify the SCHEMABINDING option. This option prevents structural changes to underlying objects while the view exists. To demonstrate what can happen without this option, run the following code to alter the view from the last example in the previous section to not include the SCHEMABINDING option:

```
CREATE OR ALTER VIEW Sales.USACusts
AS

SELECT
  custid, companyname, contactname, contacttitle, address,
  city, region, postalcode, country, phone, fax
FROM Sales.Customers
WHERE country = N'USA';
GO
```

It's important to remember that when you alter a view, either with the ALTER VIEW command, or with the CREATE OR ALTER VIEW command, you have to specify again any view attributes that you want to preserve. The main benefit in altering a view, as opposed to dropping and recreating it, is that permissions are preserved.

Now that our view does not include the SCHEMABINDING option, you're allowed to alter the underlying table definition. Run the following code to drop the address column from the table (in a transaction that you roll back to undo the change):

```
BEGIN TRAN;
  ALTER TABLE Sales.Customers DROP COLUMN address;
ROLLBACK TRAN; -- undo change
```

The code runs successfully.

Alter the view to include the SCHEMABINDING attribute:

```
CREATE OR ALTER VIEW Sales.USACusts
  WITH SCHEMABINDING
AS

SELECT
  custid, companyname, contactname, contacttitle, address,
  city, region, postalcode, country, phone, fax
FROM Sales.Customers
WHERE country = N'USA';
GO
```

Try to drop the column again:

```
ALTER TABLE Sales.Customers DROP COLUMN address;
```

This time the attempt is rejected, and you get the following errors:

```
Msg 5074, Level 16, State 1, Line 247
The object 'USACusts' is dependent on column 'address'.
Msg 4922, Level 16, State 9, Line 247
ALTER TABLE DROP COLUMN address failed because one or more objects access this column.
```

T-SQL supports a view attribute called ENCRYPTION that causes SQL Server to obfuscate the object definition that is stored internally. Without this attribute, you can get the object definition by using the OBJECT_DEFINITION function, like so:

```
SELECT OBJECT_DEFINITION(OBJECT_ID(N'Sales.USACusts'));
```

This code returns the requested view's definition. Alternatively you can use the sp_help-text procedure, or query the sys.syscomments view directly. Next, alter the view definition to include the ENCRYPTION attribute, like so (don't forget to re-specify the SCHEMABINDING option otherwise the view is altered without it):

```
CREATE OR ALTER VIEW Sales.USACusts
  WITH SCHEMABINDING, ENCRYPTION
AS

SELECT
  custid, companyname, contactname, contacttitle, address,
  city, region, postalcode, country, phone, fax
FROM Sales.Customers
WHERE country = N'USA';
GO
```

Run the following code to try and get the object definition:

```
SELECT OBJECT_DEFINITION(OBJECT_ID(N'Sales.USACusts'));
```

This time the code returns a NULL.

## Modifying data through views

You're not limited to only issuing SELECT queries against table expressions, such as views, rather, you're also allowed to issue modification statements against those. Because a table expression is a reflection of data from some underlying tables, it's those underlying tables that are affected by the modification. If you're modifying the data through a view, you do need appropriate permissions assigned to you against the view.

To demonstrate this capability, I use the Sales.USACusts view, which you create by running the following code:

```
CREATE OR ALTER VIEW Sales.USACusts
  WITH SCHEMABINDING
AS

SELECT
  custid, companyname, contactname, contacttitle, address,
  city, region, postalcode, country, phone, fax
FROM Sales.Customers
WHERE country = N'USA';
GO
```

Run the following code to add a customer to the Sales.Customers table through the view:

```
INSERT INTO Sales.USACusts(
  companyname, contactname, contacttitle, address,
  city, region, postalcode, country, phone, fax)
VALUES(
  N'Customer AAAAA', N'Contact AAAAA', N'Title AAAAA', N'Address AAAAA',
  N'Redmond', N'WA', N'11111', N'USA', N'111-1111111', N'111-1111111');
```

Query the underlying table to make sure that the new row made it there:

```
SELECT custid, companyname, country
FROM Sales.Customers
WHERE custid = SCOPE_IDENTITY();
```

You get the following output confirming that it did:

```
custid      companyname                              country
----------- ---------------------------------------- ---------------
92          Customer AAAAA                           USA
```

There are some very sensible restrictions on modifications through table expressions. One of them is that if the inner query joins multiple tables, INSERT and UPDATE statements are allowed to affect only one target table at a time. Also, you cannot insert rows through a table expression if it doesn't include at least one column from the underlying table that doesn't somehow get its values automatically (for example by allowing NULLs or having a default value).

Note that normally, you are allowed to insert and update rows through the view even if the modification contradicts the inner query's filter. In our example, you can insert customers from a non-US country, or update an existing customer's country to one other than the US. The effect seems strange because the underlying Sales.Customers table becomes modified, but when you query the view, you won't see the modified rows because they don't satisfy the view's filter anymore.

As an example, run the following code to add a customer from the UK through the view:

```
INSERT INTO Sales.USACusts(
  companyname, contactname, contacttitle, address,
  city, region, postalcode, country, phone, fax)
VALUES(
  N'Customer BBBBB', N'Contact BBBBB', N'Title BBBBB', N'Address BBBBB',
  N'London', NULL, N'22222', N'UK', N'222-2222222', N'222-2222222');
```

The code runs successfully, and the row is added to the underlying table.

Query the view to look for the new customer:

```
SELECT custid, companyname, country
FROM Sales.USACusts
WHERE custid = SCOPE_IDENTITY();
```

You get an empty set back:

```
custid      companyname                              country
----------- ---------------------------------------- ---------------
```

Query the underlying table to look for the new customer:

```
SELECT custid, companyname, country
FROM Sales.Customers
WHERE custid = SCOPE_IDENTITY();
```

This time you do get the new customer row back:

| custid | companyname | country |
| --- | --- | --- |
| 93 | Customer BBBBB | UK |

T-SQL supports an option called CHECK OPTION that prevents inserting or updating rows through the view if the change contradicts the inner query's filter. This option has a somewhat similar effect to a CHECK constraint in a table. You add it at the end of the inner query, like so:

```
CREATE OR ALTER VIEW Sales.USACusts
  WITH SCHEMABINDING
AS

SELECT
  custid, companyname, contactname, contacttitle, address,
  city, region, postalcode, country, phone, fax
FROM Sales.Customers
WHERE country = N'USA'
WITH CHECK OPTION;
GO
```

Run the following code to try again to add a customer from the UK through the view:

```
INSERT INTO Sales.USACusts(
  companyname, contactname, contacttitle, address,
  city, region, postalcode, country, phone, fax)
VALUES(
  N'Customer CCCCC', N'Contact CCCCC', N'Title CCCCC', N'Address CCCCC',
  N'London', NULL, N'33333', N'UK', N'333-3333333', N'333-3333333');
```

This time the code fails and you get the following error:

```
Msg 550, Level 16, State 1, Line 352
The attempted insert or update failed because the target view either specifies WITH
CHECK OPTION or spans a view that specifies WITH CHECK OPTION and one or more rows
resulting from the operation did not qualify under the CHECK OPTION constraint.
The statement has been terminated.
```

Curiously, the CHECK option in a view does differ from a CHECK constraint in a table in how the two handle NULLs, if those are allowed in the target column. For example, suppose that the country column allowed NULLs. A CHECK constraint based on the predicate country = N'USA' would have allowed rows with a NULL country, whereas a view with a filter based on the same predicate and the CHECK option would have regected such rows.

## Indexed views

Recall that when you query a view, SQL Server expands the view definition, and optimizes the code against the underlying tables. I demonstrated this earlier. But what if the inner query is quite expensive, and you query the view frequently? You want to avoid the repetition of the work that is involved every time you query the view. To achieve this, you create a clustered index on the view, and this way you persist the view's result within the clustered index B-tree structure. There is an extra cost every time you modify data in the underlying tables because SQL Server needs to modify the indexed view, like it would need to modify other indexes on the tables. So, similar to regular indexes, the tradeoff is faster queries at the cost of extra write cost and space.

To demonstrate the use of indexed views, I use the Sales.OrderTotals view from the previous examples, which you create by running the following code:

```
CREATE OR ALTER VIEW Sales.OrderTotals
  WITH SCHEMABINDING
AS

SELECT
  O.orderid, O.custid, O.empid, O.shipperid,  O.orderdate,
  O.requireddate, O.shippeddate,
  SUM(OD.qty) AS qty,
  CAST(SUM(OD.qty * OD.unitprice * (1 - OD.discount))
      AS NUMERIC(12, 2)) AS val
FROM Sales.Orders AS O
  INNER JOIN Sales.OrderDetails AS OD
    ON O.orderid = OD.orderid
GROUP BY
  O.orderid, O.custid, O.empid, O.shipperid, O.orderdate,
  O.requireddate, O.shippeddate;
GO
```

The first index that you create on the view has to be clustered and unique. Run the following code to try and create such an index on the view:

```
CREATE UNIQUE CLUSTERED INDEX idx_cl_orderid ON Sales.OrderTotals(orderid);
```

As it turns out, there are restrictions and requirements to allow you to create an indexed view. One of them is that the view header has to have the SCHEMABINDING attribute, which in our case is fulfilled. Another is that if the query is a grouped query, it has to include the COUNT_BIG aggregate. SQL Server needs to track the group row counts to know when a group needs to be eliminated as a result of deletes or updates of underlying detail rows. Consequently, your attempt to create the index fails, and you get the following error:

```
Msg 10138, Level 16, State 1, Line 98
Cannot create index on view 'TSQLV4.Sales.OrderTotals' because its select list does not
include a proper use of COUNT_BIG. Consider adding COUNT_BIG(*) to select list.
```

To satisfy this requirement, you alter the view definition and add the COUNT_BIG function by running the following code:

```
CREATE OR ALTER VIEW Sales.OrderTotals
  WITH SCHEMABINDING
AS

SELECT
  O.orderid, O.custid, O.empid, O.shipperid,  O.orderdate,
  O.requireddate, O.shippeddate,
  SUM(OD.qty) AS qty,
  CAST(SUM(OD.qty * OD.unitprice * (1 - OD.discount))
       AS NUMERIC(12, 2)) AS val,
  COUNT_BIG(*) AS numorderlines
FROM Sales.Orders AS O
  INNER JOIN Sales.OrderDetails AS OD
    ON O.orderid = OD.orderid
GROUP BY
  O.orderid, O.custid, O.empid, O.shipperid, O.orderdate,
  O.requireddate, O.shippeddate;
GO
```

Try to create the index again:

```
CREATE UNIQUE CLUSTERED INDEX idx_cl_orderid ON Sales.OrderTotals(orderid);
```

The attempt fails again with the following error:

```
Msg 8668, Level 16, State 0, Line 124
Cannot create the clustered index 'idx_cl_orderid' on view 'TSQLV4.Sales.OrderTotals'
because the select list of the view contains an expression on result of aggregate
function or grouping column. Consider removing expression on result of aggregate
function or grouping column from select list.
```

As it turns out, you're not allowed to manipulate the result of an aggregate calculation, and our query casts the total order value, which is computed with the SUM aggregate, to NUMERIC(12, 2). In order to be able to create the index, you need to remove the manipulation that is applied by the CAST function, like so:

```
CREATE OR ALTER VIEW Sales.OrderTotals
  WITH SCHEMABINDING
AS

SELECT
  O.orderid, O.custid, O.empid, O.shipperid,  O.orderdate,
  O.requireddate, O.shippeddate,
  SUM(OD.qty) AS qty,
  SUM(OD.qty * OD.unitprice * (1 - OD.discount)) AS val,
  COUNT_BIG(*) AS numorderlines
FROM Sales.Orders AS O
  INNER JOIN Sales.OrderDetails AS OD
    ON O.orderid = OD.orderid
GROUP BY
  O.orderid, O.custid, O.empid, O.shipperid, O.orderdate,
  O.requireddate, O.shippeddate;
GO
```

Try again to create the index:

```
CREATE UNIQUE CLUSTERED INDEX idx_cl_orderid ON Sales.OrderTotals(orderid);
```

This time the index is created successfully.

To recap, the view has to include SCHEMABINDING, the first index has to be clustered and unique, if the query is a grouped query it has to include the COUNT_BIG aggregate functions, and you're not allowed to manipulate the result of aggregate functions. You can find a more complete list of requirements and restriction at *https://msdn.microsoft.com/en-us/library/ms191432.aspx*.

Once you successfully created a clustered index on a view, you're allowed to create additional nonclustered indexes. Run the following code to create a number of nonclustered indexes on the Sales.OrderTotal view:

```
CREATE NONCLUSTERED INDEX idx_nc_custid      ON Sales.OrderTotals(custid);
CREATE NONCLUSTERED INDEX idx_nc_empid       ON Sales.OrderTotals(empid);
CREATE NONCLUSTERED INDEX idx_nc_shipperid   ON Sales.OrderTotals(shipperid);
CREATE NONCLUSTERED INDEX idx_nc_orderdate   ON Sales.OrderTotals(orderdate);
CREATE NONCLUSTERED INDEX idx_nc_shippeddate ON Sales.OrderTotals(shippeddate);
```

Run the following code to query the view:

```
SELECT orderid, custid, empid, shipperid, orderdate,
  requireddate, shippeddate, qty, val, numorderlines
FROM Sales.OrderTotals;
```

As long as you're running the code on an Enterprise or Developer edition of SQL Server, the optimizer considers using indexes on the view without any special instructions. This can be seen in the execution plan of the last query, as shown in Figure 3-2.

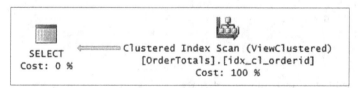

**FIGURE 3-2** Query plan with index on OrderTotals view

If you're using a non-Enterprise or Developer edition of SQL Server, you need to indicate the NOEXPAND hint against the view in order for SQL Server to not expand the view definition, but rather consider using the index on the view. The following query demonstrates using this hint:

```
SELECT orderid, custid, empid, shipperid, orderdate,
  requireddate, shippeddate, qty, val, numorderlines
FROM Sales.OrderTotals WITH (NOEXPAND);
```

Curiously, as long as you do use Enterprise or Developer edition, SQL Server considers using the indexes on the view even when you query the underlying tables. For example, consider the following query.

```
SELECT
  O.orderid, O.custid, O.empid, O.shipperid,  O.orderdate,
  O.requireddate, O.shippeddate,
  SUM(OD.qty) AS qty,
  CAST(SUM(OD.qty * OD.unitprice * (1 - OD.discount))
      AS NUMERIC(12, 2)) AS val
FROM Sales.Orders AS O
  INNER JOIN Sales.OrderDetails AS OD
    ON O.orderid = OD.orderid
GROUP BY
  O.orderid, O.custid, O.empid, O.shipperid, O.orderdate,
  O.requireddate, O.shippeddate;
```

The plan for this query is shown in Figure 3-3.

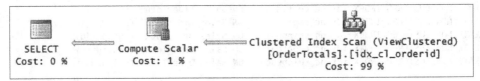

**FIGURE 3-3** Another query plan with index on OrderTotals view

Recall that you had to remove the CAST function that you originally applied to the SUM aggregate that computed the net order value in order to create the indexed view. If you want the user to be able to query a simplified view with the casted value, you could create an intermediate indexed view without the CAST expression, and then a non-indexed view with the original name that adds the CAST expression, like so:

```
-- create intermediate view
CREATE OR ALTER VIEW Sales.VOrderTotals
  WITH SCHEMABINDING
AS

SELECT
  O.orderid, O.custid, O.empid, O.shipperid,  O.orderdate,
  O.requireddate, O.shippeddate,
  SUM(OD.qty) AS qty,
  SUM(OD.qty * OD.unitprice * (1 - OD.discount)) AS val,
  COUNT_BIG(*) AS numorderlines
FROM Sales.Orders AS O
  INNER JOIN Sales.OrderDetails AS OD
    ON O.orderid = OD.orderid
GROUP BY
  O.orderid, O.custid, O.empid, O.shipperid, O.orderdate,
  O.requireddate, O.shippeddate;
GO

-- create indexes on view
CREATE UNIQUE CLUSTERED INDEX idx_cl_orderid ON Sales.VOrderTotals(orderid);
CREATE NONCLUSTERED INDEX idx_nc_custid     ON Sales.VOrderTotals(custid);
CREATE NONCLUSTERED INDEX idx_nc_empid      ON Sales.VOrderTotals(empid);
CREATE NONCLUSTERED INDEX idx_nc_shipperid  ON Sales.VOrderTotals(shipperid);
CREATE NONCLUSTERED INDEX idx_nc_orderdate  ON Sales.VOrderTotals(orderdate);
```

```
CREATE NONCLUSTERED INDEX idx_nc_shippeddate ON Sales.VOrderTotals(shippeddate);

-- create view with CAST
CREATE OR ALTER VIEW Sales.OrderTotals
  WITH SCHEMABINDING
AS

SELECT
  orderid, custid, empid, shipperid,  orderdate, requireddate, shippeddate, qty,
  CAST(val AS NUMERIC(12, 2)) AS val
FROM Sales.VOrderTotals;
GO
```

Run the following code to query the view:

```
SELECT orderid, custid, empid, shipperid,  orderdate,
  requireddate, shippeddate, qty, val
FROM Sales.OrderTotals;
```

The plan for this query is shown in Figure 3-4.

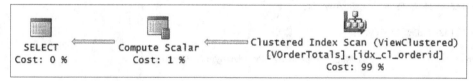

**FIGURE 3-4** Query plan with index on VOrderTotals view

Observe that the clustered index on the VOrderTotals view is used.

When you're done, run the following code for cleanup:

```
DROP VIEW IF EXISTS
  Sales.OrderTotals, Sales.VOrderTotals, Sales.CustLast5OrderDates,
  Sales.CustTop5OrderValues, Sales.OrderValuePcts, Sales.USACusts;
```

# User-defined functions

A user-defined function (UDF) is a routine that accepts parameters, applies calculations, and returns either a scalar-valued or a table-valued result. SQL Server supports developing functions using either T-SQL, or the common language runtime (CLR). The focus of the exam—and hence the book's—is the T-SQL kind.

A user-defined function can appear in places in your code where a scalar-valued or table-valued expression can appear, such as in a query, a computed column, and a CHECK constraint. It can even appear in the definition of another user-defined function. You can use a user-defined function to replace a stored procedure when you want to be able to query its result. You can use it as an alternative to a view with parameters, since views don't support parameters. You can even use a user-defined function to query an indexed view, and with parameter support, improve its functionality. You can also use a user-defined function to define a filter for a security policy as part of an implementation of row level security.

There are a number of restrictions and limitations on user-defined functions. Within user-define functions you cannot:

- Use error handling
- Modify data (other than in table variables)
- Use data definition language (DDL)
- Use temporary tables
- Use dynamic SQL

You can find a more complete list of requirements and restrictions at *https://msdn.microsoft.com/en-us/library/ms191320.aspx*.

Some of the examples in this section use a table called dbo.Employees (not to be confused with HR.Employees from the sample database). Run the following code to create this table and populate it with sample data:

```
SET NOCOUNT ON;
USE TSQLV4;
DROP TABLE IF EXISTS dbo.Employees;
GO
CREATE TABLE dbo.Employees
(
  empid    INT         NOT NULL CONSTRAINT PK_Employees PRIMARY KEY,
  mgrid    INT         NULL
    CONSTRAINT FK_Employees_Employees REFERENCES dbo.Employees,
  empname VARCHAR(25) NOT NULL,
  salary  MONEY        NOT NULL,
  CHECK (empid <> mgrid)
);

INSERT INTO dbo.Employees(empid, mgrid, empname, salary)
  VALUES(1, NULL, 'David', $10000.00),
        (2, 1, 'Eitan', $7000.00),
        (3, 1, 'Ina', $7500.00),
        (4, 2, 'Seraph', $5000.00),
        (5, 2, 'Jiru', $5500.00),
        (6, 2, 'Steve', $4500.00),
        (7, 3, 'Aaron', $5000.00),
        (8, 5, 'Lilach', $3500.00),
        (9, 7, 'Rita', $3000.00),
        (10, 5, 'Sean', $3000.00),
        (11, 7, 'Gabriel', $3000.00),
        (12, 9, 'Emilia' , $2000.00),
        (13, 9, 'Michael', $2000.00),
        (14, 9, 'Didi', $1500.00);

CREATE UNIQUE INDEX idx_unc_mgr_emp_i_name_sal ON dbo.Employees(mgrid, empid)
  INCLUDE(empname, salary);
```

T-SQL supports three kinds of user-defined functions: *scalar, inline table valued* and *multi-statement table valued*. The upcoming sections cover these three types.

## Scalar user-defined functions

A scalar user-defined function accepts parameters, applies calculations, and returns a single value. It has a body with flow that can have multiple statements, including queries, and eventually it must invoke a RETURN clause to return the result value. The header of the function defines the input parameters as well as the return type using a RETURNS clause.

As an example, the following code defines a function called dbo.SubtreeTotalSalaries:

```
CREATE OR ALTER FUNCTION dbo.SubtreeTotalSalaries(@mgr AS INT)
  RETURNS MONEY
WITH SCHEMABINDING
AS
BEGIN
  DECLARE @totalsalary AS MONEY;

  WITH EmpsCTE AS
  (
    SELECT empid, salary
    FROM dbo.Employees
    WHERE empid = @mgr

    UNION ALL

    SELECT S.empid, S.salary
    FROM EmpsCTE AS M
      INNER JOIN dbo.Employees AS S
        ON S.mgrid = M.empid
  )
  SELECT @totalsalary = SUM(salary)
  FROM EmpsCTE;

  RETURN @totalsalary;
END;
GO
```

The header of the function defines an input parameter called @mgr representing an input manager ID, and MONEY as the returned type. It specifies the SCHEMABINDING option to prevent structural changes to dependent objects (the Employees table in our case). The body of the function resides between the mandatory BEGIN and END clauses. The code in the function's body declares a local variable called @totalsalary. It then uses a recursive query that identifies the input manager's subordinates (direct and indirect). The outer statement of the CTE then assigns the total salaries of the input manager and all identified subordinates to the variable. Finally, the code returns the value stored in @totalsalary.

**EXAM TIP**

Remember that during the exam you don't have access to any online or offline resources that can help you figure out the syntax of T-SQL commands. Make sure to memorize the syntax for defining the different types of user-defined functions.

Use the following code to test the function, asking for the total salaries of the subtree of manager 8 (Lilach):

```
SELECT dbo.SubtreeTotalSalaries(8) AS subtreetotal;
```

This code returns the following output:

```
Subtreetotal
--------------------
3500.00
```

With most object types, T-SQL allows you to omit the schema name when referring to the object, in which case it uses implicit schema name resolution. With scalar UDFs, you must use the two-part name including the schema. For instance, try calling the function again, but this time without the schema:

```
SELECT SubtreeTotalSalaries(8) AS subtreetotal;
```

You get the following error:

```
Msg 195, Level 15, State 10, Line 553
'SubtreeTotalSalaries' is not a recognized built-in function name.
```

SQL Server looks for a built-in function with the specified name and since it can't find one, it fails.

As mentioned, you can invoke a user-defined function as part of a query. For example, the following code queries the Employees table, and invokes the function for each employee to return the total salaries of the respective employee's subtree:

```
SELECT empid, mgrid, empname, salary,
  dbo.SubtreeTotalSalaries(empid) AS subtreetotal
FROM dbo.Employees;
```

This code generates the following output:

| empid | mgrid | empname | salary | subtreetotal |
| --- | --- | --- | --- | --- |
| 1 | NULL | David | 10000.00 | 62500.00 |
| 2 | 1 | Eitan | 7000.00 | 28500.00 |
| 3 | 1 | Ina | 7500.00 | 24000.00 |
| 4 | 2 | Seraph | 5000.00 | 5000.00 |
| 5 | 2 | Jiru | 5500.00 | 12000.00 |
| 6 | 2 | Steve | 4500.00 | 4500.00 |
| 7 | 3 | Aaron | 5000.00 | 16500.00 |
| 8 | 5 | Lilach | 3500.00 | 3500.00 |
| 10 | 5 | Sean | 3000.00 | 3000.00 |
| 9 | 7 | Rita | 3000.00 | 8500.00 |
| 11 | 7 | Gabriel | 3000.00 | 3000.00 |
| 12 | 9 | Emilia | 2000.00 | 2000.00 |
| 13 | 9 | Michael | 2000.00 | 2000.00 |
| 14 | 9 | Didi | 1500.00 | 1500.00 |

There is an interesting difference between invoking a built-in nondeterministic function like SYSDATETIME directly in a query, and invoking it indirectly from a user-defined function that you then invoke in a query. Recall from Skill 1.3 in Chapter 1 that a *deterministic* function is guaranteed to return the same output across calls given the same inputs, and a *nondeterministic* function isn't. When you invoke a nondeterministic function directly in a query, SQL Server executes it only once for the entire query. The NEWID function is an exception to this rule because SQL Server executes it once per row. When you invoke a nondeterministic built-in function indirectly, from within a user-defined function, and then invoke the user-defined function in a query, the function gets executed once per row.

As an example, the following code queries the Sales.Orders table, and invokes the functions SYSDATETIME (returns the current date and time), RAND without a seed (returns a random float value in the range 0 through 1), and NEWID (returns a globally unique identifier) in the SELECT list:

```
SELECT orderid, SYSDATETIME() AS [SYSDATETIME], RAND() AS [RAND], NEWID() AS [NEWID]
FROM Sales.Orders;
```

This code generated the following output on my system (your result naturally differs):

```
orderid  SYSDATETIME                   RAND                NEWID
-------- ----------------------------- ------------------- ------------------------------
-----
11008    2016-11-23 09:41:20.0517170 0.115119415679133  DF00ED3F-53B9-4034-9D4D-
ABF33F3625F0
11019    2016-11-23 09:41:20.0517170 0.115119415679133  F3AB18AE-E897-4714-B7E5-
6962E26237C0
11039    2016-11-23 09:41:20.0517170 0.115119415679133  1D0D899C-8477-4617-B7C9-
797554059AA4
11040    2016-11-23 09:41:20.0517170 0.115119415679133  AF6386D7-122F-43E6-90EF-
AB432A9C03EB
11045    2016-11-23 09:41:20.0517170 0.115119415679133  EC3857B7-854A-4121-8CD5-
74B5B36DB279
...
11050    2016-11-23 09:41:20.0517170 0.115119415679133  9CAA81D2-4A3A-4B36-A8C8-
A1F92D78FC66
11055    2016-11-23 09:41:20.0517170 0.115119415679133  58E95547-DA18-4EAE-BC5C-
09252F266510
11063    2016-11-23 09:41:20.0517170 0.115119415679133  138CE9F6-7FFE-41E0-A507-
4190183CC203
11067    2016-11-23 09:41:20.0517170 0.115119415679133  CB864AFA-0D44-4435-90DA-
A718F200C85D
11069    2016-11-23 09:41:20.0517170 0.115119415679133  CC8B555C-DD9F-45C0-A2AE-
4E468ECED251
```

Observe that both SYSDATETIME and RAND return the same result in all rows even though they are nondeterministic functions. As mentioned, most nondeterministic built-in functions are invoked once per query. Also observe that NEWID behaves differently; it is invoked once per row.

T-SQL supports invoking nondeterministic built-in functions within user-defined functions, as long as they don't have any side effects on the system. The functions SYSDATETIME, RAND (without an input seed), and NEWID are all nondeterministic functions. The SYSDATETIME function doesn't have any side effects on the system and therefore is allowed in user-defined functions. As an example, run the following code to create the user-defined function MySYS-DATETIME:

```
CREATE OR ALTER FUNCTION dbo.MySYSDATETIME() RETURNS DATETIME2
AS
BEGIN
  RETURN SYSDATETIME();
END;
GO
```

The function is created successfully.

The NEWID and RAND functions both have side effects in the sense that one function call leaves a mark behind that affects a subsequent function call. Consequently, you're not allowed to invoke NEWID and RAND within user-defined functions. As an example, run the following code in attempt to create a user-defined function called MyRand that calls the built-in RAND function:

```
CREATE OR ALTER FUNCTION dbo.MyRAND() RETURNS FLOAT
AS
BEGIN
  RETURN RAND();
END;
GO
```

The attempt to create the function fails with the following error:

```
Msg 443, Level 16, State 1, Procedure MyRAND, Line 4 [Batch Start Line 516]
Invalid use of a side-effecting operator 'rand' within a function.
```

Curiously, if you invoke the built-in side-effecting function from a view, SQL Server does allow you to query the view from within a user-defined function. This allows you to circumvent the aforementioned restriction. As an example, run the following code to create a view called VRAND that invokes the built-in function RAND and returns the result as a column called myrand:

```
CREATE OR ALTER VIEW dbo.VRAND
AS

SELECT RAND() AS myrand;
GO
```

Next, run the following code to create the function MyRAND, which returns the result of a query against the view:

```
CREATE OR ALTER FUNCTION dbo.MyRAND() RETURNS FLOAT
AS
BEGIN
  RETURN (SELECT myrand FROM dbo.VRAND);
END;
GO
```

Run the following code to query the Sales.Orders table and invoke the functions MySYS-DATETIME and MyRAND:

```
SELECT orderid, dbo.MySYSDATETIME() AS mysysdatetime, dbo.MyRAND() AS myrand
FROM Sales.Orders;
```

This code generates the following output:

```
orderid     mysysdatetime                     myrand
----------- --------------------------------- ----------------------
11008       2016-11-23 09:47:46.5503588 0.0641387937377291
11019       2016-11-23 09:47:46.5518609 0.397630436473708
11039       2016-11-23 09:47:46.5518609 0.906453593195041
11040       2016-11-23 09:47:46.5518609 0.50133925878664
11045       2016-11-23 09:47:46.5518609 0.867531671551516
...
11050       2016-11-23 09:47:46.5634261 0.666663850667723
11055       2016-11-23 09:47:46.5634261 0.452951660618415
11063       2016-11-23 09:47:46.5634261 0.286359018535061
11067       2016-11-23 09:47:46.5634261 0.265970755632963
11069       2016-11-23 09:47:46.5634261 0.453168331889983
```

Observe that SQL Server executed the user-defined functions once per row, unlike earlier when you invoked the built-in functions directly, in which case SQL Server executed the functions only once for the entire query.

Note that in order to use a user-defined function in a persisted computed column or in an indexed view, the function needs to be deterministic. What this means is that the user-defined function must not call nondeterministic functions, plus you need to define it with the SCHEMABINDING attribute. As an example, run the following code to create the function ENDOFYEAR, which accepts a date as input, and returns the corresponding end of year date:

```
CREATE OR ALTER FUNCTION dbo.ENDOFYEAR(@dt AS DATE) RETURNS DATE
AS
BEGIN
  RETURN DATEFROMPARTS(YEAR(@dt), 12, 31);
END;
GO
```

Notice that the function's header does not include the SCHEMABINDING attribute. As such, the user-defined function isn't guaranteed to be deterministic. Next, run the following code in attempt to create a table with a persistent computed column that is based on the function that you just created:

```
DROP TABLE IF EXISTS dbo.T1;
GO
CREATE TABLE dbo.T1
(
  keycol INT NOT NULL IDENTITY CONSTRAINT PK_T1 PRIMARY KEY,
  dt DATE NOT NULL,
  dtendofyear AS dbo.ENDOFYEAR(dt) PERSISTED
);
```

SQL Server rejects the attempt with the following error:

```
Msg 4936, Level 16, State 1, Line 574
Computed column 'dtendofyear' in table 'T1' cannot be persisted because the column is
non-deterministic.
```

Run the following code to recreate the function, only this time with the SCHEMABINDING attribute:

```
CREATE OR ALTER FUNCTION dbo.ENDOFYEAR(@dt AS DATE)
  RETURNS DATE
WITH SCHEMABINDING
AS
BEGIN
  RETURN DATEFROMPARTS(YEAR(@dt), 12, 31);
END;
GO
```

Run the following code in attempt to create the table again:

```
CREATE TABLE dbo.T1
(
  keycol INT NOT NULL IDENTITY CONSTRAINT PK_T1 PRIMARY KEY,
  dt DATE NOT NULL,
  dtendofyear AS dbo.ENDOFYEAR(dt) PERSISTED
);
```

This time the code completes successfully.

## Inline table-valued user-defined functions

An inline table-valued user-defined function is very similar in concept to a view in the sense that it's based on a single query, and you interact with it like a table expression, only unlike a view, it supports input parameters. So you could think of such a function as a parameterized view.

The reason that it's called an *inline* function is because SQL Server inlines, or expands, the inner query definition, and constructs an internal query directly against the underlying tables. The inlining process includes replacing the inner query's references to the input parameters with the passed constants (what's known as *parameter embedding*).

As an example, run the following code to create an inline function called GetPage:

```
CREATE OR ALTER FUNCTION dbo.GetPage(@pagenum AS BIGINT, @pagesize AS BIGINT)
  RETURNS TABLE
WITH SCHEMABINDING
AS
RETURN
  WITH C AS
  (
    SELECT ROW_NUMBER() OVER(ORDER BY orderdate, orderid) AS rownum,
      orderid, orderdate, custid, empid
    FROM Sales.Orders
  )
  SELECT rownum, orderid, orderdate, custid, empid
  FROM C
  WHERE rownum BETWEEN (@pagenum - 1) * @pagesize + 1 AND @pagenum * @pagesize;
GO
```

Notice that the function's header defines the input parameters and says that it returns a table result (RETURN TABLE). There's no body to the function (no BEGIN-END block), rather just a RETURN clause with a query.

This function implements a paging solution where you pass a page number and page size, and the function returns orders from the desired page. The code defines a CTE called C based on a query that computes row numbers for orders, based on orderdate and orderid ordering. The outer query then filters only the rows from C with the row numbers that fall in the requested page. The starting row number is based on the expression (@pagenum - 1) * @pagesize + 1, and the ending row number is based on the expression pagenum * @pagesize. For example, with a page number 3, and a page size of 12, the first row number is 25, and the last row number is 36.

Run the following query to test the function, asking for page 3 with a page size of 12:

```
SELECT rownum, orderid, orderdate, custid, empid
FROM dbo.GetPage(3, 12) AS T;
```

This query generates the following output:

```
rownum  orderid  orderdate   custid  empid
------- -------- ----------- ------- ------
25      10272    2014-08-02  65      6
26      10273    2014-08-05  63      3
27      10274    2014-08-06  85      6
28      10275    2014-08-07  49      1
29      10276    2014-08-08  80      8
30      10277    2014-08-09  52      2
31      10278    2014-08-12  5       8
32      10279    2014-08-13  44      8
33      10280    2014-08-14  5       2
```

| 34 | 10281 | 2014-08-14 69 | 4 |
| 35 | 10282 | 2014-08-15 69 | 4 |
| 36 | 10283 | 2014-08-16 46 | 3 |

Recall from Chapter 1 that T-SQL supports a built-in feature for ad-hoc paging in the form of a filter called OFFSET-FETCH. With this filter, you can simplify the solution for the task at hand by using the following function definition instead:

```
CREATE OR ALTER FUNCTION dbo.GetPage(@pagenum AS BIGINT, @pagesize AS BIGINT)
  RETURNS TABLE
WITH SCHEMABINDING
AS
RETURN
  SELECT ROW_NUMBER() OVER(ORDER BY orderdate, orderid) AS rownum,
    orderid, orderdate, custid, empid
  FROM Sales.Orders
  ORDER BY orderdate, orderid
  OFFSET (@pagenum - 1) * @pagesize ROWS FETCH NEXT @pagesize ROWS ONLY;
GO
```

With this solution you don't need to use a CTE that defines row numbers and then an outer query that handles the filter, you can handle both tasks in one query. Run the following code to test the altered function:

```
SELECT rownum, orderid, orderdate, custid, empid
FROM dbo.GetPage(3, 12) AS T;
```

You get the same result as before.

As a more complex example for an inline table-valued user-defined function, suppose that you need to implement a function called GetSubtree that accepts a manager ID as input (call it @mgr), and an optional parameter to limit the number of levels (call it @maxlevels); the function should return the set of all subordinates of the input manager, applying the level limit if one was specified. The function should return a NULL as the manager ID of the input manager.

Run the following code to implement the GetSubtree function as an inline table-valued one:

```
DROP FUNCTION IF EXISTS dbo.GetSubtree;
GO
CREATE FUNCTION dbo.GetSubtree(@mgr AS INT, @maxlevels AS INT = NULL)
  RETURNS TABLE
WITH SCHEMABINDING
AS
RETURN
  WITH EmpsCTE AS
  (
    SELECT empid, CAST(NULL AS INT) AS mgrid, empname, salary, 0 as lvl,
      CAST('.' AS VARCHAR(900)) AS sortpath
    FROM dbo.Employees
    WHERE empid = @mgr
```

```
      UNION ALL

      SELECT S.empid, S.mgrid, S.empname, S.salary, M.lvl + 1 AS lvl,
        CAST(M.sortpath + CAST(S.empid AS VARCHAR(10)) + '.' AS VARCHAR(900)) AS sortpath
      FROM EmpsCTE AS M
        INNER JOIN dbo.Employees AS S
          ON S.mgrid = M.empid
          AND (M.lvl < @maxlevels OR @maxlevels IS NULL)
    )
    SELECT empid, mgrid, empname, salary, lvl, sortpath
    FROM EmpsCTE;
```

The function uses a recursive CTE to handle the task. The anchor member returns the row for the input manager, along with the constant manager ID NULL, the level 0, and a sort path that is made of a separator plus the current employee ID plus another separator.

The recursive member joins the managers from the previous round (identified with the recursive reference to the CTE name) with the Employees table to return direct subordinates, provided the level (depth) did not exceed the specified maximum number of levels, if one was specified. The subordinate's level is computed as the corresponding manager's level plus 1, and the subordinate's sort path is computed by concatenating the manager's path with the current employee ID plus a separator.

Note that corresponding columns in the anchor and the recursive queries must have identical types, including length and precision. Since the manager ID of the input manager is supposed to be set to the constant NULL, and the manager IDs of the subordinates are to be integer typed values, you need to explicitly convert the NULL constant to INT in the anchor query. Similarly, since the column sortpath in both the anchor and recursive queries have to have the same type and length, the code explicitly converts the values in both queries to VARCHAR(900).

The following example demonstrates using the function to return the subtree of manager 3, without limiting the number of levels:

```
SELECT empid, REPLICATE(' | ', lvl) + empname AS emp,
  mgrid, salary, lvl, sortpath
FROM dbo.GetSubtree(3, NULL) AS T
ORDER BY sortpath;
```

This code generates the following output:

```
empid  empname                mgrid  salary    lvl  sortpath
------ ---------------------- ------ --------- ---- -----------
3      Ina                    NULL   7500.00   0    .
7      | Aaron                3      5000.00   1    .7.
11     | | Gabriel           7      3000.00   2    .7.11.
9      | | Rita              7      3000.00   2    .7.9.
12     | | | Emilia          9      2000.00   3    .7.9.12.
13     | | | Michael         9      2000.00   3    .7.9.13.
14     | | | Didi            9      1500.00   3    .7.9.14.
```

Ordering the result by the sortpath column guarantees that the presentation order of the result reflects *topological sort order*, meaning that a manager always shows up before his or her subordinates. Using the REPLICATE function the code replicates a string lvl times to achieve a visual indentation effect that reflects the level of the current node with respect to the root of the subtree. It's pretty!

> **MORE INFO    ROW-LEVEL SECURITY**
>
> You can also use inline table-valued user-defined functions as a filter predicate for a security policy as part of a solution for row-level security. You can find the details at *https://msdn.microsoft.com/en-us/library/dn765131.aspx.*

## Multistatement table-valued user-defined functions

A multistatement table-valued user-defined function is a table function, so from the user's perspective, it's used as a source table in a query much like an inline table-valued function is used. However, instead of being based on a single query, the multistatement function declares a returned table variable in its header, and then its body is responsible for filling the returned table variable with rows. Whenever you query the function, behind the scenes SQL Server creates the table variable that is defined in the function's header, runs the flow in the function's body to fill it with rows, and then as soon as the function executes the RETURN command, SQL Server hands the table variable to the calling query.

As an example, run the following code to create an alternative implementation of the Get-Subtree function, this time as a multistatement table-valued function:

```
DROP FUNCTION IF EXISTS dbo.GetSubtree;
-- cannot use CREATE OR ALTER to change the function type
GO
CREATE FUNCTION dbo.GetSubtree (@mgrid AS INT, @maxlevels AS INT = NULL)
RETURNS @Tree TABLE
(
  empid    INT          NOT NULL PRIMARY KEY,
  mgrid    INT          NULL,
  empname  VARCHAR(25)  NOT NULL,
  salary   MONEY        NOT NULL,
  lvl      INT          NOT NULL,
  sortpath VARCHAR(892) NOT NULL ,
  INDEX idx_lvl_empid_sortpath NONCLUSTERED(lvl, empid, sortpath)
)
WITH SCHEMABINDING
AS
BEGIN
  DECLARE @lvl AS INT = 0;

  -- insert subtree root node into @Tree
  INSERT INTO @Tree(empid, mgrid, empname, salary, lvl, sortpath)
    SELECT empid, NULL AS mgrid, empname, salary, @lvl AS lvl, '.' AS sortpath
    FROM dbo.Employees
    WHERE empid = @mgrid;
```

```
WHILE @@ROWCOUNT > 0 AND (@lvl < @maxlevels OR @maxlevels IS NULL)
BEGIN
  SET @lvl += 1;

  -- insert children of nodes from prev level into @Tree
  INSERT INTO @Tree(empid, mgrid, empname, salary, lvl, sortpath)
    SELECT S.empid, S.mgrid, S.empname, S.salary, @lvl AS lvl,
      M.sortpath + CAST(S.empid AS VARCHAR(10)) + '.' AS sortpath
    FROM dbo.Employees AS S
      INNER JOIN @Tree AS M
        ON S.mgrid = M.empid AND M.lvl = @lvl - 1;
END;

  RETURN;
END;
GO
```

The header of the function defines a table variable called @Tree as the returned value. Then the code in the body of the function (observe the BEGIN-END block) starts by declaring a level counter called @lvl and initializes it with 0. The code continues to insert the row for the input manager into the table variable along with the just initialized level and initial sort path. The code then defines a loop that keeps iterating as long as the number of rows affected by the previous insert is nonzero, and we haven't yet reached the maximum number of levels if one was specified. In each round, the loop increments the level counter and inserts the next level of subordinates into the table variable. Finally, the code executes the RETURN command, causing the function to exit and hand the table variable to the calling query.

Use the following code to test the function:

```
SELECT empid, REPLICATE(' | ', lvl) + empname AS emp,
  mgrid, salary, lvl, sortpath
FROM dbo.GetSubtree(3, NULL) AS T
ORDER BY sortpath;
```

This code generates the following output:

```
empid  empname              mgrid  salary    lvl  sortpath
------ -------------------- ------ --------- ---- -----------
3      Ina                  NULL   7500.00   0    .
7      | Aaron              3      5000.00   1    .7.
11     | | Gabriel          7      3000.00   2    .7.11.
9      | | Rita             7      3000.00   2    .7.9.
12     | | | Emilia         9      2000.00   3    .7.9.12.
13     | | | Michael        9      2000.00   3    .7.9.13.
14     | | | Didi           9      1500.00   3    .7.9.14.
```

If you're wondering why bother implementing a task as a multistatement function instead of an inline one, there could be a number of reasons. The recursive query in the inline function uses a spool (worktable) to store the intermediate results, but you have no control over the indexing on that spool. With the multistatement function, you control the definition of the table variable, including indexing. Furthermore, the inline function is only allowed to return a query, whereas the multistatement function can have complete flow with procedural logic. It just so happens that the task in our specific example can be handled with both kinds of functions, so you can try them both, and compare their performance to see which one works better for you. But some tasks cannot be handled with a single query, rather require a multi-step procedural solution.

When you're done, run the following code for cleanup:

```
DROP TABLE IF EXISTS dbo.T1;

DROP VIEW IF EXISTS dbo.VRAND;

DROP FUNCTION IF EXISTS dbo.MySYSDATETIME, dbo.MyRAND, dbo.ENDOFYEAR,
    dbo.SubtreeTotalSalaries, dbo.GetPage, dbo.GetSubtree;

DROP TABLE IF EXISTS dbo.Employees;
```

## Stored procedures

Stored procedures are routines that support flow with multiple steps. They support many T-SQL elements that user-defined functions don't, like modifying data in the database and even applying data definition changes to database objects (DDL), using temporary tables, dynamic SQL, error handling, and more. These are clear advantages compared to user-defined functions; however, unlike with functions, stored procedures cannot be embedded in queries.

Stored procedures support input and output parameters and can also return result sets of queries. SQL Server caches the execution plans of the stored procedure's queries, and typically reuses them in subsequent executions of the procedure to save the time, CPU and memory resources that are associated with optimizing the queries.

Stored procedures provide many benefits compared to implementing the business logic in the application. They encapsulate the logic to allow reusability and hiding of complexity. It's much easier to apply changes to a stored procedure with a simple ALTER PROC command compared to deploying changes in the application. Also, with stored procedures you tend to have less network traffic because when you call a stored procedure from the application, all that is passed through the network is just the procedure name and its parameters. The flow runs in the database engine, and then only the final result is sent to the application. When you implement the logic in the application, you usually get more roundtrips between the application and the database, and consequently more network traffic.

Stored procedures also simplify handling security in the database. Often you don't want to grant users with permissions to directly query and modify data in tables, rather you want them to be able to achieve such tasks only indirectly through stored procedures. To achieve this, grant the users with EXECUTE permissions on the stored procedure while not granting them direct access to underlying objects.

The upcoming sections cover working with stored procedures, using dynamic SQL within procedures, using output parameters and modifying data, and also using cursors within stored procedures. Later in the chapter, Skill 3.2 covers error handling within stored procedures.

## Working with stored procedures

A stored procedure is a reusable routine that supports input and output parameters, and even returning result sets of queries. This section starts with a simple example for using input parameters and returning a result set of a query. I demonstrate using output parameters in a later section.

Suppose that you are given a task to create a stored procedure that handles what's called *dynamic search conditions* to query and filter data from the Sales.Orders table. The procedure should have four optional input parameters for filtering the orders by order ID, order date, customer ID, and employee ID. The executing user determines which combination of columns to filter by. The way you make the input parameters optional is by defining them with a default NULL. If the user doesn't specify a value for an input parameter, it is set to the default NULL, telling you that you're not supposed to apply a filter to the corresponding column.

Run the following code to create the GetOrders stored procedure, which handles the task at hand:

```
CREATE OR ALTER PROC dbo.GetOrders
  @orderid   AS INT  = NULL,
  @orderdate AS DATE = NULL,
  @custid    AS INT  = NULL,
  @empid     AS INT  = NULL
AS

SET XACT_ABORT, NOCOUNT ON;

SELECT orderid, orderdate, shippeddate, custid, empid, shipperid
FROM Sales.Orders
WHERE (orderid   = @orderid   OR @orderid   IS NULL)
  AND (orderdate = @orderdate OR @orderdate IS NULL)
  AND (custid    = @custid    OR @custid    IS NULL)
  AND (empid     = @empid     OR @empid     IS NULL);
GO
```

Observe the header of the stored procedure with the definition of the input parameters and the syntax for defining default values. Some people like to place the parameter definitions within parentheses, as in:

```
CREATE OR ALTER PROC dbo.GetOrders
(
  @orderid   AS INT  = NULL,
  @orderdate AS DATE = NULL,
  @custid    AS INT  = NULL,
  @empid     AS INT  = NULL
)
AS...
```

As for the body of the stored procedure, notice that there's no mandatory BEGIN-END block like in multistatement user-defined functions, but you can use one if that's your styling preference, as in:

```
BEGIN

  SET XACT_ABORT, NOCOUNT ON;

  SELECT orderid, orderdate, shippeddate, custid, empid, shipperid
  FROM Sales.Orders
  WHERE (orderid   = @orderid   OR @orderid   IS NULL)
    AND (orderdate = @orderdate OR @orderdate IS NULL)
    AND (custid    = @custid    OR @custid    IS NULL)
    AND (empid     = @empid     OR @empid     IS NULL);

END;
```

The stored procedure's code starts by setting the options XACT_ABORT and NOCOUNT to ON. The XACT_ABORT option determines the effect of run-time errors raised by T-SQL statements. When this option is OFF (the default in most cases), some errors cause an open transaction to roll back and the execution of the code to be aborted, whereas other errors leave the transaction open. To get a more reliable and consistent behavior, I consider it a best practice to set this option to ON, and this way all errors cause an open transaction to be rolled back and the execution of the code to be aborted. The NOCOUNT option suppresses messages indicating how many rows were affected by data manipulation statements. When it's OFF (the default), those messages can degrade query performance due to the network traffic that they generate, plus this causes trouble for client applications that perceive those as query results.

The code then invokes a query against the Sales.Orders table that filters the data based on the specified parameters. For each parameter the query's WHERE clause has the following *disjunction* of predicates (predicates separated by an OR operator):

```
column = @parameter OR @parameter IS NULL
```

When the user doesn't specify an input value, the parameter is set to the default NULL. In such a case the predicate @parameter IS NULL is true, and therefore the disjunction of predicates is true, so no filtering is applied. When the user does specify an input value, the predicate @parameter IS NULL is false, and it is left to the predicate column = @parameter to determine whether to keep the row or discard it.

Run the following code to test the procedure, asking to filter orders placed on November 11, 2015 by customer 85:

```
EXEC dbo.GetOrders @orderdate = '20151111', @custid = 85;
```

This code generates the following output:

```
orderid     orderdate   shippeddate custid      empid       shipperid
----------- ----------- ----------- ----------- ----------- -----------
10737       2015-11-11  2015-11-18  85          2           2
```

Note that you can also execute the procedure, passing input values without specifying the target parameter names, but then you need to know the positions of the parameters in the procedure's header. Here's the equivalent to the above procedure execution passing inputs by position:

```
EXEC dbo.GetOrders DEFAULT, '20151111', 85, DEFAULT;
```

Using named parameters is considered a best practice because you need to specify only the applicable parameters, and you don't need to know in what order they are defined in the procedure's header. The code is also much clearer.

Execute the procedure again, asking to filter the order with order ID 42:

```
EXEC dbo.GetOrders @orderid = 42;
```

Such an order doesn't exist and therefore the procedure returns an empty set:

```
orderid     orderdate   shippeddate custid      empid       shipperid
----------- ----------- ----------- ----------- ----------- -----------
```

## Stored procedures and dynamic SQL

The previous section demonstrated using a stored procedure to handle a dynamic search conditions task to query and filter data from the Sales.Orders table using a static query. This section describes an alternative solution that uses *dynamic SQL*, which is a technique that involves building a batch of code as a character string, usually in a variable, and then telling SQL Server to execute the code that resides in that variable.

Using a static query in our case is not ideal in terms of query performance. The reason for this has to do with the fact that SQL Server caches the execution plan for the query for reuse in subsequent executions of the stored procedure. The cached plan has to incorporate all filter predicates and not just the ones that are related to the parameters that are applicable in the execution that gets optimized. Otherwise, SQL Server would not be able to reuse the plan in subsequent executions that specify a different set of applicable parameters. This tends to result in a generalized plan that cannot really be optimal for all possible combinations of parameters.

One way to get efficient plans is to add the query option RECOMPILE, as in:

```
<query> OPTION(RECOMPILE);
```

With this option, in every execution of the stored procedure SQL Server optimizes the query from scratch, after applying *parameter embedding* (replacing the parameters with constants) and normalizing the query to remove the redundant parts. For instance, if you execute the procedure, providing an input value only to the @orderid parameter (say, 10248), effectively the query that gets optimized is:

```
SELECT orderid, orderdate, shippeddate, custid, empid, shipperid
FROM Sales.Orders
WHERE orderid   = 10248;
```

As you can realize, the likelihood to get efficient plans with this solution is quite high. But this comes at the cost of recompiling the query in every execution of the stored procedure. If you want to both get optimal plans and optimal cached query plan reuse behavior, you need to use a different solution. One of the ways to achieve this is to dynamically build the query string with only the relevant parameterized predicates, and execute the code that you built with the sp_executesql procedure. Here's the solution code that implements this approach:

```
CREATE OR ALTER PROC dbo.GetOrders
  @orderid   AS INT  = NULL,
  @orderdate AS DATE = NULL,
  @custid    AS INT  = NULL,
  @empid     AS INT  = NULL
AS

SET XACT_ABORT, NOCOUNT ON;

DECLARE @sql AS NVARCHAR(MAX) = N'SELECT orderid, orderdate, shippeddate, custid, empid,
shipperid
FROM Sales.Orders
WHERE 1 = 1'
  + CASE WHEN @orderid   IS NOT NULL THEN N' AND orderid   = @orderid  ' ELSE N'' END
  + CASE WHEN @orderdate IS NOT NULL THEN N' AND orderdate = @orderdate' ELSE N'' END
  + CASE WHEN @custid    IS NOT NULL THEN N' AND custid    = @custid   ' ELSE N'' END
  + CASE WHEN @empid     IS NOT NULL THEN N' AND empid     = @empid    ' ELSE N'' END
  + N';'

EXEC sys.sp_executesql
  @stmt = @sql,
  @params = N'@orderid AS INT, @orderdate AS DATE, @custid AS INT, @empid AS INT',
  @orderid    = @orderid,
  @orderdate  = @orderdate,
  @custid     = @custid,
  @empid      = @empid;
GO
```

The code declares a variable called @sql to store the dynamic query string. It constructs it with the fixed SELECT and FROM parts first. It starts the WHERE clause with the predicate 1 = 1, which is always true, to avoid needing to deal differently with the first applicable element that needs to be concatenated versus the nonfirst ones. Then, using a CASE expression, for each applicable parameter (one that is not NULL), the code concatenates a parameterized predicate to the filter, otherwise an empty string.

The code then executes the dynamically built query by using the sp_executesql procedure. The first part of the procedure is the @stmt parameter, where you provide the string with the code that you want to execute (@sql variable in our case). The second part is the @params parameter, where you declare all of the dynamic batch parameters. In our case, we declare a corresponding dynamic batch parameter for each of the stored procedure's parameters. It's quite all right if you wish to use the same names for the dynamic batch parameters and the stored procedure's parameters as is done in our example. The last part is a series of assignments of the stored procedure's parameters to the corresponding dynamic batch parameters.

Use the following code to test the stored procedure:

```
EXEC dbo.GetOrders @orderdate = '20151111', @custid = 85;
```

You get the following output:

```
orderid     orderdate   shippeddate custid      empid       shipperid
----------- ----------- ----------- ----------- ----------- -----------
10737       2015-11-11  2015-11-18  85          2           2
```

Each unique query string (same combination of parameters) that is used gets optimized separately, and SQL Server is able to reuse a previously cached plan when the query string matches.

There's a certain caveat related to security when using dynamic SQL. Earlier I mentioned that SQL Server supports a security model where you grant users EXECUTE permissions on a stored procedure without granting them direct permissions against the underlying objects. This way users are able to perform the task only through the stored procedure and not directly. This capability is known as *ownership chaining*. However, ownership chaining is limited only to SELECT, INSERT, UPDATE, and DELETE statements using static SQL, and only when the owner of the calling and the called objects is the same. Because in our case the code is executed using dynamic SQL, ownership chaining doesn't apply and the executing user needs direct SELECT permissions against the Sales.Orders table. Before I provide a workaround, I demonstrate the fact that when using dynamic SQL, only EXECUTE permission on the stored procedure isn't sufficient.

Run the following code to create a login called login1, and an associated user in the database called user1:

```
CREATE LOGIN login1 WITH PASSWORD = 'J345#$)thb';
GO
CREATE USER user1 FOR LOGIN login1;
GO
```

Next, run the following code to grant EXECUTE permission on the stored procedure to user1:

```
GRANT EXEC ON dbo.GetOrders TO user1;
```

Use the following code to display the current execution context:

```
SELECT SUSER_NAME() AS [login], USER_NAME() AS [user];
```

You should get output similar to the following, with your login name, of course:

```
login                            user
-------------------------------- -----
MicrosoftAccount\<your acount>   dbo
```

Run the following code to set the execution context to login1:

```
EXECUTE AS LOGIN = 'login1';
```

Run the following code to display the current execution context again:

```
SELECT SUSER_NAME() AS [login], USER_NAME() AS [user];
```

You get the following output indicating that your context indeed changed to login1 as the login, and user1 as the database user:

```
login   user
------- ------
login1  user1
```

Run the following code in attempt to execute the stored procedure:

```
EXEC dbo.GetOrders @orderdate = '20151111', @custid = 85;
```

You get the following permission error:

```
Msg 229, Level 14, State 5, Line 882
The SELECT permission was denied on the object 'Orders', database 'TSQLV4', schema
'Sales'.
```

Run the following code to revert back to original execution context:

```
REVERT;
```

As a workaround, you can define the stored procedure with an EXECUTE AS clause, to impersonate the security context of the procedure's execution to that of the specified entity. For example, using the option EXECUTE AS OWNER impersonates the security context to that of the stored procedure's owner. Alternatively, you can provide a specific user name that has the right permissions. Run the following code to recreate the stored procedure using the EXECUTE AS OWNER option:

```
CREATE OR ALTER PROC dbo.GetOrders
  @orderid   AS INT  = NULL,
  @orderdate AS DATE = NULL,
  @custid    AS INT  = NULL,
  @empid     AS INT  = NULL
```

```
WITH EXECUTE AS OWNER
AS

SET XACT_ABORT, NOCOUNT ON;

DECLARE @sql AS NVARCHAR(MAX) = N'SELECT orderid, orderdate, shippeddate, custid, empid,
shipperid
FROM Sales.Orders
WHERE 1 = 1'
  + CASE WHEN @orderid   IS NOT NULL THEN N' AND orderid   = @orderid  ' ELSE N'' END
  + CASE WHEN @orderdate IS NOT NULL THEN N' AND orderdate = @orderdate' ELSE N'' END
  + CASE WHEN @custid    IS NOT NULL THEN N' AND custid    = @custid   ' ELSE N'' END
  + CASE WHEN @empid     IS NOT NULL THEN N' AND empid     = @empid    ' ELSE N'' END
  + N';'

EXEC sys.sp_executesql
  @stmt = @sql,
  @params = N'@orderid AS INT, @orderdate AS DATE, @custid AS INT, @empid AS INT',
  @orderid   = @orderid,
  @orderdate = @orderdate,
  @custid    = @custid,
  @empid     = @empid;
GO
```

Run the following code to set the execution context to login1:

```
EXECUTE AS LOGIN = 'login1';
```

Try to execute the stored procedure again:

```
EXEC dbo.GetOrders @orderdate = '20151111', @custid = 85;
```

This time the stored procedure runs successfully.

Run the following code to revert back to original execution context:

```
REVERT;
```

> **MORE INFO** **DYNAMIC SQL AND SECURITY IN STORED PROCEDURES**
>
> The aforementioned method to impersonate the security context of the procedure's execution is quite simple and straightforward, but not always ideal in terms of auditing and monitoring capabilities. There are more complex, yet more recommended alternatives, in which you sign the stored procedure with a certificate. You associate the certificate with a user that cannot login, and grant that user with the appropriate permissions. For more information on the topic see Erland Sommarskog's text "The Curse and Blessings of Dynamic SQL" at *http://www.sommarskog.se/dynamic_sql.html* and "Giving Permissions through Stored Procedures" at *http://www.sommarskog.se/grantperm.html*.

## Using output parameters and modifying data

If you need to return scalar values back from a stored procedure, you can do this by using output parameters. Also, unlike with user-defined functions, you can modify data in the database from stored procedures. This section demonstrates both capabilities.

To define a parameter as an output one add the keyword OUTPUT or OUT in its definition. Also, when executing the procedure, you need to provide a local variable to accept the returned value, and indicate the keyword OUTPUT or OUT again in that assignment, otherwise the parameter is actually treated as an input one.

As an example, suppose that you need to develop a solution for generating integer keys with a guarantee for no gaps between the values. For instance, perhaps you need such a solution to generate invoice numbers and you need an assurance that they are to be consecutive. You cannot use the identity property or the sequence object because these solutions do not guarantee that you won't have gaps between the keys. If you create an identity or sequence value in a transaction that ends up failing, that value is gone.

You decide to handle the task by creating a table called MySequences where you maintain your own custom sequences. For each such sequence you store a row with the sequence name and the last used value. Whenever you need a new key, you update the relevant row to increase the current value, query it, and use it in the target table. When you update a row, your session obtains an exclusive lock on the row and keeps the lock until the end of the transaction. This means that on one hand no one else can obtain a new value until your transaction is over; on the other hand, if the transaction fails, the current sequence value is undone to the original one. This way you have a guarantee for no gaps.

Use the following code to create the table dbo.MySequences:

```
DROP TABLE IF EXISTS dbo.MySequences;
GO
CREATE TABLE dbo.MySequences
(
  seqname VARCHAR(128) NOT NULL
    CONSTRAINT PK_MySequences PRIMARY KEY,
  val INT NOT NULL
    CONSTRAINT DFT_MySequences_val DEFAULT(0)
);
```

Run the following code to add a row representing a sequence for generating invoice numbers:

```
INSERT INTO dbo.MySequences(seqname, val) VALUES('SEQINVOICES', 0);
```

You name the custom sequence SEQINVOICES and initialize it with 0 so that the first value that it generates is 1.

Use the following code to create a stored procedure called GetSequenceValue to handle a request for a new value for a given sequence name:

```
CREATE OR ALTER PROC dbo.GetSequenceValue
  @seqname AS VARCHAR(128),
  @val     AS INT OUTPUT
AS

SET XACT_ABORT, NOCOUNT ON;

UPDATE dbo.MySequences
  SET @val = val += 1
WHERE seqname = @seqname;

IF @@ROWCOUNT = 0
  THROW 51001, 'Specified sequence was not found.', 1;
GO
```

Observe that the header of the stored procedure defines an input parameter called @seq-name to accept the input sequence name, and an output parameter called @val to return the newly generated sequence value. The procedure uses an UPDATE statement with a variable (covered in Chapter 1) to increment the requested sequence value by 1, and assigns the new value to the output parameter. If the requested custom sequence doesn't exist, the UPDATE statement has affected zero rows, in which case the stored procedure throws an error using the THROW command.

Use the following code to request a new invoice number:

```
DECLARE @newinvoicenumber AS INT;
EXEC dbo.GetSequenceValue @seqname = 'SEQINVOICES', @val = @newinvoicenumber OUTPUT;
SELECT @newinvoicenumber AS newinvoicenumber;
```

The code uses a local variable to absorb the returned value from the output parameter. Notice that you specify the OUTPUT keyword again in the execution; otherwise the parameter is treated as an input one.

This code generates the following output:

```
newinvoicenumber
----------------
1
```

Run the code a couple of more times, and see how the sequence value keeps advancing.

Try running the code with a sequence name that doesn't exist:

```
DECLARE @newinvoicenumber AS INT;
EXEC dbo.GetSequenceValue @seqname = 'NOSUCHSEQUENCE', @val = @newinvoicenumber OUTPUT;
SELECT @newinvoicenumber AS newinvoicenumber;
```

This time the procedure throws an error:

```
Msg 51001, Level 16, State 1, Procedure dbo.GetSequenceValue, Line 15 [Batch Start Line 978]
Specified sequence was not found.
```

Later in the chapter, Skill 3.2 covers error handling.

## Using cursors

Another example where the encapsulation provided by stored procedures is beneficial is when using cursors. A cursor allows you to iterate through rows of some query result one at a time. Solutions that use cursors tend to be lengthy because you need explicit code to define the cursor, open it, iterate through its rows, and apply some logic per row, close, and deallocate it. With a stored procedure, you can hide all that complexity. Furthermore, if at a later point you manage to find a better solution, perhaps one that doesn't use a cursor, you can simply alter the stored procedure's implementation. This is transparent to the users of the stored procedure.

The following example demonstrates the use of a stored procedure with a cursor. It involves a task called *depleting quantities*. You're given a table called Transactions, which you create and populate by running the following code:

```
DROP TABLE IF EXISTS dbo.Transactions;
GO
CREATE TABLE dbo.Transactions
(
  txid INT NOT NULL CONSTRAINT PK_Transactions PRIMARY KEY,
  qty  INT NOT NULL,
  depletionqty INT NULL
);
GO

TRUNCATE TABLE dbo.Transactions;
INSERT INTO dbo.Transactions(txid, qty)
  VALUES(1,2),(2,5),(3,4),(4,1),(5,10),(6,3),(7,1),(8,2),(9,1),(10,2),(11,1),(12,9);
```

Your task is to create a stored procedure called ComputeDepletionQuantities that processes the transactions that are stored in the Transactions table. The procedure should process the transactions in order based on the txid column. Each transaction adds a certain quantity (qty column) of some item to a container. The container has a limited capacity, which is provided as an input parameter called @maxallowedqty to the stored procedure. As soon as the cumulative quantity in the container exceeds the maximum allowed, the container needs to be depleted, and your code should write the depletion quantity to the depeletionqty column of the current transaction. At the end of the stored procedure's execution, rows in the Transactions table representing transactions where the container was depleted should have the depletion quantity stored in the depleteqty column, and all remaining rows should have a NULL in that column. Furthermore, the stored procedure should return a result set showing the transactions in order, along with the depletion quantity (depleteqty column) where applicable, and the current cumulative quantity in the container (totalqty column).

After you're done developing the stored procedure, use the following code to test it:

```
EXEC dbo.ComputeDepletionQuantities @maxallowedqty = 5;
```

The stored procedure should return the following output for the given sample data in the Transactions table and the specified maximum container capacity of 5.

```
txid        qty         depletionqty totalqty
----------- ----------- ------------ -----------
1           2           NULL         2
2           5           7            0
3           4           NULL         4
4           1           NULL         5
5           10          15           0
6           3           NULL         3
7           1           NULL         4
8           2           6            0
9           1           NULL         1
10          2           NULL         3
11          1           NULL         4
12          9           13           0
```

The following code demonstrates one way to implement the stored procedure using a cursor:

```
CREATE OR ALTER PROC dbo.ComputeDepletionQuantities
  @maxallowedqty AS INT
AS

SET XACT_ABORT, NOCOUNT ON;

UPDATE dbo.Transactions
  SET depletionqty = NULL
WHERE depletionqty IS NOT NULL;

DECLARE @qty AS INT, @sumqty AS INT = 0;

DECLARE C CURSOR FOR
  SELECT qty
  FROM dbo.Transactions
  ORDER BY txid;

OPEN C;

FETCH NEXT FROM C INTO @qty;

WHILE @@FETCH_STATUS = 0
BEGIN
  SET @sumqty += @qty;

  IF @sumqty > @maxallowedqty
  BEGIN
    UPDATE dbo.Transactions
      SET depletionqty = @sumqty
    WHERE CURRENT OF C;

    SET @sumqty = 0;
  END;

  FETCH NEXT FROM C INTO @qty;
END;
```

```
CLOSE C;

DEALLOCATE C;

SELECT txid, qty, depletionqty,
  SUM(qty - ISNULL(depletionqty, 0))
    OVER(ORDER BY txid ROWS UNBOUNDED PRECEDING) AS totalqty
FROM dbo.Transactions
ORDER BY txid;
GO
```

The code starts by updating the Transactions table, setting the depletionqty column to NULL where it currently isn't NULL.

Next, the code declares local variables called @qty and @sumqty to hold the current transaction's quantity and current cumulative quantity (initialized with 0), respectively.

The code then declares a cursor based on a query that returns the transaction quantities in order, opens it, and fetches the first transaction's quantity into the @qty variable.

Next, the code executes a loop that iterates per transaction while the last fetch was successful (@@FETCH_STATUS function returns 0, meaning we haven't reached the end of the cursor yet). In each iteration of the loop, the code increases the current cumulative quantity (@sumqty variable) by the current transaction's quantity (@qty variable). If the new cumulative quantity exceeds the maximum allowed in the container, the code applies two steps. One, it uses the syntax UPDATE <table> WHERE CURRENT OF <cursor> to update the depletion quantity of the Transactions table's row that the cursor is currently positioned on to the new cumulative quantity. Two, it resets the current cumulative quantity to 0. Before finishing the current iteration of the loop, the code fetches the next transaction's quantity into the @qty variable.

After the loop is done with all of its iterations, the code closes and deallocates the cursor.

At this point the Transactions table is updated with the correct depletion quantities in the applicable transactions. The code finally issues a query that in addition to returning the current data from the Transactions table, also computes the current total quantity in the container (totalqty column) after each transaction. The query uses the following expression based on a window function to compute the totalqty result column:

```
SUM(qty - ISNULL(depletionqty, 0))
  OVER(ORDER BY txid ROWS UNBOUNDED PRECEDING) AS totalqty
```

The computation is a running total of all transaction quantities minus the depletion quantities (or zero if NULL) based on txid ordering, from the beginning of the activity and up to the current transaction.

Run the following code to test the stored procedure with a maximum allowed capacity of 5:

```
EXEC dbo.ComputeDepletionQuantities @maxallowedqty = 5;
```

Verify that you get the correct result, which was provided earlier. Of course, feel free to test the procedure with different input values.

When you're done, run the following code for cleanup:

```
DROP USER IF EXISTS user1;
GO
DROP LOGIN login1;
GO
DROP PROC IF EXISTS dbo.GetOrders, dbo.GetSequenceValue, dbo.ComputeDepletionQuantities;
DROP TABLE IF EXISTS dbo.MySequences, dbo.Transactions;
```

# Skill 3.2: Implement error handling and transactions

Transactions and error handling are two mechanisms in SQL Server that enable you to work with a consistent database and define the course of action to take in case of errors. The two are strongly intertwined. When errors happen in transactions, the default handling of SQL Server is not always the desired one; with your own error handling, you have some degree of control over the outcome. This skill starts with coverage of transactions. It then describes the error handling constructs that T-SQL supports. It then explains how to handle errors that happen in transactions.

**This section covers how to:**

- Determine results of Data Definition Language (DDL) statements based on transaction control statements
- Implement TRY...CATCH error handling with Transact-SQL
- Generate error messages with THROW and RAISERROR
- Implement transaction control in conjunction with error handling in stored procedures

## Understanding transactions

A transaction is a unit of work with one or more activities that manipulate data, and possibly its structure (yes, unlike in some other database platforms, in SQL Server most DDL is transactional!). A transaction has, or at least should have, four main properties known collectively as the *ACID* properties. A stands for atomicity, C for consistency, I for isolation, and D for durability.

Theoretically, a transaction should be *atomic*; namely either complete in its entirety or not take place at all. In practice, this is not always the default behavior in SQL Server, and in order to achieve true atomicity, you need to add your own error handling code.

A transaction should be *consistent*; namely, it should transition the database from one consistent state to another in terms of adhering to the data model, constraints, and triggers.

A transaction should be *isolated*; this means that intermediate inconsistent states of the data are supposed to be visible only to the transaction that made the changes, but not to other transactions. You can set what's called an *isolation level* either at the session level with a SET TRANSACTION ISOLATION LEVEL option, or at the query level with a table hint to control the degree of isolation that you get.

**MORE INFO ON ISOLATION LEVELS**

You can find more information on isolation levels at *https://technet.microsoft.com/en-us/library/ms189122(v=sql.105).aspx*.

Finally, a transaction should be durable; this means that when you commit the transaction and get an acknowledge from the database that the transaction committed successfully, you can rest assured that the transaction's changes are durable. This means that the changes can survive a crash of the SQL Server process, such as a result of a power failure event.

This section explains how to define transactions, nesting of transactions, and working with savepoints.

## Defining transactions

SQL Server allows you to either explicitly define the transaction's boundaries yourself or to let it define those implicitly for you. To explicitly mark the beginning of a transaction, use the BEGIN TRANSACTION statement (or BEGIN TRAN for brevity). To end the transaction and commit its work, use the COMMIT TRANSACTION statement (supported alternatives: COMMIT TRAN, COMMIT WORK and just COMMIT). To end a transaction and roll back its work, undoing all of its changes, use the ROLLBACK TRANSACTION statement (supported alternatives: ROLLBACK TRAN, ROLLBACK WORK and just ROLLBACK).

You can query a function called @@TRANCOUNT to know whether you're currently in an open transaction or not. If you're in an open transaction the function returns a value greater than zero, otherwise, it returns zero. I provide more details about this function later under the topic Nesting of transactions.

As an example, the following code uses an explicit user transaction to add a new order to the TSQLV4 sample database:

```
USE TSQLV4;
SET XACT_ABORT, NOCOUNT ON;

-- start a new transaction
BEGIN TRAN;

-- declare a variable
DECLARE @neworderid AS INT;

-- insert a new order into the Sales.Orders table
INSERT INTO Sales.Orders
    (custid, empid, orderdate, requireddate, shippeddate,
     shipperid, freight, shipname, shipaddress, shipcity,
     shippostalcode, shipcountry)
  VALUES
    (1, 1, '20170212', '20170301', '20170216',
     1, 10.00, N'Shipper 1', N'Address AAA', N'City AAA',
     N'11111', N'Country AAA');

-- save the new order id in the variable @neworderid
SET @neworderid = SCOPE_IDENTITY();

PRINT 'Added new order header with order ID ' + CAST(@neworderid AS VARCHAR(10))
  + '. @@TRANCOUNT is ' + CAST(@@TRANCOUNT AS VARCHAR(10)) + '.';

-- insert order lines for new order into Sales.OrderDetails
INSERT INTO Sales.OrderDetails(orderid, productid, unitprice, qty, discount)
  VALUES(@neworderid, 1, 10.00, 1, 0.000),
        (@neworderid, 2, 10.00, 1, 0.000),
        (@neworderid, 3, 10.00, 1, 0.000);

PRINT 'Added order lines to new order. @@TRANCOUNT is '
  + CAST(@@TRANCOUNT AS VARCHAR(10)) + '.';

-- commit the transaction
COMMIT TRAN;
```

The examples in this section use ad-hoc batches for simplicity, but in a later section you will encapsulate the code in a stored procedure. The code starts by setting the XACT_ABORT and NOCOUNT options to ON. As a reminder, when the XACT_ABORT setting is off (the default), not all run-time errors cause the transaction to roll back, and execution of the code to abort. By setting this option to on, you provide a more consistent and expected behavior from transactions whereby all errors cause the transaction to roll back and execution of the code to abort. By setting the NOCOUNT option to ON you request to suppress messages reporting how many rows were affected by DML statements.

The code uses a single transaction to add both an order header to the Sales.Orders table, and corresponding order lines to the Sales.OrderDetails table. After inserting the order header row to Orders, the code saves the order ID that was just generated by the identity property to a variable, and then uses the variable when adding the order line rows to OrderDetails.

This code prints the state of the transaction after each of the INSERT statements, generating the following output:

```
Added new order header with order ID 11078. @@TRANCOUNT is 1.
Added order lines to new order. @@TRANCOUNT is 1.
```

In case you already ran code that added orders previously, the new order ID that SQL Server creates for your new order may be different than in the earlier example. Remember that you can always run the code that creates the sample database TSQLV4 to start with a clean copy.

Remember that because you set the XACT_ABORT setting to ON, if there had been a run-time error after any of the INSERT statements, the transaction would have rolled back in its entirety and execution of the code would have been aborted. In our case, the transaction completed successfully. If you now query the Orders and OrderDetails tables, you find the data for the new order, including both the order header and its corresponding order lines. Run the following code to achieve this (use the order ID that you got in case it's different than the one in this example):

```
SELECT orderid, orderdate, custid, empid
FROM Sales.Orders
WHERE orderid = 11078;

SELECT orderid, productid, qty
FROM Sales.OrderDetails
WHERE orderid = 11078;
```

This code generates the following output:

```
orderid      orderdate   custid       empid
-----------  ----------  -----------  -----------
11078        2017-02-12  1            1

orderid      productid   qty
-----------  ----------  ------
11078        1           1
11078        2           1
11078        3           1
```

Next, run the following code to try adding an order with an invalid order line where the discount is greater that 1:

```
SET XACT_ABORT, NOCOUNT ON;

BEGIN TRAN;

DECLARE @neworderid AS INT;

INSERT INTO Sales.Orders
    (custid, empid, orderdate, requireddate, shippeddate,
     shipperid, freight, shipname, shipaddress, shipcity,
     shippostalcode, shipcountry)
  VALUES
    (2, 2, '20170212', '20170301', '20170216',
     2, 20.00, N'Shipper 2', N'Address BBB', N'City BBB',
     N'22222', N'Country BBB');

SET @neworderid = SCOPE_IDENTITY();

PRINT 'Added new order header with order ID ' + CAST(@neworderid AS VARCHAR(10))
    + '. @@TRANCOUNT is ' + CAST(@@TRANCOUNT AS VARCHAR(10)) + '.';

INSERT INTO Sales.OrderDetails(orderid, productid, unitprice, qty, discount)
  VALUES(@neworderid, 1, 20.00, 2, 2.000), -- CHECK violation since discount > 1
        (@neworderid, 2, 20.00, 2, 0.000),
        (@neworderid, 3, 20.00, 2, 0.000);

PRINT 'Added order lines to new order. @@TRANCOUNT is '
    + CAST(@@TRANCOUNT AS VARCHAR(10)) + '.';

COMMIT TRAN;
```

The first INSERT statement, which adds the order header row, completes successfully. However, the second INSERT statement, which attempts to add the order lines, fails due to a CHECK constraint violation because one of the order lines has a discount value that is greater than 1. The table has a CHECK constraint that limits the discount to the range 0 through 1. You can see the constraints that are defined on the table by running the following code:

```
EXEC sys.sp_helpconstraint 'Sales.OrderDetails';
```

Because the XACT_ABORT setting is turned on, the error causes the transaction to roll back and execution of the code to abort. The execution of the code generates the following output:

```
Added new order header with order ID 11079. @@TRANCOUNT is 1.
Msg 547, Level 16, State 0, Line 86
The INSERT statement conflicted with the CHECK constraint "CHK_discount". The conflict
occurred in database "TSQLV4", table "Sales.OrderDetails", column 'discount'.
```

Query both tables looking for the rows that are related to the new order:

```
SELECT orderid, orderdate, custid, empid
FROM Sales.Orders
```

```
WHERE orderid = 11079;

SELECT orderid, productid, qty
FROM Sales.OrderDetails
WHERE orderid = 11079;
```

You get empty sets back from both queries:

```
orderid      orderdate  custid      empid
-----------  ---------- ----------- -----------


orderid      productid  qty
-----------  ---------- ------
```

If you don't explicitly define the transaction boundaries, SQL Server uses an *autocommit* mode where each individual statement is considered a separate transaction, as if it's preceded by a BEGIN TRAN statement and followed by a COMMIT TRAN statement. Note that with most statements, the individual statement must be atomic, meaning that the single statement either completes in its entirety or not take place at all. For instance, suppose that you issue a DELETE statement that deletes 100 rows from a table under autocommit mode. If the statement fails before completion, say after 17 rows were deleted, SQL Server undoes the change. Either all 100 rows get deleted, or none at all.

 **EXAM TIP**

The types of statements that are considered *transactional statements* include DML statements (such as SELECT against a table, INSERT, UPDATE, DELETE, TRUNCATE, MERGE), many DDL statements such as creating, altering and dropping tables, DCL statements like GRANT and REVOKE, and others. Assigning values to variables as well as modifying data in table variables are not transactional operations, so if you applied such activities in a transaction that ended up rolling back, those activities are not undone.

In our example of adding an order, it's not a good idea to use the autocommit mode because under this mode the statements that add the order header and order lines are treated as two separate transactions. If the first succeeds and the second fails, you end up with the order header added without related order lines. The following code demonstrates this:

```
SET XACT_ABORT, NOCOUNT ON;

DECLARE @neworderid AS INT;

INSERT INTO Sales.Orders
    (custid, empid, orderdate, requireddate, shippeddate,
     shipperid, freight, shipname, shipaddress, shipcity,
     shippostalcode, shipcountry)
  VALUES
    (3, 3, '20170212', '20170301', '20170216',
     3, 30.00, N'Shipper 3', N'Address CCC', N'City CCC',
     N'33333', N'Country CCC');

SET @neworderid = SCOPE_IDENTITY();
```

```
PRINT 'Added new order header with order ID ' + CAST(@neworderid AS VARCHAR(10))
   + '. @@TRANCOUNT is ' + CAST(@@TRANCOUNT AS VARCHAR(10)) + '.';

INSERT INTO Sales.OrderDetails(orderid, productid, unitprice, qty, discount)
   VALUES(@neworderid, 1, 30.00, 3, 2.000), -- CHECK violation since discount > 1
        (@neworderid, 2, 30.00, 3, 0.000),
        (@neworderid, 3, 30.00, 3, 0.000);

PRINT 'Added order lines to new order. @@TRANCOUNT is '
   + CAST(@@TRANCOUNT AS VARCHAR(10)) + '.';
```

This code generates the following output:

```
Added new order header with order ID 11080. @@TRANCOUNT is 0.
Msg 547, Level 16, State 0, Line 126
The INSERT statement conflicted with the CHECK constraint "CHK_discount". The conflict
occurred in database "TSQLV4", table "Sales.OrderDetails", column 'discount'.
```

Notice that this time you were not in an open transaction after adding the order header row. Query the tables to see if any rows related to the new order survived:

```
SELECT orderid, orderdate, custid, empid
FROM Sales.Orders
WHERE orderid = 11080;

SELECT orderid, productid, qty
FROM Sales.OrderDetails
WHERE orderid = 11080;
```

This code generates the following output:

```
orderid     orderdate   custid      empid
----------- ----------- ----------- -----------
11080       2017-02-12  3           3

orderid     productid   qty
----------- ----------- ------
```

Observe that the order header row exists, but there are no corresponding order lines. That's obviously an undesirable outcome, which is why it's important to perform both activities in a single transaction and not in two separate ones.

The SQL standard defines an *implicit transactions* mode, which is supposed to be the default mode for working with transactions. Under this mode, when you issue a transactional statement, if a transaction is not open at that point, the system is supposed to open an implicit transaction for you. However, unlike under the default autocommit mode in SQL Server, under the standard implicit transactions mode you are responsible for explicitly closing the transaction by either committing it or rolling it back. You enable the standard implicit transactions mode by setting the session option IMPLICIT_TRANSACTIONS to ON, like so (make sure you run this code for the next demo to work):

```
SET IMPLICIT_TRANSACTIONS ON;
```

Assuming you enabled this option, run the following code to add another order to the system:

```
SET XACT_ABORT, NOCOUNT ON;

DECLARE @neworderid AS INT;

-- following statement triggers the opening of a transaction but doesn't close it
INSERT INTO Sales.Orders
    (custid, empid, orderdate, requireddate, shippeddate,
     shipperid, freight, shipname, shipaddress, shipcity,
     shippostalcode, shipcountry)
  VALUES
    (4, 4, '20170212', '20170301', '20170216',
     1, 40.00, N'Shipper 1', N'Address AAA', N'City AAA',
     N'11111', N'Country AAA');

SET @neworderid = SCOPE_IDENTITY();

PRINT 'Added new order header with order ID ' + CAST(@neworderid AS VARCHAR(10))
  + '. @@TRANCOUNT is ' + CAST(@@TRANCOUNT AS VARCHAR(10)) + '.';

INSERT INTO Sales.OrderDetails(orderid, productid, unitprice, qty, discount)
  VALUES(@neworderid, 1, 40.00, 4, 0.000),
        (@neworderid, 2, 40.00, 4, 0.000),
        (@neworderid, 3, 40.00, 4, 0.000);

PRINT 'Added order lines to new order. @@TRANCOUNT is '
  + CAST(@@TRANCOUNT AS VARCHAR(10)) + '.';

-- must explicitly commit the transaction
COMMIT TRAN;
```

Notice that this time there's no explicit BEGIN TRAN statement because you're relying on the implicit transactions mode, but there is an explicit COMMIT TRAN statement. This code generates the following output:

```
Added new order header with order ID 11081. @@TRANCOUNT is 1.
Added order lines to new order. @@TRANCOUNT is 1.
```

This time both the addition of the order header and the addition of the order lines ran in a single implicit transaction. If there had been a failure in any of the statements, the entire transaction would have rolled back. In our case, the transaction completed successfully. Query the tables to see the data that was added:

```
SELECT orderid, orderdate, custid, empid
FROM Sales.Orders
WHERE orderid = 11081;

SELECT orderid, productid, qty
FROM Sales.OrderDetails
WHERE orderid = 11081;
```

This code generates the following output:

```
orderid     orderdate   custid      empid
----------- ----------- ----------- -----------
11081       2017-02-12  4           4

orderid     productid   qty
----------- ----------- ------
11081       1           4
11081       2           4
11081       3           4
```

Run the following code to turn the implicit transactions mode back off:

```
SET IMPLICIT_TRANSACTIONS OFF;
```

Having implicit transactions turned on is usually a bad idea. It increases the likelihood that transactions stay open for long periods, or worse, just stay open until someone realizes that that's the case and manually intervenes. Long open transactions can cause performance problems in the system, including blocking and others. Also, your code has to be written differently to work with implicit transactions.

Remember that both DML and DDL are transactional in SQL Server. However, assignment of values to variables as well as changes to table variables are not transactional, other than each individual statement having to complete in its entirety or not take place at all. Run the following code to see that DDL is transactional:

```
DROP TABLE IF EXISTS dbo.T1;

BEGIN TRAN;

CREATE TABLE dbo.T1(col1 INT);
INSERT INTO dbo.T1(col1) VALUES(1),(2),(3);
PRINT 'In transaction';
SELECT col1 FROM dbo.T1;

ROLLBACK TRAN;

PRINT 'After transaction';
SELECT col1 FROM dbo.T1;
```

This code generates the following output under Results to Text (Ctrl + T):

```
In transaction
col1
-----------
1
2
3

After transaction
Msg 208, Level 16, State 1, Line 206
Invalid object name 'dbo.T1'.
```

As you can see, the table creation and population were both undone when the transaction was rolled back. As a result, the attempt to query the table after the ROLLBACK TRAN statement was submitted generates an error because the table doesn't exist at that point.

Run the following code to see that changes to a table variable are not undone when a transaction is rolled back:

```
BEGIN TRAN;

DECLARE @T1 AS TABLE(col1 INT);
INSERT INTO @T1(col1) VALUES(1),(2),(3);
PRINT 'In transaction';
SELECT col1 FROM @T1;

ROLLBACK TRAN;

PRINT 'After transaction';
SELECT col1 FROM @T1;
```

This code generates the following output, again, under Results to Text:

```
In transaction
col1
-----------
1
2
3

After transaction
col1
-----------
1
2
3
```

As you can see, the table variable itself, as well as the data that you inserted into it, are still present after the transaction was rolled back. As mentioned, you would get the same behavior when assigning values to regular variables in a transaction.

## Nesting of transactions

SQL Server doesn't support a true concept of nested transactions where you can have an inner transaction that is completely independent of an outer one. Rather, in SQL Server you're either in a transaction or not. When you issue a BEGIN TRAN statement, SQL Server increases the value of @@TRANCOUNT in order to know when it needs to truly open a transaction—when @@TRANCOUNT changes from zero to a greater-than-zero value. Issuing a BEGIN TRAN statement when @@TRANCOUNT is already greater than zero has no real effect other than increasing the @@TRANCOUNT value. When you issue a COMMIT TRAN statement SQL Server decreases the @@TRANCOUNT value by 1. SQL Server truly commits the transaction only if you issue a COMMIT TRAN statement when @@TRANCOUNT is 1 prior to committing. However, if you issue a ROLLBACK TRAN statement in an open transaction, never mind the current value of @@TRANCOUNT, SQL Server rolls back the entire transaction.

Run the following code to test the behavior of nested BEGIN TRAN statement:

```
SET NOCOUNT ON;
DROP TABLE IF EXISTS dbo.T1;
GO
CREATE TABLE dbo.T1(col1 INT);

PRINT '@@TRANCOUNT before first BEGIN TRAN is '
  + CAST(@@TRANCOUNT AS VARCHAR(10)) + '.';

BEGIN TRAN;

PRINT '@@TRANCOUNT after first BEGIN TRAN is '
  + CAST(@@TRANCOUNT AS VARCHAR(10)) + '.';

BEGIN TRAN;

PRINT '@@TRANCOUNT after second BEGIN TRAN is '
  + CAST(@@TRANCOUNT AS VARCHAR(10)) + '.';

BEGIN TRAN;

PRINT '@@TRANCOUNT after third BEGIN TRAN is '
  + CAST(@@TRANCOUNT AS VARCHAR(10)) + '.';

INSERT INTO dbo.T1 VALUES(1),(2),(3);

COMMIT TRAN; -- this doesn't really commit

PRINT '@@TRANCOUNT after first COMMIT TRAN is '
  + CAST(@@TRANCOUNT AS VARCHAR(10)) + '.';

ROLLBACK TRAN; -- this does roll the transaction back

PRINT '@@TRANCOUNT after ROLLBACK TRAN is '
  + CAST(@@TRANCOUNT AS VARCHAR(10)) + '.';

SELECT col1 FROM dbo.T1;
```

This code generates the following output:

```
@@TRANCOUNT before first BEGIN TRAN is 0.
@@TRANCOUNT after first BEGIN TRAN is 1.
@@TRANCOUNT after second BEGIN TRAN is 2.
@@TRANCOUNT after third BEGIN TRAN is 3.
@@TRANCOUNT after first COMMIT TRAN is 2.
@@TRANCOUNT after ROLLBACK TRAN is 0.
col1
-----------
```

Observe that every BEGIN TRAN statement increased the @@TRANCOUNT value by 1, but as soon as the ROLLBACK TRAN statement was issued, @@TRANCOUNT dropped to 0. Also, observe that the INSERT statement that added three rows to the table T1 was rolled back even though you issued a COMMIT TRAN statement after it, because that statement did not really commit the transaction.

**EXAM TIP**

The point in supporting nested BEGIN TRAN-COMMIT TRAN statements is to allow you to issue those statements within a stored procedure without needing to check first if a transaction is already open. If your procedure actually opens the transaction, its COMMIT TRAN statement is supposed to also actually commit it as well. However, if a transaction was opened by an outer module or batch, it's not supposed to be the inner procedure's choice to actually commit it, rather the outer module's choice. Just make sure to remember that if you issue a ROLLBACK TRAN statement at any point, even if you do so from an inner module that was not the one that actually opened the transaction, this causes the entire transaction to truly roll back and all of its changes to be undone. The following example demonstrates this.

Normally, you would encapsulate the logic of the previously demonstrated task of adding an order within a stored procedure. You can pass the order header info to the stored procedure as scalar input parameters. However, because the order lines info should be passed as a set, you would probably want to work with a table valued parameter, or a TVP in short. Before using a TVP you need to prepare a table type, which is a table definition that you store as an object in the database and later use as a type for table variables and TVPs. Run the following code to create the type dbo.OrderLines for this purpose:

```
DROP TYPE IF EXISTS dbo.OrderLines;
GO
CREATE TYPE dbo.OrderLines AS TABLE
(
  productid INT           NOT NULL PRIMARY KEY,
  unitprice MONEY         NOT NULL CHECK (unitprice >= 0),
  qty       SMALLINT      NOT NULL CHECK (qty > 0),
  discount  NUMERIC(4, 3) NOT NULL CHECK (discount BETWEEN 0 AND 1)
);
```

Run the following code to create the stored procedure dbo.AddOrder:

```
CREATE OR ALTER PROC dbo.AddOrder
  @custid         AS INT,
  @empid          AS INT,
  @orderdate      AS DATE,
  @requireddate   AS DATE,
  @shippeddate    AS DATE,
  @shipperid      AS INT,
  @freight        AS MONEY,
  @shipname       AS NVARCHAR(40),
  @shipaddress    AS NVARCHAR(60),
  @shipcity       AS NVARCHAR(15),
  @shipregion     AS NVARCHAR(15),
  @shippostalcode AS NVARCHAR(10),
  @shipcountry    AS NVARCHAR(15),
  @OrderLines     AS dbo.OrderLines READONLY,
  @neworderid     AS INT OUT
AS
```

```
SET XACT_ABORT, NOCOUNT ON;

BEGIN TRAN;

-- add order header
INSERT INTO Sales.Orders
    (custid, empid, orderdate, requireddate, shippeddate,
     shipperid, freight, shipname, shipaddress, shipcity,
     shippostalcode, shipcountry)
  VALUES
    (@custid, @empid, @orderdate, @requireddate, @shippeddate,
     @shipperid, @freight, @shipname, @shipaddress, @shipcity,
     @shippostalcode, @shipcountry);

SET @neworderid = SCOPE_IDENTITY();

-- add order lines
INSERT INTO Sales.OrderDetails(orderid, productid, unitprice, qty, discount)
  SELECT @neworderid, productid, unitprice, qty, discount
  FROM @OrderLines;

COMMIT TRAN;
```

The first 13 parameters contain the order header's attributes. The 14th parameter is a TVP named @OrderLines and is of the OrderLines table type. Notice that it has to be marked as READONLY, meaning that you cannot apply changes to its contents. In our case, it is sufficient as a read-only parameter. The 15th parameter is an output parameter through which you return the newly generated order ID to the caller.

The procedure starts by setting XACT_ABORT and NOCOUNT to ON as suggested earlier. You want to make sure that if any errors occur, you never leave the transaction open. The code then performs the addition of the order header and order lines in an explicit transaction. What's currently missing is error handling code, but I take care of this in the section Error handling with TRY-CATCH.

To execute the stored procedure from T-SQL, you first need to declare a table variable of the OrderLines table type and populate it with rows. You then assign the table variable to the TVP when you call the stored procedure. You also prepare a variable to collect the newly generated order ID from the output parameter. Here's an example for executing the stored procedure:

```
DECLARE @MyOrderLines AS dbo.OrderLines, @myneworderid AS INT;

INSERT INTO @MyOrderLines(productid, unitprice, qty, discount)
  VALUES(1, 50.00, 5, 0.000),
        (2, 50.00, 5, 0.000),
        (3, 50.00, 5, 0.000);

EXEC dbo.AddOrder
  @custid        = 5,
  @empid         = 5,
  @orderdate     = '20170212',
  @requireddate  = '20170301',
```

```
@shippeddate      = '20170216',
@shipperid        = 2,
@freight          = 50.00,
@shipname         = N'Shipper 2',
@shipaddress      = N'Address BBB',
@shipcity         = N'City BBB',
@shipregion       = N'Region BBB',
@shippostalcode   = N'22222',
@shipcountry      = N'Country BBB',
@OrderLines       = @MyOrderLines,
@neworderid       = @myneworderid OUT;

PRINT 'Added new order with order ID '
  + CAST(@myneworderid AS VARCHAR(10)) + '.';
```

This code generates the following output:

```
Added new order with order ID 11082.
```

Run the following code to query the data for the new order:

```
SELECT orderid, orderdate, custid, empid
FROM Sales.Orders
WHERE orderid = 11082;

SELECT orderid, productid, qty
FROM Sales.OrderDetails
WHERE orderid = 11082;
```

This code generates the following output:

```
orderid     orderdate  custid      empid
----------- ---------- ----------- -----------
11082       2017-02-12 5           5

orderid     productid   qty
----------- ----------- ------
11082       1           5
11082       2           5
11082       3           5
```

Next, run the following code to execute the stored procedure from an explicit transaction, and then roll the transaction back:

```
BEGIN TRAN;

DECLARE @MyOrderLines AS dbo.OrderLines, @myneworderid AS INT;

INSERT INTO @MyOrderLines(productid, unitprice, qty, discount)
  VALUES(1, 60.00, 6, 0.000),
        (2, 60.00, 6, 0.000),
        (3, 60.00, 6, 0.000);

EXEC dbo.AddOrder
  @custid      = 6,
  @empid       = 6,
```

```
@orderdate       = '20170212',
@requireddate    = '20170301',
@shippeddate     = '20170216',
@shipperid       = 3,
@freight         = 60.00,
@shipname        = N'Shipper 3',
@shipaddress     = N'Address CCC',
@shipcity        = N'City CCC',
@shipregion      = N'Region CCC',
@shippostalcode  = N'33333',
@shipcountry     = N'Country CCC',
@OrderLines      = @MyOrderLines,
@neworderid      = @myneworderid OUT;

PRINT 'Added new order with order ID '
  + CAST(@myneworderid AS VARCHAR(10)) + '.';

ROLLBACK TRAN;
```

This code generates the following output:

```
Added new order with order ID 11083.
```

The COMMIT TRAN statement within the stored procedure doesn't truly commit the transaction because it doesn't reduce @@TRANCOUNT to zero. Because the outer batch issues a ROLLBACK TRAN statement, the work that added the header and lines of order 11083 was undone. Query the tables to look for the data of the new order:

```
SELECT orderid, orderdate, custid, empid
FROM Sales.Orders
WHERE orderid = 11083;

SELECT orderid, productid, qty
FROM Sales.OrderDetails
WHERE orderid = 11083;
```

This code generates the following output:

```
orderid     orderdate   custid      empid
----------- ----------- ----------- -----------


orderid     productid   qty
----------- ----------- ------
```

Note that if you insist on actually committing the transaction in your stored procedure irrespective of whether you started it or not, you can use a loop that keeps committing until @@TRANCOUNT drops to zero, like so:

```
WHILE @@TRANCOUNT > 0
  COMMIT TRAN;
```

This isn't considered a very good practice because someone who started a transaction and then called your procedure also expects to be able to control whether to commit it or roll it back. Also, if there's a mismatch between the @@TRANCOUNT values when the procedure starts and when it finishes, SQL Server generates error 266 indicating the mismatch. Though this error doesn't terminate an open transaction and doesn't abort the execution of the code even if XACT_ABORT is set to ON.

To demonstrate this I use a stored procedure called dbo.Proc1 that uses an explicit transaction to create a table called dbo.DoIExist, with a loop that keeps committing until @@TRANCOUNT drops to zero. Run the following code to create the stored procedure:

```
CREATE OR ALTER PROC dbo.Proc1
AS

SET XACT_ABORT, NOCOUNT ON;

BEGIN TRAN;

PRINT 'In transaction in proc. @@TRANCOUNT is '
  + CAST(@@TRANCOUNT AS VARCHAR(10)) + '.';

CREATE TABLE dbo.DoIExist(col1 int);

WHILE @@TRANCOUNT > 0
  COMMIT TRAN;

PRINT 'Still in proc. @@TRANCOUNT is '
  + CAST(@@TRANCOUNT AS VARCHAR(10)) + '.';
GO
```

Use the following code to test the procedure without first opening a transaction in the outer batch:

```
DROP TABLE IF EXISTS dbo.DoIExist;

EXEC dbo.Proc1;

IF OBJECT_ID('dbo.DoIExist') IS NOT NULL
  PRINT 'DoIExist exists.'
ELSE
  PRINT 'DoIExist does not exist.';

PRINT 'Still in batch. @@TRANCOUNT is '
  + CAST(@@TRANCOUNT AS VARCHAR(10)) + '.';
```

This code generates the following output, as expected:

```
In transaction in proc. @@TRANCOUNT is 1.
Still in proc. @@TRANCOUNT is 0.
DoIExist exists.
Still in batch. @@TRANCOUNT is 0.
```

Now execute the stored procedure from an outer transaction that you wish to roll back:

```
DROP TABLE IF EXISTS dbo.DoIExist;

BEGIN TRAN;
```

```
EXEC dbo.Proc1;

PRINT 'Still in batch. @@TRANCOUNT is '
  + CAST(@@TRANCOUNT AS VARCHAR(10)) + '.';

IF @@TRANCOUNT > 0
  ROLLBACK TRAN;

IF OBJECT_ID('dbo.DoIExist') IS NOT NULL
  PRINT 'DoIExist exists.'
ELSE
  PRINT 'DoIExist does not exist.';
```

This code generates the following output:

```
In transaction in proc. @@TRANCOUNT is 2.
Still in proc. @@TRANCOUNT is 0.
Msg 266, Level 16, State 2, Procedure dbo.Proc1, Line 0 [Batch Start Line 436]
Transaction count after EXECUTE indicates a mismatching number of BEGIN and COMMIT
statements. Previous count = 1, current count = 0.
Still in batch. @@TRANCOUNT is 0.
DoIExist exists.
```

The stored procedure actually committed the transaction even though it wasn't the one that opened it. You get an error indicating the mismatch in the @@TRANCOUNT values when entering and leaving the procedure, but this error doesn't stop the execution of the code and doesn't cause the transaction to roll back. The table creation gets committed and the outer batch's ROLLBACK TRAN statement doesn't get the chance to execute.

## Working with named transactions, savepoints, and markers

T-SQL supports indicating a name as part of the ROLLBACK TRAN[SACTION] statement, as in:

```
ROLLBACK TRAN SomeName;
```

The name has to have a binary match either with an outermost transaction name that you assigned earlier with the statement BEGIN TRAN[SACTION] <name>, or a savepoint name that you assigned earlier with the statement SAVE TRAN[SACTION] <name>.

The idea behind rolling back to a transaction name is to verify that you're explicitly rolling back the outermost transaction. If that's not the case, you get an error. As an example, run the following code:

```
SET XACT_ABORT OFF;
BEGIN TRAN OutermostTran;
BEGIN TRAN InnerTran1;
BEGIN TRAN InnerTran2;
ROLLBACK TRAN OutermostTran;
PRINT '@@TRANCOUNT is ' + CAST(@@TRANCOUNT AS VARCHAR(10)) + '.';
```

Because there's a match between the names in the ROLLBACK TRAN statement and the outermost BEGIN TRAN statement, the outermost transaction is rolled back successfully. This code generates the following output:

@@TRANCOUNT is 0.

As another example, run the following code, this time specifying an inner transaction name in the ROLLBACK TRAN statement:

```
SET XACT_ABORT OFF;
BEGIN TRAN OutermostTran;
BEGIN TRAN InnerTran1;
BEGIN TRAN InnerTran2;
ROLLBACK TRAN InnerTran1;
PRINT '@@TRANCOUNT is ' + CAST(@@TRANCOUNT AS VARCHAR(10)) + '.';
GO
ROLLBACK TRAN;
```

The attempt to roll the transaction back fails, the transaction remains open, and the code continues execution. This code generates the following output:

```
Msg 6401, Level 16, State 1, Line 472
Cannot roll back InnerTran1. No transaction or savepoint of that name was found.
@@TRANCOUNT is 3.
```

Keep in mind, though, that the above examples are executed with XACT_ABORT set to OFF, as is the case by default. If you follow best practices and set this option to ON, in the second example the error—not the ROLLBACK TRAN statement itself—causes the open transaction to roll back and the execution of the code to abort.

If you issue a ROLLBACK TRAN statement without a name, it behaves as usual irrespective of whether you named transactions or not; namely, it rolls the entire transaction back.

You can also specify a transaction name in the COMMIT TRAN[SACTION] statement, as in COMMIT TRAN SomeName, but with this command the name is simply ignored.

Naming transactions is a very uncommonly used practice. This book covers it mainly for the small chance that it would appear in the exam.

T-SQL also supports a concept called savepoints. A *savepoint* is a marker within an open transaction that you can later roll back to, undoing only the changes that took place since the savepoint, and not the rest of the changes that took place in the transaction. When you roll back to a save point, the transaction remains open and the code continues execution. You mark a savepoint with the statement SAVE TRAN[ACTION] <savepoint name>, and roll back to a savepoint using the statement ROLLBACK TRAN[SACTION] <savepoint name>. You must be in an open transaction to mark a savepoint; otherwise you get an error. You are allowed to mark multiple savepoints within the same transaction. You can gradually roll back to different savepoints, but in such a case you have to keep going backwards; otherwise you get an error. For example, if you marked save points S1, S2, S3 in this order, you can later first roll back to S3 and afterwards to S1, but not the other way around.

The following example demonstrates using savepoints:

```
SET XACT_ABORT, NOCOUNT ON;
DROP TABLE IF EXISTS dbo.T1;
GO
CREATE TABLE dbo.T1(col1 VARCHAR(10));
```

```
GO

BEGIN TRAN;

SAVE TRAN S1;
INSERT INTO dbo.T1(col1) VALUES('S1');

SAVE TRAN S2;
INSERT INTO dbo.T1(col1) VALUES('S2');

SAVE TRAN S3;
INSERT INTO dbo.T1(col1) VALUES('S3');

ROLLBACK TRAN S3;

ROLLBACK TRAN S2;

SAVE TRAN S4;
INSERT INTO dbo.T1(col1) VALUES('S4');

COMMIT TRAN;

SELECT col1 FROM dbo.T1;
GO
DROP TABLE IF EXISTS dbo.T1;
```

This code generates the following output:

```
col1
----------
S1
S4
```

When the code issued the statement ROLLBACK TRAN S3, the changes that took place between S3 and that statement were undone (the insertion of the value 'S3' to the table). When the code then issued the statement ROLLBACK TRAN S2, the changes that took place between S2 and S3 were undone (the insertion of the value 'S2' to the table). So, both the insertion of the value 'S1', which happened before S2, and the insertion of the value 'S4', which happened after the last rollback to a savepoint took place, persisted.

The BEGIN TRAN[SACTION] statement also supports an option called WITH MARK <marker name>, as in BEGIN TRAN MyTran WITH MARK 'My Mark'. This option defines a marker name in the transaction log. Later on, if you apply a restore from a log backup, you can specify the option STOPATMARK <marker name> to recover the changes only until the indicated marked transaction, inclusive, or STOPBEFOREMARK <marker name> to exclude the marked transaction.

# Error handling with TRY-CATCH

Robust programming solutions always include code to handle errors. You want to make sure that you control the outcome of both anticipated and unanticipated errors to the degree that you can. This is true with any kind of programming, and of course also specifically with T-SQL. In case of an error, you do not want to leave a database in an inconsistent state. Also, you do not want an error to result in an unterminated transaction because this causes concurrency and other problems in the system.

This section describes the error handling tools that T-SQL supports. It covers the main T-SQL error handling construct—TRY-CATCH, error functions, generating error messages with THROW and RAISERROR, and handling errors in transactions.

## The TRY-CATCH construct

T-SQL uses a classic TRY-CATCH construct to handle errors, similar to what most programming languages use for error handling. You place your usual code within the TRY block, and you place any error handling code within the CATCH block. If there's no error in the TRY block, the CATCH block is skipped. If there is an error in the TRY block, control is passed to the first line of code within the CATCH block.

As the first example for using the TRY-CATCH construct I demonstrate code that adds a couple of rows to a table called T1. Run the following code to create the table T1:

```
SET NOCOUNT ON;
USE TSQLV4;

DROP TABLE IF EXISTS dbo.T1;
GO
CREATE TABLE dbo.T1
(
  keycol INT NOT NULL
    CONSTRAINT PK_T1 PRIMARY KEY,
  col1 INT NOT NULL
    CONSTRAINT CHK_T1_col1_gtzero CHECK(col1 > 0),
  col2 VARCHAR(10) NOT NULL
);
```

The following example demonstrates execution of code with no errors:

```
BEGIN TRY

  INSERT INTO dbo.T1(keycol, col1, col2)
    VALUES(1, 10, 'AAA');
  INSERT INTO dbo.T1(keycol, col1, col2)
    VALUES(2, 20, 'BBB');

  PRINT 'Got to end of TRY block.';

END TRY
BEGIN CATCH
```

```
  PRINT 'Error occurred. Entering CATCH block. Error message: ' + ERROR_MESSAGE();

END CATCH;
GO

SELECT keycol, col1, col2
FROM dbo.T1;

-- cleanup
TRUNCATE TABLE dbo.T1;
```

The code in the TRY block runs successfully and therefore the CATCH block is skipped. This code generates the following output:

```
Got to the end of the TRY block.
keycol      col1         col2
----------- ------------ ----------
1           10           AAA
2           20           BBB
```

The following example demonstrates execution of code with an error:

```
BEGIN TRY

  INSERT INTO dbo.T1(keycol, col1, col2)
    VALUES(1, 10, 'AAA');
  INSERT INTO dbo.T1(keycol, col1, col2)
    VALUES(2, -20, 'BBB');

  PRINT 'Got to the end of the TRY block.';

END TRY
BEGIN CATCH

  PRINT 'Error occurred. Entering CATCH block. Error message: ' + ERROR_MESSAGE();

END CATCH;
GO

SELECT keycol, col1, col2
FROM dbo.T1;

-- cleanup
TRUNCATE TABLE dbo.T1;
```

The first INSERT statement runs successfully and the row makes it to the table. The second INSERT statement fails due to a CHECK constraint violation when it tries to add a row with a col1 value that is not greater than zero. The second row doesn't make it to the table. The PRINT command at the end of the TRY block doesn't get to execute. Control of the code passes to the CATCH block, which in this example simply prints a message indicating that an error occurred along with the error message. This code generates the following output:

```
Error occurred. Entering CATCH block. Error message: The INSERT statement conflicted
with the CHECK constraint "CHK_T1_col1_gtzero". The conflict occurred in database
"TSQLV4", table "dbo.T1", column 'col1'.
keycol       col1        col2
-----------  ----------- ----------
1            10          AAA
```

This is hardly an example for robust error handling because this code leaves the database
in an inconsistent state with only one of the two rows making it into the target table. Normally you would place the work in a transaction and make sure that when an error happens
you roll the transaction back, but I get to this later. For now, I just wanted to demonstrate the
flow of the code with the TRY-CATCH construct when it runs successfully and when there is an
error.

If an error happens within a stored procedure and is handled by a TRY-CATCH construct,
as far as the caller of the stored procedure is concerned, there was no error. If an error happens in a stored procedure, but not in a TRY block, the error bubbles up in the call stack
until it finds a TRY block, and if one is found, it activates the corresponding CATCH block. For
example, say Proc1 calls Proc2 from within a TRY block, and Proc2 runs code without using a
TRY-CATCH construct. An error in Proc2 results in the CATCH block of Proc1 being activated.
If no TRY-CATCH construct is found along the way, the caller who initiated the code ends up
getting the error.

**EXAM TIP**

**For cases where code within the CATCH bock can potentially fail, you are allowed to nest a
TRY-CATCH construct within the CATCH block, and this way handle such errors. If an error
happens in a CATCH block, but not in a nested TRY-CATCH construct, the error behaves as
if it didn't happen in a TRY block; namely, it bubbles up.**

To demonstrate nesting of TRY-CATCH constructs I use a procedure called AddRowToT1
and a table called ErrorLog where the procedure is supposed to log errors.

Run the following code to create the table ErrorLog:

```
DROP TABLE IF EXISTS dbo.ErrorLog;
GO
CREATE TABLE dbo.ErrorLog
(
  id INT NOT NULL IDENTITY
    CONSTRAINT PK_ErrorLog PRIMARY KEY,
  dt DATETIME2 NOT NULL DEFAULT(SYSDATETIME()),
  loginname NVARCHAR(128) NOT NULL DEFAULT(SUSER_SNAME()),
  errormessage NVARCHAR(4000) NOT NULL
);
```

The table definition uses default constraints to record the time of the error and the executing login.

Run the following code to create the stored procedure AddRowToT1:

```
CREATE OR ALTER PROC dbo.AddRowToT1
  @keycol INT,
  @col1   INT,
  @col2   VARCHAR(10)
AS

SET NOCOUNT ON;

BEGIN TRY

  INSERT INTO dbo.T1(keycol, col1, col2)
    VALUES(@keycol, @col1, @col2);

  PRINT 'Got to the end of the outer TRY block.';

END TRY
BEGIN CATCH

  PRINT 'Error occurred in outer TRY block. Entering outer CATCH block.';

  BEGIN TRY

    INSERT INTO dbo.ErrorLog(errormessage) VALUES(ERROR_MESSAGE());

    PRINT 'Got to the end of the inner TRY block.';

  END TRY
  BEGIN CATCH

    PRINT 'Error occurred in inner TRY block. Entering inner CATCH block. Error message:
' + ERROR_MESSAGE();

  END CATCH;

END CATCH;
GO
```

As you can see, the stored procedure uses an outer TRY block to add a row to T1 with the values received as input parameters. If all goes well, the outer TRY block prints a message indicating that it got to the end. Note that the PRINT statements are used here only for illustration purposes to show which parts of the code got executed; normally, you would not include those in production code. In case of an error, the outer CATCH block is activated. The code in the outer CATCH block prints that it got there, and then activates an inner TRY-CATCH construct. The inner TRY block tries to write the error information into the table ErrorLog. If all goes well, the code indicates that it got to the end of the inner TRY block. If there's an error in the inner TRY block, the inner CATCH block is activated. The inner CATCH block prints a message indicating the code got there and the error message.

Use the following code to test the procedure for the first time:

```
EXEC dbo.AddRowToT1
  @keycol = 1,
  @col1 = 10,
  @col2 = 'AAA';
GO

SELECT keycol, col1, col2 FROM dbo.T1;
SELECT id, dt, loginname, errormessage FROM dbo.ErrorLog;

-- cleanup
TRUNCATE TABLE dbo.T1;
TRUNCATE TABLE dbo.ErrorLog;
```

The code runs successfully with no errors. The code generates the following output:

```
Got to the end of the outer TRY block.
keycol      col1        col2
----------- ----------- ----------
1           10          AAA

id   dt  loginname  errormessage
---- --- ---------- -------------
```

As you can see, the outer TRY block executed to completion. The code added a new row into the table T1. The outer CATCH block was skipped, and no row was added to the table ErrorLog.

Run the following code in attempt to add a row with an invalid col1 value:

```
EXEC dbo.AddRowToT1
  @keycol = 1,
  @col1 = -10,
  @col2 = 'BBB';
GO

SELECT keycol, col1, col2 FROM dbo.T1;
SELECT id, dt, loginname, errormessage FROM dbo.ErrorLog;

-- cleanup
TRUNCATE TABLE dbo.T1;
TRUNCATE TABLE dbo.ErrorLog;
```

This time there's an error when the outer TRY block attempts to add the row into T1, therefore the outer CATCH block is activated. The outer CATCH block uses an inner TRY-CATCH construct to add a row with the error information into the table ErrorLog. The inner TRY block succeeds in this task and therefore the inner CATCH block is skipped. This code generates the following output (formatted for clarity):

```
Error occurred in outer TRY block. Entering outer CATCH block.
Got to the end of the inner TRY block.
keycol      col1        col2
----------- ----------- ----------
```

```
id          dt                          loginname
----------- --------------------------- -------------
1           2017-01-24 09:44:24.1014963 <your_login>

errormessage
----------------------------------------------------------------------------------
------------------------------------------------------------------
The INSERT statement conflicted with the CHECK constraint "CHK_T1_col1_gtzero". The
conflict occurred in database "TSQLV4", table "dbo.T1", column 'col1'.
```

The new row didn't make it into T1. A row with the error info was written into ErrorLog.

To test an example for an error in the inner CATCH block, open two new connections (I refer to them as connection 1 and connection 2). Run the following code in connection 1 to obtain an exclusive table lock on the table ErrorLog within a transaction that the code leaves open:

```
BEGIN TRAN;

SELECT TOP (0) * FROM dbo.ErrorLog WITH (TABLOCKX);
```

Next, run the following code to first set the session's lock expiration time out to zero (no wait), and then to attempt to add an invalid row:

```
SET LOCK_TIMEOUT 0;

EXEC dbo.AddRowToT1
  @keycol = 1,
  @col1 = -10,
  @col2 = 'BBB';
```

The outer TRY block fails when trying to add the invalid row, activating the outer CATCH block. The outer CATCH block activates the inner TRY-CATCH construct. The inner TRY block fails when trying to add a row to the table ErrorLog because it cannot obtain a lock. Because you set the lock expiration time out to zero, the inner CATCH block is immediately activated, printing the inner error information. This code generates the following output:

```
Error occurred in outer TRY block. Entering outer CATCH block.
Error occurred in inner TRY block. Entering inner CATCH block. Error message: Lock
request time out period exceeded.
```

Run the following code in connection 1 to commit the open transaction and release the lock on ErrorLog:

```
COMMIT TRAN;
```

Run the following code in connection 2 to query the tables, clean them up, and to set the lock expiration time out back to infinity:

```
SELECT keycol, col1, col2 FROM dbo.T1;
SELECT id, dt, loginname, errormessage FROM dbo.ErrorLog;

-- cleanup
TRUNCATE TABLE dbo.T1;
```

```
TRUNCATE TABLE dbo.ErrorLog;
SET LOCK_TIMEOUT -1;
```

This code generates the following output showing that both tables are empty:

```
keycol      col1        col2
----------- ----------- ----------

id   dt  loginname  errormessage
---- --- ---------- ------------
```

Close connection 2 and return to connection 1 before continuing.

An important limitation of TRY-CATCH that you want to make sure that you're aware of, and that you plan for, is that it cannot catch compilation errors, such as referring to objects and columns that don't exist, in the same scope. However, you can catch such errors in an outer scope.

As an example, consider the following stored procedure called InnerProc:

```
CREATE OR ALTER PROC dbo.InnerProc
AS

BEGIN TRY
  SELECT nosuchcolumn FROM dbo.NoSuchTable;
END TRY
BEGIN CATCH
  PRINT 'In CATCH block of InnerProc.';
END CATCH;
GO
```

The procedure tries to query a table that doesn't exist.

Run the following code to execute InnerProc:

```
EXEC dbo.InnerProc;
```

Because the error is a compilation error, it isn't caught by the inner CATCH block. This execution generates the following error:

```
Msg 208, Level 16, State 1, Procedure dbo.InnerProc, Line 5 [Batch Start Line 703]
Invalid object name 'dbo.NoSuchTable'.
```

Use the following code to create a stored procedure called OuterProc that invokes Inner-Proc within a TRY block:

```
CREATE OR ALTER PROC dbo.OuterProc
AS

BEGIN TRY
  EXEC dbo.InnerProc;
END TRY
BEGIN CATCH
  PRINT 'In CATCH block of OuterProc.';
END CATCH;
GO
```

Use the following code to test OuterProc:

```
EXEC dbo.OuterProc;
```

This time the CATCH block of OuterProc is activated, and the execution generates the following output:

```
In CATCH block of OuterProc.
```

## Error functions

T-SQL supports six error functions that provide information about the error, and that you can query in the CATCH block. Following are the functions and their descriptions:

- ERROR_NUMBER() provides the error number.
- ERROR_MESSAGE() provides the error message.
- ERROR_SEVERITY() provides the error severity. You can catch errors with severity 11 to 19. Errors with severity 20 and up are so severe that when they happen, SQL Server terminates your connection. Any error handling code that you may have doesn't really have a chance to run. Messages with severity 0 to 9 are considered informational and are always passed to the client; they're not accessible to SQL Server. Messages with severity 10 are also informational; for compatibility reasons, SQL Server converts those to severity 0 internally. For more information about error severities, see the topic "Database Engine Error Severities" at *https://msdn.microsoft.com/en-us/library/ms164086.aspx*.
- ERROR_STATE() provides the error state. The error state is an integer in the range 1 to 255. It can be used for different custom purposes such as indicating where the error originated in cases where the error can happen in different places in the SQL Server engine's code.
- ERROR_LINE() provides the line number where the error happened.
- ERROR_PROCEDURE() provides the name of the stored procedure where the error happened. If the error did not happen in a stored procedure, this function returns a NULL.

There are a number of important things you want to keep in mind when using these functions:

- If you invoke these functions not within a CATCH block, they all return NULLs.
- If you nest TRY-CATCH constructs, whether directly or indirectly when you call one procedure from another, these functions return error information about the innermost error.
- Some failures generate a chain of errors. These functions only return information about the last error in the chain.

Conveniently, you are allowed to invoke these functions from a stored procedure for reusability. Still, the ERROR_PROCEDURE function returns the name of the stored procedure where the error happened and not the name of the procedure where you invoked the function, if different. To demonstrate this, first run the following code to create the stored procedure PrintErrorInfo, which simply prints the values of the error functions:

```
CREATE OR ALTER PROC dbo.PrintErrorInfo
AS

PRINT 'Error Number  : ' + CAST(ERROR_NUMBER() AS VARCHAR(10));
PRINT 'Error Message : ' + ERROR_MESSAGE();
PRINT 'Error Severity: ' + CAST(ERROR_SEVERITY() AS VARCHAR(10));
PRINT 'Error State   : ' + CAST(ERROR_STATE() AS VARCHAR(10));
PRINT 'Error Line    : ' + CAST(ERROR_LINE() AS VARCHAR(10));
PRINT 'Error Proc    : ' + COALESCE(ERROR_PROCEDURE(), 'Not within proc');
GO
```

Next, run the following code to alter the AddRowToT1 procedure to run the PrintErrorInfo procedure in the CATCH block when an error happens in the attempt to insert the row into T1 in the TRY block:

```
CREATE OR ALTER PROC dbo.AddRowToT1 -- proc name
  @keycol INT,
  @col1   INT,
  @col2   VARCHAR(10)
AS

SET NOCOUNT ON;

BEGIN TRY

  INSERT INTO dbo.T1(keycol, col1, col2) -- line 11
    VALUES(@keycol, @col1, @col2);

END TRY
BEGIN CATCH

  EXEC dbo.PrintErrorInfo;

END CATCH;
GO
```

Run the following code to execute the AddRowToT1 procedure with an invalid value for col1:

```
EXEC dbo.AddRowToT1
  @keycol = 1,
  @col1 = -10,
  @col2 = 'AAA';
```

This code generates the following output:

```
Error Number  : 547
Error Message : The INSERT statement conflicted with the CHECK constraint "CHK_T1_col1_
gtzero". The conflict occurred in database "TSQLV4", table "dbo.T1", column 'col1'.
Error Severity: 16
Error State   : 0
Error Line    : 11
Error Proc    : dbo.AddRowToT1
```

Notice that the stored procedure name where the error actually happened was captured correctly. Also notice that the line number reported is the line number where the error happened within the stored procedure.

## The THROW and RAISERROR commands

The THROW and RAISERROR (yes there's only one E in there) commands allow you to raise an error. Both allow you to raise a user defined error, but only THROW allows you to re-throw an original error that was caught by a TRY-CATCH construct.

### THE THROW COMMAND

The THROW command has two supported syntaxes. One is without parameters, with which you use the command in a CATCH block to re-throw the error that originally activated that CATCH block. The re-thrown error behaves like the original one, with the same error number, severity, and state. Also, if the failure normally generates a chain of error messages, the re-thrown error does too. Irrespective of whether the original error is a batch-aborting one or not, the THROW command aborts the batch and bubbles up, unless you call it from a nested TRY-CATCH construct, in which case it activates the inner CATCH block.

The following procedure demonstrates using THROW without parameters:

```
CREATE OR ALTER PROC dbo.Divide
  @dividend AS INT,
  @divisor  AS INT
AS

SET NOCOUNT ON;

BEGIN TRY

  SELECT @dividend / @divisor AS quotient, @dividend % @divisor AS remainder;

END TRY
BEGIN CATCH

  PRINT 'Error occurred when trying to compute the division '
    + CAST(@dividend AS VARCHAR(11)) + ' / ' + CAST(@divisor AS VARCHAR(11)) + '.';

  THROW;

  PRINT 'This doesn''nt execute.';

END CATCH;
GO
```

The procedure Divide uses a TRY block to invoke a query that computes the quotient and remainder of integer division applied to the two input parameters. If all goes well, the query returns the result of the calculations. In case of an error, the CATCH block is activated. The CATCH block first prints a message indicating that an error occurred with the attempted calculation, and then re-throws the original error assuming that you want it to bubble up to the caller. To show that the THROW command aborts the batch, the CATCH block has a PRINT statement after the THROW command, but this statement never gets to execute.

Use the following code to first test the procedure with valid inputs:

```
EXEC dbo.Divide @dividend = 11, @divisor = 2;
```

The procedure executes successfully, generating the following output:

```
quotient    remainder
----------- -----------
5           1
```

Execute the procedure again, but this time with zero as the divisor:

```
EXEC dbo.Divide @dividend = 11, @divisor = 0;
```

This code generates the following output:

```
quotient    remainder
----------- -----------

Error occurred when trying to compute the division 11 / 0.
Msg 8134, Level 16, State 1, Procedure dbo.Divide, Line 8 [Batch Start Line 799]
Divide by zero error encountered.
```

A *divide by zero* error happened. The CATCH block was activated. The CATCH block printed a message saying "Error occurred when trying to compute the division 11 / 0." The CATCH block then re-threw the error, at which point SQL Server aborted the batch and passed the error to the caller. Then next line of code in the CATCH block after the THROW command didn't get to execute.

You should be aware of potential parsing ambiguity with code that has an unterminated statement preceding the THROW command. As an example, run the following code to alter the definition of the procedure Divide, and execute it with zero as the divisor:

```
CREATE OR ALTER PROC dbo.Divide
  @dividend AS INT,
  @divisor  AS INT
AS

SET NOCOUNT ON;

BEGIN TRY

  SELECT @dividend / @divisor AS quotient, @dividend % @divisor AS remainder;

END TRY
BEGIN CATCH

  SELECT 'What comes next is an alias'

  THROW;

END CATCH;
GO
```

```
EXEC dbo.Divide @dividend = 11, @divisor = 0;
GO
```

This code generates the following output:

```
quotient    remainder
----------- -----------

THROW
---------------------------
What comes next is an alias
```

Notice that SQL Server didn't re-throw the error because the parser assumed that the code uses THROW as a column alias for the expression in the preceding unterminated query, as if the intended query was:

```
SELECT 'What comes next is an alias' THROW;
```

As another example for ambiguity, run the following code to alter the procedure definition again, and execute it:

```
CREATE OR ALTER PROC dbo.Divide
  @dividend AS INT,
  @divisor  AS INT
AS

SET NOCOUNT ON;

BEGIN TRY

  SELECT @dividend / @divisor AS quotient, @dividend % @divisor AS remainder;

END TRY
BEGIN CATCH

  IF @@TRANCOUNT > 0 ROLLBACK TRAN

  THROW;

END CATCH;
GO

EXEC dbo.Divide @dividend = 11, @divisor = 0;
```

Here your goal in the CATCH block is to roll back an active transaction if one was opened by calling code before you re-throw the error. However, because the preceding ROLLBACK TRAN statement isn't terminated, the parser thinks that THROW is a transaction or savepoint name, rather than being a command of its own, as if the statement was ROLLBACK TRAN THROW. In the above execution, there's no transaction open, so the ROLLBACK TRAN THROW statement doesn't get to execute, and the problem silently goes unnoticed. The error is not re-thrown. This code generates the following output:

```
quotient    remainder
----------- -----------
```

Next, execute the code from within a user transaction:

```
BEGIN TRAN;

EXEC dbo.Divide @dividend = 11, @divisor = 0;

PRINT '@@TRANCOUNT is ' + CAST(@@TRANCOUNT AS VARCHAR(10)) + '.';
```

This time the CATCH block tries to execute the command ROLLBACK TRAN THROW, but because it cannot find a transaction or savepoint name called THROW, it generates an error indicating as much, and does not re-throw the original divide by zero error. Worse, it leaves the transaction open! This code generates the following output:

```
quotient    remainder
----------- -----------

Msg 6401, Level 16, State 1, Procedure dbo.Divide, Line 15 [Batch Start Line 58]
Cannot roll back THROW. No transaction or savepoint of that name was found.
@@TRANCOUNT is 1.
```

Run the following code to roll back the currently open transaction:

```
ROLLBACK TRAN;
```

Clearly, this ambiguity can get you into quite a lot of trouble. The official documentation for THROW states that a statement preceding the command must be terminated. If indeed you terminate the preceding statement, there is no ambiguity. If you have a coding policy to terminate all statements, you avoid ambiguity anyway. The reality though is that most people simply don't follow the best practice to terminate all statements, so most T-SQL code out there isn't properly terminated. To be on the safe side, some people developed a practice to always precede the THROW command with a terminator, as if the command was actually ;THROW. This way you don't need to worry about whether the preceding statement is, or might be, terminated.

A very similar ambiguity exists with the WITH clause which can be used to define a CTE as well as for other purposes like specifying a table hint in a query. Therefore, the documentation indicates that you must terminate a statement preceding a WITH clause that defines a CTE. Similar to the unofficial practice to prefix THROW with a terminator, some people also regularly prefix a WITH clause that defines a CTE with a terminator, as in ;WITH.

The second syntax for the THROW command is with parameters. You use this syntax to throw a user-defined error. You can use it both inside and outside a CATCH block. The general form of THROW with parameters is:

```
THROW errornumber, message, state;
```

All three parameters can be either constants or variables.

Here's an example for using THROW with constant parameters:

```
THROW 50000, 'This is a user-defined error.', 1;
```

This code generates the following output:

```
Msg 50000, Level 16, State 1, Line 865
This is a user-defined error.
```

The first parameter is a user specified integer error number that must be greater than or equal to 50000. The error number does not need to be recorded anywhere previously.

The second parameter is a user specified error message. The THROW command does not support parameter markers in the message directly. If you want to embed the percent sign (%) as part of the message, you need to escape it by indicating two percent signs (%%). If you want to embed input values as part of the message, you need to construct the message ahead in a variable by applying string concatenation, or by using the FORMATMESSAGE function, which supports using parameter markers. I demonstrate this shortly.

The third parameter is a user specified integer state in the range 1 to 255. You usually use this value to provide custom information like which place in the code the error originated from.

The THROW command does not support specifying a severity. It always generates an error with severity 16.

Here's an example of using a variable for the error message parameter:

```
DECLARE @msg AS NVARCHAR(2048) =
  'This is a user-define error that occurred on ' + CONVERT(CHAR(10), SYSDATETIME(),
121) + '.';

THROW 50000, @msg, 1;
```

This code generates the following output, with the date reflecting your execution date, of course:

```
Msg 50000, Level 16, State 1, Line 872
This is a user-define error that occurred on 2017-02-12.
```

As an alternative to constructing the message with string concatenation techniques, you can use the FORMATMESSAGE function, which allows you to embed in the message text parameter markers like the ones used by the printf function in C, like so:

```
DECLARE @msg AS NVARCHAR(2048) =
  FORMATMESSAGE('This is a user-define error that occurred on %s.',
    CONVERT(CHAR(10), SYSDATETIME(), 121));

THROW 50000, @msg, 1;
```

Commonly used markers are %s for a string and %d for an integer.

In the example above the first parameter to FORMATMESSAGE is the message text with the parameter markers, followed by values for the parameter markers. You can use an alternative syntax where the first parameter is an ID of a message stored in the sys.messages table. You can store user defined messages in sys.messages using the sp_addmessage stored procedure. See the official documentation for details at *https://msdn.microsoft.com/en-us/library/ms186788.aspx*.

If you execute the THROW command with parameters outside a TRY-CATCH construct, it always aborts the batch. If you execute it in a TRY block, it causes the corresponding CATCH block to be activated.

The following example demonstrates the batch-abort behavior:

```
THROW 50000, 'This is a user-defined error.', 1;
PRINT 'This code in the same batch doesn''t execute.';
GO
PRINT 'This code in a different batch does execute.';
```

This code generates the following output:

```
Msg 50000, Level 16, State 1, Line 884
This is a user-defined error.
This code in a different batch does execute.
```

Notice that the PRINT statement that appears right after the THROW command in the same batch doesn't get to execute, but the subsequent PRINT statement in a separate batch does.

When XACT_ABORT is off and you execute THROW while in an open transaction, the transaction remains open and committable.

When XACT_ABORT is on and you execute THROW while in an open transaction, if you're not using TRY-CATCH, SQL Server aborts the transaction, and if you are using TRY-CATCH, SQL Server dooms the transaction. I explain what doomed transactions are in the next section.

The following code demonstrates calling THROW when XACT_ABORT is set to off:

```
SET XACT_ABORT OFF;

BEGIN TRAN;

THROW 50000, 'Hello from THROW.', 1;
PRINT 'This doesn''t execute.';
GO

PRINT 'New batch... @@TRANCOUNT is ' + CAST(@@TRANCOUNT AS VARCHAR(10)) + '.';
IF @@TRANCOUNT > 0
  ROLLBACK TRAN;
```

This code generates the following output:

```
Msg 50000, Level 16, State 1, Line 894
Hello from THROW.
New batch... @@TRANCOUNT is 1.
```

Notice that the execution of the THROW command terminated the batch but not the transaction.

Run the code again, this time setting XACT_ABORT to on:

```
SET XACT_ABORT ON;
```

```
BEGIN TRAN;

THROW 50000, 'Hello from THROW.', 1;
PRINT 'This doesn''t execute.';
GO

PRINT 'New batch... @@TRANCOUNT is ' + CAST(@@TRANCOUNT AS VARCHAR(10)) + '.';
IF @@TRANCOUNT > 0
  ROLLBACK TRAN;
```

This code generates the following output:

```
Msg 50000, Level 16, State 1, Line 908
Hello from THROW.
New batch... @@TRANCOUNT is 0.
```

This time the execution of THROW caused both the batch and the transaction to abort.

The THROW command doesn't support an option to request to log the error in the SQL Server error log or the Windows application log.

### THE RAISERROR COMMAND

The RAISERROR command is the predecessor to the THROW command. Some still find it useful even when writing new code because it supports certain options that THROW doesn't.

The RAISERROR command has the following syntax:

```
RAISERROR ( { message | messageid }, severity, state [, arguments for parameter markers
] ) [ WITH options ];
```

The parameters can be either constants or variables.

Here's an example for using the RAISERROR command:

```
RAISERROR( 'This is a user-define error with a string parameter %s and an integer
parameter %d.', 16, 1, 'ABC', 123 );
```

This code generates the following output:

```
Msg 50000, Level 16, State 1, Line 926
This is a user-define error with a string parameter ABC and an integer parameter 123.
```

The first parameter can be a message text, with optional parameter markers using C-like printf syntax (details can be found at *https://msdn.microsoft.com/en-us/library/ms178592. aspx*), such as in the above example. In such a case, the error number is always 50000. The parameters positioned fourth and on are the values that the command uses to replace the parameter markers. In our example, ABC replaces %s and 123 replaces %d. If you want to include the percent sign (%) in the message text, you need to escape it by specifying two percent signs (%%). Alternatively, the first parameter can be an ID of a user-defined message with a number greater than 50000 that you created earlier with the sp_addmessage stored procedure, and that was stored in the sys.messages table. You can also emulate system errors for error numbers that are greater than or equal to 13000.

The second parameter is the error severity. The outcome of raising an error with a certain severity is similar to the outcome of a system generated error with the same severity. Namely, messages with severities 0 to 10 are considered informational, and are always sent to the client, with severity 10 getting internally converted to 0 for compatibility reasons. With severities 0 and 10, the message prints without a header. With severities 1 to 9, the message prints with a header.

The following example demonstrates raising an error with severity 0:

```
RAISERROR( 'This is a message with severity 0.', 0, 1 );
```

This code generates the following output:

```
This is a message with severity 0.
```

The following example demonstrates raising an error with severity 1 to 9:

```
RAISERROR( 'This is a message with severity 1 to 9.', 1, 1 );
```

This code generates the following output:

```
This is a message with severity 1 to 9.
Msg 50000, Level 1, State 1
```

Errors with a severity level lower than 11 are not catchable. Errors with severities 11 to 19 are catchable. Errors with severities 20 to 25 terminate the connection. To raise an error with severity 19 and up you have to add the option WITH LOG, which logs the error in the SQL Server error log as well as the Windows application log. To use the WITH LOG option you must be a member of the sysadmin role or have the ALTER TRACE permission.

The third parameter is an integer state value in the range 1 to 255, similar to the state value you specify with the THROW command.

There are additional options that you can specify as part of the WITH clause of the RAISERROR command. The two most commonly used ones are LOG and NOWAIT. I already explained what the LOG option does and the required permissions to use it. The NOWAIT option causes SQL Server to send the message immediately to the client without waiting for its internal buffer to first fill up. Developers often use this option when running long scripts to report the progress of the code in intermediate milestones. The following example demonstrates using the NOWAIT option:

```
RAISERROR( 'First message.', 0, 1 ) WITH NOWAIT;
WAITFOR DELAY '00:00:05';
RAISERROR( 'Second message.', 0, 1 ) WITH NOWAIT;
```

Both messages are sent immediately to the client when the corresponding RAISERROR command executes. The first immediately prints when the code starts executing and the second after five seconds. Run the following code, which does not use the NOWAIT option:

```
RAISERROR( 'First message.', 0, 1 );
WAITFOR DELAY '00:00:05';
RAISERROR( 'Second message.', 0, 1 );
```

This time both messages get printed only after five seconds when the code completes executing.

The following example demonstrates raising an error with severity 20 using the WITH LOG option:

```
RAISERROR( 'This is a message with severity 20.', 20, 1 ) WITH LOG;
```

The message gets logged. Also, because the specified severity is 20, SQL Server terminates the connection, generating the following output:

```
Msg 50000, Level 20, State 1, Line 945
This is a message with severity 20.
Msg 596, Level 21, State 1, Line 944
Cannot continue the execution because the session is in the kill state.
Msg 0, Level 20, State 0, Line 944
A severe error occurred on the current command.  The results, if any, should be
discarded.
```

At this point you are disconnected; however, next time you execute a batch of T-SQL code, SSMS 2016 will restore the connection.

The THROW command does not support options similar to LOG and NOWAIT, giving RAISERROR an advantage when you need those.

Note that other than errors with severity 20 and up, which terminate the connection, if you raise an error with a severity that is lower than 20 this doesn't terminate the batch, nor does this terminate or doom the transaction, irrespective of the state of the XACT_ABORT option. This is one of the drawbacks of the RAISERROR command. The following code demonstrates this:

```
SET XACT_ABORT ON;

BEGIN TRAN;

RAISERROR( 'This is a user-defined error.', 16, 1 );
PRINT 'This code in the same batch executes. @@TRANCOUNT is ' + CAST(@@TRANCOUNT AS
VARCHAR(10)) + '.';

IF @@TRANCOUNT > 0
  ROLLBACK TRAN;
```

This code generates the following output:

```
Msg 50000, Level 16, State 1, Line 953
This is a user-defined error.
This code in the same batch executes. @@TRANCOUNT is 1.
```

As you can see, the batch continued executing after raising the error and the transaction remained open despite the fact that XACT_ABORT was on.

Since RAISERROR is a reserved keyword, unlike THROW, with the former a preceding statement doesn't have to be terminated, though it is still a good practice to do so.

If your exam includes questions involving RAISERROR and THROW, chances are that you are expected to know how to pick between the two based on the differences between them. For your convenience, Table 3-1 provides a comparison summary between the two tools. Make sure you understand and memorize all items in the table.

Table 3-1 has a comparison between THROW and RAISERROR.

**TABLE 3-1** Comparison between THROW and RAISERROR

| Proprty | THROW | RAISERROR |
| --- | --- | --- |
| Can re-throw original system error | Yes | No |
| Activates CATCH block | Yes | Yes, for 10 < severity < 20 |
| Always aborts batch when not using TRY-CATCH | Yes | No |
| Aborts/dooms transaction if XACT_ABORT is off | No | No |
| Aborts/dooms transaction if XACT_ABORT is on | Yes | No |
| If error number is passed, it must be defined in sys.messages | No | Yes |
| Supports printf parameter markers directly | No | Yes |
| Supports indicating severity | No | Yes |
| Supports WITH LOG to log error to error log and application log | No | Yes |
| Supports WITH NOWAIT to send messages immediately to the client | No | Yes |
| Preceding statement needs to be terminated | Yes | No |

The next section covers handling errors that happen in transactions.

## Error handling with transactions

When errors happen in transactions, there are additional considerations and complexities that you need to be aware of beyond what the previous sections already covered. Your course of action in case of an error could depend on the state of the transaction after the error. This section covers error handling with transactions.

As mentioned earlier, there are quite a lot of possible outcomes of errors in T-SQL. Some errors abort the batch and some don't. Some errors abort the transaction and some don't. Some errors even terminate the connection. You can achieve better consistency and some degree of control over the outcome of errors by turning the XACT_ABORT option to on, and by using the TRY-CATCH construct. This results in more robust solutions.

The following example demonstrates a divide by zero error, which normally doesn't abort the batch and doesn't terminate the transaction:

```
SET XACT_ABORT OFF;

BEGIN TRAN;

DECLARE @i AS INT = 10/0;
PRINT 'Batch wasn''t aborted.';
GO

PRINT '@@TRANCOUNT is ' + CAST(@@TRANCOUNT AS VARCHAR(10)) + '.';

IF @@TRANCOUNT > 0
  ROLLBACK TRAN;
```

This code generates the following output:

```
Msg 8134, Level 16, State 1, Line 967
Divide by zero error encountered.
Batch wasn't aborted.
@@TRANCOUNT is 1.
```

The following example demonstrates a conversion error, which aborts both the batch and the transaction:

```
BEGIN TRAN;

DECLARE @i AS INT = CAST('1,759' AS INT);
PRINT 'Batch wasn''t aborted.';
GO

PRINT '@@TRANCOUNT is ' + CAST(@@TRANCOUNT AS VARCHAR(10)) + '.';

IF @@TRANCOUNT > 0
  ROLLBACK TRAN;
```

This code generates the following output:

```
Msg 245, Level 16, State 1, Line 980
Conversion failed when converting the varchar value '1,759' to data type int.
@@TRANCOUNT is 0.
```

As you can see, it's not like a conversion error is considered more severe than a divide by zero error, at least as far as the formal severity level is concerned. But the two errors have very different outcomes. If you set the XACT_ABORT option to on, you get a more consistent behavior in the sense that most errors that normally don't terminate the transaction and/or batch, with this option turned on terminate the batch and rollback the transaction.

To demonstrate this, run the example with the divide by zero error again, after turning on the XACT_ABORT option:

```
SET XACT_ABORT ON;

BEGIN TRAN;
```

```
DECLARE @i AS INT = 10/0;
PRINT 'Batch wasn''t aborted.';
GO

PRINT '@@TRANCOUNT is ' + CAST(@@TRANCOUNT AS VARCHAR(10)) + '.';

IF @@TRANCOUNT > 0
  ROLLBACK TRAN;
```

This code generates the following output:

```
Msg 8134, Level 16, State 1, Line 995
Divide by zero error encountered.
@@TRANCOUNT is 0.
```

This time the error caused both the batch and the transaction to abort.

As you've seen, when you're not using TRY-CATCH, the transaction state after an error can be either open or not, and you can check the state using the @@TRANCOUNT. If it is open, you can determine whether you want to commit it or roll it back. The problem with cases where the transaction is aborted is that any changes done by the transaction are lost. What if as part of your error handling logic you wish to investigate data that was created by the transaction before you eventually roll it back. To this end, errors that normally cause the transaction to abort when you're not using TRY-CATCH, cause the transaction to enter a special *doomed* state (also known as *failed*, and *uncommittable* state). Under this state, you're not allowed to change data other than in table variables, but you are allowed to read data. You're not allowed to commit a doomed transaction, rather you have to eventually roll it back. You're not allowed to roll the transaction back to a savepoint, rather it has to be a full transaction rollback.

So when using TRY-CATCH, there could be three possible outcomes of an error in terms of the state of the transaction. The transaction could be open and committable, open and uncommittable (doomed), and no open transaction. If you want your error handling code to react differently depending on the transaction state, it's not enough to check the @@TRAN-COUNT value because it only tells you whether a transaction is open or not; it doesn't tell you whether it's open and committable or doomed. T-SQL supports an alternative function called XACT_STATE that does make the distinction between the three states. It returns 0 when no transaction is open (equivalent to @@TRANCOUNT being 0), 1 when the transaction is open and committable, and -1 (minus one) when the transaction is doomed.

The following example demonstrates the outcome of a nondooming error when using TRY-CATCH:

```
SET XACT_ABORT OFF;

BEGIN TRY

  BEGIN TRAN;

  DECLARE @i AS INT = 10/0;
  -- normally there would be work here that warrants a transaction
```

```
    COMMIT TRAN;

END TRY
BEGIN CATCH

  PRINT
    CASE XACT_STATE()
      WHEN  0 THEN 'No open transaction.'
      WHEN  1 THEN 'Transaction is open and committable.'
      WHEN -1 THEN 'Transaction is doomed.'
    END;

  IF @@TRANCOUNT > 0
    ROLLBACK TRAN;

END CATCH;
```

This code generates the following output:

```
Transaction is open and committable.
```

The following example demonstrates the outcome of a dooming error when using TRY-CATCH:

```
SET XACT_ABORT OFF;

BEGIN TRY

  BEGIN TRAN;

  DECLARE @i AS INT = CAST('1,759' AS INT);
  -- normally there would be work here that warrants a transaction

  COMMIT TRAN;

END TRY
BEGIN CATCH

  PRINT
    CASE XACT_STATE()
      WHEN  0 THEN 'No open transaction.'
      WHEN  1 THEN 'Transaction is open and committable.'
      WHEN -1 THEN 'Transaction is doomed.'
    END;

  IF @@TRANCOUNT > 0
    ROLLBACK TRAN;

END CATCH;
```

This code generates the following output:

```
Transaction is doomed.
```

If you turn on the XACT_ABORT option, as recommended, most errors are treated as dooming errors. For instance, the example before the last with the divide by zero error results in a doomed transaction with XACT_ABORT turned on.

Remember, though, that in case an error with severity 20 and up happens, the connection is terminated, so any error handling code that you have doesn't have a chance to run.

**MORE INFO ON CLASSIFICATION OF ERRORS AND THEIR OUTCOMES**

Erland Sommarskog has a nice summary of the different classification of errors and their possible outcomes at *http://www.sommarskog.se/error_handling/Part2.html#classification*.

If you do not wish to deal differently with open and committable and doomed transactions, rather react the same in both cases, to check whether you're in an open transaction you could either check that @@TRANCOUNT is greater than zero or that XACT_STATE is different than zero. Just make sure that whatever you do, you don't leave a transaction open other than in very special, controlled, circumstances.

For example, suppose that you wanted to add error handling code to the AddOrder procedure, which you created in an earlier section. In the CATCH block you simply want to make sure that in case there's an open transaction you roll it back, and re-throw the error to the caller. Use the following code to achieve this:

```
CREATE OR ALTER PROC dbo.AddOrder
  @custid         AS INT,
  @empid          AS INT,
  @orderdate      AS DATE,
  @requireddate   AS DATE,
  @shippeddate    AS DATE,
  @shipperid      AS INT,
  @freight        AS MONEY,
  @shipname       AS NVARCHAR(40),
  @shipaddress    AS NVARCHAR(60),
  @shipcity       AS NVARCHAR(15),
  @shipregion     AS NVARCHAR(15),
  @shippostalcode AS NVARCHAR(10),
  @shipcountry    AS NVARCHAR(15),
  @OrderLines     AS dbo.OrderLines READONLY,
  @neworderid     AS INT OUT
AS

SET XACT_ABORT, NOCOUNT ON;

BEGIN TRY

BEGIN TRAN;

  -- add order header
  INSERT INTO Sales.Orders
      (custid, empid, orderdate, requireddate, shippeddate,
       shipperid, freight, shipname, shipaddress, shipcity,
       shippostalcode, shipcountry)
```

```
    VALUES
        (@custid, @empid, @orderdate, @requireddate, @shippeddate,
        @shipperid, @freight, @shipname, @shipaddress, @shipcity,
        @shippostalcode, @shipcountry);

    SET @neworderid = SCOPE_IDENTITY();

    -- add order lines
    INSERT INTO Sales.OrderDetails(orderid, productid, unitprice, qty, discount)
        SELECT @neworderid, productid, unitprice, qty, discount
        FROM @OrderLines;

    COMMIT TRAN;

END TRY
BEGIN CATCH

    IF @@TRANCOUNT > 0
        ROLLBACK TRAN;

    THROW;

END CATCH;
GO
```

Note that because you turned on the XACT_ABORT option, even if you didn't explicitly roll the transaction back in the CATCH block, the THROW command would. However, it's a good practice to keep this check in place in case someone changes the procedure in the future and removes the code that sets XACT_ABORT to on.

If you need to write any error information to a log table, make sure that you do so after the ROLLBACK TRAN statement and before the THROW command. If you try to do so before rolling the transaction back, you get an error saying that writes are not allowed under a doomed transaction. Furthermore, even if it was allowed, the ROLLBACK TRAN statement would have rolled back any such changes. Also, if you need to log data that was created by the transaction, make sure you first write it to a table variable before issuing the ROLLBACK TRAN statement, and then copy it from the table variable to the log table after rolling the transaction back. Remember that writes to a table variable are not undone when a transaction rolls back. Your catch block would look like this:

```
BEGIN CATCH
    ... declare a table variable and write what's needed into it ...
    IF @@TRANCOUNT > 0
        ROLLBACK TRAN;
    ... write what's needed to a log table, including copying data from the table variable
...
    THROW;
END CATCH;
```

When you're done, run the following code for cleanup:

```
DELETE FROM Sales.OrderDetails WHERE orderid > 11077;
DELETE FROM Sales.Orders WHERE orderid > 11077;
```

```
DBCC CHECKIDENT('Sales.Orders', RESEED, 11077);
DROP PROC IF EXISTS dbo.AddRowToT1, dbo.OuterProc, dbo.InnerProc,
  dbo.PrintErrorInfo, dbo.Divide, dbo.AddOrder, dbo.Proc1;
DROP TABLE IF EXISTS dbo.T1, dbo.ErrorLog;
```

Before continuing to the next section, remember my earlier recommendation to make sure that you read at least the first two parts in Erland Sommarskog's coverage of error handling, which you can find in his website at *http://sommarskog.se/error_handling/Part1.html.*

# Skill 3.3: Implement data types and NULLs

This skill covers data types, data type conversions, and handling NULLs using the ISNULL and COALESCE functions. If some of these topics seem familiar, that's because I found it impor- tant to already cover them at least to some extent earlier in the book. For instance, I already covered some aspects of data type conversions, including implicit ones, as well as handling of NULLs, and the COALESCE and ISNULL functions in Chapter 1. Consider the coverage here as an opportunity to review these important topics again and have another chance to practice them.

---

**This section covers how to:**

- Evaluate results of data type conversions
- Determine proper data types for given data elements or table columns
- Identify locations of implicit data type conversions in queries
- Determine the correct results of joins and functions in the presence of NULL values
- Identify proper usage of ISNULL and COALESCE functions

---

## Working with data types

When defining columns in tables, parameters in procedures and functions, and variables in T-SQL batches, you need to choose a data type for those. The data type constrains the data that is supported, in addition to encapsulating behavior that operates on the data, exposing it through operators and other means. Because data types are such a fundamental component of your data—everything is built on top—your choices of data types have dramatic implica- tions for your application at many different layers. Therefore, this is an area that should not be taken lightly, but instead treated with a lot of care and attention.

The upcoming sections provide recommendations for choosing the appropriate data type for different database elements, choosing a data type for keys, and data type conversions.

# Choosing the appropriate data type

Choosing the appropriate data types for your attributes is probably one of the most important decisions that you make regarding your data. SQL Server supports many data types from different categories: exact numeric (INT, NUMERIC), character strings (CHAR, VARCHAR), Unicode character strings (NCHAR, NVARCHAR), approximate numeric (FLOAT, REAL), binary strings (BINARY, VARBINARY), date and time (DATE, TIME, DATETIME2, SMALLDATETIME, DATETIME, DATETIMEOFFSET), and others. There are many options, so it might seem like a difficult task, but as long as you follow certain principles, you can be smart about your choices, which results in a robust, consistent, and efficient database.

One of the great strengths of the relational model is the importance it gives to enforcement of data integrity as part of the model itself, at multiple levels. One important aspect in choosing the appropriate type for your data is to remember that a type is a constraint. This means that it has a certain domain of supported values and does not allow values outside that domain. For example, the DATE type allows only valid dates. An attempt to enter something that isn't a date, like 'abc' or '20170230', is rejected. If you have an attribute that is supposed to represent a date, such as birthdate, and you use a type such as INT or CHAR, you don't benefit from built-in validating of dates. An INT type won't prevent a value such as 99999999 and a CHAR type won't prevent a value such as '20170230'.

Much like a type is a constraint, NOT NULL is a constraint as well. If an attribute isn't supposed to allow NULLs, it's important to enforce a NOT NULL constraint as part of its definition. Otherwise, NULLs find their way into your attribute.

Also, you want to make sure that you do not confuse the formatting of a value with its type. Sometimes, people use character strings to store dates because they think of storing a date in a certain format. The formatting of a value is supposed to be the responsibility of the application when data is presented. The type is a property of the value stored in the database, and the internal storage format shouldn't be your concern. This aspect has to do with the *physical data independence* principle in the relational model.

A data type encapsulates behavior. By using an inappropriate type, you miss all the behavior that is encapsulated in the type in the form of operators and functions that support it. As a simple example, for types representing numbers, the plus (+) operator represents addition, but for character strings, the same operator represents concatenation. If you chose an inappropriate type for your value, you sometimes have to convert the type (explicitly or implicitly), and sometimes juggle the value quite a bit, in order to treat it as what it is supposed to be.

Another important principle in choosing the appropriate type for your data is size. Often one of the major aspects affecting query performance is the amount of I/O involved. A query that reads less simply tends to run faster. The bigger the type that you use, the more storage it uses. Tables with many millions of rows, if not billions, are commonplace nowadays. When you start multiplying the size of a type by the number of rows in the table, the numbers can quickly become significant. As an example, suppose you have an attribute representing test scores, which are integers in the range 0 to 100. Using an INT data type for this purpose is overkill. It would use 4 bytes per value, whereas a TINYINT would use only 1 byte, and is therefore the more appropriate type in this case. Similarly, for data that is supposed to represent dates, many people have a tendency to use the legacy DATETIME type, which uses 8 bytes of storage.

If the value is supposed to represent a date without a time, you should use DATE, which uses only 3 bytes of storage. Moreover, if the value is supposed to represent both date and time, you should consider DATETIME2. It requires storage between 6 to 8 bytes (depending on precision), and as an added value, provides a wider range of dates and improved, controllable precision. In short, you should use the smallest type that serves your needs. Though of course, this applies not in the short run, but in the long run. For example, using an INT type for a key in a table that at one point or another grows to a degree of billions of rows is a bad idea. You should be using BIGINT. But using INT for an attribute representing test scores or DATETIME for dates are both bad choices even when thinking about the long run.

Be very careful with the imprecise types FLOAT and REAL. The first two sentences in the documentation describing these types should give you a good sense of their nature: "Approximate-number data types for use with floating point numeric data. Floating point data is approximate; therefore, not all values in the data type range can be represented exactly." The benefit in these types is that they can represent very large and very small numbers beyond what any other numeric type that SQL Server supports can represent. So, for example, if you need to represent very large or very small numbers for scientific purposes and don't need complete accuracy, you may find these types useful. They're also quite economic (4 bytes for REAL and 8 bytes for FLOAT). But do not use them for things that are supposed to be precise.

I had a customer case who initially tried to use FLOAT to represent barcode numbers of products, and was then surprised by not getting the right product when scanning the products' barcodes.

To demonstrate the trickiness of these types, consider the following query, which converts a FLOAT value to NUMERIC:

```
DECLARE @f AS FLOAT = 29545428.022495;
SELECT CAST(@f AS NUMERIC(28, 14)) AS numericvalue;
```

Can you guess what the output of this code is? Here's what I got on my system:

```
numericvalue
---------------------------------------
29545428.02249500155449
```

As mentioned, some values cannot be represented precisely.

In short, make sure you use exact numeric types when you need to represent values precisely, and reserve the use of the approximate numeric types only to cases where you're certain that it's acceptable for the application.

Another important aspect in choosing a type has to do with choosing fixed types (CHAR, NCHAR, BINARY) vs. dynamic ones (VARCHAR, NVARCHAR, VARBINARY). Fixed types use the storage for the indicated size; for example, CHAR(30) uses storage for 30 characters, whether you actually specify 30 characters or less. This means that updates don't require the row to physically expand, and therefore no data shifting is required. So for attributes that get up-dated frequently, where the update performance is a priority, you should consider fixed types. Note that when compression is used—specifically row compression—SQL Server stores fixed types like variable ones, but with less overhead.

Variable types use the storage for what you enter, plus a couple of bytes for offset infor-mation (or 4 bits with row compression). So for widely varying sizes of strings, if you use vari-able types you can save a lot of storage. As already mentioned, the less storage used, the less there is for a query to read, and the faster the query can perform. So variable length types are usually preferable in such cases when read performance is a priority.

With character strings, there's also the question of using regular character types (CHAR, VARCHAR) vs. Unicode types (NCHAR, NVARCHAR). The former use 1 byte of storage per character and support only one language (based on collation properties) besides English. The latter use 2 bytes of storage per character (unless compressed) and support multiple languages. If a surrogate pair is needed, a character requires 4 bytes of storage. So if data is in multiple languages and you need to represent only one language besides English in your data, you can benefit from using regular character types, with lower storage requirements. When data is international, or your application natively works with Unicode data, you should use Unicode data types so you don't lose information. The greater storage requirements of Unicode data are mitigated with Unicode compression.

When using types that can have a length associated with them, such as CHAR and VAR-CHAR, T-SQL supports omitting the length and then uses a default length. However, in differ-ent contexts, the defaults can be different. It is considered a best practice to always be explicit about the length, as in CHAR(1) or VARCHAR(30).

## Choosing a data type for keys

When defining a key based on an existing attribute that already serves some purpose beyond being a key, there's usually no question about which data type to use because you've already made that choice previously. But when you need to create a new attribute solely for the purpose of being used as a key, you need to determine an appropriate data type, as well as a mechanism to generate the key values. The reality is that you hear many different opinions as to what is the best solution. Different systems and different workloads could end up with different optimal solutions. What's more, in some systems, write performance might be the priority, whereas in others, the read performance is. One solution can make the inserts faster but the reads slower, and another solution might work the other way around. At the end of the day, to make smart choices, it's important to learn the theory, learn about others' experi-ences, but eventually make sure that you run benchmarks in the target system.

The typical options people use to generate keys are:

- **The identity column property** A property that automatically generates keys in an at-tribute of a numeric type with a scale of 0; namely, any integer type (TINYINT, SMALL-INT, INT, BIGINT) or NUMERIC/DECIMAL with a scale of 0.

- **The sequence object** An independent object in the database from which you can obtain new sequence values. Like identity, it supports any numeric type with a scale of 0. Unlike identity, it's not tied to a particular column; instead, as mentioned, it is an independent object in the database. You can also request a new value from a sequence object before using it.

- **Nonsequential GUIDs** You can generate nonsequential global unique identifiers to be stored in an attribute of a UNIQUEIDENTIFIER type, which uses 16 bytes of storage. You can use the T-SQL function NEWID to generate a new GUID, possibly invoking it with a default expression attached to the column. You can also generate one from any-where—for example, the client—by using an application programming interface (API) that generates a new GUID. The main advantage of GUIDs is that they are guaranteed to be unique across space and time. Their disadvantages are that they use a lot of stor-age and are quite awkward to work with.

- **Sequential GUIDs** You can generate sequential GUIDs within the machine by using the T-SQL function NEWSEQUENTIALID. This function is only allowed in a default con-straint that is associated with a column.

- **Custom solutions** If you do not want to use the built-in tools that SQL Server provides to generate keys, you need to develop your own custom solution. The data type for the key then depends on your solution. An example would be storing the last used value in a table, and every time you need a new value, incrementing the existing value in the table with an UPDATE statement and using the new value when you insert a row into the target table.

One thing to consider regarding your choice of a key generator and the data type involved is the size of the data type. The bigger the type, the more storage is required, and hence the slower the reads are. A solution using an INT data type requires 4 bytes per value, BIGINT requires 8 bytes, UNIQUEIDENTIFIER requires 16 bytes, and so on. The storage requirements for your key can have a cascading effect if your clustered index is defined on the same key columns (the default for a primary key constraint). The clustered index key columns are used by all nonclustered indexes internally as the means to locate rows in the table. So if you de-fine a clustered index on a column x, and nonclustered indexes—one on column a, one on b, and one on c—your nonclustered indexes are internally created on columns (a, x), (b, x), and (c, x), respectively. In other words, the effect is multiplied.

Regarding the use of sequential keys (as with identity, sequence, and NEWSEQUENTIALID) vs. nonsequential ones (as with NEWID or a custom randomized key generator), there are several aspects to consider.

Starting with sequential keys, all rows go into the right end of the index. When a page is full, SQL Server allocates a new page and fills it. This results in less fragmentation in the index, which is beneficial for read performance. Also, insertions can be faster when a single session is loading the data, and the data resides on a single drive or a small number of drives. However, with high-end storage subsystems, the situation can be different. When loading data from multiple sessions, such as in typical OLTP workloads like order entry systems, you end up with a performance problem known as the rightmost page latch contention. Latches are objects used to synchronize access to database pages. In this scenario, you have a bottleneck when multiple threads try to obtain a latch against the rightmost index page and end up being queued since only one thread at a time can obtain the latch. This bottleneck prevents use of the full throughput of the storage subsystem and in systems with a high volume of small insert transactions often results in serious performance problems. As an interesting aside, the rightmost page latch contention problem exists when using the traditional disk-based architecture for data. The problem is completely eliminated when using the In-Memory OLTP feature because it uses an architecture with no locking or latching.

Consider nonsequential keys, such as random ones generated with NEWID or with a custom solution. When trying to force a row into an already full page, SQL Server performs a classic page split—it allocates a new page and moves half the rows from the original page to the new one. A page split has a cost, plus it results in index fragmentation. Index fragmentation can have a negative impact on the performance of reads. However, when using a high-end storage subsystem and loading data from multiple sessions, the random order can result in much better performance than sequential despite the splits. That's because there's no hot spot at the right end of the index, and you use the storage subsystem's available throughput better. Page splits and index fragmentation can be mitigated by periodic index rebuilds as part of the usual maintenance activities.

If for aforementioned reasons you decide to rely on keys generated in random order, you still need to decide between GUIDs and a custom random key generator solution. As already mentioned, GUIDs are stored in a UNIQUEIDENTIFIER type that is 16 bytes in size; that's large. But one of the main benefits of GUIDs is the fact that they can be generated anywhere and not conflict across time and space. You can generate GUIDs not just in SQL Server using the NEWID function, but anywhere, using APIs. Otherwise, you could come up with a custom solution that generates smaller keys that are generated in a random-like order as far as the insertions are concerned. The solution can even be a mix of a built-in tool and some tweaking on top. For example, you can find a creative solution by Wolfgang 'Rick' Kutschera at *http:// dangerousdba.blogspot.com/2011/10/day-sequences-saved-world.html*. Rick uses the SQL Server sequence object, but flips the bits of the values so that the insertion is distributed across the index leaf.

To conclude this section about keys and types for keys, remember that there are multiple options. Smaller is generally better, but then there's the question of the hardware that you use, and where your performance priorities are. Also remember that although it is very important to make educated guesses, it is also important to benchmark solutions in the target environment.

## Data type conversions

This section covers both explicit and implicit data type conversions and is mainly provided as a review of previously discussed topics.

You want to make sure that when indicating a literal of a type, you use the correct form. For example, literals of regular character strings are delimited with single quotation marks, as in 'abc', whereas literals of Unicode character strings are delimited with a capital N, and then single quotation marks, as in N'abc'. When an expression involves elements with different types, SQL

Server needs to apply implicit conversion when possible, and this may result in performance penalties. Note that in some cases the interpretation of a literal may not be what you think intuitively. In order to force a literal to be of a certain type, you may need to apply explicit conversion with functions like CAST, CONVERT, PARSE, or TRY_CAST, TRY_CONVERT, and TRY_PARSE. As an example, the literal 1 is considered an INT by SQL Server in any context. If you need the literal 1 to be considered, for example, a BIT, you need to convert the literal's type explicitly, as in CAST(1 AS BIT). Similarly, the literal 4000000000 is considered NUMERIC and not BIGINT. If you need the literal to be the latter, use CAST(4000000000 AS BIGINT). The difference between the functions without the TRY and their counterparts with the TRY is that those without the TRY fail if the value isn't convertible, whereas those with the TRY return a NULL in such a case. For example, the following code fails.

```
SELECT CAST('abc' AS INT);
```

It generates the following output:

```
-----------
Msg 245, Level 16, State 1, Line 28
Conversion failed when converting the varchar value 'abc' to data type int.
```

Conversely, the following code returns a NULL.

```
SELECT TRY_CAST('abc' AS INT);
```

As for the difference between CAST, CONVERT, and PARSE, with CAST, you indicate the expression and the target type; with CONVERT, there's a third argument representing the style for the conversion, which is supported for some conversions, like between character strings and date and time values. For example, CONVERT(DATE, '1/2/2017', 101) converts the literal character string to DATE using style 101 representing the United States standard. With PARSE, you can indicate the culture by using any culture supported by the Microsoft .NET Framework. For example, PARSE('1/2/2017' AS DATE USING 'en-US') parses the input literal as a DATE by using a United States English culture.

**EXAM TIP**

As mentioned in Chapter 1, the PARSE function is significantly slower than the CONVERT and CAST functions. So, in real life, I recommend staying away from it unless at some point Microsoft fixes the performance issue. However, when taking the exam make sure that you understand carefully what the questions are about. If presented with a conversion task and asked which solutions are correct (as opposed to efficient), by all means, you should consider using PARSE if presented with the option.

When using expressions that involve operands of different types, SQL Server usually converts the one that has the lower data type precedence to the one with the higher. Consider the expression 1 + '1' as an example. One operand is INT and the other is VARCHAR. If you look in Books Online under "Data Type Precedence (Transact-SQL)," at *https://msdn.microsoft.com/en-us/library/ms190309.aspx*, you find that INT precedes VARCHAR; hence, SQL Server implicitly converts the VARCHAR value '1' to the INT value 1, and the result of the expression is therefore 2 and not the string '11'. Of course, you can always take control by using explicit conversion.

If all operands of the expression are of the same type, that's also going to be the type of the result, and you might not want it to be the case. For example, the result of the expression 5 / 2 in T-SQL is the INT value 2 and not the NUMERIC value 2.5, because both operands are integers, and therefore the result is an integer. If you were dealing with two integer columns, like col1 / col2, and wanted the division to be NUMERIC, you would need to convert the columns explicitly, as in CAST(col1 AS NUMERIC(12, 2)) / CAST(col2 AS NUMERIC(12, 2)).

Curiously, T-SQL handles conversions from NUMERIC to INT differently than between NUMERIC with a higher scale to a lower one. With the former, T-SQL truncates the value, with the latter, it rounds it. The following example demonstrates this:

```
SELECT
  CAST(10.999 AS NUMERIC(12, 0)) AS numeric_to_numeric,
  CAST(10.999 AS INT) AS numeric_to_int;
```

This code generates the following output:

```
numeric_to_numeric                    numeric_to_int
------------------------------------- --------------
11                                    10
```

When converting a character string to a date and time type or a date and time type with a higher precision to one with a lower precision, you get rounding—not truncation. The following example demonstrates this:

```
DECLARE
  @s AS CHAR(21) = '20170212 23:59:59.999',
  @dt2 AS DATETIME2 = '20170212 23:59:59.999999';

SELECT
  CAST(@s AS DATETIME) AS char_to_datetime,
  CAST(@dt2 AS DATETIME) AS char_to_datetime;
```

This code generates the following output:

```
char_to_datetime        char_to_datetime
----------------------- -----------------------
2017-02-13 00:00:00.000 2017-02-13 00:00:00.000
```

The above conversion behavior applies whether the conversion is explicit or implicit.

When defining attributes that represent the same thing across different tables—especially ones that are later used as join columns (like the primary key in one table and the foreign key in another)—it's very important to be consistent with the types. Otherwise, when comparing one attribute with another, SQL Server has to apply implicit conversion of one attribute's type to the other, and this could have negative performance implications, like preventing efficient use of indexes.

# Handling NULLs

Chapter 1 already covered in detail the trickiness and complexity of dealing with NULLs in different T-SQL elements and provided recommendations for proper handling of NULLs. This section gives you an opportunity to practice what you know by going over a number of examples. The two main areas that this section demonstrates are using the ISNULL and CO-ALESCE functions, and handling NULLs when combining data from different tables.

## The ISNULL and COALESCE functions

The ISNULL and COALESCE functions are both commonly used functions that return the first value that is not NULL among their inputs. There are quite a few differences between them that you should be aware of before you decide which of the two is more appropriate for you to use.

The first important difference between ISNULL and COALESCE is that the former supports only two input parameters, whereas the latter supports more than two. Here's a simple example demonstrating their use:

```
SET NOCOUNT ON;
USE TSQLV4;

DECLARE
  @x AS INT = NULL,
  @y AS INT = 1759,
  @z AS INT = 42;

SELECT COALESCE(@x, @y, @z);
SELECT ISNULL(@x, @y);
```

Both expressions return the value 1759 because in both cases it's the first value that is not NULL.

The ISNULL function is a proprietary T-SQL feature whereas the COALESCE function is defined by the ISO/ANSI SQL standard. So if there is a policy in your organization to use standard code whenever possible, you should prefer COALESCE in such a case.

The previous section in this skill discussed data type conversions, including implicit conversions. There's a curious difference between ISNULL and COALESCE in terms of how the data type of the returned value is determined and how implicit conversion is handled. With ISNULL, the data type of the result is determined like so:

1. If the first input has a data type (as opposed to being an untyped NULL literal), the result type is the type of the first input.

2. If the first input is an untyped NULL literal, and the second input has a data type, the result type is the type of the second input.

3. If both inputs are untyped NULL literals, the result data type is INT.

With COALESCE, the type is determined like so:

1. If at least one of the inputs has a type, the result type is the type with the highest precedence among the inputs.

2. If all inputs are untyped NULL literals, you get an error.

Consider the following example:

```
DECLARE
  @x AS VARCHAR(3) = NULL,
  @y AS VARCHAR(10) = '1234567890';

SELECT ISNULL(@x, @y) AS ISNULLxy, COALESCE(@x, @y) AS COALESCExy;
```

Before you actually run it, can you guess what each of the functions return?

This code generates the following output:

```
ISNULLxy COALESCExy
-------- ----------
123      1234567890
```

Notice that with ISNULL the first input determines the type, which is VARCHAR(3), and since the first input is NULL and the second input isn't, the function returns the second input value after implicitly converting it to the first input's type. Consequently, the string gets truncated after the first three characters. With COALESCE, the type of the result is the type with the highest precedence among the inputs, meaning VARCHAR(10) in our example, so the returned value doesn't get truncated.

Consider another example:

```
SELECT ISNULL('1a2b', 1234) AS ISNULLstrnum;
GO
SELECT COALESCE('1a2b', 1234) AS COALESCEstrnum;
GO
```

Again, before actually running this code, can you guess the outcome of both function calls?

With the ISNULL function, the type of the result is based on the first input, so you get the first input value with its original type as the result: '1a2b'. With the COALESCE function, the type with the highest precedence among the inputs is INT, therefore the function tries to implicitly convert the first input value to INT before returning it and fails since the value doesn't covert. This code generates the following output:

```
ISNULLstrnum
------------
1a2b

COALESCEstrnum
--------------
Msg 245, Level 16, State 1, Line 85
Conversion failed when converting the varchar value '1a2b' to data type int.
```

Another difference between the two functions has to do with the nullability of the result column when using them in a SELECT INTO statement. With ISNULL, if any of the input expressions is nonnullable, the result column is defined as NOT NULL. If both inputs are nullable, the result is a column defined as allowing NULLs. With COALESCE, only if all inputs are nonnullable, the result column is defined as NOT NULL, otherwise, it is defined as allowing NULLs.

The following code demonstrates the difference between the two functions in terms of the nullability of the result:

```
DROP TABLE IF EXISTS dbo.TestNULLs;
GO
SELECT empid,
  ISNULL(region, country) AS ISNULLregioncountry,
  COALESCE(region, country) AS COALESCEregioncountry
INTO dbo.TestNULLs
FROM HR.Employees;

SELECT
  COLUMNPROPERTY(OBJECT_ID('dbo.TestNULLs'), 'ISNULLregioncountry',
    'AllowsNull') AS ISNULLregioncountry,
  COLUMNPROPERTY(OBJECT_ID('dbo.TestNULLs'), 'COALESCEregioncountry',
    'AllowsNull') AS COALESCEregioncountry;

DROP TABLE IF EXISTS dbo.TestNULLs;
```

The region column in the HR.Employees table allows NULLs and the country column doesn't. With ISNULL, because at least one input is defined as not allowing NULLs, the result column is defined as NOT NULL. With COALESCE, because at least one input allows NULLs, the result column allows NULLs as well. Here's the output of this code indicating the nullability of the two result columns:

```
ISNULLregioncountry COALESCEregioncountry
------------------- ---------------------
0                   1
```

Another important difference between the two functions has to do with performance when using subqueries. That is, when comparing an expression such as ISNULL((<subquery>), 0) with COALESCE((<subquery>), 0). The ISNULL function evaluates the subquery only once. If its result is not NULL, it returns its result. If it is NULL, it evaluates the second input and returns its result. With COALESCE, according to the SQL standard, the expression is translated to:

```
CASE WHEN (<subquery>) IS NOT NULL THEN (<subquery>) ELSE 0 END
```

If the result of the execution of the subquery in the WHEN clause isn't NULL, SQL Server executes it a second time in the THEN clause. In other words, in such a case it executes it twice. Only if the result of the execution in the WHEN clause is NULL, SQL Server doesn't execute the subquery again, rather returns the ELSE expression. So when using subqueries, the ISNULL function has a performance advantage.

***EXAM TIP***

If your exam includes questions involving ISNULL and COALESCE, chances are that you are expected to know how to pick between the two based on the differences between them. For your convenience, Table 3-2 provides a comparison summary between the two functions. Make sure you understand and memorize all items in the table.

**TABLE 3-2** Comparison between ISNULL and COALESCE

| aspect | isnull | coalesce |
|---|---|---|
| Number of supported parameters | 2 | > 2 |
| Standard | No | Yes |
| Data type of result | 1. If first input has a type, that's the type of the result. 2. Otherwise, if second input has a type, that's the type of the result. 3. If both inputs are untyped NULL literals, the result type is INT. | 1. If at least one input has a type, the result type is the type with the highest precedence. 2. If all inputs are untyped NULL literals, you get an error. |
| nullability of result | If any input is nonnullable, result is defined as NOT NULL, otherwise as NULL. | If all inputs are nonnullable, result is defined as NOT NULL, otherwise as NULL. |
| Might execute subquery more than once | No | Yes |

## Handling NULLs when combining data from multiple tables

When you need to combine data from multiple tables you use tools like joins, subqueries, and set operators. You always want to check if NULLs are possible in the tables you're combining, especially when it concerns the columns that you're comparing between the sides. If NULLs are possible in the data, you want to make sure that you have the right logic in place in your code to get the behavior that you consider as correct. This section demonstrates NULL handling when combining data from multiple tables with all three tools.

The examples in this section query tables called TableA and TableB. Run the following code to create these tables and populate them with sample data:

```
DROP TABLE IF EXISTS dbo.TableA, dbo.TableB;
GO
CREATE TABLE dbo.TableA
(
  key1 CHAR(1) NOT NULL,
  key2 CHAR(1) NULL,
  A_val VARCHAR(10) NOT NULL,
  CONSTRAINT UNQ_TableA_key1_key2 UNIQUE CLUSTERED (key1, key2)
);

INSERT INTO dbo.TableA(key1, key2, A_val)
  VALUES('w', 'w', 'A w w'),
        ('x', 'y', 'A x y'),
        ('x', NULL, 'A x NULL');
```

```
CREATE TABLE dbo.TableB
(
  key1 CHAR(1) NOT NULL,
  key2 CHAR(1) NULL,
  B_val VARCHAR(10) NOT NULL,
  CONSTRAINT UNQ_TableB_key1_key2 UNIQUE CLUSTERED (key1, key2)
);

INSERT INTO dbo.TableB(key1, key2, B_val)
  VALUES('x', 'y', 'B x y'),
        ('x', NULL, 'B x NULL'),
        ('z', 'z', 'B z z');
```

Joins and subqueries behave similarly in terms of NULLs when you compare key columns between the two sides of the operation in the join predicate or the subquery's WHERE clause. When comparing two columns using an equality operator (=), if either side is NULL, the outcome of the comparison is the logical value *unknown*. As part of a join predicate, the case is considered a nonmatch, and as part of a filter, the result row is discarded. If you want to get a match/keep the row when both sides are NULL, you need to add explicit special handling.

I'll demonstrate this behavior first with joins and then with subqueries. The following example joins TableA and TableB and compares both key1 (nonnullable) and key2 (nullable) from both sides:

```
SELECT A.A_val, B.B_val
FROM dbo.TableA AS A
  INNER JOIN dbo.TableB AS B
    ON A.key1 = B.key1
    AND A.key2 = B.key2;
```

Only rows with proper key values that match are returned. That is, only rows where both keys are not NULL and equal are considered matches and therefore are returned. This code generates the following output:

```
A_val      B_val
---------- ----------
A x y      B x y
```

Notice that even though both sides have a row where key1 is x and key2 is NULL, such a case is not considered a match, and therefore a result row is not returned for it. If you want such a case to be considered a match, you need to add special handling of the NULLs. One way to achieve this is to add a predicate that checks for the option that both sides are NULL, like so:

```
SELECT A.A_val, B.B_val
FROM dbo.TableA AS A
  INNER JOIN dbo.TableB AS B
    ON A.key1 = B.key1
    AND (A.key2 = B.key2 OR A.key2 IS NULL AND B.key2 IS NULL);
```

This special handling is only required for the nullable columns; therefore, you only need it for key2, but not for key1. This code generates the following output:

```
A_val        B_val
----------   ----------
A x NULL     B x NULL
A x y        B x y
```

This form is considered order-preserving by the optimizer, meaning that it enables efficient use of indexing.

Another common solution is to use the ISNULL or COALESCE functions to replace a NULL with a value that cannot normally appear in the data in both sides. This way, when both sides are NULL, you get a match. Here's how you use this technique in our example:

```
SELECT A.A_val, B.B_val
FROM dbo.TableA AS A
  INNER JOIN dbo.TableB AS B
    ON A.key1 = B.key1
    AND COALESCE(A.key2, '<N/A>') = COALESCE(B.key2, '<N/A>');
```

This code generates the following output:

```
A_val        B_val
----------   ----------
A x NULL     B x NULL
A x y        B x y
```

Unfortunately, this form is not considered order-preserving by the optimizer, and therefore might result in a less optimal plan compared to the previous solution. But as mentioned several times in this guide, during the exam make sure you understand carefully what the exact requirements of the questions are. When only asked about the correctness of a solution and not its efficiency, use of such techniques is fair game. When considering which solution to use in production code, you want to stay away from such techniques.

As mentioned, subqueries behave very similar to joins in terms of NULL handling. Consider the following example:

```
SELECT A.A_val
FROM dbo.TableA AS A
WHERE EXISTS
  ( SELECT * FROM dbo.TableB AS B
    WHERE A.key1 = B.key1
      AND A.key2 = B.key2 );
```

Like with the first example with the join, without any special NULL handling, only rows from TableA with proper key values (ones that are not NULL) that match all compared columns in TableB are filtered. The row in Table A where key1 is x and key2 is NULL is not returned, despite the fact that Table B also has a row where key1 is x and key2 is NULL. This code generates the following output:

```
A_val
----------
A x y
```

If you are supposed to return such rows, just like with joins, you need to add special ex-plicit NULL treatment. Here's an example demonstrating the order-preserving technique with the extra predicate:

```
SELECT A.A_val
FROM dbo.TableA AS A
WHERE EXISTS
  ( SELECT * FROM dbo.TableB AS B
    WHERE A.key1 = B.key1
      AND (A.key2 = B.key2 OR A.key2 IS NULL AND B.key2 IS NULL) );
```

This code generates the following output:

```
A_val
----------
A x NULL
A x y
```

And here's an example demonstrating the technique that is not order-preserving, and therefore typically less efficient, with the COALESCE function:

```
SELECT A.A_val
FROM dbo.TableA AS A
WHERE EXISTS
  ( SELECT * FROM dbo.TableB AS B
    WHERE A.key1 = B.key1
      AND COALESCE(A.key2, '<N/A>') = COALESCE(B.key2, '<N/A>') );
```

This code generates the following output:

```
A_val
----------
A x NULL
A x y
```

Using a set operator, like INTERSECT, the comparison between the two inputs uses a concept of distinctness instead of equality. With distinctness, when you compare two NULLs you get *true* and not *unknown* as the result. That is, it is true that one NULL isn't distinct from another NULL.

Here's an example combining the rows with key1 and key2 from the two tables using the INTERSECT operator:

```
SELECT key1, key2 FROM dbo.TableA
INTERSECT
SELECT key1, key2 FROM dbo.TableB;
```

This code generates the following output:

```
key1 key2
---- ----
x    NULL
x    y
```

As you can see, there's no need here for special handling of NULLs if you want to get a true when comparing two NULLs. That's the behavior of set operators by design. The one drawback that set operators have compared to the alternative tools is that with set operators you're limited to returning only the columns that you're comparing.

In Chapter 1 I described a technique that brings together all three tools to combine data between tables in a manner that is order-preserving, allows returning elements from both sides and that uses distinctness-based semantics. Here's the technique applied to our example:

```
SELECT A.A_val, B.B_val
FROM dbo.TableA AS A
  INNER JOIN dbo.TableB AS B
    ON EXISTS( SELECT A.key1, A.key2
                INTERSECT
                SELECT B.key1, B.key2 );
```

This code generates the following output:

```
A_val       B_val
----------  ----------
A x NULL    B x NULL
A x y       B x y
```

This beautiful technique is considered pretty advanced and is not very well known, and hence it's not very likely that it will show up in the exam. However, if you do understand it well, you should have a pretty good grasp of the fundamental querying tools that it's based on. And what could be a nicer way to end the book than with this example?

When you're done, run the following code for cleanup:

```
DROP TABLE IF EXISTS dbo.TableA, dbo.TableB;
```

# Chapter summary

- Views are reusable table expressions that don't support parameters. Inline table valued functions (TVFs) are like views, but with parameter support. You should think of inline TVFs as parameterized views.
- Scalar user-defined functions (UDFs) accept parameters and return a single value. You cannot change data from UDFs or have any side effects on the database. T-SQL does not support error handling in UDFs.
- Multistatement table-valued UDFs define a table variable that they return in their header. The responsibility of the UDF's body is to fill the returned table variable with data. When you query such a UDF, SQL Server internally creates the table variable, runs the function's flow to fill it with data, and hands it to the calling query. The benefit of UDFs is that unlike with stored procedures you can interact with them as part of a query.

- Stored procedures are reusable routines that allow you to encapsulate logic. Unlike UDFs, stored procedures can modify data in the database, use dynamic SQL, and support error handling. They help you hide the complexity of your tasks. They also help you better control permissions by granting EXECUTE permissions to the user on the procedure without granting permissions to perform the underlying activities directly. Unlike UDFs, stored procedures cannot appear in a query.

- SQL Server supports doing work as transactions with full ACID properties (atomicity, consistency, isolation and durability).

- T-SQL supports a TRY-CATCH construct for error handling purposes. Using this construct appropriately, combined with making sure that you don't leave a transaction open in case of errors, allows you to provide consistent error handling solutions.

- By turning the XACT_ABORT option to on you get a more consistent outcome in terms of an open transaction when an error happens. When not using TRY-CATCH, an open transaction is rolled back and the batch is aborted. When using TRY-CATCH, the transaction is doomed and control passes to the CATCH block.

- The ISNULL and COALESCE functions return the first value that is not NULL among their inputs.

- When combining data from multiple tables you use tools like joins, subqueries and set operators. If NULLs are possible in the key columns that you're matching, you need to think about the desired outcome of the comparison. If you wish to get a match when comparing two NULLs, with joins and subqueries you need to add special handling, whereas with set operators you don't.

# Thought experiment

In this thought experiment, demonstrate your skills and knowledge of the topics covered in this chapter. You can find the answer to this thought experiment in the next section.

You are a member of a database development team of a large retail company. There seems to be some confusion among the developers in terms of which tools to use for which tasks, resulting in inconsistent choices. Your team has a meeting where different members raise questions with regards to the recommended tools and practices to use. You are asked about your opinion concerning the following questions:

1. Some of the developers argue against implementing logic in database routines like stored procedures. Do you have any arguments in favor of using those?

2. Some of the developers argue that there's no need for error handling in T-SQL, rather all error handling should be done in the application. Can you provide any arguments in favor of handling errors in T-SQL, and any recommendations for consistent error handling?

3. There's some inconsistency in the choice of data types for columns that represent the same thing in different tables. Making a change in the type of a column involves some refactoring, and in some cases downtime. What are the benefits and arguments in favor of creating a plan for more consistent use of data types for attributes that represent the same thing?

4. Currently there's a lot of inconsistency in using ISNULL and COALESCE. If the dev team had to pick one of the two to be consistent, which of the two should it be? Also, are there special cases where an exception should be made?

5. When joining data with keys that support NULLs, developers regularly use the ISNULL function in both sides of the join to replace a NULL with an alternative value, and this way get a match when both sides are NULL. However, users complain about bad performance for those queries. Can you suggest an alternative solution?

# Thought experiment answer

This section contains the solution to the thought experiment.

1. Stored procedures allow you to encapsulate logic in a reusable database routine. Compared to implementing logic in the application, it's much easier to deploy a change in a stored procedure. You simply alter the procedure with the new code, and from that moment everyone starts using the new version. Stored procedures also tend to result in less network traffic since the application passes through the network only the procedure name and its arguments; the flow runs in the database, and the stored procedure returns only the final result through the network. Stored procedures also make it easy to handle security because you grant the user only EXECUTE permissions on the stored procedure, without needing to grant the user direct permissions for the underlying activities.

2. The two don't have to be mutually exclusive. For highly robust solutions you want to handle errors in both the application and the T-SQL code. You always want to check the inputs in the application and avoid submitting any unnecessary activity to the database. Once the request is submitted to the database, when an error happens, T-SQL doesn't behave very consistently by default in terms of the transaction and batch state. Using the TRY-CATCH construct, plus turning on the XACT_ABORT option, you can achieve a more consistent behavior. When an error happens, the transaction is doomed and control passes to the CATCH block. After doing what you need to do in the CACTH block, you typically want to roll back the transaction, if still open, and rethrow the error to the caller. You can then do what you need to do in the application with the error.

3. Columns that represent the same thing in different tables are often used as join columns, such as in a foreign key-primary key relationship. Such columns are typically used as join columns. Inconsistency in the data types between the sides of the join causes SQL Server to implicitly convert the type of one of the sides to the other. With implicit conversion, the data loses its original ordering property, preventing SQL Server from being able to rely on index ordering to support the join. Therefore, it's important to use consistent types, and if currently inconsistent, to create a plan for altering the types so that eventually they are consistent.

4. The ISNULL function is proprietary whereas COALESCE is standard. Furthermore, IS-NULL supports only two inputs whereas COALESCE supports more than two. For these reasons, if you had to choose only one for consistency, COALESCE should be preferred. The one exception is when you do have only two inputs, and the first is a subquery, the ISNULL function executes the subquery only once whereas the COALESCE function might execute it twice (when the result is not NULL). So, if performance is a concern, in this exceptional case it's recommended to use ISNULL.

5. Once you apply manipulation to a column like with the ISNULL and COALESCE functions, the data loses its original ordering property—at least as far as the optimizer is concerned. This means that you prevent the optimizer from being able to rely on the ordering of supporting indexes. So instead of COALESCE(T1.key1, <somevalue>) = COALESCE(T2.key1, <somevalue>), you should prefer T1.key1 = T2.key1 OR (T1.key1 IS NULL AND T2.key1 IS NULL).

# Index

## Symbols

@@IDENTITY function 82
@maxallowedqty parameter 260
@parameter IS NULL 253
@params parameter 255
@qty variable 262
@@ROWCOUNT function 80
@sql variable 255
@stmt parameter 255
@sumqty variable 262
@@TRANCOUNT function 265, 272, 277–278, 279, 302, 304

## A

add (+) operator 83
aggregate functions 84–86, 153–155
  window 168–172
aggregation element 160
aliases
  column 19
  table 18
aliasing 18–20, 48
  columns 145
  external 145
  inline 223
  internal 145
all-at-once concept 106–107
ALL predicate 131
ALL subclause 191
ALTER PROC command 250
ALTER TABLE statement 122–124
ALTER VIEW command 229
American National Standards Institute (ANSI) 3
AND operator 24
Anti Semi Join optimization 137

ANY predicate 131–132
application-time period tables 177
APPLY operator 105, 137–141, 167, 201
  CROSS APPLY 138–140
  OUTER APPLY 140–141
  vs. joins 137
arithmetic operators 83–84, 85–86
arrays 207, 211
AS clause 8–9
AS OF clause 188
AS OF @dt 187
asterisk (*) 18
atomic transactions 264
atomic values 198, 200
at sign (@) 21
AT TIME ZONE function 71–72, 72, 191
attribute-centric presentation 193
attributes 8, 18
  aliasing 19
  renaming 19
  view 229–230
  XML 193
autocommit mode 268
AUTO option 195
AVG function 84–85, 86
Azure SQL Database 2

## B

BEGIN TRANSACTION statement 265, 270, 272–274, 281
BIGINT value 84

## C

CASE expressions 76–79
case-sensitive Unicode text 193

# D

indexes 170
 XML 205
indexing
 foreign key columns 50
inline aliasing 223
inline table-valued functions 148–150
inline table-valued user-defined functions 244–248
inner joins 48–52
IN predicate 131
input parameters 81, 241, 251–252
INSERT EXEC statement 97–98
inserting data 93–100
INSERT SELECT statement 96
INSERT statement 80, 231, 267, 273
 with OUTPUT clause 116–117
INSERT VALUES statement 94–95, 95–96
internal aliasing 145
International Organization for Standards (ISO) 3
INTERSECT operator 43–44, 320–321
INT type 313
ISJSON function 216
IS NOT NULL operator 23
ISNULL function 60–62, 73, 78–79, 98, 162, 306,
 314–317, 319
IS NULL operator 23, 24, 89
isolation levels 264
iterations 6

## J

JOIN keyword 52
joins 45–67
 APPLY operator vs. 137
 composite 58–65
 cross 46–48
 DELETE statement with 110
 derived tables 145–146
 inner 48–52
 multi-join queries 65–67
 NULLs in 58–65
 outer 52–57
 set operators and 64
 subqueries vs. 134–137
 UPDATE statement with 102–103
JSON
 data types 207, 208, 216
 special characters 207
 specification 206
 syntax 207

JSON data 205–216
 converting to tabular format 212–216
 members 207
 producing output from queries 207–212
JSON_MODIFY function 215–216
JSON_QUERY function 215
JSON_VALUE function 215

## K

keyed-in order 11
keys
 choosing data type for 309–311
 nonsequential 311
 sequential 310
key-value pairs 81

## L

LAG function 174–175
LAST_VALUE function 175–176
latches 310–311
LEAD 174–175
LEFT function 74, 88
LEFT OUTER JOIN keywords 52–54
LEN function 74
LIKE predicate 25–26
literals 25
logical query processing 1, 10–17, 48, 170
 phases 11
LOWER function 75
LTRIM function 75

## M

markers 279–281
markup, XML 193
mathematics 2, 5
members, JSON 207
MERGE algorithm 61–65
MERGE statement 4, 110–115
 with OUTPUT clause 118–119
metadata 194
Microsoft Visual Basic 3
Microsoft Visual C# 3
modify() method 200, 201
modulo (%) operator 83, 85
multi-join queries 65–67

# P

parameter embedding 245, 254
parameters 81, 241, 251–252, 253
  input 241, 251–252
  named 253
  output 241, 258–259
parentheses 24
PARSE function 68, 312
PATH option 196
PATINDEX function 74
PERCENT keyword 34
physical data independence 307
pivoting data 160–164
PIVOT operator 160–164, 225
plus (+) operator 72–73
POC index 170
precedence rules 24
predicate logic 4–5
predicate pushdown 48
predicates 9
  ALL 131
  ANY 131–132
  combining 23–25
  disjunction of 252
  EXISTS 133
  filtering data with 21–28
    search arguments 86–90
  IN 131
  LIKE 25–26
  seek 63
  SOME 131–132
  three-valued-logic and 21–23
presentation order 16
primary keys 45, 48–49
primitive data types 207
PRINT statement 184, 296
programmability objects 221–263
  stored procedures 250–263
  user-defined functions 237–250
  views 222–237
prolog 198
pseudo functions 24

# Q

QName 198
queries 6

APPLY operator 137–141
group and pivot data using 150–176
grouped 15, 151–160
JSON data 205–216
keyed-in order 11
logical query processing 10–17
multi-join 65–67
on mutiple tables 45–67
pivot 160–164
search arguments 86–90
SELECT 1–45
static 253–254
subqueries 130–137, 316
temporal data 176–192
using table expressions 141–150
using wildcards 26
windowed 85
XML data 192–205
query() method 200, 201

# R

RAISERROR command 291, 297–300
RAND function 91, 242
RANGE option 171
RANK function 173
RAW option 194–195
REAL data type 308
RECOMPILE option 254
records 10
relational database management systems (RDBMSs) 2
relational model 4–9, 307
relational operators 40
REPLACE function 75
REPLICATE function 75
RETURN clause 150, 239, 245
RIGHT function 74
RIGHT OUTER JOIN keywords 55–56
ROLLBACK TRANSACTION statement 265, 272, 277, 280–281, 305
ROLLUP clause 157–158, 160
ROOT clause 210
root node 193
ROWCOUNT_BIG function 80
row-level security 248
ROW_NUMBER function 144, 145, 172–173
rowpattern 196

# About the author

 **ITZIK BEN-GAN** is a T-SQL instructor for and co-founder of SolidQ. A Microsoft Data Platform MVP (Most Valuable Professional) since 1999, Itzik has delivered numerous training events around the world focused on T-SQL querying, query tuning, and programming. Itzik has authored many T-SQL books as well as a monthly column for SQL Server Pro. Itzik's speaking activities include SQLPASS, SQLBits, IT/Dev Connections, and various user groups around the world. Itzik is the author of SolidQ's Advanced T-SQL Querying, Programming and Tuning, and T-SQL Fundamentals courses, along with being a primary resource within the company for its T-SQL-related activities.